ILLINI
Legends, Lists, & Lore

Second Edition

GREATEST MOMENTS OF
UNIVERSITY OF ILLINOIS ATHLETICS

by Mike Pearson

Audio CD narrated by Brian Barnhart, produced by Ed Bond

Foreword by Ron Guenther

Epilogue by Jim Turpin

Sports Publishing L.L.C.
Champaign, Illinois

Director of production: Susan M. Moyer
Project manager: Tracy Gaudreau
Interior design: Jennifer Polson & Tracy Gaudreau
Copy editor: Cindy McNew
Dust jacket design: Joseph Brumleve

ISBN: 1-58261-347-8

We have made every effort to trace the ownership of copyrighted photos. If we have failed to give adequate credit, we will be pleased to make changes in future printings.

Printed in the United States

To my wife and children, who make me smile.

Table of Contents

Acknowledgments

Most authors will readily admit that writing the acknowledgments is one of the most difficult parts of the project. From the individuals who've answered simple questions during my research to those who worked hand-in-hand with me throughout the process, I express my heartfelt gratitude.

First, thanks to the tremendous staff at the University of Illinois' Division of Intercollegiate Athletics, admirably directed by Ron Guenther. Assistant athletic directors Kent Brown and Dave Johnson have provided especially enthusiastic support, and I'm very fortunate to be able to count them as trusted friends. Other athletic staffers who provided valuable assistance during the last several months include Cassie Arner, Dick Barnes, Derrick Burson. Marcia Goldenstein, Terry Neutz-Hayden, Mike Koon, Dave Reiter, Kara Stachowiak, Michelle Warner, and their talented student staff. Thanks also to Warren Hood and Marty Kaufmann in the DIA's corporate relations office, and longtime friends such as Dana Brenner, Terry Cole, Lenny Willis, Shawn Wax, Ken Zimmerman, Steve Greene, Mike Hatfield, Andy Dixon, Al Martindale, Cheryl Cain, Tom Michael, Rod Cardinal, and Mary Ann McChesney. This is just a small portion of the DIA's all-star roster.

Next, my appreciation goes out to the fabulous Fighting Illini coaching staff and athletes who have produced such consistent success, particularly in recent years. All those who wear Orange & Blue are very proud of your efforts. Keep it going!

The staff at University Archives went well beyond the call of duty in helping me. Thanks to Maynard Brichford, William Maher, Chris Prom , Bob Chapel, and John Franch for helping me gather audio clips for the CD, photos and various other nuggets. Thanks also to Jim Keene and University Bands for allowing me to use their inspiring Illini music.

Also, regarding the audio portion of this project, I tip my hat to Sid Rotz of WSOY Radio, Dave Eanet of WGN Radio, Larry Miller, Roger Huddleston, Mark and Julie Herman, and Ted Patterson for allowing me to access personal clips that I'm able to share with Illini fans. And to the various "Voices of the Illini"—Jim Turpin, Larry Stewart, Dick Martin, Loren Tate, Neil Funk, Jim Grabowski, Will Tieman, and Dave Loane —for their wonderful descriptions of Illini history.

And, for their expertise with the production of the CD, special kudos to narrator Brian Barnhart—the new "voice"—producer Ed Bond, and WDWS Radio's Stevie Jay. Great job, guys.

Special thanks to Jim and Joan Sheppard, who time after time have opened their doors to me, and provided fresh linen at the Sheppard Suites. True friends.

Photography-wise, I salute the talented Mark Jones for his fantastic help and friendship. Artist Jack Davis, the photo staff of the Champaign News-Gazette, and the UI News Bureau also provided the magical images that are included inside these pages.

To the great staff at Sports Publishing in Champaign, once again you have come through with flying colors. Thanks to Joe Bannon, Sr., Peter Bannon, Joe Bannon, Jr., Susan Moyer, Tracy Gaudreau, Joseph Brumleve, Scott Rauguth, Dave Kasel, Walter Pierce, Maurey Williamson, Cindy McNew, and many others.

And last, but certainly not least, thanks to my family for their special support. Wife Laura, son Tony and his wife Stephanie, son Tom, daughter Paige, son Parker, my Mom and my "much older"" sisters all have played a major role in any success that I've attained. Hugs to all of you.

Foreword

For the past 10 years, I have had the privilege of serving the University of Illinois as the Director of Athletics, but my affiliation with this great institution goes back nearly 40 years to my freshman year of 1963. My first exposure to the UI came during my high school years at York when I followed the basketball team to the state tournament at Huff Gym. I was fortunate enough to be recruited to play football at the UI by Pete Elliott and Burt Ingwersen, and have met, played and worked with some of the great names of Illinois lore, all of whom are mentioned in this book.

The changes made on this campus over the last 40 years in the realm of athletics are truly amazing, but the names associated with the Fighting Illini will live on forever. They read like a Who's Who of collegiate athletics – Huff, Zuppke, Grange, Butkus, Caroline, Eddleman, Weatherspoon, Phillip, Boudreau, Harper, Kerr, Buford, Mondie-Milner, Virgin, Laz, Richards, Polk, Eggers, Stricker and Norman. The list goes on and on. In *Illini Legends, Lists and Lore*, Mike Pearson gives you a look at these and many more of the individuals and teams that make up the rich history of Illini athletics.

One of the things that makes athletics so interesting is to follow the student-athletes and coaches today who will be the legends of tomorrow. Which of the current Illini coaching staff that includes Ron Turner, Theresa Grentz, Don Hardin and Bill Self will be considered legends by future generations? Stars from 2001-02 including Perdita Felicien, Kurt Kittner, Andy Dickinson and Frank Williams all have their names listed in the record books. Who will be a part of the next generation of Illini greats?

Over the last 10 years, we have added women's soccer and softball to our list of varsity sports, seen the construction of the Bielfeldt Athletic Administration Building, the Irwin Academic Center, the Ubben Basketball Practice Facility, the Irwin Indoor Practice Facility and Eichelberger Field. Future plans include a Multipurpose Olympic Training Center and Arena, completions to the UI Soccer and Track Stadium, additions to the Atkins Tennis Center and a championship golf course. But, just as these facilities are important in giving UI student-athletes a place to train and compete, most important is the caliber of person we have as coaches and athletes. Our philosophy for Illini Excellence is based on integrity, academic performance, balanced budget, championship program, gender and ethnic equity, facilities and caring community.

I have known Mike for many years, and I am confident that no one has ever been more diligent than he's been while doing the research for this book. I know he is immensely proud of this work. I hope the memories relived from the stories told in this book remind us all how fortunate we are to be affiliated with, and fans of, the University of Illinois. I'm proud to be a part of it. I hope you are too.

Ronald E. Guenther

Ronald E. Guenther

"No other individual had the esteem and affection of so many alumni, students, and friends than George Huff. He stood for everything that was right and honorable, not only in his administration and direction of athletics, but in all of his activities. His personal code of honor and of sportsmanship was based upon a philosophy of life that should inspire any man or woman. The influence of his career on all who knew him and the ideals he has left us will be a cherished heritage."

— A.C. Willard, President,
University of Illinois,
upon the death of George Huff

1895-96

AMERICA'S TIME CAPSULE

Oct. 4, 1895	Newport (Rhode Island) Golf Club hosted the first U.S. Open golf tournament.
Jan. 4, 1896	Utah became the 45th state in the Union.
April 6, 1896	The first modern Olympic Games opened in Athens, Greece.
April 23, 1896	The first public showing of a moving picture was presented in New York City.
June 4, 1896	Assembly of the first Ford automobile was completed by Henry Ford in Detroit.

ILLINI MOMENT

The Palmer House, Chicago, Illinois, late 1800s.

FORMATION OF THE BIG TEN CONFERENCE:

The date was February 8, 1896. At the Palmer House in Chicago, Illinois, seven men were meeting to establish standards and regulations for the administration of intercollegiate athletics. These faculty representatives from seven of the Midwest's finest universities designated themselves as the "Intercollegiate Conference of Faculty Representatives." Professor Henry H. Everett represented the University of Illinois. Today, the organization is known as the "Big Ten Conference," although its bulky original label is still the official title. The seven charter members of the conference included the Universities of Illinois, Chicago, Michigan, Minnesota, Wisconsin, plus Northwestern University and Purdue University. Indiana and Iowa were admitted in 1899, and Ohio State gained entrance in 1912. Chicago formally withdrew from the conference in 1946 due to its inability to "provide reasonable competition," reducing the Big Ten to the Big Nine. Three years later, it was once again the Big Ten when Michigan State was admitted by the membership. Most recently, in 1989, an invitation of Big Ten membership was made to and accepted by Penn State.

ILLINI SCRAPBOOK

Illinois' first football team in 1890, featured future coach and athletic director, George Huff (back row, center).

A TOTAL OF 40 MEN won varsity letters for the University of Illinois' three athletic teams (football, baseball, and track) during the 1895-96 season. Three men—Harry Hadsall, Paul Cooper, and Harvey Sconce—earned letters in both football and baseball. It should be noted that the "I" letters weren't officially awarded to those men until November 3, 1923.

(Left to right) Harry Hadsall, Harvey Sconce and Paul Cooper each earned varsity letters in both football and baseball.

Illini Lists

ILLINI FOOTBALL SUCCESS (DECADE BY DECADE)

Decade	W	L	T	PCT
1890-1899	45	26	8	.620
1900-1909	61	27	6	.681
1910-1919	49	15	7	.739
1920-1929	55	19	3	.734
1930-1939	38	39	5	.494
1940-1949	38	49	5	.440
1950-1959	48	37	6	.560
1960-1969	36	59	1	.424
1970-1979	38	67	4	.367
1980-1989	63	48	4	.565
1990-1999	50	63	2	.443
2000-2001	15	8	0	.652
Total	536	457	51	.538

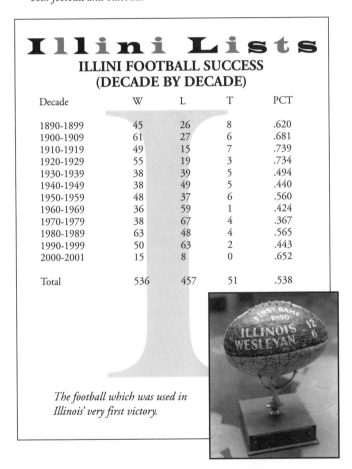

The football which was used in Illinois' very first victory.

Illini Legend

GEORGE HUFF

When George Huff entered the University of Illinois as a student in 1887, he had no idea how much of an impact he would make upon his hometown of Champaign over the next half century. Not only was "G" a member of the school's first football team in 1890, he also molded the lives of hundreds of other young men through his roles as Fighting Illini coach and director of athletics. The rotund Huff lettered twice in football as the team's center and three times as a multi-position player in baseball. As head coach of the Fighting Illini football team from 1895-1899, "G" was only mildly successful (21-16-3). However, as skipper of the Illini baseball squad, Huff dominated his opponents, winning nearly 70 percent of the 544 games he coached from 1896-1919. "G" directed the Illini nine to a record 11 Big Ten championships. As UI's athletic director from 1901-36, Huff's contributions were monumental. He had a knack of hiring outstanding coaches (Bob Zuppke, Carl Lundgren, Craig Ruby, and Harry Gill). He helped build a phenomenal athletic plant (Memorial Stadium and Huff Gymnasium). But George Huff will be best known as a man who devoted his life to the honor and glory of the University of Illinois with honesty and fair play. On October 1, 1936, uremic poisoning claimed the life of "The Father of Fighting Illini Athletics" at the age of 64.

ILLINI LORE

During the 1895-96 school year, the University of Illinois had nine instructional buildings and 84 faculty members. Of President Andrew Draper's 855 total students, nearly 80 percent were males, and nearly a third of the student body majored in either English or Electrical Engineering.

1896-97

AMERICA'S TIME CAPSULE

July 7, 1896	The city of Chicago hosted the Democratic National Convention, which nominated William Jennings Bryan as its candidate.
Oct. 1, 1896	The Federal Post Office established free rural delivery.
Nov. 3, 1896	William McKinley won the U.S. presidency in a landslide.
March 17, 1897	Bob Fitzsimmons defeated "Gentleman Jim" Corbett for the world heavyweight boxing title.
April 19, 1897	John McDermott won the first Boston Marathon in a time of two hours, 55 minutes, and 10 seconds.

ILLINI MOMENT

Amos Alonzo Stagg directed the University of Chicago to a victory in Illinois' first Big Ten football game.

ILLINOIS' FIRST CONFERENCE FOOTBALL GAME—OCTOBER 31, 1896:

"It not infrequently happens," reported the University of Illinois' student newspaper, *The Illini,* "that a team which is manifestly superior to that lined up against it, comes out the loser. If there ever was a game in which the weaker of the two elevens gained the victory, it was in the contest between Chicago and Illinois on Marshall Field when Stagg's aggregation of hirelings managed to win, 12 to 0. The rotten state of athletics at Chicago is well known and her name has become synonymous for corruption in that branch of college life." What made this game particularly momentous was that it was the Fighting Illini football team's very first conference game. Coach Amos Alonzo Stagg's Maroons defeated Illinois that afternoon, with an alleged "professional," Frederick Nichols, directing the Maroons to two touchdowns (worth four points each), and two goals after touchdown (two points each).

Illinois Field served as the home of Fighting Illini football teams beginning in 1891 until the last game on October 13, 1923.

Captain William Fulton hit .302 for the 1897 Illini baseball team.

THREE FIGHTING ILLINI baseball players—second baseman William Fulton, shortstop Hugh Shuler, and centerfielder Harry Hadsall—were selected to the 1897 All-Western team by *Harper's Weekly*. Fulton (.302) and Shuler (.304) both hit well, but Hadsall batted just .160 for the year.

Illini Legend

Henry Everett

The University of Illinois' third athletic director and first faculty representative was Henry Houghton Everett. A native of Chicago, Everett was an all-star athlete for the University of Chicago Maroons, participating in football, track, and wrestling. He left UC to become assistant superintendent of the Chicago Y.M.C.A., but after only a year he quit to enroll at Northwestern University's medical school. Medicine soon took a back seat to Everett's intense interest in athletics, and he was on the move again, this time to the University of Wisconsin as an instructor in UW's gymnasium. In 1895, the University of Illinois hired the 31-year-old Everett as its director of athletics, faculty representative, and track coach. Perhaps his greatest contribution was as UI's representative at the January 11, 1895 meeting in Chicago, which formed the Big Ten Conference. Everett gave way to George Huff after one year as AD, but coached Illini track for three seasons, from 1896-98. He returned to his career in medicine, serving at both Rush Medical College and at Chicago's Presbyterian Hospital. Henry Everett died in 1928 at the age of 61.

Illini Lists

ILLINI ATHLETIC DIRECTORS

- 1892-1894   Edward K. Hall
- 1894-1895   Fred H. Dodge
- 1895-1898   Henry H. Everett
- 1898-1901   Jacob K. Shell
- 1901-1936   George A. Huff
- 1936-1941   Wendell S. Wilson
- 1942-1966   Douglas Mills
- 1967-1972   E.E. (Gene) Vance
- 1972-1979   Cecil N. Coleman
- 1979   Ray Eliot (interim)
- 1980-1988   Neale R. Stoner
- 1988   Ronald E. Guenther (interim)
- 1988   Dr. Karol A. Kahrs (interim)
- 1988-1991   John Mackovic
- 1991-1992   Robert Todd (interim)
- 1992-   Ronald E. Guenther

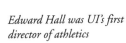

Edward Hall was UI's first director of athletics

ILLINI LORE

Dedicated June 8, 1897, the University of Illinois library—renamed Altgeld Hall in 1940—served students for nearly 30 years as the campus's main resource center. The original structure cost $380,000 and featured a distinctive 132-foot tower, from which a daily chimes concert emanates. Additions to the building were made in 1914, 1919, 1926, and 1956. After its service as the home of the library, it was the headquarters for the College of Law for 28 years, and in 1955 was assigned to the Department of Mathematics.

1897-98

AMERICA'S TIME CAPSULE

Sept. 21, 1897   In response to a letter from young Virginia O'Hanlon, a *New York Sun* editorial declared, "Yes, Virginia, there is a Santa Claus."

July 2, 1897   A coal miners' strike put 75,000 men out of work in Pennsylvania, Ohio, and West Virginia.

Feb. 15, 1898   An explosion destroyed the battleship *Maine*. 260 crew members perished.

April 24, 1898   The United States declared war on Spain, and the Spanish-American War began.

June 1, 1898   Congress passed the Erdman Arbitration Act, making government mediation in railroad disputes legitimate.

ILLINI MOMENT

1897 football team

ILLINOIS' FIRST INDOOR FOOTBALL GAME-NOVEMBER 20, 1897:

The University of Illinois' first night game and its first game played indoors came against the Carlisle Indians at the old Chicago Coliseum. The contest, called by one journalist "hair raising in its recklessness," pitted East (Carlisle) against West (Illinois) on a gridiron of sand and sawdust. Though the great Jim Thorpe had already graduated, Carlisle remained a powerhouse team. The Fighting Illini began like a prairie whirlwind, scoring the first touchdown after a series of rushes down the field. Halftime's intermission saw Illinois ahead, 6-5, but that lead evaporated in the second half as the Indians tallied three unanswered touchdowns. After the game, the two teams traveled together by train to Champaign-Urbana, where the Carlisle squad stayed until the following Wednesday as guests of the University.

University Hall

ILLINI SCRAPBOOK

1897-98 track and field team

ILLINOIS' TRACK AND FIELD team placed fifth among five teams at the first Indoor Western Intercollegiate meet, held in Chicago. J.K. Hoagland of Illinois won the 880-yard walk to become the school's first individual conference track champion.

Illini Legend

Fred Smith

During the infancy of college athletics in the late 1800s, it was very common for one individual to hold more than one position within the athletic department. Such was the case with athletic director/baseball coach/football coach George Huff. "G" decided that the multiple responsibilities were diluting his efficiency and affecting his health, so in 1900 he submitted his resignation as the Illini grid mentor. Huff chose former Illini assistant coach Fred Smith as his successor in 1900, a man who had performed the bulk of the head coaching duties for Huff in 1897 and '98. Smith starred as a quarterback at Princeton, directing the Tigers to a 10-0-1 record and the mythical national championship. During his lone season as Illinois' official head coach, Smith guided the Illini to a very respectable 7-3-2 record, including a victory over Purdue. Altogether, Illinois registered eight defensive shutouts in 12 games, a mark that equals the most in Illinois football history during a single season. Smith eventually settled in New York City, where he doubled as an engineer with the Department of Public Works and as head football coach at Fordham College. He died in 1923 at the age of 50.

Illini Lists

ILLINI SINGLE-SEASON FOOTBALL SHUTOUTS

- 1900 — 8 (in 12 games)
- 1902 — 8 (in 13 games
- 1910 — 7 (in 7 games)
- 1901 — 7 (in 10 games)
- 1904 — 7 (in 12 games)
- 1917 — 6 (in 8 games)
- 1903 — 6 (in 14 games)

The 1900 Illini football team posted eight shutouts in 12 games.

ILLINI LORE

In April of 1897, Charles W. Spalding, treasurer for the University of Illinois, was charged with embezzling University funds of $460,000. About 95 percent of that total had been secretly invested by Spalding in land deals in the state of Idaho. Two months after he had been caught, the Illinois state legislature appropriated money to cover the deficit caused by Spalding's actions. On December 1, 1897, Spalding was sent to the state penitentiary to begin a four-year sentence.

1898-99

AMERICA'S TIME CAPSULE

Aug. 1, 1898	The United States estimated that 4,200 servicemen fighting in Cuba suffered from yellow fever or typhoid.
Nov. 8, 1898	Rough Rider Teddy Roosevelt was elected governor of New York.
Dec. 10, 1898	A peace treaty was signed in Paris by the United States and Spain, ending the Spanish-American War.
Feb. 14, 1899	Congress approved the use of voting machines for federal elections.
June 9, 1899	Jim Jeffries knocked out Bob Fitzsimmons for the world heavyweight boxing title.

ILLINI MOMENT

Illinois' 1898 football team

ILLINI'S 11-10 FOOTBALL WIN AT MINNESOTA, NOVEMBER 24, 1898:

Coach George Huff's Illini limped into Minnesota with a three-game losing streak, so no one gave the visitors much of a chance that cold and snowy Thanksgiving Day. Only a day after being shut out by the Carlisle Indians, the Illinois party set off on its exceedingly long and tedious trip to the Land of 10,000 Lakes. The first ever matchup between the two schools began predictably, as Minnesota jumped off to a 10-0 first-quarter lead. Illinois battled back, scoring a five-point touchdown just before the whistle sounded to trail 10-5 at the intermission. In the final 25 minutes, the Illini successfully navigated the treacherous field by rushing the ball. All-star fullback A.R. Johnston, the Illini captain, scored the game-tying TD, then kicked the point after for the eventual 11-10 victory.

Action from Illinois' upset victory over Minnesota.

ILLINI SCRAPBOOK

This "I" sweater from 1898 belonged to Illini player and later head football coach, Arthur Hall.

Illini Item

IN DECEMBER OF 1898, the UI's Athletic Association began issuing blue sweaters with the orange block "I" to members of the Illini football, baseball, and track teams who won either a contest or an individual event against teams representing the universities of Chicago, Michigan, Wisconsin, or Minnesota, or to Illini who won a point in the annual field meet of the Western Intercollegiate Athletic Association.

Illini Lists

JUSTA LINDGREN'S ALL-TIME ILLINI FOOTBALL TEAM (chosen in 1943)

- Ends: Chuck Carney and Claude Rothgeb
- Tackles: Walter Crawford and Butch Nowack
- Guards: Ralph Chapman and Jim McMillin
- Center: Bob Reitsch
- Quarterback: Potsy Clark
- Halfbacks: Red Grange and Harold Pogue
- Fullback: Jack Crangle

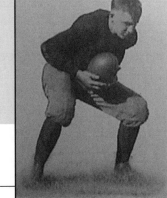

George "Potsy" Clark was the quarterback on Justa Lindgren's all-time Illini football team.

Illini Legend

JUSTA LINDGREN

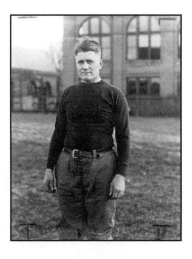

For 40 consecutive years plus a few more, the name Justa Lindgren was synonymous with Fighting Illini football. "Lindy," as he was known to the legion of players he coached and his many friends, first joined the University of Illinois as a freshman lineman from Moline in 1898. Four letter-winning seasons later, he graduated from the UI and was contacted by Cornell College in Mt. Vernon, Iowa, to become the school's head football coach. After only two seasons in Iowa, Lindgren returned to Urbana-Champaign as one of four graduates in George Huff's alumni coaching system. He served for one season as the Illini's head coach, 1906, but the conservative, detail-minded Lindgren felt more comfortable as an assistant, serving as line coach under Arthur Hall, Bob Zuppke, and Ray Eliot through 1943. Lindgren developed seven All-American players at Illinois during that span and was an integral member of eight Big Ten championship teams. He died in 1951 at the age of 72.

ILLINI LORE

On May 5, 1899, the University of Illinois' Board of Trustees decided to erect a $150,000 agriculture building. The facility, which opened for use September 10, 1900, eventually came to be known as Davenport Hall, in honor of the College of Agriculture's dean, Eugene Davenport.

1899-00

AMERICA'S TIME CAPSULE

Oct. 14, 1899   William McKinley became the first president to ride in an automobile.

Nov. 21, 1899   Vice President Garret Hobart died. New York Governor Theodore Roosevelt was nominated as Hobart's replacement. Roosevelt first declined the nomination, but later relented at the Republican National Convention.

March 14, 1900   Congress standardized the gold dollar as the unit of monetary value in the United States.

May 14, 1900   Carrie Nation began her anti-liquor campaign.

July 4, 1900   The Democratic Party nominated William Jennings Bryan of Nebraska as its presidential candidate.

ILLINI MOMENT

ILLINOIS' FIRST WESTERN CONFERENCE TITLE:

The beginning of the 20th century trumpeted the arrival of the University of Illinois' very first Western Conference title. Coach George Huff's 1900 baseball squad returned most of its members from the 1899 Big Ten runner-up and began its preseason with a series of exhibition games against the Chicago White Sox. After winning three and tying one of the nine games, Huff knew he had the makings of a championship club. His standout players included pitchers Carl Lundgren and Harvey McCollum, second baseman Billy Fulton, third baseman Carl Steinwedell, and center fielder Jimmy Cook—all members of Huff's all-time Illinois baseball team. The Illini won seven of their first eight conference games, winding up with an 11-2 record.

ILLINI SCRAPBOOK

A collection of Illinois' most treasured football memorabilia.

I Illini Item

Illini Lists

ALL-TIME BIG TEN BASEBALL VICTORIES
(Through 2002 season)

1.	889 wins	ILLINOIS (1896)
2.	871 wins	Michigan (1896)
3.	798 wins	Minnesota (1906)
4.	731 wins	Ohio State (1913)
5.	615 wins	Iowa (1906)
6.	565 wins	Wisconsin (1896*)
7.	557 wins	Indiana (1906)
8.	536 wins	Purdue (1906)
9.	513 wins	Northwestern (1898)
10.	443 wins	Michigan State (1951)
11.	221 wins	Chicago (1896**)
12.	143 wins	Penn State (1992)

*Dropped baseball as varsity sport following 1991 season
**Withdrew from Big Ten following 1946 season

Illini Legend

Carl Lundgren

The immortal George Huff called him "the greatest of all college baseball coaches." An early sports magazine, *Athletic World*, praised him as "the peer of all college baseball instructors." In any case, the name Carl Leonard Lundgren is permanently linked with University of Illinois success on the baseball diamond. As a pitcher on the Fighting Illini nines of 1899-1902, "Lundy" led Illinois to Big Ten championships his sophomore and senior seasons. The esteem in which he was held by his fellow students was displayed by his election not only to the baseball team's captaincy, but also to the presidency of UI's senior class. Lundgren went directly from Illinois into professional baseball, pitching for the Chicago Cubs for seven seasons. Twice the Cubbies were world champs, due in great part to his spectacular pitching which accounted for 92 career victories. After leaving the Cubs, he began his brilliant coaching career at Princeton as freshman coach, then went to Michigan as varsity coach, where he coached future Hall of Famer George Sisler. Huff lured Lundgren back to Champaign to coach the Illini in 1921, where he directed Illinois to five conference titles in 12 seasons. Lundgren died on August 24, 1934, of a heart attack at the age of 54.

ILLINI LORE

. . . .

On September 20, 1899, the University of Illinois' student-operated newspaper, *The Illini*, began publishing on a thrice-weekly basis. For the previous five years, the *Illini* was printed just once per week. The newspaper expanded to printing five times per week during the 1902-03 school year.

1900-01

AMERICA'S TIME CAPSULE

Sept. 8, 1900   A hurricane ravaged Galveston, Texas, killing 6,000 people and causing property damages of $20 milliion.
Nov. 6, 1900   William McKinley won the presidency for a second term.
Jan. 10, 1901   A well near Beaumont, Texas, brought in oil, the first evidence of oil from that region.
March 3, 1901   The United States Steel Corporation was incorporated in New Jersey.
June 15, 1901   Willie Anderson won the U.S. Open golf tournament.

ILLINI MOMENT

Second baseman Jimmy Cook led the Illinois effort against the Chicago Cubs.

ILLINOIS VS. THE CUBS—APRIL 3-16, 1901:

Before the days of spring training sites in warm climates, major league baseball teams frequently would hook up for a series of practice games against teams from the local universities. Such was the case in 1901, when manager Tom Loftus brought his Chicago Cubs to Champaign-Urbana for a nine-game series. The Cubbies featured future Hall of Famer Frank Chance, he of the famous baseball triumvirate "Tinker-to-Evers-to-Chance." Coach George Huff's Illini surprisingly won four games against the National League club, paced by the hitting of second baseman Jimmy Cook and catcher Jake Stahl. Illinois used the exhibition series as a springboard to a second-place finish in the Big Ten, but the Cubs ultimately finished 37 games behind the Pittsburgh Pirates in the NL race.

A turn of the century campus scene.

ILLINI SCRAPBOOK

ROBERT "RED" MATTHEWS, the nation's first acrobatic cheerleader, served as the University of Illinois' first cheerleader from 1899-1900. Said Matthews later, "I just busted out on the sidelines like the measles, and started hollering with my head up, my arms waving, and my legs jumping." Matthews was an institution at the University of Tennessee from 1907-49, serving on the engineering faculty and initiating UT's first cheerleading program. At age 95, he attended Illinois' 1973 Homecoming game and joined the Illini cheerleading squad on the sidelines. Matthews died in 1978 at the age of 99.

Illini Legend

Dr. Jacob Shell

Dr. Jacob Kinzer Shell's tenure as the University of Illinois' athletic director from 1898-1901 was generally accented by achievement. Though football and track successes were minimal, the baseball team won a Western Conference (Big Ten) championship in 1900, the school's first ever. Shell also had a hand in welcoming Indiana and Iowa into the conference, and he helped establish the Urbana-Champaign campus as the training quarters for the Chicago Cubs. During his undergraduate days at the University of Pennsylvania in the early 1880s and during his graduate career at Swarthmore College, Shell was a fantastic athlete. "Doc" starred in football, baseball, gymnastics, track, lacrosse, boxing, and won America's middleweight wrestling championship. Shell resigned his post as UI's director of athletics on May 29, 1901, opening the door for his successor, George Huff. He was one of the founders of the American Athletic Union, serving 34 years for the AAU in numerous capacities. Shell died on December 10, 1940, at the age of 78.

Illini Lists

ALL-TIME BIG TEN CHAMPIONSHIPS
(Men's and Women's Sports)
(Through 2000-01 season)

1.	Michigan	271
2.	ILLINOIS	214
3.	Ohio State	155
	Wisconsin	155
5.	Indiana	153
6.	Minnesota	124
7.	Iowa	95
8.	Chicago	73
9.	Michigan State	65
10.	Purdue	63
11.	Northwestern	59
12.	Penn State	19

ILLINI LORE

University of Illinois seniors first wore caps and gowns at commencement exercises on June 12, 1901. The procession of students marched up Burrill Avenue to the old Armory. After diplomas were received, the seniors marched back to the lawn south of Green Street, where they sang "Auld Lang Syne." A total of 174 degrees were issued at the Urbana-Champaign campus in 1900-01, the most in the history of the University at the time.

1901-02

AMERICA'S TIME CAPSULE

Sept. 6, 1901	President McKinley was shot as he attended a reception in Buffalo. He died of his wounds eight days later.
Sept. 14, 1901	Forty-two-year-old Theodore Roosevelt took the presidential oath of office.
Jan. 1, 1902	Michigan defeated Stanford in the first Rose Bowl game at Pasadena, California.
May 12, 1902	Nearly 140,000 United Mine Workers went on strike.
May 20, 1902	Four years after the end of the Spanish-American War, Cuban independence was achieved.

ILLINI MOMENT

1901 football team

1901 ILLINOIS-CHICAGO FOOTBALL GAME —OCTOBER 19, 1901:

Coach Edgar Holt's Illini were unstoppable through the first four games of the season, rolling up 135 points. Their defensive play was particularly impressive, allowing nary a single opponent to penetrate their end zone. But now came the real test, against Coach Amos Alonzo Stagg's University of Chicago club, on the Maroons' home field. Nearly half of the crowd of 7,000 cheered on the Illini from the east bleachers. Though the first half was scoreless, the orange and blue controlled play with a steady ground game that ultimately accounted for 560 total yards by game's end. Illinois continued its dominance in the second half, with Jake Stahl following the blocks of lineman Justa Lindgren for UI's first two scores. The Illini won the game, 24-0, chalking up their fifth consecutive shutout. On the following Monday evening, the team was honored with a parade and a 24-gun salute and was presented with a key to the city of Urbana.

ILLINI SCRAPBOOK

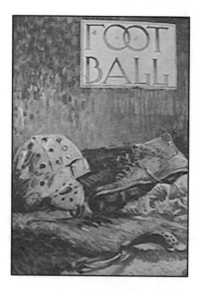

Artwork from the Illio *yearbook.*

Center Fred Lowenthal earned All-Western honors in 1901.

I Illini Item

ILLINOIS' 1901 FOOTBALL TEAM posted seven shutouts in 10 games, allowing an average of less than four points per game. Against Western Conference competition, Coach Edgar Holt's squad won four of six league games, allowing just 39 total points. Guard Jake Stahl and center Fred Lowenthal won All-Western honors for the Fighting Illini.

Illini Lists

ILLINOIS' ALL-TIME SINGLE-SEASON BATTING AVERAGES

- Darrin Fletcher, 1987 .497
- Ben Lewis, 1933 .473
- Boyd Bartley, 1943 .460
- John Toncoff, 1933 .460
- Jerry Jordan, 1926 .447
- Jake Stahl, 1903 .444
- Jake Stahl, 1901 .443
- Fred Major, 1926 .441
- Larry Sutton, 1991 .434
- Ruck Steger, 1950 .429

Jake Stahl in action.

Illini Legend

GARLAND "JAKE" STAHL

During his era, Garland "Jake" Stahl was a man among boys at the University of Illinois. He was an All-America tackle in football, leading the Illini to 25 victories in his last three seasons on the gridiron. As a catcher on the baseball team, Stahl played a level above his teammates, averaging well over .400 from the plate the last three years. His 400-foot, bases-loaded home run against Michigan, May 9, 1903, off the tree in deep right center field at Illinois Field remains as one of the most legendary single plays in Illini baseball history. Stahl's senior-year batting average of .444 stood as a school record for 23 seasons. But as it turned out, that was only the beginning. Stahl took his act into major league baseball, enjoying a magnificent career. Included among the highlights of his eight-year career were two World Series championships with the Boston Red Sox (1903 and 1912), the last one as the manager, and an American League-leading 10 home runs in 1910. Stahl died on September 18, 1922, at the age of 43.

ILLINI LORE

On April 6, 1902, University of Illinois president Andrew Sloan Draper was seriously injured when he was thrown from his horse-drawn carriage. Three days later, doctors amputated his leg. President Draper didn't return to the university until October 1.

AMERICA'S TIME CAPSULE

Oct. 11, 1902	Lawrence Auchterlonie won the U.S. Open golf tournament.
Nov. 4, 1902	In congressional elections, the Republicans maintained their Senate majority over the Democrats, 57-33.
Jan. 22, 1903	A 99-year lease was signed by the United States and Columbia giving America sovereignty over a canal zone in Panama.
July 4, 1903	President Roosevelt sent a message around the world and back in 12 minutes through use of the first Pacific communications cable.
Aug. 8, 1903	Great Britain defeated the United States to capture tennis's Davis Cup.

ILLINI MOMENT

Illinois' 1902 football squad

ILLINOIS-OHIO STATE FOOTBALL GAME- NOVEMBER 15, 1902:

Tying a game, it has been said, is like kissing your sister. But Illinois' 0-0 stalemate with Ohio State in the first-ever engagement between the sister institutions was more like a spat. The Buckeyes had not yet become a member of the Big Ten, though they regularly played against conference schools. The Illinois contingent traveled to Columbus expecting an easy victory, since OSU had been pummeled by Michigan earlier in the year by an 86-0 count. Several times during the game, Illinois threatened the Buckeye end zone, but fumbles and two failed field goals did in the Illini. Coach Edgar Holt's Illini squad wound up the season with a 10-2-1 record, placing fourth in the conference behind Michigan's famous point-a-minute team.

Garland "Jake" Stahl, shown at bat, connected on one of the most famous home runs in Illini history, May 9, 1903. With the bases loaded, Stahl's grand slam belt was estimated at approximately 400 feet, into a tree in deep right center field.

Four-year-old Red Grange.

ON A SEASONABLY MILD DAY—June 13,1903—at their home in Forksville, Pennsylvania, Sadie Grange gave birth to a bouncing baby boy named Harold Edward Grange. Little did she know that the youngster would grow up to revolutionize the sport of football.

Illini Legend

Edgar Holt

Before the turn of the century, it was Harvard and Princeton who were two of the kingpins of college football. So, thought Illini athletic director George Huff, why not hire an Eastern coach to turn the sluggish Illinois football program into a winner? Huff's choice was Edgar Garrison Holt, a product of both the Harvard and Princeton systems. Holt had toiled as a lineman during his playing days, so he spent the bulk of his time tutoring UI front-line players such as "Jake" Stahl, Fred Lowenthal, and Justa Lindgren. In two seasons, 1901 and '02, Holt guided Illinois to its first two winning records in Big Ten play and a cumulative record of 18-4-1. Holt died April 19, 1924 at the age of 49.

Illini Lists

MOST BIG TEN CHAMPIONSHIPS BY A SCHOOL IN A SINGLE SPORT
(Through 2000-01 season)

1.	Michigan (football)	40
2.	Michigan (men's tennis)	36
3.	Wisconsin (men's cross country)	34
4.	Michigan (baseball)	31
	Michigan (men's swimming)	31
6.	ILLINOIS (men's fencing)	30
	Michigan (men's track)	30

1951 Big Ten Championship fencing team.

I L L I N I L O R E

. . . .

The University of Illinois' new $289,000 Chemical Building opened to students September 28, 1902. At that time, the 165,000-square-foot facility was said to be the largest building in the country devoted exclusively to chemistry. An addition was made to the structure in 1916, and on May 13, 1939, the laboratory was named in honor of longtime department head William Noyes.

1903-04

AMERICA'S TIME CAPSULE

Oct. 13, 1903	The Boston Red Stockings defeated the Pittsburgh Pirates in baseball's first World Series.
Dec. 17, 1903	Orville and Wilbur Wright made their first successful flight in a crude flying machine at Kitty Hawk, North Carolina.
Jan. 4, 1904	The Supreme Court ruled that Puerto Ricans are not aliens and must not be refused admission into the United States.
June 1, 1904	President Theodore Roosevelt was nominated as the Republican candidate at the national convention in Chicago.
July 6, 1904	The Democrats convened in St. Louis to nominate Alton Parker for president.

ILLINI MOMENT

ILLINI "9" CAPTURES CONFERENCE TITLE:

Nobody gave Coach George Huff's 1904 Fighting Illini baseball team much of a chance to defend the Big Ten title it had won the season before. After all, how would Illinois ever replace such stalwarts as Jake Stahl and Jimmy Cook, both .400 hitters in 1903? Huff's club played a very ambitious nonconference schedule but lost just one of 13 games. In conference play, the Illini battled Wisconsin for the top spot, ultimately outdistancing the Badgers with an impressive 11-3 record. The title clincher came on May 28th when Illinois defeated the University of Chicago, 11-0, behind the two-hit pitching of Frank Pfeffer and two home runs by Captain Roy Parker. The leading Illini hitters in 1904 were left fielder Claude Rothgeb at .351 and third baseman R.L. Pitts at .350.

(seated, far right) Frank Pfeffer pitched a two-hitter in Illinois' title clincher against Chicago.

ILLINI SCRAPBOOK

Baseball captain Roy Parker

Football coach George Woodruff

Harry Gill

HARRY GILL, who debuted as the Fighting Illini track and field coach in 1904, was America's premier decathlon performer in 1900. A native Canadian, Gill defeated three-time United States champion Ellery Clark in a one-on-one contest in New York to earn that distinction.

Illini Legend

Claude Rothgeb

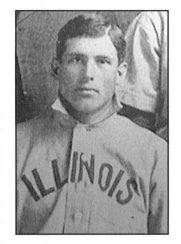

One way to gauge the accomplishments of an athlete is to measure the success of his teams. During the 1903-04 season, the most successful Fighting Illini teams were found over at Illinois Field. The Illinois football teams, though they never were champions, racked up a cumulative record of 44 victories, 15 losses, and four ties from 1900 through 1904. In baseball, the 1904 and '05 clubs were 37-9. The sparkplug of those teams was a talented young man named Claude Rothgeb. As an end for the football squad, Rothgeb lettered four times and served as captain of the 1903 team. So outstanding was he that during his senior year he became only the third Illini gridder to earn All-American honors. As the left fielder for George Huff's baseball team, Rothgeb was the leading hitter (.351) for the 1904 Big Ten champs and the captain of the 1905 conference runner-up. Rothgeb also lettered four times for the Illini track team as a sprinter and shot putter, winning a Big Ten individual title in the latter event.

Illini Lists

MULTIPLE LETTERWINNERS (1878-1925)

- A.W. Merrifield   11 letters (baseball & track)
- Claude Rothgeb   10 letters (football, baseball & track)
- Burt Ingwersen   9 letters (football, basketball & baseball)
- James Cook   8 letters (football & baseball)
- Don Sweney   8 letters (football & track)
- Charles Carney   7 letters (football & basketball)
- Ira Carrithers   7 letters (football, baseball & track)
- George Huff   7 letters (football & baseball)
- Arthur Johnston   7 letters (football & baseball)
- Garland "Jake" Stahl   7 letters (football & baseball)
- Lawrence Walquist   7 letters (football & basketball)

Ira Carrithers

ILLINI LORE

On August 23, 1904, Dr. Edmund James, president of Northwestern University, was elected to the University of Illinois presidency. James replaced President Andrew Draper who resigned in January to accept a position as Commissioner of Education for the state of New York. By 1909, James had become a national figure, and by 1916, he was being discussed as a candidate for the presidency of the United States.

AMERICA'S TIME CAPSULE

Oct. 8, 1904	Automobile racing as an organized sport began with the Vanderbilt Cup race on Long Island, New York.
Oct. 27, 1904	The first section of New York City's subway system was opened to the public.
Nov. 8, 1904	Theodore Roosevelt was reelected president of the United States, defeating Alton Parker by nearly two million votes.
April 17, 1905	The Supreme Court found a New York state law that limited maximum hours for workers unconstitutional, ruling that such a law interfered with the right to free contract.
May 5, 1905	Boston's Cy Young threw baseball's first-ever perfect game, retiring 27 consecutive Philadelphia Athletic batters.

ILLINI MOMENT

1904 football squad

ILLINI TIE STAGG'S MAROONS:

Illinois' 1904 football team was coached by Justa Lindgren, Arthur Hall, Fred Lowenthal, and Clyde Mathews who led the Illini to a perfect record through their first seven games. On October 29, hundreds of Illini fans filled UC's Marshall Field to witness the Illini vs. Coach Amos Alonzo Stagg's Chicago Maroons. The Illini clearly outplayed their hosts in the first half, but neither team was able to score. In the third quarter, Illinois made its only mistake of the game as quarterback William Taylor fumbled the ball on his own 27-yard line. Chicago's left tackle, Glenn Parry, gathered up the loose pigskin, and with an extra-point kick, gave the Maroons a 6-0 lead. On the ensuing kickoff, Illinois' Claude Rothgeb ran the ball back to Chicago's 20-yard line. Charles Fairweather then scored a five-point touchdown and Charles Moynihan kicked the point for a 6-6 final score. Illinois continued its aggressive play against the highly favored Maroons, but time ran out and the game ended in a tie. Back in Champaign, Illini fans frolicked in the streets until midnight.

"Pushball" was a hotly contested event between the various UI classes.

Claude Rothgeb

COACH GEORGE HUFF'S Fighting Illini baseball team got only one hit against Wisconsin, May 27, 1905, but they made the most of it and defeated the Badgers, 1-0, at Illinois Field. In the second inning, clean-up hitter Claude Rothgeb smacked a curve ball far into right field. By the time the Badger fielders retrieved it from the bleachers and relayed it home, Rothgeb had rounded the bases, crossed the plate, and was sitting on the bench. The victory secured second place in the Big Ten standings for Illinois behind eventual champion Michigan.

Illini Legend

Harry Gill

It was a Canadian who brought the University of Illinois to prominence as an American collegiate track power. During a 29-year coaching career at Urbana-Champaign from 1904-29, then again from 1931-33, Harry Gill's Fighting Illini churned out an amazing 19 Big Ten championships—11 titles outdoors and eight indoors. On the national scene, Gill's teams won NCAA titles in 1921 and 1927, plus three Spalding Cups, at an annual invitational meet that attracted the nation's top colleges. The height of Gill's coaching career came in 1924 when his Illinois athletes—Harold Osborn, Dan Kinsey, and Horatio Fitch—scored more track and field points in the 1924 Summer Olympic Games than any other nation. In addition to those stars, Gill developed all-time greats Avery Brundage, longtime president of the International Olympic Federation, and "Tug" Wilson, former Olympic performer and Big Ten commissioner. Gill died in 1956 at the age of 80. The Harry Gill Company, a sporting goods manufacturer specializing in track equipment, remains in Urbana.

Illini Lists

POINTS SCORED BY HARRY GILL'S ILLINI TRACK TEAMS IN BIG TEN OUTDOOR MEETS (1904-29)

- ILLINOIS   914 pts
- Michigan   587 1/3 pts
- Chicago   541 1/2 pts
- Wisconsin   514 1/2 pts
- Iowa   328 pts
- Ohio State   211 pts
- Minnesota   186 1/3 pts
- Northwestern   151 1/2 pts
- Purdue   136 1/3 pts
- Indiana   101 1/2 pts

One of Coach Harry Gill's championship relay teams.

ILLINI LORE

Around 1894, University of Illinois students began displaying their individual class colors by wearing ribbons on their shirts around campus. There was great disdain for the lowly freshmen, especially from the sophomores. Consequently, the two classes engaged in an annual physical battle called the "class rush." The reigning champions defended a greased flagpole from which a flag of their class colors flew. As many as 300-400 students locked arms and encircled the pole, while the challengers used any means to remove their opponent's flag. University officials eventually channeled the students' energy toward a game called push-ball, which only resulted in more injuries than the color rush. Another contest, called the sack rush, was then instituted, but eventually in 1914, Illinois students discontinued these dangerous traditional rivalry games.

1905-1914

1905-06

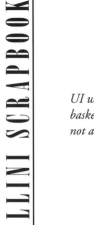
AMERICA'S TIME CAPSULE

Sept. 22, 1905   Willie Anderson won his third consecutive U.S. Open golf tournament championship.

Oct. 14, 1905   The New York Giants defeated the Philadelphia Athletics to win baseball's second World Series.

Feb. 23, 1906   Tommy Burns won the world heavyweight boxing title.

April 7, 1906   The first successful transatlantic wireless transmission was made from New York City to a receiving station in Ireland.

April 18, 1906   A massive earthquake rocked San Francisco, as some people were killed and more than 500,000 others were left homeless.

ILLINI MOMENT

Illinois' very first basketball team

ILLINOIS' FIRST BASKETBALL GAME:

The first official intercollegiate basketball game occurred at the University of Illinois some 15 years after it was introduced in Springfield, Massachusetts by Dr. James Naismith. Three hundred twenty-five fans, many of whom were probably watching the game for the very first time, saw their Fighting Illini defeat Indiana, 27-24. When a goal was made, a spectator had to retrieve the ball out of the closed basket so that the game could resume. The Illini starting lineup featured Roy Riley at the center position, Floyd Talmage and V.C. Kays at the forwards, and E.G. Ryan and Arthur Ray at the guards. Indiana jumped off to a 5-0 lead, before Talmage finally scored Illinois' historic first basket. Talmage continued his sharp-shooting, scoring seven field goals and two free throws for 16 of UI's 27 total points.

UI women also played basketball in 1906, though not at the varsity level.

1906 water polo squad

I Illini Item

THE UNIVERSITY OF ILLINOIS' WATER POLO TEAM (later called water basketball) made its debut on February 17, 1906, by defeating the University of Chicago, 2-1. For the next 33 years, the Illini dominated the sport in the Midwest, winning 10 Big Ten championships and registering a dual-meet record of 95-39-3. The sport discontinued competition at Illinois during the war years of 1941-46 and was never resumed.

Illini Lists

MARCHING ILLINI BAND HIGHLIGHTS

- June 6, 1872: The UI band performed for the first time
- February, 1892: UI Military Band presented its first annual concert
- March 3, 1906: "Illinois Loyalty" first performed
- Fall, 1910: Debut of "Oskee-Wow-Wow" and "Hail to the Orange"
- Oct. 15, 1910: Band first formed "Block I"
- Oct. 15, 1921: Band sang "Hail to the Orange" a capella for the first time
- Nov. 4, 1922: First mass bands performance at Illinois
- Nov. 3, 1923: Band first formed the word "Illini"
- Oct. 30, 1926: First performance of Chief Illiniwek
- Sept. 11, 1943: Idelle Stitch became first female to portray Chief Illiniwek
- Sept. 1, 1948: Austin Harding, director of bands, retired, ending 43-year career at UI
- Jan. 1, 1952: UI band's first performance in Tournament of Roses Parade
- September, 1970: First female members of Marching Illini
- June, 1976: Everett Kissinger ended 27-year career as director of Marching Illini; succeeded by Gary Smith
- Fall, 1976: Debut of Illinettes, Big Ten's first women's dance team
- September, 1977: Deborah Soumar became first female drum major in Big Ten
- Winter, 1980: First collegiate band to use a giant school flag

Illini Legend

Thatcher Guild

It's a name even the most avid Fighting Illini fan doesn't know. But if the University of Illinois ever establishes an athletic Hall of Fame, Thatcher Howland Guild's name needs to be included. Guild didn't score any touchdowns or hit any home runs, but his contribution to the University—"Illinois Loyalty"—has been sung thousands of times at every home Illini football and basketball game for more than 90 years. Much like Schubert's "Unfinished Symphony," Guild brought the lyrics and melody to the Urbana-Champaign campus with him from his alma mater, Brown University. His original first line ran: We're loyal to you, men of Brown. A newly hired English instructor, Guild took his tune to UI's longtime band director Austin Harding, and the two men refined the now legendary melody. After more than six months of work, "Illinois Loyalty" was finally performed before the UI student body at Harding's First Anniversary Concert on March 3, 1906. Guild died at the tender age of 35 in 1914 from a heart attack, during a hot summer's day tennis match.

ILLINI LORE

On October 16, 1905, the University of Illinois' Women's Building was dedicated. Designed by the celebrated architectural firm of McKim, Mead, and White, it became a stately element along the University's principal mall. The $330,000 structure, now known as the English Building, features a central colonnade and twin-domed towers.

1906-07

AMERICA'S TIME CAPSULE

Oct. 14, 1906	The Chicago White Sox beat the Chicago Cubs to win the third World Series.
Nov. 9, 1906	Theodore Roosevelt became the first president to travel abroad, journeying to Panama to inspect the progress on the Panama Canal.
Dec. 24, 1906	Reginald Fessenden made the first known radio broadcast of voice and music from his Branch Rock, Massachusetts experiment station.
Feb. 20, 1907	President Roosevelt signed the Immigration Act of 1907, restricting immigration by Japanese laborers.
March 21, 1907	U.S. Marines were sent to Honduras to quell a political disturbance.

ILLINI MOMENT

The 1907 Western Conference champs.

ILLINOIS' FIRST BIG TEN TRACK & FIELD TITLE:

The University of Illinois track and field team had traveled a rocky road during the first three seasons of the Harry Gill coaching era, finishing no higher than fifth in the Western Conference championship outdoor meet. So, on that cold first day of June, 1907, the Illini could only be cautiously optimistic about what would ultimately turn out to be the greatest day in the history of the sport at Illinois. Illini football star Wilbur Burroughs was the star of the day, capturing individual titles in both the shot put and the hammer throw and accounting for nearly one-third of the team's points. Billy May finished first in the 100-yard dash and second in the 220-yard dash, which gave the Illini eight more valuable points, allowing Illinois to edge host Chicago, 31-29, for the school's very first conference championship in track and field.

ILLINI SCRAPBOOK

"G" Huff encourages his Red Sox squad during an exhibition game at Illinois Field.

Jake Stahl (left) and George Huff as members of the Red Sox.

Louis Cook filled in as Illini baseball coach during George Huff's brief stint with the Boston Americans.

I Illini Item

THE ILLINI BASEBALL TEAM won its second consecutive Western Conference title in 1907, capturing all seven of its league games. On April 14, just three days before the regular season was to begin, Coach George Huff accepted an offer from the Boston Americans to manage that professional club, so Louis Cook hastily took over for Huff to direct Illinois to its fourth conference baseball title in the last five years. After only 13 days in Boston, Huff sent a telegram to UI President Edmund James, stating, "Have received my release. Will be back Saturday. This is final and positive."

Illini Lists

ILLINI COACHES WITH THE LONGEST REIGNS
(through 2001-02 season)

- Gary Wieneke, cross country   35 years (1967-02)#
- Ed Manley, swimming   33 years (1920-52)
- Bob Zuppke, football   29 years (1913-41)
- Leo Johnson, track   28 years (1938-65)
- Max Garret, fencing   27 years (1941-72)*
- Lee Eilbracht, baseball   27 years (1952-78)
- Harry Gill, track   26 years (1904-29)
- George Huff, baseball   24 years (1896-1919)
- Don Sammons, swimming   23 years (1971-93)
- Ralph Fletcher, golf   23 years (1944-66)
- Leo Johnson, cross country   23 years (1938-60)

*UI did not sponsor fencing from 1943-46 and Garret did not coach in 1970
#Still active as UI coach

Coach Gary Wieneke

Illini Legend

AVERY BRUNDAGE

He was best known for his 20-year reign as the controversial president of the International Olympic Committee (IOC), but few know that Avery Brundage began his career in the world of sports at the University of Illinois as an athlete. Brundage, a native of Detroit, earned varsity letters with the Fighting Illini basketball team and track squad. He was the center for the 1908 basketball squad that won 20 of 26 games, and an outstanding shot putter and discus thrower for the Illini thinclads, winning an individual title in the latter event at the 1909 Western Conference track meet. Brundage competed in the 1912 Olympic decathlon with the legendary Jim Thorpe. In 1916 and 1918, he won the national all-around decathlon championship. Brundage served as president of the Amateur Athletic Union from 1928-35 and for the U.S. Olympic Committee from 1929-33. As the IOC's most famous administrator, he fought a fierce battle to maintain the Olympic ideals of amateurism. A longtime member of the UI President's Club, he established a scholarship bearing his name in 1974. Brundage died of a heart attack May 8, 1975, at the age of 87. His papers in the University Archives continue to attract scholars from around the world.

ILLINI LORE

On May 18, 1907, the last saloon in Champaign-Urbana closed. The editor of the University of Illinois' *Alumni Quarterly* applauded the move. "Though it cannot be expected that the closing of the saloons will put an end to drinking in the two cities," the *Quarterly* said, "it must, in a large degree, mitigate the effect. With the saloons gone, Champaign and Urbana are undoubtedly safer places for young men than they have previously been."

1907-08

AMERICA'S TIME CAPSULE

Sept. 12, 1907	The *Lusitania*, the world's largest steamship, completed its maiden voyage between Ireland and New York.
Oct. 12, 1907	The Chicago Cubs swept the World Series from the Detroit Tigers.
Nov. 16, 1907	Oklahoma became the 46th state.
Dec. 6, 1907	Three hundred sixty-one miners were killed in a West Virginia coal mine explosion.
May 10, 1908	Mother's Day was first celebrated.

ILLINI MOMENT

The 1908 Fighting Illini baseball team won 11 of 14 conference games en route to its third consecutive league title.

ILLINI DEFEAT MINNESOTA TO WIN TITLE:

Winning Western Conference baseball titles had become commonplace for the University of Illinois, but the game that clinched the Illini's 1908 championship was one of the most decisive victories ever registered at Illinois Field. Minnesota, which eventually wound up as the conference's runner-up, was the Illini victim on that 23rd day of May. To say that Illinois merely won that day would be an understatement, for the 16-0 romp over the Gophers was never competitive. Pitcher Ernie Ovitz not only blanked Minnesota on the mound, allowing just one hit, he also scored runs in all four of his official times at the plate. The deadly combination of 14 Illini hits and nine Gopher errors resulted in an average of two runs every inning and the most lopsided shutout victory in four conference seasons.

Five University of Illinois athletes were members of the 1912 United States Olympic Track & Field Team. Illini Olympians included (left to right) Avery Brundage (lettered at UI in 1908-09), Jack Case (1912-13), Frank Murphy (1910-11-12) and Ed Lindberg (1906-07-08-09), and (seated) Perry MacGillivray (attended UI from 1911-12, but did not letter).

Coach Fletcher Lane

Illini Legend

Arthur Hall

The architect of the University of Illinois' first-ever Big Ten football title was Coach Arthur Hall, an Illini athlete himself from 1898-1900. Hall's greatest season came in 1910 when his Fighting Illini team became only the second conference team, and only the 13th in college football history, to be undefeated and unscored upon. In six seasons at Illinois from 1907-12, Hall coached the Illini gridders to a record of 27-10-3. Incredibly, coaching football wasn't Hall's only profession. His "day" job was practicing law in Danville, Illinois. At the end of the 1912 season, Hall decided that the pace was too hectic, so he resigned his position at the University of Illinois and went into law full time. Athletic Director George Huff replaced Hall with the immortal Bob Zuppke. Artie Hall served as Vermilion County (Illinois) probate court judge until his retirement in 1954. He was also instrumental in developing the state of Illinois' "hard road" system. Hall died in 1955 at the age of 86.

Illini Lists

ILLINOIS' MOST DOMINANT FOOTBALL TEAMS

- 1910 7-0-0, outscored its opponents 89-0
- 1914 7-0-0, outscored its opponents 224-22
- 1915 5-0-2, outscored its opponents 183-25
- 1923 8-0-0, outscored its opponents 136-20
- 1927 7-0-1, outscored its opponents 152-24
- 1951 9-0-1, outscored its opponents 220-83

(left to right) Ray Eliot, Arthur Hall and Bob Zuppke were architects of the six most dominant football teams in Illini history.

ILLINI LORE

On November 4 and 5, 1907, the University of Illinois dedicated its new $152,000 auditorium, which provided an adequate place for convocations, lectures, concerts, and other large gatherings. Constructed of brick and Indiana limestone, the facility was remodeled in 1915 to correct its accoustical deficiencies. The structure was rededicated as the Foellinger Auditorium April 26, 1985, named for benefactor Helene Foellinger ('32). Among those who have performed or lectured at the auditorium are John Phillip Sousa (1909), Amelia Earhart (1935), Duke Ellington (1948), and Eleanor Roosevelt (1956).

1908-09

AMERICA'S TIME CAPSULE

Oct. 1, 1908	The Model T was introduced by Henry Ford.
Nov. 3, 1908	William Howard Taft was elected president of the United States.
April 6, 1909	Robert Peary reached the North Pole.
July 12, 1909	Congress proposed an amendment to authorize a national income tax.
July 27, 1909	Orville Wright set a flight-duration record of just more than one hour.

ILLINI MOMENT

GILL'S MEN ROMP AWAY WITH TRACK TITLE:

On June 5, 1909, at Chicago's Marshall Field, Coach Harry Gill directed the University of Illinois track and field squad to its second Western Conference title in three years. Though it was the official conference meet, nonconference schools such as Stanford, Michigan Agricultural College, and Notre Dame also participated in the festivities. Illinois won three individual firsts, including Roger Stephenson in the broad jump (22'6 1/4"), Lud Washburn in the high jump (5'10"), and Avery Brundage in the discus throw (43'2 1/2"). The meet was clinched by the Illini mile relay team. Altogether, Illinois athletes scored in 11 of the 15 events, claiming four firsts, four seconds, and four thirds.

ILLINI SCRAPBOOK

The University of Illinois band performed often at the Auditorium.

THOUGH PURDUE denied Illinois its fourth consecutive Western Conference baseball title, the 1909 season was nevertheless considered a grand success. The Boilermakers' 7-2 conference record was just a few percentage points better than the Illini's 9-3 league mark. Coach George Huff issued a challenge to Purdue to determine a true champion, but the Boilermakers reportedly refused.

Illini Legend

Forest Van Hook

Forest Van Hook, captain of the 1908 Illini football team, was the first University of Illinois athlete to earn All-Western honors each of the three seasons he lettered. An outstanding guard for coach Arthur Hall, Van Hook and his teammates had their best performance in 1908 during his senior season. The 5-1-1 Illini lost their only game, 11-6, at the University of Chicago and eventually placed second in the Western Conference standings to the undefeated Maroons. Van Hook was a burly, dark-haired man weighing around 230 pounds, a huge person in those days. Walter Eckersall, longtime sports editor of the *Chicago Tribune* and college football's most noted critic, said that despite his size, "Van" could have starred at any position on the field. Van Hook was a medical general practitioner in his hometown of Mount Pulaski until his death in 1937 from diabetes at the age of 52.

Illini Lists

BEST ILLINI DEFENSIVE PERFORMANCES (VS. BIG TEN BASKETBALL OPPONENTS)

- 1909 Illinois 30, Indiana 2
- 1909 Illinois 35, Northwestern 4
- 1913 Illinois 35, Iowa 9
- 1915 Illinois 27, Purdue 8
- 1914 Illinois 21, Ohio State 10
- 1920 Illinois 41, Michigan 14
- 1921 Illinois 17, Wisconsin 9
- 1926 Illinois 17, Minnesota 8
- 1993 Illinois 52, Michigan State 39
- 2000 Illinois 51, Penn State 50

1913 basketball team

ILLINI LORE

The University of Illinois observed the 100th anniversary of the birth of Abraham Lincoln on February 8, 1909, with a campus-wide celebration. The exercises included a convocation, an exhibit of Lincoln memorabilia, and addresses on several aspects of Lincoln's service as U.S. president.

1909-10

AMERICA'S TIME CAPSULE

Oct. 16, 1909   The Pittsburgh Pirates defeated the Detroit Tigers in the sixth World Series.

Feb. 6, 1910   The Boy Scouts of America organization was chartered by Chicago publisher William Boyce.

March 16, 1910   Auto racer Barney Oldfield set a land speed record of 133 miles per hour.

June 19, 1910   Spokane, Washington became the first city to celebrate Father's Day.

July 4, 1910   Jack Johnson successfully defended his world heavyweight boxing championship against Jim Jeffries.

ILLINI MOMENT

John Buzick pitched all 17 innings in Illinois' baseball marathon vs. Chicago.

ILLINI "9" BEATS CHICAGO IN 17-INNING MARATHON:

The May 20, 1910, baseball matchup between the Universities of Illinois and Chicago was described by the UI campus newspaper as "...the most brilliant game ever played on Illinois Field." When the three-hour, twenty-minute marathon ended, Coach George Huff's Illini won their 10th consecutive game, a streak that would eventually climax at 14-0 and result in a Western Conference championship. Illinois' John Buzick went the entire distance on the mound, as did his counterpart, UC's Pat Page. With the score tied at one run apiece, Page lost the game in the bottom of the 17th inning when Illinois' Ray Thomas led off with a double, moved to third on a sacrifice by E.B. Righter, then scored when Page uncorked a wild pitch. The Illini went on to win their final four games and wound up as the first conference baseball team in history to finish with an unblemished overall record.

The University of Illinois' YMCA building finished in 1909 is shown here during the 1930s.

ILLINI SCRAPBOOK

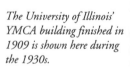

Frank Murphy pole vaulted to a height of 12' 4 7/8" at the 1910 conference meet and was the only Illini athlete to win an event.

I Illini Item

THE FIRST WESTERN CONFERENCE outdoor track and field meet held at a site other than Chicago came on June 4, 1910, at Champaign. Though Illinois was the top-finishing conference team, it placed third behind Notre Dame and Stanford. It wasn't until l 1926 that only conference teams were allowed to participate in the outdoor championship meet.

Illini Lists

HOMECOMING THRILLERS

- Oct. 15, 1910 — Illinois 3, Chicago 0
  (UI's first-ever Homecoming game, the nation's first of its kind)
- Nov. 3, 1923— Illinois 7, Chicago 0
  (UI's first-ever game at Memorial Stadium; Red Grange scores touchdown)
- Oct. 18, 1924 — Illinois 39, Michigan 14
  (Dedication game of Memorial Stadium)
- Nov. 4, 1939 — Illinois 16, Michigan 7
  (UI beat UM and future Heisman Trophy winner–Tom Harmon)
- Oct. 27, 1956 — Illinois 20, Michigan State 13
  (UI beat ninth-ranked Spartans)
- Oct. 26, 1968 — Ohio State, Illinois 24
  (No. 2 Buckeyes score winning TD with 1:30 left)
- Oct. 15, 1983 — Illinois 17, Ohio State 13
  (Illini beat No. 6 Buckeyes)
- Oct. 20, 1990 — Illinois 15, Michigan State 13
  (Doug Higgins kicks game-winning field goal with :42 left)

Illini Legend

Clarence Williams & Elmer Ekblaw

Clarence Williams (left) and Elmer Ekblaw (right) aren't familiar names to even the most ardent Fighting Illini fans, but their accomplishment back in 1910 definitely earns them a niche in University of Illinois history. Williams, better known as "Dab," and Ekblaw, the editor of the *Daily Illini*, conceived the very first Homecoming during the fall of 1909. They presented the idea to Shield and Trident, a senior honorary society, then called upon UI President Edmund James and Dean Thomas Arkle Clark. A year later, during that first Homecoming weekend—October 14-16, 1910—more than 1,500 UI graduates returned to campus, nearly one-third of the school's alumni. The culmination of the inaugural Homecoming weekend was a 3-0 victory by the Illini football team over the University of Chicago. Illinois' Otto Seiler kicked a field goal to provide the final margin.

ILLINI LORE

On August 10, 1909, the cornerstone of Lincoln Hall was laid. President William Abbott of the Board of Trustees presided. Three and a half years later on February 12, 1913, the 104th anniversary of Abraham Lincoln's birth, Lincoln Hall was dedicated by the University of Illinois.

1910-11

AMERICA'S TIME CAPSULE

Nov. 8, 1910	In congressional elections, the Democratic party took control of Congress for the first time in 16 years.
Nov. 14, 1910	The first successful attempt of a naval aircraft launching from the deck of a warship was made off the cruiser *Birmingham*.
March 25, 1911	One hundred forty-six persons perished in a New York City industrial fire.
May 11, 1911	The Supreme Court ordered Standard Oil dissolved because it violated the antitrust law.
May 30, 1911	Ray Harroun won the first Indianapolis 500 automobile race.

ILLINI MOMENT

1910 football team

1910 BIG TEN FOOTBALL CHAMPIONS:

The University of Illinois football team's unbeaten, unscored upon season of 1910 is a feat that's been duplicated only 19 times in the history of college football. Though Coach Arthur Hall's squad wasn't an offensive juggernaut, averaging just 13 points a game, it was an immovable force when it came to playing defense. In fact, their opponents rarely crossed Illinois' 50-yard line the entire season! The Illini opened their campaign with easy nonconference victories over Millikin and Drake before the school's historic first Homecoming game on October 15th, a 3-0 win over Chicago. Two weeks later, Illinois shut out Purdue, then blanked Indiana and Northwestern on consecutive Saturdays to wrap up the school's very first Western Conference title. Otto Seiler kicked his third game-winning field goal of the year in the season finale at home against Syracuse to give the Illini a perfect 7-0 record.

Action from UI's first Homecoming game.

ILLINI SCRAPBOOK

Harry Geist

I Illini Item

THE UNIVERSITY OF ILLINOIS won its first men's Western Conference gymnastics title on April 22, 1911 over host Chicago, 1104.50 to 1016.25. Illinois' Edward Styles, R.J. Roarke, Edward Hollman, and Harry Geist all captured individual championships.

Illini Lists

FOOTBALL GAMES WON IN FINAL MINUTE BY A FIELD GOAL

- Oct. 15, 1910: Illinois 3, Chicago 0 — Otto Seiler, 38 yards (exact time not available)
- Nov. 5, 1910:   Illinois 3, Indiana 0 — Otto Seiler (exact distance and time not available)
- Nov. 22, 1919: Illinois 9, Ohio State 7—— Bob Fletcher, 20 yards, :12 remaining
- Oct. 30, 1926: Ilinois 3, Pennsylvania 0 — Frosty Peters, 14 yards (exact time not available)
- Sept. 13, 1980: Illinois 20, Michigan State 17 — Mike Bass, 38 yards, :00 remaining
- Oct. 23, 1982: Illinois 29, Wisconsin 28 — Mike Bass, 46 yards, :03 remaining
- Oct. 5, 1985: Illinios 31, Ohio State 28 –– Chris White, 38 yards, :00 remaining
- Oct. 17, 1987: Illinois 16, Wisconsin 14 — Doug Higgins, 34 yards, :54 remaining
- Oct. 20, 1990: Illinois 15, Michigan State 13 — Doug Higgins, 48 yards,:59 remaining
- Oct. 22, 1991: Illinois 10, Ohio State 7 –– Chris Richardson, 41 yards, :36 remaining

Otto Seiler

Illini Legend

GLENN BUTZER

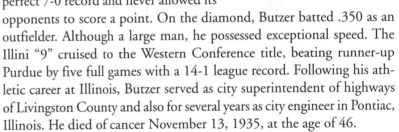

The premier performer during the 1910-11 athletic season at the University of Illinois was a young man whose teams tasted defeat only twice in 27 contests. Not only did Glenn Butzer captain Illinois' greatest football team ever in 1910, he also was the leading hitter on the 1911 Western Conference champion baseball team. On the gridiron, the Hillsdale, Illinois, native was a Walter Camp All-American as one of the game's finest linemen. The 1910 Illini football squad posted a perfect 7-0 record and never allowed its opponents to score a point. On the diamond, Butzer batted .350 as an outfielder. Although a large man, he possessed exceptional speed. The Illini "9" cruised to the Western Conference title, beating runner-up Purdue by five full games with a 14-1 league record. Following his athletic career at Illinois, Butzer served as city superintendent of highways of Livingston County and also for several years as city engineer in Pontiac, Illinois. He died of cancer November 13, 1935, at the age of 46.

ILLINI LORE

United States President William Howard Taft visited the University of Illinois on February 11, 1911. Taft arrived at 8:50 a.m. and was driven to Illinois Field, where he reviewed the cadet regiment. He then took a tour of the campus grounds, made a five-minute address at the Illinois Central Station, and left for Springfield, all in less than an hour.

1911-12

AMERICA'S TIME CAPSULE

Oct. 26, 1911	The American League's Philadelphia Athletics defeated the New York Giants to win the World Series.
Nov. 10, 1911	Andrew Carnegie established the Carnegie Corporation with an endowment of $125 million.
Feb. 14, 1912	Arizona was admitted to the union as the 48th U.S. state.
April 15, 1912	About 1,500 persons were killed when the British liner *Titanic* struck an iceberg and sank off the coast of Newfoundland.
July 22, 1912	The Olympic Games came to a close in Stockholm, Sweden. Among the American gold medal winners was decathlete Jim Thorpe.

ILLINI MOMENT

ILLINOIS WINS ITS FIRST SWIMMING TITLE:

The University of Illinois' men's swimming program had traditionally languished at or near the bottom of the Big Ten standings. But for the first three seasons of conference meets from 1911-13, Coach Ed Manley's Illini set the standard of excellence. Perhaps Illinois' greatest team was its 1912 squad, winner of the Western Conference championship by 17 points over second-place Northwestern. The Illini weren't a one-man team that year, but it would be difficult to overlook the monumental contribution by captain Bill Vosburgh. The Illini junior accounted for four individual titles—at 40, 100, 220, and 440 yards—and was the anchor of Illinois' championship relay squad. Vosburgh also took third place in a since-discontinued event called "plunge for distance."

This 1911 trophy was presented to Coach Ed Manley's Fighting Illini swimming team.

ILLINI SCRAPBOOK

High hurdles champion John Case.

EDWARD STYLES won his second consecutive individual all-around championship on April 11, 1911, leading the University of Illinois gymnastics squad to its second straight team title, 1174.75 to 957.25, over Wisconsin.

Illini Legend

ED MANLEY

For 41 years, the name Ed Manley was synonymous with University of Illinois swimming. He was lured to Champaign-Urbana by UI athletic director George Huff in 1912 from Springfield, Missouri, where he served as an aquatic instructor. Manley's Illini swimming teams captured Western Conference titles his first two years at Illinois and placed among the top five in the league 24 times. He also developed 20 conference champions in the sports of water polo and water basketball, and directed those teams to dual-meet victories nearly 75 percent of the time. Manley called 1930's performer Chuck Flachmann his greatest single performer. The veteran coach was honored posthumously in 1975 when the university named the historic Huff Gym natatorium the Edwin Manley Memorial Pool. Manley died in 1962 at the age of 75.

Illini Lists

ILLINOIS' BIG TEN MEN'S TEAM TITLES (THROUGH 2001-02)

- Fencing — 30 titles
- Men's Outdoor Track — 28 titles
- Baseball — 27 titles
- Men's Gymnastics — 22 titles
- Men's Indoor Track — 22 titles
- Wrestling — 16 titles
- Football — 15 titles
- Men's Basketball — 15 titles
- Men's Tennis — 14 titles

Illinois' 1912 track and field team

ILLINI LORE

In response to a request from the athletic department that its needs be given more consideration in future planning of the campus, Professor James White, supervising architect of the University of Illinois, submitted a new campus scheme to the Board of Trustees on October 5, 1911. Extensive additions to the university's land holdings were proposed, with particular view to providing playgrounds to compensate for the utilization of the area south of the Auditorium for building sites. White suggested that the entire tract of land between the campus and the Illinois Central railroad be acquired. Less than 10 years later, a portion of that tract was reserved for the construction of Memorial Stadium.

1912-13

AMERICA'S TIME CAPSULE

Oct. 14, 1912   Presidential candidate Theodore Roosevelt was shot in an assassination attempt in Milwaukee, Wisconsin.

Oct. 16, 1912   The Boston Red Sox won the ninth annual baseball World Series over the New York Giants.

Nov. 5, 1912   Democrat Woodrow Wilson won the U.S. presidency in a landslide victory.

May 31, 1913   The Seventeenth Amendment, providing for the popular election of U.S. senators, went into effect.

July 28, 1913   The U.S. won the Davis Cup tennis challenge for the first time in 11 years.

(front row, left to right) Elston, Gage, Lansche, Simison, Meyers (back row, left to right) Jones, Brunkow, Colombo, Leichsenring, Schroeder, Featherstone

ILLINI MOMENT

ILLINOIS WINS CONFERENCE WRESTLING CHAMPIONSHIP:

Illinois and Minnesota shared the title at the first-ever Western Conference Wrestling Championship, held April 19, 1913, at Madison, Wisconsin. Junior lightweight G.W. Schroeder, Illinois' captain, was his team's only individual winner, defeating Albert Gran of Iowa. Illini wrestlers M.F. Leichsenring, a middleweight, and J.B. Colombo, wrestling in the "special" division, both were runners-up at their weights. It was the final season of Illinois coach Alexander Elston's brief two-year career. The Illini wrestling program went on to dominate the conference through the 1930s, capturing 13 team titles, more than any other school.

ILLINI SCRAPBOOK

The UI's mammoth Armory nears completion.

I Illini Item

ILLINI SWIMMER BILL VOSBURGH wrapped up his sensational career at the 1913 Western Conference championships by capturing three individual titles and anchoring the first-place UI relay squad. During his three years at Illinois, Vosburgh claimed 10 individual conference championships and swam on two relay winners, an all-time record at that time.

Illini Lists

WINNINGEST MARGINS BY ILLINOIS FOOTBALL TEAMS

- 84 pts — Illinois 87, Ill. Wesleyan 3 (10/5/12)
- 80 pts — Illinois 80, Iowa 0 (11/27/1902)
- 79 pts — Illinois 79, Ill. College 0 (10/19/1895)
- 73 pts — Illinois 79, Ill. Normal 6 (9/16/44)
- 68 pts — Illinois 75, Rolla Mines 7 (10/9/15)
- 67 pts — Illinois 67, Butler 0 (10/3/42)

1912 Illini football team

Illini Legend

Ralph Chapman

His parents presented him with the distinguished appellation of Ralph Dwyer Clinton Chapman. His classmates knew him best as "Slouie." And Bob Zuppke, the legendary coach of the Fighting Illini, touted him as one of the greatest players he ever coached. Whatever you called him, it would be difficult not to call Ralph "Slouie" Chapman the University of Illinois' best athlete of his day. A native of Vienna, Illinois, the 180-pound Chapman was named by the legendary Walter Camp as a consensus All-American performer following his sensational senior season in 1914. The captain of Illinois' first national championship club was known for his speed, aggressiveness, and fighting spirit. Following his graduation in 1915, Chapman answered the call to arms when the United States entered World War I. He was wounded in action and underwent a series of operations. Upon his discharge, Chapman entered the brokerage business in Chicago, and he once served as vice president of the UI Foundation. Chapman died in 1969 at the age of 77.

ILLINI LORE

Ground was broken September 18, 1912, for the University of Illinois' Armory. Completed in 1915 at a cost of $702,000, the 98-foot-high roof is supported by 14 three-hinged arches. The outer section of military offices and classrooms was not completed until 1927. The Armory has been the site of Fighting Illini track meets since 1916.

1913-14

AMERICA'S TIME CAPSULE

| Oct. 11, 1913 | The Philadelphia Athletics defeated the New York Giants to capture the 10th annual World Series. |

Oct. 11, 1913 — The Philadelphia Athletics defeated the New York Giants to capture the 10th annual World Series.

Dec. 23, 1913 — President Woodrow Wilson reformed the American banking system by establishing the Federal Reserve System.

April 22, 1914 — Mexico severed diplomatic relations with the United States.

May 7, 1914 — A congressional resolution established the second Sunday in May to be celebrated as Mother's Day.

Aug. 15, 1914 — Australia defeated the United States to win the Davis Cup tennis challenge.

ILLINI MOMENT

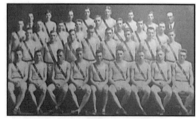

UI's 1914 track and field team

MEN'S TRACK TEAM DOMINATES CONFERENCE MEETS:

The University of Illinois track and field program had become a dominant force in the Western Conference under Coach Harry Gill. It was a rare occasion when the talented Illini lost a dual meet, and equally rare when they failed to win the conference title. During the 1914 season, Illinois performed at a level that allowed the team to cruise to both the indoor and outdoor conference championships. The Illini were a superbly balanced outfit, scoring points in nearly every event. Indoors at Evanston, Illinois waltzed to a nine-point victory over Wisconsin. Outdoors at Chicago, the Illini's winning margin was 22 points, led by Fred Henderson's victories in the 440- and 880-yard runs. "You have a wonderful track team," wrote Cornell coach John Moakley to Gill. And who could argue with that?

The 1914 baseball squad won the Big Ten title.

Artwork from the Illio.

WOMEN'S ATHLETICS

Walt Halas

I Illini Item

ILLINOIS' BASEBALL TEAM defeated league-leading Chicago, 4-3, on May 29, 1914, to win the conference title for the first time in three years. Illini pitcher Walt Halas, the older brother of football immortal George Halas, went the distance on the mound in a driving rainstorm.

Illini Legend

Illini Lists

ILLINI FOOTBALL COACHES' FIRST CONTRACTS

• Bob Zuppke	$1,500 (1913)
• Ray Eliot	$6,000 (1942)
• Pete Elliott	$18,000 (1960)
• Jim Valek	$18,500 (1967)
• Bob Blackman	$25,000 (1971)
• Gary Moeller	$35,000 (1977)
• Mike White	$50,000 (1980)
• John Mackovic	$70,000 (1988)
• Lou Tepper	$120,000 (1992)
• Ron Turner	$150,000 (1997)

Bob Zuppke's first UI coaching contract was one one-hundreth the size of Ron Turner's.

Bob Zuppke

Robert Carl Zuppke was introduced to the world in 1879, just 10 years after college football's very first game in New Brunswick, New Jersey. Thirty-five years later, the native of Berlin, Germany, would establish the University of Illinois as the home of the 1914 national football champions. By the time he retired in 1941, Zuppke's 29 teams captured three more national titles—1919, 1923, and 1927—and seven Big Ten crowns. He was football's most innovative coach, being credited with such originations as the huddle, the screen pass, and the "flea flicker." Among the stars Zuppke tutored were consensus All-Americans Chuck Carney, "Red" Grange, and Bernie Shively. He was honored in 1951 by being selected a charter member of college football's Hall of Fame. Zuppke died in 1957 at the age of 78. On November 12, 1966, Memorial Stadium's playing field was named in his honor.

ILLINI LORE

Edward A. Doisy, a 1914 graduate of the University of Illinois, shared the Nobel Prize in medicine in 1943 for isolating and determining the composition of vitamin K. This vitamin stimulates the production of prothrombin as a major element in blood clotting. Seventeen years earlier in 1926, Doisy isolated estrone, a sex hormone. He died October 23, 1986, at the age of 92.

1914-15

AMERICA'S TIME CAPSULE

Oct. 13, 1914   The National League's Boston Braves completed their sweep of the Philadelphia Athletics to win baseball's World Series.

Jan. 25, 1915   Alexander Graham Bell placed the first successful transcontinental telephone call from New York City to San Francisco.

Feb. 8, 1915   D. W. Griffith's famous motion picture, *Birth of a Nation*, opened in Los Angeles.

April 5, 1915   Jess Willard defeated Jack Johnson in 23 rounds to win the world heavyweight boxing title.

May 7, 1915   A German submarine sank the British steamship *Lusitania* and nearly 1,200 drowned.

ILLINI MOMENT

ILLINI BASKETBALL TEAM NIPS CHICAGO:

Home of the 1914-15 Illini basketball team.

On March 6, 1915, Illinois' undefeated basketball team faced its biggest challenge of the season, a game at the University of Chicago against the second-place Maroons. Coach Ralph Jones's Illini trailed by a score of 11-9 at the halftime intermission, and the teams traded baskets for most of the second half, with the lead going back and forth. Only a minute remained when Chicago star George Stevenson threw in a field goal, and the Maroon fans began to celebrate the apparent upset victory over their downstate rivals. However, the Illini regained the lead 30 seconds later when senior Frank Bane wove through the Chicago defense for the game-winning basket. Illinois' 19-18 triumph improved its league record to 11-0 and clinched the school's first-ever Western Conference basketball title. Their 16-0 overall record that season marks the only time in Illini history that perfection has been achieved.

UI's championship pin

Illinois' football team wound up beating Chicago by the score shown on the scoreboard.

Edward Williford

EDWARD WILLIFORD, the leading scorer of the 1915 Fighting Illini basketball team, was the University of Illinois' first Big Ten Conference Medal of Honor recipient. The award has been given annually since that year at each conference institution to the student athlete who demonstrates proficiency in scholarship and academics.

Illini Legend

Perry Graves

At 5'6" and 148 pounds, Perry Graves looked more like a gymnast than an All-America football player. Even back when he played in 1913 and 1914, Graves was small by Big Ten standards, but all who went against him quickly realized he was a powerhouse. During his senior season, Coach Bob Zuppke's Fighting Illini posted a perfect 7-0 record, won the Big Ten championship, and shared the national title with Army. A native of Rockford, Graves played freshman ball at the University of Pittsburgh, but returned to his home state to compete for Illinois. He also played baseball for Coach George Huff's Illini, starring as a shortstop and a third baseman as Illinois went on to win the Big Ten title. Graves was the owner and operator of the Robinson (Illinois) Lumber & Coal Company for several years, and served as a Big Ten football official for 22 seasons. He died in 1979 at the age of 89.

Illini Lists

ILLINOIS NATIONAL CHAMPIONS (TEAMS)

- Men's Gymnastics   9 (1939, '40, '42, '50, '55, '56, '58, '89)
- Men's Track & Field   5 (1921, '27, '44, '46, '47)
- Football   4 (1914, '19, '23, '27)
- Fencing   2 (1956, '58)

1914 National Champion football team

ILLINI LORE

During the summer of 1915, the west addition of what is now known as the Henry Administration Building was completed. The $1.45 million office space served as home of the registrar and dean of men on the first floor, the architect and the comptroller on the second floor, and as headquarters for President Edmund James and the Alumni Association on the third floor.

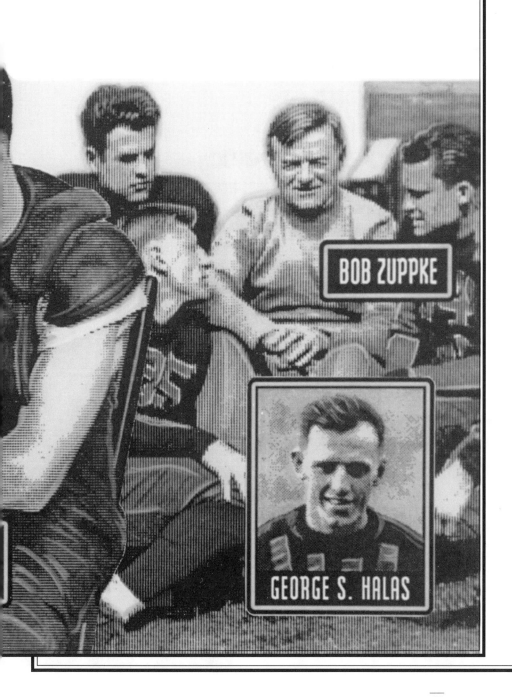

BOB ZUPPKE

GEORGE S. HALAS

1915-16

AMERICA'S TIME CAPSULE

Oct. 13, 1915	The Boston Red Sox won the World Series from the Philadelphia Phillies.
Dec. 10, 1915	The millionth Model T rolled off Ford's assembly line in Detroit.
March 9, 1916	Legendary Mexican bandit "Pancho" Villa led 1,500 guerrillas across the border, killing 17 Americans in New Mexico.
June 30, 1916	Charles Evans won the U.S. Open golf tournament.
Aug. 4, 1916	The United States purchased the Virgin Islands from Denmark for $25 million.

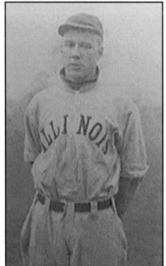

ILLINI MOMENT

"RED" GUNKEL'S NO-HITTER:

Coach George Huff's 1916 Fighting Illini pitching staff was nearly flawless during its Western Conference slate, allowing a total of just 10 runs in nine league games. The strongest arm belonged to a wiry, red-headed senior named Woodward "Red" Gunkel. Red's finest game came on May 5, 1916, at Illinois Field when he no-hit the Ohio State Buckeyes, 4-0. Gunkel pitched to only 28 men in his nine innings of work, striking out 12 batters, while notching his third of four consecutive shutouts. The Illini wound up taking the conference title that season with an 8-1 record.

"Red" Gunkel no-hit Ohio State in 1916, pitching to only 28 men in nine innings.

Football star Jack Watson

1916 Western Conference baseball champs.

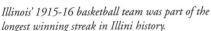

Illinois' 1915-16 basketball team was part of the longest winning streak in Illini history.

Illini Item

ILLINOIS' BASKETBALL TEAM won 25 games in a row from February 21, 1914, through February 9, 1916, a record that still stands. Included in the streak were 17 consecutive Western Conference victories in which Illinois' competition averaged less than 14 points per contest.

Illini Legend

RAY WOODS

Nowadays, Ray Woods's name is outshone by such basketball luminaries as George Mikan, Bill Russell, and Oscar Robertson. But in 1917, the spotlight was on him, when he was recognized as America's greatest college basketball player. As a three-year Fighting Illini letterman under Coach Ralph Jones from 1915-17, Woods became the University of Illinois' very first first-team All-American. Though he never led his team in scoring or shooting as did his twin brother Ralf, no one was a better all-around ball-handler or defender or leader than Ray Woods. The crafty guard from Evanston led the Illini to a cumulative record of 42 victories against only six losses in three seasons. Two of those three teams—1915 and 1917—were Western Conference champions, while the 1916 club finished as the league runner-up. Woods died in Berwyn, Illinois in 1965 at the age of 70.

Illini Lists

LONGEST ILLINI MEN'S BASKETBALL WINNING STREAKS IN CONFERENCE PLAY

- 17   February 21, 1914 thru February 9, 1916
- 15   January 20, 1951 thru February 2, 1952
- 14   March 7, 1942 thru January 3, 1944
- 13   February 23, 1924 thru February 21, 1925
- 13   February 26, 1955 thru February 20, 1956
- 9   February 24, 1941 thru February 7, 1942

The 1951-52 Illini basketball team built up a 15-game conference winning streak.

ILLINI LORE

On April 14, 1916, former University of Illinois regent Thomas J. Burrill died of pneumonia, 11 days short of his 77th birthday. He served on the UI faculty from 1868 to 1912, rising from a position as a horticulture instructor to acting head of the University in just 11 years. Burrill served as the official regent (president) from 1891-94, establishing the UI's graduate school during that tenure.

1916-17

AMERICA'S TIME CAPSULE

Sept. 30, 1916   The New York Giants' 26-game winning streak, baseball's longest ever, was halted by the Boston Braves.

Nov. 7, 1916   Woodrow Wilson was reelected president of the United States.

Feb. 3, 1917   The United States severed diplomatic relations with Germany due to increased submarine warfare.

March 2, 1917   The Jones Act made Puerto Rico a U.S. territory.

April 2, 1917   President Wilson requested a declaration of war against Germany.

Bart Macomber (top) and Ren Kreft scored TDs in UI's upset of Minnesota's "perfect team".

ILLINI MOMENT

THE ILLINI UPSET MINNESOTA'S "PERFECT TEAM":

The November 5th edition of the *Chicago Record-Herald* screamed out in bold type: "HOLD ON TIGHT WHEN YOU READ THIS!" And for good reason. In one of the greatest upsets in college football history, Coach Bob Zuppke's undermanned Illinois club had handed Minnesota's "perfect team" its only loss of the 1916 season, 14-9. The Illini led 14-0 at halftime on first-quarter touchdowns by Bart Macomber and Ren Kraft. Minnesota narrowed the gap in the third quarter by scoring a touchdown and adding a safety, but Zuppke's men hung on in the final stanza for the victory at Minneapolis. Just how good were the Gophers? Well, other than its loss to Illinois that year, Minnesota compiled a flawless 6-0 record by outscoring its opponents 339-14.

Walter Becker not only captured the Big Ten tennis singles title in 1917, he also teamed with Ernest McKay for the conference doubles crown.

UI's tennis courts in 1916-17.

ILLINI SCRAPBOOK

Illinois' 1916-17 men's basketball team

ILLINOIS SHARED the Western Conference basketball title with Minnesota in 1917, with each team recording a mark of 10-2. Coach Ralph Jones's squad won its last six games of the season, including an 18-17 victory over the cochampion Gophers on February 10 at Urbana.

Illini Legend

GEORGE HALAS

George Halas became famous by his moniker "Papa Bear," but his athletic career at the University of Illinois spanned much further than just the football field. He lettered in baseball, basketball, and football for the Illini from 1916-18, starring in each sport. Halas was graduated from the UI in 1918 with a degree in civil engineering, but his life took a detour when he enlisted in the Navy for service in World War I. When the war ended, he played major league baseball for a season with the New York Yankees. However, an injury ended his baseball career, and Halas turned to his first love—football. He was a driving force in giving birth to the National Football League in 1920, and brought credibility to the league five years later when he signed Illini running back "Red" Grange to a $100,000 Chicago Bears contract. During his 40-year coaching career with the Bears, Halas won more games (326) than any other NFL coach in history. He died October 31, 1983, at the age of 88.

Illini Lists

GEORGE HALAS CHRONOLOGY

1895 — Born February 2 in Chicago
1918 — Graduated from University of Illinois
1919 — Named player of the game in the 1919 Rose Bowl, playing for Great Lakes
1919 — Baseball career ends with New York Yankees (replaced by Babe Ruth)
1920 — Organized the American Professional Football Association, forerunner of the NFL, which involved his Decatur Staleys
1925 — Signed Red Grange from the University of Illinois
1933 — Led Bears to NFL Championship
1940 — Coached Bears to 73-0 massacre over Washington in NFL title game
1963 — Won his final NFL championship, 14-10, over New York Giants
1968 — Retired permanently as coach of the Bears
1983 — Succumbed to cancer on October 31

ILLINI LORE

· ·

Nearly five million Americans served their country during World War I, including 9,442 faculty, staff, and students from the University of Illinois. Of about 17,000 Americans who died, 183 men and one woman from the Urbana-Champaign and Chicago campuses lost their lives. The names of those 184 individuals are commemorated on the columns of Memorial Stadium.

1917-18

Od. 15, 1917   The Chicago White Sox defeated the New York Giants to win the World Series.
Nov. 3, 1917   U.S. forces engaged in their first World War I battle in Europe.
Dec. 18, 1917 The U.S. Constitution's 18th amendment was passed, outlawing the manufacture
               and sale of alcoholic liquors.
May 15, 1918   Airmail service began between New York City and Washington, D.C.
June 25, 1918 American forces halted the Germans in the Battle of Belleau Wood in France.

ILLINI MOMENT

Illinois' 1917 football team

FIGHTING ILLINI ATHLETICS AND WORLD WAR I:

World War I put a crimp in the University of Illinois' athletic program during the 1917-18 season, as only football, basketball, baseball, and track were among the teams that competed on a varsity level. None of the four squads were conference champions, though baseball and outdoor track both finished runners-up to Michigan. Illinois' other sports—gymnastics, wrestling, tennis, cross country, and fencing—were all suspended during the war years, with most not reinstated for competition until the 1919-20 season. Among Illinois' most famous World War I servicemen was three-sport star George Halas, who enlisted in the navy in January of 1918. The university would later honor its war dead with the construction of Memorial Stadium.

ILLINI SCRAPBOOK

Military Day at the University of Illinois.

Homer Dahringer

Illini Legend

John Depler

One of the premier football players at the University of Illinois during the war years was a center from Lewistown, Illinois, named John Depler. Depler's All-American career with Coach Bob Zuppke's Illini was dotted with success; he was a key member of the 1918 and 1919 Western Conference champions. Illini teams won 14 of 17 conference games during his playing career. Following his graduation in 1919 from UI, Depler coached for eight seasons at Columbia University. In 1930, he organized and was co-owner of the Brooklyn Dodgers professional football team. Depler spent several years of his life operating hotels and restaurants. Upon his retirement, he wrote a newspaper column for the *Fulton County* (Illinois) *News* and was presented with the Illinois State Historical Society's "Individual Award for Regional History Writing." Depler died in 1970 at the age of 71.

Illini Lists

BOB ZUPPKE'S CONSENSUS ALL-AMERICAN FOOTBALL PLAYERS

- 1914   Ralph Chapman, G
- 1914   Perry Graves, E
- 1915   Bart Macomber, HB
- 1918   John Depler, C
- 1920   Charles Carney, E
- 1923   Jim McMillen, G
- 1923-25 Harold "Red" Grange, HB
- 1926   Bernie Shively, G

Jim McMillen earned consensus All-American honors in 1923.

ILLINI LORE

In the November 15, 1917, edition of the *Alumni Quarterly*, the University of Illinois announced that "plans for an elaborate celebration of the 50th birthday of the university have been abandoned," due to World War I. The celebration was to have centered around a "great pageant" to depict the history of the institution that opened for business March 2, 1868. Instead, the UI was asked to raise $20,000 as its share in the state of Illinois' effort to collect $3 million for support of American servicemen.

1918-19

Sept. 11, 1918   The Chicago Cubs lost the World Series to the Boston Red Sox.
Nov. 9, 1918   Kaiser Wilhelm II of Germany abdicated.
Nov. 11, 1918   World War I ended on the I Ith hour of the I Ith day of the I Ith month.
June 11, 1919   Walter Hagen won the U.S. Open golf tournament.
July 4, 1919   Jack Dempsey won the world heavyweight boxing title with a technical knockout
                 against the defending champion, Jess Willard.

ILLINI MOMENT

A capacity crowd at Illinois Field saw the Illini beat Ohio State, 13-0, for the Big Ten football title.

ILLINI GRIDDERS CLAIM CONFERENCE TITLE:

Just five days after the Germans surrendered to end World War I, University of Illinois students had cause to celebrate another major event. On November 16, two-time defending Big Ten champion Ohio State came to Illinois Field to face Coach Bob Zuppke's Fighting Illini. Illinois took charge immediately, marching down the field for a touchdown on its first possession. That 7-0 halftime lead was increased to the eventual final score of 13-0 in the third quarter. The Illini wrapped up a perfect 4-0 Big Ten season (all four wins coming by shutouts) the following Saturday with a 29-0 win over Chicago. Zuppke wanted to play undefeated Michigan for an unscheduled winner-take-all game on December 7, but the proposed playoff game was vetoed by UI's Council of Administrators. Ohio State coach Jack Wilce told the press afterwards, "We met both Illinois and Michigan, and there is no comparison. Illinois is, by far, the better."

ILLINI SCRAPBOOK

Seven of Illinois' greatest athletes gathered for this group photo. (left to right) George Halas, Doug Mills, Dike Eddleman, Red Grange, Bob Richards, Lou Boudreau and Tug Wilson.

1918 Illinois football team

ON OCTOBER 26, 1918, Illinois hosted the Municipal Pier football team in a game at Illinois Field in Urbana. The Fighting Illini lost the game, 7-0, but no one complained. That's because the game was played behind closed gates, due to an influenza epidemic in Champaign-Urbana.

Illini Lists

WINNINGEST ILLINI MEN'S BASKETBALL COACHES (BY PERCENTAGE)

	W	L	Pct.
• Ralph Jones (1913-20)	85	34	.714
• Doug Mills (1937-47)	151	66	.696
• Harry Combes (1948-67)	316	150	.678
• Lou Henson (1976-96)	423	224	.654
• Craig Ruby (1923-36)	148	97	.604
• Harv Schmidt (1968-74)	89	77	.536

Ralph Jones's .714 winning percentage is tops among Illini men's basketball coaches.

Illini Legend

Kenneth "Tug" Wilson

Kenneth "Tug" Wilson admitted that it was a long way from Atwood to Antwerp, but that's exactly where his athletic career led him. Born in Atwood, Illinois, a little town 30 miles south of the University of Illinois, Wilson enrolled at the UI in the fall of 1916 after two years of teaching at a country school near his home. He was a fantastic athlete, winning five varsity letters in basketball and track and field. On the hardwood, Wilson led the Illini in scoring as a junior and was the team's captain his senior year. Athletically, his greatest accomplishment came in the summer of 1920 when he was a member of the United States Olympic team, competing at Antwerp, Belgium, in the javelin and discus. Wilson began his career in athletic administration at Illinois under George Huff, then spent three years at Drake and 21 years at Northwestern as athletic director. In 1945, he resigned from NU to become Major John Griffith's successor as Commissioner of the Big Ten Conference. Tug Wilson died February 1, 1979, at the age of 82.

ILLINI LORE

An entertaining part of campus life at the University of Illinois during the first three decades of the 20th century was the annual Interscholastic Circus. The 1919 version of the circus, described by UI's *Alumni Quarterly* magazine as "a roaring furnace of farce," attracted more than 7,000 students, faculty, and staff. Highlights of the May 31st festivities included clowns, acrobats, and swimming coach Ed Manley's "plunge from a dizzy height of 50 feet into a shimmering, seething tank of fiery water."

1919-20

AMERICA'S TIME CAPSULE

Sept. 26, 1919   President Wilson suffered a stroke during a national tour.
Oct. 9, 1919   The Chicago White Sox lost the World Series to the Cincinnati Reds.
April 20, 1920   The Olympic Games began in Antwerp, Belgium.
July 3, 1920   Bill Tilden won the men's singles title at the Wimbledon tennis championships.
July 5, 1920   Governor James Cox of Ohio became the Democrats' presidential nominee.

ILLINI MOMENT

Bob Fletcher (third row, far left) came off the bench to kick the first field goal of his career.

FLETCHER FIELD GOAL BEATS OHIO STATE:

The Illini traveled to Ohio State for the 1919 season finale with both the Big Ten championship and the national title on the line. Coach Bob Zuppke's men trailed the Buckeyes 7-6 with just five minutes left in the game. Quarterback Lawrence Walquist and end Chuck Carney connected for three pass completions, putting the Illini deep into Ohio State territory. With only 12 seconds remaining in the game and Illinois place kicker Ralph Fletcher out of the game with an ankle injury, Coach Zuppke called upon Ralph's younger brother, Bob, to kick a game-winning 25-yard field goal—*the first field goal he'd ever attempted in a game!* The 9-7 victory gave Illinois its second national championship.

First baseman Burt Ingwersen stretches high for a throw in this 1920 game.

The 1920 Illini wrestling team was the Big Ten champion. Two UI wrestlers, heavyweight H.A. Whitson and 175-pounder H.L. Hoffman, captured individual titles.

ILLINI SCRAPBOOK

Illini Item

ON MARCH 20, 1920, Illinois' mile-relay team of Phil Donohoe, John Prescott, Phil Spink, and Bob Emery set an indoor conference record of 3:29 in the final event, giving the Illini track team the conference title over Michigan, 31 5/8 to 27 1/2.

Captain Bob Emery (front row, fourth from left) was a member of the mile relay unit that gave Illinois the conference title.

Illini Lists

LONGEST CONTINUOUS TENURES AS ILLINI ASSISTANT FOOTBALL COACH

- Justa Lindgren   40 years (1904-43)
- Ralph Fletcher   22 years (1942-63)
- Burt Ingwersen   20 years (1945-64)
- Leo Johnson   15 years(1942-56)
- Mel Brewer   13 years (1947-59)
- Greg McMahon   12 years (1992-present)
- Robert King   11 years (1947-57)
- Milt Orlander   11 years (1924-34)
- Gene Stauber   11 years (1960-70)
- J.C. Caroline   10 years (1967-76)

Justa Lindgren's (right) career as an assistant coach at Illinois stretched over a span of five decades.

Illini Legend

Burt Ingwersen

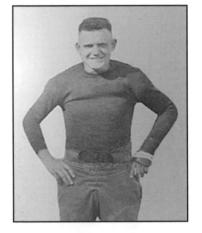

Burt Ingwersen was, literally, a man for all seasons at the University of Illinois. After the Fighting Illini football season was completed, he'd lace up his sneakers for duty with Coach Ralph Jones's basketball team. And after the basketball stopped bouncing, Ingwersen would race back out to Illinois Field to play first base for Coach George Huff's Illini baseball squad. He earned nine varsity letters altogether from 1917-20, earning all-star acclaim in football. Following graduation, Ingwersen joined the UI coaching staff, handling the freshman football and baseball squads. In 1924, Ingwersen succeeded Howard Jones as Iowa's head football coach, compiling a record of 33-27-4 in eight seasons as the Hawkeye mentor. After Iowa, he made assistant coaching stops at Louisiana State and Northwestern. In February of 1943, Ingwersen was commissioned a lieutenant commander in the U.S. Navy, serving as head football coach. Two years later, he was transferred to the Naval Air Technical Training Center in Chicago, where he also served a brief stint as athletic director. Ingwersen rejoined Coach Ray Eliot's UI football staff in the fall of 1945, retiring in 1965. He died on July 17, 1969, at the age of 70.

ILLINI LORE

Formal instruction in athletic coaching began during the fall of 1919 as a regular department in the University of Illinois' College of Education. Athletic Director George Huff had been running successful coaching sessions for several summers, but up until this time, students in those classes never received actual course credit. Out of 136 credit hours that were required for graduation, students enrolled in the athletic curriculum had to complete studies in 34 hours of practical coaching and physical education. Among the graduates were: Floyd "Shorty" Stahl, who went on to coach basketball at Ohio State; Otto Vogel, head baseball coach at Iowa; and Bernie Shively, athletic director at Kentucky for 30 years.

1920-21

AMERICA'S TIME CAPSULE

Sept. 28, 1920   Eight members of the Chicago White Sox were indicted on charges of having taken bribes to throw the 1919 World Series.

Nov. 2, 1920   Warren Harding was elected U.S. president by a landslide margin.

Nov. 2, 1920   Radio station KDKA in Pittsburgh broadcast the results of the presidential election, the first time that happened.

June 29, 1921   Elizabeth Ryan and Bill Tilden claimed Wimbledon tennis titles.

July 2, 1921   Jack Dempsey successfully defended his heavyweight boxing title against Georges Carpentier.

ILLINI MOMENT

George Huff (front row, far right) and Bob Zuppke (second row, third from left) were members of the Stadium Committee.

FUND DRIVE FOR NEW STADIUM:

The old gym annex looked like the Chicago Coliseum during the Republican convention on that 25th day of April, 1921. Every seat was filled as bands played and horns tooted. On the platform were university executives and distinguished Illini athletes and coaches. President David Kinley first spoke to the masses, then Athletic Director George Huff followed. When the ovation ceased, Huff said, "I want to see a great stadium at the University of Illinois. The stadium will be many things—a memorial to Illini who have died in the war, a recreational field, and an imposing place for our varsity games. But it will also be an unprecedented expression of Illinois spirit." Then football coach Bob Zuppke spoke, his hands rigidly clasped begind his back. After a few minutes, Zup ended with his request for voluntary donations of $1,000 for the stadium. Finally, following a few seconds of silence, a Latin-American student named R.L. Cavalcanti shouted out, "I will give, sir!" Within 10 minutes, more than $700,000 of the $2.5 million needed to build the great structure had been pledged by the undergraduate body.

UI's Smith Music Hall

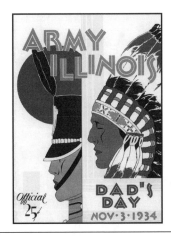

Dad's Day football program, 1934.

FIRST DAD'S DAY GAME: The University of Illinois hosted intercollegiate football's first "Dad's Day" on November 20, 1920. Unfortunately, Coach Bob Zuppke's Illini dropped a 7-0 decision to Western Conference champion Ohio State at Illinois Field.

Illini Legend

Chuck Carney

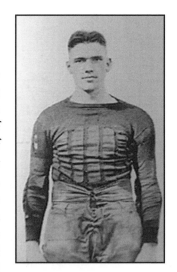

The greatest of athletes are honored following their careers by being selected to their particular sport's Hall of Fame. It's inconceivable that one man could be honored by two different sports' Hall of Fames, but that's exactly what former University of Illinois football and basketball star Chuck Carney could proudly claim. At 6'1" and 196 pounds, Carney was an outstanding receiver for Bob Zuppke's Illini from 1918-21, earning consensus All-America honors his junior year. On the basketball court his sophomore year, he set a Western Conference record by scoring 188 points in 12 league games, a record that stood for 22 years. Carney also led the conference in scoring his senior season and was named college basketball's player of the year. He coached football at Northwestern, Wisconsin, and Harvard before entering the investment banking business at the New York Stock Exchange. Carney died in 1984 at the age of 84.

Illini Lists

ILLINI NCAA TRACK & FIELD TEAM CHAMPIONSHIPS

Illinois won the NCAA's very first outdoor track & field championship on June 18, 1921, even though it didn't win a single individual title.

YEAR	CHAMPION	RUNNER-UP	SITE
1921	Illinois, 20 1/4 pts	Notre Dame, 16 3/4 pts	Chicago
1927	Illinois, 35 2/5 pts	Texas, 29 1/2 pts	Chicago
1944	Illinois, 79 pts	Notre Dame, 43 pts	Milwaukee
1946	Illinois, 78 pts	Southern Cal, 42 85/100 pts	Minneapolis
1947	Illinois, 59 2/3 pts	Southern Cal, 34 1/6 pts	Salt Lake City

1921 Championship Track Team

ILLINI LORE

President David Kinley began his 10-year term at the University of Illinois September 1, 1920. The 60-year-old Scottish-born professor of economics was vice president and dean of the graduate school during the term of his predecessor, Edmund James. The Kinley period was highlighted by the completion of several projects begun by James. Among the facilities constructed in Kinley's decade of service were Memorial Stadium, Smith Music Hall, the Library, and McKinley Hospital.

1921-22

Sept. 8, 1921	Margaret Gorman of Washington, D.C. won the title of the first Miss America.
Nov. 11, 1921	The "Unknown Soldier" of World War I was buried at Arlington National Cemetery.
Feb. 21, 1922	An explosion of the airship *Roma* killed 34 of its 45-man crew.
May 30, 1922	The Lincoln Memorial, designed by UI student Henry Bacon, was dedicated in Washington, D.C.
July 15, 1922	Gene Sarazen won the U.S. Open golf tournament.

Illini third baseman Harry McCurdy.

ILLINI MOMENT

CROWD OF 15,000 SEES ILLINI "9" BEAT MICHIGAN:

The boisterous crowd of 15,000 that gathered to watch their heroes at Illinois Field that 20th day of May, 1922, totally encircled the baseball diamond. And Coach Carl Lundgren's Illini didn't disappoint the faithful throng, pounding three Michigan hurlers for 12 hits en route to a 7-3 victory over the conference leaders. Third baseman Harry McCurdy was the hitting star for the Illini that afternoon, drilling two of Illinois' seven doubles. Wally Roettger relieved UI starter C.L. Jackson on the mound in the seventh inning, shutting out the Wolverines the rest of the way. Illinois clinched its second consecutive Western Conference title three days later at home, defeating Purdue 5-3.

ILLINI SCRAPBOOK

During the spring of 1923, workers went about their task, and George Huff's great dream began to rise from the prairie.

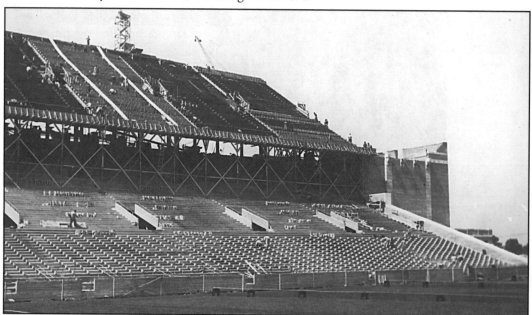

Red Grange (left) and Bob Zuppke.

I Illini Item

BOB ZUPPKE first met Red Grange on May 20, 1922, when Grange was on the University of Illinois campus participating in a high school track meet. After witnessing Grange win the 220-yard dash, Zuppke commented to the youngster, "I think you have a chance to make our team."

Illini Lists

ZUPPKEISMS

- The hero of a thousand plays becomes a bum after one error.
- All quitters are good losers.
- A man has to lose before he can appreciate winning.
- If the team wins all of its games, the alumni are loyal.
- Victory in football is 40 percent ability and 60 percent spirit.
- I don't care how big or how strong our opponents are, as long as they're human.
- My definition of an All-American is a player who has weak opposition and a poet in the press box.
- Never prophesy a great football future for any back until he has gained his first yard and taken his first bump.
- No athletic director holds office longer than two unsuccessful football coaches.
- Never let hope elude you. That is life's biggest fumble.

Illini Legend

Paul Prehn

The most prosperous University of Illinois coach in terms of Big Ten success was wrestling mentor Paul Prehn. During his coaching career from 1920-28, Prehn's Fighting Illini grapplers dominated the sport in conference action. Illinois won Big Ten titles seven times in nine seasons and had an impressive dual-meet record of 42-5. Among Prehn's individual stars were Illini wrestling legends Allie Morrison and Hek Kenney. When he left Illinois, Prehn began a highly successful restaurant business in Champaign-Urbana. He also served as chairman of the Illinois Athletic Commission for four years, a period that included the Jack Dempsey-Gene Tunney "Battle of the Century" boxing match in Chicago. Prehn also served as the state director for Illinois' Republican Party for 10 years. The World War I veteran from Mason City, Iowa, died on May 10, 1973, at the age of 80.

ILLINI LORE

In the spring of 1922, a 400-watt transmitter using the call letters WRM went into operation in the University of Illinois' Electrical Engineering Laboratory. The listeners' favorite programming included the bands, the glee clubs, and the scores of Fighting Illini athletic teams, but the few alumni who owned radio sets asked for more. In 1926, Boetius Sullivan, a wealthy UI alumnus, presented the university with a radio station in memory of his father. The station was later shifted to 890 KC, and the call letters were changed to WILL.

1922-23

AMERICA'S TIME CAPSULE

Oct. 4, 1922   Famed sportswriter Grantland Rice reported the first radio play-by-play coverage of the World Series.

Oct. 8, 1922   John McGraw's New York Giants won their second consecutive World Series title against the New York Yankees.

March 13, 1923   Motion pictures with sound were first demonstrated in New York City.

July 15, 1923   Golf amateur "Bobby" Jones won the U.S. Open.

Aug. 2, 1923   President Warren Harding died of an embolism while recovering from an attack of ptomaine poisoning.

ILLINI MOMENT

Big Ten medalist Rial Rolfe (far right) led Illinois to its first-ever conference golf championship.

ILLINOIS' FIRST CONFERENCE GOLF TITLE:

The first of seven all-time Big Ten golf championships for the University of Illinois was registered by Coach George Davis's team on June 19, 1923. Evanston Golf Club was the site for Illinois' five-stroke victory over defending champ Chicago, 643 to 648. The Maroons whittled nine strokes off the Illini's first-day, 14-stroke lead, but the one-two punch of UI's Rial Rolfe and John Humphreys was ultimately too much to overcome. Rolfe, a product of Chicago Senn High School, also captured Illinois' first-ever individual title, defeating teammate Gustav Novotny by four strokes.

Otto Vogel, a letter winner in both baseball and football, was selected as the University of Illinois' Big Ten Conference Medal of Honor winner in 1923.

Coach Harry Gill (center) and four of his 1923 track stars.

I Illini Item

ILLINOIS' TRACK AND FIELD SQUAD lost the Western Conference outdoor meet to host Michigan on June 2, 1923, 57 1/2 to 57. Despite a victory by the Illini in a conference-record time of 3:20 in the mile relay, the meet's final event, the referee ordered the race rerun when a misplaced hurdle caused a Michigan runner to miss a step and fall. Coach Harry Gill's Illini refused to run again, and the referee eventually canceled the event altogether, handing Michigan the team championship.

Illini Lists

ILLINI TRACK & FIELD OLYMPIC GOLD MEDALISTS

1912   Ed Lindberg, 1,600-meter relay (second leg), 3:16.6
1924   Harold Osborn, High Jump, 6' 5 15/16"
        Harold Osborn, Decathlon, 7710.755 points
1952   Bob Richards, Pole vault, 14' 11 1/4"
        Herb McKenley*, 1,600-meter relay (second leg), 3:03.9
1956   Bob Richards, Pole vault, 14' 11 1/2"
        *Member of Jamaican Olympic team

Dan Kinsey (left in white uniform) won an Olympic gold medal in 1924.

Illini Legend

Harold Osborn

Just how outstanding a track and field athlete was the University of Illinois' Harold Osborn? He was so good that he was one of 26 persons selected as charter members of the National Track and Field Hall of Fame, joining such greats as Ralph Boston, Bob Mathias, Wilma Rudolph, and Jesse Owens. Osborn is the only competitor in Olympic history ever to win an individual event gold medal (the high jump), as well as the gold medal in the decathlon, registering a world record in both events! While a member of the Illini track team, Osborn led Illinois in indoor and outdoor Western Conference crowns in 1920, '21, and '22. From 1922 to 1933, Osborn was a coach and teacher at Champaign High School. He was an osteopathic physician in Champaign from 1939 until his retirement. Osborn died in 1975 at the age of 75.

ILLINI LORE

During the 1922-23 school year, the University of Illinois ranked as America's third largest institution of higher learning. A total of 9,285 full-time students were enrolled at Illinois, a total higher than any other U.S. university except the University of California (14,061) and Columbia University (10,308). The Universities of Michigan and Minnesota ranked fourth and fifth. At the time, Illinois had more architecture students than any other (237) and ranked second in the country in terms of its number of commerce students (2,044).

1923-24

AMERICA'S TIME CAPSULE

Sept. 14, 1923   Jack Dempsey retained his heavyweight boxing crown with a second-round knockout of
                  Luis Angel Firpo, the "Wild Bull of the Pampas."

Oct. 15, 1923   The Yankees won the World Series over the Giants in an all-New York City showdown.

Jan. 25,1924   The first Winter Olympics were held in Chamonix, France, as the Americans finished
                  fourth in the unofficial team standings.

June 30, 1924   The Teapot Dome oil leasing scandal indicted several oil company presidents on charges
                  of bribery and conspiracy to defraud the United States.

July 21, 1924   Life sentences were given to Nathan Leopold and Richard Loeb for the highly publicized
                  murder of Bobby Franks.

ILLINI MOMENT

1923 UI-Chicago football game

MEMORIAL STADIUM MAKES ITS DEBUT:

Illinois' football team made its debut at Memorial Stadium a successful one, defeating the University of Chicago, 7-0, November 3, 1923. Construction of the stadium, begun just 14 months before, was not totally completed, but athletic director George Huff had pledged that the imposing structure would be ready for the Illini Homecoming game of 1923. Red Grange—who else—scored the first and only touchdown in that inaugural game, rushing 24 times on the muddy field for 101 yards. It rained hard all afternoon, and because the stadium's walkways weren't yet completed, several hundred of the 60,632 fans were forced to abandon their shoes and boots in the mud. Tickets, priced at $2.50 each, yielded record gate-sale receipts of more than $132,000 to the UI Athletic Association.

ILLINI SCRAPBOOK

Horatio Fitch, immortalized in the movie Chariots of Fire, *wins this 1924 race on the UI track.*

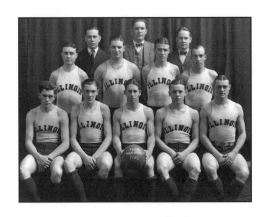

COACH CRAIG RUBY'S Illini basketball team clinched a tie for the Western Conference title on March 10, 1924, with a 31-19 victory over Minnesota. Senior Leland "Slim" Stilwell, in the final game of his career, was blanked from the field, but converted 11 free throws. Stilwell later returned to the University of Illinois to serve as the school's team physician.

Illini Legend

HAROLD "RED" GRANGE

Illini Lists

MEMORIAL STADIUM CONSTRUCTION STATISTICS

- 2,700 tons of steel
- 800 tons of reinforcing bars
- 4.8 million bricks
- 50,000 barrels of cement
- 7,200 tons of cut stones
- 17 miles of seats, covered by 21 acres of paint
- 404 miles of lumber

George Huff (right) and friends in front of the Memorial Stadium skeleton.

Those who call Harold Edward "Red" Grange the greatest college football player of all time have plenty of facts to back up their braggadocio. They'll point out that he was the very first winner of the *Chicago Tribune's* Silver Football Award as the Big Ten's Most Valuable Player. They'll mention that he was a charter member of both college and professional football's Hall of Fame. And they'll conclude that the Galloping Ghost was a unanimous selection on the all-time All-America team. So talented was Grange that the number 77 he wore on his back during his career at Illinois from 1923-25 was immediately retired by the university. So recognizable was his name that, in his very first game as a pro, Grange turned a normal Chicago Bears' gathering of less than 5,000 into a standing-room-only crowd of 36,000. Upon Grange's death in January of 1991 at the age of 87, UI athletic director John Mackovic summed up Grange's life by saying, "Red Grange has been, and will always be, one of the largest legends in the game of football. His presence will continue to be felt as long as the game is played."

ILLINI LORE

The cornerstone for the University of Illinois' new McKinley Memorial Hospital was laid May 10, 1924. The original structure, completed in the fall of 1925 at a cost of $225,000, didn't include its current wings on the north and south sides. Senator W.B. McKinley, a student at the UI in the 1870s, was the benefactor of the campus's first health facility. Each student that joined the hospital association that first year paid fees of $3 per semester and was afforded a maximum of 28 days of free care.

AMERICA'S TIME CAPSULE

Oct. 10, 1924	The Washington Senators, led by pitcher Walter Johnson, defeated the New York Giants, four games to three, in the World Series.
Nov. 4, 1924	Calvin Coolidge was reelected president of the United States, defeating Democrat John Davis.
Jan. 5, 1925	Mrs. William B. Ross was inaugurated governor of Wyoming, becoming the first woman governor in U.S. history.
July 21, 1925	Tennessee teacher John Scopes, a former University of Illinois student, was convicted for teaching the theory of evolution to his students.
Aug. 24, 1925	Helen Wills and Bill Tilden successfully defended their singles titles at the U.S. Lawn Tennis championships.

ILLINI MOMENT

THE WHEATON ICEMAN GALLOPS OVER MICHIGAN:

October 18, 1924, is, quite understandably, the most memorable single day in University of Illinois sports history. Not only was it the afternoon the university's imposing Memorial Stadium was officially dedicated, but it was also the day when one of America's greatest football legends—Red Grange—was christened. During the first 12 minutes of the game, the Wheaton Iceman scored touchdowns the first four times he touched the ball, on runs of 95, 67, 56, and 44 yards. He later returned to score a fifth TD on an 11-yard run and also threw for a sixth Illini score. When the final gun sounded, Grange had piled up 276 yards of total offense and had 126 yards in kickoff returns. Illinois beat mighty Michigan by the unlikely score of 39-14.

ILLINI SCRAPBOOK

The game program for the 1924 contest between Illinois and Chicago.

The University of Chicago

STAGG FIELD

Saturday, November 8, 1924

ILLINOIS
VERSUS
CHICAGO

REFEREE—	UMPIRE—
J. C. MASKER	H. NELLY
Northwestern	West Point
FIELD JUDGE—	HEAD LINESMAN—
M. MORTON	F. H. YOUNG
Michigan	Illinois Wesleyan

OFFICIAL PROGRAM

Compliments of

THE CHICAGO DAILY NEWS

Copyright 1924 By The Chicago Daily News Co.

Earl Britton, a letter winner in both football and basketball, kicked the very first 50-yard field goal in Illinois history.

I Illini Item

THE CHICAGO TRIBUNE AWARDED the very first Silver Football Trophy to the University of Illinois' Red Grange following the 1924 season, honoring him as the Big Ten's Most Valuable Player. Grange rushed for a career-high 743 yards on only 113 carries and scored a school record 13 touchdowns.

Red Grange won the Big Ten's first-ever Silver Football Trophy.

Illini Lists

ILLINI WHO PLAYED (OR COACHED) IN THE WORLD SERIES

- Fred "Cy" Falkenberg (1903, Pittsburgh)
- Garland "Jake" Stahl (1903, 1912-manager, Boston)
- Carl Lundgren (1906, 1907, 1908, Chicago Cubs)
- Frank Pfeffer (1910, Chicago Cubs)
- Wally Roettger (1928, St. Louis)
- Lou Boudreau (1948, Cleveland)
- John Brittin (1950, Philadelphia)
- Lou Skizas (1959, Chicago White Sox)
- Tom Haller (1962, San Francisco)
- Ed Spiezio (1964, 1967, 1968, St. Louis)
- Ken Holtzman (1972, 1973, 1974, Oakland)

Tom Haller

Illini Legend

Wally Roettger

Like George Huff and Carl Lundgren before him, the University of Illinois' Wally Roettger became the third consecutive Fighting Illini baseball coach to return to his alma mater. Roettger was an outstanding player at Illinois from 1922-24, with a career batting average over .300. As a junior in 1923 he hit .409, the fifth-best single-season average ever at that time. Major league scouts quickly noticed Roettger, and in six big-league seasons for his hometown St. Louis Cardinals, the New York Giants, and the Cincinnati Reds, he batted a respectable .277 in 468 games. Roettger also helped the Cardinals win the World Series title over the Philadelphia Athletics. He retired from the majors following the 1932 season to coach the baseball and basketball teams at Illinois Wesleyan. In 1934, Roettger's life changed dramatically when Carl Lundgren, his mentor at Illinois, died suddenly of a heart attack. It didn't take long for Fighting Illini athletic director George Huff to choose Lundgren's successor. In the next 17 years, Roettger won four Big Ten titles and finished among the top three eight other times; his record with the Illini baseball team was 212-111-7. However, all was not well with Roettger, and in 1951, he took his own life at the age of 49.

ILLINI LORE

In the fall of 1924, the University of Illinois' Alumni Association conducted a random survey of its graduates, polling them regarding their occupations, their incomes, and their spending habits. Of the 264 people who responded, the survey concluded that the alumnus's average annual income was $7,031. Graduates who went on to become manufacturers led the way with an average yearly salary of $27,100, followed by architects ($14,960), physicians ($13,831), and bankers ($12,014). One hundred and eight of the 264 respondents owned their homes, while 86 were renters. Those who owned automobiles preferred Fords (47), a choice nearly three times the total of the second-most preferred cars, Buicks and Dodges (17 each).

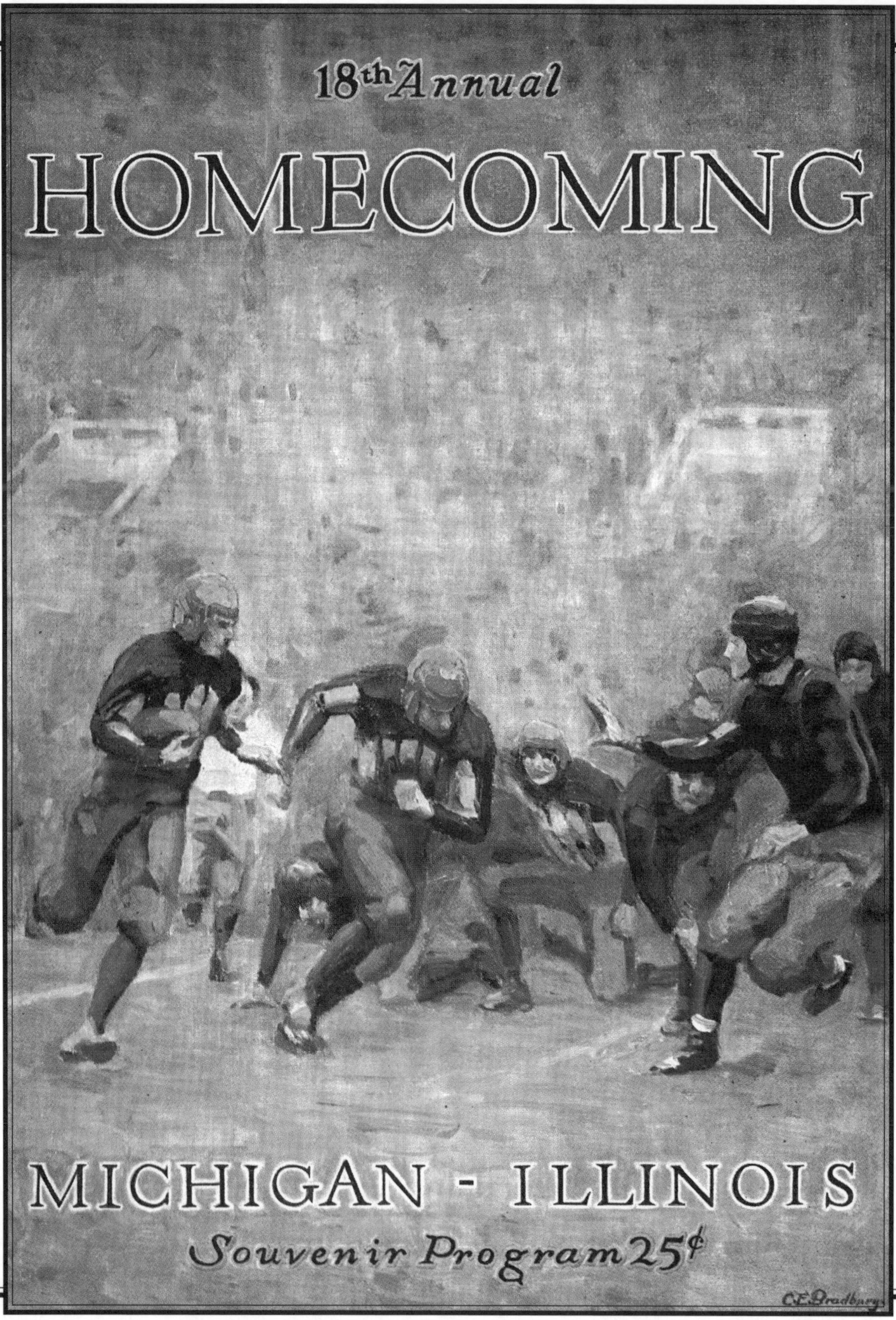
18th Annual
HOMECOMING
MICHIGAN - ILLINOIS
Souvenir Program 25¢
C.E. Bradbury

LAST MINUTE PHOTOS
ILLINI'S BIG THREE!

Photo shows, left to right: Earl Britten, Harold (Red) Grange, and Frank Rokusek, three aces of the Illinois football team.
(Underwood & Underwood Photos.)

With Britten, a punting and passing star; Grange, a superb open field runner, and Captain Rokusek, one of the best linemen in the business, Zuppke hopes to lead his fighting Illini to a western conference championship.

THE NEWS OF THE WORLD IN PICTURES
EVERY DAY IN THE

Chicago Tribune
THE WORLD'S GREATEST NEWSPAPER

1925-26

AMERICA'S TIME CAPSULE

Sept. 3, 1925	The U.S. Army dirigible *Shenandoah* was wrecked in a storm near Ava, Ohio, killing 14 people.
Oct. 15, 1925	Baseball's World Series was won by the Pittsburgh Pirates in seven games over the Washington Senators.
March 7, 1926	The American Telephone and Telegraph Company successfully demonstrated the first transatlantic radio-telephone conversation between New York City and London.
May 9, 1926	Rear Admiral Richard Byrd made the first successful flight over the North Pole.
Aug. 6, 1926	Nineteen-year-old Gertrude Ederle of New York City became the first woman to swim the English Channel.

ILLINI MOMENT

Illini captain Red Grange (right) meets his Penn adversary for the pregame coin flip.

ILLINI GRIDDERS VICTORIOUS AT PENN:

Red Grange's most famous college football game, of course, was his 1924 dismantling of Michigan at Memorial Stadium. But just as impressive was his performance on October 31, 1925, against the powerful University of Pennsylvania, gridiron rulers of the East. Bolstered by the 160-man UI marching band who had made the cross-country trip to Philadelphia, Coach Bob Zuppke's Illini handed their hosts a stunning 24-2 loss. The muddy Franklin Field turf didn't slow down Grange, who rushed for 237 yards on 28 carries, the best performance of his career. Besides scoring three touchdowns, Grange returned two kickoffs for 79 yards and caught two passes for 35 yards. Wrote Walter Eckersall of the *Chicago Tribune* afterwards, "Whatever doubt there was in the minds of Eastern gridiron critics and coaches regarding the quality of Red Grange was settled once and for all today."

The ticket and game program from Illinois' rematch in 1925 vs. Michigan, a contest won by the Wolverines, 3-0.

ILLINI SCRAPBOOK

Promoter C.C. "Cash & Carry" Pyle (right) helped turn Red Grange into one of sports' first successfful endorsers.

Illini Item

TWO DAYS AFTER his final game with the University of Illinois football team—November 23, 1921—"Red" Grange signed a $100,000 contract to play football for Coach George Halas's fledgling Chicago Bears. Including his royalties for endorsements, Grange was reportedly making thousands of dollars per week during his peak, but he asked his agent, C.C. Pyle, to limit him to a drawing account of a flat $100 per week.

Illini Lists

RED GRANGE'S BARNSTORMING TOUR

In an effort to capitalize on the lure of their new star—Red Grange—George Halas and the Chicago Bears quickly arranged a 19-game nationwide barnstorming tour. Here are the stops that Grange and the Bears made during their 66-day road trip.

Nov. 26, 1925: GAME 1—Grange made his pro debut at Cubs Park. A crowd of 20,000 was expected, but a throng of more than 70,000 crashed the gates to watch a 0-0 tie between the Bears and the Chicago Cardinals. (Grange: 96 yards rushing, intercepted pass)

Nov. 29, 1925: GAME 2—Bears beat Columbus Tigers in Chicago before 28,000 fans. (Grange: 140 yards rushing, 22-yard touchdown pass)

Dec. 2, 1925: GAME 3—Grange and Bears crush the Donnelly Stars in St. Louis. Crowd of 8,000. (Grange: scored four TD)

Dec. 5, 1925: GAME 4—Bears top Frankford Yellow Jackets in Philadelphia before 35,000 fans. (Grange: scored two TD)

Dec. 6, 1925: GAME 5—Crowd of 73,000 watch Bears play New York Giants at Polo Ground. (Grange: 35-yard interception return for TD)

Dec. 8, 1925: GAME 6—Bears beat Washington All-Stars in front of 7,000 fans. (Grange: dropkick PAT)

Dec. 9, 1925: GAME 7—Babe Ruth visited with Grange after Bears lost to Providence Steam Rollers. (Grange: 18 yards rushing on five attempts)

Dec. 10, 1925: GAME 8—Pittsburgh All-Stars shut out Bears as 6,000 watched. (Grange left game after 10 plays due to arm injury)

Dec. 12, 1925: GAME 9—Grange didn't play against Detroit Panthers due to injury. Most of crowd of 4,000 demanded their money back.

Dec. 13, 1925: GAME 10—New York Giants topped Bears in Chicago. Grange sat out second consecutive game, but 15,000 still attended game.

Dec. 25, 1925: GAME 11—Crowd of 5,000 watched Grange and Bears beat Miami All-Stars in Florida. (Grange: 98 yards rushing, one TD)

Jan. 1, 1926: GAME 12—Bears beat Tampa Cardinals in front of 8,000 fans. (Grange: 85 yards rushing, including a 70-yard TD)

Jan. 2, 1926: GAME 13—Bears continued Florida swing with a victory over the Jacksonville All-Stars in Florida before 6,700 fans. (Grange: threw 30-yard TD pass)

Jan. 10, 1926: GAME 14—Chicago shut out Southern All-Stars in New Orleans. (Grange: 136 yards rushing, 51-yard punt return)

Jan. 16, 1926: GAME 15—Crowd of 75,000 watched Bears defeat Los Angeles Tigers in California. (Grange: two TD)

Jan. 17, 1926: GAME 16—Chicago beat Cline's Californians in San Diego. (Grange: one TD)

Jan. 24, 1926: GAME 17—Bears lost to San Francisco Tigers before 23,000 fans. (Grange: 41 rushing yards)

Jan. 30, 1926: GAME 18—Chicago beat Longshoremen in Portland, Oregon. (Grange: 93 rushing yards, 20 passing yards, 23 receiving yards, two TD)

Jan. 31, 1926: GAME 19—Bears concluded 66-day road trip by topping Washington All-Stars before crowd of 5,000. (Grange: 99 rushing yards, two TD)

Illini Legend

Tim O'Connell

The University of Illinois' tennis program had until recently, enjoyed only moderate team success during its history, but one Fighting Illini player still tops the Big Ten singles' list for individual achievement. Until tennis legend Marty Riessen came along at Northwestern in the early 1960s, the name Tim O'Connell of Illinois stood alone. O'Connell's serve-and-volley game won three consecutive Big Ten singles titles from 1926-28, leading the Illini to team championships each of those seasons. He also was a two-time Big Ten doubles champ, giving him five individual titles altogether, second only to Riessen's six crowns. O'Connell continued his tennis pursuits after graduating from Illinois, earning amateur titles both as a singles and a doubles player. He worked for Union Carbide for nearly 40 years. O'Connell died in June of 1987 in San Mateo, California at the age of 82.

ILLINI LORE

The University of Illinois' "New Gymnasium," later to be known as Huff Gym, opened for business with a basketball game between the Illini and Butler, December 12, 1925. The building was completed at a cost of $500,000—20 cents per cubic foot. A $225,000 South wing, which included a swimming pool, was added a year later. Huff Gym had a capacity of 7,000, double the size of its predecessor, the Men's Old Gym Annex. From 1925 through 1963, when the Assembly Hall opened, Illini basketball teams compiled a record of 339 victories against only 121 losses at Huff Gym.

Red Grange
An Original Superstar

The Legend of Harold "Red" Grange and his contributions to the University of Illinois and American society are almost larger than life. Here are some rarely seen photographs of the most famous Fighting Illini athlete of all time.

Red Grange, shown here on the practice field east of Memorial Stadium, was one of the heroes of America's Golden Era of Sports.

Shown here in a Bears uniform, Grange was a charter member of the Pro Football Hall of Fame.

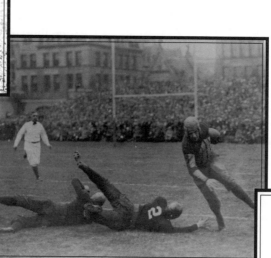

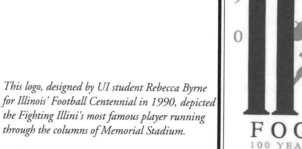

Grange deftly eludes a Penn defender in the 1925 game at Philadelphia, a contest many experts called his greatest individual effort.

Resplendent in the garb of the 1920s, this was one of the final photos taken of Red Grange as a University of Illinois student. He served as a member of the University's Board of Trustees from 1951-55.

This logo, designed by UI student Rebecca Byrne for Illinois' Football Centennial in 1990, depicted the Fighting Illini's most famous player running through the columns of Memorial Stadium.

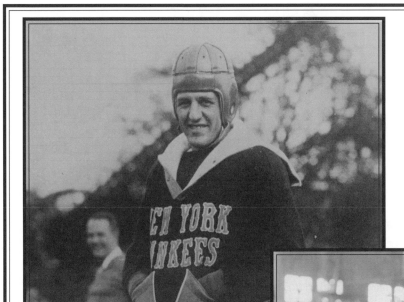

In 1926, Grange left the Bears for a fifty-fifty interest in the New York Yankees of the fledgling American Professional Football League.

Centerfielder Red Grange batted a paltry .091 for Coach Carl Lundgren's 1924 Illinois baseball team.

Grange's jersey 77 is one of sports' most immortal numbers.

The Galloping Ghost scores his second touchdown against Michigan in the 1924 Memorial Stadium dedication game.

Babe Ruth (right) met Red Grange for the first time in a New York City hotel room during the Chicago Bears' 1925-26 barnstorming tour. The Bambino said, "Kid, I want to give you two pieces of advice: Don't pay any attention to what they say or write about you. And don't pick up too many checks."

1926-27

AMERICA'S TIME CAPSULE

Sept. 18, 1926	Nearly 400 people were killed and 6,000 injured as a hurricane swept through Florida and other Gulf states.
Sept. 23, 1926	Challenger Gene Tunney defeated boxing champ Jack Dempsey in a ten-round heavyweight title fight in Philadelphia.
April 7, 1927	Television was demonstrated for the first time in New York City, as Secretary of Commerce Herbert Hoover was seen and heard from his office in Washington, D.C.
May 20, 1927	Aviator Charles Lindbergh took off from Long Island, New York for Paris, France, in his monoplane, *The Spirit of St. Louis*. He successfully landed 33 1/2 hours later.
Aug. 2, 1927	President Calvin Coolidge declined nomination for a second term.

ILLINI MOMENT

CHIEF ILLINIWEK DEBUTS:

The first appearance of the University of Illinois' symbol, Chief Illiniwek, was October 30, 1926, at Memorial Stadium. UI assistant marching band director Ray Dvorak is credited with starting the tradition, which officially began at halftime of the 1926 Illinois-Pennsylvania football game. Sophomore Lester Leutwiler, a UI student interested in Indian lore, was selected as the first Chief. In his recollection of that first performance, Leutwiler wrote, "As the band marched into the formation (spelling out the word "Penn"), the Chief ran from a hiding place north of the Illinois stands and led the band with his frenzied dance. The band stopped in the center of the field and played 'Hail Pennsylvania' while the chief saluted the Penn rooters. William Penn, impersonated by George Adams (the Illinois drum major), came forward and accepted the gesture of friendship. Together, we smoked the peace pipe and walked arm in arm across the field to the Illinois side, amidst a deafening ovation." Leutwiler's performance was so well received that he was asked to continue his performances at future Fighting Illini football games.

ILLINI SCRAPBOOK

Track and field's Doran Rue won the 1927 Conference Medal of Honor.

I Illini Item

UNIVERSITY OF ILLINOIS SENIOR John Sittig set an American collegiate record with a time of 1:54.4 in the 880-yard run as the Fighting Illini track and field team captured the sixth annual NCAA championship in Chicago, June 1, 1927.

Illini Legend

Bernie Shively

When a list of the University of Illinois' finest all-around athletes is compiled, the name Bernie Shively always appears. Perhaps most famous as a guard running interference for the immortal Red Grange, Shively was selected as the Fighting Illini's eighth consensus All-America football player following the 1926 season. He was inducted into the College Football Hall of Fame in 1982. The former prep star from Paris, Illinois, also excelled on the wrestling mat, grappling to a draw with his heavyweight opponent from Indiana in the 1926 Big Ten championship match, but losing on a coin toss. Shively also was a three-time letterman for the UI track and field squad, placing twice in conference championship competition as a hammer thrower. Altogether, he won eight varsity letters at Illinois. Following his graduation in 1927, Shively began a distinguished career at the University of Kentucky, culminating in a 30-year career as director of athletics. He died in 1967 at the age of 64.

Illini Lists

CHIEF ILLINIWEK FACTS

- Total number of Chief Illiniweks: 34 (as of 2001-02)
- First Chief Illiniwek: Lester Leutwiler, 1926
- First Chief to appear in authentic American Indian regalia: Webber Borchers, 1930
- First female Chief (Princess): Idelle Stitch, 1943
- First brothers to perform as Chief: John Forsyth, 1957-59 & Ben Forsyth, 1960-63
- First father-son to perform as Chief: Robert Bitzer, 1945-46 & John Bitzer, 1970-73
- Most common home states of Chiefs: Illinois (27 times) & Missouri (4 times)

Chief Mike Gonzalez met UI's first Chief Illiniwek, Leutwiler, September 25, 1976.

ILLINI LORE

Famed sculptor Lorado Taft laid the cornerstone for the new $500,000 University of Illinois architecture building, November 16, 1926. In Taft's remarks at the ceremony, he paid homage to Professor Nathan C. Ricker, the father of Illinois architecture. The structure, located at the south end of the campus, brought together the instructors not only of architecture, but also of art, design, sculpture, and other branches of the fine arts. The site of the three-story structure was formerly an apple orchard.

1927-28

AMERICA'S TIME CAPSULE

Sept. 30, 1927	Babe Ruth slugged his record-setting 60th home run for the New York Yankees.
Oct. 6, 1927	The world's first talking motion picture—*The Jazz Singer*—using the sound-on-film process was released. The movie was based on a play by Illinois alumnus Samson Raphaelson.
Nov. 13, 1927	The Holland Tunnel, America's first underwater tunnel, was opened to traffic, linking New Jersey with Manhattan. Its ventilation system was designed by Illinois professor Arthur Willard.
May 25, 1928	Amelia Earhart became the first woman to fly an airplane across the Atlantic.
July 30, 1928	George Eastman demonstrated the world's first color motion pictures at Rochester, New York.

ILLINI MOMENT

ILLINI GRIDDERS CLAIM THE NATIONAL CHAMPIONSHIP:

A rock-ribbed defense was the hallmark of Coach Bob Zuppke's 1927 University of Illinois national championship football team. In five of its eight games, the Fighting Illini defensive unit had shutout efforts, while in two other games, it yielded only a single touchdown. A 12-12 tie with Iowa State was Illinois' only flaw. The stars of Zuppke's team included All-America linemen Bob Reitsch, Russ Crane, and "Butch" Nowack. Among the key performers on the steady but unspectacular offensive team were backs Doug Mills, Frank Walker, and Fred Humbert, and end Jud Timm. Illinois' 5-0 Big Ten Conference record was good for first place ahead of 3-0-4 Minnesota.

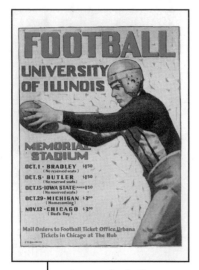

UI's 1927 football poster

The University of Illinois' Dave Abbott (far right) was a two-time NCAA track champion in 1928 and '29 in the two-mile run.

ILLINI SCRAPBOOK

74

All-America lineman "Butch" Nowack and his coach, Bob Zuppke.

I Illini Item

THE FIGHTING ILLINI FOOTBALL TEAM made a trip to Evanston, Illinois, October 22, 1927, to take on the Northwestern Wildcats at NU's brand-new Dyche Stadium. Illinois defeated Northwestern, 7-6, on a Bud Jolley touchdown and "Butch" Nowack's successful point after touchdown. The Illini victory snapped a seven-game Wildcat winning streak.

Illini Legend

Allie Morrison

One of the University of Illinois' greatest athletes in the sport of wrestling was Allie Morrison, the gold medalist at 135 pounds at the 1928 Olympic Games in Amsterdam. A native of Marshalltown, Iowa, Morrison was unbeaten as a 135-pound Fighting Illini wrestler from 1928-30, compiling a perfect 22-0 record. He also won three consecutive national AAU individual titles. Team-wise, his three Illini squads won two Big Ten championships (1928 and '30) and finished second once (1929). He began a long coaching career immediately afterwards. Among his coaching stops were Penn State and Doane College, then at the high school level in Omaha, Nebraska, where he produced four state titles in five years. A member of the Helms Foundation Amateur Wrestling Hall of Fame, Morrison died in 1966 at the age of 62.

Illini Lists

ILLINI ATHLETES WHO LATER BECAME UI ATHLETIC DIRECTORS

	Years as UI athlete	Years as UI AD
George Huff	1890-93	1896-1935
Wendell S. Wilson	1924-26	1936-41
Douglas R. Mills	1926-30	1941-66
E.E. (Gene) Vance	1942-47	1967-72
Raymond Eliot (interim)	1929-31	1979
Ronald E. Guenther	1963-66	1992-present

Athletic Director Gene Vance

ILLINI LORE

During the fall of 1927, St. John's Catholic Church was completed at the corner of Sixth Street and Armory Avenue. The church accommodated a congregation of between 1,500 and 2,000 and featured marble altars from Italy and stained glass windows from Germany. UI band leader Ray Dvorak served as the church's organist and choir director. Two additional residence halls, comprised of 180 rooms for 360 male students, were attached to the church. The Reverend Monsignor Edward Duncan has served as chaplain to the Catholic students and director of the Newman Foundation since October 1943.

1928-29

AMERICA'S TIME CAPSULE

Oct. 9, 1928   The St. Louis Cardinals were swept in four straight games by the New York Yankees at the World Series.

Nov. 6, 1928   In a landslide Republican victory, Herbert Hoover defeated Alfred Smith for the presidency of the United States.

Feb. 14, 1929   The mass murder known as the St. Valentine's Day Massacre took place on Chicago's North Side.

May 16, 1929   *Wings* was selected as Best Picture at the first Academy Awards.

June 30, 1929   Bobby Jones won the U.S. Open golf tournament over runner-up Al Espinosa.

ILLINI MOMENT

Illini quarterback Frosty Peters scored UI's only touchdown vs. Ohio State in 1928.

ILLINI CLINCH BIG TEN FOOTBALL TITLE WITH VICTORY OVER OHIO STATE:

November 24th, 1928, was a day when Illinois' football team needed all the "ifs" to come true, and that's exactly what happened. Coach Bob Zuppke's Fighting Illini and Ohio State entered the 1928 season finale at Memorial Stadium with identical 3-1 conference records, one-half game behind undefeated Wisconsin. The combatants would need not only a victory over the other, but also a win by Minnesota over the league-leading Badgers. After the dust had settled, the unlikely scenario played out perfectly to the Illini's advantage, as Illinois beat OSU, 8-0, and the Gophers beat Wisconsin, 6-0. That combination of results allowed Illinois to finish atop the Western Conference standings with a 4-1 record, its second consecutive league title. "Frosty" Peters scored the only Illini touchdown of the afternoon late in the first half on a quarterback sneak.

Max Abramowitz (left inset), a 1929 UI graduate, was the architect for many prominant structures, including the Assembly Hall.

ILLINI SCRAPBOOK

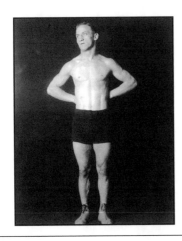

Joe Sapora was one of Illinois' first two NCAA wrestling champions.

I Illini Item

I

UNIVERSITY OF ILLINOIS WRESTLERS Joe Sapora and George Minot won individual titles at the second annual NCAA championship, held in Columbus, Ohio. Sapora, a 115-pounder, and Minot, at 135 pounds, were Illinois' first two NCAA wrestling champs.

Illini Lists

ILLINOIS' SPORTS INFORMATION DIRECTORS

1922-43	L.M. "Mike" Tobin
1943-56	Charles "Chuck" Flynn
1956-70	Charles "Charlie" Bellatti
1970-74	Norm Sheya
1974-89	Tab Bennett
1980-85	Lani Jacobsen (women's SID)
1985-87	Tom Boeh (women's SID)
1987-89	Mary Fowler (women's SID)
1989-95	Mike Pearson
1996-99	Dave Johnson
1999	Barbara Butler
2000-present	Kent Brown

Former Sports Information Directors (left to right) Charlie Bellatti, Chuck Flynn, and Tab Bennett.

Illini Legend

L.M. "Mike" Tobin

The greatest of Fighting Illini fans can easily recite the legends of "Red" Grange and the "Whiz Kids," but nary a one probably knows L.M. "Mike" Tobin, the man whose diligent work made those athletes household names. The Danville, Illinois, native was the first full-time collegiate athletic publicist in the country, and it was his initial task to spread the word about a red-headed youngster from Wheaton who became the most famous collegiate football player ever—Red Grange. For more than 20 years from his tiny office in Huff Gymnasium, Tobin pounded out thousands of stories about the Illini on his manual typewriter. Every sportswriter in the Midwest relied upon Tobin to supply them with information about the nationally prominent University of Illinois athletic program. Upon Tobin's death in 1944 at the age of 64, Bob Zuppke said that Illinois had lost "its most loyal of loyal friends. We owe him more than we ever could have repaid."

ILLINI LORE

Lorado Taft's Alma Mater Statue, the $25,000 gift of the University of Illinois classes of 1923-29, was formally dedicated June 12, 1929. Originally located just south of the Auditorium, the statue was moved to the Altgeld Hall lawn in August of 1962. The central image of the three-figure bronze, inspired by Daniel Chester French's "Alma Mater" at Columbia University, welcomes visitors to the Urbana-Champaign campus. The figures at the rear, their hands clasped, represent learning and labor. Inscribed at the statue's granite base are the words, "To thy happy children of the future, those of the past send greetings."

1929-30

AMERICA'S TIME CAPSULE

Oct. 29, 1929	A record 16,410,000 shares were traded for whatever they would bring, signaling the beginning of the American Depression.
Nov. 29, 1929	Lt. Commander Richard E. Byrd completed the first flight over the South Pole.
March 13, 1930	The planet Pluto was identified from an observatory in Flagstaff, Arizona.
June 7, 1930	Gallant Fox captured horse racing's Triple Crown with a victory at the Belmont Stakes.
June 12, 1930	Germany's Max Schmeling defeated Jack Sharkey to win the world heavyweight boxing championship.

ILLINI MOMENT

Fred Siebert (second from left), Otto Haier (sixth from left), and "Doc" Gross (second from right) all won Big Ten fencing titles in 1930.

"PERFECT" ILLINI WIN BIG TEN FENCING CHAMPIONSHIP:

Everything went "perfectly" for Coach H.W. Craig's Fighting Illini fencing team at the Western Conference's 1930 fencing championships in Chicago. Not only did Craig's squad capture the team title, all three of the young men who accompanied him on the trip to Chicago came home individual champions. Shattering all conference records as well as their own, the Illini fencing triumvirate of Otto Haier, Fred Siebert, and Chalmer "Doc" Gross recorded the league's first perfect score—-a 15. Captain Haier won the foil title, his second consecutive crown in that weapon; Siebert was king of the epeeists, and Gross finished first among the sabremen. It was the second in a string of five consecutive team titles for the Illini fencers.

The UI president's residence was completed in 1930.

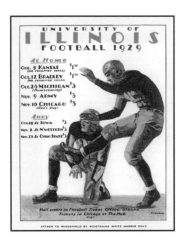

UI's 1929 football poster.

Illini Item

ON NOVEMBER 9, 1929, underdog Illinois up-ended powerful Army, 17-7, before a crowd of nearly 70,000 in the first matchup between the two teams. Illinois' Arnold Wolgost scored the eventual game-winning touchdown on a 75-yard dash from scrimmage, while the Illini defense completely corralled Army's future Hall of Famer "Red" Cagle.

Illini Legend

DOUG MILLS

The 40-year athletic career of Doug Mills at the University of Illinois must be discussed in three different chapters: as an athlete, as a coach, and as an administrator. From 1927-30, Mills's career as a football and basketball athlete was highlighted by both individual and team success. He was a two-time all-conference basketball player and a three-year letterman on the gridiron, leading his teammates to a pair of Big Ten football titles. As a coach, Mills guided the Illini cagers to three conference championships in 11 seasons. Illini basketball reached its peak with Mills shortly before World War II, when four in-state athletes—Gene Vance, Ken Menke, Andy Phillip, and Jack Smiley—formed the nucleus of a team that was known simply as the "Whiz Kids." Following the 1946-47 season, Mills retired from the coaching ranks to devote himself as full-time Illinois athletic director, a job he inherited in 1941 at the age of 33. The last years of Mills's administration were marred by a Big Ten investigation, and he gave up his post in November 1966. He died on August 12, 1983, at the age of 75.

Illini Lists

ILLINOIS' FIRST AFRICAN-AMERICAN MALE ATHLETES

- 1904 Football (Roy Young)
- 1904 Track & Field (Hiram Hanibal Wheeler)
- 1929 Tennis (Douglas Turner)
- 1947 Swimming (Ralph Hines)
- 1950 Fencing (John Cameron)
- 1951 Basketball (Walt Moore)
- 1963 Wrestling (Al McCullum)
- 1965 Baseball (Trenton Jackson)
- 1982 Gymnastics (Charles Lakes)

Trenton Jackson

ILLINI LORE

The University of Illinois' Library Building was dedicated October 18, 1929. The library was constructed in three sections and cost a total of $1.75 million. At that time, the facility contained more than 758,000 volumes and nearly 157,000 pamphlets. In 2002, the library houses more than ten million volumes.

AMERICA'S TIME CAPSULE

Sept. 27, 1930	Bobby Jones became the first player to capture golf's Grand Slam when he won the U.S. Amateur tournament.
Dec. 11, 1930	The powerful Bank of the United States closed in New York City, due to the deepening economic crisis.
Jan. 7, 1931	The President's Emergency Committee for Unemployment Relief announced that between four and five million Americans were out of work.
March 3, 1931	President Herbert Hoover signed a congressional act making "The Star Spangled Banner" the USA's national anthem.
May 1, 1931	The Empire State Building, the world's tallest building, opened in New York City.

ILLINI MOMENT

Coach Zuppke (left) and running back Gil Berry.

A "BERRY" GOOD PERFORMANCE:

A young sophomore halfback from Abingdon, Illinois, wearing the number "7" on his back, stole the show for Illinois' football team on October 11, 1930, reminding fans of a redhead named Grange who had galloped the Memorial Stadium turf just five years before. Though he didn't wind up his career with as much acclaim as his famous predecessor, Gilbert Berry—for one game, at least—showed ghost–like moves on that cool autumn afternoon. His touchdown runs of 60 and 80 yards led the Fighting Illini to a 27-0 shutout of Butler. Berry touched the ball only 19 times for 227 yards of total offense. Rushing-wise, he averaged better than 20 yards per carry, gaining 183 yards on nine attempts. The Illini victory would turn out to be one of only three for Coach Bob Zuppke's club that season.

Webber Borchers of Decatur, Illinois was the second man to portray Chief Illiniwek, and the first to appear in authentic American Indian regalia. In 1929, he began a campaign to raise funds to replace his homemade outfit with an authentic one, but in the depths of the Depression, he received only $30. However, Champaign merchant Isaac Kuhn stepped forward with a $500 gift, and Borchers finally had enough money to pay for the outfit. He traveled to the Pine Ridge reservation in South Dakota where a Sioux Indian woman and two younger women fashioned the costume. In New York's Yankee Stadium--November 8, 1930--Illinois' football team played Army. It was there that Borchers made the first appearance of Chief Illiniwek in that outfit.

Buster Fuzak hit for the "cycle" against Northwestern on April 11, 1931.

I Illini Item

COACH CARL LUNDGREN'S Fighting Illini baseball team won its Big Ten season opener April 11, 1931, crushing Northwestern 15-4 at Illinois Field. The hitting star for the Illini was senior Buster Fuzak, who hit for the cycle against the Wildcats. Fuzak connected for a single, a double, two triples, and a home run, while scoring three runs himself.

Illini Lists

ILLINI CODE OF SPORTSMANSHIP

In 1930, George Huff, Director of Athletics at the University of Illinois, instituted the Illini Code of Sportsmanship.

A true Ilini sportsman…

1. Will consider all athletic opponents as guests and treat them with all of the courtesy due to friends and guests.
2. Will accept all decisions of officials without question.
3. Will never hiss or boo a player or official.
4. Will never utter abusive or irritating remarks from the sideline.
5. Will applaud opponents who make good plays or show good sportsmanship.
6. Will never attempt to rattle an opposing player.
7. Will seek to win by fair and lawful means, according to the rules of the game.
8. Will love the game for its own sake and not for what winning may bring him.
9. Will 'do unto others as he would have them do unto him.'
10. Will 'win without boasting and lose with out excuses.'

Illini Legend

DICK MARTIN

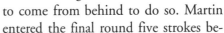

While Walter Hagen and Bobby Jones were dominating professional golf, the kingpin of the Big Ten Conference was Illinois' Dick Martin. A letterman for Coach J.H. Utley's Fighting Illini from 1929-31, Martin captured conference medalist honors as a junior in 1930 at Westmoreland Country Club in Evanston, winning by one stroke and leading his teammates to the Big Ten title. As a senior, he again became the Big Ten medalist, but he had to come from behind to do so. Martin entered the final round five strokes behind Ohio State's Johnny Florio. He played through a continual downpour to pass Florio on the 12th hole, then had birdies on his final two holes to pull away. Once again, the Illini won the team title, by five strokes over host Michigan. Both years, Illinois placed fifth at the NCAA championships. Martin probably would have won three consecutive Big Ten titles, but Illinois did not compete in the conference meet his sophomore year due to finals scheduled on the day of the meet. Martin has been "lost" in the Alumni Association's records since graduation.

ILLINI LORE

Dr. Harry Woodburn Chase assumed duties as the sixth president of the University of Illinois, July 5, 1930, taking over from David Kinley. He came from the University of North Carolina where he had served as president from 1919-30. Chase was called to take over administration at the Urbana-Champaign campus during a time that a major construction program was ending. Construction on campus during his tenure included Freer Gymnasium, the Ice Skating Rink, and the president's residence. Chase resigned July 1, 1933, to become chancellor of New York University.

1931-32

AMERICA'S TIME CAPSULE

Oct. 25, 1931	The George Washington Bridge, connecting Manhattan with New Jersey across the Hudson River, was opened to traffic.
March 1, 1932	Charles A. Lindbergh, Jr., 20-month-old son of the famous aviator, was kidnapped from his home at Hopewell, New Jersey.
May 2, 1932	Pearl Buck's *The Good Earth* was awarded a Pulitzer prize in the category of fiction.
July 2, 1932	Franklin Roosevelt accepted the Democratic party's nomination for president and announced his plan for a "new deal."
Aug. 14, 1932	The United States won the unofficial team championship at the Summer Olympic games in Los Angeles by claiming the last of its 16 gold medals.

ILLINI MOMENT

Cas Bennett (front row, left) and Red Owen (front row, fourth from left) were the Illini heroes in a 1932 victory over Purdue.

ILLINI CAGERS DERAIL BOILERMAKERS:

Purdue ruled Big Ten basketball during the 1930s, but the Fighting Illini teams of Coach Craig Ruby always seemed to have the Boilermakers' number. Such was the case on January 9, 1932, when Illinois beat Purdue, 28-21, at the New Gym (soon to be called Huff Gym). Ward "Piggy" Lambert's Boilers showed a perfect 6-0 record coming into the game, relying on a fast-break style of play. However, Illinois' defense applied the brakes to the Boilermaker Express in the first half, claiming a 19-5 lead at halftime. Purdue All-American Johnny Wooden, who later became college basketball's most dominant coach at UCLA, led a strong comeback by scoring a game-high 10 points. However, the Illini held on to win behind the sterling play of Cas Bennett and "Red" Owen. The loss would turn out to be the only blemish in 18 games for Purdue that season, which ended with a 17-1 record.

Baseball's Edward Gbur won the UI's Conference Medal of Honor in 1932.

ILLINI SCRAPBOOK

ILLINOIS' 1932 MEN'S TENNIS TEAM shared the Big Ten Conference championship with Indiana in a showdown at Bloomington, Indiana, on May 18. Illini senior Eddie Lejeck beat Ohio State's Carl Dennison for the singles title, while he and Fred Hands were runners-up in doubles competition.

Eddie Lejeck (fourth from left) won the Big Ten singles title, and he teamed up with Fred Hands (second from left) as doubles finalists.

Illini Lists

ILLINOIS' TOP TEN CAREER BASEBALL HITTERS
(Through 2001 season)

1.	Darrin Fletcher, 1985-87	.392
2.	Andy Schutzenhofer, 2000-01	.383
3.	Dave Payton, 1984-87	.374
4.	Tim Richardson, 1980-83	.372
5.	Herb Plews, 1947-50	.367
6.	Ed Tryban, 1930-32	.365
7.	Sean Mulligan, 1989-91	.364
8.	Luke Simmons, 1999-01	.362
9.	Ben Lewis, 1933-35	.361
10.	Mike Murawski, 1967-69	.356

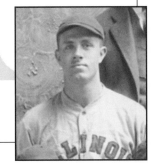

Ed Tryban had a .365 career batting average from 1930-32 at Illinois.

Illini Legend

Craig Ruby

Known as one of the great basketball strategists of his time, Craig Ruby directed University of Illinois' basketball team for 14 years (1923-36), a span that saw the Fighting Illini claim 13 upper-division finishes in Big Ten play. Illinois won two conference titles during that span—1923-24 and 1934-35—second only to Purdue, which won five championships during Ruby's reign in Champaign. In each of the four campaigns that Illinois played Purdue during Boilermaker championship seasons, Ruby's club upset the Riveters at least once. His teams played slow-break basketball, relying on a pivot and passing style. Ruby left coaching in 1936 to enter the greeting card business. He resided in Kansas City, Missouri, until his death in 1980 at the age of 84.

ILLINI LORE

James "Scotty" Reston (left in photo), a 1932 graduate of the University of Illinois, is one of the school's most influential alumni. The native of Scotland worked as a student assistant in UI's sports information office and competed in varsity golf and soccer. Reston moved to the New York Times in 1939 following a seven-year stint with The Associated Press, becoming one of America's most noted journalists. *Time* magazine said in a 1960 edition, "Politicians and other newsmen watch Reston's tone and are influenced by it." Reston won two Pulitzer prizes for national reporting. He retired as vice president of the *Times* in December of 1974.

1932-33

AMERICA'S TIME CAPSULE

Oct. 2, 1932   The Chicago Cubs were swept in four straight games by the New York Yankees at the 29th annual World Series.

Nov. 8, 1932   In a landslide victory over Herbert Hoover, Franklin Roosevelt was elected president of the United States.

March 13, 1933   United States banks began to reopen across the country, following a prolonged depression.

May 27, 1933   Chicago's Century of Progress Exposition began, in honor of that city's centennial celebration.

July 6, 1933   Babe Ruth hit a home run at major league baseball's first All-Star game, as the American League defeated the National League, 4-2, at Chicago's Comiskey Park.

ILLINI MOMENT

Coach Zuppke (left) and quarterback Jack Beynon.

ILLINOIS GRIDDERS WIN DOUBLEHEADER:

The only football doubleheader in University of Illinois history was played at Memorial Stadium on October 1, 1932. Coach Bob Zuppke divided his squad into two entirely separate units, one playing the first half of both games and one playing the second half of both. In game one, Illinois cruised to a 20-7 victory over Miami of Ohio, thanks to a pair of touchdown passes from quarterback Jack Beynon to halfback Dave Cook. The "nightcap," which began at 3 p.m., resulted in a 13-0 shutout by the Fighting Illini over Coe College. Though they were blanked, Coe proved to be the tougher adversary of Illinois, shutting out their hosts for most of the first half. Pete Yanuskus's touchdown just before halftime proved to be the only score the Illini would need. The biggest disappointment was that only 4,568 fans showed up on that beautiful, 70-degree fall afternoon, causing the UI Athletic Association to incur a $3,600 loss after expenses.

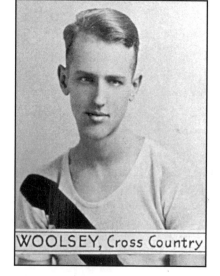

WOOLSEY, Cross Country

Illinois' Dean Woolsey won the individual title at the 1932 Big Ten cross-country meet. Unfortunately, Indiana runners finished second, third, and fourth, and the Hoosiers edged the Illini for the team championship.

ILLINI SCRAPBOOK

Coach Harry Gill

COACH HARRY GILL directed the Fighting Illini track and field squad for his 30th and final season in 1932-33. During those three decades, Gill directed Illinois' program to 11 Big Ten outdoor team championships and eight indoor titles.

Illini Legend

Ralph Epstein

The only fencer in Fighting Illini history to win Big Ten individual titles in three consecutive seasons was Ralph Epstein. The foil specialist from Chicago won championships in 1932, '33, and '34, leading Illinois to team honors during his sophomore and junior seasons. Epstein was also a standout in the classroom, becoming the 20th Illini athlete to be honored as the UI's Big Ten Conference Medal of Honor winner. As a serviceman in World War II, he helped the United States Air Corps design this nation's very first jet airplane. After the war, Epstein returned to the Chicago architectural engineering firm of Epstein & Sons International, where he retired as president. He died on August 11, 1986, at the age of 72.

Illini Lists

MULTIPLE BIG TEN FENCING CHAMPIONS

Robert Tolman	3 titles (Foil: 1920-21; Sabre: 1921)
Ralph Epstein	3 titles (Foil: 1932-33-34)
Francis Van Natter	2 titles (Sabre: 1916; Epee: 1916)
Otto Haier	2 titles (Foil: 1929-30)
Fred Siebert	2 titles (Epee: 1930; Foil: 1931)
E. Perella	2 titles (Sabre: 1932-33)
William Chiprin	2 titles (Foil: 1935-42)
Herman Velasco	2 titles (Foil: 1954-56)
Larry Kauffman	2 titles (Epee: 1955-56)
Art Schankin	2 titles (Foil: 1957; Sabre: 1958)
Nate Haywood	2 titles (Epee: 1972-73)
Mark Snow	2 titles (Foil: 1981-82)
Eric Schicker	2 titles (Foil: 1986-87)

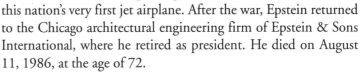

Larry Kauffman (left) and Herman "Pete" Velasco won two titles each in the mid 1950s.

ILLINI LORE

On December 26, 1932, President Chase announced that the University of Illinois would reduce its legislative request for operating expenses by a million dollars, as compared to its last appropriation. Salaries of UI faculty and administrative staff were reduced by 10 percent, and deans and department heads were asked to boil down their budgets as never before. Ultimately, the state's appropriation to the university was reduced much more severely than expected. UI's $11.3 million budget during the 1931-32 and '32-33 school years was cut to $7.8 million during 1933-34 and '34-35, a reduction of 31 percent.

1933-34

AMERICA'S TIME CAPSULE

Dec. 5, 1933	Probibition in the United States was repealed when Congress adopted the 21st Amendment.
Dec. 17, 1933	The Chicago Bears defeated the New York Giants, 23-21, winning the first National Football League championship playoff.
May 23, 1934	Dr. Wallace Carothers of DuPont Laboratories first developed a synthetic fiber called nylon.
June 14, 1934	Max Baer scored a technical knockout over Primo Camera to win the world heavyweight boxing championship.
July 22, 1934	John Dillinger, America's public enemy number one, was shot and killed in Chicago by FBI agents.

ILLINI MOMENT

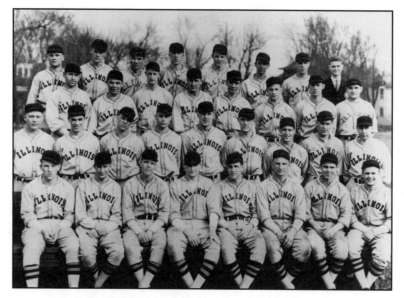

ILLINI SPOIL BOILERS' CHAMPIONSHIP SEASON:

Coach "Piggy" Lambert's Purdue Boilermakers had wrapped up their Big Ten championship a few days before with a home-court victory over Indiana. So perhaps they had little more than pride to play for when they came to Champaign on March 5, 1934, for the season finale against Illinois. The Illini, however, had a different outlook on the game, hoping to send out their senior quartet of Huddie Hellmich, Fred Fencl, and Chin and Jake Kamm on a winning note against the 17-2 Boilermakers. The game was nip-and-tuck all the way and came down to the final hair-raising 20 seconds. With the Illini ahead by one point, UI's Hellmich fouled Purdue All-American Ray Eddy. Fortunately for Illinois, the Big Ten's individual scoring champion missed both of his free throws, allowing the Illini to escape with a 27-26 win.

(Left to right) Fred Fencl, Chin Kamm and Huddie Hellmich helped the Illini spoil Purdue's championship season.

Illinois' 1934 baseball team, champions of the Western Conference.

DR. LELAND "SLIM" STILWELL was named team physician for the University of Illinois' Athletic Association in 1933. A basketball letterman for the Fighting Illini from 1922-24, he was known to UI student athletes as "Doc" Stilwell for 35 years. He was named UI's Varsity I Award winner in 1971.

Illini Legend

Frank Froschauer

From September of 1932 through March of 1935, the name Frank Froschauer dominated the sports pages at the University of Illinois. As a member of Coach Bob Zuppke's Fighting Illini football team, the Lincoln, Illinois, native was a prominent contributor from his halfback position. With Coach Craig Ruby's basketball squad, Froschauer led the team in scoring for three consecutive years, averaging eight points per game in an era when the entire team only scored 30 points a game. He also paced the Big Ten in scoring his senior season. Froschauer served as a coach and athletic director for 37 years in the south suburban Chicago area. He was involved with football, swimming, and golf at Thornton of Harvey over a period of 25 years and became Thornridge's first athletic director in 1960, serving until 1972 when he was succeeded by Ron Ferguson. Froschauer died April 28, 1985, at the age of 75.

Illini Lists

FAMOUS ILLINI "33s"

- Kenny Battle, men's basketball
- Dee Dee Deeken, women's basketball
- Bill Erickson, men's basketball
- Chris Green, football
- Eddie Johnson, men's basketball
- Ken Norman, men's basketball
- Lonnie Perrin, football
- Harv Schmidt, men's basketball
- John Valente, baseball
- Kevin Turner, men's basketball
- Damir Krupalija, men's basketball

Captain Bill Erickson wore jersey number 33.

ILLINI LORE

Arthur Cutts Willard took over as the ninth president of the University of Illinois July 1, 1934, succeeding Arthur Daniels. He had been head of the UI's Mechanical Engineering department and acting dean of the College of Engineering. In 1921, Willard had received international recognition for his research work, which provided engineering principles for the ventilation system of the Holland Tunnel under the Hudson River connecting Manhattan, New York, with Jersey City, New Jersey. After 12 years of service, during a period when a depressed economy gripped his campus and the rest of America, Willard retired.

1934-35

AMERICA'S TIME CAPSULE

Oct. 9, 1934	Dizzy Dean and the St. Louis Cardinals won the World Series over the Detroit Tigers.
Dec. 9, 1934	The Chicago Bears lost the NFL championship game to the New York Giants, 30-13.
May 6, 1935	The Works Progress Administration (WPA) began operation, giving jobs to millions of Americans.
May 24, 1935	More than 20,000 fans at Cincinnati's Crosley Field watched their Reds beat the Philadelphia Phillies in baseball's first-ever night game.
Aug. 14, 1935	President Roosevelt signed the Social Security Act, establishing payment of benefits to senior citizens.

ILLINI MOMENT

Bob Reigel (front row, center) scored nine points in Illinois' 36-22 victory over Michigan.

ILLINI CAGERS BEAT MICHIGAN, CLAIM BIG TEN TITLE:

Illinois athletic teams traveled to Ann Arbor three times during the 1934-35 season, returning each time with a victory. In football, the Illini beat Michigan, 7-6. In baseball, Illinois triumphed 1-0 at Ferry Field. But perhaps its most satisfying conquest in Michigan came on March 4, when the Illini basketball team beat their hosts, 36-22, to claim a share of the Big Ten title. Illinois exploded out of the blocks, scoring the first 15 points of the game, behind Captain Frank Froschauer who ended the contest with nine points. Bob Riegel (nine points), Harry Combes (eight), and Roy Guttschow (seven) tallied 24 of the remaining 25 points. Illinois wound up tying for the title with Purdue and Wisconsin, all finishing with 9-3 league records.

ILLINI SCRAPBOOK

Coach Hartley Price led the Fighting Illini gymnastics team to the 1935 Big Ten Championship at a meet held in Champaign.

ON OCTOBER 20, 1934, when Illinois squared off against Michigan's football team at Ann Arbor, Illini team members didn't realize that they were lining up against a future president of the United States. Wolverine center Gerald Ford became president 40 years later in 1974, when he succeeded Richard Nixon.

Michigan's Gerry Ford

Illini Legend

Charles Flachmann

One of Illinois' most brilliant athletes during the mid-1930s was swimmer Charles Flachmann. Lettering for the Fighting Illini from 1934-35 for Coach Ed Manley, Flachmann dominated the freestyle events in Big Ten championship competition. He swept the 50- and 100-yard races both years and also captured the 220-yard event his junior year.

Nationally, Flachmann also won titles in all three events. Following his athletic career at Illinois, he served as a captain in the army during World War II. When Flachmann returned to civilian life, he worked as an insurance broker in St. Louis and was also an amateur artist. Flachmann died in 1983 at the age of 69.

Illini Lists

NCAA WRESTLING CHAMPIONS

- 1929-30 Joe Sapora, 115 pounds
- 1929 George Minot, 135 pounds
- 1932 Joe Puerta, 121 pounds
- 1935 Ralph Silverstein, 175 pounds
- 1938 John Ginay, 165 pounds
- 1938 Allen Sapora, 126 pounds
- 1939 Archie Deutschman, 136 pounds
- 1946 David Shapiro, 165 pounds
- 1956 Larry TenPas, 157 pounds
- 1957-58 Bob Norman, heavyweight
- 1991 Jon Llewellyn, heavyweight
- 1995 Steve Marianetti, 150 pounds
- 1995 Ernest Benion, Jr., 158 pounds
- 1998 Eric Siebert, 150 pounds
- 2000 Carl Perry, 141 pounds
- 2001 John Lockhart, heavyweight
- 2001 Adam Tirapelle, 149 pounds

Ralph "Ruffy" Silverstein won the 175-pound NCAA championship in 1935.

ILLINI LORE

On February 9, 1935, the University of Illinois' Board of Trustees approved the formation of the UI Foundation to encourage the giving of more gifts to the University, not only by alumni but by citizens in general. An organization called the Alumni Fund, the predecessor to the Foundation, managed to raise only $48,000 after coming into being in 1921. Over the past 65 years, the UI Foundation has accepted more than $2 billion in gifts and contributions.

RAY ELIOT
"Mr. Illini"

DIKE ED

CLAUDE "BUDDY" YO

ALEX AGASE

1935-36

AMERICA'S TIME CAPSULE

Sept. 8, 1935   Powerful Louisiana politician Huey Long was assassinated in the corridor of the state capitol in Baton Rouge.

Oct. 7, 1935   The Chicago Cubs lost baseball's World Series to the Detroit Tigers, four games to two.

Nov. 9, 1935   The Committee for Industrial Organization (CIO) was established by John L. Lewis.

June 12, 1936   Kansas governor Alf Landon and Col. Frank Knox of Illinois were nominated by the Republican National Convention as its candidates for president and vice president.

Aug. 16, 1936   The Summer Olympic Games, featuring American track star Jesse Owens, ended in Berlin, Germany.

ILLINI MOMENT

ILLINI BURY WOLVERINES IN MUD:

The Michigan "Football Express" roared into Illinois' Memorial Stadium on a four-game winning streak, but the combination of a stingy Illini defense and a muddy field buried the Wolverines in their tracks, November 9, 1935. The mud-encrusted right foot of Illini kicker Lowell Spurgeon accounted for the only score of the day, a 31-yard field goal in the second quarter, as Illinois beat Michigan, 3-0. The Wolverine offense never got started; in fact, it never carried the ball as far as the middle of the field. Gaining only 16 total yards, the only first down Michigan managed the entire afternoon was courtesy of an Illini penalty. The mud didn't seem to bother Illini quarterback "Wib" Henry, though, as he rushed for a net gain of 123 yards.

Lowell Spurgeon's 31-yard field goal beat Michigan in 1935.

ILLINI SCRAPBOOK

Aviator Amelia Earhart (right) was hosted at the University of Illinois campus in 1935 by UI First Lady Sarah Williard, wife of President Arthur Willard.

Thirty-nine-year-old Craig Ruby announced his resignation in 1936, saying, "I do not choose to face the prospect of coaching basketball at 50 or 60 years of age."

I Illini Item

BASKETBALL COACH CRAIG RUBY concluded his 14-year career at the University of Illinois by announcing his resignation on February 7, 1936. "My reason for resigning," said the 39-year-old Ruby, "is that I believe it is unwise for my family and myself to depend upon the game of basketball entirely in the later years of my life. I do not choose to face the prospect of coaching basketball at 50 or 60 years of age."

Illini Lists

HEISMAN AWARD WINNERS
WHO PLAYED AGAINST ILLINOIS

(Performances in the year they won the award)

- Jay Berwanger of Chicago (11/23/35)
  26 rushes for 106 yards, 1 TD
- Tom Harmon of Michigan (10/19/40)
  21 rushes for 58 yards, 1 TD, 1 FG
- Bruce Smith of Minnesota (10/11/41)
  Yardage unavailable, 2 TD
- Angelo Bertelli of Notre Dame (10/23/43)
  5 of 7 passes for 82 yards, 1 TD pass
- Les Horvath of Ohio State (11/18/50)
  22 rushes for 109 yards, 2 TD
- Vic Janowicz of Ohio State (11/18/50)
  21 rushes for 90 yards, 5 of 12 passes for 59 yards, 1 TD
- Howard Cassady of Ohio State (10/8/55)
  18 rushes for 95 yards, 2 TD
- Archie Griffin of Ohio State (11/2/74)
  20 rushes for 144 yards, 2 TD
- Archie Griffin of Ohio State (11/8/75)
  23 rushes for 127 yards, 1 TD
- Desmond Howard of Michigan (11/16/91)
  7 catches for 80 yards, 1 TD
- Eddie George of Ohio State (11/11/95)
  36 rushes for 314 yards, 3 TD

Illini Legend

Harry Combes

For 24 years, the name Harry Combes was synonymous with University of Illinois basketball. The Monticello, Illinois, native played guard and forward on the Fighting Illini teams of 1935, '36, and '37, twice leading Illinois to Big Ten Conference titles. An All-Big Ten selection his junior and senior seasons, Combes also won the Conference Medal of Honor for proficiency in athletics and scholarship his final year. Two years after his graduation, he began a highly successful nine-year prep coaching career at Champaign High School. Combes succeeded Doug Mills as Illinois' basketball coach in 1947 and led the Illini to Big Ten titles in three of his first five seasons. In 1949, '51, and '52, UI basketball clubs finished third at the NCAA tournament each year. Combes's 20-year coaching record at Illinois was 316 wins and 150 losses, a mark that stood as the Illini record until it was broken by Lou Henson. He died November 13, 1977, at the age of 62.

ILLINI LORE

In December of 1935, after four months of negotiations, the State of Illinois approved an appropriation of $1.2 million to the University of Illinois for a major addition to the Medical Center on Polk Street in Chicago. For a time, the depression halted progress on the center's east tower. But finally, in 1937, construction was eventually completed through the federal Public Works Administration.

1936-37

AMERICA'S TIME CAPSULE

Nov. 3, 1936   Franklin Roosevelt was elected president of the United States in a crushing victory over Republican Alf Landon.

May 6, 1937   The dirigible *Hindenburg* burst into flames at Lakehurst, New Jersey, marking the virtual end of lighter-than-air transportation.

May 12, 1937   Americans listened to the coronation of King George IV of England in radio's first worldwide broadcast.

June 5, 1937   Jockey Charles Kurtsinger rode War Admiral to victory at the Belmont Stakes, thus winning horse racing's Triple Crown.

June 22, 1937   Joe Louis knocked out Jim Braddock to capture the heavyweight boxing title in a match held at Chicago's Soldier Field.

ILLINI MOMENT

Hale Swanson's tip-in salvaged the Illini comeback against Purdue.

ILLINI CAGERS SNAP 14-YEAR JINX AT PURDUE:

In one of the most raucous basketball battles ever played between Illinois and Purdue, it took a rebound basket by Illini reserve center Hale Swanson with just five seconds left to secure a 38-37 victory. The January 18, 1937, win was Illinois' first at West Lafayette in 14 seasons and moved the Illini into a first-place tie in the Big Ten standings. Trailing 23-11 early in the second half, Illinois steadily whittled away at the Boilermaker advantage and took the lead with six minutes remaining. Purdue regained the lead in the final minute, but fouled Illini star Lou Boudreau with just five seconds left in the game. Boudreau missed both free-throw attempts, but Swanson's tip-in salvaged the Illini comeback. Illinois went on to win six of its last seven games to tie Minnesota for the Big Ten title.

Fighting Illini wrestler John Ginay won the 195-pound Big Ten title in both 1937 and '38, leading Illinois to the team championship as a junior.

ILLINI SCRAPBOOK

ILLINOIS

The Fighting Illini basketball team, coached by Bill Self (second from right), won back-to-back Big Ten titles in 2001 and 2002.

Illinois' Carl Perry realized his dream in March of 2000 when he captured the NCAA championship at 141 pounds.

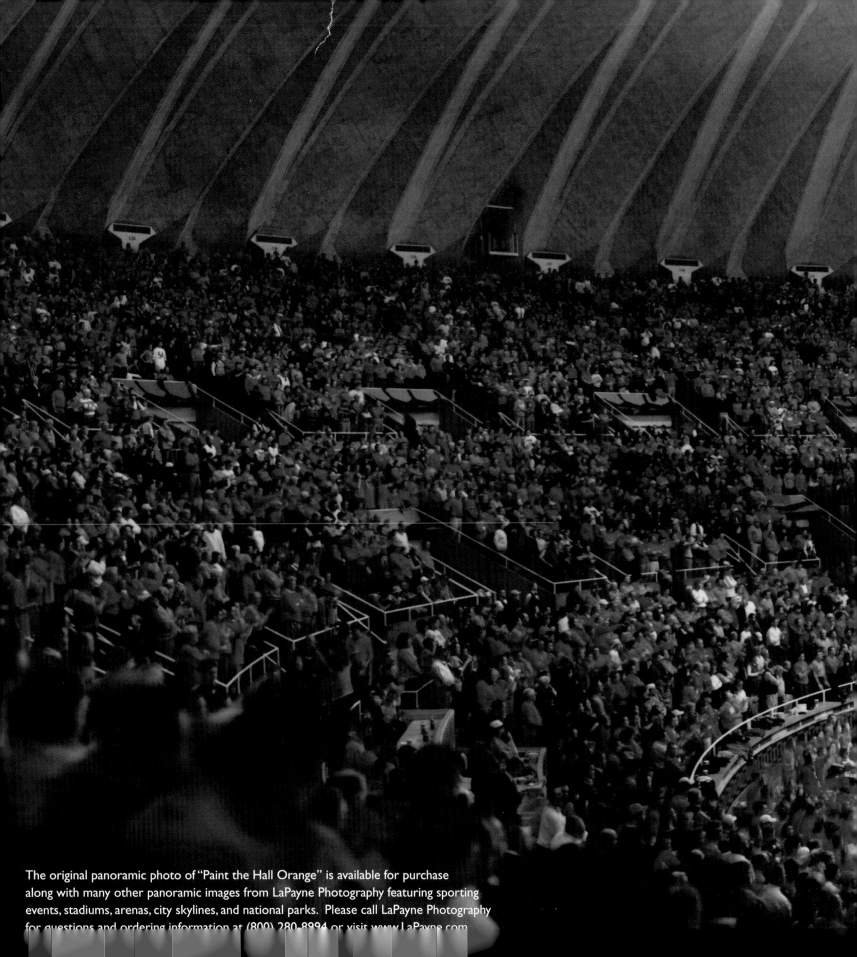

The original panoramic photo of "Paint the Hall Orange" is available for purchase
along with many other panoramic images from LaPayne Photography featuring sporting
events, stadiums, arenas, city skylines, and national parks. Please call LaPayne Photography
for questions and ordering information at (800) 280-8994 or visit www.LaPayne.com

Eichelberger Field, the home of Fighting Illini softball, was dedicated March 27, 2001.

LEFT

Illinois' Andy Dickinson was the Big Ten Conference's Pitcher of the Year in 2001.

RIGHT

Craig Tiley, shown here with UI athlete Brian Wilson, has led the Fighting Illini men's tennis team to six consecutive Big Ten championships.

LEFT

More than 350 students comprise the Marching Illini band each year.

RIGHT

Women's basketball coach Theresa Grentz (left) and her star athlete, Ashley Berggren, won respective Coach of the Year and Player of the Year awards following the 1996-97 season.

LEFT

Quarterback Kurt Kittner (left) and Head Coach Ron Turner led the Fighting Illini to the 2001 Big Ten title and an appearance in the Sugar Bowl on New Year's Day, 2002.

RIGHT

Chief Illiniwek

Dick Butkus's jersey number 50 is one of only two football numbers retired by the University of Illinois.

WENDELL "WEENIE" WILSON, Illinois varsity football letter winner in 1925 and '26, was officially appointed director of athletics February 27, 1937, replacing the late George Huff. He was only 31 years old at the time of his appointment.

Illini Legend

Lou Boudreau

The folks at Harvey Thornton High School probably knew that Lou Boudreau would end up in the Hall of Fame. However, they figured it would be in the sport of basketball, not baseball, where their favorite son would make his greatest impression. Boudreau did enjoy great success on the hardcourts at Illinois, earning All-America honors as a junior, averaging nearly nine points per game. However, the major league baseball scouts also liked what they saw of Boudreau in 1937, hitting .347 while leading the Illini to the Big Ten title. The very next spring, he joined the Cleveland Indians. Four years later at age 24, Boudreau was named player-manager of the Indians. His greatest success on the baseball diamond came in 1948 when he guided Cleveland to the World Series title while earning American League MVP honors. During his 15-year major league career with Cleveland and the Boston Red Sox, Boudreau hit .295 with 68 home runs and 789 RBI. In addition to managing Cleveland, he also was the skipper for the Red Sox, the Kansas City Athletics, and the Chicago Cubs. He served as a television and radio announcer for the Cubs for more than two decades, and was inducted into Baseball's Hall of Fame in 1970. The University of Illinois retired baseball jersey number five in his honor on April 18, 1992. Boudreau died in 2001.

Illini Lists

ALL-TIME COLLEGE BASEBALL "DREAM TEAM"

(As selected in 1990 by Collegiate Baseball)

- **Lou Boudreau, Illinois**
- Mickey Cochrane, Boston U.
- Jackie Robinson, UCLA
- George Sisler, Michigan
- Eddie Collins, Columbia
- Joe Sewell, Alabama
- Frankie Frisch, Fordham
- Thurman Munson, Kent State
- Mike Schmidt, Ohio U.
- Harvey Kuenn, Wisconsin
- Ethan Allen, Cincinnati
- Tony Gwynn, San Diego State
- Lou Gehrig, Columbia
- Reggie Jackson, Arizona State
- Carl Yastrzemski, Notre Dame
- Dave Winfield, Minnesota
- Christy Mathewson, Bucknell
- Eddie Plank, Gettysburg

Illinois' Lou Boudreau was a member of college baseball's Dream Team.

ILLINI LORE

"If every professor on the campus were as good in his line as Illini Nellie is in hers," the Illinois *Alumni News* said in a June, 1937 story, "what a university we would have!" The dairy department's super-cow was the world's record holder for production, setting seven marks during a 12-month period. Nellie produced 1,200 pounds of butterfat and 29,569 pounds of milk, as compared to the average cow (161 pounds of butterfat). The nine-year-old, pure-bred brown Swiss cow's average daily diet consisted of 25 pounds of hay, 15 pounds of grain, 20 pounds of beet pulp, and five pounds of silage.

1937-38

AMERICA'S TIME CAPSULE

Dec. 12, 1937   The Chicago Bears lost the NFL championship game to the Washington Redskins, 28-21.
April 10, 1938   The German army occupied and annexed Austria.
May 2, 1938   Thornton Wilder's "Our Town" won a Pulitzer Prize for drama.
June 25, 1938   President Franklin Roosevelt signed the Wage and Hours Act, raising the minimum wage for workers engaged in interstate commerce from 25 cents to 40 cents per hour.
July 1, 1938   Don Budge and Helen Wills Moody captured Wimbledon tennis titles.

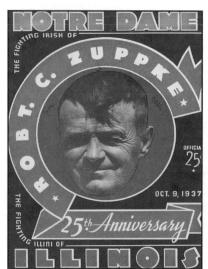

ILLINI MOMENT

FIGHTING ILLINI BATTLE IRISH TO STANDSTILL:

The scoreboard at the end of the game read Illinois-0, Notre Dame-0, but none of the 45,000 fans in attendance at Memorial Stadium that mild afternoon of October 9, 1937, went home disappointed. They'd just seen one of the most magnificent defensive efforts ever by their Fighting Illini, holding Coach Elmer Layden's Irish juggernaut to little more than 100 total yards. Jack Berner, who punted 10 times for an average of 35 yards, was also a bulwark on defense, lending a hand in stopping almost every Notre Dame run. Mel Brewer missed what would have been the game-winning field goal, a 14-yarder, in the first quarter, but the Illini never generated another true scoring threat. Notre Dame wound up the season with a 6-2-1 record, while Illinois finished at 3-3-2.

Pitcher Ray Poat compiled a perfect 10-0 record for the Illini baseball team in 1937 and '38.

Illinois' "Pick" Dehner

I Illini Item

ILLINOIS' LEWIS "PICK" DEHNER tied Big Ten basketball's individual scoring record January 15, 1938, with a 29-point performance against the University of Chicago. The record was set originally by Joe Reiff of Northwestern in 1933 and tied by Jewell Young of Purdue in 1937. Only a weakness at the free-throw line (5 of 10) kept Dehner from setting a record.

Illini Legend

Hek Kenney

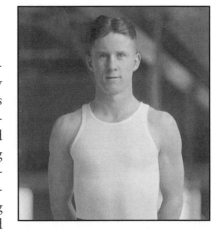

Harold Eugene "Hek" Kenney is remembered as the man for whom Kenney Gym on the University of Illinois campus was named. However, it was his accomplishments in the sport of wrestling that gained him his initial fame. A two-time wrestling captain during his Illini career from 1924-26 under Coach Paul Prehn, Kenney succeeded his mentor as coach of UI grappling in 1929. For the next 15 years, he guided the Illini to a dual-meet record of 91-28-2 and four Big Ten titles. It was not uncommon for Kenney's teams to wrestle before crowds of more than 3,000 fans. Among his standout pupils were the Sapora brothers, Joe and Al, Ralph "Ruffy" Silverstein, and Archie Deutschman. So respected was Kenney that he served two terms as president of the National Wrestling Coaches and Officials Association. He was a member of UI's physical education faculty until his retirement in 1967. Two years later, he was honored as the first recipient of the College of Physical Education's "Distinguished Alumnus Award." Kenney died in 1972 at the age of 69. On April 25, 1974, the building in which he had toiled for most of his life was renamed in his honor.

Illini Lists

Pat Harmon, historian of the National Football Foundation and College Football Hall of Fame, worked as a sportswriter and later served as sports editor of the *Champaign News-Gazette* from 1934 to 1947. Here's his list of the 10 most memorable Illini athletes of that period:

1. Dike Eddleman — won 11 letters in football, basketball, and track
2. Lou Boudreau — a star in baseball and basketball
3. Ralph "Ruffy" Silverstein— a colorful showman for the Illini wrestling team
4. Alex Agase — a football All-American
5. Andy Phillip — the best basketball player of his era
6. Buddy Young — superstar of Illini football and track
7. Harry Combes — one of Illini basketball's greatest leaders
8. Lee Eilbracht — Illinois' best in baseball
9. Herb McKenley — the nation's best in the 440-yard dash
10. Wib Henry — a three-sport star in football, basketball, and baseball

ILLINI LORE

On March 11, 1938, the 70th anniversary of the opening of the University of Illinois, workers began razing Old University Hall. The facility, completed in 1873 at a cost of $150,000, represented 65 years of history to UI alumni and there was much resistance from them towards tearing it down. However, building experts indicated that the cost of leveling the structure would run as much as constructing a new classroom. Salvaged from the historic building was the Memorial Clock, a gift from the Class of 1878, which today graces the cupola of the Illini Union.

1938-39

AMERICA'S TIME CAPSULE

Oct. 9, 1938   The New York Yankees defeated the Chicago Cubs in four straight games for the World Series title.

Oct. 30, 1938   American radio listeners panicked as Orson Welles staged his play *War of the Worlds*. They mistook the realistically performed "news reports" for an actual invasion from Mars.

June 8, 1939   King George VI and Queen Elizabeth of Great Britain visited President Roosevelt at the White House.

June 12, 1939   Byron Nelson captured the U.S. Open golf tournament championship.

June 28, 1939   The Pan American Airways airliner *Dixie Clipper* began regular transatlantic passenger service.

ILLINI MOMENT

Coach Hartley Price (front row, far right) and the 1939 gymnastics team.

NATIONAL CHAMPS:

Coach Hartley Price's University of Illinois gymnasts were on top of the world during the 1938-39 season. They roared through their dual-meet schedule unbeaten, then hosted the Western Conference Meet at the Old Gym on March 11. The Fighting Illini didn't disappoint their hometown fans that day, outdistancing runner-up Minnesota by 22 points, 111.5 to 89.5. A month later came the national meet at the University of Chicago, and Illinois again wound up on top, claiming their first-ever NCAA title. Leading the way for the Illini was junior All-American Joe Giallombardo, who won the individual all-around championships at both the conference and national meets. Other UI stars included Paul Fina, Marvin Forman, and Harry Koehnemann.

Harry Koehnemann (left) and Paul Fina

FIGHTING ILLINI WRESTLING CAPTAIN Archie Deutschman was a two-way star during the 1938-39 season. On the wrestling mat for Coach Hek Kenney, he won both the Big Ten and NCAA titles at the 136-pound classification. As a reward for his proficiency in the classroom, Deutschman was honored as Illinois' Big Ten Conference Medal of Honor winner.

Archie Deutschman (left) with Coach Hek Kenney.

Illini Legend

Joe Giallombardo

At first glance, Joe Giallombardo could hardly be mistaken for a dominant athlete. However, packed inside his stocky five-feet four-inch, 155-pound frame were tightly wound, spring-loaded muscles. While Jesse Owens, his Cleveland East Tech High School classmate, was making headlines as a track man, Giallombardo became the premier athlete in the sport of gymnastics. During his three years at the University of Illinois from 1938-40, "Little Joe" won every individual title there was to win. He was a three-time all-around champion in the Big Ten, helping the Fighting Illini win the 1939 team title. Among his record seven NCAA titles were three all-around crowns, three tumbling championships, and a first-place finish on the rings. Giallombardo coached gymnastics at New Trier and New Trier West high schools from the time he graduated until his retirement in 1975. He now lives in Wheeling, Illinois.

Illini Lists

ILLINI WHOSE NUMBERS HAVE BEEN RETIRED IN PROFESSIONAL SPORTS

No. 5	Lou Boudreau, Cleveland Indians
No. 7	George Halas, Chicago Bears
No. 22	Buddy Young, Baltimore Colts
No. 51	Dick Butkus, Chicago Bears
No. 66	Ray Nitschke, Green Bay Packers
No. 77	Red Grange, Chicago Bears

George Halas

ILLINI LORE

· ·

The cornerstone of Gregory Hall was laid June 10, 1939, by Alfred Gregory, son of the man for whom the memorial was being made—John Milton Gregory, first president of the University of Illinois. The structure originally housed the College of Education, the School of Journalism, and classrooms for students enrolled in Liberal Arts and Sciences. A copper box containing, among other items, the photograph and biography of President Gregory was placed inside the cornerstone.

1939-40

AMERICA'S TIME CAPSULE

Sept. 3, 1939	The nations of France and Great Britain declared war on Germany, while President Roosevelt said that the United States would remain neutral.
Dec. 10, 1939	The Green Bay Packers defeated the New York Giants, 27-0, to win the NFL championship.
March 30, 1940	Indiana won its first NCAA basketball title, beating Kansas, 60-42.
May 6, 1940	John Steinbeck won a Pulitzer Prize for his book *The Grapes of Wrath*.
May 15, 1940	The first successful helicopter flight in the United States took place.

ILLINI MOMENT

Illini fans celebrated their heroes' upset of Michigan.

ILLINOIS SHOCKS MICHIGAN:

Winless Illinois wasn't given much hope against Coach Fritz Crisler's Michigan Wolverine football squad, starring eventual Heisman Trophy winner Tom Harmon. Michigan came to Champaign averaging 41 points per game, but on that unseasonably mild November 4 afternoon, the Wolverines managed only a single touchdown. Though Harmon did net 72 yards rushing, his performance was stymied by a brilliant effort from Coach Bob Zuppke's defensive unit. Illinois' two touchdowns were scored by George Rettinger following a 48-yard pass and by Jim Smith on a three-yard run. One of the unsung heroes for the Illini was lineman Mel Brewer, who dedicated the game to his mother who had died earlier that week. The nation's sportswriters later selected the game as the biggest upset of the 1939 season. Illinois wound up the year with a 3-4-1 record as compared to Michigan's 6-2 overall mark.

ILLINI SCRAPBOOK

The Illini Union opened its doors to the public in 1941.

Illini baseball player Hoot Evers also threw the javelin for the track squad.

I Illini Item

SOPHOMORE WALTER "HOOT" EVERS was the most versatile Fighting Illini athlete of 1939-40, lettering in basketball, baseball, and track. On the hardcourts, "Hoot" was Illinois' second-leading scorer. As a center fielder in baseball, Evers hit a cool .353 in Big Ten play. Illini track coach Leo Johnson pulled Evers off the baseball diamond to compete in the Big Ten outdoor meet as a javelin thrower. Despite practicing only a week, "Hoot" placed second in the conference meet. At the end of the season, Evers received numerous offers to quit college and play professional baseball, which he turned down. However, in midterm of the 1940-41 school year, Evers failed a history course and was declared ineligible for college athletics. He signed with Detroit and went on to a long and successful career in the major leagues.

Illini Legend

Bill Hapac

Quick now—what does former Illinois basketball star Bill Hapac have in common with Andy Phillip, Terry Dischinger, Jimmy Rayl, Dave Schellhase, and Rick Mount? If you guessed that they all once set the Big Ten single-game scoring record, you get the grand prize. Hapac's night in the spotlight came against Minnesota on February 10, 1940, when he scored a then unheard-of 34 points. The Cicero, Illinois, native was the conference's leading scorer his senior year, averaging nearly 14 points per game. Besides lettering three times in basketball, Hapac also earned three varsity monograms in baseball. Twice he scored five runs in a game, a mark that's still a school record. Hapac served as an officer in the air corps during World War II, then played pro basketball for several years. A consensus basketball All-American at Illinois, he coached the sport at Morton East High School until his death in 1967 at the age of 49.

Illini Lists

SHORTEST ILLINI MEN'S BASKETBALL PLAYERS

Joe Frank, a Fighting Illini letter from 1938-40, was one of the shortest men ever to play basketball at the University of Illinois. Here's a list of the tiniest Illini hoopsters.

5'7"	Joe Frank, Vandalia, 1940
5'7"	Seymour Gantman, Chicago, 1952
5'8"	Phil Flanigan, Tuscola, 1959
5'8"	John Easterbrook, Champaign, 1960
5'8"	Bob Meadows, Collinsville, 1965
5'9"	Bill Ridley, Taylorville, 1956
5'9"	Halim Abdullah, Jersey City, N.J. 1997
5'10"	Tony Wysinger, Peoria, 1987
5'10"	P.J. Bowman, Champaign, 1990
5'10"	Jelani Boline, Chicago, 1998

Joe Frank

ILLINI LORE

The world's first betatron, an atom-smasher for high-energy physics exploration into the nucleus of the atom, was introduced in 1940 by University of Illinois physicist Donald Kerst. Kerst's first betatron was 19 inches long, 20 inches high, eight inches thick, and weighed 200 pounds. It produced x-rays with an energy of two and one-half million electron volts. The electrons reached their energy by spinning around many times within a doughnut-shaped vacuum tube.

1940-41

AMERICA'S TIME CAPSULE

Sept. 16, 1940	Congress passed the Selective Service Act, requiring all men between the ages of 20 and 36 to register for the armed services .
Nov. 5. 1940	Franklin Roosevelt defeated Republican Wendell Willkie for a second term as president.
Dec. 8, 1940	The Chicago Bears beat the Washington Redskins, 73-0, in the NFL championship game.
June 22, 1941	Germany invaded the U.S.S.R.
July 17, 1941	Joe DiMaggio's incredible baseball hitting streak of 56 consecutive games was ended by the Cleveland Indians.

ILLINI MOMENT

(left to right) Captain Alex Welsh, John Holmstrom, John Buzick, Bill Usinger, Dick Wolfley, and Ross Reed.

ILLINI GOLFERS CAPTURE BIG TEN CROWN:

When Coach Winsor Brown's Fighting Illini golf team captured its second consecutive Big Ten championship on June 19, 1941, it helped the University of Illinois to become the winningest conference school ever in the sport at that time. Led by individual medalist Alex Welsh, the Illini outdistanced runners-up Ohio State and Michigan for their sixth all-time team crown. Besides Welsh, other members of the team included John Holmstrom, John Buzick, Dick Wolfley, and Bill Usinger. A week later, the Illini golf squad traveled to to the NCAA championship meet and placed fourth. Since 1941, Illini golfers have won only one Big Ten team title.

Brothers Paul and Tiz Bresee shared public address duties at Fighting Illini football and basketball games, beginning in the early 1930s and ending with their joint retirement in 1972. This photo is of their ground-level booth, used in the early portion of their PA career.

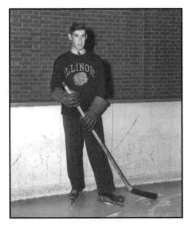

Coach Vic Heyliger

I Illini Item

ILLINOIS WAS THE UNOFFICIAL national champion of college ice hockey in 1941, recording a mark of 17-3-1. In competition against Big Ten foes, the Illini were 6-1-1. The stars of coach Vic Heyliger's team were Norbert Sterle, Aldo Palazarri, and Arno Bessone. Bessone later became a successful coach at Michigan State, leading the Spartans to the 1966 NCAA title.

Illini Legend

Leo Johnson

If the measure of success of a coach is quantified in championships, then longtime University of Illinois coach Leo Johnson was a giant of his era in the sport of track and field. From the time he was hired as coach of the Illini in 1938 until his retirement at age 70 in 1965, Johnson guided Fighting Illini teams to 17 Big Ten titles and three national championships. Since 1944, when Johnson's Illini won the NCAA title, he is one of only four coaches outside the Sun Belt states to win a national championship. His athletes captured 27 individual NCAA titles and 158 conference firsts during his 28 years at Illinois. A member of numerous track and field Halls of Fame, Johnson was also known in Illini football history as one of the game's finest scouts. A college football and track star at Millikin College in Decatur, Johnson served as a lieutenant in World War I. When the war ended, he played pro football briefly with George Halas' Decatur Staleys, then became head coach of all sports at Millikin in 1923. Johnson died in 1982 at the age of 87.

Illini Lists

ILLINI MEN'S ATHLETIC TRAINERS

—— to 1913	William "Willie" McGill
1913-26	Dr. Samuel Bilik
1916-47	David M. "Matt" Bullock
1947-51	Elmer "Ike" Hill
1951-57	Richard Klein
1957-69	Robert Nicollette
1969-73	Robert Behnke
1973-83	John "Skip" Pickering
1983-present	Al Martindale

ILLINI WOMEN'S ATHLETIC TRAINERS

1975-78	Dana Gerhardt
1978-80	Ellen Murray
1980-present	Karen Lehl-Morse

Matt Bullock served as Illinois' head athletic trainer from 1916-47.

ILLINI LORE

The Illini Union officially opened its doors at the University of Illinois on February 8, 1941. Interest in building a facility intensified in 1934 when A.C. Willard was inaugurated as president of the university. One of the president's first official acts was to appoint a committee to investigate construction of a Union building. When the UI decided to raze University Hall—the site on which the Illini Union was built—the decision of the committee was unanimous. An addition to the $1.2 million structure was completed at a cost of nearly $7 million in 1963. More than 40 volumes of illustration of colonial architecture were used in preparing the preliminary drawings of the Illini Union. The distinctive feature of the building is a 30-foot open-arched cupola and its 11-foot bronze weather vane. In the belfry of the cupola is the University's historic chapel bell and, at its base, is the 124-year-old clock that once stood in University Hall.

1941-42

AMERICA'S TIME CAPSULE

Dec. 7, 1941	About 3,000 Americans lost their lives when the Japanese attacked Pearl Harbor, Hawaii.
Dec. 11, 1941	Germany and Italy declared war against the United States.
Dec. 21, 1941	The Chicago Bears won the NFL championship, defeating the New York Giants 37-9.
Jan. 9, 1942	Joe Louis successfully defended his world heavyweight boxing title for the 20th time, knocking out Max Baer in the first round.
April 18, 1942	American bombers, under the command of Maj. Gen. James Doolittle, conducted a successful air raid on Tokyo.

ILLINI MOMENT

WHIZ KIDS:

Doug Mills, coach of the University of Illinois' most famous basketball team, placed his "Whiz Kids" in a class of their own. "Of all the players I ever coached," Mills recalled later, "only Lou Boudreau could have played with them. That's how good they were." Four finely tuned athletes, all around 6'3", formed the heart of the "Whiz Kids." In three seasons together, the quartet of future Hall of Famer Andy Phillip, Jack Smiley, Gene Vance, and Ken Menke, along with two-year Whiz Kid Art Mathisen, fashioned a cumulative Big Ten record of 33-6 in 1942, '43, and '47, winning two conference titles and finishing second as seniors. The 1943 club finished the year with an overall record of 17-1 and was undefeated in conference play (12-0), but didn't play in the national tournament because of service in World War II. "Uncle Sam had our draft rights," said Vance, and the war took precedence over the five-year-old NCAA championship playoffs. "I'm 99 percent sure we would have won," said Menke. When the group reunited for the 1946-47 campaign, all four players returned to starting positions for Mills, but it wasn't quite the same. "The war had taken something out of them," recalled Mills. "They had gone through terrible war experiences, and they had changed." Still, in the history of Fighting Illini basketball, there has never been a team quite like the "Whiz Kids."

The Whiz Kids, coached by Doug Mills (left), were comprised of (left to right) Art Mathisen, Jack Smiley, Gene Vance, Ken Menke and Andy Phillip.

ILLINI SCRAPBOOK

UI's fraternity houses transformed into army barracks during the second World War. These soldiers stayed in the living room at the Sigma Pi fraternity.

Coach Bob Zuppke gives instructions to an Illini player during this scene from 1941.

Illini Item

ON NOVEMBER 17, 1941, five days before his team's season finale at Northwestern, veteran Fighting Illini football coach Bob Zuppke announced his retirement. Under pressure from alumni and the University of Illinois' Board of Trustees, Zuppke stepped down "for the good of Illinois." Unfortunately, Zuppke's team ended the season on a sour note, losing to the Wildcats, 27-0.

Illini Lists

RECIPIENTS OF THE VARSITY "I" AWARD

1970	Claude "Buddy" Young ('46)	Football/Track
1971	Leland Stilwell ('24)	Basketball
1972	Barton Cummings ('35)	Football/Track
1973	Ray Eliot ('32)	Football/Baseball
1974	Robert Wright ('36)	Football/Track
1975	Willard Franks ('49)	Football/Track
1976	Perry Graves ('15)	Football/Baseball
1977	George Halas ('18)	Football/Basketball/Baseball
1978	Charles Bennis ('35)	Football
1979	Charles Carney ('22)	Football/Basketball
1980	Duane Cullinan ('37)	Track
1981	Wayne Paulson ('66)	Football
1982	Cirilo McSween ('54)	Track
1983	Dwight "Dike" Eddleman ('49)	Football/Basketball/Track
1984	Thomas Stewart ('50)	Football
1985	Russell "Ruck" Steger ('48)	Football/Baseball
1986	Willard Thomson ('55)	Track
1987	Louis Boudreau ('87)	Basketball/Baseball
1988	David Downey ('63)	Basketball
1989	Thomas Riggs ('41)	Football
1990	Richard Butkus ('65)	Football
1991	Thomas Haller ('59)	Football/Basketball/Baseball
1992	William Butkovich ('47)	Football/Baseball
1993	Jerry Colangelo ('93)	Basketball/Baseball
1994	Bobby Mitchell ('58)	Football/Track
1995	Tal Brody ('65)	Basketball
1996	Joe Tanner ('72)	Swimming
1997	Eddie Johnson ('81)	Basketball
1998	John Wright Sr. ('67)	Football/Track
1999	Doug Mills ('62)	Football/Basketball/Baseball
2000	Joel Hirsch ('63)	Golf
2001	Arthur Wyatt ('49)	Golf

Illini Legend

Andy Phillip

The magnificent career of Fighting Illini basketball star Andy Phillip can be summed up in just two words: record-setting. Besides setting University of Illinois basketball records for points in a game, in a season, and in a career, the Granite City, Illinois, native also put his name in the record book beside several Big Ten marks. Following the 1945 season, he was named first-team All-American and was honored as the Big Ten's Most Valuable Player. Phillip and his "Whiz Kids" teammates won back-to-back Big Ten titles in 1942 and '43, compiling an unbelievable 25-2 record in conference play over that span. After the end of the '43 season, Phillip was called to active duty with the Marine Corps for three years. When World War II ended, he returned to Illinois with three other "Whiz Kids" (Jack Smiley, Gene Vance, and Ken Menke) in 1947, when they settled for a second-place finish in the conference. For the next 11 years, Phillip played professional basketball in the National Basketball Association, including two seasons with the world champion Boston Celtics. A five-time NBA All-Star, he was named to the Basketball Hall of Fame in 1961. Phillip has spent all of his postbasketball life in California, retiring in 1987 after 24 years as supervising officer for the Riverside County Probation Department. He died on April 28, 2001, at the age of 79.

ILLINI LORE

During its first 12 months of operation, the $1.7 million Abbott Power Plant in 1941-42 proved to be more efficient than University of Illinois officials hoped it would be. The new plant was built adjacent to the Illinois Central railroad tracks, just northwest of Memorial Stadium, and close to the expanding University. A comparison of the facility's performance in 1921-22 to 1932-33 showed that nearly 10 percent less coal was burned and that 13 percent more cubic feet of space was heated.

1942-43

AMERICA'S TIME CAPSULE

Dec. 1, 1942   Nationwide gasoline rationing went into effect.
Dec. 13, 1942   The Chicago Bears were defeated in the NFL championship game by
                    the Washington Redskins, 14-6.
May 1, 1943   Count Fleet, with jockey Johnny Longden, won the 69th annual Kentucky Derby.
May 5, 1943   Postmaster Frank Walker inaugurated a postal-zone numbering system to speed
                    up mail delivery.
July 19, 1943   More than 500 Allied planes bombed Rome.

ILLINI MOMENT

Lineman Alex Agase scored two touchdowns for the Illini to beat defending national champion Minnesota.

ILLINI END MINNESOTA'S 18-GAME WINNING STREAK:

The 24,000 fans who attended Illinois' 32nd annual Homecoming Game witnessed one of the greatest Illini football upsets ever. First-year coach Ray Eliot inspired his troops with a pregame pep talk and snapped defending national champion Minnesota's 18-game winning streak. The unlikely Illini hero that afternoon was junior guard Alex Agase who scored two of his team's three touchdowns. With the score tied 13-13 late in the fourth quarter, Agase scored the game-winning TD by pouncing on an errant Gopher snap in the end zone. Illinois' 20-13 victory was its first over a Big Ten foe since 1939.

Illinois' Herb Matter won both the pole vault and the broad jump title at the 1943 Big Ten indoor track and field championships.

Coach Doug Mills (right) and his "Whiz Kids" gathered for a reunion in the 1960s.

Illini Item

ILLINOIS' "WHIZ KIDS" beat Northwestern, 86-44, at the Chicago Stadium on February 27, 1943, before a record crowd of 19,848. The triumph marked the school's largest margin of victory ever on the road and was the 11th of 12 in a row as the Illini wrapped up a perfect record in conference play.

Illini Lists

WHIZ KIDS' MOST MEMORABLE GAMES

In June 1994, the University of Illinois' famous Whiz Kids basketball team of the 1940s was surveyed to find out what they considered to be their most memorable games. Ken Menke, Andy Phillip, Art Mathisen, Gene Vance, and Jack Smiley were asked to rank their top 10 selections in order, with 10 points awarded for their first selection, nine points for their second choice, etc. Four of the five men selected Illinois' game vs. Great Lakes on December 19, 1942 as their most memorable game. In that contest, the "Whiz Kids" came from behind to beat a team of former pros, 57-53.

1.	12/19/42 vs. Great Lakes	48 pts.
2.	2/27/43 at Northwestern	39 pts.
3.	1/3/42 at Wisconsin	26 pts.
4.	1/2/43 vs. Stanford	24 pts.
5.	2/28/42 at Northwestern	23 pts.
6.	3/1/43 vs. Chicago	17 pts.
7.	2/23/42 vs. Wisconsin	16 pts.
8.	1/11/43 at Wisconsin	13 pts.
9.	1/13/47 vs. Ohio State	13 pts.
10.	12/9/41 vs. Marquette	12 pts.

Nearly 50 years after they had performed there as athletes, the Whiz Kids returned to Huff Gym to participate in a 1990 re-dedication ceremony. Pictured here are (left to right) Andy Phillip, Ken Menke, Art Mathisen, Jack Smiley and Gene Vance.

Illini Legend

Ray Eliot

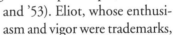

During his days as a Fighting Illini football player under Bob Zuppke in the 1930s, he was listed on the roster as No. 38, Ray Nusspickle. As Zuppke's replacement from 1942 to 1959, he was introduced as head coach Ray Eliot. However, to the thousands of loyal fans who grew to love him, he was best known by the simple moniker "Mr. Illini." A football and baseball letter winner at Illinois, Eliot's greatest fame came after he coached the Illini to Rose Bowl victories in 1947 over UCLA and in 1952 over Stanford. Three times, he won Big Ten championships (1946, '51, and '53). Eliot, whose enthusiasm and vigor were trademarks, served as associate athletic director from 1960 until his retirement in 1973. He represented the Illini program in an honorary capacity after that, before being called upon in the spring of 1979 to become interim athletic director. Eliot was a dynamic speaker who was best known for his inspiring speech "The Proper State of Mind." He died on February 24, 1980, at the age of 75, and was buried in Mt. Hope Cemetery, across Fourth Street from Memorial Stadium.

ILLINI LORE

The University of Illinois focused much of its effort toward wartime preparedness during the 1942-43 academic year. About 1,100 persons, including the physical plant staff and several faculty members, were actively engaged in a program of wartime civilian defense. University enrollment dropped nine percent, but more than 2,000 Navy School trainees were on campus, using Newman Hall and the ice rink as barracks. The UI taught 42 special war courses, ranging from training in Red Cross and Civilian Defense to the structural design of airplanes. A total of 20,276 alumni served in the armed forces during World War 11, with 29 former varsity athletes and 709 others with UI ties losing their lives in service.

1943-44

AMERICA'S TIME CAPSULE

Dec. 24, 1943   General Dwight D. Eisenhower was appointed Supreme Commander of Allied forces for the European invasion.

Dec. 26, 1943   Coach George Halas's Chicago Bears won the NFL title by defeating the Washington Redskins, 41-21.

March 6, 1944   U.S. pilots dropped 2,000 tons of bombs on Berlin.

June 6, 1944   More than 4,000 ships, 3,000 planes, and 4 million Allied troops began the Normandy invasion.

Aug. 25, 1944   Paris was liberated as the Germans surrendered.

ILLINI MOMENT

ILLINI ATHLETICS DURING THE WAR:

World War II had a dramatic effect upon the University of Illinois' intercollegiate athletics program in 1943-44. Of the 81 men who earned varsity letters during the 1942-43 season, only wrestling letterman Robert Hughes and track and field monogram winners Marce Gonzalez and Robert Phelps returned to the '43-44 rosters. Among the more than 150 eligible athletes who left school to serve in the United States' armed forces were such Illini stars as basketball "Whiz Kids" Andy Phillip and Gene Vance, football's Alex Agase and Tony Butkovich, and baseball's Lee Eilbracht. The war forced the Athletic Association to totally drop its gymnastics and fencing programs from 1943-46, while ice hockey was eliminated from varsity status altogether. However, Athletic Director Doug Mills decided that "athletics in wartime should be carried on in as nearly prewar fashion as possible. Certainly, material is not plentiful, coaches may feel their task at times is insurmountable, and gate receipts may decline seriously. But none of these factors should influence us from the conviction that the basic values of the athletic program must remain alive."

Tony Butkovich

Illinois' talented Robert Kelley won the 880-yard run at both the Big Ten indoor and outdoor meets, and at the NCAA championship.

The 1943 Illini football team.

I Illini Item

ILLINOIS LOST ITS ONLY opportunity to salvage a dismal football season on November 13, 1943, when it traveled to Ohio State. When Buckeye quarterback Dean Sensenbaugher's last-ditch pass fell incomplete in Illinois' end zone, the two teams went disappointedly to their dressing rooms, tied at 26 all. However, a game official had signaled the Illini off sides and put two seconds back on the clock. Both teams were brought back on the field, and OSU placekicker John Stungis kicked a 23-yard field goal to give the Buckeyes a 29-26 victory.

Illini Lists

LONGEST RUNS FROM SCRIMMAGE

Buddy Young, Illinois' lightning-quick dynamo from Chicago, played more than a half century ago, but still ranks as the Fighting Illini's most electrifying running back. Of UI football's 10 longest runs from scrimmage, Young owns three of those lengthiest dashes, including two in the very same game.

1. 93 yards Buddy Young vs. Great Lakes, 9/30/44
2. 92 yards Buddy Young vs. Pittsburgh, 10/21/44
3. 89 yards Harry Jefferson vs. Syracuse, 10/23/54
4. 84 yards Ray Nitschke vs. Northwestern, 11/23/57
5. 83 yards John Karras vs. Indiana, 10/27/51
6. 82 yards Buddy Young vs. Pittsburgh, 10/21/44
7. 82 yards Red Grange vs. Chicago, 11/8/24
8. 80 yards Cyril Pinder vs. Duke, 10/23/65
9. 80 yards Edgar Nichol vs. Coe, 10/13/28
10. 78 yards Howard Griffith vs. Utah, 9/17/88

Buddy Young

Illini Legend

Claude "Buddy" Young

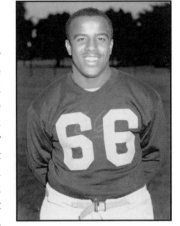

The University of Illinois' first nationally famous African-American athlete stood only five feet, four inches tall, but the legacy he established is immeasurable. Claude "Buddy" Young came to Champaign-Urbana from Chicago Phillips High School, where he was a state champion sprinter and an all-star halfback in football. In his very first competition with the Fighting Illini track team on February 5, 1944, Young won the 60-yard dash at New York's prestigious Millrose Games. He lost very few races that freshman year, tying the world indoor record of 6.1 seconds in the 60 and capturing two sprint titles at the NCAA outdoor meet. On the football field, little number 66 was equally magnificent. The 1944 season saw Young tie Red Grange's school record for touchdowns (13) and average nearly nine yards every time he rushed the ball. He served in the navy in 1945, but was able to return to the Illini football team in 1946, winning MVP honors in the '47 Rose Bowl. Young left Illinois after that season to sign a football contract with the New York Yankees. His Hall of Fame career in pro football ended after 10 seasons, and he became the first Baltimore Colts player to have his jersey—No. 22—retired. In 1964, Young became the first black executive to be hired by the National Football League. He stayed at that post until his death in an automobile accident on September 4, 1983.

ILLINI LORE

On June 1, 1944, the University of Illinois' Board of Trustees approved a proposal to establish a College of Veterinary Medicine and Surgery. Twenty-five years earlier, in 1919, establishment of the college had been authorized by the Illinois General Assembly, but no appropriations followed. The first course in veterinary medicine was actually taught at the UI in 1870.

1944-45

AMERICA'S TIME CAPSULE

Oct. 9, 1944	The St. Louis Cardinals beat the St. Louis Browns, four games to two, in the 41st World Series.
Nov. 7, 1944	Franklin Roosevelt was reelected president of the United States for a record fourth term. He died five months later—April 12, 1945—at the age of 63, and was succeeded by Harry Truman.
Dec. 16, 1944	The last major German offensive of World War II—the Battle of the Bulge—began.
May 8, 1945	The Germans unconditionally surrendered, ending the European phase of World War II
Aug. 6, 1945	The city of Hiroshima, Japan, was destroyed by the first atomic bomb to be used in war. Nine days later, the Japanese surrendered to the Allies.

ILLINI MOMENT

WALKER LEADS ILLINI TO TRACK TITLE:

Scoring in 12 of the 14 events, Coach Leo Johnson's Fighting Illini track and field squad ended Michigan's two-year reign as Big Ten champions, May 26, 1945. Illinois' star performers included two veterans and a pair of freshmen. Junior captain Marce Gonzalez captured the 220-yard dash while grad student Bob Kelley repeated his conference outdoor titles in the 440- and 880-yard runs. Illini rookie George Walker accounted for 15 of his team's 65 1/2 points, taking first place in the 100-yard dash, the 120-yard high hurdles and the 220-yard low hurdles. Fellow freshman Henry Aihara won the broad jump and tied for fourth in the high jump. Two weeks later at the NCAA meet in Milwaukee, the Illini placed second behind Navy, 62 to 57 3/4. Walker captured both hurdles events, Aihara won the broad jump, and Bob Phelps took top honors in the pole vault.

George Walker accounted for 15 of Illinois' 65 1/2 points and led the Illini track and field team to the 1945 Big Ten outdoor championship.

ILLINI SCRAPBOOK

Basketball's Donald Dellaney won the University of Illinois' coveted Conference Medal of Honor in 1945.

Buddy Young (66) rushed three times for 100 yards in his Illini football debut.

I Illini Item

TO SAY THAT THE FOOTBALL debut of Buddy Young, September 16, 1944, was impressive would be a mammoth understatement. The nation's fastest halfback played nine and one-half minutes for Illinois against Illinois State, averaging more than 28 yards every time he touched the ball. Young lost four yards on his very first carry, then scored touchdowns of 22 and 82 yards on his next two attempts. He also ran 51 yards for a TD, only to have it called back by a clipping penalty. The final score: Illinois 79, ISU 0.

Illini Lists

ILLINI FOOTBALL PLAYERS IN HEISMAN TROPHY BALLOTING

1944	Buddy Young, 5th
1951	John Karras, 6th
1953	J.C. Caroline, 7th
1959	Bill Burrell, 4th
1963	Dick Butkus, 6th
1964	Dick Butkus, 3rd
1965	Jim Grabowski, 3rd
1980	Dave Wilson, 10th
1982	Tony Eason, 8th
1989	Jeff George, 35th
2001	Kurt Kittner, 12th

John Karras (#48)

Illini Legend

Walton Kirk

It was a star-studded cast of nominees for the *Daily Illini's* annual "Illini Athlete of the Year" award in 1944-45, but in the end, a junior basketball guard nicknamed "Junior" ran away from his competition. Unanimous All-Big Ten selection Walton "Junior" Kirk was the students' first choice, outdistancing two-sport standout Howie Judson by a two-to-one margin. The native of Mt. Vernon, Illinois, was the Most Valuable Player of Doug Mills's Illinois cagers, averaging nearly 11 points per game. His best effort of the '44-45 campaign came at Michigan in a 55-37 victory when he scored a season-high 21 points. Kirk went into the service at Fort Lewis in June of 1945, then returned to Illinois for the 1946-47 season. He then signed a $10,000 NBA contract with the Fort Wayne Pistons, joining teammates Jack Smiley and Ken Menke. Kirk scored 907 points during his 163-game NBA career with Fort Wayne, Tri-Cities, and Milwaukee. In 1952, he began a long high school coaching career, which saw him make stops at Harvard and Salem, Illinois, and at Dubuque, Iowa. Now retired, he and his wife reside in Dubuque.

ILLINI LORE

George Dinsmore Stoddard was appointed as the University of Illinois' 10th president May 26, 1945, replacing Arthur Cutts Willard as the chief executive officer. Stoddard was the University's chief executive officer during a construction boom on campus, but he also found himself mired in controversy. UI's Board of Trustees and state legislators disapproved of Stoddard's frequent trips abroad and of his ongoing debates with various members of the school's faculty. Stoddard resigned July 24, 1953, under pressure from the Board of Trustees following a 6-3 vote of "no confidence."

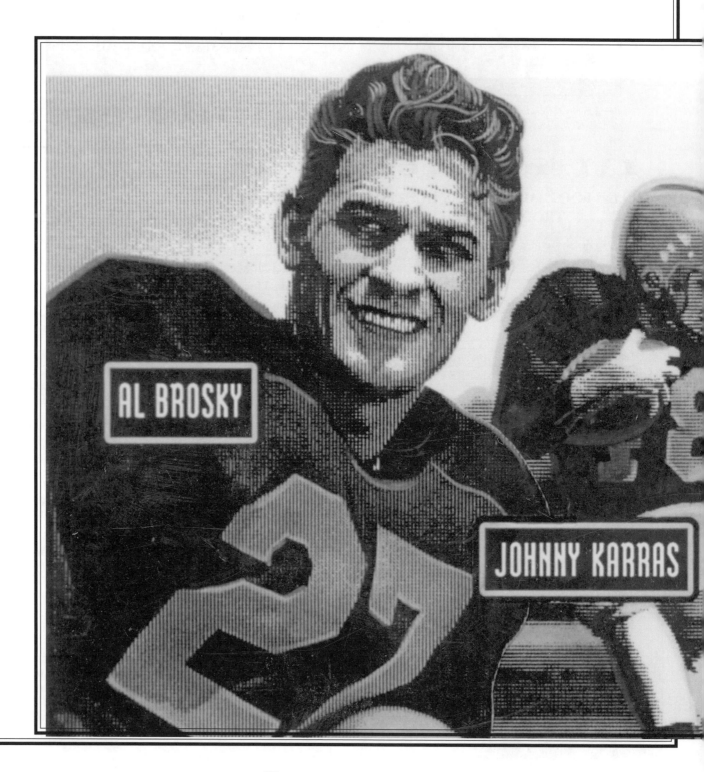

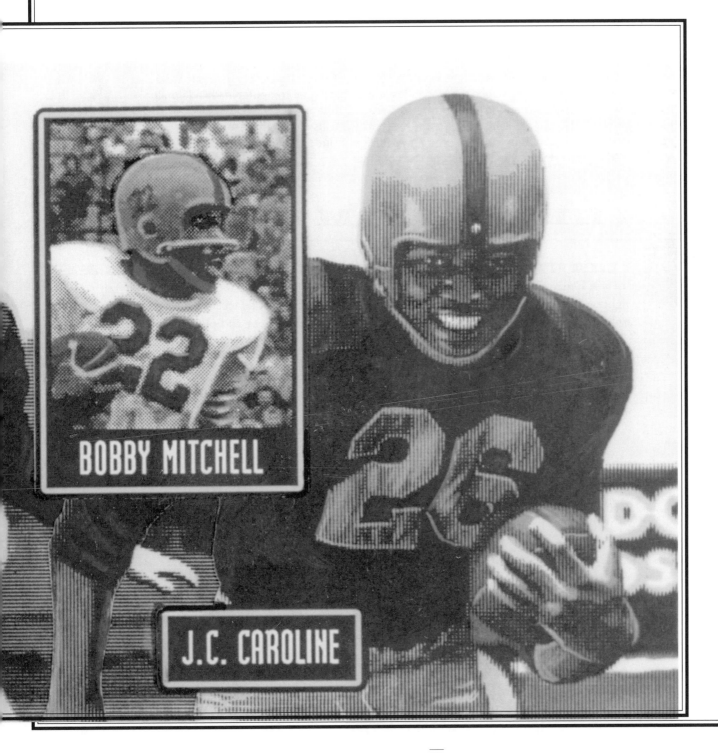

BOBBY MITCHELL

J.C. CAROLINE

1945-46

AMERICA'S TIME CAPSULE

Sept. 2, 1945	Japan signed the formal document of surrender aboard the U.S.S. *Missouri* in Tokyo Bay.
Oct. 10, 1945	The Chicago Cubs lost the World Series to the Detroit Tigers, four games to three.
Feb. 15, 1946	Scientists developed the world's first electronic digital computer in Philadelphia.
June 25, 1946	Fire destroyed the LaSalle Hotel in Chicago. 61 people lost their lives.
July 2, 1946	African-Americans voted for the first time in Mississippi primaries.
July 4, 1946	President Harry Truman proclaimed Philippine independence.
Aug. 25, 1946	Ben Hogan won the PGA golf tournament.

ILLINI MOMENT

The 1946 Illini tennis team won its first Big Ten title in 14 years. Pictured here (left to right) are Jim Gates, Fred Steers, Ben Migdow, Coach Howard Braun, Melvin Rondoll, Roger Downs, and Ray Von Spreckelsen.

ILLINI TEAMS WIN FOUR BIG TEN TITLES:

Though they finished second to Ohio State in the all-sports standings among Big Ten schools, Fighting Illini teams won more conference titles than any other conference member during the 1945-46 athletic season. Illinois took top honors in the sports of both indoor and outdoor track, wrestling, and tennis. The latter two were especially pleasing, since several years had lapsed in between championships. Nine years had passed since the Illini grapplers last won a title, and 14 years had gone by since the tennis squad ended up on top of the league standings. Coach Leo Johnson's track and field team made the biggest news, however. Not only did they sweep titles in both Big Ten seasons, they also took top honors nationally, winning the NCAA outdoor title in Minneapolis.

Fred Green (#19) went on to become a member of the post-World War II "Whiz Kids"

ILLINI SCRAPBOOK

Coach Ray Eliot climbs aboard the TWA Airliner.

THE VERY FIRST "FLYING ILLINI" team took to the airways November 16, 1945, when Coach Ray Eliot's football squad chartered a flight from Willard Airport to Ohio State. Eliot and 19 of his top players departed Savoy at 1 p.m., landing an hour and a half later in Columbus in their TWA airliner. It was the first large passenger takeoff from the new airport, dedicated just three weeks before. Illinois' starting left tackle Bill Kolens, a navy fighter pilot, voluntarily gave up his seat on the plane to let someone else experience his first flight. The balance of the Illini football team rode a New York Central train for seven hours to the Ohio capital city. The entire squad returned to Champaign via the railways following their 27-2 loss.

Illini Legend

Herb McKenley

His coach, Leo Johnson, once compared Herb McKenley to "a golf ball bouncing down a concrete road." That statement probably doesn't do justice to how good Illinois' greatest quarter-miler actually was. McKenley rarely met defeat during his two-year track career at the University of Illinois, setting some sort of standard every time he ran. He ran 34 races as an Illini, excluding relays, winning 31 and setting 18 records. Three of McKenley's 18 marks were world records. As a junior in 1946 and a senior in '47, no one was ever able to beat him in a 440-yard race at the Big Ten and NCAA meets. He swept to six titles. The Jamaican speedster, who came to Illinois after a two-year stop at Boston College, also led his native country to a gold medal victory over the United States at the 1952 Olympics. McKenley later became coach and director of Jamaica's Olympic track squad. One of his athletes, George Kerr, later broke McKenley's world record at Illinois. Now retired, McKenley still resides in Jamaica.

Illini Lists

MULTIPLE ILLINI BIG TEN INDIVIDUAL MEN'S TRACK CHAMPIONS
(since 1945)

1. Charlton Ehizuelen — 12 titles (includes one relay title)
2. George Walker — 10 titles
3. Mike Durkin — 9 titles
4. Herb McKenley — 9 titles (includes three relay titles)
5. Willie Williams — 9 titles
6. Marko Koers — 9 titles (includes one relay title)
7. Tim Simon — 8 titles (includes four relay titles)
8. Bobby True — 8 titles (includes four relay titles)
9. Sherman Armstrong — 8 titles (includes three relay titles)
10. George Kerr — 7 titles (includes two relay titles)
11. Don Laz — 7 titles
12. Dorian Green — 7 titles (includes four relay titles)

George Kerr won seven Big Ten track titles during his career from 1958-60.

ILLINI LORE

Less than four years after President Arthur Willard first addressed the University of Illinois' Board of Trustees about securing an appropriation of $200,000 for the purchase of land in Savoy, the University's new airport was dedicated October 26, 1945. The 762-acre airport featured three mile-long concrete runways, making it the nation's foremost university-owned facility. It was renamed UI Willard Airport on October 18, 1961, after the former president.

1946-47

AMERICA'S TIME CAPSULE

Oct. 15, 1946	The St. Louis Cardinals defeated the Boston Red Sox in the World Series, four games to three.
Dec. 15, 1946	Coach George Halas's Chicago Bears won the NFL championship, beating the New York Giants 24-14.
April 11, 1947	Jackie Robinson made his debut with the Brooklyn Dodgers as major league baseball's first black player.
April 16, 1947	Some 500 persons died in a ship explosion at Texas City, Texas.
June 23, 1947	Despite President Truman's veto, the controversial Taft-Hartley Labor Act was passed by Congress.

Coach Ray Eliot savors the moment as Illinois wins the Rose Bowl.

ILLINI SCRAPBOOK

ILLINI MOMENT

ILLINI SMELL THE ROSES:

The road to Pasadena was a long and winding one for the University of Illinois. Illini players traveled familiar highways through such Midwestern cities as Bloomington, Ann Arbor, and Iowa City, but also detoured through much less familiar sites such as Germany and Okinawa. Nearly 300 men, most of whom were returning from military duty in World War II, turned out for Coach Ray Eliot's opening practice in 1946. The Illini split their first four games, but stepped on the gas at the end. Illinois consecutively disposed of Wisconsin, Michigan, Iowa, Ohio State, and Northwestern to wind up with a 6-1 Big Ten record and a berth in the Rose Bowl. It marked the first game in the pact between the Big Ten and the Pacific Eight conferences. Though it marked UI's first-ever trip to Pasadena for the New Year's Day classic, the Illini weren't greeted with open arms. California's media didn't respect the 11-point underdogs, predicting a huge victory by third-ranked UCLA. The Bruins led 7-6 after the first quarter, but it was all Illinois during the final three periods. Illini running backs Julius Rykovich and Buddy Young rushed for 103 yards apiece, and seven different players each scored a touchdown. The final score: Illinois 45, UCLA 14.

Action from the 1947 Rose Bowl.

George Walker

IN ADDITION to the Fighting Illini football team, four other Illinois athletic teams finished on top of their respective Big Ten standings. Coach Leo Johnson's track team swept to titles both indoors and out, led by Bob Rehberg, Bob Richards, John Twomey, Bill Mathis, Herb McKenley, Dike Eddleman, and George Walker. The Illini baseball team, coached by Wally Roettger, got big seasons from pitcher Marv Rotblatt and catcher Lee Eilbracht, winning their conference race by one game over Ohio State. Finally, the Illinois wrestling squad saw Dave Shapiro and Lou Kachiroubas successfully defend their Big Ten titles, en route to the team championship.

Illini Legend

Alex Agase

In 1990, to commemorate the 100th anniversary of Walter Camp's first All-American football team, the New Haven (Connecticut) *Register* selected a 24-member All-Century Team. Among the two dozen players chosen, the University of Illinois led the way with three honorees. Two were predictable—Red Grange and Dick Butkus—but the third Illini—Alex Agase—was probably a surprise to some. However, when one considers that the 205-pound guard from Evanston, Illinois was the only college player to be a three-time All-American for two different teams—Illinois and Purdue—his selection makes perfect sense. In addition to earning MVP honors at Illinois in 1946, Agase also was selected as the Big Ten's top player, leading the Illini to the 1947 Rose Bowl championship. Following a pro football career in Chicago, Cleveland, and Baltimore, Agase entered the coaching ranks. He served as head coach for both Northwestern and Purdue, earning Coach of the Year honors in 1970. Agase is now retired and lives in Florida.

Illini Lists

ILLINOIS FOOTBALL PLAYERS WHO WERE BIG TEN MVPS

The Chicago Tribune has presented the Silver Football award to the Big Ten's Most Valuable Player each year since 1924. Here are the six Illinois gridders who've been so honored:

1924	Harold "Red" Grange, halfback	
1946	Alex Agase, guard	
1959	Bill Burrell, guard	
1963	Dick Butkus, linebacker	
1965	Jim Grabowski, fullback	
1983	Don Thorp, defensive tackle	

Dick Butkus was selected as the Big Ten's Most Valuable Player in 1963.

ILLINI LORE

The University of Illinois received the largest gift in its history in June of 1946, when wealthy land owner Robert Allerton presented the UI with more than 6,000 acres of farmland, located just west of Monticello, Illinois. The gift more than doubled UI's land holdings. Allerton Park was eventually opened to the general public, with the exception of the mansion, which Allerton stipulated to be used for general University purposes. During the Bob Blackman era, the Illinois football team stayed at Allerton House the night before home games.

1947-48

AMERICA'S TIME CAPSULE

Oct. 14, 1947   Captain Chuck Yeager piloted the world's first supersonic aircraft.

Dec. 5, 1947   Heavyweight boxing champion Joe Louis earned a split decision over "Jersey Joe" Walcott.

March 8, 1948   The Supreme Court ruled that religious education in public schools was a violation of the First Amendment.

May 3, 1948:   James Michener's *Tales of the South Pacific* and Tennessee Williams's *A Streetcar Named Desire* earned Pulitzer Prizes.

Aug. 16, 1948   Babe Ruth, baseball's greatest player, died of cancer.

ILLINI MOMENT

Cadets of the U.S. Military Academy parade on the turf of Yankee Stadium before the 1947 game between Illinois and Army.

ILLINOIS & ARMY BATTLE TO SCORELESS TIE:

New York's historic Yankee Stadium, the site of many of baseball's greatest games, hosted one of college football's top battles on October 11, 1947. The combatants were a powerful Army team, unbeaten in 30 consecutive games, and Illinois, looking for its third win in three outings. Coach Ray Eliot's Fighting Illini carried the fight through the entire game, out-gaining their highly favored opponents 212 yards to 162. Illinois' best opportunity to score came late in the first half when it moved the ball 51 yards from its own 27 to the Army 22. Illini placekicker Don Maechtle came in to try a field goal, but a low snap ruined UI's only chance to score all day. Army, which had only nine total first downs, never came close to denting the Illini end zone, and the game ended in a 0-0 tie.

Illini baseball's Herb Plews ended his career with an all-time best average of .367, then went on to a four-year stint in the majors with Washington and Boston.

(left to right) Head Coach Harry Combes and assistant coaches Art Mathisen and Howie Braun.

Illini Item

THE 1947-48 BASKETBALL SEASON marked the first of 20 years in the saddle for Illinois hoops coach Harry Combes. Combes, who'd spent the year before as head coach at Champaign High School, won his first seven games as the Illini mentor. His Illini were nearly perfect in contests at Huff Gym that season, winning 11 of 12 games, losing only to eventual Big Ten champion Michigan.

Illini Lists

ILLINOIS' GREATEST STRIKE-OUT PITCHERS (CAREER)
(through 2001 season)

1.	Brett Weber (1995-98)	292
2.	Marv Rotblatt (1946-48)	286
3.	John Ericks (1986-88)	210
4.	Jason Anderson (1998-00)	197
5.	Carl Jones (1984-87)	196
	Greg McCollum (1984-87)	196
7.	Jeff Innis (1981-83)	178
8.	Bubba Smith (1989-91)	171
9.	John Oestriech (1992-95)	169
10.	Mark Dressen (1989-92)	162

Brett Weber

Illini Legend

Marv Rotblatt

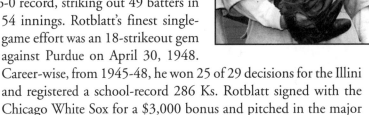

Though he stood only five-feet-seven-inches tall, southpaw Marv Rotblatt was one of college baseball's greatest pitchers in the 1940s. Relying on his wicked curve ball, Rotblatt set a plethora of records in 1947 and '48, many of which still stand. In six Big Ten appearances during the '47 campaign, the lefty from Chicago's Von Steuben High School compiled a perfect 6-0 record, striking out 49 batters in 54 innings. Rotblatt's finest single-game effort was an 18-strikeout gem against Purdue on April 30, 1948. Career-wise, from 1945-48, he won 25 of 29 decisions for the Illini and registered a school-record 286 Ks. Rotblatt signed with the Chicago White Sox for a $3,000 bonus and pitched in the major leagues for three seasons. Nowadays, he lives in Chicago.

John Phillip Sousa (left) and A.A. Harding

ILLINI LORE

. . . .

During the 1947-48 academic year, Professor Albert Austin Harding completed 43 years as director of University of Illinois bands. A 1906 UI graduate, Harding helped "Illinois Loyalty" composer Thatcher Howland Guild arrange the school's fight song. Harding was widely acclaimed for his work with university bands, and due to his admiration of Harding's work, famed "March King" John Philip Sousa donated his massive band collection to the university.

1948-49

Nov. 2, 1948 In a major political upset, Harry Truman defeated Thomas Dewey for the U.S. presidency.

Dec. 15, 1948 Former State Department official Alger Hiss was indicted by a federal grand jury on two counts of perjury.

April 4, 1949 NATO was formed when the North Atlantic Treaty was signed in Washington, D.C.

April 20, 1949 The discovery of cortisone, the hormone promised to bring relief to sufferers of rheumatoid arthritis, was announced.

June 22, 1949 Ezzard Charles defeated "Jersey Joe" Walcott to become the new heavyweight boxing champion.

ILLINI MOMENT

ILLINI NEED TWO OVERTIMES TO BEAT HOOSIERS:

Coach Harry Combes and his 1948-49 Illini basketball team.

Fred Green needed nearly 50 minutes to score his only basket of the game, but it proved to be the biggest one of his career and the biggest shot of the 1948-49 Illini basketball season. Playing before a sellout crowd in Bloomington January 8, 1949, Illinois and Indiana battled back and forth through a 37-37 tie at regulation time and 40-all at the end of the first overtime. With 14 seconds left in the second OT and the ball belonging to the Illini out-of-bounds under Indiana's goal, Bill Erickson slowly brought the ball down the court and shot a pass in to Green, deep in the lane. The 6'7" senior from Urbana wheeled to his left and shot with his right hand, threading the ball through the hoop with just four seconds remaining. Illinois' 44-42 victory was its second of what would eventually be a league-leading 10 wins that season, enough for the school's first Big Ten title in six years.

ILLINI SCRAPBOOK

Professor Joseph Tykociner retired from the UI faculty in 1949

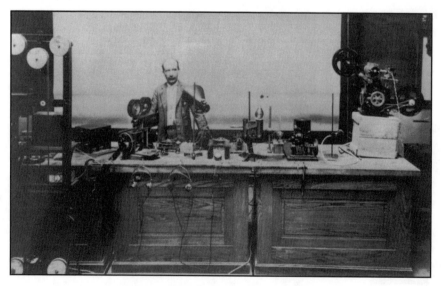

THOUGH IT WAS THE ONLY time in his first dozen seasons that he didn't win the Big Ten title, Charlie Pond made his debut as head coach of the University of Illinois gymnastics team in 1948-49. Pond's success with the Illini was accentuated by 11 conference championships and four NCAA titles.

Illini Legend

Dike Eddleman

In the fall of 1992, the University of Illinois honored the greatest all-around athlete in its history by naming its "Athlete of the Year" award after the incomparable Dike Eddleman. No other man can claim the amazing feats accomplished by the pride of Centralia, Illinois, during his Illini career. Not only was Eddleman a member of Illinois' first Rose Bowl championship team in 1947 and the leading scorer on UI's first Final Four basketball team in 1949, he also won a silver medal as a high jumper in the 1948 Olympic games. Dike's 11 varsity letters at Illinois also stand as a record. He starred in the classroom as well, being awarded the Big Ten Conference Medal of Honor as an Illini senior. Following his graduation, Eddleman played in the NBA with the Tri-City Blackhawks and the Fort Wayne Pistons. In 1970, Dike returned to Illinois as the executive director of the Athletic Association's Grants-in-Aid program, retiring in 1992. He died on August 1, 2001, at the age of 79.

Illini Lists

LONGEST ILLINI PUNTS

1. 88 yards   Dike Eddleman vs. Iowa, 11/6/48
2. 86 yards   Dike Eddleman vs. Ohio State, 11/13/48
    86 yards   Bill Butkovich vs. Michigan, 10/27/45
4. 85 yards   Ryan Tabloff vs. Purdue, 10/25/97
    85 yards   Phil Vierneisel vs. Michigan State, 10/19/74
6. 82 yards   Phil Vierneisel vs. Ohio State, 11/2/74
7. 80 yards   Brett Larsen vs. Arizona, 9/16/95
8. 78 yards   Steve Fitts vs. Wisconsin, 10/17/98
9. 75 yards   Steve Fitts vs. Minnesota, 10/16/99
10. 74 yards   Steve Fitts vs. Arkansas State, 9/4/99
    74 yards   Dike Eddleman vs. Iowa, 11/6/48

Dike Eddleman's 88-yard punt vs. Iowa is the longest in Illini football history.

ILLINI LORE

Professor Joseph Tykociner, developer of sound movies, retired in 1949 after 27 years at the University of Illinois. He was born in Russian Poland in 1877 and studied in German technical institutes before coming to the United States in 1920. Following a year with Westinghouse, Tykociner joined the UI staff, and a year later, on June 9, 1922, gave his first public demonstration of movies with sound. Tykociner's developmental budget was less than $ 1,000. By coincidence, the first full-length sound picture, *The Jazz Singer*, was written by UI alumnus Samson Raphaelson.

1949-50

Oct. 9, 1949   The New York Yankees beat the Brooklyn Dodgers to win baseball's World Series.

Oct. 24, 1949   The United Nations' headquarters were dedicated in New York.

Jan. 31, 1949   President Truman authorized development of the hydrogen bomb.

April 23, 1950   The Minneapolis Lakers, starring George Mikan, beat the Syracuse Nationals to win the first National Basketball Association championship.

June 27, 1950   President Truman ordered U.S. armed forces to Korea to help South Korea repel the North Korean invasion.

ILLINI MOMENT

THE ARGO EXPRESS:

Johnny Karras was known as "The Argo Express."

Johnny Karras originally reported to the University of Illinois football camp in the fall of 1946, but he quickly discovered that his opportunity to be a first-team running back was limited by the presence of an abundance of returning war veterans, including Buddy Young and Paul Patterson. Karras decided to return to his hometown of Argo, Illinois, and enlist in the army, spending 18 months in the service. It turned out to be one of the smartest decisions he ever made, for when he came back to Illinois in 1949 as a mature, 20-year-old sophomore, he exploded into prominence, earning first-team All-Big Ten honors. In nine games that season, the Argo Express averaged 6.5 yards per rush and 31 yards per kickoff return, scoring an Illini-high seven touchdowns. For that performance, he was named Illinois' Most Valuable Player. Karras's success continued in 1950 and '51, as he eventually earned All-American laurels his senior year.

Walt "Ox" Osterkorn led the Fighting Illini basketball team in scoring with 15.1 points per game in 1950, earning team MVP honors.

ILLINI SCRAPBOOK

Dick Raklovits

DICK "ROCKY" RAKLOVITS was one of Illinois' most brilliant performers in the early 1950s, starring on both the football field and the baseball diamond. He and Ruck Steger are the only two Fighting Illini athletes in the last 50 years to earn first-team All-Big Ten honors in both of those sports in the same season (1950-51).

Illini Lists

ILLINI ATHLETES WHO BECAME MEMBERS OF THE BOARD OF TRUSTEES

*James W. Armstrong, football/track	1923-35
David J. Downey, basketball	1991-93
Harold E. Grange, football	1951-55
Wirt Herrick, track	1949-61
Robert Z. Hickman, football	1949-55
*Harold A. Pogue, football/track	1935-41
Russell W. Steger, football/baseball	1969-75
Frederick L. Wham, football	1925-27

*Served as president of UI's Board of Trustees

Russell "Ruck" Steger served on UI's Board of Trustees from 1969-75.

Illini Legend

Ruck Steger

Russell "Ruck" Steger was a born entertainer. As an athlete, he thrilled Fighting Illini fans with battering-ram runs and tape-measure clouts. Off the field, Ruck mesmerized his audience by strumming a guitar and singing "The Wabash Cannonball." In addition to combining brawn and charm, the native of St. Louis also had his share of brains, maintaining a B average in the classroom and eventually earning the Big Ten Conference Medal of Honor. Uncle Sam put the finger on Ruck for two years before he could begin his athletic career at the University of Illinois. But once he put on an Illini uniform, there was no holding him back. In football, Steger was a first-team All-Big Ten running back, leading Illinois rushers in 1947 and '48. As an outfielder for Wally Roettger's UI baseball squad, Ruck had a career .317 average, en route to winning all-conference and Illini Athlete of the Year honors in 1950. His success didn't stop there, as he enjoyed a prosperous career in insurance and other businesses. Steger also served as a member of UI's Board of Trustees and is now semi-retired in Chicago.

This scene from 1948 shows workers dredging out a pond for the new golf course in Savoy.

ILLINI LORE

The University of Illinois' new 18-hole golf course, built at a cost of $250,000 entirely from Athletic Association funds, opened May 13, 1950, in Savoy. Constructed on 170 acres of rich farmland donated by Hartwell Howard, the 6,884-yard course was designed and built by C.D. Wagstaff, a 1918 UI alumnus.

1950-51

AMERICA'S TIME CAPSULE

Sept. 26, 1950   U.S. troops recaptured Seoul, the capital of South Korea.

Oct. 7, 1950   The New York Yankees defeated the Philadelphia Phillies to win the World Series, four games to none.

Feb. 26, 1951   Congress adopted the 22nd Amendment to the U.S. Constitution, stipulating that no person may be elected to the presidency for more than two terms.

April 11, 1951   President Truman relieved Gen. Douglas MacArthur of his post as supreme commander.

June 25, 1951   The Columbia Broadcasting System (CBS) presented television's first commercial color broadcast.

Rod Fletcher helped lead Illinois to the 1951 Big Ten basketball title.

ILLINI MOMENT

FLETCHER'S HEROICS LEAD ILLINI TO BIG TEN TITLE:

Trailing by four points in the Big Ten season finale with only four and a half minutes left on the Jenison Field House clock, Illinois' prospects for an undisputed conference basketball crown certainly didn't look very promising ... that is, until Rod Fletcher stepped forward to put on a dazzling one-man show for the Illini. During the next 60 seconds, he picked the pockets of two Michigan State dribblers and cashed them into baskets, tying the score at 43-all. With 3:30 left, the backcourt whiz from Champaign rose at the free-throw line to can a jumper, and a minute later tapped in a left-handed rebound to give Illinois a four-point lead and its eventual 49-43 victory. Fletcher's heroics gave Harry Combes's troops a nearly perfect 13-1 record in Big Ten play, a half-game better than runner-up Indiana, sending them to the NCAA tournament. In postseason play, the Illini lost the opening-round game at New York's Madison Square Garden to Kansas State, then rebounded in game two to defeat Columbia. Illinois then beat North Carolina State and lost to champion-to-be Kentucky by two points. The Illini salvaged third place in the Final Four by beating Oklahoma A&M at Minneapolis, giving them a final overall record of 22-5.

Bob Hope, who last appeared on campus in 1990, regularly came to the University of Illinois in the 1950s and became a close friend of Illini football coach Ray Eliot. He made an impromptu appearance at the January 20, 1951 Illini basketball game vs Iowa, when the Hawkeyes were delayed nearly three hours by a blizzard.

Don Laz

I Illini Item

ON MAY 25, 1951, Don Laz's unusual double victory in the pole vault and the broad jump led Illinois to the Big Ten Outdoor Track and Field Championships at Dyche Stadium in Evanston, Illinois. Laz's amazing feat marked the first time in the 51-year history of the conference championships that the same man had captured individual titles in those two events in the same meet.

Illini Legend

Don Sunderlage

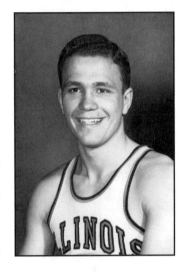

The 1951 Big Ten basketball season featured an abundance of stars, including Indiana's Bill Garrett and Minnesota's Whitey Skoog, but the league's Most Valuable Player that year was a senior guard from the University of Illinois named Don Sunderlage. The Illini captain led the conference in scoring with an average of 17.4 points per game. Many of Sunderlage's points came from the charity stripe, setting Illini records for both free throws made (171) and attempted (218). Those marks stood for 42 years at Illinois until Kiwane Garris broke them in 1993-94. Sunderlage wound up his college career as Illinois' all-time scoring leader, tallying 777 points in three seasons. He spent two seasons in the NBA, one year each with Milwaukee and Minnesota, averaging nearly eight points per game. Sunderlage was a member of the West squad in the 1954 NBA All-Star game. His life came to a tragic end at the age of 31 on July 15, 1961, when he and his wife, Janice, were killed in an automobile crash.

Illini Lists

ILLINI FOOTBALL'S GREATEST PERFORMANCES VS. NO. 1-RANKED TEAMS

- Nov. 5, 1955   Illinois 25, Michigan 6
- Nov. 18, 1950 Illinois 14, Ohio State 7
- Oct. 27, 1956 Illinois 20, Michigan State 13
- Oct. 30, 1948 Michigan 28, Illinois 20
- Oct. 1, 1966   Michigan State 26, Illinois 10
- Oct. 24, 1970 Ohio State 48, Illinois 29

Illinois upset the No. 1-ranked Ohio State Buckeyes in 1950.

ILLINI LORE

The first coed cheerleaders for a University of Illinois athletic event appeared September 30, 1950, when the Fighting Illini football team hosted Ohio University at Memorial Stadium. The group included Marilyn Lowe of Springfield, Dorothy Rich of Manteno, Mary Lou Schaeflein of Chicago, and Marilyn Berger of Chicago.

AMERICA'S TIME CAPSULE

Nov. 10, 1951   The first transcontinental direct dial telephone service took place when a call was placed from New Jersey to California.

Dec. 20, 1951   A station in Idaho began producing electricity from the first atomic-powered generator.

April 8, 1952   A presidential order prevented a shutdown of the nation's steel mills by strikers.

July 11, 1952   Gen. Dwight Eisenhower and Sen. Richard Nixon were nominated as the presidential ticket for the Republicans.

July 26, 1952   Illinois governor Adlai Stevenson was nominated at the Democratic National Convention as that party's presidential candidate.

ILLINI MOMENT

Bill Tate

MORE ROSES:

Coach Ray Eliot's 1951 squad is the last University of Illinois football team to be undefeated during an entire season. They won their first seven games of the campaign, then played to a scoreless tie at Ohio State. Illinois' Rose Bowl-clinching victory came in the regular-season finale at Northwestern, thanks to the toe of Sammy Rebecca, who kicked a 16-yard field goal. The New Year's Day showdown against Stanford, America's first college football game to be nationally telecast, proved to be a defensive struggle through the first half, with the Indians leading the Illini by a single point, 7-6. However, Illinois exploded for 34 unanswered points in the second half, capitalizing on a pair of Stan Wallace defensive interceptions and a strong running attack from game MVP Bill Tate (150 yards) and Johnny Karras. The 40-7 victory capped a 9-0-1 season and allowed the Illini to finish third in the national rankings.

Coach Harry Combes (left) and Rod Fletcher.

ILLINI SCRAPBOOK

*Illini pole vaulter
Bob Richards*

ON JANUARY 2, 1952, former University of Illinois pole vaulter Bob Richards was named winner of the Sullivan Award, symbolic of the nation's top amateur athlete. The 25-year-old preacher was the first choice on 174 of the 487 ballots cast by a nationwide panel of sports authorities, easily outdistancing teenage tennis sensation Maureen Connolly. Richards was the reigning Olympic champion in both the pole vault and the decathlon events, and the only two-time gold medal winner in his event (1952 and '56) in Olympic competition. For several years, Richards was the spokesman for Wheaties cereal.

Illini Legend

Chuck Boerio

Linebacker Chuck Boerio typified the group of players who made up the University of Illinois' 1952 Rose Bowl team. At five feet, eleven inches and 190 pounds, Boerio was Coach Ray Eliot's star linebacker, earning first-team All-Big Ten honors. As the Illini's defensive signal caller, the Kincaid, Illinois, walk-on was the leader of a unit that allowed its six Big Ten foes an average of only five points per game during the 1951 campaign. Boerio, named Illini Athlete of the Year for 1951-52, was selected defensive captain of the 1952 College All-Stars in their game against the NFL champion Los Angeles Rams. His pro football career lasted only half a season with the Green Bay Packers, primarily due to his lack of size and speed. Boerio returned to the UI in 1956 and coached under Eliot for three seasons. He served as an assistant at the University of Colorado from 1959-61, helping guide the Buffaloes to the school's first Big Eight title that final year. Boerio was a teacher and coach in the Boulder, Colorado school district for 28 years, retiring in 1990.

Illini Lists

MOST BIG TEN MEN'S TEAM CHAMPIONSHIPS IN A SINGLE SEASON
(through 2000-01 season)

- 8 Illinois, 1951-52
- 8 Michigan, 1943-44
- 6 Illinois, 1921-22
- 6 Michigan, 1922-23
- 6 Illinois, 1923-24
- 6 Michigan, 1960-61
- 6 Indiana, 1972-73
- 6 Indiana, 1973-74
- 5 Michigan, 8 times
- 5 Illinois, 6 times
- 5 Michigan State, 1970-71

Pitcher Gerry Smith compiled a perfect 5-0 record with a 1.40 earned run average in 1952, leading the Illini baseball team to the Big Ten championship.

Dennis Swanson was a manager for the Illini basketball team in the 1950s.

ILLINI LORE

The University of Illinois' School of Journalism celebrated its silver anniversary May 9, 1952. Among the individuals who have studied journalism at the UI are *Chicago Sun-Times* movie critic Roger Ebert, *New York Times* columnist and former Illini golfer, James "Scotty" Reston, *Sports Illustrated's* William Nack, the *Wall Street Journal's* Frederick Klein, and WNBC-TV's general manager Dennis Swanson.

1952-53

AMERICA'S TIME CAPSULE

Sept. 23, 1952   Rocky Marciano won his 43rd consecutive bout without a loss, defeating "Jersey Joe" Walcott for the world heavyweight boxing title.

Nov. 4, 1952   Dwight Eisenhower defeated Illinois governor Adlai Stevenson for the presidency of the United States.

Jan. 2, 1953   Wisconsin senator Joseph McCarthy, known for his charges of communist infiltration in various organizations, was accused by a senate subcommittee of "motivation by self-interest."

March 18, 1953   Baseball's Boston Braves moved to Milwaukee, Wisconsin.

May 4, 1953   Author Ernest Hemingway was awarded a Pulitzer Prize for his book *The Old Man and the Sea*.

ILLINI MOMENT

Willie Williams helped Illinois' track team dominate the Big Ten in 1952-53.

MORE TITLES IN 1952-53:

At no time in University of Illinois history was its athletic program prospering more than in the early 1950s under Athletic Director Doug Mills. In fact, from the 1950-51 season through the 1953-54 campaign, Fighting Illini teams captured 23 of the Big Ten Conference's possible 48 championships—nearly 50 percent! The 1952-53 athletic year saw Illinois ring up five titles. Lee Eilbracht's baseball team averaged only .223 at the plate in 13 conference games that season, but the strong pitching of Clive Follmer, Carl Ahrens, and Gerry Smith rang up a combined record of 9-2 on the mound as Illinois tied Michigan. Charlie Pond's Illini gymnastics team reigned as Big Ten champs for the fourth consecutive season and placed second in the NCAA meet, behind the consistent performances of Frank Bare, Jeff Austin, and Bob Sullivan. The Illini track teams, directed by Leo Johnson, once again dominated the conference cinders both indoors and out, thanks to sprinter Willie Williams, middle-distance star Stacey Siders, and high hurdler Joel McNulty. In fencing, it was business as usual, with Illinois winning its fourth consecutive Big Ten crown under Coach Max Garret. Sabreman John Cameron slashed his way to an individual title in his specialty.

Ron Ultes (left) and Coach Lee Eilbracht led the Illini "9" to the Big Ten title in 1953.

Clive Follmer

ILLINOIS' TOP TWO-SPORT ATHLETE of 1952-53 was basketball/baseball star Clive Follmer from Forrest, Illinois. Follmer averaged 11.8 points per game in hoops as a senior starter, helping the Illini to an 18-4 overall record and a second-place finish in the Big Ten. As a pitcher for the baseball team that season, he had a 6-1 overall record, striking out 51 batters in 68 innings, and allowing little more than two earned runs per outing. The current Urbana, Illinois, attorney was awarded five UI varsity letters during his career—three in basketball and two in baseball—and was a member of four Big Ten championship clubs.

Illini Legend

Al Brosky

The record Al Brosky achieved as a defensive back for the Fighting Illini football team is difficult to measure accurately. It might be akin to Joe DiMaggio hitting in 56 consecutive games or Harry Broadbent's record of scoring a goal in 16 straight National Hockey League contests. However, Brosky's NCAA record of an interception in 15 consecutive games is significantly more impressive in that opposing quarterbacks purposely threw their passes away from him, knowing his proficiency as a defender. The youngest of 12 children of immigrant Czechoslovakian parents, Brosky attended Harrison Tech High School in Chicago. Upon his graduation, Brosky enlisted in the army and served for more than 15 months. He was discharged in 1948 and enrolled at St. Louis University, but left after a semester and came to the University of Illinois. During the next three seasons, Brosky was simply amazing, developing into the greatest Illini pass defender ever. In 28 career games at Illinois, he picked off a national record 30 interceptions. Besides being captain and Most Valuable Player of the 1952 squad, Brosky also was an All-Big Ten and All-America selection. A severe back disorder as well as other complications never allowed him to pursue a career in professional football, so he went into business for himself. Nowadays, Brosky resides in Naperville.

Illini Lists

ILLINI ON ALL-TIME PRO BASKETBALL SCORING LIST*
(through 2000-01 season)

1. 19,202 points — Eddie Johnson (1982-99)
2. 16,006 points — Derek Harper (1984-99)
3. 12,480 points — John "Red" Kerr (1955-66)
4. 12,233 points — Don Freeman (1968-76)
5. 11,549 points — Don Ohl (1961-70)
6. 11,469 points — Nick Anderson (1990-01)
7. 11,204 points — Kendall Gill (1991-01)
8. 8,717 points — Ken Norman (1988-97)
9. 7,922 points — Rich Jones (1970-77)
10. 6,384 points — Andy Phillip (1948-58)

*includes NBA, ABA, NPBL

Don Ohl scored 11,549 points during a 10-year career in the NBA.

ILLINI LORE

In February of 1953, the Federal Communications Commission assigned television channel 12, later to become WILL-TV, to the University of Illinois. Coordinated by the UI's new TV-Motion Picture unit, channel 12's original studio was located just inside Gate 24 on the west side of Memorial Stadium. Also located in the southwest tower of the stadium were the station's offices, control room, projection booths, and film editing facility. Often, Fighting Illini fans who were unable to secure a ticket to sold-out basketball games at Huff Gym were given the opportunity to watch the events on closed-circuit TV inside the Great West Hall of the stadium. WILL-TV officially began TV broadcasts August 1, 1955, as the nation's 14th education station. The broadcasts were initially limited from 6:45 p.m. to 8:30 p.m., Monday through Friday.

1953-54

AMERICA'S TIME CAPSULE

Oct. 5, 1953	The New York Yankees won baseball's World Series for the fifth consecutive time, defeating the Brooklyn Dodgers.
Feb. 23, 1954	Inoculation of school children against polio began for the first time.
March 1, 1954	An explosion of a hydrogen bomb in the Marshall Islands exceeded all estimates of its power.
March 20, 1954	Bradley was defeated by La Salle in the NCAA basketball championship game.
May 17, 1954	The Supreme Court declared racial segregation in public schools unconstitutional.

ILLINI MOMENT

J.C. Caroline (left) and Mickey Bates were known as "Mr. Zoom and Mr. Boom."

CAROLINE, BATES, & CO. JET PAST BUCKEYES:

One veteran Ohio sportswriter said that Illinois' October 10, 1953, performance against Ohio State was "the wildest first half in Ohio Stadium history, leaving Buckeye fans stunned." Though Illinois led by only one point at halftime, 21-20, it was all Illini in the second half, with the final score showing them on top, 41-20. Two jet-powered halfbacks, J.C. Caroline and Mickey Bates, combined for an unheard-of 339 yards rushing from scrimmage, 192 by Caroline and 147 by Bates. Afterwards, bewildered OSU coach Woody Hayes, said, "They just ran us to death, that's the whole story." Illinois continued its rampage through the Big Ten, with the No. 3-ranked Illini stumbling only at Wisconsin and tying Michigan State for the Conference football title. Since the Illini and the Spartans hadn't faced each other in 1953, Big Ten athletic directors were forced to choose the league's Rose Bowl representative. Unfortunately, they picked MSU, and the Illini spent their holidays at home.

Former Illini football player Peter Palmer (third from left) starred on Broadway as "Li'l Abner".

Johnny "Red" Kerr was the Big Ten's basketball MVP in 1954.

I Illini Item

Illini Lists

ILLINOIS' FIRST-ROUND NFL/AFL DRAFT PICKS

1944	Tony Butkovich, RB, Los Angeles Rams, 11th pick
1954	Stan Wallace, DB, Chicago Bears, 6th pick
1954	John Bauer, G, Cleveland Browns, 12th pick
1959	Rich Kreitling, WR, Cleveland Browns, 11th pick
1961	Joe Rutgens, DT, Oakland Raiders, AFL, 4th pick
	Joe Rutgens, DT, Washington Redskins, 3rd pick
1965	Dick Butkus, LB, Chicago Bears, 3rd pick
1965	George Donnelly, DB, San Francisco 49ers, 13th pick
1966	Jim Grabowski, RB, Green Bay Packers, 9th pick
	Jim Grabowski, RB, Miami Dolphins, AFL, 1st pick
1981	Dave Wilson, QB, New Orleans Saints, 1st pick*
1983	Tony Eason, QB, New England Patriots, 15th pick
1988	Scott Davis, DE, Los Angeles Raiders, 25th pick
1990	Jeff George, QB, Indianapolis Colts, 1st pick
1991	Henry Jones, DB, Buffalo Bills, 26th pick
1992	Brad Hopkins, OT, Houston Oilers, 13th pick
1996	Kevin Hardy, LB, Jacksonville Jaguars, 2nd pick
1996	Simeon Rice, LB, Arizona Cardinals, 3rd pick

*Supplemental draft

Illini Legend

J.C. Caroline

Though he played only for two seasons, J.C. Caroline made a tremendous impact on the college football scene, ultimately being honored as a Hall of Famer. The personable South Caro-linian made headlines as a sophomore, rushing for a Big Ten record 1,256 yards in 1953, shattering Red Grange's Illini single-season mark. Of the myriad of stars Ray Eliot coached during his 18 years at Illinois, the veteran mentor rated Caroline at the very top. Since he averaged six yards per carry from scrim-mage—1,696 on 287 attempts—who can argue with Eliot's choice? Caroline's All-America career at Illinois ended when he dropped out of school before his senior season to sign with Montreal of the Canadian Football League. In 1956, coach George Halas of the Chicago Bears inked Caroline after only one year in the CFL, converting him into a defensive back. He retired as a player in 1965 after 10 seasons with the Bears, earning All-Pro honors and playing on three championship teams. Caroline served as an assistant coach at Illinois from 1967-76, then coached briefly at Urbana High School. He continues to live in Urbana and works as a teacher in that city's school system.

ILLINI LORE

On February 1, 1954, Dr. Lloyd Morey became the seventh president and 11th chief executive officer of the University of Illinois. Morey had been appointed acting president five months earlier when President George Stoddard was forced to resign by UI's Board of Trustees. Morey had been on the staff for 42 years and held the position of comptroller at the time of his appointment.

1954-55

Oct. 15, 1954   Hurricane Hazel killed 99 Americans and 249 Canadians.

Nov. 8, 1954   Baseball's Philadelphia Athletics moved to Kansas City.

Dec. 2, 1954   In a vote by U.S. Senators, Sen. Joseph McCarthy was condemned for activities in his anticommunist witch hunt.

May 2, 1955   A Pulitzer prize was awarded to Tennessee Williams for his drama *Cat on a Hot Tin Roof.*

May 23, 1955   The Presbyterian Church approved the ordination of women ministers.

Among the members of the 1955 Illini gymnastics team were (front row, left to right) Tony Hlinka, Charles Highsmith, Captain Tom Gardner, Coach Charlie Pond, Jeff Austin, and manager Larry Cross; (back row, left to right) Jon Culbertson, Dan Lirot, Richard Jirus, Eric Stattin and Kenneth Stone.

ILLINI SCRAPBOOK

ILLINI MOMENT

ILLINI GYMNASTS CLAIM FIRST OF TWO CONSECUTIVE NATIONAL TITLES:

Coach Charlie Pond's outstanding Illini gymnastics teams of the 1950s strung together a since-unmatched chain of 11 consecutive Big Ten crowns, but the pinnacle of their success came during the 1955 and '56 seasons when Illinois won back-to-back NCAA championships. The first of the two national titles in 1955 at Los Angeles was achieved without one single Illini gymnast winning an individual championship. Illinois placed at least two scorers in every event with the exception of the rings, with Jeff Austin coming the closest to a title with a runner-up finish on the trampoline. Illini captain Tom Gardner (fifth), Tony Hlinka (sixth), and Dick Jirus (seventh) all placed among the top seven all-arounders, as Illinois clipped second-place Penn State, 82.5 to 69, for the team crown. Pond's Illini traveled to Chapel Hill, North Caroina for the 1956 team title, nearly doubling runner-up Penn State's score, 123.5 to 67.5. Illinois' 56-point decision still is the second-biggest margin of victory ever for a gymnastics team in an NCAA championship meet. Don Tonry in the all-around and Dan Lirot in the tumbling event claimed individual championships that year.

Vic Petreshene led the Big Ten with six home runs in 1955.

Pitcher Dick Vorreyer paced the conference with a 1.29 earned run average.

I Illini Item

WILLARD THOMSON of the Fighting Illini track team hurdled his way to three Big Ten championships during the 1954-55 season. Thomson won the 70-yard high hurdles indoors, then swept both the 120 highs and the 220 lows outdoors. Altogether during his career at Illinois, Thomson accounted for six individual conference hurdles titles.

Willard Thomson

Illini Lists

TOP 10 RUSHING PLAYS AT MEMORIAL STADIUM

1.	89 yards	Harry Jefferson of Illinois vs. Syracuse, 10/23/54
2.	84 yards	Ray Nitschke of Illinois vs. Northwestern, 11/23/57
	84 yards	Billy Taylor of Michigan, 11/8/69
4.	83 yards	Emil Sitko of Notre Dame, 9/28/46
5.	80 yards	Cyril Pinder of Illinois vs. Duke, 10/23/65
	80 yards	Edgar Nichol of Illinois vs. Coe, 10/13/28
7.	78 yards	Howard Griffith of Illinois vs. Utah, 9/17/88
	78 yards	Keith Jones of Illinois vs. Nebraska, 9/20/86
9.	76 yards	Rex Kern of Ohio State, 10/24/70
10.	75 yards	Phil Colella of Notre Dame, 9/28/46

Harry Jefferson's 89-yard run vs. Syracuse in 1954 still ranks as the longest in Memorial Stadium history.

Illini Legend

Paul Judson

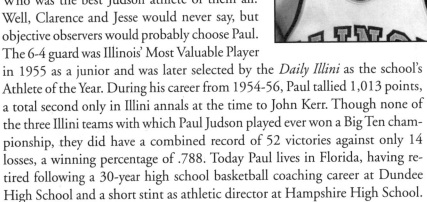

Four different members of Clarence and Jesse Judson's family wore Fighting Illini basketball uniforms during a 36-year period, starting in 1944 with son Howard and ending in 1980 with grandson Rob. The Judsons' twin boys, Paul and Phil, also lettered during the mid 1950s for Coach Harry Combes's Illini cagers, starring first on the University of Illinois campus in 1952 when they led tiny Hebron High to the state championship at UI's Huff Gym. Who was the best Judson athlete of them all? Well, Clarence and Jesse would never say, but objective observers would probably choose Paul. The 6-4 guard was Illinois' Most Valuable Player in 1955 as a junior and was later selected by the *Daily Illini* as the school's Athlete of the Year. During his career from 1954-56, Paul tallied 1,013 points, a total second only in Illini annals at the time to John Kerr. Though none of the three Illini teams with which Paul Judson played ever won a Big Ten championship, they did have a combined record of 52 victories against only 14 losses, a winning percentage of .788. Today Paul lives in Florida, having retired following a 30-year high school basketball coaching career at Dundee High School and a short stint as athletic director at Hampshire High School.

ILLINI LORE

On December 14, 1954, David Dodds Henry accepted an offer from the University of Illinois' Board of Trustees to succeed Dr. Lloyd Morey as the school's president. The 49-year-old Henry, a graduate of Pennsylvania State University, came to Champaign-Urbana from New York University, where he had served as that institution's vice chancellor since 1952. Henry began his appointment at the UI September 1, 1955, at a salary of $30,000.

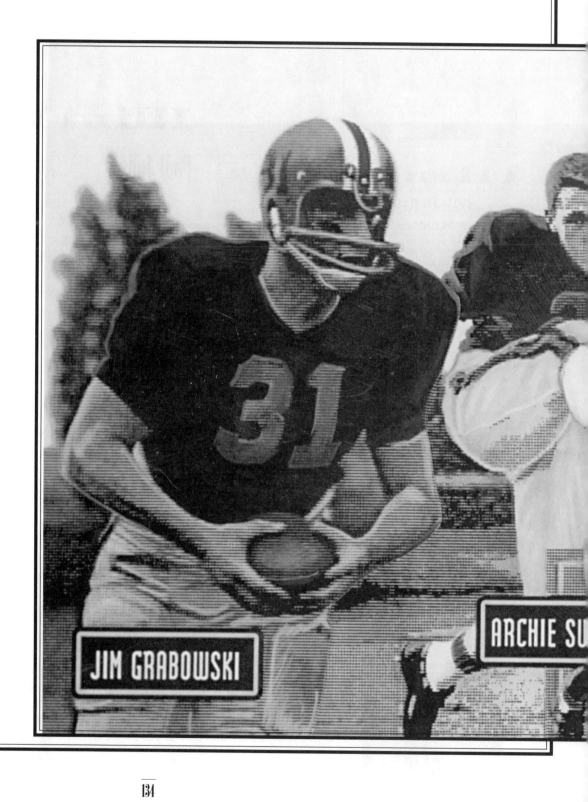

JIM GRABOWSKI

ARCHIE SU

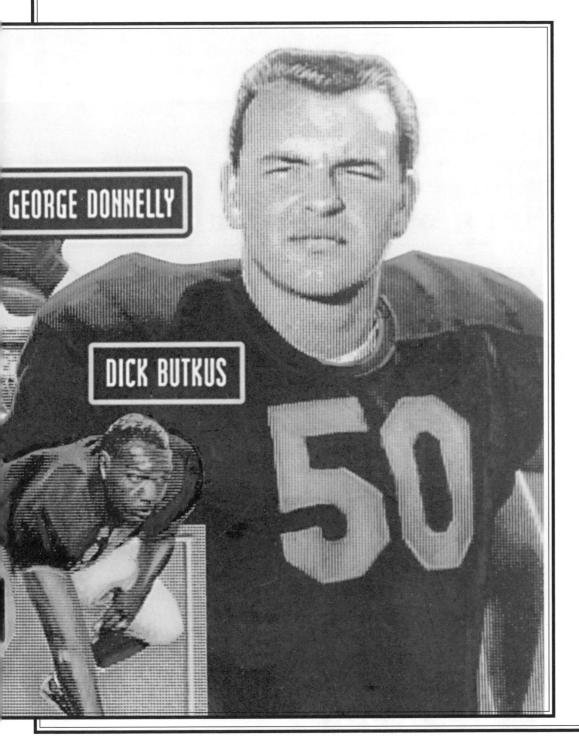

GEORGE DONNELLY

DICK BUTKUS

1955-56

AMERICA'S TIME CAPSULE

Sept. 21, 1955	Rocky Marciano defeated Archie Moore to retain the heavyweight boxing title.
Oct. 4, 1955	The Brooklyn Dodgers beat their crosstown rivals, the Yankees, in game seven of the World Series.
Feb. 6, 1956	The University of Alabama's first black student, Autherine Lucy, was suspended, ending three days of campus violence.
April 19, 1956	American actress Grace Kelly was married to Prince Rainier of Monaco.
June 16, 1956	Dr. Cary Middlecoff defeated Ben Hogan and Julius Boros by one stroke to win the U.S. Open golf tournament.

ILLINI MOMENT

ILLINI GRIDDERS UP-END
NO. 1 MICHIGAN:

Illini football fans who attended the November 5, 1955 matchup at Memorial Stadium between 3-3 Illinois and 6-0 Michigan were probably pessimistic about their hometown heroes' chances against the nation's No. 1-rated team. However, when the Illini battled the Wolverines on even terms after the first half, 6-6, there was a little more cause for optimism. A fake field-goal attempt that turned into a screen pass to Abe Woodson late in the third quarter gave the Illini a 12-6 lead. Then Illinois put its bag of tricks away to rely upon its fleet-footed halfback, Bobby Mitchell. The speedy sophomore from Hot Springs, Arkansas, who accounted for 173 rushing yards on only 10 attempts that afternoon, nailed the Michigan coffin shut with a 64-yard sprint to the end zone, giving the Illini an insurmountable lead and their eventual 25-6 upset win. Afterward, Illini coach Ray Eliot called his squad's effort "a great team victory. It best exemplified what is meant by the words Fighting Illini. Every kid did a magnificent job. They were all heroes."

Bobby Mitchell (#22) rushed for 173 yards vs. Michigan in 1955.

Illinois' 1956 basketball team compiled an 18-4 overall record, finished second in Big Ten play, and placed seventh in the national rankings. On Feb. 11, 1956, UI set a single-game scoring mark with a 111-64 victory over Ohio State at Huff Gym.

ILLINI SCRAPBOOK

Em Lindbeck

EM LINDBECK was selected as the University of Illinois' Athlete of the Year for 1955-56, in the *Daily Illini's* annual end-of-the-season contest. The native of Kewanee earned Most Valuable Player honors in both football and baseball. As a quarterback, Lindbeck led the Illini past No.1-ranked Michigan, earning honorable mention All-Big Ten acclaim. On the baseball diamond, he batted .382 for the Illini, winning second-team All-Big Ten laurels as a center fielder.

Illini Legend

Art Schankin

If you asked the man on the street to name the world's most famous fencer, you might end up with a blank stare. But if you asked a sports trivia expert about the greatest fencer in the history of the U of I, Art Schankin's name would probably be at the top of the list. Though toiling in relative anonymity, Schankin ruled the world of collegiate fencing from 1956 through 1958. He tied for fifth nationally in the sabre event as a sophomore, finished third in foil as a junior, and swept the NCAA sabre title as a senior, becoming the first intercollegiate fencer to win a national championship with an unbeaten mark. Schankin continued to compete in the sport after his graduation in 1958, being nationally ranked. In 1964, six weeks before his wedding day, he was in an automobile accident that ended his fencing career but began his highly successful coaching tenure with the Illini. From 1973-93, Schankin's UI teams amassed a dual-meet record of 391 wins and 51 losses, including seven Big Ten champions. In addition to being Illini fencing coach, he was also a sales supervisor for Collegiate Cap and Gown. Schankin resides in Champaign.

Illini Lists

MEN'S BASKETBALL SCORING LEADERS OF THE 1950s

1949-50	15.1 ppg	Wally Osterkorn
1950-51	17.4 ppg	Don Sunderlage
1951-52	13.7 ppg	John Kerr
1952-53	17.5 ppg	John Kerr
1953-54	25.3 ppg	John Kerr
1954-55	16.5 ppg	Paul Judson
1955-56	22.9 ppg	George Bon Salle
1956-57	18.8 ppg	Harv Schmidt
1957-58	19.6 ppg	Don Ohl
1958-59	17.9 ppg	Roger Taylor

Roger Taylor

ILLINI LORE

A pair of distinguished University of Illinois alumni—Dr. Vincent du Vigneaud and Dr. Polykarp Kusch—were awarded Nobel prizes in November of 1955. Dr. du Vigneaud, who received his bachelor's degree in 1923 and his master's in 1924 from the UI, won the $36,720 award for chemistry for his work on two hormones that assist in childbirth and keep a check on vital organs. He was on the staff of Cornell University's medical college at the time. Dr. Kusch, who earned his master's in 1933 and his Ph.D. in 1936 from the UI, split the Nobel physics award with Dr. W.E. Lamb of Stanford. Kusch, who then taught at Columbia University, won his prize for work in calculating the properties of the atom.

1956-57

AMERICA'S TIME CAPSULE

Oct. 8, 1956   Don Larsen of the New York Yankees hurled the first perfect game in World Series history.

Nov. 4, 1956   Political demonstrations against Communist rule in Hungary led to a surprise attack by Soviet Armed forces, resulting in the deaths of 32,000 persons.

Nov. 6, 1956   Dwight Eisenhower defeated Illinois governor Adlai Stevenson in the presidential election.

Jan. 21, 1957   NBC carried the first nationally televised videotaped broadcast, a recording of the presidential inauguration ceremonies.

July 12, 1957   Surgeon General Leroy Burney reported that a link between cigarette smoking and lung cancer had been established.

ILLINI MOMENT

NO. 1 FALLS AGAIN TO ILLINI:

For the second consecutive season, a No. 1-rated football team from the state of Michigan was brought to its knees at Memorial Stadium, as Illinois beat top-ranked Michigan State, 20-13, on October 27, 1956. As big a thorn as Bobby Mitchell was to Michigan in 1955, so was Abe Woodson to the Spartans in 1956. Trailing 13-0 at halftime, prospects for another Fighting Illini upset looked bleak. But that's when the Austin Express got rolling. Woodson narrowed the margin to 13-6 midway through the third quarter on a two-yard touchdown. Then, in the fourth quarter, he tied the game with 1:42 gone on a 70-yard gallop around right end. Nine minutes later, Woodson scored the game winner when he grabbed a screen pass from sophomore quarterback Bill Offenbecher on the 18-yard line and dashed 82 yards. All told, Woodson touched the ball 20 times for 271 yards, marking an individual performance that ranks among Illinois' best ever.

Abe Woodson (#40)

The 1957 Illini gymnastics team won the Big Ten championship and was runner-up at the NCAA meet.

ILLINI SCRAPBOOK

George Bon Salle

I Illini Item

THE UNIVERSITY OF SAN FRANCISCO'S basketball team tasted defeat for the first time in more than two years on December 17, 1956, when Illinois beat the defending national champions, 62-33, at Huff Gym. Coach Harry Combes's Illini broke USF's national-record 60-game winning streak behind a strong defensive effort and 19 points from center George BonSalle.

Illini Lists

ILLINI FOOTBALL'S RUSHING LEADERS OF THE 1950s

1950	Dick Raklovits	709 yards
1951	John Karras	650 yards
1952	Pete Bachouros	484 yards
1953	J.C. Caroline	1,256 yards
1954	J.C. Caroline	440 yards
1955	Harry Jefferson	514 yards
1956	Abe Woodson	599 yards
1957	Ray Nitschke	514 yards
1958	Marshall Starks	303 yards
1959	Bill Brown	504 yards

Marshall Starks

Illini Legend

Abe Woodson

Abe Woodson had a lot to live up to when he inherited football jersey number 40 at the University of Illinois. The two men who wore those numerals before him were Dike Eddleman, Illinois' greatest all-time athlete, and Stan Wallace, a gridiron star in his own right at Illinois. Well, when Woodson's eligibility expired in 1956, the former star from Chicago's Austin High School had proven he was more than worthy. Woodson, of course, is best known for his role in Illinois' 1956 upset of No. 1-ranked Michigan State. He wound up his three-year career as the school's fifth leading rusher with 1,276 yards and twice led Illinois in pass receiving. Abe was also a terror on the track, winning two Big Ten titles as a 50-yard hurdler and tying the world's indoor mark twice in that event. After being selected as UI's Athlete of the Year in 1956-57, Woodson enjoyed a nine-year career in the National Football League with San Francisco and St. Louis. He hung up his cleats in 1967 and worked briefly for S&H Green Stamps. Woodson then began a 20-year career as a life insurance agent in the San Francisco area. In 1991, he enrolled as a student at the Southern California School of Evangelism. Today, Woodson is a Church of Christ minister in Las Vegas, Nevada and has developed a prison ministry in Indian Springs, Nevada.

ILLINI LORE

The University of Illinois' John Bardeen was one of three American scientists to be awarded the 1956 Nobel prize in physics for their development of the transistor. Bardeen, a professor of electrical engineering and physics since 1951, perfected the micro-amplifiers with William Shockley of Pasadena, California and Walter Brattain of Murray Hill, New Jersey at the Bell Telephone Laboratories. In 1972, he again shared a Nobel prize for a theory on superconductivity.

1957-58

AMERICA'S TIME CAPSULE

Sept. 25, 1957   President Eisenhower sent 1,000 army paratroopers to Little Rock, Arkansas to enforce the desegregation of Central High School.

Oct. 4, 1957   The Soviet Union launched Sputnik 1, the first Earth satellite.

Oct. 10, 1957   The Milwaukee Braves beat the New York Yankees in game seven of the 54th World Series.

Jan. 31, 1958   Explorer I, the first U.S. Earth satellite, was launched from Cape Canaveral, Florida.

March 25, 1958   Sugar Ray Robinson regained the world middleweight boxing title for an unprecedented fifth time, defeating Carmen Basilio.

Coach Garret (left) with his three star fencers, (left to right) Abbey Silverstone, Lee Sentman and Art Schankin.

ILLINI SCRAPBOOK

ILLINI MOMENT

ILLINI FENCERS AND GYMNASTS WIN NCAA CROWNS:

University of Illinois athletes captured a pair of national team championships during the 1957-58 season, with Illini fencers and gymnasts bringing home top honors. Coach Mac Garret's swordsmen travelled all the way to Lubbock, Texas on March 21-22, edging Columbia, Yale, and Navy for the NCAA title. Illinois' fencers earned 47 points altogether, including 21 in sabre from individual champion Art Schankin, 14 in foil from Abbey Silverstone, and 12 in epee from Lee Sentman. The Illini gymnasts tied Michigan State for the national title on April 11-12, with each team scoring 79 points at MSU's Jenison Field House. Illinois got predicted individual championships in the horizontal bars and free exercise events from Abie Grossfeld, but it was a junior tumbler named Allan Harvey who provided the Illini with their biggest surprise. For the first time in his competitive career, Harvey executed the difficult double back somersault, a performance that netted him second place in tumbling. A shoulder injury suffered by UI's Bob Diamond on the first night of competition probably cost Illinois an undisputed team title, as Diamond was counted on to place well on the side horse.

Not only was Bobby Mitchell a brilliant football player, he also ran track for the Fighting Illini, winning the 100- and 200-yard sprints in Big Ten championship action.

Ray Nitschke was inducted into the Pro Football Hall of Fame in 1978.

Illini Item

Illini Legend

Illini Lists

ILLINOIS' MULTIPLE BIG TEN WRESTLING CHAMPIONS

3—Jon Llewellyn, heavyweight (1989-90-91)
2—Joe Sapora, 115 pounds (1929-30)
2—Bob Emmons, 126 pounds (1932-33)
2—Lou Kachiroubas, 128 pounds (1946-47)
2—Archie Deutschman, 136 pounds (1938-39)
2—Norton Compton, 137 pounds (1952-53)
2—Jack McIlvoy, 145 pounds (1935-37)
2—Werner Holzer, 147 & 157 pounds (1957-58)
2—John Ginay, 165 pounds (1937-38)
2—Dave Shapiro, 165 pounds (1943-47)
2—Ralph Silverstein, 175 pounds & heavyweight (1935-36)
2—Bob Norman, heavyweight (1957-58)

Werner Holzer

Bob Norman

His dream was to play varsity football for the University of Illinois, but a knee injury during his freshman year never allowed Bob Norman to realize his boyhood ambition. So after sitting out the balance of that season and all of his sophomore year, Norman turned to his second love—the sport of wrestling. What resulted were two consecutive Big Ten and NCAA heavyweight championships and a nearly perfect 36-0-1 record. The 6'4" 225-pounder's senior campaign in 1958 was particularly impressive, recording 14 pins during a flawless 21-0 performance. Norman earned entrance into the Amateur Wrestling Hall of Fame in 1978. Following his graduation from Illinois with a degree in horticulture, Norman entered the construction business in Chicago. Norman worked several years as an engineer for Cook County and the state of Illinois, and currently owns his own carpentry business in Winfield, Illinois. His son, Tim, lettered in football at Illinois from 1977-80.

President Dodds show UI students his building plan.

ILLINI LORE

Details of a 10-year, $198.5 million building program for the University of Illinois were announced at a July 1957 meeting of the Board of Trustees. The previous comprehensive building program for the UI took place more than a quarter of a century earlier, when, during the 1920s, the University expanded its facilities to handle rising enrollments. Among the facilities planned were plant services buildings. More than $5 million of the 1957 request was for remodeling and renovation of existing structures.

1958-59

AMERICA'S TIME CAPSULE

Sept. 30, 1958	Arkansas Gov. Orval Faubus defied the Supreme Court's ruling against racial segregation in public schools.
Dec. 28, 1958	The Baltimore Colts won the NFL championship by defeating the New York Giants.
Jan. 3, 1959	President Dwight Eisenhower proclaimed Alaska the 49th state.
Feb. 3, 1959	Rock and roll stars Buddy Holly and Richie Valens died in an airplane crash.
May 28, 1959	The U.S. Army launched two monkeys into space. They were recovered unhurt from the Caribbean Sea after a 300-mile-high flight.
Aug. 21, 1959	Hawaii was admitted to the union as the 50th state.

ILLINI MOMENT

Coach Harry Combes (left) and his starters (left to right) Mannie Jackson, Al Gosnell, Govoner Vaughn, Roger Taylor and John Wessels upset first-place Indiana in 1959.

ILLINI RALLY DERAILS FIRST-PLACE HOOSIERS:

The odds seemed overwhelming against Illinois' basketball team derailing league-leading Indiana at Bloomington, February 9, 1959. The ninth-place Illini, mired in the throes of a five-game losing streak, faced a Hoosier club that featured 6'11" center Walt Bellamy and an array of other talented sophomores. During the first four and a half minutes, Indiana ran off to a 15-0 lead and had visions of resetting the single-game scoring record of 122 points that it had compiled one week before at Ohio State. The Hoosiers lost their momentum, however, and the Illini played on even terms for the balance of the first half. In the last period, Illinois rode the hot shooting of Govoner Vaughn to finally take the lead, 68-67. From that point on, Illinois never trailed, winding up with a come-from-behind 89-83 victory.

ILLINI SCRAPBOOK

Coach Charlie Pond's Illini gymnasts won the 1959 Big Ten crown and placed second nationally.

Rich Kreitling caught touchdown passes of 83 and 64 yards at Minnesota.

THE FIGHTING ILLINI FOOTBALL TEAM beat Minnesota 20-8 on October 18, 1958, recording its first victory on the Gophers' home field since 1919. Quarterback Bob Hickey and wide receiver Rich Kreitling combined for touchdowns of 83 and 64 yards, as Illinois won for the first time on the road in 12 tries.

Illini Legend

Abie Grossfeld

Abie Grossfeld was a Big Ten champion, a national champion and a two-time Olympian, but he said that being chosen as UI's Athlete of the Year marked one of the most special moments in his gymnastics career. "In 1959, when I received that award from the *Daily Illini*, I was the first person to win who wasn't a football or a basketball player. I was very proud to be picked as Illinois' Athlete of the Year." From 1957-59, Grossfeld won seven Big Ten titles and was a member of three conference championship teams. Grossfeld also earned the Big Ten Conference Medal of Honor as Illinois' top scholar-athlete. After earning his bachelor's and master's degrees at Illinois, Grossfeld entered the coaching world; he's been the head coach at Southern Connecticut State University since 1963. Grossfeld, currently the longest tenured collegiate gymnastics coach, directed SCSU to three national titles and 29 individual national titles. His greatest athlete at SCSU was Peter Kormann, a bronze medalist in the 1976 Olympics. Grossfeld was the head coach of the U.S. Olympic Gymnastics Team in 1972, '84 and '88, and was an assistant coach in 1964 and '68. Today, the gymnastics Hall of Famer resides in Woodbridge, Connecticut.

Illini Lists

ILLINOIS GYMNASTICS BIG TEN ALL-AROUND CHAMPIONS

- E.B. Styles   1910-11-12
- A.W. Ziegler   1920
- Joe Giallombardo   1938-39
- Frank Dolan   1950
- Bob Sullivan   1952
- Don Tonry   1956
- Abie Grossfeld   1957-58-59
- Ray Hadley   1960-62
- Charles Lakes   1984-85
- Dominick Minicucci   1988

Ray Hadley earned Big Ten all-around championships in 1960 and '62.

ILLINI LORE

Charles "Chilly" Bowen stepped down from his post as executive director of the Alumni Association in June of 1959 following 17 years of service for the organization. A 1922 graduate of the University of Illinois, Bowen began his 32-year stint with the UI as ticket manager and business manager for the Athletic Association. In 1942, he was appointed as the Alumni Association's first executive director. Alumni membership grew from less than 3,000 to more than 19,000 during Bowen's time in that position.

1959-60

Sept. 15, 1959   Soviet Premier Nikita Khrushchev arrived in the United States for meetings with President Eisenhower.

Oct. 18, 1959   The Chicago White Sox were beaten by the Los Angeles Dodgers for the World Series title.

Jan. 4, 1960   The United Steel Workers and the nation's steel companies agreed on a wage increase to settle a six-month strike.

May 1, 1960   A United States U-2 reconnaissance plane was shot down inside the U.S.S.R., causing Soviet Premier Khrushchev to cancel a planned summit meeting in Paris.

June 20, 1960   Floyd Patterson knocked out Ingemar Johansson to become the first boxer in history to regain the heavyweight championship.

ILLINI MOMENT

The Ray Eliot era at Illinois ended in 1959 with a victory over Northwestern.

ILLINI END ELIOT ERA WITH VICTORY:

The Ray Eliot era at Illinois concluded with a storybook finish November 21, 1959, as the Fighting Illini football team swept past Northwestern, 28-0, at Memorial Stadium. Playing against the school that had inflicted so many thorns in his side during 18 years on the sidelines, Eliot and his charges were in control all the way, out-gaining the Wildcats 365 yards to 142. Three hundred forty-eight of Illinois' yards came on the ground as fullback Bill Brown (164 yards) and halfback Mel Counts (109 yards) averaged more than eight yards a carry. The Illini defensive unit, led by Bill Burrell, allowed Northwestern to penetrate the 50-yard line only once all day. When the final gun sounded, UI students rushed the field, and along with Illini players, hoisted the broadly smiling Eliot and carried him off the field.

Illini track star George Kerr repeated as NCAA 880-yard champion in 1960, running the event in a time of 1:46.4.

ILLINI SCRAPBOOK

Govoner Vaughn

I Illini Item

FIGHTING ILLINI BASKETBALL STAR Govoner Vaughn saved his best until last, scoring a career-high 30 points in his final game at Huff Gym, February 29, 1960. The senior forward from Edwardsville hit 14 out of 17 shots from the field, including all nine of his attempts in the second half, to lead Illinois to a 90-61 victory over Michigan.

Illini Legend

Bill Burrell

The 1959 Heisman Trophy balloting, long recognized as a barometer of individual greatness in college football, ranked Bill Burrell as the nation's fourth-best overall player and No. 1 defensive performer his senior year. He was named a consensus All-American linebacker and was a three-time first-team all-conference selection. The *Chicago Tribune* even named Burrell as Big Ten football's Most Valuable Player in 1959. But today, despite all those laurels, Bill Burrell probably still doesn't receive the credit due him. Ray Nitschke, a teammate and one of the Illini linebackers ranked above Burrell, recently called him Illinois' "forgotten man." The fact that he was one of only a handful of blacks playing college football in the late 1950s lends credence to the charge that racism has robbed Burrell of his recognition. However, to his Illini teammates, it is impossible to masquerade No. 68 as anything less than the best UI player of his time. Burrell died in 2001.

Illini Lists

LEO JOHNSON'S ALL-TIME ILLINI TRACK TEAM

Leo Johnson coached the University of Illinois track and field squad for 28 years, from 1938-65. Here, based on the Big Ten championship titles they won, is who Johnson might have chosen on his Fighting Illini outdoor track and field "Dream Team" (two men per individual event).

100-yard dash: Willie Williams and Claude "Buddy" Young
220-yard dash: Herb McKenley and Willie Williams
440-yard run: Cirilo McSween and Herb McKenley
880-yard run: Stacey Siders and George Kerr
One-mile run: Bob Rehberg and Jim Bowers
Two-mile run: Waldemar Karkow and Ken Brown
120-yard high hurdles: George Walker and Willard Thomson
220-yard low hurdles: George Walker and Willard Thomson
High jump: Dike Eddleman and Al Urbanckas
Pole vault: Don Laz and Bob Richards
Discuss: Bogie Redmon and Marv Berschet
Shot put: Bill Brown and Norm Wasser
Long Jump: Paul Foreman and Don Laz
One-mile relay team: Herb McKenley, Bob Rehberg, Cirilo McSween and Stacey Siders

ILLINI LORE

Presidential candidate John F. Kennedy campaigned on Wright Street in the spring of 1960. Kennedy wound up carrying the state of Illinois over Vice President Richard Nixon, winning the state's 27 electoral votes.

1960-61

AMERICA'S TIME CAPSULE

Sept. 26, 1960	Sen. John Kennedy and Vice President Richard Nixon participated in the first of a series of televised presidential campaign debates.
Oct. 13, 1960	Bill Mazeroski of Pittsburgh slammed a game-winning home run against the New York Yankees to give the Pirates the World Series championship.
Nov. 8, 1960	John Kennedy was elected president of the United States in a narrow victory over Richard Nixon.
April 17, 1961	Nearly 2,000 CIA-trained anti-Castro Cuban exiles landed at the Bay of Cochinos in Cuba, in what came to be known as the Bay of Pigs invasion.
May 5, 1961	Alan Shepard made a successful flight aboard the Project Mercury capsule Freedom Seven to become the first American in space.

ILLINI MOMENT

ELLIOTT DEBUTS AS WINNER:

On September 24, 1960, just 10 months after the Eliot era had concluded, the Elliott era began at the University of Illinois' Memorial Stadium. And as Ray Eliot's career had ended, so too did Pete Elliott's career begin—with an Illini football victory. Illinois' victim on this warm September afternoon was Indiana, recently suspended from conference competition due to its violation of recruiting rules. For the first seven minutes of the game, Indiana appeared to be in complete control, marching for an 80-yard touchdown on the opening drive. Thereafter, it was all Illinois as Elliott's option attack punctured the Hoosier defense for two touchdowns and a field goal while the Illini defense limited IU to just two first downs the balance of the game. Illinois' individual star was Champaign senior quarterback Johnny Easterbrook who twice ran options around left end for TDs and led the team in rushing with 74 yards. The final score: Illinois 17, Indiana 6.

Quarterback John Easterbrook (#11) helped Illinois beat Indiana in 1960.

Brothers Pete (left) and Bump Elliott coached against each other seven times when they were at Illinois and Michigan, respectively. Bump held a 6-1 edge in those Illini–Wolverine gridiron confrontations.

ILLINI SCRAPBOOK

Bill Small's layup against Michigan State helped the Illini beat the Spartans.

I Illini Item

ILLINOIS' BASKETBALL TEAM spotted Michigan State a 14-0 lead, but fought back to win, 93-92, at Hull Gym on January 30, 1961. Bill Small's layup with 21 seconds left gave the Illini their first lead of the game at 91-90, and two pressure-packed free throws by Dave Downey with eight seconds remaining provided Illinois with its final margin.

Illini Lists

PETE ELLIOTT'S MOST UNDERRATED ILLINI PLAYERS

Pete Elliott, coach of the Fighting Illini football team from 1960-66, was asked to select his 10 most underrated players at Illinois. Here, in no particular order, are his choices and comments about those players:

- Ernie McMillan ——"an outstanding player in college and as a pro"
- Ed O'Bradovich ——"a standout later with the Chicago Bears"
- Mike Taliaferro ——"outstanding on Rose Bowl team and very good in pro ball"
- Jim Warren ——"excellent on offense and defense; became a fine pro defensive back"
- Dick Deller ——"captain of the Rose Bowl team"
- Ron Acks——"a fine athlete who had an excellent pro career"
- Gregg Schumacher——"a big, agile player who could do a lot of things"
- Bob Trumpy ——"later became a standout with the Cincinnati Bengals"
- Sam Price ——"a three-year starter and an excellent power halfback"
- Cyril Pinder——"though he was plagued with injuries, he was one of Illinois' finest talents"

Illini Legend

Bill Brown

The term "battering ram" probably never more aptly described a football player than it did Illinois' Bill Brown. At 5-11, 210 pounds, the all-state fullback from Mendota, Illinois was never known as a flashy player, but there were few who were more productive. From 1958-60, Brown ground out a total of 1,269 yards to become Illinois' sixth-leading rusher of all time. When his Illini offensive unit ran out of downs, Brown stayed on the field as a defensive linebacker. And when he wasn't playing offense or defense, Brown starred as a punter, winding up his career with a UI-record average of more than 40 yards per punt. When football season ended, Brown headed for the Armory to compete for Leo Johnson's track team as a shot putter. He lettered twice in track, holding the school's outdoor record in the shot put (54' 8 1/2") and winning the 1960 Big Ten indoor title. Brown was drafted by the NFL's Chicago Bears in 1961, but spent 12 of his 13 years in the pros with the Minnesota Vikings. He led the Vikings in rushing five times and played in three Super Bowls. After he hung up his cleats, Brown entered the insurance business for 10 years, but for the last 25 years he has directed the sales force of John Roberts Printing Co. in Minneapolis, Minnesota.

ILLINI LORE

On May 20, 1961, the University of Illinois' Krannert Art Museum was dedicated. Mr. and Mrs. Herman Krannert, benefactors of $430,000, were on hand to open the university's first real home for UI's permanent art collection. Previously the Architecture Building was the campus site for art displays.

1961-62

AMERICA'S TIME CAPSULE

Oct. 1, 1961 Roger Maris of the New York Yankees hit his 61st home run, breaking Babe Ruth's single-season record.

Feb. 10, 1962 Jim Beatty became the first American to break the four-minute mile indoors, registering a time of 3:58.9 in Los Angeles.

Feb. 20, 1962 Astronaut John Glenn became the first American to orbit the Earth, circling the globe three times aboard Friendship 7.

March 2, 1962 Wilt Chamberlain of the Philadelphia Warriors became the first NBA player to score 100 points in a game.

Aug. 5, 1962 Actress Marilyn Monroe, 36, died in her Los Angeles home of an apparent overdose of sleeping pills.

ILLINI MOMENT

Coach Lee Eilbracht and captain Tony Eichelberger

ILLINI BASEBALL TEAM IS UNDISPUTED CHAMPION:

Behind the flawless pitching of Tom Fletcher and Doug Mills and the timely hitting of Lloyd Flodin and Tony Eichelberger, Illinois' 1962 baseball team captured its first undisputed Big Ten title in 15 years. Only Indiana and Northwestern were able to hand the Fighting Illini losses in 15 Big Ten games, as Illinois finished a half-game better than runner-up Michigan. The clincher came on May 19 at Illinois Field when the Illini swept a doubleheader from Iowa, while the league-leading Wolverines were dropping a pair at Wisconsin. Fletcher and Mills both went to the mound five times during the Big Ten season, and each man recorded a perfect 5-0 win-loss mark. Illinois' top hitters were Flodin (.370), the team's catcher, and shortstop Eichelberger (.365). Right fielder Bud Felichio led the Illini in home runs and runs batted in during conference play, with two and 13, respectively. In NCAA tournament action, Coach Lee Eilbracht's troops beat the University of Detroit in their opening game (2-1), but lost their next two to Western Michigan (10-2) and Michigan (5-1) to be eliminated.

The 1962 Big Ten baseball champions.

Mike Toliuszis

Illini Item

SENIOR MIKE TOLIUSZIS became the first University of Illinois golfer since 1942 to win medalist honors at the Big Ten Championships, May 18-19, 1962. Toliuszis trailed Purdue's Steve Wilkinson by five strokes after 36 holes, but pulled into a first-place tie after the third round. In the fourth and final round, the Illini star shot a 73 to wind up six strokes better than the second-place Wilkinson.

Illini Legend

Doug Mills

Though he is no relation to his namesake, Douglas C. Mills had a lot in common with the longtime Illini athlete, coach and athletic director. Both men were multiple-sport stars as undergraduates, and both were huge successes after their playing days were through. The younger Mills, a native of Galesburg, lettered in football, basketball, and baseball during his career at the Urbana-Champaign campus, earning six monograms altogether. His greatest individual achievements came as a pitcher for Coach Lee Eilbracht's UI baseball squad. As a senior, Mills appeared on the mound five times in Big Ten play and won all five decisions, helping Illinois capture its first undisputed conference baseball title in 15 years. Though Mills' basketball and football performances were less spectacular, he did average nearly four points per game as a substitute guard for Coach Harry Combes. Illinois' 1962 Athlete of the Year has enjoyed a remarkable career in the banking industry, rising to his current position as Chairman of the Board of Urbana's First Busey Corporation. In 1998, Mills, his wife, Linda, and their children, David and Rob, gave a gift which endows the salary of the head football coach at The University of Illinois.

Illini Lists

MOST POINTS BY
BIG TEN BASKETBALL PLAYERS
VS. ILLINOIS

1.	49 points	Glenn Robinson, Purdue (3/13/94)
	49 points	Gary Bradds, Ohio State (2/10/64)
3.	48 points	Mike Woodson, Indiana (3/3/79)
4.	45 points	Terry Dischinger, Purdue (1/8/62)
	45 points	Terry Dischinger, Purdue (2/17/62)
6.	43 points	Robin Freeman, Ohio State (2/25/56)
	43 points	Terry Dischinger, Purdue (1/11/60)
8.	42 points	Walt Bellamy, Indiana (2/22/60)
9.	41 points	Dave Schellhase, Purdue (2/6/65)
	41 points	Steve Downing, Indiana (2/12/73)

Terry Dischinger

ILLINI LORE

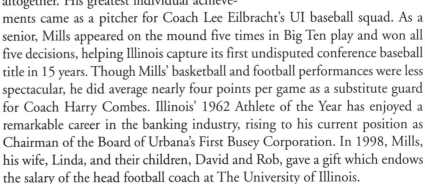

James Brady, former press secretary to President Ronald Reagan, earned a degree in journalism in 1962. The Centralia, Illinois native served as president of Sigma Chi fraternity as a University of Illinois student and also wrote for the *Daily Illini*. Just three months after his appointment as the presidential press secretary, Brady was critically injured in the March 1981 assassination attempt on the president. He received the UI Alumni Association's Alumni Achievement Award in 1991 and now serves as vice chairman of the National Organization on Disability in Washington, D.C. Brady resides in Arlington, Virginia.

1962-63

AMERICA'S TIME CAPSULE

Oct. 1, 1962   James Meredith, escorted by U.S. marshals, became the first black to attend classes at the University of Mississippi. Two men were killed in the ensuing mob violence.

Oct. 22, 1962   President Kennedy addressed the nation on television regarding the Cuban missile crisis. The missile bases were dismantled by the Soviet Union I I days later.

May 7, 1963   The communications satellite Telstar 2 was launched from Cape Canaveral, Florida, and began relaying television signals between the United States and Europe.

June 26 ,1963   President Kennedy spoke to a crowd of more than one million adjacent to the Berlin Wall in Germany.

Aug. 28, 1963   Dr. Martin Luther King presented his "I Have a Dream" speech to a crowd of 200,000 from the steps of the Lincoln Memorial in Washington, D.C.

ILLINI MOMENT

ILLINI CAGERS CLINCH BIG TEN TITLE AT NEW ASSEMBLY HALL:

The 1962-63 basketball season was an unforgettable one for the University of Illinois. First, the Fighting Illini played their 38th and final season at Huff Gym, winning all nine of their games in that storied facility. Second, Illinois opened its futuristic new palace, the Assembly Hall, on March 4, 1963, with a nail-biting 79-73 victory over Northwestern. But the most thrilling chapter of 1962-63 came on March 9, when in the regular-season finale at Champaign, Illinois defeated Iowa, 73-69, to claim a share of the Big Ten title. Illinois went on to the NCAA tournament for the first time since 1952. Illinois travelled up to East Lansing, Michigan for the Mideast Regional games, defeating Bowling Green in the opener, then losing to eventual champ Loyola in game two. The Illini heroes that season included starting forwards Bob Starnes and Dave Downey, center Bill Burwell, and guards Bill Small and Tal Brody. Skip Thoren, Bill Edwards and Bogie Redmon were valuable members of the team off the bench for Coach Harry Combes's 20-6 club.

Though the ticket indicates that the site of this matchup between Illinois and Northwestern would be played at Huff Gym, the contest was actually the first to be played at the brand new Assembly Hall.

ILLINI SCRAPBOOK

Illinois' 1963 Big Ten basketball champs.

Ken Zimmerman (#20) and Head Coach Pete Elliott.

ON NOVEMBER 3, 1962, the University of Illinois football team broke the longest losing streak in modern Big Ten history—15 in a row—with a 14-10 upset victory over Purdue at West Lafayette, Indiana. Coach Pete Elliott's Illini shocked the Purdue Homecoming crowd when they took the lead on a 23-yard pass from Mike Taliaferro to Thurman Walker in the second quarter, and built the margin to 14-3 on a 30-yard gallop by Ken Zimmerman on the final play of the third period. When the team returned by bus from West Lafayette, it was greeted by thousands of fans lined up on Cunningham and Florida Avenues.

Illini Legend

Dave Downey

Dave Downey's association with the University of Illinois has seen him rise from the status of a student athlete, to that of assistant coach, to a role as a color analyst on the Illini basketball telecasts, and, finally, to an appointment from the governor as a member of the UI's Board of Trustees. For Downey, the challenge of combining a career of athletics and academics was seemingly never difficult, as witnessed by his earning the prestigious Big Ten Conference Medal of Honor as a senior in 1963. He was best known for his Illini exploits on the basketball court, a three-year stretch from 1960-63 in which he was named team MVP every season. Downey set nearly every UI scoring record, including marks for a single game (53 points vs. Indiana on February 16, 1963) and for a career (1,360 points). A charter member of the Illinois Coaches Association High School Hall of Fame, the Canton, Illinois High School graduate earned All-Big Ten and All-American honors at Illinois. Downey was the recipient of the Varsity "I" Award in 1988, saluting his marvelous performance as an athlete and his successful career as president of Champaign's Downey Planning Services.

Illini Lists

PRO FOOTBALL HALL OF FAME

On January 29, 1963, the National Football League elected its charter class for the new Pro Football Hall of Fame in Canton, Ohio. Two men with Illini ties were among the group of 16:

- Sammy Baugh, QB
- Bert Bell, contributer
- Joe Carr, contributer
- "Dutch" Clark, QB
- **Harold "Red" Grange, RB**
- **George Halas, player/coach**
- Mel Hein, C
- Cal Hubbard, T
- Don Hutson, E
- "Curly" Lambeau, player/coach
- Tim Mara, contributer
- George Marshall, contributer
- Johnny "Blood" McNally, RB
- "Bronko" Nagurski, RB
- Ernie Nevers, RB
- Jim Thorpe, RB

The Assembly Hall begins to rise from the ground.

ILLINI LORE

A massive building program begun in 1958 at the University of Illinois saw the completion of numerous structures during the 1962-63 school year. Among the facilities opened to students included the $1.35 million Student Services Building, $1.96 million Entomology Building, the $2.3 million Physics Building, the $5.75 million Pennsylvania Residence Halls, the $6.9 million Illini Union addition, and the $8.3 million Assembly Hall.

1963-64

AMERICA'S TIME CAPSULE

Oct. 2, 1963   Pitcher Sandy Koufax of the Los Angeles Dodgers set a World Series record by striking out 15 New York Yankees in the opening game.

Nov. 22, 1963   President John F. Kennedy was killed by an assassin's bullet in Dallas, Texas.

Dec. 31, 1963   The Chicago Bears won the NFL championship by defeating the New York Giants, 14-0.

Feb. 7, 1964   The Beatles arrived in New York City for an appearance on the *Ed Sullivan Show*.

Feb. 25, 1964   Challenger Cassius Clay defeated Sonny Liston for the world heavyweight boxing title.

July 2, 1964   The Civil Rights Act of 1964 was signed by President Lyndon Johnson.

Three of Illinois football's biggest stars in 1963 were Mike Taliaferro (#19), Jim Grabowski (#31) and Dick Butkus (snapping ball).

ILLINI MOMENT

PRESIDENT'S ASSASSINATION DELAYS ILLINI CHAMPIONSHIP:

For the University of Illinois football team, it was the worst of times and it was the best of times. Forced to postpone its season-ending showdown at Michigan State for five days due to the shocking assassination of President John Kennedy, Coach Pete Elliott's Illini made a second trip to East Lansing to play the fourth-ranked Spartans on Thanksgiving Day 1963. State's roster was stocked with All-Americans such as halfback Sherman Lewis, but the Illini countered with a stifling defense led by the incomparable Dick Butkus. In the end, Illinois' defenders were the difference, causing the Spartans to cough up three fumbles and throw four interceptions, resulting in a 13-0 Illini victory. UI's offensive attack was led by sophomore fullback Jim Grabowski, who rushed for 85 yards against the heretofore impenetrable Spartan defense. The triumph gave Illinois its 12th football championship and its third trip to the Rose Bowl.

The 1964 Rose Bowl victors.

ILLINI SCRAPBOOK

Illinois' George Donnelly (#26)

I Illini Item

THE FIGHTNG ILLINI FOOTBALL TEAM made it three Rose Bowl victories in a row on January 1, 1964, by defeating Washington 17-7. In a game witnessed by nearly 97,000 fans, including former president and Tournament of Roses Grand Marshal Dwight Eisenhower, the Illini rebounded from a 7-0 deficit behind the methodical running of game MVP Jim Grabowski, who rushed for 125 yards.

Illini Legend

Pete Elliott

One of the most popular men to ever don Fighting Illini coaching apparel, Pete Elliott took his team from the brink of destruction to the pinnacle of success during his career from 1960-66. Elliott's initial years at the University of Illinois were clouded with failure, losing a modern Big Ten record 15 games in a row from November 19, 1960 to October 27, 1962. But in 1963, Elliott troops made Cinderella's story pale in comparison, capturing the 1963 Big Ten title and defeating Washington in the 1964 Rose Bowl. "We knew as we went through the losses that we didn't have a good team," Elliott told the Champaign-Urbana *News-Gazette* in 1977. "But we were confident because our athletes were devoted and they helped us recruit top prospects. They were tremendous emissaries for the school." On March 18, 1967, Elliott and basketball coach Harry Combes resigned from the UI staff as a result of the "slush fund" scandal. Elliott served as athletic director at the University of Miami for several years, and executive director of the Pro Football Hall of Fame from 1979 until he retired on October 31, 1996.

Illini Lists

NAISMITH AWARD WINNERS' PERFORMANCES VS. ILLINOIS

1971	Austin Carr, Notre Dame, 23 points on 1/30/71 (Illinois won, 69-66)
1973	Bill Walton, UCLA, 20 points on 12/30/72 (UCLA won, 71-64)
1976	Scott May, Indinana, 27 points on 1/17/76 (Indiana won 83-55); and 6 points on 2/14/76 (Indiana won, 58-48)
1988	Danny Manning, Kansas, 28 points on 11/29/87 (Illinois won, 81-75)
1993	Calbert Cheaney, Indiana, 30 points on 1/16/93 (Indiana won, 83-79); and 29 points on 2/17/93 (Indiana won, 93-72)
1994	Glenn Robinson, Purdue, 49 points on 3/13/94 (Purdue won, 87-77)
2001	Shane Battier, Duke, 11 points on 11/28/00 (Duke won, 78-77)

Duke's Shane Battier

ILLINI LORE

A 1964 graduate of the University of Illinois and a native of Urbana, famed film critic Roger Ebert had his first professional newspaper job when he was 15, as a sports writer for *The News-Gazette* in Champaign. An employee of the *Chicago Sun Times* since 1967, he was the first-ever recipient of a Pulitzer Prize for film criticism (1975) and is best known for his TV work with the late Gene Siskel on the shows *At the Movies* and *Siskel and Ebert*. Ebert has authored numerous books about the cinema and is also a highly acclaimed screenwriter. He often returns to Champaign-Urbana, including annual summer visits for his popular weekend film festival.

1964-65

AMERICA'S TIME CAPSULE

Sept. 27, 1964   The Warren Commission on the assassination of John Kennedy reported that there was no conspiracy and that Lee Harvey Oswald alone was responsible for the shooting of the president.

Oct. 15, 1964   Bob Gibson and the St. Louis Cardinals defeated the New York Yankees for the World Series title.

Nov. 3, 1964   Lyndon Johnson defeated Barry Goldwater in the presidential election.

March 8, 1965   The first United States combat forces landed in South Vietnam to guard the U.S. Air Force base at Da Nang.

June 5, 1965   Astronaut Edward White successfully completed a 20-minute walk in space, the first by an American.

ILLINI MOMENT

Jim Grabowski pounded out a Big Ten-record 239 yards vs. Wisconsin in 1964.

GRABOWSKI SETS BIG TEN RECORD:

Jim Grabowski is eternally grateful to men such as Archie Sutton, Ed Washington, Ron Acks and Dave Mueller, a few of the numerous teammates who opened the holes for his 239-yard rushing performance vs. Wisconsin, November 14, 1964. But the man to whom No. 31 owes the biggest debt of gratitude might be Illini publicity man Charlie Bellatti. It was Bellatti who sent word to his sideline spotters that Grabowski needed only 19 more yards in the final quarter to set a Big Ten record. "I wasn't going to put Jim back in the next series," head coach Pete Elliott told reporters afterwards, "but a man deserves a shot at a record like that." Badger coach Milt Bruhn, gracious despite Wisconsin's 29-0 defeat, praised Grabowski's ability to explode off the mark. "He keeps this head of steam up and blasts right through the man who is trying to tackle him," Bruhn said. Grabowski needed only 33 attempts to set the record, two of which resulted in touchdowns.

Bogie Redmon, shown here in a recent photo, played basketball and was a three-time letter winner in track and field. He combined his athletic prowess with classroom intelligence and was the University of Illinois' 1965 Big Ten Conference Medal of Honor winner.

ILLINI SCRAPBOOK

Skip Thoren led Illinois to a victory against defending national champion UCLA, Dec. 4, 1964.

I Illini Item

COACH HARRY COMBES'S Fighting Illini basketball team demolished defending national champion UCLA, 110-83, on December 4, 1964, severing the Bruins' 30-game-winning streak. Though UCLA guard Gail Goodrich tossed in a game-high 25 points, the Illini countered with a balanced attack that had six men score in double figures, paced by 20 points from center Skip Thoren.

Illini Legend

Dick Butkus

Just how good was Illinois linebacker Dick Butkus? Consider the following:

- An award in his name is given annually to the nation's top college football linebacker.
- He was a two-time consensus All-American and All-Big Ten selection for the Fighting Illini from 1962-64.
- He was the Big Ten's Most Valuable Player in 1963.
- He finished third in the Heisman Trophy balloting as a senior, unheard of for a defensive player.
- His jersey, number 50, was retired at Illinois alongside Red Grange's immortal 77.
- He's a member of every all-time all-star squad in existence and was a first-ballot selection into the College and Pro Football Halls of Fame.
- During his nine-year career with the Chicago Bears, he was an All-Pro pick eight times.

George Halas, who coached Butkus with the Bears, says, "Dick Butkus remains the standard for defensive players to strive for." Nowadays, Butkus is a TV and movie actor. He resides in Rancho Mirage, California.

Illini Lists

LEADING SINGLE-GAME RUSHERS IN BIG TEN HISTORY

When Jim Grabowski broke the Big Ten's single-game football rushing record on November 14, 1964, he put his name atop a list that included many of the conference's greatest stars.

239 yards	Jim Grabowski of Illinois, vs. Wisconsin, 1964
216 yards	Bill Daley of Michigan, vs. Northwestern, 1943
212 yards	Harold "Red" Grange of Illinois, vs. Michigan, 1924
207 yards	Tony Butkovich of Purdue, vs. Illinois, 1943
205 yards	J.C. Caroline of Illinois, vs. Minnesota, 1953
200 yards	Alan Ameche of Wisconsin, vs. Minnesota, 1951
199 yards	Dick Gordon of Michigan State, vs. Wisconsin, 1964

Jim Grabowski (foreground) bested six other Big Ten greats, including the legendary Red Grange (background).

ILLINI LORE

The College of Education dedicated its new $3.3 million building November 6-7, 1964, before an overflow group of students, alumni and other guests. The facility brought together departments that had been spread out over 27 campus locations. The education building was one of the first structures on campus to have extensive use of glass and to be fully air conditioned.

DAN BEAVER

"TAB" BENNETT

1965-1974

SCOTT STUDWELL

MIKE WELLS

1965-66

AMERICA'S TIME CAPSULE

Oct. 28, 1965   Workers topped out the Gateway Arch in St. Louis, Missouri.

Nov. 9, 1965   Millions of people in the Northeast were affected by a massive 13-hour power blackout.

Jan. 31, 1966   President Lyndon Johnson announced that American pilots had resumed their bombing raids on North Vietnam after a 38-day hiatus in hopes of furthering peace negotiations.

April 28, 1966   The Boston Celtics beat the Los Angeles Lakers in game seven of the NBA championship series, enabling coach Red Auerbach to retire with his eighth successive title.

June 8, 1966   The National and American football leagues merged, effective in 1970, setting up a Super Bowl game between the league champions.

ILLINI MOMENT

COMBES WINS HIS 300TH ILLINI VICTORY OVER MICHIGAN:

Illinois' most memorable basketball victory of the 1965-66 season came on February 1, 1966, before a sellout crowd of 7,350 at Michigan's Yost Field House. The 99-93 triumph not only got Illinois back in the Big Ten race, it also marked UI's first win in Ann Arbor in 11 years and gave Coach Harry Combes his 300th win as the Illini coach. Trailing by three points at the half, Illinois shot a school-record .697 from the field in the second half (23 of 33) to create a three-team logjam atop the conference standings. Illinois' offensive heroes were Don Freeman (33 points) and Rich Jones (31), while defensive kudos went to Preston Pearson, who despite playing the entire second half with four fouls, "held" Michigan's Cazzie Russell to 33 points.

Rich Jones' 31 points vs. Michigan helped Illinois give Coach Harry Combes his 300th Illini victory.

Former Illini athlete, coach and athletic director, Doug Mills, who was forced to step down as the University of Illinois' AD, was honored at a UI basketball game in the 1980s.

ILLINI SCRAPBOOK

Don Freeman

I Illini Item

CHICAGO STADIUM scoring records fell on January 18, 1966, when Illinois' basketball team defeated Notre Dame, 120-92. The Illini, led by Don Freeman's 33 points, just missed the school record of 121 points set twice a year before against Purdue and Michigan State. Illinois averaged more than 87 points per game that season, the fourth-highest average in its history.

Illini Lists

TOP BIG TEN TITLE WINNERS AMONG ILLINI COACHES

20 titles   Harry Gill, track & field (1904-29 and 1931-33)
18 titles   Leo Johnson, cross country (1938-60) and track & field (1938-65)
17 titles   Maxwell Garret, fencing (1941-72)
12 titles   Gary Wieneke, cross country (1967-present) and track & field (1974-present)
11 titles   George Huff, baseball (1896-1919)
11 titles   Charlie Pond, gymnastics (1949-61 and 1962-73)
9 titles   Gary Winckler, women's track & field (1986-present)
8 titles   Art Schankin, fencing (1973-93*)
7 titles   Bob Zuppke, football (1913-41)
6 titles   Paul Prehn, wrestling (1921-28)
6 titles   Hek Kenney, wrestling (1929-43 and 1946-47)
6 titles   Craig Tiley, tennis (1997-present)

*Fencing was discontinued as a Big Ten-sponsored sport following the 1985-86 season

Coach Leo Johnson (holding trophy) won 18 Big Ten championships as track and field coach at Illinois.

Illini Legend

Jim Grabowski

He broke nearly all of Red Grange's rushing records and played in the first two Super Bowls during a six-year career in the National Football League, but Jim Grabowski will be remembered for much more than just his prowess on the athletic field at the University of Illinois. The personable native of Chicago was an all-star in the classroom as well, earning Academic All-America acclaim in 1964 and '65 and the Big Ten Conference Medal of Honor in 1966. Grabowski was inducted into the Academic All-America Hall of Fame in 1993, joining such notables as Princeton's Bill Bradley, Notre Dame's Joe Theismann and Southern Cal's Pat Haden.

Pat Harmon presents Jim Grabowski (right) with his Hall of Fame plaque.

No. 3 in the Heisman Trophy balloting of 1965, Grabowski finished his brilliant Illini career as the Big Ten's career rushing leader with 2,878 yards. He was the first-round pick of the Green Bay Packers in 1966, retiring after the 1971 season following a series of knee injuries. In January of 1995, Grabowski was selected to become a member of the College Football Hall of Fame. Grabowski has served as color commentator for the Illini Football Radio Network since the 1970s.

ILLINI LORE

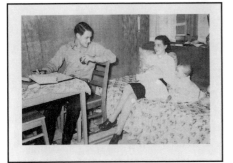

Early in 1966, wrecking crews began to remove the University of Illinois' temporary housing units known to their tenants as Illini Village and Stadium Terrace. The 41-story buildings, which once served as housing at an Indiana plant during World War 11, provided housing for 762 families of married students. War veterans attending school on the G.I. bill, and many others over the next two decades, remember these hastily built structures as brutally hot in the summer and bone-chillingly cold in the winter.

1966-67

AMERICA'S TIME CAPSULE

Oct. 13, 1966   U.S. bombers made their heaviest air strike of the war on North Vietnam.

Nov. 11, 1966   The last mission of the Gemini space series was launched as astronauts Jim Lovell and "Buzz" Aldrin successfully rendezvoused with an Agena target vehicle.

Jan. 15, 1967   The Green Bay Packers defeated the Kansas City Chiefs in the first-ever Super Bowl, 35-10.

March 25, 1967   Sophomore center Lew Alcindor led UCLA to the NCAA basketball championship over Dayton, 79-64.

July 23, 1967   Forty-three people were killed in Detroit as the worst race riot in U.S. history erupted.

Doug Mills (top) and Mel Brewer

ILLINI SCRAPBOOK

ILLINI MOMENT

SLUSH FUND SCANDAL ROCKS ILLINOIS:

March 19, 1967: "I have received today and have accepted the resignations of Pete Elliott, head football coach, Harry Combes, head basketball coach, and Howard Braun, assistant basketball coach." With those 26 words, UI President David Dodds Henry brought an end to one of the darkest sagas in Fighting Illini athletic history. Henry's actions came three months after he had asked the Big Ten Conference to make an investigation of alleged irregularities in assistance to athletes. On December 23, 1966—two days before Christmas—Big Ten Commissioner Bill Reed announced confirmation that illegal funds did exist. "These funds were completely apart from the operation of the University's grants-in-aid program," Reed said. "They were created with the knowledge of the director of athletics (Doug Mills) and of the assistant director of athletics (Mel Brewer), and disbursements were made at the direction of the respective head coaches." Twelve Illini football and basketball athletes were identified by the Big Ten and suspended from any further intercollegiate competition. It would take Illinois 16 years to win its next Big Ten football title and 17 years to claim its next conference basketball championshp.

Harv Schmidt, an Illini letterman from 1955-57, replaced Harry Combes as UI's basketball coach in 1967.

Fencing coach Max Garret won 17 Big Ten titles during his distinguished career at Illinois.

Illini Lists

ILLINI WHO HAVE PLAYED IN THE SUPER BOWL

The first Super Bowl was played in January of 1967 between the Green Bay Packers and the Kansas City Chiefs. Two former Illini, Ray Nitschke and Jim Grabowski, played in that inaugural battle between the American and National Football Leagues. Here's a list of all the Illinois football players who have Super Bowl experience.

Ed Brady, Cincinnati — XXIII
Bill Brown, Minnesota — IV, VII, IX
Darryl Byrd, L.A. Raiders — XVIII
Tony Eason, New England — XX
Jim Grabowski, Green Bay — I, II
Henry Jones, Buffalo — XXVI, XXVII, XXVIII
Jim Juriga, Denver — XXIV
Adam Lingner, Buffalo — XXV, XXVI, XXVII, XXVIII
Ray Nitschke, Green Bay — I, II
Preston Pearson, Baltimore — III; Pittsburgh— IX; Dallas — X, XII, XIII
Jack Squirek, L.A. Raiders — XVIII
Calvin Thomas, Chicago — XX
Howard Griffith, Denver — XXXII, XXXIII
Robert Holcombe, St. Louis — XXXIV
Brad Hopkins, Tennessee — XXXIV

Preston Pearson

Illini Legend

Jim Dawson

Jim Dawson's selection as the Big Ten most valuable basketball player in March of 1967 was a curious one. He wasn't the league's top scorer (25.5 points per game); that distinction belonged to Minnesota's Tom Kondla. He wasn't the conference's best rebounder or shooter; Ohio State's Bill Hosket easily won those titles. And he didn't lead his team to the Big Ten championship, as had Indiana's Butch Joyner. What earned Jim Dawson the MVP title was his ability to perform in the face of adversity, and no one endured more adversity than did the University of Illinois at that time. The "slush fund" scandal had brought about the ineligibilities of a trio of exceptional Illini players—Rich Jones, Steve Kuberski and Ron Dunlap—and stripped away Illinois' opportunity at a national title. Big Ten coaches clearly recognized the fact that, without Dawson, the 6 and 8 Illini might not have won a conference game. Following a one-year stint with the ABA's Indiana Pacers, the six-foot guard from Elmhurst York High School took that same determined approach in the business world, moving from New York's Wall Street to California, and, in 1992, to a management position with Victoria Investors in Winnetka, Illinois.

ILLINI LORE

. . . .

The University of Illinois observed its centennial celebration beginning February 28, 1967. UI's Board of Trustees met at the Capitol in Springfield to witness the issuance of an executive proclamation by Governor Otto Kerner. On campus that morning, the Altgeld Hall chimes played a brief anniversary concert, followed by the band's performance of the National Anthem and Illinois Loyalty. A total of 3,567 UI students received degrees in June of 1967, as compared to 20 in the first senior class of 1872.

1967-68

AMERICA'S TIME CAPSULE

Oct. 2, 1967	Thurgood Marshall was sworn in as the United States' first black Supreme Court justice.
Oct. 12, 1967	The St. Louis Cardinals won game seven of the World Series, defeating the Boston Red Sox.
Jan. 23, 1968	North Korea seized the naval intelligence ship U.S.S. *Pueblo* off its coast. Its crew of 83 was released on December 23.
April 4, 1968	Dr. Martin Luther King Jr. was assassinated by a sniper at the Lorraine Motel in Memphis, Tennessee, setting off a week of rioting in several urban black ghettos.
June 5, 1968	Presidential candidate Robert Kennedy was fatally shot in Los Angeles after delivering a speech to acknowledge his victory in the California primary.

Jim Valek

ILLINI MOMENT

VALEK WINS HOME DEBUT:

It would prove to be one of only four home-field victories he'd capture over the next four years, but new Fighting Illini football coach Jim Valek truly enjoyed his first appearance on the sidelines of Memorial Stadium, September 30, 1967. Valek's troops had lost their debut a week earlier at Florida, but this one belonged to the Illini from start to finish, defeating Pittsburgh, 34-6. Quarterback Bob Naponic directed Illinois to scoring drives of 46, 71 and 60 yards as the Illini beat Pitt for the sixth time in as many meetings. UI's workhorse out of the backfield was junior fullback Rich Johnson who gained 116 yards in just 17 attempts. Illinois' defense, bolstered by interceptions from Ron Bess and Ken Kmiec, halted Panther runners to an average of less than two yards per try and allowed only eight of 23 passes to be caught. It would be more than a year later—November 16, 1968—before Illinois would win again at home.

The Morrow Plots, located near the library, have been ground for continuous experiment since 1876.

Ron Bess

Illini Legend

John Wright

It was during game five of his junior season, versus Indiana, that John Wright became the leading pass receiver in University of Illinois football history. From that point on, every time he caught a pass he set a record. During his three years at Illinois from 1965-67, the split end from Wheaton set Big Ten records of 159 catches for 2,284 yards, more than twice the previous UI record totals of Rex Smith (70 catches) and John "Rocky" Ryan (1,041 yards). To put his accomplishments even more into perspective, consider that during his three years at Illinois, Wright caught 28 more passes than all the rest of his teammates combined! Nationally, only four men—topped by all-time leader Howard Twilley from Tulsa (261 catches)—had more career receptions than did Illinois' No. 45. He also lettered twice in track as a hurdler. Academically, Wright grabbed even more honors, including Academic All-American laurels in 1966. Following college, he played for the NFL's Detroit Lions for three seasons, then began a highly successful career in insurance. Wright, whose father Bob and son John Jr. also played for the Illini, now lives near St. Joseph, Illinois.

Illini Lists

BIG TEN SINGLE-SEASON RECEIVING LEADERS
(from 1965-67)

1. 50 recs.   Jack Clancy, Michigan, 1966
2. 47 recs.   Jim Beirne, Purdue, 1966
3. 44 recs.   Al Bream, Iowa, 1967
4. 41 recs.   Jim Berline, Michigan, 1967
5. 38 recs.   JOHN WRIGHT, ILLINOIS, 1965
    38 recs.   Tom McCauley, Wisconsin, 1966
    38 recs.   Roger Murphy, Northwestern, 1966
8. 37 recs.   Jack Clancy, Michigan, 1965
    37 recs.   Billy Anders, Ohio State, 1966
10. 36 recs.   JOHN WRIGHT, ILLINOIS, 1966
11 36 recs.   JOHN WRIGHT, ILLINOIS, 1967

Three generations of excellence (right to left) John II, Robert and John Wright.

ILLINI LORE

On June 15, 1966, the University of Illinois' Board of Trustees formally approved the establishment of the administrative post designated Chancellor of the Urbana-Champaign campus. Chosen as UIUC's first chancellor was 43-year-old Jack Peltason, who previously served as vice chancellor for academic affairs at the University of California at Irvine. Peltason remained at Illinois until August of 1977, when he became President of the American Council on Education.

1968-69

AMERICA'S TIME CAPSULE

Oct. 10, 1968   The Detroit Tigers won the World Series for the first time since 1945, defeating the
                 St. Louis Cardinals in seven games.

Nov. 5, 1968   Republican Richard Nixon won the presidential election, beating Hubert Humphrey
                 by only 500,000 votes.

July 16, 1969   U.S. space capsule Apollo 11 landed on the moon at 4:17 p.m. EDT. Astronaut Neil
                 Armstrong became the first person to set foot on the moon.

July 18, 1969   Senator Edward Kennedy was involved in an auto accident on Chappaquiddick Island,
                 Massachusetts, resulting in the death of his passenger, Mary Jo Kopechne.

Aug. 15, 1969   The Woodstock Music and Art Fair began, drawing a crowd estimated at nearly a half
                 million people.

ILLINI MOMENT

ILLINI CAGERS BATTLE FOR
BIG TEN CROWN:

Coach Harv Schmidt's 1968-69 basketball team fought to an impressive 19-5 overall record and a spot in the Top 20 national ranking, but could do no better than finish four games behind champion Purdue in the Big Ten standings. Illinois won its first 10 in a row before losing to Rick Mount's juggernaut at West Lafayette in game two of the conference season. The Illini turned a disappointing 4-4 conference start into a 9-5 final league record by winning five of its last six Big Ten games. UI's balanced attack was paced by senior forward Dave Scholz (19.1 points per game) and sophomore center Greg Jackson (16-4). Guards Mike Price (12.4) and Jodie Harrison (10.6) also were consistent scorers for the Illini. Illinois' 19 victories were the most since the 1962-63 season when that club won the Big Ten title with 20 overall wins.

Greg Jackson was a valuable member of Illinois' 19-5 basketball team in 1968-69.

IN MEMORIAL STADIUM
$6.00 — 1:30 P.M.

Sept. 21 . . . . Kansas
("I" Men's Day)

Sept. 28 . . . . Missouri
(Chicago Campus Day)

Oct. 26 . . . . Ohio State
(58th Annual Homecoming)

Nov. 16 . . . . Northwestern
(49th Annual Dad's Day)

Nov. 23 . . . . Iowa

GAMES AWAY

Oct. 5—At Indiana 1:30, $6.00
Oct. 12—At Minnesota 1:30, $5.50
Oct. 19—At Notre Dame 1:30, $7.00
Nov. 2—At Purdue 1:30, $6.00
Nov. 9—At Michigan 1:30, $6.00

Mail Orders, Home and Away Games,
To: FOOTBALL TICKET OFFICE,
100 ASSEMBLY HALL, CHAMPAIGN, ILL.

ILLINOIS
FOOTBALL
1968

The 1968 football season is one that Fighting Illini fans would probably rather forget. Illinois lost its first eight games that season, before finally putting it all together to shut out Northwestern, 14-0, in game nine. UI lost the season finale at the hands of Iowa, finishing with a 1-9 overall record.

ILLINI SCRAPBOOK

AN INDOOR TRACK AND FIELD DUAL MEET against Wisconsin at the University of Illinois' Armory on February 22, 1969 was the site for a record-breaking performance by Illini pole vaulter Ed Halik. Halik cleared the bar at 16' 3/4", becoming the first Illinois vaulter and only the third Big Ten athlete to clear a height over 16 feet.

Illini Legend

Dave Scholz

Today, a humble Dave Scholz tells his friends that "I really didn't have the ability to play major college basketball." So how did the six-eighter from Decatur end up as the University of Illinois' all-time leading scorer? "I was on the receiving end of a lot of good passes," he says. Still, scoring a total of 1,459 points against such superstars as Lew Alcindor and Rudy Tomjanovich takes some coordination. In fact, of the nearly 400 men who've lettered in basketball at Illinois, only Scholz (20.5 points per game), Nick Weatherspoon (20.9), and Don Freeman (20.1) have averaged better than 20 points per contest. No. 40's biggest night came on February 24, 1968, when he drilled home 42 points against Northwestern, a single-game total second only to Dave Downey's 53-point masterpiece vs. Indiana. Following a brief tour of the pros, Scholz returned to the UI to obtain his master's degree in accountancy. In 1980, he began the first of six years in Saudi Arabia with the Arabian American Oil Co., then moved to Nashville, Tennessee, where he still resides.

Illini Lists

IF ILLINI ATHLETES WERE KNOWN BY THEIR GIVEN FIRST NAMES

Nelison (Nick) Anderson
Theodore (Tab) Bennett
Casper (Cap) Boso
Burie (Shelly) Clark
George (Potsy) Clark
Talib (Ty) Douthard
Charles (Tony) Eason
Thomas (Dike) Eddleman
Walter (Hoot) Evers
Morris (Moe) Gardner
Harold (Red) Grange
Rausell (Rocky) Harvey
Richard (Itch) Jones
Harold (Hek) Kenney
Duane (Skip) Thoren
Charles (Bubba) Smith
Dennis (D.J.) Svihlik
Russell (Ruck) Steger
Ellis (Gene) Vance
Thomas (T.J.) Wheeler
Kenneth (Tug) Wilson
Claude (Buddy) Young

Russell "Ruck" Steger

ILLINI LORE

The $21 million Krannert Center for the Performing Arts opened its doors to the University of Illinois community April 1920, 1969. Donated to the UI by philanthropists Mr. and Mrs. Herman C. Krannert, Krannert Center was conceived with a twofold purpose. First, it would provide the most up-to-date facilities for the training of UI students in the performing arts, and it would also provide a modern cultural center for the community. The facility features three auditoriums: The Great Hall, seating 2,100, was designed for music presentations; the Festival Theatre, with a capacity of 965, was planned for singing performances; and the Playhouse, seating nearly 700, was designed specifically for acting.

1969-70

AMERICA'S TIME CAPSULE

Sept. 22, 1969   Willie Mays of the San Francisco Giants hit his 600th career home run, becoming only the second major leaguer other than Babe Ruth to reach that plateau.

Nov. 16, 1969   More than 450 Vietnam villagers were slain by a U.S. infantry unit in what would be known as the My Lai massacre.

March 18, 1970   The first major postal workers' strike began in the United States.

April 29, 1970   U.S. and South Vietnamese troops invaded Cambodia.

May 4, 1970   Four Kent State University students were killed by National Guard troops during an antiwar demonstration.

ILLINI MOMENT

ILLINI SHATTER SHOOTING RECORD:

Coach Harv Schmidt's 1969-70 Fighting Illini basketball squad, known more for its defensive prowess, shot the proverbial lights out against Indiana on January 6, 1970 at Illinois' Assembly Hall. Illinois' .679 shooting performance from the field (40 of 59) obliterated its former high mark of .613, set against Iowa in 1967. Individually, the Illini outside shooters were paced by Rick Howat and Mike Price who hit 16 of their 24 long-bomb attempts. Inside, the triumvirate of Randy Crews, Fred Miller and Greg Jackson connected on nearly 71 percent of their shots. Illinois' 94-74 victory over the Hoosiers was the second of the young Big Ten season. Illinois went on to win three more games in a row to improve its record to 12-2. They couldn't keep up their momentum, however, winding up with an overall mark of 15-9.

Mike Price

ILLINI SCRAPBOOK

Thousands of protesters marched down Green Street in the Fall of 1969, displaying their opposition of the Vietnam War.

Hall of Famer Lou Boudreau (right), joined by interim athletic director Bob Todd, had his jersey No. 3 retired at Illinois.

I Illini Item

ON JULY 27, 1970, former Fighting Illini baseball and basketball standout Lou Boudreau was inducted into Cooperstown's Baseball Hall of Fame. Also included in Cooperstown's Class of 1970 with the former Cleveland Indians star were pitcher Jess Haines and outfielder Earl Combs.

Illini Legend

Randy Crews

The University of Illinois may never honor Randy Crews with a spot in its Hall of Fame, but the kid from Bradley-Bourbonnais High School will probably get some write-in votes for his athletic versatility. With a career-scoring average of little more than eight points per game for Coach Harv Schmidt's Illini basketball team, Crews was noted for his defense rather than his offense, frequently being assigned to the opponent's top scorer. The 6-6 first baseman was even more intimidating on the baseball diamond, finishing his career among Illinois' top ten all-time hitters with a .315 batting average. He was chosen to the Big Ten's 1970 all-star baseball squad his senior year, hitting .361 for the season. Nowadays, Crews resides in Tallahassee, Florida.

Illini Lists

ILLINI FOOTBALL ACADEMIC ALL-AMERICANS

(first-team slections)

1952	Bob Lenzini, DT
1964-65	Jim Grabowski, FB
1966	John Wright Sr., E
1970	Jim Rucks, DE
1971	Bob Bucklin, DE
1980-81-82	Dan Gregus, DL
1991	Mike Hopkins, DB
1992	John Wright Jr., WR
1994	Brett Larsen, P
1999-00	Josh Whitman, TE

Jim Rucks of Illinois was an Academic All-American selection in 1970.

ILLINI LORE

The month of May, 1970, will be remembered by students and faculty as a period of great unrest at American universities. Stoked by President Nixon's announcement that American troops would be sent to Cambodia and ignited by the killing of four Kent State University students on May 4, UI students and thousands of others at campuses across the country called for a nationwide strike. A rally jammed the UI Auditorium on May 5, and action began the moment the gathering ended. The "trashing" of the campus business district and some University buildings started soon after UI Chancellor Jack Peltason denounced the violence and refused to close the university, but only 60 percent of the classes went on as scheduled. From May 5-10, police made 221 arrests, and damage totaled more than $26,000.

1970-71

AMERICA'S TIME CAPSULE

Nov. 8, 1970   Tom Dempsey of the New Orleans Saints kicked an NFL-record 63-yard field goal.
Dec. 2, 1970   The Environmental Protection Agency, established in July, was activated.
Dec. 23, 1970   The World Trade Center was topped in New York City to become the world's largest building.
Jan. 25, 1971   Charles Manson and three of his followers were convicted of the 1969 murders of actress Sharon Tate and six others.
March 29, 1971 William Calley was convicted of the murder of 22 South Vietnamese people at My Lai.
July 30, 1971   Astronauts David Scott and Jim Irwin became the fourth American space team to explore the moon's surface, making their tour in a four-wheeled lunar rover.

ILLINI MOMENT

ILLINI GRIDDERS END LOSING STREAK:

It had been nearly two years since Illinois had won a Big Ten Conference football game, so the odds of coach Jim Valek's squad beating Purdue in PU's Homecoming game (October 31, 1970) would have tested even the bravest gambler. The Boilermakers jumped off to a 14-0 lead at halftime, thanks to a 62-yard touchdown pass from quarterback Gary Danielson to halfback Otis Armstrong. Illinois bounced back to take a 17-14 advantage early in the fourth quarter, but Purdue regained the lead, 21-17, with 4:01 remaining. Illini quarterback Mike Wells then engineered a game-winning, seven-play, 69-yard drive, combining his own passes to Doug Dieken with the brilliant running of Darrell Robinson. The 23-21 Illinois victory brought an end to the school's 11-game Big Ten losing streak. It would be the last win in Valek's Illini coaching career.

Quarterback Mike Wells (top) and tight end Doug Dieken helped the Illini snap an 11-game Big Ten losing streak.

Rick Howat earned second-team All-Big Ten honors for the Fighting Illini basketball team during the 1971 conference season.

ILLINI SCRAPBOOK

Tim McCarthy was recognized for his heroics at halftime of the 1981 football game between Illinois and Wisconsin.

I Illini Item

TIM McCARTHY, who used to deliver hard hits as a safety on the Fighting Illini football team, took one for his country on March 30, 1981. The former walk-on from Chicago's Leo High School lettered for Illinois in both 1969 and 1970, but his greatest notoriety came as a Secret Service agent that afternoon in Washington, D.C. McCarthy stepped in front of a bullet aimed at President Ronald Reagan and was wounded in the abdomen. On January 11, 1982, the National Collegiate Athletic Association honored him with its Award of Valor.

Illini Legend

Lee LaBadie

Though he won only one individual conference title during his three-year career at the University of Illinois, Lee LaBadie's name will always have a prominent place in Big Ten track and field lore. On May 11, 1971 in a dual meet against Southern Illinois, he became the first Big Ten Conference undergraduate to break the four-minute barrier in the mile run. LaBadie ran his first 440 yards in 60 seconds, but his pace slowed to 2:03 after the first half mile. Then he began to pour on the coals, touring the next quarter mile in :57.5. LaBadie ran the final 440 yards in :58.3, finishing in a record time of 3:58.8. He was also a key member of a world record-tying two-mile relay squad at Illinois, a unit that won the 1972 NCAA indoor title. He served as cross-country and track coach at Parkland College from 1976-85, and in 1985 LaBadie became head coach of Bowling Green State's women's cross-country and track programs. From 1989-92, he was Ohio State's assistant men's cross-country and track coach and helped Buckeye runner Mark Croghan to the NCAA steeplechase title. LaBadie left OSU following the 1992 season, joining his wife, Diane, in a Westerville, Ohio real estate business.

Illini Lists

ILLINOIS' FASTEST MILERS

1. 3:53.47   Marko Koers, 1996
2. 3:56.7   Mike Durkin, 1975
3. 3:58.8   Lee LaBadie, 1971
4. 4:00.4   Rick Gross, 1972
5. 4:00.56i   Len Sitko, 1991
6. 4:00.68i   Tom Stevens, 1982
7. 4:00.8   Jeff Jirele, 1976
8. 4:00.94i   Greg Domantay, 1983
9. 4:01.49i   Jon Schmidt, 1982
10. 4:02.30i   Mike Patton, 1985

i — indicates mark accomplished indoors

Mike Durkin ran an all-time Illini record 3:56.7 in the mile.

ILLINI LORE

On February 13, 1971, the Board of Trustees elected 46-year-old Dr. John Corbally as the 13th president of the University of Illinois, replacing the retiring David Henry. Corbally came to the Urbana-Champaign campus from Syracuse University where he served as president and chancellor. He remained at the UI until September 1, 1979.

1971-72

AMERICA'S TIME CAPSULE

Sept. 13, 1971	A prison riot at Attica State Correctional Facility in New York ended after claiming 43 lives.
Sept. 21, 1971	Baseball's Washington Senators announced that the franchise would move to Texas for the beginning of the 1972 season.
Feb. 21, 1972	President Nixon began his historic visit to mainland China.
May 26, 1972	Soviet secretary Leonid Brezhnev and President Nixon signed a treaty on anti-ballistic missile systems.
June 17, 1972	Police arrested five men involved in a burglary of Democratic Party headquarters, beginning the famed Watergate affair.

Bob Blackman

ILLINI SCRAPBOOK

ILLINI MOMENT

BOB BLACKMAN HIRED:

The hiring of Bob Blackman as the Fighting Illini football coach on December 23, 1970 was greeted with open arms by the Champaign-Urbana community and University of Illinois fans all around the state. The entire Illini athletic program had been submerged in the dregs of the infamous "slush fund," and Blackman's glowing 16-year record at Dartmouth was hoped to be the antidote that would cure the school's football ills. The Blackman era began slowly. After losing their first six games of 1971, including their first three by shutouts, the Illini bounced back to win their last five in a row. Again in 1972, Blackman's squad began poorly, losing its first seven games, before salvaging three of its last four contests. That mediocre trend continued for the balance of Blackman's six-year career at Illinois, with only 1974's 6-4-1 record breaking the sub-.500 pattern. There were several bright spots, however, during Blackman's reign. Despite going 0-12 against the Big Ten's "Big Two" of Michigan and Ohio State during his Illini career, Blackman's Illini amassed a cumulative record of 24-11-1 against the other seven conference opponents.

IMPE pool opened in time for the 1971-72 swimming season.

Rick Gross

RICK GROSS concluded an outstanding career in cross-country and track and field in 1972 at the University of Illinois. An All-American and 1971 Big Ten runner-up in cross-country, Gross set Illini varsity records in the steeple-chase (8:41.8) and the 10,000-meter run (29:17.4), and nearly broke the magic four-minute barrier in the mile run (4:00.4).

Illini Legend

Tab Bennett

To become a college football All-American, it is almost always a necessity that one's team be ranked among the nation's elite. But that certainly wasn't the case in 1972 for Illinois' standout defensive end Theodore Anthony "Tab" Bennett. The Illini's 3-8 mark didn't draw attention to Bennett's individual talent as Nebraska's nearly perfect record had done for All-America middle guard Rich Glover, but it was difficult to disguise Bennett's outstanding abilities. The native of Miami, Florida lettered once under Coach Jim Valek and twice for Bob Blackman, and earned All-Big Ten honors both his junior and senior seasons. Bennett's 231 career tackles ranked second only to Dick Butkus at the time. An ankle injury prevented him from continuing his career in the NFL, so Bennett turned his sights toward a profession in college athletic administration at his alma mater. A meteoric rise saw him named as Illinois' Sports Information Director in 1974, becoming the Big Ten Conference's first-ever African-American SID. Bennett continued in that role until 1989, when a life-threatening automobile accident forced him to retire. He died March 13, 1994, at the age of 42.

Illini Lists

DIKE EDDLEMAN'S FAVORITE ATHLETES

Illinois' greatest athlete of all time chose his favorite Illini

- Alex Agase, football
- Kenny Battle, basketball
- Dick Butkus, football
- Dave Downey, basketball
- Tony Eason, football
- Jill Estey, basketball
- Darrin Fletcher, baseball
- Jim Grabowski, football
- Abie Grossfeld, gymnastics
- Renee Heiken, golf
- Dana Howard, football
- Lou Kachiroubas, wrestling

- John "Red" Kerr, basketball
- Herb McKenley, track
- Bob Norman, wrestling
- Ken Norman, basketball
- Andy Phillip, basketball
- Bob Richards, track
- Tina Rogers, volleyball
- Steve Stricker, golf
- Nancy Thies, gymnastics
- Deon Thomas, basketball
- Willard Thomson, track
- Buddy Young, football & track

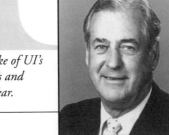

Dike Eddleman, namesake of UI's annual award to its men's and women's Athletes of the Year.

ILLINI LORE

The $11.2 million Intramural-Physical Education Building opened for use at the University of Illinois during the fall semester of the 1971-72 academic year. UI students paid the major portion of the bill—$9.1 million—through an activity fee of $18 per semester. Highlighting the facility were four large gymnasiums, indoor and outdoor swimming pools, a three-court tennis complex, 23 handball courts and seven squash courts. Estimated usage by students that first year was more than 548,000, with a record 734,000 student usage in 1987-88.

1972-73

AMERICA'S TIME CAPSULE

Nov. 7, 1972   The Republican Party enjoyed its greatest landslide victory ever with the reelection of President Richard Nixon.

Dec. 18, 1972   Paris peace negotiations reached an impasse and full-scale bombing of North Vietnam was resumed by American pilots.

Jan. 22, 1973   An agreement to end the war in Vietnam was signed in Paris by representatives of the United States and North and South Vietnam.

June 9, 1973   Secretariat, called the greatest race horse ever, won the Belmont Stakes and became the ninth Triple Crown winner.

July 16, 1973   The existence of the Watergate tapes was revealed.

ILLINI MOMENT

PERRIN PUTS ON A SHOW AS ILLINI DAZZLE INDIANA:

Lonnie Perrin put on a one-man show vs. Indiana in 1972.

November 11, 1972 marked one of the greatest individual performances in Fighting Illini football history, as Illinois' Lonnie Perrin set a Big Ten total offense record against the Indiana Hoosiers. The sophomore halfback from Washington, D.C. rushed 142 yards in 12 carries, completed two passes to Garvin Roberson for 94 yards, and grabbed three aerials from Mike Wells for an additional 35 yards. Perrin's 14 rushes and passes averaged 16.86 yards per play, erasing a four-year-old mark held by Iowa's Ed Podolak. The most exciting play in Illinois' 37-20 victory over the Hoosiers was Perrin's long, cross-field lateral to George Uremovich who sprinted down the west sideline to complete a 96-yard kickoff return. "I really didn't feel up for the game," said Perrin afterwards in the locker room, "but after my first play (a 16-yard gain) I was ready."

George Uremovich vs. Indiana

ILLINI SCRAPBOOK

172

Art Schankin

Illini Legend

Nick Weatherspoon

Illini Lists

GREATEST MEN'S BASKETBALL DEBUTS

Points
1. 30 pts   Jeff Dawson vs. DePauw, 12/2/72
2. 23 pts   Govoner Vaughn vs. Marquette, 12/2/57
3. 21 pts   Deon Thomas vs. American-Puerto Rico, 11/23/90
4. 20 pts   James Griffin vs. Texas-Arlington, 11/24/78
5. 20 pts   Cory Bradford vs. Wake Forest, 11/10/98

Rebounds
1. 13 rebs   Greg Jackson vs. Butler, 12/2/68
2. 12 rebs   Bill Burwell vs. Creighton, 12/1/60
3. 11 rebs   Dave Downey vs. Creighton, 12/1/60
   11 rebs   Don Freeman vs. Butler, 11/30/63
5. 10 rebs   Nick Anderson vs. Baylor, 11/27/87
   10 rebs   Efrem Winters vs. Vanderbilt, 11/26/82

Jeff Dawson scored 30 points in his Illini debut.

Team-wise, Nick Weatherspoon's college basketball career at the University of Illinois was only moderately successful, but individually, very few Fighting Illini basketball players were more proficient than "The Spoon." The former Ohio prep player of the year from Canton McKinley High School ruled Coach Harv Schmidt's Assembly Hall court from 1971-73, setting Illini records for points (1,481) and rebounds (806). His career averages of 20.9 points and 11.4 rebounds are still tops at Illinois. Weatherspoon seemed to peak when the Illini played Michigan, averaging nearly 26 points and 14 rebounds in his five career games against the Wolverines. "Spoon" was the 13th pick in the first round of the 1973 NBA draft, going to the Washington Bullets. His eight-year NBA career also included stints with the Seattle Supersonics, the Chicago Bulls and the San Diego Clippers. The 6'7" forward scored 4,086 points and grabbed 2,232 rebounds in 453 career NBA games. Today, Weatherspoon is semiretired, but continues to direct his own insurance company in Bolingbrook, Illinois.

ILLINI LORE

The Levis Faculty Center began operation during the 1972-73 academic year. Made possible by a $1.2 million gift from Mrs. Margaret Levis, a 1914 graduate, the center's primary purpose was to serve as an intellectual gathering place for the faculty and staff of the University of Illinois. The facility replaced the University Club on Oregon Street that UI faculty had previously used.

1973-74

AMERICA'S TIME CAPSULE

Dec. 6, 1973   Gerald Ford was sworn in as vice president, filling the void created by Spiro Agnew's resignation on October 10.

Dec. 16, 1973   O.J. Simpson of the Buffalo Bills set an NFL single-season rushing record, breaking the mark held by Jim Brown.

Feb. 5, 1974   Patricia Hearst was kidnapped from her California apartment by a group calling itself the Symbionese Liberation Army.

April 8, 1974   Hank Aaron of the Atlanta Braves hit his 715th career home run, breaking Babe Ruth's legendary record.

Aug. 8, 1974   President Richard Nixon announced in a televised address that he would resign, with Gerald Ford sworn in as president the following day.

ILLINI MOMENT

Illini basketball coach Harv Schmidt.

THE HARV SCHMIDT ERA ENDS:

Harv Schmidt's University of Illinois basketball coaching career ended in 1973-74 as stormily as it began. The former Illini standout from Kankakee was hired as his alma mater's head coach in 1967, taking over for Harry Combes who resigned in the aftermath of the infamous "slush fund." Schmidt's first team, headed by Dave Scholz, Randy Crews and Mike Price, managed only an 11-13 overall record. Illinois' success under Schmidt reached its zenith in 1968-69, streaking to a second-place finish in the Big Ten and a 19-5 season mark. The Illini fans fondly embraced their coach, rising to their feet at his mere appearance from the Assembly Hall tunnel. Harv's third Illini team in 1969-70 jumped off to a terrific 12-2 start, but managed only three more wins in its final 10 games that season. Despite that late-season slump, Illinois basketball fans turned out in record numbers during the '70-71 campaign, setting an NCAA-record attendance average of 16,128 per game. Schmidt's final four Illini teams from 1970-71 to 1973-74 compiled a sub-.500 mark of 44 wins and 50 losses, and he was replaced in 1974 by Gene Bartow.

WOMEN'S MILESTONES

MAY 15, 1974

The Board of Trustees of the University of Illinois, chaired by Earl Hughes, took action to put intercollegiate athletics for women under the auspices of the Athletic Association. Dr. Karol A. Kahrs became the UI's first assistant director for women's athletics on June 1, 1974.

Dan Beaver

Illini Item

ON SEPTEMBER 29, 1973, a red-headed missionary's son from Africa began his assault on the University of Illinois football record book. Dan Beaver's 37-yard field goal against West Virginia was the first of 38 three-pointers he'd kick during his career from 1973-76. Two weeks later against Purdue, the soccer-style kicker booted a Big Ten-record five field goals. Beaver kicked four placements of 50 yards or more, including a conference record-tying 57-yarder versus Purdue his junior year. He became Illinois' all-time leading scorer on November 20, 1976, breaking Red Grange's 51-year-old record with a four-year total of 198 points.

Illini Lists

ILLINOIS' LONGEST FIELD GOALS
(in chronological order)

50 yards   by Earl Britton vs. Iowa, 10/23/23
51 yards   by Dan McKissic vs. Purdue, 11/4/67
52 yards   by Lonnie Perrin vs. Penn State, 10/7/62
57 yards   by Dan Beaver vs. Purdue, 10/18/75

OPPONENTS' LONGEST FIELD GOALS
VS. ILLINOIS
(in chronological order)

57 yards   by Pat O'Dea of Wisconsin, 11/11/1899
59 yards   by Tom Skladany of Ohio State, 11/8/75
61 yards   by Ralf Mojsiejenko of Michigan State, 9/11/82

Earl Britton kicked Illinois' first 50-yard field goal in 1923.

Illini Legend

Charlton Ehizuelen

Twenty years have passed, but Big Ten track and field aficionados can still find Charlton Ehizuelen's name at the top of the conference's all-time lists in the long jump. The "kangaroo" from Benin City, Nigeria dominated the conference competition during his career from 1974-77 at Illinois. Ehizuelen missed the 1974 Big Ten meet due to a bout with malaria and was absent from the 1976 conference championships due to his suspension from the team. However, in the six Big Ten track meets in which he did compete, the amazing African captured 11 of a possible 12 conference titles. Ehizuelen also won four NCAA championships, including three long jump titles. After graduation in 1977, Ehizuelen held all-time Big Ten best performances in both the long jump (27-1 1/4 indoors, 26-10 outdoors) and the triple jump (54-9 1/2 indoors, 55-2 1/4 outdoors), breaking Jesse Owens's record on one occasion. Though he performed for Coach Gary Wieneke, the 6'0", 160-pound Ehizuelen was actually recruited by Wieneke's predecessor, Bob Wright, who brought him to Champaign-Urbana with the help of Nigerian coach Awoture Eleyae, a UI post-graduate student. Today, Ehizuelen lives with his family in Surulere, Lagos, Nigeria.

ILLINI LORE

A $1.65 million capital fund campaign "to keep Memorial Stadium beautiful for the next 50 years" was announced by the University of Illinois at a meeting of the UI Foundation in October of 1973. Priorities for the campaign were to replace Zuppke Field's natural grass with an artificial turf, to install lighting for night activities at the stadium, and to renovate the locker rooms and training facilities. Directing the "Golden Anniversary Fund Campaign" were chairman William Karnes and honorary chairman Harold "Red" Grange.

1974-75

AMERICA'S TIME CAPSULE

Sept. 8, 1974	President Ford pardoned former President Nixon for any crimes he may have committed while in office, calling for an end to the Watergate episode.
Oct. 30, 1974	Muhammad Ali recaptured the heavyweight boxing title with an eighth-round knockout of George Foreman in Zaire.
Feb. 21, 1975	Former White House aides H. R. Haldeman and John Ehrlichman, and former attorney general John Mitchell, were each sentenced to 30 months' imprisonment for their roles in the Watergate affair.
July 5, 1975	Arthur Ashe became the first African-American to win the men's singles title at England's Wimbledon tennis championships.
July 31, 1975	Former Teamsters leader James Hoffa was reported missing.

ILLINI MOMENT

Red Grange returned to Memorial Stadium 50 years after galloping to glory against Michigan.

THE ICE MAN RETURNETH:

Fifty years to the day after his greatest Illinois triumph, October 18, 1974, Harold "Red" Grange returned to Memorial Stadium. A half century earlier, he'd galloped against Michigan, leading Illinois to a 39-14 victory. But on this afternoon, the 71-year-old football legend spoke to Coach Bob Blackman's 1974 Illini squad. "Football is a game that demands teamwork," Grange told the young Illini. "It is natural, I suppose, for the scorer to get all the publicity. But it isn't fair. At Illinois, I was just a cog in a good machine." That evening, the Galloping Ghost was feted by a packed house of nearly 700 fans at the Ramada Inn's Convention Center. George Halas, Grange's coach with the Chicago Bears, told the $20-a-plate crowd that "Red Grange had more impact on the game of football than any single individual in this century." The next day at Memorial Stadium, between halves of the Illinois-Michigan State game, which ended in a 21-21 tie, Grange was presented the UI Board of Trustees' highest award, the Trustee Medallion. Then the Wheaton Iceman addressed his adoring fans. "I've always said that this is the most beautiful stadium in the world and that Illinois fans are the most beautiful people in the world."

WOMEN'S MILESTONES

JULY 7, 1974

Betsy Kimpel became the first coach of the Fighting Illini women's fledgling varsity athletic program. She was hired by associate director of athletics Karol Kahrs at a 10-month salary of $2,900 to coach the women's golf team.

Mike Durkin

I Illini Item

THE UNIVERSITY OF ILLINOIS' 12-year drought without a Big Ten championship in any sport other than fencing ended on May 17, 1975, when the Illini track and field squad nipped runner-up Indiana by a point-and-a-half. Senior captain Mike Durkin paved the way with a double victory in the steeplechase and the 880-yard run. The meet was undecided heading into the triple jump finals, but Illini star Charlton Ehizuelen sewed up the team championship with a title-winning 50' 6/4" leap. Up to then—dating all the way back to a football title by the 1963 Illini--11 UI athletic teams, with the exception of the fencing squad, had entered 130 consecutive Big Ten championship competitions without a victory.

Illini Legend

Karol Kahrs

When the United States Congress passed Title IX regulations in 1972, mandating equal opportunity for women, the face of intercollegiate athletics began to change at the University of Illinois. On June 1, 1974—just nine days after UI's Board of Trustees approved the Athletic Association's recommendation to include women's athletics—Dr. Karol Kahrs was hired by athletic director Cecil Coleman to oversee Illinois' seven-sport women's program. Kahrs's initial budget was $82,500 in 1974-75. Women's athletics were incorporated into the Big Ten Conference during the 1981-82 season, and since that time, Illini teams have won 15 league titles in four different sports. In 1988, Kahrs served as director of internal affairs for the AA, helping with its merger into the University in 1989 as the Division of Intercollegiate Athletics (DIA). In 1992, her contributions to intercollegiate athletes were recognized by the National Association of College Women Athletic Administrators when she was named NACWAA Administrator of the Year for District V. Her last two years at the DIA were spent in the Development Office. Kahrs retired from The University of Illinois on August 31, 2000, after 36 years of service.

Illini Lists

ILLINI CAREER TACKLES LEADERS
(through 2001 season)

1. 595   Dana Howard (1991-94)
2. 501   John Sullivan (1974-78)
3. 483   Darrick Brownlow (1987-90)
4. 441   John Gillen (1977-80)
5. 436   John Holecek (1991-94)
6. 381   Danny Clark (1996-99)
7. 374   Dick Butkus (1962-64)
8. 371   Steve Glasson (1976-89)
9. 342   Scott Studwell (1972-76)
10. 331   Tyrone Washington (1992-95)

Scott Studwell

ILLINI LORE

The operating budget for Director of Athletics Cecil Coleman and the Athletic Association in 1974-75 was $2.47 million, a 91 percent increase from the budget total of $1.29 million just 10 years earlier. The expenses rose 241 percent to $8.43 million from 1974-75 to 1984-85, and another 95 percent to $16.4 million from 1984-85 to 1994-95, and to $35 million in 2001-02.

1975-1984

1975-76

AMERICA'S TIME CAPSULE

Sept. 5, 1975   President Gerald Ford escaped the first of two assassination attempts in a little more than two weeks. Lynette "Squeaky" Fromme was apprehended.

Sept. 18, 1975   A 19-month FBI search ended when Patricia Hearst was captured in San Francisco.

Oct. 1, 1975   Heavyweight boxing champion Muhammad Ali defeated Joe Frazier in the "Thrilla in Manilla".

Feb. 13, 1976   Dorothy Hamill won a gold medal in figure skating at the Winter Olympics in Innsbruck, Austria.

July 4, 1976   The bicentennial of United States independence was celebrated.

July 20, 1976   Viking 1, launched 11 months earlier, landed on Mars.

ILLINI MOMENT

ILLINI CAGERS UPSET MICHIGAN:

1975-76 Basketball Poster

Fourteenth-ranked Michigan came to Champaign-Urbana with a nearly perfect 6-1 Big Ten record. Coach Johnny Orr's line-up included future NBA stars Phil Hubbard and Rickey Green, plus former Chicago prep star John Robinson. "I've never seen a line-up with the speed and quickness that Michigan has," said first-year Illini coach Lou Henson, who countered with blue-collar seniors like Nate Williams, Mike Washington and Otho Tucker. Despite a subpar shooting performance, Michigan controlled play for the first 39 minutes, and led 75-72 following a Wayman Britt jumper with 55 seconds left. Illinois' Williams was fouled 17 seconds later when his 15-foot turnaround jumper cut the Michigan lead to 75-74. And when he missed the free throw attempt, 6'9" sophomore Rich Adams soared high to tip in the ball for what would ultimately be the winning goal. Orr's talented Wolverines had a flurry of attempts in the closing seconds, but a tip-in by Robinson came a split-second after the final buzzer. Michigan bounced back from that defeat to become an NCAA finalist, while Henson's Illini were limited to four victories in their last 10 games.

WOMEN'S MILESTONES

DECEMBER 4-5, 1975

The University of Illinois women's gymnastics team, coached by Allison Milburn, won the first unofficial Big Ten women's championship in any sport. The Fighting Illini edged runner-up Michigan State, 102.55 to 97.10. Illinois' Nancy Thies won not only the all-around title, but also each of the other four events.

Becky Beach

BECKY BEACH was one of the University of Illinois' premier female athletes during the infancy of women's intercollegiate athletics. Besides winning golf medalist honors at the 1976 Big Ten Championships, she also starred on the basketball court from 1976-78, finishing as the Illini's all-time leader in points, assists and rebounds. Nowadays, the daughter of former Illini basketball star Ted Beach is the assistant golf professional at Lincolnshire Fields Country Club in Champaign.

Illini Lists

LOU HENSON'S ALL-OPPONENT TEAM
(1975-96)

Starting Five:
G—Magic Johnson, Michigan State
G—Isiah Thomas, Indiana
C—Mychal Thompson, Minnesota
F—Glen Rice, Michigan
F—Glenn Robinson, Purdue

Bench:
Juwan Howard, Michigan
Jimmy Jackson, Ohio State
Ronnie Lester, Iowa
Shawn Respert, Michigan State
Jalen Rose, Michigan
Steve Smith, Michigan State
Chris Webber, Michigan

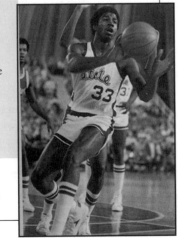

MSU's Magic Johnson

Illini Legend

Lou Henson

It took University of Illinois athletic director Cecil Coleman just three days to name a basketball coaching successor for Gene Bartow, and his April 5, 1975 announcement of Lou Henson stunned the media gathered that day at UI's Varsity Room. Among the names bandied about by the press were those of Bartow's assistants, Tony Yates and Leroy Hunt, plus Virginia Tech's Don Devoe and Kansas State's Jack Hartman, but never once mentioned was the 43-year-old head coach from New Mexico State. In 1975-76, Henson's first season as the Illini mentor, Illinois won its first five games en route to posting a 14-13 record. His first big year in Champaign-Urbana was 1978-79 when the Illini started out 15-0, including a two-point thriller over Magic Johnson and Michigan State. Henson's Illini made it to the semifinals of the NIT in 1979-80, while the '80-81 club qualified for the NCAA tournament for the first time in 18 years. Henson's other major accomplishments since coming to Illinois include an NCAA Final Four appearance in 1989, 11 seasons of 20 or more victories, 11 NCAA Tournament appearances and Big Ten Coach of the Year honors in 1993. He retired as head coach of the Illini following the 1995-96 season and accumulated a record of 423-224 in 21 seasons. He is currently the head coach at New Mexico State.

ILLINI LORE

The Medical Sciences building made its debut at the University of Illinois campus during a dedication ceremony October 15, 1975. The ultra-modern, $10 million facility became the newest structure in the Life Sciences complex, joining Morrill and Burrill Halls. The School of Basic Medical Sciences, while located at the Urbana-Champaign campus, actually is a part of the College of Medicine at the Medical Center in Chicago.

1976-77

AMERICA'S TIME CAPSULE

Sept. 12, 1976   Jimmy Connors joined Chris Evert as U.S. Open tennis champion.
Nov. 2, 1976   Jimmy Carter defeated incumbent Gerald Ford in the presidential election.
Dec. 14, 1976   ABC-TV aired Barbara Walters's first special, featuring interviews with Jimmy Carter
                 and Barbra Streisand.
Jan. 17, 1977   A 10-year halt on capital punishment ended in the U.S. when Gary Gilmore was
                 executed by a Utah firing squad.
July 28, 1977   The trans-Alaska pipeline went into full operation.
Aug. 10, 1977   New York City police arrested David Berkowitz as the Son of Sam killer.

ILLINI MOMENT

*1977 NCAA Track
Championship Program*

ILLINI HOST 1977 NCAA TRACK MEET:

For five days in the spring of 1977, the University of Illinois' Memorial Stadium became the mecca for track and field fans. The 56th annual NCAA championship drew a talented field of competitors, including lightning-fast sprinters such as Harvey Glance of Auburn, Johnny Jones of Texas and Herman Frazier of Arizona State. Illinois native Gregory Foster, who wore the blue and gold uniform of UCLA, was the meet's most celebrated hurdler. Africans Samson Kimombwa and Henry Rono paced the distance runners, while five-foot five-inch high jumper Franklin Jacobs of Farleigh Dickinson and pole vaulter Earl Bell of Arkansas State were premier performers in the field events. The Illini contingent was led by distance star Craig Virgin, who placed second in the 10,000-meter run and fourth in the 5,000; pole vaulter Doug Laz, who finished fourth with a respectable effort of 16'6"; and Charlton Ehizuelen, who placed second in the long jump and third in the triple jump. Arizona State beat runner-up Texas-El Paso, 64-50, for the team title on June 4, before a crowd of between 15,000-20,000 at Memorial Stadium. Illinois meet officials so impressed their guests and NCAA officials that the meet was granted again to the UI in 1979.

Ann Pollock

WOMEN'S MILESTONES

FEBRUARY 25-26, 1977

Coach Ann Pollock's Illini women's swimming team won the IAIAW state title, defeating Southern Illinois, 655 to 577. Mary Paterson led the way by winning individual titles in the 50-yard freestyle, the 50- and 100-yard butterfly and the 100-yard individual medley, as well as anchoring the 200- and 400-yard freestyle relay championships. Becky McSwine captured the 100- and 200-yard backstroke titles.

Nancy Thies

Illini Item

PERHAPS THE GREATEST FEMALE GYMNAST in University of Illinois history grew up in Urbana. Nancy Thies (Marshall), who made the United States Olympic team as a 14-year-old ninth grader, competed for the Fighting Illini gymnastics squad in 1976 and '77. She won the Big Ten's all-around title both years, as well as individual championships on the vault, the uneven parallel bars, the balance beam and the floor exercise. Thies also served as the UI's Homecoming Queen in 1978.

Illini Legend

Craig Virgin

It's shocking to learn that Craig Virgin, the University of Illinois' greatest distance runner ever, almost never made it past age five. Following surgery for a bladder ailment, the young farm boy's condition worsened, affecting his kidneys. Doctors weren't optimistic, but, slowly, Virgin got stronger. As a scrawny high school freshman, his fame as a distance runner began to grow, luring Illini cross-country coach Gary Wieneke to Virgin's hometown of Lebanon, Illinois. Virgin ultimately ended up at the UI, enjoying a four-year career that included every honor imaginable. He became the Big Ten's first four-time cross-country champion from 1973-76 and captured the NCAA title in that sport his junior year. On the track, he became America's premier distance runner, setting the United States collegiate record for the 10,000-meter run in 1976 (27:59.4). Following his graduation from UI's College of Communications in 1977, Virgin continued to run. He was a member of the U.S. Olympic Team in 1976, 1980 and 1984, and competed for the U.S. International Cross-Country Team from 1978-88, twice winning the world title. Virgin launched an unsuccessful campaign for the Illinois State Senate in 1992, and currently serves as president of Front Runner Inc., a sports marketing company based in Lebanon, Illinois.

Illini Lists

ILLINI BIG TEN
CROSS-COUNTRY CHAMPIONS

1928	David Abbott
1945	Victor Twomey
1962	Allen Carius
1963	Allen Carius
1973	Craig Virgin
1974	Craig Virgin
1975	Craig Virgin
1976	Craig Virgin

Allen Carius captured individual honors at the 1962 and '63 Big Ten Cross-Country Championships.

ILLINI LORE

James R. Thompson, a former student at the University of Illinois' Chicago Undergraduate Division at Navy Pier, became the first UI alumnus to win election as the state's governor, November 2, 1976. One other alumnus, Samuel Shapiro '29, advanced from lieutenant governor to the governorship when Gov. Otto Kerner resigned to become a federal judge in 1968.

1977-78

AMERICA'S TIME CAPSULE

Sept. 13, 1977   The first diesel-engine automobiles were introduced by General Motors.

Feb. 8, 1978   Egyptian President Anwar el-Sadat began a six-day visit to the United States to
                   hasten a Middle East peace settlement.

Feb. 15, 1978   Leon Spinks won a 15-round decision over Muhammad Ali to capture the heavyweight
                   boxing title.

June 10, 1978   Affirmed, ridden by jockey Steve Cautben, won horse racing's Triple Crown with a
                   victory at the Belmont Stakes.

Aug. 4, 1978   Evacuation of the Love Canal area of Niagara Falls, a dumping ground for toxic waste
                   in the 1940s and '50s, began.

ILLINI MOMENT

MOELLER REPLACES BLACKMAN:

Coach Gary Moeller

Just 13 days after Bob Blackman received word that his six-year reign as Illinois' head football coach had ended, the University of Illinois secured one of its archenemies' brightest young assistants. On December 2, 1976, 35-year-old Michigan defensive coordinator Gary Moeller became Illinois' third coach in seven seasons. Illini athletic director Cecil Coleman interviewed eight men for the position, including Chuck Studley, Don James and Jim Young, but settled on Bo Schembechler's top assistant. "I want to have a winning program and see the players benefit from it," said Moeller at his introductory press conference. "We will throw the ball, if I feel we can do it successfully, but very few passing teams are consistent winners." Moeller's christening as a head coach came September 10, 1977, against Michigan and his former mentor. The Illini took a 3-0 lead that afternoon, but ended up losing, 37-9. Unfortunately, Moeller's luck at Illinois never changed as his teams struggled to consecutive records of 3-8, 1-8-2 and 2-8-1. On November 20, 1979, he was fired by athletic director Neale Stoner.

Lynette Robinson (#43)

WOMEN'S MILESTONES

MAY 2, 1978

Lisa and Lynette Robinson of Annawan, Illinois became the first women athletes in University of Illinois history to sign full scholarships. Four years later, they ended their careers as Illinois' top two career basketball scorers of all time.

Lisa Robinson (#34)

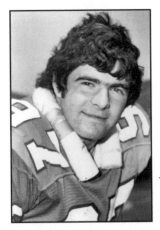

John Sullivan

LINEBACKER JOHN SULLIVAN was Most Valuable Player of the 1977 and 1978 Fighting Illini football teams. He finished his career as Illinois' all-time leading tackler, breaking Dick Butkus' 14-year-old record. It should be pointed out, however, that Sullivan needed 36 games to break a mark that Butkus had established in just 26. Sullivan's record of 501 total stops was broken in 1994 by Dana Howard.

Illini Legend

Lee Eilbracht

From 1952 to 1978, 14 different men served as manager of the Chicago Cubs. During that same 27-year span, the University of Illinois had one baseball coach: Lee Eilbracht. Appointed acting head coach in 1952 following the death of Wally Roettger, Eilbracht's position was made permanent at the end of the season. "The Swami," as he was affectionately called by his players, recorded more coaching victories than any of his five Illini predecessors. His career record of 519-397-6 included Big Ten championships in 1952, '53, '62 and '63. Eilbracht coached two athletes to All-American honors, 12 to first-team All-Big Ten laurels, and 34 others to All-Star mention. Catcher Tom Haller and pitcher Ken Holtzman, who went on to the major leagues, were two of his most famous pupils. Eilbracht earned three varsity letters at Illinois and was named the Illini's Most Valuable Player in 1946 and 1947. He hit .484 during the 1946 Big Ten season, the fourth-best average in conference history, and had a career average of .330. After his retirement following the 1978 season, Eilbracht served as the executive director of the American Association of College Baseball Coaches. Eilbracht and his wife, Euline, reside in Champaign.

Illini Lists

TOP MEMORIAL STADIUM RUSHING PERFORMANCES

1. 289 yards — Ron Dayne, Wisconsin, 11/23/96
2. 266 yards — Kent Kitzmann, Minnesota, 11/12/77
3. 263 yards — Howard Griffith, Illinois vs. Northwestern, 11/24/90
4. 239 yards — Jim Grabowski, Illinois vs. Wisconsin, 11/14/64
5. 231 yards — Leroy Keyes, Purdue, 11/4/67
6. 228 yards — Anthony Thomas, Michigan, 9/23/00
7. 215 yards — Rocky Harvey, Illinois vs. Mid. Tenn. St., 9/12/98
8. 212 yards — Red Grange, Illinois vs. Michigan, 10/18/24
9. 209 yards — Antwaan Randle El, 11/4/00
10. 208 yards — Howard Griffith, Illinois vs. Southern Illinois, 9/22/90

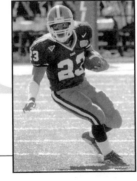

Rocky Harvey

ILLINI LORE

. . . .

On his 48th birthday, September 9, 1977, William P. Gerberding was introduced as the new chancellor for the University of Illinois at Urbana-Champaign. He came from UCLA where he served for 16 years, first as a faculty member and then as executive vice chancellor. Gerberding left the UI in 1979 to become president at the University of Washington.

1978-79

AMERICA'S TIME CAPSULE

Sept. 15, 1978   Muhammad Ali regained the heavyweight boxing title with a 15-round decision over Leon Spinks.

Nov. 18, 1978   More than 900 people, including 211 children, were found dead in Guyana. Jim Jones, leader of a religious sect, led the group in a mass suicide by poison.

March 26, 1979   Magic Johnson and Michigan State defeated Larry Bird and Indiana State in the NCAA basketball championship game at Salt Lake City.

March 28, 1979   Three Mile Island, near Harrisburg, Pennsylvania, was the site of a nuclear near-disaster.

May 25, 1979   An American Airlines DC-10 jet crashed shortly after takeoff in Chicago, killing all 272 passengers on board and three other people on the ground.

ILLINI MOMENT

ILLINI VICTORY PROVES TO BE BETTER THAN MAGIC:

Eddie Johnson's jump shot nestles through the twine with just four seconds left to send Michigan State home with a 57-55 loss.

A record Assembly Hall crowd of 16,209 was on hand January 11, 1979 to watch their third-ranked Fighting Illini (14-0) against No. 1 Michigan State (9-1). The Johnson boys—MSU's Earvin and Illinois' Eddie—were their respective teams' stars, but despite his opponent's famous nickname, it was Eddie who was "magic" on this particular night. The Spartans vaulted off to a 24-13 lead after the first 10 minutes of play, but the Illini sizzled in the last 10 minutes, outscoring their guests 19-4. The second half was like a see-saw, as the lead changed hands eight times. A Mike Brkovich jumper with 2:27 left pulled State even at 55-55, and Illini coach Lou Henson called time out with just :37 left on the clock to set up his team's final shot. UI's Steve Lanter penetrated the lane, forcing MSU's Greg Kelser to abandon Eddie Johnson. Lanter then dished the ball out to the right baseline where No. 33 was in position for an uncontested 18-foot jumper. With six seconds left, Johnson set himself, flicked his wrist, and sent the ball arcing toward the hoop. Nothing but net! The 57-55 victory improved the Illini record to 15-0, but, unfortunately, that perfection would last only for another 36 hours.

Mary Charpentier's nearly flawless performance helped Illinois beat Southern Illinois for the state championship.

WOMEN'S MILESTONES

FEBRUARY 23-24, 1979

Illinois' women's gymnastics team stunned everyone by defeating perennial powerhouse Southern Illinois at the state championship meet, 130.95 to 130.70. It was the first defeat SIU had suffered at home in 11 years. Mary Charpentier led the way for the Illini, finishing first in the vault (8.80), second on the beam (8.55) and fourth in all-around competition (33.25).

Cecil Coleman

CECIL COLEMAN'S seven-year tenure as athletic director at the University of Illinois came to an end April 27, 1979 when the Athletic Association's board of directors voted to dismiss him. Hired in 1972 to improve the school's image with the NCAA and to balance a budget which had a $1 million deficit, Coleman achieved both of those objectives. He was often criticized for his hard-nosed approach, but he probably never received credit for a series of other accomplishments, including the hiring of basketball coach Lou Henson and the establishment of UI's women's athletic program. He died February 27, 1988.

Illini Lists

ALMOST NO. 1

Lou Henson's club of 1978-79 started the season with 15 consecutive victories, including its monumental win over Magic Johnson's No. 1-rated Michigan State team at the Assembly Hall on January 11, 1979. Illinois' streak was finally snapped by a talented Ohio State team, two days after the Illini victory over the Spartans. Here's the entire list:

1. Illinois 109, Texas-Arlington 74 (H—11/24/78)
2. Illinois 81, Denver 57 (H—11/28/78)
3. Illinois 65, Tulane 60 (A—12/2/78)
4. Illinois 69, Missouri 57 (A—12/5/02)
5. Illinois 64, South Carolina 57 (H—12/8/78)
6. Illinois 86, Centenary 60 (H—12/9/78)
7. (#18) Illinois 82, Kent State 44 (A—12/16/78)
8. (#15) Illinois 82, (#8) Syracuse 61 (N—12/22/78)
9. (#15) Illinois 71, (#17) Texas A&M 57 (N—12/23/78)
10. (#6) Illinois 84, Western Michigan 79 (N—12/28/78)
11. (#6) Illinois 88, Ozarks 82 (N—12/29/78)
12. (#6) Illinois 92, Alaska-Anchorage 80 (A—12/30/78)
13. (#4) Illinois 65, Indiana 61 (H—1/4/79)
14. (#4) Illinois 74, Northwestern 56 (A—1/6/79)
15. (#4) Illinois 57, (#1) Michigan State 55 (H—1/11/79)
    Ohio State 69, (#4) Illinois 66 (OT) (H—1/13/79)

Illini Legend

Mark Smith

Even though he was voted Most Valuable Player of the 1978-79 Fighting Illini basketball squad, Mark Smith could have easily developed a Rodney Dangerfield complex. Classmate Eddie Johnson got the bulk of the publicity during their four years together at Illinois from 1978-81, but Smith's accomplishments were nothing short of sensational. It's true that Eddie wound up as UI's all-time leading scorer with 1,692 points, but there was Mark with just 39 fewer points. Johnson was the Illini's career rebounding leader, but Mark averaged just one rebound less per game. Though Johnson was considered the better shooter, it was Smith who posted better percentages from both the field (.525 to .454) and at the free-throw line (.781 to .671). And when it came to passing the ball, the former Peoria Richwoods star had nearly twice as many career assists (350 to 209). During Smith's four years at Illinois, the Illini won nearly 62 percent of their games. He died June 27, 2001 in his hometown of Peoria.

ILLINI LORE

On May 4, 1979, John E. Cribbet was named interim chancellor at the Urbana-Champaign campus of the University of Illinois, replacing William Gerberding who had left to become president at the University of Washington. Seven months later, December 12, 1979, the dean of UI's College of Law was chosen from a field of 114 candidates to become the full-time chancellor.

1979-80

AMERICA'S TIME CAPSULE

Sept. 9, 1979	John McEnroe and 16-year-old Tracy Austin won singles titles at the U.S. Tennis Open.
Nov. 4, 1979	Iranian revolutionaries seized the U.S. embassy in Teheran, taking some 90 hostages, including 65 Americans.
Jan. 20, 1980	President Carter announced that the U.S. Olympic Team would boycott the 1980 Summer Olympics in Moscow in protest against the Soviet invasion of Afghanistan.
Feb. 22, 1980	The U.S. hockey team beat the heavily favored Soviet Union, 4-3, advancing to the finals where it defeated Finland for the gold medal.
May 18, 1980	Mt. St. Helens, a volcano that had been dormant since 1857, erupted in Washington, leveling about 120 square miles of forest.

ILLINI MOMENT

Illini legend Ray Eliot (left) congratulates Neale Stoner on his appointment as Illinois' athletic director.

STONER BEGINS INITIAL SEASON AS ATHLETIC DIRECTOR:

Californian Neale Stoner became athletic director of the University of Illinois on September 27, 1979, boldly proclaiming that "the '80s belong to the Illini." Stoner had extraordinary success as AD at Cal State-Fullerton, but rebuilding Illinois into an athletic power would be the most challenging task of his career. After less than three months on the job, he replaced Gary Moeller as head football coach with another Californian, Mike White. White's successful passing attack helped raise Illinois' average football attendance from 45,000 per game in 1979 to more than 76,000 in 1984. Grant-in-aid support rose from around $400,000 a year in the 1970s to between $2 million and $3 million in the mid-1980s. Other accomplishments during the Stoner era included a capital campaign that produced new offices for the football staff and new facilities for baseball and outdoor track and field. The beginning of the end for Stoner came during the summer of 1988 when media questioned his use of Athletic Association funds and his miscalculation of AA income and expenses, which resulted in a $1.45 million shortfall during the 1987-88 fiscal year. On July 12, 1988, Stoner submitted his resignation as UI's athletic director "so that accusations will no longer interfere with the effective operation of the Athletic Association."

WOMEN'S MILESTONES

MARCH 7, 1980

Long jumper Becky Kaiser became the University of Illinois' first female athlete to win All-American honors. The sophomore from Charleston, Illinois went 20' 5/2" to place second at the Association of Intercollegiate Athletics for Women indoor track and field championship, held in Columbia, Missouri.

(left to right) Levi
Cobb, Lou Henson
and Neil Bresnahan

Illini Item

ILLINOIS' MEN'S BASKETBALL TEAM reached the 20-victory plateau and qualified for postseason play for the first time in 17 years during the 1979-80 season. Coach Lou Henson's squad, led by junior forward Eddie Johnson, won 10 of its first 12 games and finished the regular season portion of its schedule at 18-12. The Illini beat Loyola, Illinois State and Murray State in their first three games of the National Invitation Tournament, qualifying for a Final Four trip to New York City. Minnesota beat Illinois in the semifinals, 65-63, but Henson's Illini ended their season on an up note by defeating UNLV in the consolation game.

Illini Lists

ILLINI MEN'S BASKETBALL
SINGLE-GAME SCORING LEADERS

1. 53 points   Dave Downey at Indiana, 2/16/63
2. 46 points   Andy Kaufmann vs. Wisconsin-Milwaukee, 12/3/90
3. 42 points   Dave Scholz vs. Northwestern, 2/24/68
4. 40 points   Andy Kaufmann vs. Eastern Illinois, 12/1/90
   40 points   Andy Phillip at Chicago, 3/1/43
6. 39 points   Rich Adams vs. Arizona, 11/28/77
   39 points   Deon Thomas vs. Illinois-Chicago, 12/30/91
8. 38 points   John Kerr at Ohio State, 1/16/54
   38 points   Eddie Johnson vs. Long Beach State, 12/8/79
   38 points   Dave Scholz at Northwestern, 2/10/68

*Rich Adams poured in 39 points
vs. Arizona in 1977.*

Illini Legend

Eddie Johnson

Much has been written about Eddie Johnson's record-breaking career at the University of Illinois from 1978-81, but much more could be written about his teams' successes during that period. Though Johnson and his teammates registered a sub-.500 record during his freshman season, results dramatically improved during his last three campaigns. Illinois nearly grabbed the nation's No. 1 ranking during his sophomore year, winning its first 15 games in a row before finally winding up with a 19-11 record. The Illini qualified for the National Invitation Tournament his junior year, and were just one victory shy of winning the NIT championship. And in Johnson's senior season, Illinois made it to the NCAA tournament, the first time it had accomplished that since 1963. No. 33 did become the school's all-time leading scorer (1,692 points) and rebounder (831 rebounds), and forever will be remembered in Illini history for his shot that beat No. 1 Michigan State on January 11, 1979. He was the 29th selection in the 1981 NBA draft by the Kansas City Kings, and in 1994 wound up a 17-year career with an average of 17 points per game. Johnson's total of more than 19,000 points placed him 30th on the all-time NBA scoring list, making him the highest-ranked NBA scorer who never played in an all-star game.

ILLINI LORE

Forty-four-year-old Stanley O. Ikenberry began what was to become a 16-year term as the president of the University of Illinois on September 1, 1979. The University's 14th chief executive officer came from Pennsylvania State University where he had served for eight years as senior vice president. Ikenberry replaced Dr. John Corbally, who a year earlier had announced his resignation and a desire to return to teaching.

1980-81

AMERICA'S TIME CAPSULE

Nov. 4, 1980   Ronald Reagan won the presidential election in a landslide over incumbent Jimmy Carter.
Nov. 21, 1980   More than half of America's television audience tuned in Dallas to see "Who Shot J.R.?"
Jan. 20, 1981   The Iranian hostage crisis ended when Iran released American captives who were seized
                at the U.S. embassy in Teheran 14 months before.
April 14, 1981 The space shuttle Columbia successfully touched down on Earth following a 54-hour
                maiden flight in space.
May 24, 1981   The 65th Indianapolis 500 auto race ended in controversy. The next day, Mario Andretti
                was proclaimed the winner over Bobby Unser because Unser had broken a rule on the
                race course. Four and a half months later, on October 8, the U.S. Auto Club reversed its
                decision and gave the victory to Unser.

ILLINI MOMENT

WILSON SETS NCAA PASSING MARK:

One Chicago sportswriter called it "the most incredible passing performance in collegiate history." That phrase, as well as any, accurately summed up the effort put forth by Illinois' senior quarterback Dave Wilson at Ohio State on November 8, 1980. In setting and tying 44 different Illini, Big Ten and NCAA records, Wilson completed 43 of 69 passes to 10 different receivers for an amazing 621 yards and six touchdowns, agamst a Buckeye team that had ranked first in the league in pass defense. Following Wilson's sixth TD pass with 11 seconds left that made the final score Ohio State 49, Illinois 42, Buckeye fans rose from their seats to give the Illini signal-caller a standing ovation. One loyal OSU fan even handed Wilson his Scarlet and Gray hat as a souvenir. "What makes it such a tremendous accomplishment," said Illini coach Mike White afterwards, "was that it came against a quick, aggressive Ohio State defense. Maybe Dave just plain wore them out." Completely overshadowed by Wilson's statistical extravaganza was Buckeye quarterback Art Schlichter, who completed all but four of his 21 pass attempts for 284 yards.

WOMEN'S MILESTONES

JANUARY 12-14, 1981

The 76th annual NCAA convention at Miami, Florida featured the landmark decision to include women's athletic programs within the NCAA governing structure, sounding a death knell for the Association for Intercollegiate Athletics for Women. A prolonged debate on the constitutional amendment finally resulted in approval by nearly 70 percent of the record 551 delegates. Twenty-nine NCAA-sponsored championships for women were first conducted during the 1981-82 academic year.

Kevin McMurchie's second-place finish on the still rings helped Illinois win its first Big Ten gymnastics title in 21 years.

I Illini Item

ILLINOIS' MEN'S GYMNASTICS TEAM won its first Big Ten Conference title in 21 years March 14, 1981 at Columbus, Ohio, outscoring five-time defending champion Minnesota by just one-tenth of a point, 539.50 to 539.40. Coach Yoshi Hayasaki's Illini built up a six-point lead during the first day's optional competition, behind the performances of Kevin McMurchie, Gilberto Albuquerque and Gilmarcio Sanches, who were respectively second in the still rings, vault and floor exercise. Kari Samsten was third in all-around and parallel bar competition, and Steve Lechner was third on the horizontal bar.

Illini Lists

WOMEN'S BASKETBALL SINGLE-SEASON SCORING LEADERS

1. 689 points — Ashley Berggren, 1995-96 (28 games, 24.6 ppg)
2. 658 points — Lisa Robinson, 1980-81 (31 games, 21.2 ppg)
3. 627 points — Jonelle Polk, 1986-87 (29 games, 21.6 ppg)
4. 624 points — Jonelle Polk, 1985-86 (30 games, 20.8 ppg)
5. 599 points — Allison Curtin, 1999-00 (34 games, 17.6 ppg)
6. 588 points — Kendra Grant, 1982-83 (28 games, 21.0 ppg)
7. 571 points — Ashley Berggren, 1996-97 (32 games, 17.8 ppg)
8. 554 points — Ashley Berggren, 1997-98 (30 games, 18.1 ppg)
9. 532 points — Susan Blauser, 1998-99 (31 games, 17.2 ppg)
10. 530 points — Allison Curtin, 2000-01 (33 games, 16.1 ppg)

Lisa Robinson

Illini Legend

Mike White

On December 14, 1979, 43-year-old Mike White began his tempestuous career as head football coach at the University of Illinois. The San Francisco 49ers assistant inherited a program that sorely needed an injection of adrenaline, and for the next seven years White provided plenty of excitement. Compared to the "vanilla" offensive system of his predecessor, Gary Moeller, White's style was strictly "neapolitan." In White's first season alone, 1980, Illinois had an 11-game passing yardage total of 3,227, compared to Moeller's 33-game total of 3,300 aerial yards. His best team was the 1983 Big Ten championship club,

which registered 10 victories, including a record 9-0 mark against conference foes. For that performance, White was recognized as college football's Coach of the Year. His Illini appeared in the Liberty Bowl (1982), the Rose Bowl (1984), and the Peach Bowl (1985), but never won a postseason game. Attendance at Illini football games averaged nearly 69,000 during White's reign from 1980-88. However, despite all of the successes, Mike White's career was also marred by controversy with the NCAA. And on January 18, 1988, he tendered his resignation to Athletic Director Neale Stoner. "While I was unaware of the [NCAA] violations [that were taking place]," White said in his resignation statement, "I take full responsibility for the allegations in my capacity as the University of Illinois' head football coach." Today, White is director of football administration for the Kansas City Chiefs.

ILLINI LORE

The Alma Mater sculpture made only its second journey in 52 years, August 11, 1980, when the campus landmark was removed from its base for a 10-day respite of restoration at the Physical Plant Services Building. Its first trip came in 1962 when the Alma Mater was transferred from a grove of evergreens south of the Auditorium to its present site north of Altgeld Hall. Nature's elements had rusted the iron bolts that secured the sections, so art professor Robert Youngman and his team of workers replaced what they could reach with stainless steel bolts and sprayed the remainder of the bronze sculpture with rust inhibitor. Physical Plant workers returned the refurbished Alma Mater by crane to her granite base on August 21, 1980.

AMERICA'S TIME CAPSULE

Sept. 21, 1981   Sandra Day O'Connor became the first female member of the Supreme Court.

Jan. 8, 1982   An eight-year antitrust suit by the Justice Department ended when the American Telephone and Telegraph Company (AT+T) agreed to divest itself of its 22 Bell Telephone operating systems.

March 29, 1982   Michael Jordan and North Carolina defeated Patrick Ewing and Georgetown in the NCAA basketball finals.

June 25, 1982   Secretary of State Alexander Haig resigned following disagreements with President Ronald Reagan.

July 3, 1982   Martina Navratilova won her first Wimbledon tennis championship.

ILLINI MOMENT

Illinois' Diane Eickholt puts up a shot against Ohio State in UI's Big Ten home debut.

WOMEN'S ATHLETICS BEGIN IN BIG TEN:

Until May 15, 1974, women's athletics were under the auspices of the Department of Physical Education at the UI. At that time, the budget for the women's program amounted to $14,110. Nearly 26 months after the Equal Rights Amendment was passed by the U.S. Senate, the UI Board of Trustees placed intercollegiate athletics for women under the auspices of the Athletic Association. Seventeen days later, on June 1, Dr. Karol Kahrs was hired by the AA as the first assistant director for women's athletics. Immediately, the recruitment of part-time coaches began. There were no scholarships in the 1974-75 season, but steps were taken the following year to upgrade to tuition and fees. Finally, in May of 1978, the first full-scholarship athletes began signing. On August 1, 1981, after much discussion, the UI women's athletic program officially became part of the Big Ten Conference, and competition began in 1981-82. In March of 1982, the women's basketball team finished second in the conference standings and qualified for the first NCAA women's basketball championship. Through the first 21 seasons of Big Ten competition, Fighting Illini women's teams won or shared 15 conference titles.

1986 volleyball team

WOMEN'S MILESTONES

MARCH 31, 1982

In a letter directed to Chancellor John Cribbet, the Office for Civil Rights of the U.S. Department of Education declared that the University of Illinois' intercollegiate athletic program complied with Title IX requirements for equal opportunities for women athletes. Cribbet praised the efforts of athletic director Neale Stoner and assistant director Karol Kahrs. "Illinois has been a leader in the Big Ten and nationally in promoting women's athletics," Cribbet said. "I am especially pleased that their hard work and commitment to excellence in women's athletics have been confirmed by the Department of Education."

Tim Richardson

I Illini Item

FIGHTING ILLINI FIRST BASEMAN Tim Richardson amassed terrific statistics during his junior baseball season in 1982. Playing a record 72 games, he batted .400, becoming the first Illinois player since Ruck Steger in 1952 to crack that magic average. Additionally, Richardson stroked school records for hits (104), triples (11) and total bases (163). At the end of the season, Big Ten coaches accorded him first team all-conference honors.

Illini Legend

Tony Eason

The name Charles Carroll Eason IV sounds more as if it belongs to a Bostonian socialite than to a quarterback from Walnut Grove, California. However, the guy his Illini teammates called "Tony" was very much a quarterback; in fact, he was one of the greatest signal-callers in University of Illinois football history. Eason was recruited in 1980 by Coach Mike White along with another junior college QB, Dave Wilson. Wilson beat out Eason for the starting job that first season, but "Champaign Tony" was a smash hit

in 1981, breaking nine Big Ten records by passing for 3,360 yards and 20 touchdowns. His senior season in 1982 was even more brilliant, accounting for 3,671 yards and earning first-team All-Big Ten honors for a second consecutive year as the Illini qualified for the Liberty Bowl. Named the Fighting Illini Player of the Decade for the 1980s, Eason enjoyed a successful career in the National Football League, quarterbacking the New England Patriots to a berth against the Chicago Bears in Super Bowl XX. He stayed with the Patriots for seven seasons (1983-89), ranking as that franchise's third-leading passer of all-time with 10,732 yards and 60 TD passes. Eason retired from the NFL following the 1990 season with the New York Jets. Eason started a business called "Athletic Enhancements," training athletes to be more proficient. He lives in San Marcos, California.

Illini Lists

ALL-TIME BIG TEN
WOMEN'S SPORTS CHAMPIONSHIPS
(Through 2001-02 season)

1.	Michigan	52
2.	Wisconsin	36
3.	Ohio State	35
4.	Indiana	33
5.	Iowa	23
6.	Northwestern	18
7.	Penn State	17
8.	ILLINOIS	15
9.	Purdue	12
10.	Minnesota	11
11.	Michigan State	8

Illini volleyball teams have won four of UI's 15 Big Ten titles.

ILLINI LORE

The Big Ten Conference began one-year sanctions against the University of Illinois' intercollegiate football program on August 6, 1981. The original penalties, imposed in May, were partially a result of Illini quarterback Dave Wilson's legal struggle against the conference. The Big Ten faculty representatives voted to prohibit the Illini from playing in a postseason Bowl game in 1981 and denied the University a share of the conference receipts from televised football games. On September 3, Governor James Thompson signed into law a bill that created a special lottery that helped offset an estimated $500,000 loss in football TV revenue. The lottery, originally sponsored by State Senator Stanley Weaver of Urbana and State Representative Virgil Wikoff of Champaign, eventually netted UI's Athletic Association $850,000.

1982-83

AMERICA'S TIME CAPSULE

Sept. 29, 1982	Seven persons in the Chicago area died from cyanide placed in Tylenol capsules.
Oct. 20, 1982	The St. Louis Cardinals won the seventh and deciding game of the World Series, defeating the Milwaukee Brewers.
Dec. 2, 1982	Barney Clark was the first successful recipient of an artificial heart transplant. He died on March 23, 1983.
March 2, 1983	More than 125 million viewers watched the final television episode of *M*A*S*H*.
April 12, 1983	Democratic congressman Harold Washington became the first African-American mayor of Chicago.

ILLINI MOMENT

ILLINI GRIDDERS BATTLE THE BEAR:

Illinois' Mike White and Alabama's Paul "Bear" Bryant.

The 1982 Fighting Illini football season will be remembered for many reasons. The year began with a highly successsful "Tailgreat" promotion and a big win over Northwestern in Memorial Stadium's first-ever night game. It was the season Tony Eason established an all-time record for passing proficiency. And it was the year that Illinois went "Bowling" for the first time in 19 years. The Fighting Illini met Alabama at the Liberty Bowl December 29 in Memphis, a game that would turn out to be the final one for the Crimson Tide's legendary Paul "Bear" Bryant. Bryant, who won more games than any other coach in college football, announced his retirement two weeks before, making the otherwise second-rate bowl game one of the season's top attractions. The night was clear, and the 34-degree weather favored Alabama's wishbone attack. Illinois trailed the Tide by a score of 7-6 at the half, as Alabama defenders repeatedly pummeled Eason with a ferocious pass rush. On three occasions, crushing Alabama tackles forced Eason from the game. "My eyes were bobbing up and down," the Illini quarterback said afterwards. "I couldn't even find the ground." Despite a record 423 yards passing by Eason, Illinois dropped a 21-15 decision, giving the Bear his 323rd and final collegiate victory.

WOMEN'S MILESTONES

SEPTEMBER 26, 1983

Fighting Illini golfer Mary Ellen Murphy became the first UI female athlete to earn an NCAA Post-graduate Scholarship. A two-time national qualifier and 1983 honoree as winner of the Big Ten Conference Medal of Honor, Murphy used the $2,000 scholarship prize to earn a degree in physical therapy at Northwestern University's Medical Center.

Illini Item

DISTANCE RUNNER Marianne Dickerson was the University of Illinois' Female Athlete of the Year for 1982-83. She set numerous records in cross-country and track and field, and twice won All-American honors. During her Fighting Illini career, Dickerson recorded eight of the top 10 cross-country marks, and set UI varsity records in the two- and three-mile runs and 5,000- and 10,000-meter runs. She was also an excellent student, graduating with a 4.5 grade-point average (on a 5.0 scale) in engineering.

Illini Legend

Derek Harper

If Lou Henson is ever asked to select his all-time Fighting Illini defensive team, chances are that Derek Harper will be among his starting five. The 6'4" guard from West Palm Beach, Florida consistently shut down the Big Ten's premier perimeter scorers during his career from 1981-83. Harper led the conference in steals his sophomore and junior seasons, averaging more than two per game against such conference luminaries as Michigan State's Sam Vincent, Minnesota's Darryl Mitchell and Michigan's Mike McGee. Though he wasn't known as a shooter, Harper set a Big Ten record by making 19 consecutive field goal attempts during his final campaign in 1983. His best single effort was a 29-point outing against Michigan that season. During his three years at Illinois, the Illini averaged 20 victories per season and qualified twice for the NCAA tournament. Harper left Illinois following the 1982-83 season and was a first-round pick for the Dallas Mavericks in the 1983 NBA draft. He played in Dallas for 12 seasons, winding up as the Mavericks' No. 3 all-time scorer (12,597 points), No. 1 all-time assist man (5,111) and No. 1 in career steals (1,841). He was traded to the New York Knicks late in the 1993-94 season and starred in the NBA finals against the eventual champion Houston Rockets.

Illini Lists

ILLINI FEMALE ATLETES OF THE YEAR

1982-83 Marianne Dickerson, track/cross country
1983-84 Karen Brems, gymnastics
1984-85 Kelly McNee, track/cross country
1985-86 Jonelle Polk, basketball
1986-87 Mary Eggers, volleyball
1987-88 Mary Eggers, volleyball
1988-89 Mary Eggers, volleyball
1989-90 Laura Bush, volleyball
1990-91 Renee Heiken, golf
1991-92 Renee Heiken, golf and Tonja Buford, track
1992-93 Tonja Buford, track
1993-94 Tina Rogers, volleyball
1994-95 Tonja Williams, track
1995-96 Tonja Williams, track
1996-97 Ashley Berggren, basketball
1997-98 Ashley Berggren, basketball and Yvonne Harrison, track
1998-99 Cristy Chapman, volleyball
1999-00 Jessica Aveyard, swimming
2000-01 Perdita Felicien, track
2001-02 Perdita Felicien, track

Tonya Williams, 1994-95 and '95-96 Female Athlete of the Year.

ILLINI LORE

Following two years of intense debate and examination, the Circle and Medical Center campuses at Chicago began a unified effort during the 1982-83 academic year. University of Illinois President Stanley Ikenberry, in his recommendation to the Board of Trustees for acceptance of the consolidation, said the merger would give the new UI Chicago "the ability to compete in the Chicago-area academic arena and contribute to the strengthening of the university as a whole."

1983-84

AMERICA'S TIME CAPSULE

Sept. 1, 1983	A Soviet fighter plane shot down a South Korean airliner, killing all 269 people aboard.
Oct. 23, 1983	An explosive-laden truck blew up outside the U.S. Marine headquarters in Beirut, Lebanon, taking the lives of 241 Marine and Navy personnel.
April 23, 1984	Federal researchers announced the identification of a virus thought to cause acquired immune deficiency syndrome (AIDS).
May 8, 1984	The U.S.S.R. Olympic Committee withdrew from the 1984 Olympics, to be held in Los Angeles, California.
July 28, 1984	The Summer Olympic games began in Los Angeles, highlighted by the performances of Carl Lewis and Mary Lou Retton.

ILLINI MOMENT

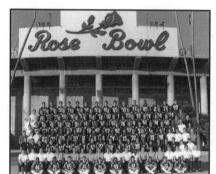

1983 football team ('84 Rose Bowl)

ILLINI FOOTBALL TEAM WINS BIG TEN:

Between 1896 and 1982, 50 of the first 87 Big Ten championship teams wound up unbeaten and untied. In 1983, Coach Mike White's Fighting Illini football team defied the odds by becoming the first Big Ten club to ever post victories over all nine of its conference foes. Game by game, momentum stayed in Illinois' corner. First, unbeaten Michigan State bit the dust (20-10), then fourth-ranked Iowa (33-0) and rugged Wisconsin (27-15). Sixth-ranked Ohio State battled the Illini tooth-and-nail at Memorial Stadium, before finally succumbing, 17-13. Illinois improved its conference mark to 5-0 with a 35-21 win at Purdue, setting up its showdown against unbeaten Michigan before a record crowd at Champaign. The bone-crushing Illini defense was at its best that day, holding the eighth-ranked Wolverines without a touchdown en route to a 16-6 victory. All that separated Illinois from the Rose Bowl were a trio of conference doormats: Minnesota, Indiana and Northwestern. Despite a lackluster effort at the Metrodome, the Illini disposed of the Golden Gophers, 50-23, to improve their conference record to 7-0. On November 12, more than 73,000 fans were on hand at Memorial Stadium to see their Illini clinch their first Rose Bowl berth in 20 years with a convincing 49-21 triumph over Indiana. About 30,000 Illini faithful showed up at Northwestern's Dyche Stadium for the regular-season finale, and White's troops toyed with the Wildcats, 56-24, to post their Big Ten-record ninth victory. Before Illinois' Rose Bowl battle against Pac-10 champion UCLA, the team collected a bushel of accolades. Six Illini players earned first-team all-conference honors, including defensive tackle Don Thorp, who was named the Big Ten's Most Valuable Player. White was honored by nearly everyone as their Coach of the Year. On January 2, 1984, a lovely 84-degree day welcomed the teams to Pasadena. Unfortunately, the weather was the high point of the day for Illinois. UCLA built up a 28-3 lead and wound up with a 45-9 victory over the fourth-ranked Illini, the most lopsided Rose Bowl score since 1960. An otherwise sweet season had been ruined by one very sour performance.

WOMEN'S MILESTONES

In 1983-84, University of Illinois women's gymnast Karen Brems became the first Fighting Illini athlete to be named as the school's Athlete of the Year and the Big Ten Conference Medal of Honor award winner in the same season. She's now a computer engineer in California and a world-class bicycle racer.

Bruce Douglas

ILLINOIS CLAIMED A SHARE of the Big Ten basketball title in 1983-84 by winning 15 of 18 conference games, including its last four in a row. Highlighting the regular season was a four-overtime victory at the Assembly Hall January 28 over Michigan, 75-66. Guard Bruce Douglas, a consensus first-team All-Big Ten selection, played all 60 minutes. The Illini won their first two games in NCAA tournament play, beating Villanova and Maryland, to advance to a quarterfinal showdown against powerful Kentucky at Lexington. The Wildcats had beaten Illinois in a Christmas Eve game at the Assembly Hall, 56-54, and the rematch was equally close, with the Illini finally losing by a score of 54-51. Illinois wound up the year with a 26-5 record, but were 0-2 against Kentucky.

Illini Item

Illini Legend

Don Thorp

Illini Lists

ILLINOIS FOOTBALL'S MOST PROLIFIC SCORING TEAMS

The 1983 Fighting Illini football team is the school's most prolific scoring squad ever in terms of Big Ten Conference games. Here's the entire list:

	PPG	Team (leading passer/receiver/rusher)
1.	33.7 ppg	1983 (Trudeau/D. Williams/Rooks)
2.	32.4 ppg	2001 (Kittner/Lloyd/Harvey)
3.	30.4 ppg	1984 (Trudeau/D. Williams/Rooks)
4.	30.3 ppg	1982 (Eason/Martin/Beverly)
5.	29.9 ppg	1989 (George/Bellamy/Griffith)
6.	29.3 ppg	1981 (Eason/D. Smith/Thomas)
7.	25.8 ppg	1995 (Johnson/Dulick/Holcombe)
	25.8 ppg	1947 (Moss/Zatkoff/Steger)
9.	25.7 ppg	1953 (Falkenstein/Ryan/Caroline)
10.	25.6 ppg	1999 (Kittner/Dean/Havard)

Jack Trudeau

As a youngster, Don Thorp attended Chicago Bears games with his father, idolizing their star linebacker, Dick Butkus. So in 1983-exactly 20 years after Butkus was named the Big Ten's Most Valuable football player-the University of Illinois' defensive tackle from Buffalo Grove appropriately matched his hero's accomplishment, capturing the *Chicago Tribune's* Silver Football Award. Thorp easily outdistanced Iowa quarterback Chuck Long for the honor, garnering nine of the 14 first-place votes and placing second on two other ballots. Ever the big-play specialist, he registered 17 tackles for losses his senior year, bringing his career total to a school-record 37. Thorp, a member of Coach Mike White's first recruiting class at Illinois, was the stalwart for a defensive unit that was primarily reponsible for his team's perfect 9-0 Big Ten record. He was rewarded with first-team All-America laurels and, more importantly to him, Most Valuable Player honors from his teammates. Nowadays, Don Thorp is an administrator for Greenfield Thorp Company in Chicago.

ILLINI LORE

William Warfield, University of Illinois professor of voice from 1974 to 1990, was awarded a Grammy Award by the National Academy of Recording Arts and Sciences in April of 1984 for his narration of Abraham Lincoln in Aaron Copland's composition, "A Lincoln Portrait." Warfield, a bass baritone, became nationally recognized for his role as Porgy in George Gershwin's *Porgy and Bess*, and for his rendition of "Ol' Man River" in the 1951 movie *Showboat*.

1984-85

AMERICA'S TIME CAPSULE

Oct. 7, 1984   Steve Garvey led the San Diego Padres to the National League pennant over the Chicago Cubs.

Nov. 6, 1984   Ronald Reagan was reelected president over Walter Mondale in the greatest Republican landslide ever.

March 4, 1985   The Environmental Protection Agency ordered a ban on leaded gasoline.

April 8, 1985   The government of India sued the Union Carbide Corporation in connection with a plant disaster that killed 1,700 and injured as many as 200,000 others.

July 13, 1985   President Reagan underwent surgery to remove a cancerous tumor from his colon.

ILLINI MOMENT

Bruce Douglas (left) and Efrem Winters.

ILLINI BID BOBBY "GOOD KNIGHT":

Illinois took advantage of a freshman-dominated Indiana lineup January 27, 1985, and administered a 52-41 spanking to Coach Bobby Knight's young Hoosiers. The perfection-driven coach from Bloomington brought only 12 players with him on the bus to Champaign, leaving veterans Winston Morgan and Mike Giomi at home because he was so disgusted with their performance in a two-point loss at Ohio State a few nights before. Knight even left All-American Steve Alford on the bench all afternoon, underlining his slightly bizarre statement to his team. Fortunately for the Illini, Knight's psychological ploy backfired. So dominating was the Illini defensive effort that night at the Assembly Hall that Indiana managed only five baskets and two free throws in the first half. The final box score showed Eftem Winters and George Montgomery pacing Illinois with 12 and 10 points, respectively, while Anthony Welch grabbed 10 rebounds. Aside from 7'2" Uwe Blab, the six Hoosiers in the game were freshmen.

Kelly McNee

Afterwards, Illini guard Doug Altenberger summed up the afternoon. "The game was just weird," he said. Was Illini coach Lou Henson disappointed he didn't get a chance to coach against Indiana's best? "It would suit me fine if they didn't play when we go over to Bloomington," he said. As it turned out, the Illini won again February 21 at IU, 66-50, propelling them to a second-place finish in the Big Ten in 1985.

WOMEN'S MILESTONES

OCTOBER 27, 1984

The Fighting Illini women's cross country team placed second at the Big Ten Championship meet, its highest finish of all time. Illinois, directed by interim head coach Patty Bradley, was runner-up to defending champion Wisconsin, 27 to 79. Junior Kelly McNee earned All-Big Ten honors by placing sixth individually. Three other Illini runners—Ruth Sterneman, Margaret Vogel and Colleen Hackett—all finished among the meet's top 17. McNee went on to represent Illinois at the NCAA championship, where she finished 21st of 150 runners and earned All-America honors.

Ty Wolf paced the Illini cross-country team to Illinois' only Big Ten team title in 1984-85.

I Illini Item

FIGHTING ILLINI MEN'S TEAMS completed one of their finest overall seasons in school history during the 1984-85 campaign. Illinois outscored Michigan in total points, 87.5 to 84.5, based on a 10-9-8 points system for a 1st-2nd-3rd finish in the Big Ten's 12 championships. The Illini cross-country squad was the only team to win a title, but four other sports-football, indoor track, fencing and basketball-placed second. Four Illinois teams placed among the NCAA's top 30 finishers-cross-country, 14th; men's basketball, round of 16; fencing, 17th; and indoor track, 27th. The Illini men's gymnastics team was ranked among the nation's top 20, the baseball team won the Big Ten's West Division title, and the tennis team finished seventh in the National Invitation postseason tournament.

Illini Legend

Mike Hebert

While the Fighting Illini football and men's basketball teams were winning Big Ten championships during the 1983-84 season, a 39-year-old volleyball coach named Mike Hebert was in the early stages of his career at the University of Illinois. Hebert's first season started unceremoniously with just five victories in 30 matches, but more than a decade later the California native had proven to be one of the Illini's winningest coaches ever. From 1983 through 1995, Hebert's Illini captured 323 victories against only 127 losses, a winning percentage of .718. That's more efficient than Lou Henson or Bob Zuppke or most any other Illini coaching legend. Including the 1994 season, Hebert's teams qualified for the NCAA tournament 10 consecutive years, including back-to-back Final Four appearances in 1987 and 1988, and have won four Big Ten championships. Over the past few seasons, as a result of that success, Illini volleyball has attracted more fans than any other school in the nation, leading the nation in attendance in both 1992 and 1993. Several of Hebert's athletes have earned All-American acclaim, including first teamers Mary Eggers and Kirsten Gleis. Hebert was named National Volleyball Coach of the Year in 1985.

Illini Lists

MIKE HEBERT'S VOLLEYBALL MVPs

1983	Laurie Watters
1984	Denise Fracaro
1985	Denise Fracaro
1986	Mary Eggers
1987	Mary Eggers and Nancy Brookhart
1988	Mary Eggers
1989	Laura Bush
1990	Petra Laverman
1991	Lorna Henderson
1992	Kirsten Gleis
1993	Tina Rogers
1994	Julie Edwards
1995	Erin Borske

Denise Fracaro was Most Valuable Player of the Illini volleyball team in 1984 and '85.

ILLINI LORE

At a news conference May 22, 1984, President Stanley Ikenberry introduced Thomas Everhart, 52, as the chancellor-elect of the Urbana-Champaign campus. Everhart, dean of Cornell University's College of Engineering, succeeded John Cribbet who returned to teaching in UI's College of Law. "This is truly a great university," Everhart told the media, "one of the four or five premier public campuses in the country. The opportunity to assume the chancellorship of this distinguished campus is compelling." Everhart served the UI until 1988.

Deon Thomas (left) and Dana Howard.

ILLINOIS

1989-90

1985-1994

ILLINOIS

1988-89 Basketball

1985-86

AMERICA'S TIME CAPSULE

Sept. 9, 1985	President Reagan announced trade sanctions against South Africa to protest that country's policy of apartheid.
Sept. 11, 1985	Cincinnati's Pete Rose broke Ty Cobb's major league baseball record for hits when he collected his 4,192nd hit against San Diego.
Oct. 27, 1985	The Kansas City Royals defeated the St. Louis Cardinals, four games to three, to win the World Series.
Jan. 26, 1986	Coach Mike Ditka's Chicago Bears beat the New England Patriots, 46-10, to win Super Bowl XX.
Jan. 28, 1986	Seven astronauts were killed when the space shuttle Challenger exploded just 74 seconds after liftoff at Cape Canaveral, Florida.

ILLINI MOMENT

CHRIS WHITE'S FIELD GOAL BEATS OHIO STATE:

Chris White

Illinois coach Mike White called it "the sweetest victory I can remember in my coaching career," and none of the 76,343 Illini fans assembled at Memorial Stadium that windy October 5th afternoon could argue with his statement. Shouldering the burden of both a disappointing 1-2 start and a 28-14 second-half deficit to their guests from Ohio State, the Fighting Illini football team rose from the dead to register a stunning 31-28 win over the fifth-ranked Buckeyes. The decisive play came when the coach's son, Chris White, drilled a 38-yard field goal as the clock ran out. However, there were more Illini heroics prior to that, and quarterback Jack Trudeau was primarily responsible for the stunning rally. Completing 28 of his 40 passes, Trudeau relied on a short passing game against the wind. His quick shovel passes to fullback Thomas Rooks and timely catches by Stephen Pierce for 131 yards nickel-and-dimed the traditionally tough Buckeye defense to death. Chris White's game-winning kick came following a pair of timeouts, the second called by Ohio State in an attempt to unnerve the senior placekicker. "I've got a lot of faith in that son of mine," the elder White told the media afterwards. "His temperament is unbelievable. I don't think that ball was six inches off center."

Thomas Rooks

WOMEN'S MILESTONES

MARCH 8, 1986

Junior center Jonelle Polk became the first University of Illinois women's basketball player to earn first-team honors on the All-Big Ten squad. Polk led the conference in scoring with an average of 21.9 points per game and also ranked among the leaders in numerous other statistical categories. Despite being named Big Ten Player of the Week four times in 1985-86, Polk was edged out by Ohio State's Tracy Hall as league Player of the Year.

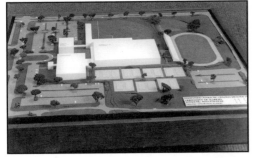

Illinois' plans for construction of new athletic facilities were unveiled in 1982 and begun in 1985.

AT A LATE JULY 1982 MEETING in Robinson, Illinois the Athletic Association's Board of Control approved Director Neale Stoner's long-range plan for construction of new athletic facilities. About 33 months later--April 15, 1985--construction began on $34 million worth of improvements. Of the total, $7 million was targeted toward upgrading football facilities, including the resurfacing of Zuppke Field, expansion of the football headquarters, and installation of an air-support structure that was eventually nicknamed "The Bubble." Construction on the new baseball and track stadiums began in June of 1985.

Illini Legend

David Williams

The soft hands of All-America receiver David Williams were once described by a sportswriter as "bean bags used to catch bullets." During his illustrious career at the University of Illinois from 1983-85, Williams's hands caught 262 passes for 3,392 yards, mostly from the skillful arm of Illini quarterback Jack Trudeau. In the history of college football, only Tulsa's Howard Twilley was a more proficient receiver than the young man from Los Angeles, California. Season-wise, Williams's top effort came in 1984 when he became the first (and only) Illini receiver to catch more than 100 passes (101). Statistically, Illinois' No. 1 had his best individual game October 12, 1985 against Purdue when he set an Illini record with 16 catches for 164 yards. David was one of three Williams brothers who played for the Illini during the 1980s, including older brother Oliver (1981-82) and younger sibling Steven (1985-89). David, who was drafted in the third round of the 1986 NFL draft by the Chicago Bears, played with Tampa Bay and the Los Angeles Raiders his first two seasons as a pro. In 1988, he began a seven-year career in the Canadian Football League, playing with British Columbia, Ottawa, Toronto and Winnipeg. During that span in Canada, Williams played in 101 CFL games, catching 439 passes for 7,197 yards and 79 touchdowns. In the fall of 1995, he returned to the University of Illinois to complete his bachelor's degree.

Illini Lists

ILLINI MEN'S AND WOMEN'S BIG TEN GOLF MEDALISTS

1923	Rial Rolfe	1986	Steve Stricker
1930	Richard Martin	1988	Steve Stricker
1931	Ricahrd Martin	1989	Steve Stricker
1941	Alex Welsh	1991	Renee Heiken
1942	James McCarthy	1992	Becky Biehl
1962	Mike Toliuszis	1993	Jamie Fairbanks
1982	Mike Chadwick	1993	Renee Heiken
		1999	Larry Nuger

Becky Biehl was the Big Ten's medalist at the 1992 women's golf championships.

ILLINI LORE

It wasn't a university-sponsored event, nor was it an athletic event, but probably the most noteworthy campus event of 1985-86 occurred at Memorial Stadium, September 22, 1985. The event's official name was "FarmAid," and it was undoubtedly one of the most diversified collections of musical talent to ever gather at the Urbana-Champaign campus. The 14-hour concert was marred by rain and cold temperatures, but that didn't much bother the 78,000 fans who filled the stadium. Among the more than 50 stars of rock and roll, blues and country who performed on the giant stage located at the north end of Zuppke Field were coorganizer Willie Nelson, Johnny Cash, Alabama, Billy Joel, the Beach Boys, Van Halen, B.B. King, and Kenny Rogers. More than $9 million in ticket sales, corporate donations and private pledges was eventually used for cash grants to needy farmers.

1986-87

AMERICA'S TIME CAPSULE

Nov. 3, 1986   The Iran-Contra affair became public when a Lebanese magazine revealed that the United States had been secretly selling arms to Iran in hopes of securing the release of hostages held in Lebanon.

Nov. 22, 1986   Twenty-year-old Mike Tyson became the youngest heavyweight boxing champion in history when he knocked out Trevor Berbick.

March 19, 1987   TV evangelist Jim Bakker admitted that he had an extramarital affair with his church secretary. He was dismissed as minister of the Assemblies of God on May 6.

April 12, 1987   Larry Mize sank a 50-yard wedge shot on the second hole of a three-way playoff against Greg Norman and Seve Ballesteros to win the Masters golf tournament.

Aug. 16, 1987   A Northwest Airlines jet crashed on takeoff from the Detroit Metropolitan Airport, killing 156 of 157 passengers.

ILLINI MOMENT

VOLLEYBALL WINS BIG TEN TITLE:

Perfection in an 18-match, round-robin format had never before been accomplished by a Big Ten volleyball team, but that all changed in 1986. Coach Mike Hebert's Fighting Illini sailed through the conference portion of the season, sweeping to victory an unprecedented 18 straight times, including three-games-to-none shutouts in 13 of those matches. During the regular season, the Illini dropped matches to only fourth-ranked San Jose and sixth-ranked Nebraska. Heading into the NCAA tournament with its 34-2 record, Illinois sported a 24-match winning streak. The Mideast Region's No. 2 seed easily disposed of Northern Iowa and Western Michigan in the first two rounds, but the Illini were eliminated in the semifinals by Nebraska in three consecutive games. Illinois athletes dominated the All-Big Ten squad as Player of the Year Mary Eggers, Disa Johnson, and Sally Rea all were named as first-teamers. Eggers also won first-team All-American honors.

Leticia Beverly

Disa Johnson won first-team All-Big Ten honors for the 1986 Fighting Illini volleyball team.

WOMEN'S MILESTONES

MAY 23-24, 1987

The Fighting Illini track team placed second to Purdue at the Big Ten Outdoor Track and Field Championships in Iowa City, Iowa, its highest finish ever to that point. Coach Gary Winckler's squad racked up a school-record 112 points, just three points behind the Boilermakers. Sophomore Leticia Beverly claimed two individual titles, winning the 100-meter hurdles and the long jump, as well as leading off the victorious 400-meter relay unit. Victoria Fulcher was the only other Illini athlete who captured an individual championship, winning the 400-meter hurdles.

Ken Norman

Illini Item

ILLINOIS BASKETBALL STAR Ken "Snake" Norman had a marvelous season in 1986-87, earning first-team All-Big Ten and second-team All-American honors. The Fighting Illini MVP averaged nearly 21 points and 10 rebounds per game, leading the conference in the latter category.

Illini Legend

Darrin Fletcher

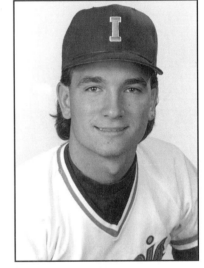

If ever there was an All-American family at the University of Illinois, it was the Fletcher clan from tiny Oakwood, Illinois. Not only were dad Tom and son Darrin outstanding citizens and model student athletes for the Fighting Illini, they were, quite literally, All-Americans in the sport of baseball. A first-team All-American selection as a pitcher in 1962, the elder Fletcher still holds the Illini records for lowest earned run average (0.38) and most shutouts (four). Darrin excelled as a catcher, but his greatest notoriety came as a batsman, hitting a school-record .392 from 1985-87, including a stunning .497 average his junior year. Fletcher held eight UI marks altogether, and was named the 1986-87 Fighting Illini Male Athlete of the Year. He was chosen as the Big Ten's baseball player of the year, hitting .432 in conference play. Darrin was a sixth-round draft choice of the Los Angeles Dodgers in 1987, earning a spot on the parent club late in the 1989 season. He was traded to Philadelphia in 1990, and a year later was dealt from the Phillies to the Montreal Expos. The crowning moment of Fletcher's major league career came in 1994 when he was selected as a member of the National League all-star team.

Illini Lists

ILLINI WOMEN'S TRACK & FIELD
MULTIPLE BIG TEN INDIVIDUAL TITLISTS
(through 2000-01)

1.	25 titles	Tonja Buford (1990-93)
2.	20 titles	Tonya Williams (1993-96)
3.	19 titles	Celena Mondie-Milner (1987-90)
4.	14 titles	Renee Carr (1986-90)
5.	11 titles	Leticia Beverly (1986-89)
6.	9 titles	Angela McClatchey (1986-89)
7.	8 titles	Carmel Corbett (1992-95)
	8 titles	Benita Kelley (1995-98)
9.	7 titles	Althea Thomas (1989-90)
	7 titles	Dawn Riley (1993-96)
	7 titles	Aspen Burkett (1995-98)

Celena Mondie-Milner captured 19 Big Ten track titles during her Fighting Illini career from 1987-90.

ILLINI LORE

On November 8, 1986, a gala ball at Lincoln Hall capped off a week of festivities that marked the 75th anniversary of the World Heritage Museum. The museum's early development occurred under curators Neil Brooks and Arthur Pease. Its first full-time director was Oscar Dodson in the 1960s. Among the museum's most notable pieces are an original fragment from the Bible's Book of James, a large display of medieval and Renaissance armor, a page from the Gutenberg Bible, and Olympic memorabilia from the collection of University of Illinois graduate and track star Avery Brundage.

1987-88

AMERICA'S TIME CAPSULE

Oct. 19, 1987   The worst stock crash in the recent history of the New York Stock Exchange occurred when the Dow Jones industrial average fell 508 points.

Nov. 18, 1987   President Reagan was blamed for failing in his constitutional duty by the congressional committee report on the Iran-Contra affair.

Feb. 5, 1988   A federal grand jury in Miami indicted Panamanian General Manuel Noriega in connection with illegal drug dealings.

April 23, 1988   A ban on smoking in passenger planes went into effect.

Aug. 8, 1988   The first night baseball game in the history of Chicago's Wrigley Field took place, though it was rained out.

ILLINI MOMENT

WHITE OUT/MACKOVIC IN:

John Mackovic replaced Mike White as the Illini football coach on Feb. 3, 1988.

Just 16 days expired between the firing of Fighting Illini head football coach Mike White and the hiring of his replacement, John Mackovic. The furious chain of events began January 18, 1988, when White submitted his resignation to Director of Athletics Neale Stoner. An NCAA investigation into alleged recruiting violations prompted White's action. Said Interim Chancellor Morton Weir,"The Athletic Association's Board of Directors and I believe that Coach White has responded appropriately by tendering his resignation." The search for White's replacement began immediately, with the list of candidates including Illini defensive coordinator Howard Tippett, former Northwestern coach Dennis Green, Boston College's Jack Bicknell, and Stoner's personal choice, ex-Kansas City Chiefs coach John Mackovic. The AA's board convened for more than three hours on February 2 before arriving at the decision to hire Mackovic. The 44-year-old Wake Forest graduate immediately went about hiring a staff and salvaging a nearly impossible recruiting scenerio by signing eventual Illini standouts Brad Hopkins, Jason Verduzco, and John Wright.

Heather Singalewitch

WOMEN'S MILESTONES

MARCH 24-25, 1988

Heather Singalewitch became the first Illinois women's athlete to be honored as the Big Ten Conference's Gymnast of the Year. She shared the honor with Minnesota's Marie Roethlisberger. The Illini sophomore tied Minnesota's Lisa Wittwer for the all-around championship with a 38.10 score, tied for second on the uneven bars (9-40), took third on the balance beam (9.60) and tied for third in the vault (9.50).

Illini coach Ed Beard (right) and his star golfer, Steve Stricker.

I Illini Item

ILLINOIS' MEN'S GOLF TEAM ended a 47-year championship drought May 16, 1988, when it defeated six-time Big Ten titlist Ohio State by 20 strokes. Illini junior Steve Stricker was named the conference's Player of the Year for firing a 72-hole total 279 to out distance teammate Mike Small and OSU's Chris Smith by 14 shots. The triumph by Ed Beard's squad came at home on Savoy's Orange Course. Said Stricker afterwards, "I don't think you could ask for anything more than winning the Big Ten championship on your home course with your family and friends watching."

Illini Lists

ILLINOIS' GREATEST FOREIGN ATHLETES

Illinois' grand tradition in athletics has been bolstered by several athletes who were products of foreign countries.

Robert Archibald, basketball, Scotland
Darren Boyer, football, Canada
Carmel Corbett, track, New Zealand
Charlton Ehizuelen, track, Nigeria
Victor Feinstein, gymnastics, Israel
Perdita Felicien, track, Canada
Oliver Freelove, tennis, England
Kirsten Gleis, volleyball, Holland
Jenny & Susanna Kallur, track, Sweden
George Kerr, track, Jamaica
Marko Koers, track, Holland
Andy Kpedi, basketball, Nigeria
Damir Krupalija, basketball, Yugoslavia
Petra Laverman, volleyball, Holland
Graeme McGufficke, swimming, Australia
Iveta Marcauskaite, basketball, Lithuania
Herb McKenley, track, Jamaica
Cirilo McSween, track, Panama
Lindsey Nimmo, tennis, England
Kari Samsten, gymnastics, Finland
Gilmarcio Sanches, gymnastics, Brazil

Illini Legend

Mary Eggers

Wrote one sports journalist, Mary Eggers "stalks the court with an icy look of controlled violence that combines the cool of Star Trek's Mr. Spock with the rage of a pit bull." That analogy aptly described the woman who went on to become the most prolific player in University of Illinois volleyball history. From Big Ten Freshman of the Year in 1985 to conference MVP from 1986-88, no one individual dominated the court quite like Eggers. She led the nation in hitting percentage her sophomore and senior seasons and set Fighting Illini career records for aces, blocks, kills and attack percentage. The four Illini teams on which she played had a cumulative record of 136 victories against only 17 losses for a winning percentage of .889. Eggers's crowning glory came following her senior season in 1988 when she earned the Honda Broderick Award, symbolic of the nation's top collegiate volleyball player. Following her graduation in 1991, she played professional volleyball in Europe. Currently, Mary Eggers Tendler is an assistant volleyball coach at James Madison University.

Nigeria's Andy Kpedi

ILLINI LORE

Morton W. Weir, interim chancellor at the Urbana-Champaign campus since August of 1987, was unanimously approved as permanent chancellor by the University of Illinois' Board of Trustees, April 14, 1988. His appointment vacated the post left by former chancellor Thomas Everhart, who left the UI to become president of Cal Tech. Weir also served as UI's acting chancellor between the terms of former chancellors Jack Peltason and William Gerberding. Among the previous positions held by Weir at the UI were head of the psychology department, vice chancellor of administrative affairs, and vice president of academic affairs. He stepped down as chancellor in 1992 to return to classroom duties.

1988-89

AMERICA'S TIME CAPSULE

Sept. 29, 1988   NASA launched its first manned space flight in 32 months, carrying a $100 million communications satellite.

Nov. 8, 1988   Vice President George Bush defeated Governor Michael Dukakis of Massachusetts in the presidential election.

Jan. 22, 1989   The San Francisco 49ers defeated the Cincinnati Bengals, 20-16, in Super Bowl XXIII. Joe Montana passed for a record 357 yards as the 49ers won their third Super Bowl title.

March 24, 1989   The oil tanker Exxon Valdez struck a reef in Prince William Sound, Alaska, leaking more than a million barrels of crude oil into the water.

Aug. 10, 1989   President Bush nominated Army General Colin Powell to be chairman of the Joint Chiefs of Staff. Powell became the first African-American to hold the nation's highest military post.

ILLINI MOMENT

THE FLYING ILLINI:

To many Illini fans, the 1988-89 men's basketball squad is the standard by which other Illini teams are measured. Coach Henson's athletes rolled through the regular season with a 27-4 record, including victories in their first 17 games. That 17th win, a 103-92 double-overtime victory against Georgia Tech at the Assembly Hall on January 22, catapulted the Illini to the top of the national rankings. Unfortunately, the bad news in that contest against the Yellowjackets was an injury to Kendall Gill, which triggered three Illinois losses in the next four games. Strong play by fellow all-star Nick Anderson, cocaptains Kenny Battle and Lowell Hamilton, and sophomore Marcus Liberty kept the Illini going until Gill returned with two games left in the regular season. The Illini beat Iowa and Michigan, finishing with a 14-4 conference record, and entered the NCAA tournament as the No. 1 seed in the Midwest Regional. There they easily disposed of McNeese State and Ball State. In the third-round battle against Louisville, a strong effort by Liberty helped Illinois overcome an injury to Hamilton, and the Illini beat the Cardinals, 72-60. In the regional finals against Syracuse, Anderson came up with his most impressive game, scoring 24 points and grabbing 16 rebounds as Illinois beat the Orangemen, 89-86, to qualify for the Final Four in Seattle. The April 1 semifinal pitted the Illini against Michigan, a team they had already overcome twice during the regular season. Unfortunately, the third time was a charm for the Wolverines, and Michigan prevailed 83-81 to knock the Illini out of their chance to win a national title. After the season, Anderson, Illinois' most valuable player, announced that he was going to forego his final year of college eligibility to enter the NBA draft.

Nick Anderson (left), Coach Lou Henson and Kenny Battle triumphantly exit the Metrodome floor.

Women's Milestones
The quartet of (left to right) Angela McClatchey, Celena Mondie-Milner, Renee Carr, and Leticia Beverly combined to win the Big Ten's 400-meter relay title.

WOMEN'S MILESTONES

Illinois' women's track and field squad captured the 1989 outdoor title at IUPUI Track Stadium in Indianapolis with a record-setting 169 points, 31 more than any other previous champion had registered in the eight-year history of the meet. Fighting Illini athletes captured titles in 11 of the 19 events, including four by Celena Mondie-Milner (100- and 200-meter dashes and 400- and 1,600-meter relays). Predictably, eight of the 16 athletes who earned All-Big Ten honors were Illini. Joining Mondie-Milner were Shayla Baine, Lisa Balagtas, Leticia Beverly, Renee Carr, Cindy Lawrence, Angela McClatchey, and Debbie Smith.

Shawn Wax's touchdown grab pulled the Illini within range of overtaking Indiana.

I Illini Item

WITH ONLY THREE AND A HALF MINUTES left in the game and Illinois trailing Indiana by 11 points, 20-9, Fighting Illini football fortunes looked hopeless at Memorial Stadium November 5, 1988. Coach John Mackovic's squad didn't give up, though, narrowing the Hoosier lead to 20-15 on a spectacular shoe-string grab by Shawn Wax from quarterback Jeff George with 1:27 remaining. On the first play of Indiana's final possession, Illini defensive back Chris Green knocked the ball loose from IU's Dave Schnell and into the arms of linebacker Julyon Brown. George confidently directed the Illini drive down the field by mixing runs and passes, and with just 26 ticks left on the clock, George threw a game-winning TD pass to Mike Bellamy. The Illini escaped with a one-point victory, 21-20.

Illini Legend

David Zeddies

The most well known individual athletic award presented to an intercollegiate athlete during any particular year is undoubtedly the Heisman Trophy, symbolic of the outstanding college football player in America. Perhaps the least known single prize in college athletics might be the Nissen Award, emblematic of the top male gymnast. So during the 1988-89 season, while Oklahoma State gridiron star Barry Sanders was picking up his hardware in New York City, Illinois gymnast David Zeddies was doing much the same April 12, 1989 in Lincoln, Nebraska. Zeddies, a native of Union Springs, New York, became the Illini's first Nissen Award winner since it was initially presented in 1966. He combined his marvelous athletic ability with sportsmanship and leadership and was also an outstanding scholar. Zeddies excelled on the rings and the parallel bars, earning 1988 Big Ten Gymnast of the Year honors and helping to lead Coach Yoshi Hayasaki's Illini squad to the 1989 NCAA title. He earned his doctorate at Northwestern University and currently serves as a research associate at Loyola of Chicago's Parmly Hearing Institute.

Nick Anderson

Illini Lists

JIMMY COLLINS AND DICK NAGY'S TOP TEN MEMORIES OF THE 1988-89 SEASON

Lou Henson's longtime assistants, Jimmy Collins and Dick Nagy, chose their top ten memories of the 1988-89 "Flying Illini".

1. March 26 vs. Syracuse: The Illini earn a spot in the Final Four.
2. December 19 vs. Missouri: Kenny Battle scores 28 as UI improves record to 8-0. The Illini overcame an 18-point deficit.
3. March 4 at Indiana: Nick Anderson hits a miracle three-pointer to beat Hoosiers.
4. March 24 vs. Louisville: Illinois wins its 30th game behind Anderson's 24 points.
5. January 22 vs. Georgia Tech: Illini earn No. 1 ranking with two-overtime win.
6. December 22 at LSU: Illini crush the Tigers by 27 points in Baton Rouge, scoring school-record 127 points.
7. March 11 at Michigan: UI wins school-record 27th game at Ann Arbor.
8. February 9 vs. Ohio State: Stephen Bardo holds Buckeye star Jay Burson to nine points.
9. January 25 vs. Indiana: Illini snap league-leading Indiana's 13-game victory streak.
10. March 8 vs. Iowa: Lowell Hamilton, Battle and Anderson play final home game. Kendall Gill returned to lineup.

ILLINI LORE

. . . .

The Beckman Center was dedicated April 7, 1989, just two and one-half years after the ground-breaking ceremonies. The new home for the executive and scientific staffs of the National Center for Supercomputing Applications had a $50 million price tag, $40 million of which was donated by philanthropist Arnold Beckman ('22). Located on University Avenue between Wright and Mathews Streets, the 310,000 square-foot facility is on the same site as Illinois Field, home of Illini football through most of 1923 and Illini baseball through 1987.

1989-90

AMERICA'S TIME CAPSULE

Sept. 21, 1989   Hurricane Hugo ravished Charleston, South Carolina, causing more than a billion dollars in damages.

Oct. 17, 1989   An earthquake measuring 6.9 on the Richter scale hit the San Francisco Bay area, killing more than 60 people.

Feb. 28, 1990   Black nationalist Nelson Mandela met with President Bush, just two weeks after his release from a 27-year imprisonment in South Africa.

May 31, 1990   Mikhail Gorbachev met with President Bush in a Washington summit.

Aug. 7, 1990   American troops, responding to the crisis in the Middle East, left for Saudi Arabia as Operation Desert Storm began.

ILLINI MOMENT

ILLINI BOWL OVER VIRGINIA:

For the first time in more than a quarter of a century, Illinois' football team began its season with a win and ended it with a bowl-game victory. At one time, the 1989 campaign was scheduled to begin several thousand miles away in Moscow with the first-ever Glastnost Bowl, but a last-minute change in plans placed the Fighting Illini instead at the Los Angeles Coliseum against highly ranked Southern Cal. A national television audience on Labor Day night witnessed one of the most exciting comebacks in UI history when quarterback Jeff George tossed a pair of fourth-quarter touchdowns to Shawn Wax and Steven Williams. The 14-13 triumph over the Trojans began a string of seven Illini successes in its first eight games, highlighted by Illinois' second straight win over Ohio State, George's triumphant return to Purdue, a miracle victory at Michigan State, and a decisive 31-7 pasting of the Iowa Hawkeyes at Kinnick Stadium. On November 11 at Memorial Stadium, Illinois hosted Michigan for the inside track to the Big Ten championship. However, for the second year in a row the Illini stumbled, forcing them to refocus their sights on a second-place conference finish and a berth in the Florida Citrus Bowl. Mackovic's talented troops, led by a defensive unit that featured five future pros (Moe Gardner, Henry Jones, Mel Agee, Chris Green, and Darrick Brownlow), easily disposed of Indiana and Northwestern, and the Illini began packing for Orlando. The Illini climbed on the plane at Champaign, where the wind chill was a brutal 50 degrees

Jeff George in action

below zero, and were similarly greeted by Florida's worst cold snap in years. But, like the weather, the Illini eventually warmed up to their task, defeating 10-1 Virginia by a score of 31-21. The pinpoint passes of game MVP George to his trusty receiver, Mike Bellamy, ended a 26-year bowl victory drought and lifted the Illini to 10th in the final national rankings with a 10-2 record. It would prove to be the final time that Jeff George would wear an Illini uniform, as he declared for the NFL draft and became the first overall pick of his hometown Indianapolis Colts.

1990 women's gymnastics team

WOMEN'S MILESTONES

MARCH 23-24, 1990

The Fighting Illini women's gymnastics team captured its first-ever official Big Ten title, nipping Michigan State and Minnesota in a championship where only four points separated the first and last place teams. Coach Bev Mackes's squad boasted four individual titlists, including Denise Lamborn in the vault, Peggy Pullman and Laura Knutson on the balance beam, and Heather Singalewitch in floor exercise. Mackes earned honors as Big Ten Coach of the Year.

Andy McVey

I Illini Item

ON JANUARY 19, 1990, the Fighting Illini men's swimming and diving team defeated Coach "Doc" Councilman's powerful Indiana Hoosiers, 60-53, marking Illinois' first dual-meet victory over IU since 1957. Illini coach Don Sammons got the most out of "Senior Night" at the IMPE Pool as final-year swimmers Andy McVey (50- and 100-yard freestyle) and Jim Mackin (200-yard butterfly) had first-place finishes. McVey and Mackin also were key members of the winning 400-yard medley relay unit.

Illini Legend

Kendall Gill

ESPN's Dick Vitale (left) and Kendall Gill.

Kendall Gill joined Coach Lou Henson's Fighting Illini basketball team as the sleeper of Illinois' 1985 recruits, hidden behind the press clippings of fellow classmates Larry Smith and Steve Bardo. Four years later, he left as the Big Ten's scoring leader and a first-team All-American. You'd be hard-pressed to find a more beloved player in Illini basketball history than the charismatic kid from Matteson, Illinois. Gill proved to be one of the sparkplugs on Illinois' famed "Flying Illini" team of 1988-89. That squad glided to a 17-0 start and the nation's No. 1 ranking, but a broken bone in his foot sidelined him for 12 games, and the Illini juggernaut became just another team. Upon Gill's return to the lineup, the Illini quickly regrouped and rolled through Indianapolis and Minneapolis into the Final Four. During his sensational senior season at Illinois in 1989-90, Gill averaged 20 points per game and wound up his career as the school's seventh all-time leading scorer with 1,409 points. Selected in the first round of the 1990 NBA draft by the Charlotte Hornets, he was traded to Seattle in September of 1993, then back to Charlotte in 1995. In the spring of 1994, Gill generously donated $300,000 to the Cunningham Children's Home in Urbana.

Illini Lists

ILLINI WHO WERE FIRST-ROUND NBA DRAFT PICKS

1970   Mike Price, 17th pick, New Jersey Knicks
1973   Nick Weatherspoon, 13 pick, Washington Bullets
1983   Derek Harper, 11th pick, Dallas Mavericks
1987   Ken Norman, 19th pick, Los Angeles Clippers
1989   Nick Anderson, 11th pick, Orlando Magic
1989   Kenny Battle, 27th pick, Detroit Pistons
1990   Kendall Gill, 5th pick, Charlotte Hornets
2002   Frank Williams, 25th pick, Denver Nuggets.

Kenny Battle slams vs. Wisconsin, Dec. 12, 1989

ILLINI LORE

The 94-year-old University of Illinois Observatory earned the designation of a National Historic Landmark in the spring of 1990, placing it alongside the Brooklyn Bridge, Carnegie Hall and the Alamo. The Observatory's 12-inch refracting telescope, first used in 1896, is still being used by UI students for viewing the heavens and for instruction in general astronomy.

1990-91

AMERICA'S TIME CAPSULE

Nov. 8, 1990   President Bush doubled U.S. forces in the Persian Gulf region to nearly half a million troops.

Jan. 16, 1991   U.S. and allied planes attacked Iraq's communications systems and chemical weapons plants.

Feb. 27, 1991   The United States and allied forces claimed an overwhelming victory, pushing back the Iraqi army.

March 3, 1991   Los Angeles policemen stopped and beat African-American motorist Rodney King, and an observer recorded the event on videotape.

June 12, 1991   Michael Jordan led the Chicago Bulls to their first-ever NBA championship, beating the Los Angeles Lakers, four games to one.

ILLINI MOMENT

Among the players named to Illinois' All-Century Football Team were (front row, left to right) Alex Agase (#59), Johnny Karras (#48), J.C. Caroline (#26) and Al Brosky (#27), plus (back row, left to right) Mike Bass, Doug Dieken, Ed O'Bradovich, Dick Butkus, Dike Eddleman, Don Thorp, Jeff George and Jim Grabowski.

Women's Milestones: The famed "Whiz Kids" participated in the ribbon-cutting ceremony at the rededication of Huff Hall. Shown here are (left to right) Jack Smiley, Ken Menke, Andy Phillip, Barb Winsett, Laura Bush, Art Mathisen, Gene Vance and Mike Hebert.

ILLINI FOOTBALL CELEBRATES ITS CENTENNIAL SEASON:

Coach John Mackovic's Fighting Illini shared the Big Ten football title with Iowa, Michigan and Michigan State in 1990, but that championship isn't what that season will be remembered for by most University of Illinois gridiron fans. The 1990 season was highlighted by the centennial celebration of Illini football, the largest athletic promotion ever staged at the Urbana-Champaign campus. The symbol of the event was a logo designed by UI student Rebecca Byrne, depicting a silhouette of Red Grange and the columns of Memorial Stadium. Among the key elements of the Centennial were: a traveling display of Illini football memorabilia that visited 44 locations around the state of Illinois; an historical book and video; banners on the street lights surrounding and leading to the stadium that featured each of the 100 years of Illini football; and a 25-man All-Century Team that was selected by more than 10,000 UI fans. For each of the six home games in 1990, a different segment of Illini football was honored, with more than 500 former UI gridiron stars ultimately returning to their alma mater and being individually introduced to their adoring fans. Said one Illini football alumnus, "It was a thrill to once again walk onto the field, this time in the presence of my wife, son and daughter."

WOMEN'S MILESTONES

On September 4, 1990, the Fighting Illini volleyball team christened historic George Huff Hall as its new home. On hand for the festivities were the five men who provided the old gymnasium with its greatest basketball memories--Illinois' famed "Whiz Kids." The quintet of Jack Smiley, Ken Menke, Andy Phillip, Art Mathisen, and Gene Vance joined volleyball cocaptains Barb Winsett and Laura Bush and Coach Mike Hebert at center court for the traditional ribbon-cutting. The Illini spikers then disposed of Southern Illinois in four games.

Bubba Smith

I Illini Item

THE APRIL 30, 1991 PERFORMANCE by Illinois' 28-17 baseball team over UI-Chicago produced some awesome numbers, but none were more incredible than those generated by first baseman Bubba Smith. The junior from Riverside, California had seven official at-bats, collected hits a record-tying six times, including a record four home runs, scored a record-tying five times, drove home a record 10 RBIs, and accumulated a record 18 total bases.

Illini Legend

Jon Llewellyn

As a freshman wrestler at Hinsdale Central High School in suburban Chicago, Jon Llewellyn was a 98-pound weakling. But seven years later, he rose to the title of NCAA heavyweight champion. "I took my lumps as a 98-pounder," Llewellyn confessed. "I never dreamed of becoming a national champion. I put in my time lifting weights and working out. I would eat all the time, even when I didn't want to." From 1988-91, the 240-pound heavyweight was the only shining light in the Illini wrestling program. Three times—as a sophomore, junior and senior—Llewellyn won the league title, setting an Illinois record in that weight class. His most glorious season came as a senior in '90-91 when he rolled through his competition with a perfect 33-0 record, boosting his career record to 97 wins against only 23 losses and three draws. Llewellyn's ultimate accomplishment came March 13, 1991 when he beat defending champion Kurt Angle of Clarion State, 6-3, at the NCAA championships in Iowa City, Iowa. Later that spring, he was honored as Illinois' Male Athlete of the Year, beating out two-time football All-American Moe Gardner. Today Llewellyn and his family reside in Manteno, where he works as structural engineer for the firm of Sargent and Lundy.

Illini Lists

HOWARD GRIFFITH'S NCAA RECORD EIGHT TOUCHDOWNS

On September 22, 1990, Illinois' Howard Griffith became the first player in NCAA Division IA football to score eight touchdowns in a single game. He broke the record of seven TDs by Mississippi's Arnold Boykin, set against Mississippi State in 1951. Here's a score-by-score description of Griffith's explosion versus Southern Illinois at Memorial Stadium:

First TD: 5-yard burst off right tackle, 10:06 left in 1st quarter.
Second TD: 51-yard up-the-middle sprint, 8:50 left in 2nd quarter.
Third TD: 7-yard up-the-middle run, 4:53 left in 2nd quarter.
Fourth TD: 41-yard dash off the left side, 3:10 left in 2nd quarter.
Fifth TD: 5-yard run off right tackle, 12:34 left in 3rd quarter.
Sixth TD: 18-yard, tackle-breaking zigzagger, 10:10 left in 3rd quarter.
Seventh TD: 5-yard run off right tackle, 6:07 left in 3rd quarter.
Eighth TD: 3-yard dive off right tackle, 1:25 left in 3rd quarter.

Howard Griffith (#29) strikes a pose alongside a cardboard image of Red Grange.

ILLINI LORE

On November 7, 1990, despite finding Illinois not guilty of any of the original charges brought against the men's basketball program, the NCAA levied harsh penalties against the University of Illinois. Based on what it called "lack of institutional control" and a third appearance by the school in the previous six years before the infractions committee, the NCAA issued a three-year probation of Coach Henson's program. The coaching staff was originally accused of offering money and a car to recruit Deon Thomas, but was eventually exonerated of any unethical conduct. Chancellor Morton Weir acknowledged some procedural and administrative shortcomings in the basketball program, but was disturbed by the NCAA's labeling of "lack of institutional control." "Over the past five years or so," said Weir, "the university has taken extraordinary measures to ensure the integrity of intercollegiate athletics on this campus. Our record in recent years demonstrates that we do not hesitate to take the strongest actions when they are warranted."

1991-92

AMERICA'S TIME CAPSULE

Sept. 9, 1991   Boxing champ Mike Tyson was indicted on rape charges by a Marion County (Indiana) grand jury.

Nov. 7, 1991   Basketball's Magic Johnson retired after announcing that he had tested positive for the HIV virus.

Dec. 25, 1991   Mikhail Gorbachev resigned his position as leader of the Soviet Union.

May 1, 1992   President Bush ordered federal troops to enter riot-torn Los Angeles. The unrest was triggered when a jury acquitted four policemen charged with beating Rodney King.

May 22, 1992   More than 50 million TV viewers tuned in to watch Johnny Carson's final appearance on the "Tonight Show."

ILLINI MOMENT

Lou Tepper and his Illini take the field at the John Hancock Bowl in El Paso, Texas.

TEPPER PROMOTED AFTER MACKOVIC LEAVES FOR TEXAS:

In a whirlwind 24-hour period, Illinois' football program lost one head coach and hired another. Rumors had constantly circulated around the status of athletic director/head coach John Mackovic, and on December 12, 1991, the highly regarded Illini mentor was hired by the University of Texas. Quickly, Chancellor Morton Weir and interim AD Bob Todd promoted Lou Tepper the very next day as Mackovic's replacement. "We knew we had the right person right here on campus," said Weir. "Lou is a man of integrity, with a strong orientation toward the academic success of student athletes." The 46-year-old Tepper pledged his long-term commitment toward the University, saying, "If I had just wanted to be a head coach, I could have done so several years ago. That was not my goal. My goal was to be a head coach at a prestigious institution and to be at one institution for a very long time." Tepper didn't need to wait the customary nine months to coach his first game, as he directed the Illini 18 days later in their December 31 John Hancock Bowl matchup against UCLA. The Illini lost to the Bruins by a score of 6-3. Tepper would coach five full seasons at Illinois, recording a 25-31-2 mark.

Big Ten Commissioner Jim Delaney spoke at a 10th anniversary luncheon at the U of I.

WOMEN'S MILESTONES

SEPTEMBER 28, 1991

The University of Illinois celebrated the 10th anniversary of women's athletics in the Big Ten Conference in grand style during the 1991-92 season, honoring a multitude of athletes at a luncheon at the Illini Union. All-Decade teams were chosen for each of the eight sports, and, from that group, a 20-person all-star team was selected. Each sport also celebrated the milestone season with its own individual reunion.

Coach Gary Winckler and women's track star Tonja Buford.

I Illini Item

COACH GARY WINCKLER'S women's track team swept to Big Ten championships both indoors and out during the 1992 season. At the indoor meet February 28-29 at Columbus, Illinois outlasted Wisconsin 81-76 in a meet that went down to the final event, the 4x400-meter relay. Outdoors at Minneapolis, May 22-23, the Illini cruised to a 122-99 victory over the runner-up Badgers. Just as she had been indoors, junior Tonja Buford was selected as the Big Ten Athlete of the championship, again winning three individual events.

Illini Lists

ILLINOIS' ALL-STAR ALL-DECADE TEAM

As part of the celebration of 10 years of women's athletics in the Big Ten Conference in 1991-92, the University of Illinois selected an all-star all-decade team for its entire women's program.

- Leticia Beverly, track
- Nancy Brookhart, volleyball
- Tonja Buford, track
- Laura Bush, volleyball
- Robin Duffy, swimming
- *Mary Eggers, volleyball
- Kendra Gantt, basketball
- Renee Heiken, golf
- Heidi Helmke, gymnastics
- Disa Johnson, volleyball
- Becky Kaiser, track
- Lynette Robinson, basketball
- Heather Singalewitch, gymnastics

- Denise Lamborn, gymnastics
- Petra Laverman, volleyball
- Celena Mondi-Milner, track
- Mary Ellen Murphy, golf
- Lindsey Nimmo, tennis
- Jonelle Polk, basketball
- Lisa Robinson, basketball

*Athlete of the Decade

Robin Duffy

Illini Legend

Renee Heiken

Renee Heiken, the greatest golfer in the 20-year history of women's athletics at the University of Illinois, began honing her skills on the links at the tender age of six. The only child of John and Ronda Heiken of Metamora, Illinois didn't have the luxury of having a course in her home town, so dad had to cart young Renee to a nine-hole course in nearby Eureka. In high school, she played on the boys' team and was the most valuable player each year. Heiken came to Illinois after graduating early from high school. Her winning ways continued with the Illini as she claimed a total of 15 tournament championships during her career, including eight in 1992-93 alone. Twice, in 1991 and '93, she earned honors as the Big Ten championship medalist. Heiken played three consecutive years in the NCAA tournament, placing among the tournament's top six golfers each time. Over 127 rounds, Heiken amazingly averaged just more than 75 strokes per 18 holes, including a varsity-record 68 at Hawaii's Rainbow Wahine Invitational in 1993. The two-time Illini Female Athlete of the Year and one-time national Player of the Year is currently an assistant golf coach at Bradley University.

ILLINI LORE

The University of Illinois' 68-year-old Memorial Stadium received an $18 million facelift between November 1991 and August 1992. Among the project's main objectives was the replacement of all the concrete bleachers in both upper decks, as well as the replacement of the top 25 rows of the main stands. The stadium's electrical and drainage systems were also brought up to code. Funds for the project were raised through the issuance of revenue bonds by the UI Auxiliary Facilities System.

1992-93

AMERICA'S TIME CAPSULE

Nov. 3, 1992   Bill Clinton won the presidential election, defeating incumbent George Bush and independent candidate Ross Perot.

Dec. 8, 1992   The first United Nations-authorized troops landed in Somalia to assist the starving populace.

Feb. 26, 1993   New York City's World Trade Center was bombed by terrorists.

April 19, 1993   Nearly 100 people perished in a fire ending the 51-day standoff of David Koresh's Branch Davidians against federal agents in Waco, Texas.

June 20, 1993   The Chicago Bulls defeated the Phoenix Suns, 99-98, to win their third consecutive NBA championship.

ILLINI MOMENT

KAUFMANN'S BUZZER BEATER UPSETS IOWA:

High-flying Iowa, led by lanky Acie Earl, invaded Illinois' Assembly Hall February 4, 1993 with soaring hopes, but a miracle shot by Andy Kaufmann instead sent the Hawkeyes home minus a few tail feathers. The Illini had not defeated an opponent ranked in the Top 10 in its last 12 tries, but this night belonged to the orange and blue. Freshman sharpshooter Richard Keene kept Illinois close throughout the game by connecting on five three-pointers, but he saved the dramatics for his senior teammate from Jacksonville. After a fluke basket by Iowa with just two seconds left gave the Hawkeyes a two-point lead, Illinois immediately called time out. Illini coach Lou Henson drew up his team's last-gasp shot, calling for T.J. Wheeler to heave a three-quarter-court pass in the direction of the Illini basket. Kaufmann hauled in the pass in front of the Illinois bench, then spun, squared up and lofted a 23-footer toward the iron rim. The ball passed cleanly into the net as the buzzer sounded, sending a tumultuous throng of Illini fans onto the court in celebration of a 78-77 Illinois victory.

Andy Kaufmann's dramatic shot vs. nationally ranked Iowa set off one of the wildest postgame scenes in Assembly Hall history.

Lindsey Nimmo

Kirsten Gleis

WOMEN'S MILESTONES

A conference-record four University of Illinois women's stars earned Big Ten Athlete of the Year honors during the 1992-93 season, a feat that may never be duplicated. Volleyball All-American Kirsten Gleis dominated that sport in what would turn out to be her only season as an Illini. Tonja Buford ruled Big Ten track and field, winning nine indoor and outdoor conference titles altogether as a senior. Golfer Renee Heiken was the medalist in the 1993 conference championship, repeating as her sport's Player of the Year. Finally, on the tennis courts, no Big Ten player was better than Lindsey Nimmo. She also captured Player of the Year honors.

Renee Heiken (left) and Jamie Fairbanks

I Illini Item

ILLINOIS GOLFERS scored a rare feat during the 1993 season, as individuals from both the men's and women's teams grabbed medalist honors in their respective Big Ten championship meets. From May 7-9 at Iowa City, senior Renee Heiken shot a 72-hole total of 300 to capture women's honors. Then , a week later at Bloomington, Indiana, junior Illini golfer Jamie Fairbanks averaged 71 strokes per round to win the men's conference tournament. That allowed Illinois to become only the second school in Big Ten history to sweep individual titles in both the women's and men's championships in the same season.

Illini Legend

Tonja Buford

Tonja Buford's magnificent career at the University of Illinois is underlined by the fact that she won not only more individual Big Ten track titles than any other Illini athlete, but also more than any other women's or men's athlete in the history of the conference. Her total of 25 championships broke the record of 23 by Wisconsin distance star Suzy Favor, the namesake of the Big Ten's Female Athlete of the Year Award. From 1990-93, Buford dominated hurdles competition at league track and field meets. Buford's eight individual titles and two relay championships during her senior season may never be broken. She was a four-time Big Ten Track Athlete of the Year and was named Athlete of the Championship three times. The Dayton, Ohio native became the first Illini women's track runner to ever compete in the Olympic Games when she qualified for the 400-meter hurdles at the 1992 Summer Games in Barcelona, Spain. Buford shared Illinois' Female Athlete of the Year Award in 1992 and won it outright in 1993. Today, Tonja Buford-Bailey competes on the professional track and field circuit.

Illini Lists

ILLINI BASEBALL CAREER HOME RUN LEADERS

(through 2001 season)

1. 48 Scott Spiezio (1991-93)
2. 40 Sean Mulligan (1989-91)
3. 38 Darrin Fletcher (1985-87)
   38 Forry Wells (1991-94)
   38 Josh Klimek (1993, 95-96)
   38 Craig Marquie (1997-00)
   38 D.J. Svihlik (1997-00)
8. 35 Brian McClure (1993-96)
9. 33 Bubba Smith (1989-91)
10. 31 Tom Sinak (1992-95)

Scott Spiezio's 48 career home runs stand as Illinois' all-time record.

ILLINI LORE

Michael Aiken, 60-year-old provost at the University of Pennsylvania since 1987, was chosen as chancellor for the University of Illinois at Urbana-Champaign in early February, 1993. The native of Arkansas and University of Mississippi graduate replaced Morton Weir, who stepped down to return to the classroom. "Though some board members had emphasized a search for women and minority candidates," said Board of Trustees President Judith Calder, "we were satisfied that Aiken's experience showed his commitment to equal opportunity." Aiken retired as chancellor in 2001.

1993-94

AMERICA'S TIME CAPSULE

Oct. 6, 1993   Michael Jordan shocked professional basketball by announcing his retirement from the Chicago Bulls.

Oct. 23, 1993   Joe Carter hit a three-run homer in the bottom of the ninth inning off Philadelphia's Mitch Williams to give the Toronto Blue Jays their second consecutive World Series title.

Jan. 17, 1994   An earthquake in southern California killed 57.

June 17, 1994   Former football star O.J. Simpson, charged with two counts of murder, led a convoy of police cars on a 60-mile chase before returning to his home.

Aug. 12, 1994   Major league baseball players went on strike. The balance of the season, including the World Series, was cancelled on September 14.

ILLINI MOMENT

ILLINI SURPRISE MICHIGAN:

Quarterback Johnny Johnson (#13) sets himself for his dramatic touchdown pass to Jim Klein.

Winning football games at Michigan has never been an easy chore for Illinois, so the Fighting Illini victory at Ann Arbor October 23, 1993 was especially gratifying for Coach Lou Tepper's troops. As had been the case so many times before in contests at mammoth Michigan Stadium, Illinois trailed the 13th-ranked Wolverines entering the fourth quarter. A Ty Douthard touchdown with 11:37 remaining narrowed the Illini deficit to 21-17, but Illinois' task appeared hopeless with just more than a minute remaining and Michigan in control of the ball. Suddenly, UI's Simeon Rice stripped the ball away from maize and blue running back Ricky Powers at the Michigan 44-yard line, and a confident Illini offense raced back onto the field. Quarterback Johnny Johnson methodically guided Illinois into the end zone in six plays, capped by a fourth-down 15-yard touchdown pass to Jim Klein. The 24-21 Illini victory at Ann Arbor snapped a 27-year road jinx and presented Illinois with one of its most satisfying victories of the 1990s.

The University of Illinois' Assembly Hall is the site each spring of the Scholar-Athlete All-Star Banquet.

WOMEN'S MILESTONES

FEBRUARY 18-19, 1994

Senior swimmer Jennifer Sadler set Illinois varsity records at the 1994 Big Ten Swimming and Diving Championships in Indianapolis. She first broke the Illini mark in the 50-yard freestyle (:23.62), then the 100-yard freestyle (:51.28).

Illinois' 1993-94 senior basketball players (front, left to right) Deon Thomas and Tom Michael, (back, left to right) T.J. Wheeler and Gene Cross won 15 of 16 games at the Assembly Hall.

I Illini Item

ONLY A 74-70 LOSS to 15th-ranked Michigan spoiled an otherwise perfect men's basketball season for Illinois at the Assembly Hall in 1993-94, Coach Lou Henson's Fighting Illini scored victories in 15 of 16 games on their freshly painted home court, including a shiny 8-1 mark in Big Ten contests. Among Illinois' highlights were a Super Bowl Sunday triumph over Indiana before a national television audience, UI's 13th consecutive home court win over a talented Wisconsin club, and a senior night victory by Deon Thomas, T.J. Wheeler, and Tommy Michael over Minnesota.

Illini Lists

ORIGINAL COSTS OF ILLINOIS' CURRENT ATHLETIC FACILITIES

*$40,000	Kenney Gym (1902)
$702,000	Armory (1915)
$2.5 million	Memorial Stadium (1923)
$725,000	Huff Hall (1925)
$250,000	Savoy Golf Course (1950, original 18 holes)
$8.35 million	Assembly Hall (1963)
$2.2 million	Outdoor Track & Field Stadium (1987)
$1.64 million	Illinois Field (1988)
$5.3 million	Atkins Tennis Center (1991)
$7.2 million	Bielfeldt Athletic Administration Building (1996)
$12.5 million	Irwin Indoor Practice Facility (2000)

*Estimated cost, due to the gymnasium being included in a bid of three different buildings

The $12.5 million Irwin Indoor Practice Facility.

Illini Legend

Deon Thomas

The basketball career of Deon Thomas was a series of peaks and valleys. As a youngster, the soft-spoken Thomas survived the brutal experiences of growing up on the streets of Chicago's West Side to become one of the city's finest prep players at Simeon High School, ultimately earning academic eligibility and an athletic scholarship at the University of Illinois. Just a few months later, false allegations of NCAA recruiting violations, based on audio tapes obtained by an assistant coach at Iowa, turned Thomas's future down a road of great despair. He strongly considered leaving school, but instead stayed to prove his innocence. After sitting out his freshman season, Thomas began a brilliant career at Illinois during the 1990-91 campaign by averaging 15 points per game. His senior year, 1993-94, saw him break Fighting Illini records nearly every time he played. Not only did Thomas become the school's all-time leading scorer with 2,129 points, he also set UI marks for field goals, free throws, free-throw attempts and blocked shots, and ranked second-best in rebounds and field-goal percentage. Following his graduation from Illinois, Thomas was the first pick in the second round of the National Basketball Association draft by the Dallas Mavericks. He played professional ball in Spain during the 2001-02 season.

ILLINI LORE

On April 24-25, 1994, Monsignor Edward J. Duncan was honored for his 50 years of service as chaplain and director of The Newman Foundation. Among the guests honoring Monsignor Duncan at a gala luncheon included retired General Motors chairman Thomas Murphy and former Illini football great Dick Butkus. During the festivities, University of Illinois Director of Athletics Ron Guenther announced that the Illini football team would institute a special citizenship award to honor its longtime team chaplain. Monsignor Duncan became chaplain at St. John's Catholic Church in 1943.

1994-95

AMERICA'S TIME CAPSULE

Sept. 8, 1994	US Airways Flight 427 crashed near Pittsburgh, killing all 132 on board.
Nov. 5, 1994	Forty-five-year-old George Foreman became boxing's oldest heavyweight champion.
Nov. 8, 1994	The Republicans won control of both houses of Congress for the first time in 40 years, rebuking Democratic president Bill Clinton.
Jan. 29, 1995	The San Francisco 49ers won an unprecedented fifth Super Bowl title, beating San Diego 49-26.
March 19, 1995	Basketball's Michael Jordan came out of retirement for the Chicago Bulls, debuting in jersey No. 45. He later switched back to his original No. 23.
April 19, 1995	One-hundred sixty-eight persons, including several children, were killed when the Federal Building in Oklahoma City was bombed by terrorists. It was, at the time, the deadliest terrorist attack ever on U.S. soil.

ILLINI MOMENT

Coach Lou Tepper and the Liberty Bowl championship trophy.

Women's Milestones
Theresa Grentz

LIBERTY BOWL CHAMPS:

Lou Tepper's third full season as head football coach at the University of Illinois was just 22 agonizing points away from being a banner year. And though the painful sting of narrow losses to four bowl-qualifying teams was eased a bit in the finale when Illinois won the Liberty Bowl, Illini fans couldn't help but think about what might have been during this roller coaster of season. The campaign began disappointingly at Chicago's Soldier Field with a one-point loss to Washington State, 10-9, but Illinois rebounded well by demolishing their next two nonconference foes, Missouri and Northern Illinois, by a cumulative score of 76-10. In week four, the Illini came up 36 inches shy of a victory in the Big Ten opener against Purdue, as the game ended with tight end Ken Dilger stacked up at the one-yard line. Tepper's crew shocked Ohio State in Columbus for a fourth consecutive time the following week, 24-10, helping linebacker Dana Howard live up to his bold prediction of a victory. Illinois then won three of its next four games, sandwiching a difficult 19-14 loss to Michigan between victories over Iowa, Northwestern and Minnesota. The most exciting game of 1994 came November 12 when No. 2-ranked Penn State travelled to Memorial Stadium. A 28-14 half-time lead by the Illini ultimately evaporated into a 35-31 loss to the eventual Rose Bowl champs. A defeat in the regular season finale at Wisconsin backed the Illini into the Liberty Bowl, and doomsayers weren't optimistic that Illinois could beat pesky East Carolina in the December 31 game at Memphis. However, a dominating offensive performance by quarterback Johnny Johnson and an equally sterling defensive effort from Simeon Rice and company made New Year's Eve especially sweet for the orange and blue.

WOMEN'S MILESTONES

Theresa Grentz, the seventh-winningest women's basketball coach in NCAA history and head coach of the 1992 United States Olympic Team, was selected as the University of Illinois' sixth head women's basketball coach on May 15, 1995. The 20-year coaching veteran from Rutgers University replaced Kathy Lindsey, who coached the Fighting Illini for five years. Grentz's coaching career at Rutgers saw the Lady Knights rise toward the top of women's intercollegiate basketball. During her 20 seasons at Rutgers, from 1976-95, Grentz's teams compiled a record of 434-150 (.743), including nine consecutive NCAA tournament appearances from 1986-94. Her 1981-82 Rutgers team captured the AIAW national championship with a 25-7 record. During her collegiate playing career at Immaculata, Grentz helped establish the first national power in women's collegiate basketball. The Mighty Macs won 74 games and captured three consecutive national titles (1972, '73, '74) during her career. Grentz was named a first-team All-American each season, won 1974 AMF Collegiate Player of the Year honors, and had her #12 retired by Immaculata.

1995 NCAA wrestling champions Steve Marianetti (left) and Ernest Benion.

Illini Item

VIRTUALLY DORMANT on the national scene for 37 years, Illinois' wrestling program got the boost it was looking for March 18, 1995 when senior Steve Marianetti (150 pounds) and sophomore Ernest Benion (158) both captured individual NCAA crowns. The dramatic scene took place at the University of Iowa. Although the Hawkeye crowd saw its favorites handily win the national team title, Marianetti's stunning 13-10 victory over Iowa's two-time defending champion Lincoln McIlravy put a damper on their celebration. Illini coach Mark Johnson, in just his third year, led Illinois to a top-ten finish (ninth) for the first time since 1958. It was the first time since 1938 that two UI wrestlers won national titles in the same year.

Illini Lists

KAROL KAHRS'S MOST OUTSTANDING WOMEN ATHLETES

Dr. Karol Kahrs, Illinois' longtime associate director of athletics, was asked to choose the most outstanding Illini women athletes of the last 20 years. Here are her selections, sport by sport.

Basketball:	Lisa Robinson
Cross Country:	Kelly McNee
Golf:	Renee Heiken
Gymnastics:	Nancy Thies
Swimming & Diving:	Mary Paterson
Tennis:	Lindsey Nimmo
Track & Field:	Tonja Buford
Volleyball:	Mary Eggers

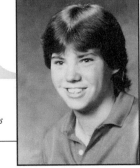

Mary Eggers

Illini Legend

Dana Howard

Illinois' reputation as "Linebacker U" gained considerable punch on December 9, 1994, when Illini senior Dana Howard earned the Butkus Award as college football's top linebacker. It was the first major individual award ever won by an Illini football player. Presenting the prize that night in Orlando, Florida was its namesake, former UI star Dick Butkus, who was celebrating his 52nd birthday. Said Howard in accepting the award, "I'd like to thank Dick Butkus for bringing that great linebacker tradition to Illinois. It gave me something to measure myself by." Howard's second consecutive All-American season was highlighted by two memorable events. First was his daring public prediction of victory and his subsequent performance at Ohio State in a 24-10 Illini victory. Howard nailed down the Butkus Award in a 35-31 loss to second-ranked Penn State when he became the Big Ten's all-time leading tackler. No. 40 topped the century mark in tackles all four seasons he played for the Illini, finishing with 595 stops, 23 more than previous record-holder Marcus Marek of Ohio State. Howard was a fifth-round draft pick of the Dallas Cowboys and played for the St. Louis Rams.

ILLINI LORE

Within a period of just 72 hours, the University of Illinois merged a Springfield-based university into its system, saw the structure of its governing board change, and gained a new president. The tumultuous three-day period began on February 28, 1995, when Governor James Edgar signed legislation to merge Sangamon State University in Springfield with the UI in January of 1996 as well as give the governor power to appoint UI trustees. Two days later, on March 2, UI-Chicago Chancellor James Stukel was named as the university's 15th president, replacing the retiring Stanley Ikenberry.

ILLINI **2001** UNIVERSITY OF ILLINOIS
orange & blue book

1995-2002

2000-01 ILLINOIS
MEN'S BASKETBALL
MEDIA GUIDE

GO ILLINI

1995-96

AMERICA'S TIME CAPSULE

Sept. 6, 1995	Baltimore Orioles shortstop Cal Ripken, Jr., played his 2,131st consecutive game before a sold-out crowd at Oriole Park at Camden Yards, breaking the record set by baseball legend Lou Gehrig in 1939.
Oct. 3, 1995	The "Trial of the Century" came to an end in Los Angeles when the jury, sequestered for 266 days, deliberated less than four hours and found O.J. Simpson not guilty of double murder.
April 3, 1996	Fingered by his brother, alleged "Unabomber" Theodore Kaczynski was arrested by FBI agents at his tiny, isolated cabin in Montana.
July 17, 1996	TWA's Flight 800 mysteriously exploded moments after taking off from New York's Kennedy International Airport, killing all 230 people on board.
Aug. 4, 1996	The Summer Olympic Games, held in Atlanta, came to a close. Highlights included Carl Lewis's fourth consecutive gold medal in the long jump, Michael Johnson's victories in the 400-meter and 200-meter races, and Muhammad Ali's lighting of the Olympic flame.

ILLINI MOMENT

Illinois' Tonya Williams (left) and Dawn Riley (right)

WOMEN'S TRACK & FIELD SQUAD TOPS ILLINI FORTUNES:

Coach Gary Winckler's women's track and field squad captured the lone Big Ten team title during the 1995-96 season among University of Illinois varsity sports. Amazingly, Illinois' convincing 18-point victory at the indoor championships, hosted by perennial favorite Wisconsin, was achieved without the benefit of an individual title by its star performer, Tonya Williams. The senior speedster had been fighting the flu and a couple of nagging injuries, but she was supported by some record-setting efforts from teammates Dawn Riley, Collinus Newsome and Benita Kelley. Riley's triple jump of 43 feet, six inches bettered the previous conference mark by almost one and a half feet. In the shot put, Newsome shattered the existing Big Ten, Camp Randall and Illinois records. And Kelley broke the Camp Randall record in the 55-meter dash with her time of :06.79. Williams was part of the 4x400-meter relay team that broke the venue record and won the event. It was the fourth team title for the Illini in the last five years. At the Big Ten outdoor meet, Illinois lost the team championship by just one point, 149-148, despite capturing nine of the 20 events, primarily in the sprints and the hurdles. Williams, who had recuperated from her maladies at the winter meet, bounced back strong in the spring championships. She was part of four different Big Ten titles. Consequently, Williams not only was named Big Ten Track and Field Athlete of the Year, but she also claimed the school's Female Athlete of the Year award.

WOMEN'S MILESTONES

Mike Hebert departed the University of Illinois athletic scene in the spring of 1996 after a sparkling 13-year career as head coach of the women's volleyball squad. From 1983 through 1995, Hebert's spikers won an unprecedented 72 percent of their games, finishing in the upper half of the Big Ten for 11 consecutive years. He was named National Coach of the Year in 1985 after leading the nation with a 39-3 record, and won Big Ten Coach of the Year honors in 1985, 1986 and 1988. Today he's the head coach at the University of Minnesota.

I Illini Item

FOR THE FIRST TIME in two decades, it was a year of transition for the Fighting Illini basketball program. Lou Henson stunned Illinois fans on February 24, 1996 by announcing that he would step down at the end of the season after a school record-breaking 21 years on the job. Athletic Director Ron Guenther responded quickly by luring Lon Kruger to Champaign-Urbana from the University of Florida, where he had guided the Gators just two years earlier to a berth in the Final Four. Though a new-found love for golf pacified Henson's retirement days for a while, an emergency call from his alma mater, New Mexico State, lured him into what was supposed to be only temporary head coaching duty. Henson continues today as coach of the Aggies while Kruger now directs the fortunes of the NBA's Atlanta Hawks.

Illini Legend

Kevin Hardy & Simeon Rice

Kevin Hardy and Simeon Rice

Despite losing Butkus Award winner Dana Howard to graduation, the linebacker corps for the 1995 Fighting Illini football team maintained its reputation as the best in the Big Ten, if not the nation. Week after week, the foursome of Kevin Hardy, Simeon Rice, John Holecek and Dennis Stallings hammered opposing offensive units with their relentless attack. Though Holecek and Stallings were amply worthy of all-star honors (and later proved their worth in the pro ranks), the flashier Hardy and Rice occupied the spotlight. Hardy served as team cocaptain and was as steady a defender as Illinois has ever had. He was equally adept in defending the run or the pass or in applying pressure to the quarterback. Rice, who came to the University of Illinois as a lightly regarded recruit, developed into a lightning-quick pass rusher. He eventually shattered the school's career records for tackles for loss (69) and quarterback sacks (44.5). Even though the Illini as a team were mediocre on the field (5-5-1) that season, bushels of honors came Hardy and Rice's way in the postseason. Kevin was a consensus first-team All-American and earned the Butkus Award as the nation's top linebacker. Simeon also won All-American honors and was a finalist for the Lombardi Award and semifinalist for the Butkus. On NFL draft day, the Illini pair were rewarded for their efforts, as Hardy was chosen second overall by the Jacksonville Jaguars and Rice went to the Arizona Cardinals on the very next pick.

Illini Lists

UI SINGLE-SEASON HOME RUN LEADERS

Illinois' Josh Klimek led the nation in home runs during the 1996 baseball season. His 26 round-trippers that year still tops the Illini single-season list.

1.	26	Josh Klimek, 1996
2.	19	Forry Wells, 1994
	19	Scott Spiezio, 1992
4.	18	Bubba Smith, 1991
5.	16	Brian McClure, 1996
	16	Scott Spiezio, 1993
	16	Mark Dalesandro, 1990
8.	15	D.J. Svihlik, 1999
	15	D.J. Svihlik, 1998
	15	Sean Mulligan, 1990
	15	Darrin Fletcher, 1987
	15	Darrin Fletcher, 1986

Josh Klimek

ILLINI LORE

Soon after he assumed the leadership in 1995, James J. Stukel made clear his four-point presidential vision for the University of Illinois: 1) to enrich undergraduate education; 2) to enhance quality throughout the University; 3) to strengthen the University's ties to the citizens of the state of Illinois; and 4) to free more money for academic purposes by streamlining business operations. Thanks in part to a $1 billion capital campaign, the University continues to meet its objectives and thrives under his rock-solid direction.

1996-97

AMERICA'S TIME CAPSULE

Nov. 5, 1996   Bill Clinton was elected to a second term as U.S. President, easily defeating former Kansas senator Bob Dole. Clinton won 31 states.

March 27, 1997   Thirty-nine members of the Heaven's Gate cult, who believed that the comet Hale-Bopp was being trailed by a spaceship that would transport them to a higher state of existence, committed mass suicide in California.

April 13, 1997   Twenty-one-year-old Tiger Woods became the youngest and the first minority golfer to win the Masters, outdistancing Tom Kite by 12 shots.

June 2, 1997   Timothy McVeigh was found guilty in the 1995 bombing of the Oklahoma City Federal Building that killed 168 people.

Aug. 31, 1997   Americans and people all over the world mourned the death of England's Princess Diana in a Paris automobile crash.

ILLINI MOMENT

(left to right) Renee Reed, Head Coach Theresa Grentz, Lavonda Wagner and Kathy McConnell-Miller

WOMEN'S BASKETBALL WINS FIRST-EVER BIG TEN TITLE:

In seasons prior to Theresa Grentz's arrival, the attendance at Fighting Illini women's basketball games could have easily been counted at a distance by the ticket manager's index finger rather than by a turnstile. On Sunday, February 23, 1997, the record-breaking crowd of 16,050 that saw UI's home game against Purdue was larger than the *total* season attendance at Illinois for every year prior to 1995. The reason? Winning basketball! The 1996-97 Illini compiled an overall record of 24-8, and tied Michigan State and Purdue for their first-ever Big Ten title. Grentz's troops were nearly perfect on the home court (11-1) and compiled an impressive 4-1 record against ranked teams. Five Illini players were accorded postseason honors, including junior Ashley Berggren, who was picked by the media as the Conference's Player of the Year. Also chosen as Big Ten all-stars were Alicia Sheeler (third-team), Krista Reinking (honorable mention), and Tauja Catchings and Katie Coleman (All-Freshman Team). Grentz was chosen as Big Ten Coach of the Year. In NCAA Tournament play, Illinois made it to the Sweet 16 for the first time and nearly upset top-ranked Connecticut in the NCAA Regional Semifinal.

WOMEN'S MILESTONES

FEBRUARY 23, 1997

A near capacity crowd of 16,050 attended the Fighting Illini women's basketball game against Purdue, setting the Big Ten's all-time single-game attendance record. It shattered the previous mark of 4,050. Though Illinois lost the game, 80-75, it was an event that made history.

Illini coach Craig Tiley (foreground) gives instructions to two of his players in NCAA tournament action.

I Illini Item

FOR THE FIRST TIME since Franklin Delano Roosevelt reigned in the White House, Illinois' men's tennis team captured the Big Ten title. Craig Tiley's team slowly climbed its way up to the conference's penthouse by recruiting talented players such as Gavin Sontag, Oliver Freelove and Cary Franklin. The league's Freshman of the Year, Franklin keyed UI's title run by beating Conference Player of the Year Alex Witt of Northwestern in the championships. The Illini wound up the 1996-97 campaign with an overall record of 18-10, including a 10-3 mark in Big Ten matches.

Illini Legend

Ernest Benion

Whether it was as a wrestler or as an a cappella singer, Ernest Benion had a star-spangled career at the University of Illinois. On the wrestling mat, the personable young man from Bolingbrook was an all-star, becoming one of only a handful of Fighting Illini grapplers to finish among the top three in the NCAA meet three different times. Benion racked up a win-loss record of 121 and 40 in four seasons at Illinois, but no victory was more important than the final match of his sophomore season when he won the national 158-pound crown. He placed second in the NCAA meet his junior year and was third as a senior. As proud as Illini coach Mark Johnson was of Benion's efforts as a wrestler, Ernest's most memorable work came outside the gymnasium. He was co-chair of the student athlete advisory board and an active member of the Fellowship of Christian Athletes. "As great an athlete as Ernest was," said Johnson, "he is an even better person. I'll always think of him as a citizen as much as anything." And when he wasn't wrestling or serving on various committees, Benion loved to sing. On numerous occasions before a variety of Illini athletic events, he used his beautiful baritone voice to sing the national anthem. He was a son every parent would love to have.

Illini Lists

THE INCREDIBLE HOLC

Despite a disappointing performance by the team, Illinois running back Robert Holcombe had an all-star season in 1996. His 315-yard rushing effort against Minnesota on November 16th set an all-time Illini record.

	Yards	Player, Opponent, Date
1.	315	Robert Holcombe, Minnesota, 11/16/96
2.	263	Howard Griffith, Northwestern, 11/24/90
3.	239	Jim Grabowski, Wisconsin, 11/14/64
4.	237	Red Grange, Pennsylvania, 10/31/25
5.	212	Red Grange, Michigan, 10/18/24
6.	215	Rocky Harvey, Middle Tenn., 9/12/98
7.	208	Howard Griffith, Southern Illinois, 9/22/90
8.	206	Robert Holcombe, Minnesota, 11/18/95
9.	205	J.C. Caroline, Minnesota, 10/17/53
10.	196	Red Grange, Chicago, 11/8/24
	196	Jim Grabowski, Wisconsin, 11/13/65

Robert Holcombe

ILLINI LORE

. . . .

On October 4, 1996, the University of Illinois' Bielfeldt Athletic Administration Building was dedicated. A $7.2 million gift from Gary and Carlotta Bielfeldt allowed nearly 100 staff members of the Division of Intercollegiate to assume residency in the 40,000-square foot structure. A Hall of Fame and a "Park of Tradition" will be featured in the future in and around Bielfeldt.

1997-98

AMERICA'S TIME CAPSULE

Nov. 19, 1997   Seven babies—four boys and three girls—were delivered by doctors to Bobbi and Kenny McCaughey in Iowa.

March 23, 1998   *Titanic* beat out *Good Will Hunting* and *As Good as it Gets* as Best Picture at the 70th annual Academy Award ceremonies in Hollywood.

May 15, 1998   Frank Sinatra died of a heart attack at the age of 82.

June 16, 1998   In what many thought would be his final game, Michael Jordan hit the game-winning shot with just :05.2 left and led the Chicago Bulls to an 87-86 victory over the Utah Jazz in the deciding game of the NBA Finals.

Aug. 17, 1998   In a televised address to the nation, President Bill Clinton admitted he had had an affair with White House intern Monica Lewinsky.

ILLINI MOMENT

ILLINI "9" COME WITHIN TWO OUTS OF COLLEGE WORLD SERIES BERTH:

D.J. Svihlik

Illinois' 1998 baseball season was truly a roller-coaster ride, ranging from a series of steep hills and sharp curves to a heart-pounding finish. As it had done in previous seasons, Coach Itch Jones's squad started painfully slowly, losing its first six games. Thanks to steady pitching and the powerful bats of second baseman D.J. Svihlik (15 home runs) and third baseman Craig Marquie (58 RBI), the Fighting Illini methodically improved, winning 13 of their first 14 games at Illinois Field. In Big Ten play, Illinois got off to a marvelous 9-1 start and came up big at the end as well, sweeping four home games against Iowa and four road games at Purdue to claim its first regular-season Big Ten championship in 35 years. The Illini placed second behind Minnesota in the conference tournament, yet earned a berth in the NCAA South Regional. In the opener at Gainesville, Florida, Wake Forest outslugged Illinois, 14-12, but the Illini won their next three against Monmouth, Baylor and Wake to qualify for the title game against host Florida. The winner would earn a spot in the College World Series. UI senior All-American Brett Weber, the Big Ten's Pitcher of the Year, hurled 7.2 gutsy innings on two days' rest against the Gators, and the game eventually went to extra innings. Illinois took a 6-5 lead into the bottom of the 11th, but surrendered two runs to Florida, losing by a score of 7-6 to bring a disappointing end to an otherwise storybook season (42-21 overall).

Coaches Tricia Taliaferro and Jillian Ellis

WOMEN'S MILESTONES

Women's soccer made its varsity debut at the University of Illinois in 1997 under the direction of Coach Jillian Ellis. It was the first women's sport to be added to the Fighting Illini athletic program since 1974. Illinois started the season with four consecutive victories, including a 4-0 win at Loyola-Chicago in its first-ever game. Perhaps its biggest triumph came on Oct. 12th when the Illini upset Northwestern at home, 3-2, in double overtime. Kelly Buszkiewicz was named the team's MVP.

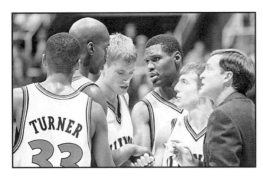

Illini Item

A SENIOR-DOMINATED Fighting Illini men's basketball team captured the school's 13th Big Ten title in 1997-98. Anchored by the upperclass starting five of Jerry Hester, Brian Johnson, Jarrod Gee, Kevin Turner and Matt Heldman, Illinois rolled through the conference schedule with a 13-3 record, including a first-ever sweep of Indiana, Iowa and Michigan. The most exciting game came on February 12th when the Illini blasted cochampion Michigan State, 84-63, at the Assembly Hall. The seniors, paced by Turner's 17.7 points per game, provided an amazing 84 percent of the team's total scoring.

Illini Legend

ASHLEY BERGGREN

Ashley Berggren stood quietly in the back of the room, listening intently, when new head coach Theresa Grentz made her introductory remarks about how she viewed the future of the University of Illinois' women's basketball program. After having suffered through a brutal freshman season in which her team had posted a 10-17 record, this was one of the first times she had been able to smile all year. Berggren blossomed beautifully under the Grentz system, setting an Illini single-season scoring record in 1995-96 while averaging 24.6 points per game. That season included a 43-point game against Minnesota, 38 points versus Northwestern, and 36 points against Purdue, three of the top 10 efforts in Illini history. Berggren's individual success continued in each of her last two seasons also, though her scoring averages weren't as lofty. But what made her most happy was the team success the Illini enjoyed. During her junior season, Illinois captured the school's first Big Ten title in women's basketball and advanced to the Sweet 16, taking top-ranked Connecticut to the limit in a five-point loss. As a senior, Berggren and the Illini again won their first two NCAA tournament games, and she became UI's all-time leading scorer (2,089 points) and a third-team All-American. Her crowning glory came when she was named Illinois' Female Athlete of the Year in 1998.

Illini Lists

THREE-TIME MVPS

In 1998, Ashley Berggren became the only Illini women's basketball player to be named the team's Most Valuable Player three times. Illinois' entire list of three-time MVPs:

Neil Adams	Men's tennis	1982-84
Ashley Berggren	Women's basketball	1996-98
Dave Downey	Men's basketball	1961-63
Mary Eggers	Volleyball	1986-88
Kiwane Garris	Men's basketball	1995-97
Mark Krajewski	Men's tennis	1989,1991-92
Steve Marianetti	Wrestling	1993-95
Justi Rae Miller	Women's golf	1987-89
Lindsey Nimmo	Women's tennis	1991-93
Deon Thomas	Men's basketball	1992-94
Tonya Williams	Women's track	1994-96

ILLINI LORE

On January 28, 1998, the day after his State of the Union address, President Bill Clinton spoke to an enthusiastic, standing-room-only crowd at the Assembly Hall. Four hundred media members accompanied the President and Vice President on their visit. The Air Force One jet that had delivered the Washington celebrities made additional news afterwards, getting stuck in the mud at Willard Airport in Savoy.

1998-99

AMERICA'S TIME CAPSULE

Sept. 8, 1998	Mark McGwire broke one of baseball's most revered records when he slugged his 62nd home run, topping the 37-year-old mark of 61 homers by Roger Maris. The St. Louis Cardinal slugger wound up the year with 70 round-trippers, while Chicago Cubs star Sammy Sosa hit 66.
Oct. 29, 1998	Seventy-seven-year-old John Glenn returned to space 36 years after becoming the first American in orbit.
Dec. 19, 1998	The United States House of Representatives impeached President Clinton on charges of perjury and obstruction of justice in the White House sex scandal.
Jan. 13, 1999	Michael Jordan, basketball's all-time greatest player, retired from the Chicago Bulls for the second time.
April 20, 1999	Two Littleton, Colorado students went on a shooting spree at Columbine High School, killing 15, including themselves.

ILLINI MOMENT

1999 Illini Tennis Team

Men's Tennis Wins Again:

It was déjà vu for the Fighting Illini men's tennis team in 1999. Not only did the team roll over its Big Ten competition to the tune of a perfect 13-0 record for a second consecutive season, head coach Craig Tiley also repeated as Big Ten Coach of the Year. The biggest improvement from the previous season was the team's record-setting 28-4 dual-meet mark and its advancement to the NCAA tournament's Elite Eight. Though the season ended on a sour note when fifth-seeded Mississippi's 4-3 victory spoiled the third-seeded Illini's hopes of a national championship, it remained an unforgettable year. Individually, senior Oliver Freelove from England won Big Ten Athlete of the Year honors. His 37-16 singles record and his 34-9 doubles record with teammate Cary Franklin made him arguably the greatest Illini single-season performer of all time. Said Tiley of Freelove, "Oliver came to Illinois as a walk-on and, in his four years, took his game to a new level." Team-wise, Illinois eventually extended its Big Ten dual-meet winning streak to 57 consecutive matches, dating from April 16, 1997 to April 29, 2001.

WOMEN'S MILESTONES

The $5.5 million Richard T. Ubben Basketball Practice Facility opened its doors to both the Fighting Illini women and men's teams in October of 1998. No longer do the Illini have to prepare for competition in poorly lit gyms across the campus nor have to share their court with intramural athletes. The building itself is divided in two equal 20,000 square foot facilities, one for the women and one for the men, including two full-length 94-by-50-foot basketball courts.

Illinois' Bill Zeman celebrates an upset victory over Iowa

I Illini Item

TWO OF ILLINOIS ATHLETICS' most memorable moments of 1998-99 came within three weeks of each other. On February 14, 1999, Griff Powell's 5-4 wrestling victory at 157 pounds gave Illinois a 20-16 upset win over powerful Iowa. The triumph broke a string of 32 consecutive losses by the Illini to the Hawkeyes. In men's basketball, from March 4th through the 7th, Coach Lon Kruger's squad stole the headlines at the Big Ten tournament. Entering play as the No. 11 seed, Illinois posted consecutive upset victories over 23rd-ranked Minnesota (67-64), 17th-ranked Indiana (82-66) and 11th-ranked Ohio State (79-77). The dream of an NCAA Tournament bid ended when the 14-17 Illini lost the title game at the hands of 2nd-ranked Michigan State (67-50).

Illini Legend

RON GUENTHER

During the years of Ron Guenther's term as Director of Intercollegiate Athletics, the 1966 University of Illinois football MVP and 1967 graduate has paid back the scholarship he was granted in a variety of ways. Using unique and systematic leadership skills and unparalleled success in hiring coaches, Guenther has guided the DIA's 19 varsity sports to a total of 10 Big Ten championships during the last decade, including a rarely achieved conference title sweep by both football and basketball in 2001-02. Academically, UI's athletes have matched the overall campus grade point average and produced more than 100 Academic All-Big Ten award winners. In terms of bricks and mortar, thanks to Guenther, the campus's athletic facilities are in their best shape in more than 75 years. Among the newest additions to the Illini landscape are a $12.5 million state-of-the-art indoor football practice facility, a nearly $6 million basketball practice facility, a $7.2 million athletic administration building, a $2.1 million academic center, and a $2 million women's softball stadium. Contributions to the Fighting Illini Scholarship are at an all-time high and Illinois is bringing in millions of dollars from licensing and a marketing/equipment agreement with Nike. According to a 1997 article in the *Chicago Sun-Times*, "Ron Guenther has the school on track to realize the expectations of unbridled athletic success, achieved the right way."

Illini Lists

ILLINOIS' BIG TEN COACHES OF THE YEAR

Baseball	Itch Jones (1998)
Men's Basketball	Lou Henson (1993)
Women's Basketball	Theresa Grentz (1997 &'98)
Football	Mike White (1983); John Mackovic (1988 & '89); Ron Turner (2001)
Men's Golf	Ed Beard (1988); Mike Small (2002)
Men's Gymnastics	Yoshi Hayasaki (1988 &"89)
Women's Gymnastics	Bev Mackes (1990)
Men's Tennis	Craig Tiley (1998, '99 & 2000)
Men's Track & Field	Gary Wieneke (1988 & '89)
Women's Track & Field	Gary Winckler (1989, '92, '93, '95 & '96)
Volleyball	Mike Hebert (1985, '86 & '88); Don Hardin (2001)
Wrestling	Mark Johnson (2001)

ILLINI LORE

The east entryway to the Urbana-Champaign campus at the corner of Lincoln Avenue and Illinois Street got a something-old-something-new look on October 8, 1998 when the Hallene Gateway Plaza was dedicated. Alumni Alan and Phyllis Hallene contributed the funds for the construction, which features the stone portal from the entrance to the first university-built classroom building, University Hall.

1999-00

AMERICA'S TIME CAPSULE

Sept. 18, 1999   Hurricane Floyd, reduced to a tropical storm as it moved up the eastern United States, left 34 dead and thousands homeless.

Nov. 12, 1999   Judge Thomas Jackson handed down a 412-paragraph decision that Bill Gates's Microsoft had an illegal monopoly over personal computer operating systems.

Jan. 1, 2000   The much-awaited turn of the century arrived with considerable celebration around the world, but without the violence or massive computer glitches that had been feared.

March 26, 2000   At the Academy Awards, *American Beauty* won five awards including Best Picture and Best Actor (Kevin Spacey).

Aug. 20, 2000   Tiger Woods won his third major tournament of the season, winning a three-hole playoff at the PGA Championship.

ILLINI MOMENT

ILLINOIS FOOTBALL GETS "OFFENSIVE":

Illinois defeated Michigan, 35-29, at UM's "Big House" in 1999, battling back from a record 27 to 7 deficit.

For the first time in a long while, the 1999 Fighting Illini football team was positively offensive, and not negatively offensive. That is to say, Illinois fans weren't offended by the performance of its team, but its opponents' defensive units definitely were. Perhaps the best way to describe the Illini offense, led by record-setting quarterback Kurt Kittner and a bevy of receivers and running backs, was by its splashy statistics. In 1999, Illinois scored a total of 388 points in 12 games (32.3 per game), more than any other team in Illini history. Coach Ron Turner's previous two squads (1997 and '98) scored a cumulative total of 268 points in 22 games (12.2). And, in the sport of football, lots of points normally mean lots of victories, and that was the case in '99, as Illinois went 8-4 and ranked 10th in the final Associated Press poll. With the exception of a heartbreaking 34-31 overtime loss at Indiana, Illinois posted wins each time it scored 29 or more points. By far, the most satisfying triumphs were at Ann Arbor against ninth-ranked Michigan, where it came back from a record 27-7 deficit to beat the Wolverines, 35-29, and at Columbus versus Ohio State, where Illinois handed the Buckeyes their worst home loss in 50 years, 46-20. In fact, no team had beaten those two schools on the road in the same season since Michigan State won a national championship in 1951. Illinois' crowning jewel came at the Micronpc.com Bowl in Miami where the Illini topped Virginia, 63-21, scoring the second-most points ever in a Bowl game by any NCAA team.

WOMEN'S MILESTONES

The University of Illinois softball team made its varsity debut in 2000, but due to the lack of a home field, Coach Terri Sullivan's players were never seen by their Illini faithful. Instead, the squad of 24, stocked primarily with freshmen, played all 30 of its games on the road. Surprisingly, the results were anything but disastrous, as Illinois produced a respectable 13-17 record. It lost a 3-2 decision to host Coastal Carolina in its first game, but rallied in the nightcap of the doubleheader for its first-ever victory by the same score. The Illini team leaders were sophomore Heather Black (.391 average) and freshman pitcher Pam Almanza (7-8 record with a 2.35 ERA).

I Illini Item

CARY FRANKLIN AND GRAYDON OLIVER captured Illinois' first-ever national tennis championship on May 28, 2000, at the University of Georgia's Dan Magill Tennis Complex, breezing past Southern California's Ryan Moore and Nick Rainey by scores of 6-4 and 6-2. The victory earned Franklin and Oliver a berth in the prestigious U.S. Open in New York later that year.

Illini Legend

JASON ANDERSON

It is not farfetched to place Jason Anderson among the greatest pitchers in University of Illinois baseball history. While there have been several outstanding Illini hurlers—including 1940s strikeout king Marv Rotblatt, 1950s ace Tom Fletcher and 1960s standout Ken Holtzman—the case for Anderson is a strong one. You could point to his cumulative 29-5 win-loss record from 1998-2000 or his 197 strikeouts in 297.1 innings, his pick to the All-American first team in 2000 or his two first-team All-Big Ten selections. But beyond his on-field accomplishments, there are the Danville, Illinois star's equally impressive credentials in the classroom. As a junior, Anderson earned first-team Academic All-American honors with B+ grades in his accounting major. During his final season at Illinois, he had a 14-3 record, setting Illini single-season marks for victories and innings pitched (134.1), while leading UI to its fifth consecutive postseason berth. That effort earned Anderson Illini Athlete of the Year honors, out-polling fellow athletic greats such as football quarterback Kurt Kittner, national doubles tennis champion Cary Franklin, and NCAA wrestling champ Carl Perry. Anderson was chosen in the 10th round of the 2000 Major League Baseball Player Draft by the New York Yankees.

Illini Lists

Kurt Kittner enjoyed the greatest season ever among Fighting Illini quarterbacks in 1999. In leading Illinois to an 8-4 record, he averaged 225 passing yards per game. Perhaps Kittner's most impressive statistic was his touchdown-to-interception ratio. UI's leaders in that category:

Rank	TD	INT	DIFF	PLAYER, SEASON
1.	24	5	+19	Kurt Kittner, 1999
2.	19	6	+13	Johnny Johnson, 1994
	27	14	+13	Kurt Kittner, 2001
4.	22	12	+10	Jeff George, 1989
	18	8	+10	Kurt Kittner, 2000
6.	18	10	+8	Jack Trudeau, 1984
7.	20	14	+6	Tony Eason, 1981
8.	16	12	+4	Jason Verduzco, 1990
	19	15	+4	Dave Wilson, 1980

Kurt Kittner

ILLINI LORE

There was an historic gathering of Chief Illiniwek supporters and detractors on April 14, 2000 at the University of Illinois' Foellinger Auditorium. Louis Garripo, a former circuit court judge in Cook County, presided over the spirited dialogue which featured anti-Chief groups from as far away as Oklahoma and legions of supportive alumni and friends. Six months later, Garripo's statistical findings were presented to the UI Board of Trustees, but it did not settle the long-standing argument over the University's 75-year-old symbol.

2000-01

AMERICA'S TIME CAPSULE

Oct. 26, 2000   The Yankees won the Subway Series by beating the Mets, claiming their third consecutive world championship.

Nov. 7, 2000   Texas Governor George W. Bush and Vice President Al Gore squared off in the closest presidential election ever, so close that a winner wasn't declared until 36 days later, on December 13.

Dec. 12, 2000   Twenty-five-year-old free agent Alex Rodriguez signed a record-high 10-year, $252 million baseball contract with the Texas Rangers.

Feb. 18, 2001   NASCAR legend Dale Earnhardt died in a crash on the final lap of the Daytona 500.

June 11, 2001   Convicted Oklahoma City bomber Timothy McVeigh was put to death, becoming the first federal prisoner to be executed in 38 years.

ILLINI MOMENT

MEN'S BASKETBALL SHARES BIG TEN TITLE, EARNS NO. 1 SEED:

(left to Right) Sergio McClain, Robert Archibald, Frank Williams and Brian Cook celebrate after Illinois' victory at Minnesota.

It is true that when Lon Kruger departed Illinois to become head coach of the Atlanta Hawks, he left the cupboard overflowing with talent for incoming coach Bill Self. Ready for action were Peoria seniors Sergio McClain and Marcus Griffin, junior three-point specialist Cory Bradford, and super sophs Frank Williams and Brian Cook. But as the old saying goes, "Championships are won on the court, not on paper," so there was plenty of pressure for the Fighting Illini to produce positive results in 2000-01. Illinois was faced with a very difficult non-conference schedule, but wound up posting victories over powerhouses Maryland, Seton Hall, Arizona and Missouri. The Big Ten portion of the slate was filled with highlights as well, including wins in six of its first seven conference games, a scintillating 11-point victory over fourth-ranked Michigan State at the Assembly Hall, and triumphs over Iowa and at Minnesota to end the regular season that allowed the Illini to share the regular-season crown. Though UI slipped unexpectedly at the Big Ten tournament, it was still rewarded with a No. 1 seed in the NCAA Tournament. Northwestern State and Charlotte were Illinois' first two victims, then at the Midwest Regional in San Antonio, Illinois opened play by spanking Kansas by 16 points, setting up a regional finals game against Arizona. However, foul problems plagued the Illini and they missed out on the Final Four by just six points. UI's 27 victories were the second-most in its history, and Williams became the first Illini player since 1967 to earn Big Ten Most Valuable Player honors. Also during the 2000-01 season. Bradford extended his consecutive games streak with a three-pointer to 88.

(Left to Right) Jenny Kallur, Camee Williams, Perdita Felicien and Susanna Kallur

WOMEN'S MILESTONES

APRIL 27, 2001

It was a world record-setting performance for four Fighting Illini women's track hurdlers at the Drake Relays in Des Moines, Iowa. The 4x100 shuttle hurdle relay quartet of Jenny Kallur, Camee Williams, Susanna Kallur and Perdita Felicien streaked around the track in an all-time best clocking of :52.85 seconds. Later that spring, Felicien was named the 2001 United States Track Coaches Association's Female Athlete of the Year.

Teddy (left) and Dike Eddleman (right) flank
Governor Jim Edgar in this May 17, 1995, photo
on Dike Eddleman Day in the state of Illinois.

I Illini Item

ILLINOIS LOST THREE of its most legendary athletes within a 105-day span when Andy Phillip (April 28, 2001), Dike Eddleman (August 1, 2001) and Lou Boudreau (August 10, 2001) all died. Phillip, 79, was a member of the Basketball Hall of Fame and Illinois' Whiz Kids; Eddleman, 78, was generally recognized as UI's greatest all-around athlete; and Boudreau, 84, was Illinois' only former athlete inducted into the Baseball Hall of Fame.

Illini Lists

MOST SUCCESSFUL FIRST-YEAR MEN'S BASKETBALL COACHES

Bill Self's debut in 2000-01 as the Fighting Illini's men's basketball coach was a spectacular one, joining Doug Mills as the only UI coaches who won Big Ten titles in their initial seasons.

Rank	Pct. (W-L)	Coach, First Season	Notable Accomplishment
1.	.778 (14-4)	Doug Mills, 1936-37	Big Ten Champion
2.	.771 (27-8)	Bill Self, 2000-01	Big Ten Champion
3.	.769 (20-6)	Fletcher Lane, 1907-08	UI's first 20-victory season
4.	.750 (15-5)	Harry Combes, 1947-48	7-0 start
5.	.688 (22-10)	Lon Kruger, 1996-97	Ranked 19th
6.	.625 (10-6)	Ralph Jones, 1912-13	Won 7 of first 8 games
7.	.611 (11-7)	Frank Winters, 1920-21	T-4th in Big Ten standings
8.	.600 (9-6)	Craig Ruby, 1922-23	T-4th in Big Ten standings
9.	.545 (12-10)	H.V. Juul, 1908-09	4-0 start
10.	.519 (14-13)	Lou Henson, 1975-76	5-0 start

Bill Self

Illini Legend
ADAM TIRAPELLE & JOHN LOCKHART

Adam Tirapelle

Since Mark Johnson's arrival as coach in 1992, the University of Illinois' wrestling program has enjoyed its best run of success since the 1920s and '30s. And while the Fighting Illini teams of that period captured an unprecedented 11 Big Ten team titles, their individual success at the national level was only slightly better than the awards the school has won during the last decade. On March 17, 2001, individual national championships by Adam Tirapelle at 149 pounds and by John Lockhart at heavyweight boosted Illinois' total to six NCAA titles since 1995. Tirapelle and Lockhart were both runners-up at the 2001 Big Ten meet, but they advanced all the way to the top step of the awards stand at the national championships in Iowa City. Tirapelle faced Lehigh's Dave Esposito and posted a 5-3 win, sealing the victory with a takedown with only 32 seconds remaining. As for Lockhart, he consistently used overtime to his advantage. The junior from Mahomet, Illinois used two overtimes in his first-round match, a single overtime in his second round match, a single-point victory in the quarterfinals, a two-overtime victory in the semis and two overtimes in the final. After a scoreless first period, the two exchanged escapes to end regulation tied at 1-1. After a scoreless overtime period, Lockhart won the coin flip and elected to start in the down position. He escaped with 11 seconds remaining in the 30-second sudden victory period to claim his crown. Team-wise, Illinois finished fifth nationally with 59.5 points, its best placing since 1946 when Glenn Law's squad finished third at the NCAA tournament.

ILLINI LORE

University of Illinois Research Park
South Center

Where for years sheep and other livestock roamed in 138 acres of grassy fields, the University of Illinois' newest research park began to sprout on the southwest corner of St. Mary's Road and First Street in the summer and fall of 2000. Officially known as the Science and Technology Engineering Technology Communications Center, these impressive structures of brick and mortar send a strong message about the UI's support of economic development. Motorola, long a corporate partner of the University, became the park's first official tenant.

AMERICA'S TIME CAPSULE

Sept. 11, 2001	Within a period of one hour and 25 minutes, 19 foreign terrorists hijacked four American passenger jets, crashing two of them into the north and south towers of New York's World Trade Center, another into the Pentagon, and a fourth plane into a vacant field southeast of Pittsburgh. A total of 3,056 people died.
Oct. 4, 2001	Robert Stevens died in Palm Beach, Florida, after contracting pulmonary anthrax. Three other American citizens also eventually died after being exposed to anthrax.
Oct. 5, 2001	Barry Bonds of the San Francisco Giants broke Mark McGwire's single-season home run record by hitting his 71st homer against Los Angeles Dodgers pitcher Chan Ho Park. He would eventually hit 73 home runs during the 2001 season.
Nov. 12, 2001	A total of 260 passengers and crew members died when American Airlines Flight 587 crashed in a Queens, New York neighborhood. Federal officials said that mechanical failure was the cause of the accident.
Feb. 8, 2002	The 19th Olympic Winter Games opened in Salt Lake City, Utah. Among the 10 American gold medal winners were figure skater Sara Hughes, sledder Jack Shea, and speed skater Derek Parra.

ILLINI MOMENT

ILLINOIS FOOTBALL ENJOYS A "SWEET" SEASON:

Coach Ron Turner

Highlighted by victories over three Top 25 teams and a perfect 6-0 record at home, Big Ten Coach of the Year Ron Turner and the Fighting Illini football team made school history in 2001, qualifying for their first-ever appearance in the Bowl Championship Series. A record-setting offensive effort and a surprisingly stingy defense yielded Illinois' first Big Ten championship since 1990 and a 10-1 regular-season record. Spoiled only by a game four loss at 17th-ranked Michigan, the Illini swept the remaining seven games of their schedule, averaging more than 34 points per game. One by one, Illinois defeated Minnesota, Indiana, Wisconsin, 15th-ranked Purdue, Penn State, 25th-ranked Ohio State and Northwestern. Two days after UI's thrilling 34-28 win over the Wildcats at Memorial Stadium on Thanksgiving Day, Ohio State did the Illini a favor by defeating Michigan at Ann Arbor, thus handing Illinois its first outright Big Ten title since 1983. UI's individual heroes included All-Big Ten first-teamers Tony Pashos (tackle) and Jay Kulaga (guard), center Luke Butkus, senior quarterback Kurt Kittner, who passed for 3,256 yards and a single-season record 27 touchdowns, and receiver Brandon Lloyd, who caught 10 TDs. Defensively, the stars included linebacker Jerry Schumacher, cornerbacks Eugene Wilson and Christian Morton, a safety Bobby Jackson. Punter Steve Fitts and placekicker Peter Christofilakos also were key contributors. Though the season ended disappointingly on New Year's Day at the Sugar Bowl in a 47-34 loss to Louisiana State, Illini fans still had a lot to smile about.

WOMEN'S MILESTONES

The University of Illinois' women's golf team, basement dwellers in the Big Ten Conference for the six previous seasons, climbed the stairs to see a brilliant sunlight in the 2002 season. After finishing fifth at the conference meet, Coach Paula Smith's squad received the school's first-ever bid to play in the NCAA Central Regional Championship at East Lansing, Michigan. There, the senior-less Fighting Illini were led by sophomore Michelle Carroll and junior Laurin Kanda and placed 13th among 21 teams.

Coach Bill Self

Illini Item

11

COACH BILL SELF'S FIGHTING ILLINI repeated as Big Ten cochampions in 2002, but it took somewhat of a miracle to record that achievement. Following a 67-61 loss to Michigan State on February 3, which snapped Illinois' 28-game home-court winning streak, Self's squad rattled off victories in its last eight conference games. The final win, a 67-66 triumph at Minnesota, was won on a shot with three seconds left by Frank Williams and enabled the Illini to win back-to-back Big Ten titles for the first time in 50 years. Illinois won its first- and second-round NCAA tournament games at Chicago but fell to Kansas in the third game, ending its season with a record of 26-9.

Illini Legend

Illini Lists

BIG TEN CHAMPIONSHIPS IN THE SAME SEASON BY FOOTBALL AND MEN'S BASKETBALL

1914-15 Football (outright), Basketball (outright)

1923-24 Football (shared with Mich.), Basketball (shared with Chi. & Wisc.)

1951-52 Football (outright), Basketball (outright)

1983-84 Football (outright), Basketball (shared with Purdue)

2001-02 Football (outright), Basketball (shared with Ind., OSU & Wisc.)

KURT KITTNER

Since 1980, the list of University of Illinois football quarterbacking greats rivals that of any other school in the Big Ten. Starting with Dave Wilson, Tony Eason and Jack Trudeau in the early '80s and continuing with Jeff George, Jason Verduzco and Johnny Johnson into the '90s, this illustrious group of Illini triggermen was joined in the 21st century by a right-handed slinger from Schaumburg named Kurt Kittner. Statistically speaking, Kittner's numbers glowed as bright as any of his fellow Illini. Though he fell just nine feet short short of Trudeau's career record of 8,725 passing yards, Kittner demolished Jack's mark for touchdown passes with 70, including a record 27 scores during the 2001 season alone. His touchdown-to-interception ratio (69 to 27) over his last three seasons was also spectacular, but all of those stats pale in comparison when Kittner's greatest achievement is revealed: a record 24 victories in 39 starts as Illinois' quarterback. Illini fans will undoubtedly remember his senior-season performances versus Wisconsin (401 yards, 4 TD) and Northwestern (387 yards, 4 TD), but Kurt's finest hour may have been as a sophomore in 1999 when he led Illinois to victories at Michigan and at Ohio State, the first time any Big Ten school had pulled off that feat in nearly half a century.

ILLINI LORE

On October 22, 2001, Chicago Bears President and CEO Ted Phillips and University of Illinois Director of Athletics Ron Guenther announced that the National Football League team would play its 2002 schedule at UI's Memorial Stadium. The move was made to allow the construction and renovation of Chicago's Soldier Field. Local economists projected that the two preseason games and the eight regular-season games would generate as much as $30 million to $40 million for Champaign and Urbana. In addition, several multimillion dollar improvements will be made at Memorial Stadium, including new training facilities and a state-of-the-art video scoreboard.

Epilogue

Back-to-back Big Ten championships in men's basketball sandwiched around an undisputed Big Ten football title and a BCS bowl game was but a dream in 1995 when I wrote of my love affair with the Illini in the Epilogue of the first edition of *Illini Legends, Lists and Lore.* The championship runs became even more important to me, personally, inasmuch as they occurred at the tail end of my long stint as play-by-play announcer for the Illini Sports Network. The end of the 2001-02 basketball season was also the end of my PBP days.

The love affair began more than a half century ago. To be specific, it was November 3, 1951. We had driven up from my hometown Olney, Illinois. It was the first Illini football game I had ever seen. Our seats were in the temporary bleachers at the north end. A 40-mile-an-hour wind blew from the south. It snowed hard. It was a blizzard. In the final five minutes, Tommy O'Connell hit Rex Smith with a short touchdown pass, and Illinois won 7-0 on the way to a 9-0-1 season, including a 40-7 Rose Bowl victory over Stanford.

When we finally found our snow-covered car, I remember plopping into the back seat, listening to the grumbling of my friends about what a lousy day it was, how cold they were, how stupid we were for making the trip. "I loved it," I said. And I still do. More now than then, more tomorrow than today.

Why do I feel that way? Why do I get chills when Chief Illiniwek dances? Why do I cry when seniors play their last games? Why can't I sleep when the Illini lose a close one? Why will I hug Mike Pearson's book and sit up long after my bedtime remembering the games, players, and coaches that have brought such joy and happiness to my life? Let me explain.

In addition to having been influenced by "just being there," I believe I caught the spirit of Illinois by observing up close those athletes with big hearts. Who can ever forget the competitiveness of Kenny Battle, Mary Eggers, Bill Brown, Dave Scholz, Craig Virgin, Matt Heldman, Lucas Johnson, Perdita Felician, Ashley Berggren, Kevin Hardy, Dana Howard, Simeon Rice and countless others who so proudly wore the orange and blue. It is no surprise that the Illini basketball team now presents two awards each year: the Kenny Battle Award goes to the most inspirational player, and the Matto (Matt Heldman) Award goes to the player who shows the most hustle.

To this day, I can feel the sense of excitement in Memorial Stadium when Dick Butkus lumbered onto the turf to snap the ball and block for the quarterback when it was 4th and short. He did it time after time. We always got the first down. Some will have other memories of Pete Elliott's 1964 Rose Bowl champions, led by Butkus and Jim Grabowski, but to me, it will always be 4th and short with the big guy comin' on to remedy the situation.

Not all memories are on the field. On October 27, 1956, this rookie reporter was a guest at Ray Eliot's Springfield Avenue residence. A few hours earlier, Abe Woodson had taken a Bill Offenbecher screen pass 82 yards for a touchdown, keying Illinois' 20-13 upset win over Michigan State. "You like that game, son?" the legendary coach asked. "Yes, sir," I mumbled. He put his hand on my shoulder and said, "Me, too. That's one we won't forget." Ray Eliot is one we won't forget, either.

One Monday noon at our Champaign Rotary Club meeting, Mike Hebert was introduced as the featured speaker. He had been named women's volleyball coach at Illinois and his mission now was to educate us. He was trying to drum up some enthusiasm for a game most of us had played at picnics in the park. Hebert's game was to be played by young women in dingy Kenney Gym. It was going to be a tough sell. Mike began his speech by saying, "This is a volleyball." We laughed at that. Then we began to learn. We began to watch. One of the greatest pleasures I've had at Illinois is watching Mike's team rise to national prominence, lead the nation in attendance, and provide thrilling season after season. Mary, Nancy, Kirsten-what a wonderful ride!

Nor will we forget the 2001 Illini football season and the 2001-02 basketball season in which Ron Turner's and Bill Self's teams made many amazing comeback victories on their way to championship seasons. And our memory bank overflows with the passing of the greatest athlete in the history of the University of Illinois—Dike Eddleman. His exploits will never be topped. Our memory of him never forgotten.

Calling the big ones on the air: sports broadcasters live for dramatic endings. Nick Anderson's last-second shot at Indiana amid a five-game victory streak against the Hoosiers ranks very near the top. So do the buzzer beaters of Andy Kaufmann against Iowa and Eddie Johnson against Michigan State. How about the remarkable twin victories over Louisville and Syracuse at Minneapolis on the road to the Final Four in 1989? And the heroics of QBs Dave Wilson, Tony Eason, Jack Trudeau, Jeff George, Jason Verduzco, Johnny Johnson and Kurt Kittner.

Even though the landscape changes with each passing year (the addition of new buildings including the football indoor practice facility, the Ubben basketball practice complex, and the renovations in Memorial Stadium) it is impossible for me not to remember how it was that day in 1951. From my office at WDWS/WHMS radio on Route 45 I can drive north to St. Mary's road, turn east, go under the viaduct, up a slight incline, and there they are: Memorial Stadium as it stood on that snowy day and the Assembly Hall, which came later, but which houses no fewer thrills and chills if you are orange and blue. Out there somewhere was where we parked our car that day: I wish I knew the exact spot. A guy should never forget exactly where he was the moment he fell in love.

Jim Turpin — August 2002

All-Time Fighting Illini Letter-Winner List

Approximately 7,500 men and women have earned varsity letters as athletes in intercollegiate athletics at the University of Illinois from 1878 through the spring of 2002. This list reflects the cumulative information contained within UI's sports summary books. Team managers, who often earned varsity letters, have not been included due to inconsistent information. Female athletes are listed by their maiden names. As with any list of this magnitude, there could be inadvertent errors or omissions. Please contact the UI Athletic Public Relations office should you discover a mistake.

KEY TO ABBREVIATIONS

BB – baseball
WBK – women's basketball
MBK – men's basketball
WCC – women's cross-country
MCC – men's cross-country
FN – fencing

FB – football
WGO – women's golf
MGO – men's golf
WGY – women's gymnastics
MGY – men's gymnastics
IHO – ice hockey

PO – polo
WSO – women's soccer
MSOC – men's soccer
SB – softball
WSW – women's swimming
MSW – men's swimming

WTN – women's tennis
MTN – men's tennis
WTR – women's track & field
MTR – men's track & field
VB – volleyball
WR – wrestling

Baseball

Adsit, Bertram W.	BB	1899,00,01
Agase, Herbert	BB	1950,51
Ahrens, Carl	BB	1951,52,53
Alcock, Warren J.	BB	1917
Alexander, Joe W.	BB	1939
Allen, Aleck M.	BB	1883
Allen, Art	BB	1965
Alley, Mike	BB	1972
Anderlik, Robert	BB	1945,47,48
Anderson, Gary	BB	1971,72,73
Anderson, Jason	BB	1998,99,00
Anderson, Jon	BB	1996,97,98,99
Anderssohn, Henry	BB	1948,49,50
Andrews, Donald H.	BB	1927,28,29
Andrews, William T	BB	1879,80,81
Antonacci, Bill	BB	1995, 96
Arbuckle, Leon	BB	1914,15,16
Arft, Kevin	BB	2000
Arlis, Patrick	BB	2001,02
Arneson, Paul	BB	1959,60,61
Arrandale, Matt	BB	1992,93
Arrasmith, William S.	BB	1919
Arthur, Ecklund	BB	1945
Ashmore, James N.	BB	1902,03
Astroth, Lavere L.	BB	1939,40,42
Atherton, George H.	BB	1891,92
Backs, Jason	BB	1988
Baker, Jerry	BB	1964
Balestri, George	BB	1943
Ballantine, Fred	BB	1949
Ballard, Brady	BB	2000,01
Bane, Frank M.	BB	1914,15

Banker, Edward H.	BB	1922
Baranski, Jerome	BB	1951,52
Barklage, Oliver F.	BB	1918,19
Barnes, Robert A.	BB	1921,22
Barnett, Scott	BB	1980
Barszcx, Casey	BB	1957,58,59
Barta, Joseph T.	BB	1925
Bartley, Boyd O.	BB	1941,42,43
Bartulis, Joe	BB	1931
Basak, Chris	BB	1998,99,00
Baum, Harvey W.	BB	1894,95
Beadle, J. Grant	BB	1885,86,87,88
Beebe, Fred L.	BB	1902,03
Belden, Edgar S.	BB	1888,89,90
Belsole, Bob	BB	1963, 64
Bennett, Cleaves	BB	1888
Bennett, Mike	BB	1970
Bennett, Sean	BB	1995
Bensko, Dusty	BB	2002
Berg, Howard M.	BB	1935,36
Berner, John R.	BB	1938
Berry, Rex	BB	1958
Bessone, Amo	BB	1941
Beyer, George F.	BB	1904,06,07
Bickhaus, Dick	BB	1961
Bickhaus, Jim	BB	1954,55,56
Biel, Joseph	BB	1981
Bills, Victor	BB	1982
Binder, Richard	BB	1967,68,69
Bisbele, Fred B.	BB	1933
Black, Marty	BB	1990,91
Blackaby, Ethan	BB	1960
Blakaslee, James W.	BB	1896

Blandy, D. C.	BB	1883
Blomquist, Brian	BB	2002
Bock, Brian	BB	1979,80,81,82
Boehler, Michael	BB	1977
Bogan, Raki	BB	1995
Bolk, Bill	BB	1956,57,58
Bonk, Bill	BB	1960
Borg, Gary	BB	1982,83,84,85
Borgialli, Dominic	BB	1978,79
Borre, Steven	BB	1977,78
Boudreau, Louis	BB	1937
Bouton, Charles S.	BB	1888,89,90,91
Bowen, Herbert L.	BB	1890
Bower, Lynn K.	BB	1929
Boyd, C. N.	BB	1879,80,81
Bozich, John	BB	1956
Brackett, Jerry	BB	1969,70,71
Bradley, John T.	BB	1914,15,16
Brenton, J. F.	BB	1912
Brewer, Joseph	BB	1951
Brewer, William R.	BB	1939,41,42
Briggs, C. W.	BB	1886,87,88
Brittin, John	BB	1943,47
Brooks, Richard A.	BB	1905,06
Brown, Donald	BB	1929,30
Brozek, Gary	BB	1982
Bruin, W. W.	BB	1931
Bunn, Charles M.	BB	1910
Bunton, F. L.	BB	1887
Burlage, Bob	BB	1996,97,98,99
Busche, Justin	BB	1995, 97
Bushnell, Howard	BB	1905,06,07
Butkovich, William	BB	1944,45

Butler, F. L.	BB	1895,96
Butzer, Glenn D.	BB	1910,11
Buzwick, John W.	BB	1908,10
Cahill, James	BB	1979
Callaghan, Rich	BB	1963,64,65
Callahan, John H.	BB	1936,37,38
Calza, Tom	BB	1968, 69
Campbell, Charles M.	BB	1941,42
Canan, Rich	BB	1985
Cann, Fremont G.	BB	1928
Caparilli, Rich	BB	1986,1987,88,89
Carlson, Clifford C.	BB	1933,34
Carnahan, David H.	BB	1892,93,95,96
Carnahan, Franklin G.	BB	1890,91,92
Carpenter, Hubert V.	BB	1896,97
Carrithers, Ira T.	BB	1906,07
Cashman, Brandon	BB	2002
Cashmore, Richard	BB	1948
Catalano, Phil	BB	1959,60
Cavallo, Ernest S.	BB	1938,39
Cawley, Mitchell	BB	1980
Champagne, Brannon	BB	1984,85,86
Chase, Morton E.	BB	1879
Chervinko, Paul	BB	1931,32,33
Christensen, Bob	BB	1987,88,89,90
Christiansen, Donald W.	BB	1938
Christopher, Ron	BB	1964
Ciaramelli, Robert	BB	1943
Cimack, Jeffrey	BB	1975
Clapp, David	BB	1979
Clark, Arthur S.	BB	1883
Clark, George	BB	1915,16
Clarkson, James F.	BB	1888,89,90

Greg Colby

Cochran, Phillip	BB	1969
Coffey, Lawrence	BB	1984,85
Cogdal, Harry F.	BB	1913,14,15
Cohick, Emmitt	BB	1989,90
Colangelo, Jerry	BB	1960
Colby, Greg	BB	1972,73,74
Colton, Seth W.	BB	1880
Conley, Frank C.	BB	1938
Conroy, Jimmy	BB	2002
Conte, Randy	BB	1979,80,81,82
Cook, Gary	BB	1973
Cook, James F.	BB	1900,01,02,03
Cook, Louis P.	BB	1903,04
Cooper, Paul H.	BB	1892,94,95,96
Cordova, Randy	BB	1971,72,73
Cortesi, Bob	BB	1971,72,73
Cox, Henry R.	BB	1917
Crangle, Walter F.	BB	1921
Crawford, Ken	BB	1993,94
Crews, Randy	BB	1968,69,70
Cross, Charles W.	BB	1889,90,91,92
Crossley, Clarence F.	BB	1920,22

John Ericks

Crotser, Max	BB	1959,60,61
Crouse, Dave	BB	1964,65,66
Cuchran, Don	BB	1988,89,90
Cvik, James	BB	1958,59
Dahlhein, Bruce	BB	1975,76,77
Dalbeck, Leon	BB	1927
Dalesandro, Mark	BB	1987,88,89,90
Dancisak, Edward J.	BB	1936
Daukus, Anthony	BB	1936
Davidson, Drew	BB	2002
Davis, John E.	BB	1915,16,17
Davis, James O.	BB	1883
Davis, John	BB	1951,52
Delveaux, Jack	BB	1958,59
Demmitt, Charles R.	BB	1905,06
DePaolis, Carl	BB	1978,80
DePew, Daren	BB	1984
Depken, Gerhard C.	BB	1933
DeVelde, H. S.	BB	1900,01,02
Devero, James	BB	1946
Dicke, Otto A.	BB	1906,07
Dickinson, Andy	BB	2000,01,02
Diehl, Harold A.	BB	1919
Dierkes, Alfred	BB	1952
Diffenbaugh, Harry	BB	1879,80,81
DiMaria, Vince	BB	2001,02
Disosway, Mark D.	BB	1907,08
Dixon, Wesley	BB	1970,71,72
Dobry, Tim	BB	1994
Dorn, Ernest F.	BB	1927,28,29
Doss, Paul C.	BB	1918,19
Doty, Dick	BB	1971,72
Dougherty, Floyd C.	BB	1921,22
Doyle, Russell	BB	1938
Drechsler, Russell E.	BB	1939,40,41
Dresson, Mark	BB	1989,90,91,92
Drish, John W.	BB	1939,40,41
Dudas, Daniel	BB	1954,55,56
Duffner, John	BB	1934,35,36
Durant, Phillip S.	BB	1921,23
Dystrup, Andrew	BB	1967
Eads, Robert	BB	1944
Edwards, James B.	BB	1918,19
Eichelberger, Tony	BB	1960,61,62
Eilbracht, Lee P.	BB	1943,46,47
Ellis, George H.	BB	1883,84,85
Emerick, Bill	BB	1971
Engle, David	BB	1970,71,72
English, Frank J.	BB	1917,20
Engvall, Phillip W.	BB	1929
Ericks, John	BB	1986,87,88
Erickson, Carl V.	BB	1925
Evans, Edwin R.	BB	1907
Evers, Walter A.	BB	1939
Eyer, Lawrence	BB	1975,76,77
Falkenburg, Fred P.	BB	1900,01,02
Farr, Alvin I.	BB	1909
Farrington, Charles E.	BB	1938

Fazzini, Pat	BB	1974,75,76,77
Feigenbutz, Vince	BB	1952,53,54
Feldman, Stanley	BB	1948,49
Felichio, Francis	BB	1960,61,62
Fencl, G. S.	BB	1930,31,32
Feuerbach, William J.	BB	1892
Filippo, Richard	BB	1980,81,82
Fillipan, John	BB	1976
Finn, Richard G.	BB	1926,27,28
Finn, Robert L.	BB	1941,42
Fischer, George	BB	1947,48
Fitzgerald, Joseph	BB	1954,55
Fleager, Clarence E.	BB	1898,99
Fletcher, Charles H.	BB	1912,13
Fletcher, Darrin	BB	1985,86,87
Fletcher, Tom	BB	1962
Flock, Ward J.	BB	1917
Flodin, Lloyd	BB	1961,62,63
Flynn, James	BB	1954,57,58
Flynn, Pat	BB	2002
Follmer, Clive	BB	1952,53
Fort, Charles	BB	1952,53,54
Foss, William	BB	1967,68,69
Frangos, John	BB	1992
Franklin, Murray	BB	1935,36,37
Frazier, Bruce	BB	1951,52,53
Frederickson, Daniel T.	BB	1894
Frederickson, George	BB	1891,92,93,94
Frederickson, Trevor	BB	2001,02
Frederickson, William	BB	1886,87,88
Frees, Herman	BB	1893,94,96
Frentz, William	BB	1956
Frew, Pete	BB	1994
Frighetto, Mark	BB	1975,76
Frillman, James	BB	1955,57
Frink, Frederick F.	BB	1932,33,34
Fritz, Alan	BB	1969,70,71
Frk, Chad	BB	2001
Fuller, James R.	BB	1887,88,89
Fulton, G. T.	BB	1892,93
Fulton, Robert B.	BB	1899,00,02
Fulton, William J.	BB	1895,96,97,98
Funk, Brian	BB	1997,98
Funk, Clarence P.	BB	1883
Furber, William A.	BB	1891
Fuzak, William G.	BB	1930,31
Galla, George	BB	1963
Gantt, Dave	BB	1959
Gasparich, Timothy	BB	1981
Gawron, William	BB	1958
Gbur, Edward F.	BB	1930,31,32
Gedvilas, Leo	BB	1944,45,46
Gellinger, Terry	BB	1958,1959,60
Gertz, Jeff	BB	1999,00,01
Gillespie, Gordon	BB	1944
Gilliland, William	BB	1887,88,89,90
Glade, Henry A.	BB	1928
Godeke, Frank B.	BB	1925

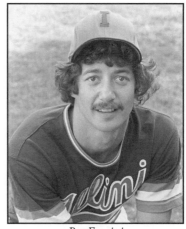
Pat Fazzini

Gold, Josh	BB	2001,02
Goldstein, Charles B.	BB	1933
Gorski, Tim	BB	2001,02
Goss, James	BB	1975,76
Gotfryd, Peter J.	BB	1943
Grant, Alan S.	BB	1939,40,41
Graves, Marvin	BB	1953,55
Graves, Perry H.	BB	1914
Gregory, Flint	BB	1968,69,70
Gregory, Gregg	BB	1966,67
Gribble, Paul A.	BB	1927
Groth, Gene	BB	1965
Gugala, John	BB	1947,48,49
Gundlach, Norman J.	BB	1926,27,28
Gunkel, Woodward W.	BB	1914,15,16
Gunn, Charles A.	BB	1891,92
Gunn, Richard	BB	1955, 1956
Gunning, Delany T.	BB	1905,06,07
Gussis, Lloyd	BB	1967,68,69
Guth, Glenn	BB	1971
Haake, Eric	BB	1988
Haas, Raymond C.	BB	1918,20

Jeff Gertz

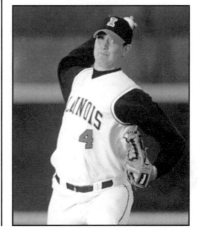

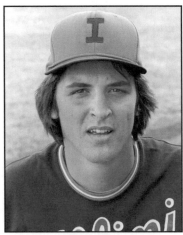

John Harshbarger

Mike Jurack

Haskell, Howard H.	BB	1893,94,95,96
Haskins, Richard	BB	1952,53
Hawkins, LeShawn	BB	1992,93,94
Hazlitt, Albert M.	BB	1897,98
Hazzard, E. M.	BB	1930,31
Heberer, Ronald	BB	1951,52
Hecht, Brian	BB	1995,96,97
Heikes, Samuel I.	BB	1920
Heinrich, Tom	BB	1971,72
Heinz, Vince	BB	1999,00
Hellstrom, Norton E.	BB	1921,22,23
Henry, Wilbur L.	BB	1935,36,37
Herzog, Shawn	BB	1994,95
Hess, G. R.	BB	1913
Hester, Jack	BB	1952
Hester, John	BB	1953,54
Higgins, Charles H.	BB	1901,02
Hill, Arthur H.	BB	1901,04
Hills, Stacy R.	BB	1894
Hinrichsen, George C.	BB	1907
Hinze, Victor H.	BB	1936,37
Hobbs, Glenn M.	BB	1890
Hodges, Bill	BB	1970,71,72,73
Hoffenberg, Earl	BB	1967
Hoffman, George O.	BB	1925,26,27
Hoffman, Thomas	BB	1949
Hoffman, William	BB	1950,51
Hohm, Harley D.	BB	1916
Holland, Pat	BB	1962,63
Holtzman, Ken	BB	1965
Hooper, Max	BB	1952,53,54
Hotchkin, Robert	BB	1935
Hotchkiss, Robert J.	BB	1894,95
Hrnyak, Nick	BB	1983
Huff, George A.	BB	1889,90,91,92
Huff, Roger G.	BB	1910
Huff, Walter W.	BB	1907
Hull, James M.	BB	1924
Hull, Thomas F.	BB	1942
Humay, Dan	BB	1965,66,67
Humphrey, Darryl	BB	1986
Huntley, Converse R.	BB	1879,80,81
Hyde, Rich	BB	1989,90,91
Iavarone, Greg	BB	1982,83,84,85
Ingle, Scott	BB	1903
Ingram, Daniel	BB	1974,75,76
Ingrum, Ronald	BB	1967,68,69
Ingwersen, Burton A.	BB	1918,19,20
Innis, Brian	BB	1982
Innis, Jeffrey	BB	1981,82,83
Ippolito, Vince	BB	1998
Irwin, Doug	BB	1992,93
Jackson, Clifford L.	BB	1921,22,23
Jackson, Matt	BB	1995, 96
Jackson, T.J.	BB	1997,98,99

Jackson, Trenton	BB	1965
Janicki, Nick	BB	1970
Jasper, Thomas	BB	1890,91,92,93
Jestes, Edmiston R.	BB	1924,25
Johansen, Bob	BB	1965
Johns, John	BB	1944,45
Johnson, Dennis	BB	1981,83
Johnson, E. Thomas	BB	1919,20,21
Johnson, Ron	BB	1961,62
Johnson, Tony	BB	1955
Johnston, Arthur R.	BB	1897,98,99,00
Jonas, Joel	BB	1964
Jones, Carl	BB	1984,85,87
Jones, Douglas	BB	1980,82,83
Jordan, Jerome J.	BB	1925,26
Journell, Jimmy	BB	1998
Joy, Samuel S.	BB	1898
Judson, Howard	BB	1944,45
Judson, Phil	BB	1955,56
Jurack, Mike	BB	1991,92,93
Jurasevich, John	BB	1958,59,60
Juul, Herbert V.	BB	1906
Kaires, Gerald	BB	1945,46,48
Kaiser, Paul W.	BB	1919
Kal, Harris	BB	1974,75,76
Kallis, Leonard	BB	1938,40
Kandel, Bruce	BB	1975,76,77
Kane, Doug	BB	1985,86,87
Kasch, Fred W.	BB	1933,34
Kasper, Ray	BB	1964,65,66
Kating, John	BB	1956,57,58
Kay, Charles J.	BB	1913
Kelso, E. L.	BB	1879
Kemman, Herbert F.	BB	1911
Kempf, George A.	BB	1911
Kilbane, James	BB	1946,47,48
Kimball, Edwin R.	BB	1883,84
Kinderman, Frederick W.	BB	1924,25,26
Kingman, Charles D.	BB	1895,96
Kinkead, David R.	BB	1887,88,89
Kirby, Marty	BB	1977
Kissinger, Donald K.	BB	1918,19,20
Klaus, Robert	BB	1957,58,59
Kleber, Doug	BB	1974,75,76,77
Klein, J. Leo	BB	1916,17,18
Klemm, Frederick	BB	1965,66,67
Klimek, Josh	BB	1993,95
Knebelkamp, Kent	BB	1983,84
Knotts, Tom	BB	1974,75
Koch, Paul	BB	1965,66
Koestner, Elmer	BB	1955
Kolb, Gary	BB	1960
Kopale, Robert	BB	1979,81,82
Kopatz, Jim	BB	1974
Kopka, John	BB	1949

Hadsall, H. H.	BB	1896,97
Haefler, Robert E.	BB	1936,37
Halas, George S.	BB	1916,17
Halas, Walter H.	BB	1914,15,16
Hall, Albert R.	BB	1899
Haller, Thomas	BB	1957
Hamstra, Daniel	BB	1980,82,83,84
Hanson, Michael	BB	1983
Hanssen, Gustav A.	BB	1887,88,89,90
Hapac, William J.	BB	1939,40
Happeny, J. Clifford	BB	1923
Hargis, Douglas	BB	1981,82
Harold, Robert	BB	1975,76
Harper, Robert H.	BB	1924
Harrington, Raymond B.	BB	1928
Harris, Newton M.	BB	1891
Harshbarger, John	BB	1977,78
Hart, Ralph W.	BB	1892
Harvey, Donald	BB	1958,59
Harvey, Ted	BB	1963

Jeff Innis

Kopp, William K.	BB	1918,19,20
Koptik, Bohumil J.	BB	1915,16,17
Kortkamp, Andy	BB	1993,94,95
Kowalski, August J.	BB	1935
Kraft, Mike	BB	1989,90
Krantz, Louis	BB	1950,51,52
Krebs, Wilbur E.	BB	1914,15,16
Krupar, Charles F.	BB	1918
Kucera, Richard K.	BB	1938,40
Kuehl, Edwin C.	BB	1923
Kuehn, Clyde	BB	1968,69,70
Kumerow, Ernie	BB	1959,60,61
Kusinski, John	BB	1926,27,29
Kvasnicka, Ryan	BB	2000,01
Lachky, Joe	BB	1972
Laing, George D.	BB	1912
Lalor, Foster M.	BB	1917,18
Lane, Josh	BB	2002
Lanter, Wayne	BB	1957
Lapins, Ron	BB	1973,74,75

Andy Kortkamp

Tim Lavery

Robert Malley

Name		Years
Larson, Lambert L.	BB	1913
Latham, E. B.	BB	1883
Laurvick, Brett	BB	1994,95
Lavery, Tim	BB	1997, 98, 99
Lawrence, Ryan	BB	2000
Lawrence, Sean	BB	1991
Leonard, Berny	BB	1966
Leonardi, Anthony	BB	1982,83
Lewis, Ben C.	BB	1933,34,35
Ligare, Edwardo	BB	1886
Light, Curtis R.	BB	1911
Lindbeck, Emerit	BB	1955,56
Linden, Frank W.	BB	1898
Long, Frank B.	BB	1884,85,86,87
Lorenz, Bob	BB	1966
Lotz, John R.	BB	1898,99,00,01
Lowes, Forrest M.	BB	1894,95
Ludlam, John S.	BB	1926
Lukaszewski, Don	BB	1955,56,57
Lundgren, Carl L.	BB	1899,00,01,02

Name		Years
Lundine, Dan	BB	1995
Lundstedt, Dave	BB	1972,73,74,75
Lymperopoulous, J.	BB	1928,29,30
Mackay, John L.	BB	1884,85
Madix, Bob	BB	1958,59,60
Maier, George	BB	1951
Majercik, Larry	BB	1970
Major, Charles F.	BB	1925,26
Maksud, Mike	BB	1954
Malley, Robert	BB	1946,47
Margolis, Ralph	BB	1924,25,26
Marquie, Craig	BB	1997,98,99,00
Marsillo, Paul	BB	1977,78,79,80
Martin, Jeff	BB	1993,94,95,96
Martin, Russell	BB	1958,59,60
Masek, Albert	BB	1934
Mason, Lou	BB	1908
Massey, Keith	BB	1984,85,86
Matejzel, August	BB	1968,69,70
Mathews, Clyde M.	BB	1899,00,01,02
Matt, John	BB	1960,61,62
Maurer, Ron	BB	1963,64,65
Maxwell, John R.	BB	1893
Mayville, Mike	BB	1974,76
Mazeika, Anthony M.	BB	1938,39
Mazurek, Dave	BB	2002
McBride, Kevin	BB	1977,78,79
McCabe, Claude P.	BB	1933
McCann, Thomas E.	BB	1921
McClure, Brian	BB	1993,94,95
McClure, Ora D.	BB	1890
McCollum, Greg	BB	1984,85,86,87
McCollum, Harvey D.	BB	1897,98,99,00
McConnell, Thomas M.	BB	1937,38,39
McCormick, Olin	BB	1892
McCully, Matt	BB	1994,95
McCune, Henry L.	BB	1880,81,83
McCurdy, Henry H.	BB	1920,21,22
McDonald, John J.	BB	1936,37
McDonald, Robert	BB	1980
McEathron, William J.	BB	1883
McGill, Ruel S.	BB	1897,98
McIlduff, Thomas E.	BB	1879,81
McKinney, Jerry	BB	1956
McMullen, Rolla	BB	1956,57
McRobie, Douglas	BB	1914
Meagher, T.F.	BB	2001,02
Mee, Julian E.	BB	1920,21
Melino, Castanzo	BB	1936
Merrifield, Albert W.	BB	1889,90,91,92
Mershon, Brian	BB	1986,87
Mershon, Mike	BB	1988
Meyer, Irwin H.	BB	1929
Meyers, William	BB	1945
Michalak, Tony	BB	1984,85,86,87

Name		Years
Miller, Fred C.	BB	1900,03
Miller, Jerome	BB	1952,53
Miller, Lester	BB	1946,47,48
Mills, Doug	BB	1960,61,62
Mills, George A.	BB	1930,31,32
Milosevich, Paul	BB	1940,41,42
Mitter, Todd	BB	1988,89
Mohr, Scott	BB	1978
Molaro, Steve	BB	1959
Moler, Jason	BB	1989,90
Moore, Barry	BB	1966
Moore, Robert	BB	1951,52,53
Morrison, John E.	BB	1907,08
Moyer, Carlisle E.	BB	1933,34,35
Mroz, Wallie	BB	1945
Muirhead, William	BB	1953
Mulligan, Sean	BB	1989,90,91
Mundt, Craig	BB	1964
Munson, Mike	BB	1985,86,87,88
Murawski, Michael	BB	1967,68,69
Murray, Bill	BB	1966,67,68
Murray, James	BB	1977,78,79
Myers, William	BB	1946,47
Naprestek, Frank J.	BB	1911
Nash, Joseph	BB	1977
Neal, John	BB	1949,50
Needham, James	BB	1892
Nelligan, Ryan	BB	1990,91
Nelson, H. A.	BB	1879,80,81
Nelson, Robert	BB	1969
Neufeldt, James	BB	1945,47
Nevins, Arthur S.	BB	1913
New, Nash	BB	1968
Newcom, Gregory	BB	1980,81
Nicholson, Garry	BB	1970,71
Nieckula, Aaron	BB	1995,96,97,98
Niezgoda, Joe	BB	1962,63
Niezyniecki, Ted	BB	1986,87
Niklewicz, F.T.	BB	1934,36,37
Noble, John	BB	1884
Noth, Charles J.	BB	1942
Nusspickel, Raymond E.	BB	1930
Nykeil, Theodore	BB	1938
O'Connor, Forrest E.	BB	1923,24
O'Connor, Kevin	BB	1989,90
O'Grady, John	BB	1928
O'Keefe, James A.	BB	1926
Oestreich, John	BB	1992,93,94,95
Offenbecher, Bill	BB	1959
Ohman, Tom	BB	1966,67
Oien, Charles	BB	1979
Olker, Joseph	BB	1982,83,84
Olson, Justin	BB	1999,00,01,02
O'Neill, Dan	BB	1996,97,98,99
Oros, James	BB	1977,78,79

Aaron Nieckula

Name		Years
Orsag, James	BB	1983,84,85
Ossola, Ken	BB	1970,71,72,73
Ovitz, Ernest G.	BB	1906,07,08
Pacotti, John B.	BB	1938,40
Palacio, Bob	BB	1990
Pall, Donn,	BB	1983,84,85
Palmer, Howard	BB	1944
Panique, Ken	BB	1973
Parenti, George	BB	1949,51
Parenti, Joe	BB	2000, 02
Parker, Edwin S.	BB	1942,43
Parker, Roy S.	BB	1902,03,04
Parks, Ryan	BB	2002
Parr, S. W.	BB	1883
Parsons, Wil	BB	1989,90
Patrick, Sean	BB	2002
Paul, Earl A.	BB	1927
Pawlow, Richard	BB	1957
Paxton, Albert E.	BB	1925
Payne, Donnie	BB	1992,93,94
Payton, David	BB	1984,85,86,87

David Payton

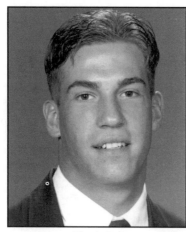

Travis Rehrer

Peach, John	BB	1976,77,78
Pearson, W. W.	BB	1889,90
Peden, Don C.	BB	1921,22
Peekel, Rick	BB	1972,73,74
Peelman, Aaron	BB	1998
Peirce, Fred D.	BB	1883
Penn, Albert	BB	1908
Penn, Henry	BB	1909,10
Perry, Loyd W.	BB	1943
Pershell, Russell M.	BB	1935
Peterson, Carl	BB	1962,63
Peterson, Mike	BB	1964,66
Peterson, Reuben W.	BB	1917
Petreshene, Victor	BB	1955,56,57
Pfeffer, Frank	BB	1904
Phelps, John C.	BB	1912,13,14
Philbrick, Alvah	BB	1883,84,85,86
Philbrick, Solon	BB	1883,84
Phillip, Andres M.	BB	1942,43,47
Pierce, Charles I.	BB	1889
Pike, Max N.	BB	1932

Danny Rhodes

Pillsbury, Arthur L.	BB	1889
Pitts, R. L.	BB	1903,04,05
Plain, Henry A.	BB	1949,50
Planert, Edward	BB	1944,45,46
Plews, Herb	BB	1948,49,50
Poat, Raymond W.	BB	1937
Pogue, Bob	BB	1966
Pollak, Mike	BB	1972
Polock, Bob	BB	1971,72,73
Ponting, Theophilus C.	BB	1925
Possehl, Louis	BB	1944
Possehl, Robert	BB	1946
Potter, Robert	BB	1952
Powers, Tim	BB	1987,88
Powers, Tom	BB	1986,87
Prentiss, William	BB	1943
Prindiville, Frank J.	BB	1912,13
Provenzano, Tony	BB	1961,62,63
Pullen, Robert	BB	1981,82,83,84
Pyrz, Anthony C.	BB	1939,40
Quarles, Samuel	BB	1975,76
Quayle, Robert H.	BB	1909,10
Quinn, E. J.	BB	1890,91
Radford, Norman H.	BB	1927
Raklovits, Richard	BB	1950,51
Ray, Hugh L.	BB	1905,06
Raymond, Brian	BB	2001, 02
Rear, David	BB	1981,82
Reed, Jim	BB	1965,66,67
Rehrer, Travis	BB	1996,97,98,99
Reichle, Richard W.	BB	1920,22
Reinhart, Freddie A.	BB	1935,36,37
Rekitzke, Philip	BB	1983
Renner, Jerry	BB	1961,62,63
Rhodes, Danny	BB	1995,96,97,98
Rhodes, Dusty	BB	1995,96,97,98
Richards, Jeff	BB	1988,89
Richards, Ronald	BB	1957
Richardson, Timothy	BB	1980,81,82,83
Rickman, T.	BB	1929
Righter, Edwin B.	BB	1908,10
Rightnowar, Brad	BB	1996
Rinaker, Lewis	BB	1888
Rizzo, Kenneth	BB	1967,68
Roberts, Brian	BB	1989,90,91
Roberts, Ralph O.	BB	1903,04
Robertson, Thomas	BB	1976
Robinson, Mark	BB	1984,87
Robinson, William B.	BB	1924
Rodgerson, Mike	BB	1965,66,67
Roettger, Walter H.	BB	1922,23,24
Rogers, Greg	BB	1984
Rommelman, Douglas	BB	1978,79
Rosenfeldt, H.	BB	1931
Rosenthal, Frank V.	BB	1929,31

Rotblatt, Marvin	BB	1945,46,47,48
Roth, Robert J.	BB	1942
Rothgeb, C. J.	BB	1904,05
Rounds, William P.	BB	1886,87
Rowe, Enos M.	BB	1912
Rowe, Ted	BB	2002
Roysdon, William I.	BB	1892,93,94,95
Rozmus, Jerrry	BB	1962
Rucks, Jim	BB	1972,73
Rudden, Kevin	BB	1996,97,98,99
Rush, Ira L.	BB	1913,14,15
Russell, Charles M.	BB	1880,81
Russell, David	BB	1966,68
Russell, Frank H.	BB	1935
Ruth, Mike	BB	1992
Ryan, Howard R.	BB	1917,19,20
Rykovich, Julius	BB	1943,47
Ryniec, Al	BB	1972,73,74
Ryniec, Dave	BB	1963,64,65
Ryniec, Lou	BB	1959,60,61,62
Ryniec, Tim	BB	1987
Sabalaskey, John	BB	1952,53,54
Sainati, Leo	BB	1938
Salter, Cody	BB	1995,96,97,98
Samuels, Jonathan H.	BB	1885,86,87,88
Sander, Matt	BB	1992,93
Sanford, Derek	BB	1967
Schaefer, Paul V.	BB	1908,09
Scharf, Albert	BB	1943,46,47
Scheidegger, Bruce	BB	1979,80
Schierer, Charles	BB	1967,68,69
Schiller, Charles L.	BB	1942
Schinker, Lee	BB	1962,63
Schlapprizzi, Lester B.	BB	1923,24
Schlueter, Bill	BB	1965
Schmitke, Todd	BB	1979,80,81,82
Schober, Max W.	BB	1905
Scholz, Mike	BB	1973,74
Schrader, Alfred C.	BB	1883,84,85
Schuckman, Meyers	BB	1937
Schuldt, James	BB	1953
Schullian, Brian	BB	1992,93,94,95
Schumacher, Greg	BB	1962
Schumaker, Jason	BB	1991,92,94
Schustek, Ivan D.	BB	1932,34
Schutzenhofer, Andy	BB	2000,01,02
Schwartz, Frank	BB	1956,57,58
Schwartz, Lloyd	BB	1910
Sconce, Harvey J.	BB	1896
Scott, Donald G.	BB	1893
Scott, Steve	BB	1974,75,76,77
Scott, Tom	BB	1953,54
Secrest, John	BB	1964,65
Seifert, Dave	BB	1992,93
Shannon, James S.	BB	1887

Brian Schullian

Shapland, Robert	BB	1969,70,71
Shaw, Joseph E.	BB	1928
Sheean, Frank T.	BB	1899
Shields, Raymond J.	BB	1908
Shlaudeman, Harry	BB	1884,85,86
Shoptaw, Robert	BB	1955,56,57
Shuler, Hugh M.	BB	1896,97,98
Shumway, Horatio G.	BB	1884
Siegel, Jeff	BB	1974,75,76
Silkman, John M.	BB	1913
Simmons, Luke	BB	1999,00,01,02
Simonetti, Robert	BB	1949
Simonich, Louis J.	BB	1924,25
Sinak, Tom	BB	1993,94,95
Sipes, Stanton	BB	1976
Siron, Jon	BB	1973,74,75
Sisco, August C.	BB	1937
Skikas, Norm	BB	1960
Skizas, Gus	BB	1949,50
Skizas, Peter	BB	1982
Slocum, Karl R.	BB	1905
Slusher, Carroll	BB	1969,70,71

Luke Simmons

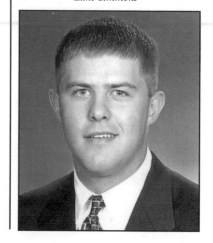

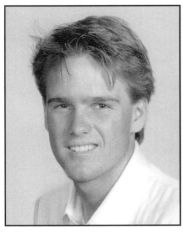

Larry Sutton

Small, Andy	BB	1989,90,91,92
Smiley, Jack	BB	1946
Smiser, Todd	BB	1991,92,93
Smith, Charles "Bubba"	BB	1989,90,91
Smith, Daniel N.	BB	1933
Smith, Gerald	BB	1953,54
Smith, Jerome	BB	1952
Smith Jr., Maurice	BB	1967
Smith, Mick	BB	1966
Smith, Reilly	BB	2001,02
Snyder, Ira D.	BB	1929
Snyder, James B.	BB	1906,07,08
Sokol, Steven	BB	1978
Sommer, Chuck	BB	1972,73
Spaulding, Tony	BB	1991
Spencer, James E.	BB	1884,85,86
Spiezio, Scott	BB	1991,92,93
Sprengard, Joe	BB	1997,2000
Stahl, Floyd S.	BB	1926
Stahl, Garland	BB	1901,02,03
Stange, Harold	BB	1946,49

Keith Toriani

Steele, Phil	BB	1886,87
Steger, Kurt	BB	1976,77,78
Steger, Peter	BB	1978
Steger, Russell	BB	1947,48,49,50
Steinwedell, Carl	BB	1900,01,02,03
Steuernagel, Fred W.	BB	1930,31,32
Stewart, James R.	BB	1926,27,28
Stewart, Paul J.	BB	1921,22,23
Stewart Jr., Thomas	BB	1974,75,76
Stierwalt, Mitchell	BB	1979,80,81
Stiles, Leroy C.	BB	1915,16
Strainis, Frank	BB	1961,62,63
Studebaker, Adam	BB	1991,94
Suter, Earl R.	BB	1913
Sutton, Larry	BB	1989,90,91,92
Svihlik, D.J.	BB	1997,98,99,00
Swakon, Larry	BB	1971,72,73,75
Swanson, Harold A.	BB	1935,36,37
Swasney, E. H.	BB	1879,80,81
Sweeney, Ira J.	BB	1926,27,28
Swikle, Charles G.	BB	1934,35,36
Switzer, Robert M.	BB	1900
Szukala, Jerry	BB	1965,66
Tangman, Horace J.	BB	1949,50
Tarajack, Bill	BB	1996
Targgart, Shawn	BB	1997,99
Tarkoff, Daniel	BB	1978,79
Taylor, Joseph W.	BB	1904,05,07
Tedesco, Robert	BB	1957,58
Theobald, William G.	BB	1933
Thienpont, Greg	BB	1984
Thomas, Glen H.	BB	1916
Thomas, Robert E.	BB	1912,13
Thomas, Raymond R.	BB	1910,11,12
Thomas, Tim	BB	1988
Thompson, Andy	BB	1991,92,93,94
Thompson, Fred L.	BB	1895,86
Thonn, Ray	BB	1956,57,58
Thornton, Robert I.	BB	1897,98
Throneburg, Derek	BB	2001
Thurlby, Burdette	BB	1948,50
Tieken, Theo	BB	1886,87
Toncoff, John	BB	1933,34
Tookey, Bill	BB	1964
Toriani, Keith	BB	1990,91,92,93
Travis, Terrence	BB	1983
Trayser, Tom	BB	1999
True, Bill	BB	1992,93
Trugillo, Glen	BB	1949,50
Tryban, Edward E.	BB	1930,31,32
Twist, Clarence C.	BB	1911
Ultes, Ronald	BB	1952,53,54
Valente, John	BB	1986,87,88
Vandagrift, Carl W.	BB	1905,06,07
Vangundy, Charles P.	BB	1886,87,88

Vangundy, Claude	BB	1910,11
VanHooreweghe, Joseph	BB	1943
Vanselow, Harold	BB	1968,69
Vayda, John	BB	1954,55,56
Venegoni, John	BB	1978,79
Vermette, Jim	BB	1958,59
Vincent, Randall	BB	1974,75,76,77
Vitacco, Alfred G.	BB	1939
Vogel, Otto H.	BB	1921,22,23
Vopicka, Jim	BB	1964,65
Vorreyer, Richard	BB	1955,56,57
Vorwald, Matt	BB	1999,00,01
Wahl, Edward C.	BB	1931,32
Wahl, Robert T.	BB	1941
Wakefield, James	BB	1945,46,47,48
Walenga, Frank	BB	1951,52
Walenwander, John	BB	1986,87,88
Walker, Harold B.	BB	1928,29
Wallace, Edward	BB	1911
Warfield, Roy M.	BB	1891
Warford, Dennis	BB	1980
Warmbier, Kenneth	BB	1982,83,84,85
Warner, Earl A.	BB	1904
Waters, Alan	BB	1965,66,67
Watts, Claude H.	BB	1911,12,13
Weber, Edward W.	BB	1934,35,36
Weber, W. Henry	BB	1910,11,12
Wedding, James	BB	1968
Weisenborn, Harold	BB	1963
Wells, Forry	BB	1991,92,93,94
Wells, Terry	BB	1983,84,85
Wentz, Brad	BB	1986,87,88
Wenzel, Rusty	BB	1979
Wernham, James I.	BB	1897,98,99
West, Ron	BB	1954
Weygandt, Jerry	BB	1962,63,64
White, Brian	BB	1980,81,82,83
White, Frank	BB	1879
Whitmore, Harold	BB	1905
Wicker, Brett	BB	2002
Wickersham, Don	BB	1971,72
Wickland, Albert	BB	1947,48
Widdersheim, John	BB	1977,78
Wiedow, Roy W.	BB	1944,45,46
Wilder, Frank S.	BB	1900
Williams, David	BB	1955,56,57
Williams, Milton L.	BB	1929,30
Williams, Sean	BB	1994,95
Wiman, Robert	BB	1954,55
Windmiller, Robert	BB	1969,70,71
Wing, Roger	BB	1952,53
Winston, Charles S.	BB	1898
Witte, Theodore C.	BB	1929,30,31
Wohlwend, Dave	BB	1992,93,94
Wojs, Dennis	BB	1966,67,68

Jason Wollard

Wollard, Jason	BB	1993,94,95
Wolters, Mike	BB	1986,87,88
Worth, John C.	BB	1925,26
Wrobke, Dewey	BB	1918,19,20
Wrobke, Floyd	BB	1932,33
Wuethrich, David	BB	1981,82
Yeaton, Frederick C.	BB	1934
Young, Everett	BB	1944
Yule, John S.	BB	1929,32,33
Yurtis, Barry	BB	1969,70
Zangerle, Adolph A.	BB	1903,04
Zeller, Roger L.	BB	1939
Ziemba, Chester J.	BB	1939,41
Zinker, Edward	BB	1950,51

Women's Basketball

Albers, Sally	WBK	1996,97,98
Allen, Jae	WBK	1975
Anderson, Betty	WBK	1975,76,77
Beach, Becky	WBK	1976,77,78
Berggren, Ashley	WBK	1995,96,97,98

Susan Blauser

Cindy Dallas

Blackburn, Brenda	WBK	2001,02
Blauser, Susan	WBK	1999,00
Bond, Kris	WBK	1995,96,97,98
Boner, Susan	WBK	1976,77,78
Booker, Tonya	WBK	1991,92,93,94
Bradley, Lisa	WBK	1985,86,87,88
Brauer, Liz	WBK	1979,80,81
Brombolich, Kim	WBK	1981,82
Carie, Doris	WBK	1987,88,89,90
Carlson, Jan	WBK	1975,76
Carmichael, Carol	WBK	1977,78,79
Catchings, Tauja	WBK	1997,98,99,00
Clinton, Anita	WBK	1993,94
Coleman, Katie	WBK	1997,98
Cundiff, Monica	WBK	1989,90,91,92
Cunningham, Mandy	WBK	1991,92,93,94
Curtin, Allison	WBK	1999,00,01
Curtin, Suzanne	WBK	2000,01
Dallas, Cindy	WBK	2001,02
Deeken, Dee Dee	WBK	1987,88,89
Dexter, Kelly	WBK	1996,97,98
Dial, Stephanie	WBK	1990

Kate Riley

Dilger, Cindy	WBK	1992,93
Dill, Marchoe	WBK	1994,95,96,97
Dluzak, Marijo	WBK	1975,76,77
Dupps, Kris	WBK	1992,93,94,95
Eickholt, Diane	WBK	1981,82,83,84
Estey, Jill	WBK	1990,91,92,93
Faulkner, Kristi	WBK	2000
Flannigan, Kathy	WBK	1977,78,79,80
Gallagher, Joyce	WBK	1979
Gamboa, Renee	WSW	1995
Gantt, Kendra	WBK	1982,83,84,85
Guarneri, Lisa	WBK	1998,99
Guth, Allison	WBK	2002
Guthrie, Tiffanie	WBK	2002
Hagberg, Karen	WBK	2000,01,02
Hanna, Cindi	WBK	1993,94,95,96
Harris, Sandra	WBK	1988,89
Haynes, Kristen	WBK	1987,88,89,90
Hemann, Jackie	WBK	1992
Henderson, Ann	WBK	1994,95,96,97
Henderson, Carrie	WBK	1986
Henry, Trisha	WSW	1995
Hofer, Lori	WBK	1983
Horvath, Cheryl	WBK	1978,79
Hudgins, Lesley	WBK	1986,87,88
Hunter, Shavonna	WBK	2000,01,02
Hutchinson, Martha	WBK	1978,79,80,81
Inman, Bridget	WBK	1993
Issenmann, Jeré	WBK	2002
Johnson, Jennifer	WBK	1985,86,87,88
Klingler, Vicki	WBK	1991,93,94
Kordas, Judy	WBK	1978,79
Lawrence, Cathy	WBK	1983
Leonhardt, Casey	WBK	1997,98
Lewis, Gia	WBK	1998
Limestall, Susan	WBK	1975,76,77
Magas, Barbella	WBK	1975,77,78
Marcauskaite, Iveta	WBK	2001,02
Martin, Kylie	WBK	1999,00
McClellan, Angie	WBK	1986,87
McClelland, Kim	WBK	1989
Means, Pam	WBK	1983,84,86
Middeler, Jenny	WBK	1983,84,85,86
Morency, Pat	WBK	1979,80,81,82
Nelson, Barbara	WBK	1975
O'Neil, Anne	WBK	2001
Parker, Melissa	WBK	1997,98,99,00
Pfeiffer, Stacey	WBK	1984
Platt, Lolita	WBK	1992,93
Polk, Jonelle	WBK	1984,85,86, 87
Preacely, Robbyn	WBK	1993
Prina, Jodi	WBK	1977,78
Reinking, Krista	WBK	1995,96,97,98
Ricketts, Diane	WBK	1982
Riley, Kate	WBK	1989,90,91,92

Roach, Arlena	WBK	1990,91
Roberts, Linda	WBK	1975,76
Robertson, Currie	WBK	1995
Robinson, Lisa	WBK	1979,80,81,82
Robinson, Lynnette	WBK	1979,80,81,82
Rodriguez, Sandra	WBK	1978
Romic, Stephanie	WBK	1983,84,85,86
Roosevelt, Rita	WBK	1977
Ruholl, Connie	WBK	1991,93
Sanderson, Lauren	WBK	1997
Shade, Susan	WBK	1975
Sharp, Sarah	WBK	1988,89,90,91
Sheeler, Alicia	WBK	1997,98,99
Shellander, Nancy	WBK	1984
Smith, Aimee	WBK	1994,95,96,97
Smith, Yolanda	WBK	2001,02
Stein, Cindy	WBK	1982,83
Steuby, Chrissy	WBK	1996
Stevenson, Nancy	WBK	1975
Taylor, Deb	WBK	1980,81
Terrien, Molly	WBK	1984,85
Thomas, Kelly	WBK	1985
Todd, Josie	WBK	1988
Tortorelli, Jeanne	WBK	1983
Travnik, Mary Pat	WBK	1976,77,78,79
Umbach, Dana	WBK	1975
Vana, Dawn	WBK	1999,00,01,02
Vandertop, Sara	WBK	1996,97,98
VanHandel, Kerry	WBK	1987,88,89,90
Vasey, Nicole	WBK	1995,96,97,98
Vossen, Michele	WBK	1981,82,83,84
Walker, Sharmella	WBK	1989,91,92
Washington, Acquanetta	WBK	1988
Waters, Sonya	WBK	1989,90,91,92
White, Liz	WBK	1983,84,85,86
Whitehead, Chenise	WBK	1983,85,86
Williams, Angelina	WBK	2002
Wilson, Holly	WBK	1999,00,01,02
Wright, Carolyn	WBK	1980,81
Wunder, Linda	WBK	1978,79,80,81
Wustrack, Sarah	WBK	1999
Yanni, Aminata	WBK	2001,02
Zurek, Elizabeth	WBK	1996,97,98

Men's Basketball

Abdullah, Halim	MBK	1997
Adams, Rich	MBK	1975,76,77,78
Altenberger, Bill	MBK	1955,56,57
Altenberger, Doug	MBK	1983,84,85,87
Altenmeyer, Vern	MBK	1959,60
Alwood, Clyde	MBK	1915,16,17
Anderson, Earl	MBK	1918
Anderson, Nick	MBK	1988,89
Anderson, Van	MBK	1948,49,50

Aimee Smith

Applegran, Clarence	MBK	1916
Archibald, Robert	MBK	1999,00,01,02
Bane, Frank	MBK	1914,15
Bardo, Stephen	MBK	1987,88,89,90
Bartholomew, Robert	MBK	1930,31,32
Battle, Kenny	MBK	1988,89
Bauer, Larry	MBK	1964
Baumgardner, Max	MBK	1951,53
Beach, Ted	MBK	1950,51
Bemoras, Irvin	MBK	1951,52,53
Benham, Harold	MBK	1935,36
Bennett, Caslon	MBK	1931,32,33
Bennett, Robert	MBK	1992,93,94,95
Bergeson, Carl	MBK	1930
Bernstein, Louis	MBK	1909,10
Beyers, Rich	MBK	1998
Beynon, Jack	MBK	1934,35
Blackwell, Glynn	MBK	1986,87,88
Blackwell, Mel	MBK	1964
Blout, Bryon	MBK	1936,37
Boline, Jelani	MBK	1997,98

Kevin Bontemps

Brian Cook

BonSalle, George	MBK	1955,56,57
Bontemps, Kevin	MBK	1980,81,82,83
Boudreau, Lou	MBK	1937,38
Bowman, P.J.	MBK	1989,90
Bradford, Cory	MBK	1999,00,01,02
Braun, Howard	MBK	1934,35,36
Bredar, James	MBK	1951,52,53
Bresnahan, Neil	MBK	1977,78,79,80
Breyfogle, Larry	MBK	1958
Britton, Earl	MBK	1924
Brody, Tal	MBK	1963,64,65
Brothers, Bruce	MBK	1954,55,56
Brown, Bob	MBK	1964,66
Brown, Cleotis	MBK	1999,00
Brundage, Avery	MBK	1908
Bunkenberg, Bruce	MBK	1958,59,60
Burmaster, Jack	MBK	1945,46,47,48
Burwell, Bill	MBK	1961,62,63
Busboom, Les	MBK	1967,68,69
Bushell, Tim	MBK	1974
Caiazza, Ted	MBK	1957
Caldwell, Herb	MBK	1996,97

Ken Ferdinand

Cann, Fremont	MBK	1928
Carmichael, Tom	MBK	1974,75
Carney, Charles	MBK	1920,21,22
Cermack, Jerome	MBK	1907
Chukwudebe, Victor	MBK	1997,98,99,00
Clarida, Doug	MBK	1992
Clark, Shelly	MBK	1994,95
Clemons, Rennie	MBK	1991,92,93
Cobb, Levi	MBK	1977,78,79,80
Cohen, Larry	MBK	1972
Colangelo, Jerry	MBK	1960,61,62
Collins, Walter	MBK	1921,22
Combes, Harry	MBK	1935,36,37
Conner, Nick	MBK	1971,72,73
Cook, Brian	MBK	2000,01,02
Craig, Hal	MBK	1946
Crane, Dudley	MBK	1914
Crews, Randy	MBK	1968,69,70
Cronk, Howard	MBK	1940
Cross, Gene	MBK	1993,94
Cross, Joe	MBK	2000,01
Curless, Jerry	MBK	1961
Dadant, Maurice	MBK	1906,07,08
Dahringer, Homer	MBK	1912,13
Daniels, Jay	MBK	1982,83
Daugherity, Russell	MBK	1925,26,27
Davidson, Marc	MBK	1992,93
Davies, Carl	MBK	1938
Davis, Arias	MBK	1998,99
Dawson, Jeff	MBK	1973,74
Dawson, Jim	MBK	1965,66,67
DeDecker, Jim	MBK	1971,72
Dehner, Lewis	MBK	1935,38,39
Deimling, Keaton	MBK	1926,27,28
Delaney, Donald	MBK	1944,45
DeMoulin, Ray	MBK	1944
Deputy, Donn	MBK	1974
Dezort, Tom	MBK	1970
Dillon, David	MBK	1941
Doolen, Bryan	MBK	1926
Dorn, Ernest	MBK	1927,28,29
Doster, Robert	MBK	1946,47
Douglas, Bruce	MBK	1983,84,85,86
Downey, Dave	MBK	1961,62,63
Drew, Earl	MBK	1928,29
Drish, John	MBK	1939,40,41
Duis, Mike	MBK	1992
Duner, Sven	MBK	1913,14,15
Dunlap, Ron	MBK	1966,67
Dutcher, James	MBK	1954,55
Eddleman, Dwight	MBK	1947,48,49
Edwards, Bill	MBK	1962,63,64
Elwell, Dan	MBK	1916
Erickson, William	MBK	1947,48,49,50
Evers, Walter	MBK	1940

Farnham, Brad	MBK	1974,75
Felmley, John	MBK	1917,20
Fencl, Fred	MBK	1934
Fencl, George	MBK	1930,31,32
Ferdinand, Ken	MBK	1976,77
Ferguson, Blandon	MBK	2002
Flessner, Deon	MBK	1966,67
Fletcher, Ralph	MBK	1919
Fletcher, Rodney	MBK	1950,51,52
Foley, Richard	MBK	1947,48,49
Follmer, Clive	MBK	1951,52,53
Follmer, Mack	MBK	1950,51
Foster, Jed	MBK	1971,72,73
Fowler, Charles	MBK	1942
Frandsen, Lee	MBK	1959,60
Frank, Joseph	MBK	1938,39,40
Freeman, David	MBK	1997,98
Freeman, Don	MBK	1964,65,66
Fronczak, Stan	MBK	1948
Froschauer, Frank	MBK	1933,34,35
Fulton, Clifton	MBK	1943,50
Gandy, Chris	MBK	1994,95,96,97
Garris, Kiwane	MBK	1994,95,96,97
Gates, Ralph	MBK	1912
Gates, William	MBK	1936
Gatewood, Roy	MBK	1950
Gedvilas, Leo	MBK	1945
Gee, Jarrod	MBK	1995,96,97,98
Geers, Tim	MBK	1990,91
Gerecke, Herbert	MBK	1951,52
Gerhardt, Tom	MBK	1976,77,78
Gibbs, Paul	MBK	1933
Gibson, Ken	MBK	1990
Gill, Kendall	MBK	1987,88,89,90
Gillespie, Gordon	MBK	1944
Gosnell, Alan	MBK	1958,59,60
Graff, Dennis	MBK	1974
Gray, Reno	MBK	1978,80
Green, Fred	MBK	1946,47,48,49
Green, Jim	MBK	1987
Greene, Royner	MBK	1934,35
Griffin, James	MBK	1979,80,81,82
Griffin, Marcus	MBK	2000,01
Guttschow, Roy	MBK	1934,35
Haffner, Scott	MBK	1985
Haines, Leonard	MBK	1924,25,26
Halas, George	MBK	1917,18
Hall, Albert	MBK	1910,12
Haller, Tom	MBK	1957
Handlon, Colin	MBK	1938,39,40
Hamilton, Lowell	MBK	1986,87,88,89
Hapac, William	MBK	1938,39,40
Harper, Charles	MBK	1929,30,31
Harper, Derek	MBK	1981,82,83
Harrington, Sean	MBK	2000,01,02

Matt Heldman

Harris, Davin	MBK	1993
Harrison, Jodie	MBK	1968,69
Hawkins, Fess	MBK	1999
Head, Luther	MBK	2002
Heldman, Matt	MBK	1995,96,97,98
Hellmich, Hudson	MBK	1932,33,34
Hellstrom, Norton	MBK	1921,23
Henry, Wilber	MBK	1935,36,37
Hester, Jerry	MBK	1994,95,96,98
Hill, Herbert	MBK	1929
Hinton, Larry	MBK	1964,65,66
Hocking, William	MBK	1940,41,42
Hoffmann, Robert	MBK	1913
Holcomb, Derek	MBK	1979,80,81
Hollopeter, Cecil	MBK	1925
Hooper, Max	MBK	1952,53,54
Hortin, Gordon	MBK	1944
How, John	MBK	1928,29
Howard, Jerrance	MBK	2001,02
Howat, Rick	MBK	1969,70,71
Humphrey, Dwight	MBK	1946,47
Ingwersen, Bert	MBK	1918,19,20

Rob Judson

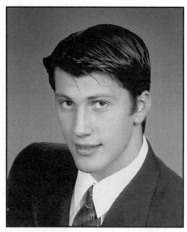

Damir Krupalija

Bill Rucks

Kawal, Ed	MBK	1930
Keene, Richard	MBK	1993,94,95,96
Keller, Charles	MBK	1986
Kerr, John	MBK	1952,53,54
Kersulis, Walt	MBK	1945,48,49,50
Kircher, Helmuth	MBK	1913,14
Kirk, Walt	MBK	1944,45,47
Klusendorf, Don	MBK	1984
Kopp, William	MBK	1919
Kpedi, Andy	MBK	1990,91
Krelle, Jim	MBK	1970,71,72
Krupalija, Damir	MBK	1999,00,01,02
Kujawa, Jens	MBK	1986,87,88
Kunz, Phil	MBK	1987,88
Landt, Louis	MBK	1959,60
Lanter, Steve	MBK	1977,79
Lasater, Harry	MBK	1938
Leddy, George	MBK	1946
Leeper, Sam	MBK	1962
Leighty, Rick	MBK	1976,77
Leo, Herbert	MBK	1911,12
Leonard, Bryan	MBK	1981,82,83
Liberty, Marcus	MBK	1989,90
Lindsay, Forrest	MBK	1926
Lipe, Cordon	MBK	1923,24,25,26
Lipe, K. Jack	MBK	1925,26
Love, John	MBK	1962,64
Lovelace, Jay	MBK	1962
Louis, Benny	MBK	1966,67,68
Lubin, Larry	MBK	1976,77,78,79
MacDonald, Mike	MBK	1989
Makovsky, Ed	MBK	1953,54
Manzke, Edward	MBK	1989
Marks, James	MBK	1948,49
Marks, John	MBK	1951
Markworth, Martin	MBK	1936
Martin, Hollie	MBK	1926
Mast, Nate	MBK	1999,00,01
Mathisen, Arthur	MBK	1941,42,43
Matthews, Audie	MBK	1975,76,77,78
Mauer, John	MBK	1924,25,26
May, Elbridge	MBK	1929,30,31
McBride, John	MBK	1973
McClain, Sergio	MBK	1998,99,00,01
McClure, Ray	MBK	1946
McKay, Ernest	MBK	1917
McKay, Robert	MBK	1927
McKeown, Bill	MBK	1964,65
Mee, Julian	MBK	1920,21
Meents, Scott	MBK	1983,84,85,86
Melton, Brett	MBK	2001
Menke, Ken	MBK	1942,43,47
Menke, Robert	MBK	1946
Mettile, Jerry	MBK	1967
Meyer, Matt	MBK	1979

Michael, Tom	MBK	1991,92,93,94
Miller, Fred	MBK	1969,70,71
Mills, Coke	MBK	1935
Mills, Doug	MBK	1961,62
Mills, Douglas	MBK	1928,29,30
Mittleman, Benjamin	MBK	1918,19
Montgomery, George	MBK	1982,83,84,85
Moore, Vernon	MBK	1932
Morris, Bill	MBK	1972
Morton, Robert	MBK	1944,45
Mroz, Wallie	MBK	1946
Nisbet, Tom	MBK	1937,38,39
Norman, Ken	MBK	1985,86,87
Notree, Bryant	MBK	1995,96,97
Ohl, Don	MBK	1956,57,58
Olson, Everette	MBK	1927
O'Neal, Alvin	MBK	1971
O'Neal, Robert	MBK	1941
Orr, John	MBK	1945
Osterkorn, Walter	MBK	1948,49,50
Otto, Gordon	MBK	1916
Owen, W. Boyd	MBK	1931,32,33
Pace, Dennis	MBK	1967,68,69
Parker, Curtis	MBK	1924
Parker, Edwin	MBK	1942
Parker, Kenneth	MBK	1943
Patrick, Stan	MBK	1944
Paul, John	MBK	1957,58
Pearson, Preston	MBK	1966,67
Penn, Albert	MBK	1908
Perry, Edward	MBK	1958,59,60
Peterson, Robert	MBK	1951,52,53
Phillip, Andrew	MBK	1942,43,47
Phillips, Charles	MBK	1938
Pierce, Scott	MBK	1991,92
Plew, Elmer	MBK	1953,54
Popken, Roland	MBK	1922,23,24
Popperfuss, Henry	MBK	1908,09,10
Poston, Emmett	MBK	1909,11
Potter, Glenn	MBK	1922,23,24
Powell, Roger	MBK	2002
Price, Mike	MBK	1968,69,70
Probst, J. S.	MBK	1918
Range, Perry	MBK	1979,80,81,82
Redmon, Bogie	MBK	1963,64,65
Reitsch, Henry	MBK	1921
Rennacker, Roy	MBK	1909
Renner, Jerry	MBK	1961
Reynolds, Kenneth	MBK	1925,26,27
Richardson, Quinn	MBK	1981,82,84
Richmond, Robert	MBK	1939,41
Ridley, William	MBK	1954,55,56
Riegel, Robert	MBK	1935,36,37
Riley, Roy	MBK	1906
Robisch, Brett	MBK	1995

Jackson, Greg	MBK	1969,70,71
Jackson, Mannie	MBK	1958,59,60
Johansen, Bob	MBK	1965,66,67
Johnson, Brian	MBK	1995,96,97,98
Johnson, Eddie	MBK	1978,79,80,81
Johnson, Howard	MBK	1974,75
Johnson, Lucas	MBK	1999,00,01,02
Jones, Mike	MBK	1978
Jones, Rich	MBK	1966,67
Jones, Rodney	MBK	1990
Judson, Howard	MBK	1944,45
Judson, Paul	MBK	1954,55,56
Judson, Phil	MBK	1955,56
Judson, Rob	MBK	1977,78,79,80
Juul, Herbert	MBK	1906,07
Kamm, Albert	MBK	1933,34
Kamm, Alfred	MBK	1934
Kamp, Elbert	MBK	1930,31,32
Kamp, Robert	MBK	1930,31,32
Karnes, T. D.	MBK	1924,25
Kassel, Charles	MBK	1925,26
Kaufmann, Andy	MBK	1990,91,93

Sergio McClain

Roberson, Garvin	MBK	1972,73
Roberts, Dave	MBK	1973,74,75
Robisch, Brett	MBK	1995
Roettger, Walter	MBK	1922,23
Roth, Steve	MBK	1992,93,94,95
Rowe, Robert	MBK	1946
Rucks, Bill	MBK	1974,75
Rucks, Jim	MBK	1972
Ryan, Edward	MBK	1906,07
Sabo, John	MBK	1921,22
Sachs, Henry	MBK	1939,40,41
Schafer, Tom	MBK	1984
Schmidt, Harv	MBK	1955,56,57
Schmidt, Rick	MBK	1973,74,75
Scholz, Dave	MBK	1967,68,69
Schroeder, C. J.	MBK	1972,73,74
Schuldt, James	MBK	1951,53
Searcy, Ed	MBK	1960
Seyler, Jim	MBK	1944,45,46
Shapiro, Harold	MBK	1939,40,41
Shapland, Bob	MBK	1970,71

Rick Schmidt

Kevin Turner

Shapland, Mark	MBK	1989
Shirley, Alton	MBK	1943
Shoaff, Oliver	MBK	1943
Small, Bill	MBK	1961, 62, 63
Small, Ervin	MBK	1988,89,90
Smiley, Arthur	MBK	1942,43,46,47
Smith, Dave	MBK	1974
Smith, Larry	MBK	1987,88,89,91
Smith, Mark	MBK	1978,79,80,81
Smith, Nick	MBK	2002
Solyom, Andrew	MBK	1928
Staab, Jake	MBK	1944,45
Starnes, Bob	MBK	1961,62,63
Sterneck, Morris	MBK	1954
Stewart, Charles	MBK	1906,07
Stilwell, Leland	MBK	1922,23,24
Storey, Awvee	MBK	1998
Stout, Hiles	MBK	1955,56,57
Swanson, Harold	MBK	1936,37
Sunderlage, Don	MBK	1949,50,51
Tabor, Hubert	MBK	1922
Tallmadge, Floyd	MBK	1906

Tony Wysinger

Tarwain, John	MBK	1930
Taylor, Brooks	MBK	1990,91,92,93
Taylor, Curtis	MBK	1986
Taylor, Paul	MBK	1918,19,20
Taylor, Roger	MBK	1957,58,59
Theobald, William	MBK	1933
Thomas, Deon	MBK	1991,92,93,94
Thomas, Derrick	MBK	1995
Thompson, Thomas	MBK	1908,09,10
Thoren, Skip	MBK	1963,64,65
Thurlby, Burdette	MBK	1948,49,50
Tucker, Craig	MBK	1981,82
Tucker, Otho	MBK	1973,75,76
Turner, Kevin	MBK	1995,96,97,98
Tuttle, Will	MBK	1992
Vail, Charles	MBK	1918,20,21
Vance, Eugene	MBK	1942,43,47
Vaughn, Govoner	MBK	1958,59,60
Vopicka, James	MBK	1936,37
Vopicka, Jim	MBK	1964,65
Walquist, Lawrence	MBK	1920,21,22
Wardley, George	MBK	1937,38,39
Washington, Mike	MBK	1975,76
Watson, Carl	MBK	1909,10
Weatherspoon, Nick	MBK	1971,72,73
Welch, Anthony	MBK	1982,83,85,86
Wente, Mike	MBK	1974
Wessels, John	MBK	1959,60,61
Westervelt, Kevin	MBK	1980
Westfall, Curtis	MBK	1907
Wheeler, T. J.	MBK	1992,93,94
Williams, Frank	MBK	2000,01,02
White, James	MBK	1911,12,13
Williams, Nate	MBK	1975,76
Williford, Edward	MBK	1913,14,15
Wilson, Kenneth	MBK	1919,20
Windmiller, Bob	MBK	1969,70
Winters, Efrem	MBK	1983,84,85,86
Woods, Ralf	MBK	1915,16,17
Woods, Ray	MBK	1915,16,17
Woodward, Reggie	MBK	1986
Woolston, William	MBK	1911,12
Wright, James	MBK	1952,53,54
Wukovits, Victor	MBK	1940,41,42
Wysinger, Tony	MBK	1984,85,86,87

Women's Cross-Country

Abrahamson, Kristen	WCC	1993
Anderson, Linda	WCC	1980
Balzer, Teresa	WCC	1980
Bethke, Breanne	WCC	1997
Bice, Marcy	WCC	2000,01
Brooks, Adrienne	WCC	1985
Braun, Joy	WCC	2001
Bruene, Carol	WCC	1985,86
Burke, Shannon	WCC	1998
Carlisle, Amy	WCC	1989

Christopher, Amy	WCC	1997
Clark, Maureen	WCC	1997
Cole, Audrey	WCC	1986
Dickerson, Marianne	WCC	1979,80,81,82
Dietzen, Cecilia	WCC	1999,00,01
Donato, Michelle	WCC	1989,90
Donohue, Kimberly	WCC	1994,95,96
Drewes, Elizabeth	WCC	1978
Elsen, Virgina	WCC	1981
Fonzino, Danielle	WCC	1996,97
Frakes, Erin	WCC	2000,01
Garrett, Rebekah	WCC	1991,94,95,96
Grabski, Erin	WCC	1998
Gross, Samantha	WCC	1991,92,93
Guard, Amy	WCC	2001
Hackett, Colleen	WCC	1983,84,85
Harpell, Danielle	WCC	1988,89,90,91
Hawkins, Leslie	WCC	1985,86, 87
Hawkins, Michelle	WCC	1988,89,90,91
Heise, Jennifer	WCC	1996
Herberger, Lynn	WCC	1997
Hoogheem, Aimee	WCC	1997
Hunt, Amber	WCC	1999,00,01
Kelleher, Rachel	WCC	1992
Kenyon, Leigh Anne	WCC	2001
Knop, Nancy L.	WCC	1977,78
Kraiss, Katherine	WCC	1994,95
Lantis, Julie E.	WCC	1982,83
LaSusa, Deanna	WCC	1981
Lehnhoff, Michelle	WCC	1985
Locascio, Sharon	WCC	1986,88,90
Madsen, Wendy	WCC	1993
Marianetti, Gina	WCC	1996
Marine, Jennifer S.	WCC	1993,95,96
Martin, Lindsay	WCC	1997,98
Mastoris, Helen	WCC	1989
Mayback, Laurie	WCC	1980
McGlone, Catherine	WCC	1980
McNee, Kelly	WCC	1983,84,85
Mendozza, Tara	WCC	1996,97,98
Meneses, Sandra	WCC	1996
Michal, Mary	WCC	1992
Morris, Karen J.	WCC	1990,91,92,93,94
Morris, Kathy A.	WCC	1991,92,93
Moyer, H. Anita	WCC	1977,78,79
Oberle, Betty	WCC	1978,79
Oberle, Elizabeth	WCC	1982
Paul, Renae	WCC	1993,94
Race, Carrie	WCC	1980
Robbins, Laura	WCC	1998
Russell, Donna	WCC	1986,87,88
Schwab, Jennifer	WCC	1992,93,94
Scigousky, Brooke	WCC	1995
Simmering, Laura	WCC	1988,89,90,91
Simpson, Casie	WCC	2001

Danielle Harpell

Sterneman, Ruth	WCC	1981,83,84,85
Stetson, Deborah	WCC	1981,82,83,85
Stevens, Lisa	WCC	1980,81,82,83
Stoltz, Christina	WCC	1980
Stoltz, Teresa	WCC	1985,86
Straza, Melissa	WCC	1986,87,88,90
Tellin, Tracy	WCC	1990,91,93
Tochihara, Tama	WCC	1993
Tomlinson, Amy	WCC	1990,91,92,94
Turilli, Jaime	WCC	2001
Tweedy, Jennifer	WCC	1990
Villagrana, Lorena	WCC	1995
Vogel, Margaret	WCC	1983,84,85
Vogel, Michelle	WCC	1981,83,84,85
Waldinger, Brenda	WCC	1979
Walter, Beth	WCC	1979
Walters, Kathy	WCC	1977,78,79
Ward, Cheryl	WCC	1981,83,84
Welch, Wendy	WCC	1990,91,93
Withrow, Loretta	WCC	1988,89,90
Zimmerman, Beth	WCC	1980
Zobel, Julie	WCC	1986,88,89,90

Laura Simmering

Kerry Dickson

Men's Cross-Country

Abbott, David	MCC	1927,28
Adams, Paul	MCC	1975
Alexander, Joe	MCC	1993,94,95,96
Allen, Bill	MCC	1972,73
Allman, John	MCC	1920
Avery, Mark	MCC	1974,75,76,77
Babb, Dick	MCC	1970
Bauer, Craig	MCC	1981,84
Baughman, Lynn	MCC	1934
Bilsbury, Norman	MCC	1988,89
Bissell, Lonnie	MCC	1979
Bolander, Harold	MCC	1913
Bowe, Christopher	MCC	1985
Bowers, James	MCC	1957,58,59
Brenneman, Bruce	MCC	1946
Bridges, Jan	MCC	1963
Bridges, Mike	MCC	1972,73,74
Brooks, Dave	MCC	1971,73
Brooks, Rich	MCC	1973,74,75
Brown, John	MCC	1958
Brown, Ken	MCC	1960
Brown, Park	MCC	1938,40
Burgoon, David	MCC	1915

Neal Gassman

Campbell, Robert	MCC	1942
Capelle, Mark	MCC	1981
Carius, Allen	MCC	1962,63
Cepulis, Wade	MCC	1983,84,85
Cherot, Tony	MCC	1968
Cleveland, Clarence	MCC	1937
Cline, Dick	MCC	1954
Close, Tim	MCC	1977,78
Cobb, Larry	MCC	1969,70,71
Cope, Walter	MCC	1912
Cox, Jeff	MCC	1975
Cullen, Joe	MCC	1980
deBeers, Jim	MCC	1990,91
Dickenson, Roger	MCC	1925
Dickison, Marc	MCC	1991,92,93
Dickson, Kerry	MCC	1979,80,81,83
Diettrich, Henry	MCC	1941
Dintleman, Bob	MCC	1955,56
Domantay, Greg	MCC	1982
Downs, Robert	MCC	1947,48,49
Duffy, Walter	MCC	1979,80,81
Dufresne, Jacques	MCC	1932,33,34
Dunn, Clarence	MCC	1941,42,46
Durkin, Mike	MCC	1971,72,73,74
Dusenberry, Paul	MCC	1921
Dykstra, Greg	MCC	1967,68,69
Eason, Ryan	MCC	1997,98,99,00
Eckburg, David	MCC	1990,92,93,94
Eicken, Jim	MCC	1975,76,77,78
Engelhorn, Rich	MCC	1966
Evans, Paul	MCC	1929,30
Fairfield, David	MCC	1925,27
Fash, Dan	MCC	1997
Ffitch, Pete	MCC	1980,81
Finney, Bruce	MCC	1971
Fisher, Ralph	MCC	1933
Flannery, Jim	MCC	1979
Francissen, Vern	MCC	1980
Frazier, Scott	MCC	1982
Fritz, Bill	MCC	1974,75,77
Gaines, Harry	MCC	1935
Galland, Michael	MCC	1933,35
Gardner, Rob	MCC	1969
Gassmann, Neal	MCC	1985,86,88,89
Gilbert, Dwight	MCC	1986,87,88
Gladding, Donald	MCC	1942
Gould, William	MCC	1930
Gow, Nick	MCC	2000
Gray, Dan	MCC	1985
Grinter, Caleb	MCC	1999,00
Gross, Rick	MCC	1969,70,71
Hall, Dick	MCC	1967,68
Hall, Melvin	MCC	1923
Halle, Dave	MCC	1984,85,86,87
Hamer, Paul	MCC	1944
Harris, Harold	MCC	1957,58
Hartman, Bill	MCC	1963
Hedgcock, Frank	MCC	1956,57
Henson, Eric	MCC	1992,93,94
Herning, Lance	MCC	1962
Hill, Greg	MCC	1984
Hiserote, Kim	MCC	1971
Homoly, Andy	MCC	1988,89,91
Horyn, Dan	MCC	1997,98,00

Howse, Ken	MCC	1968,69,70
Hughes, Eric	MCC	1945
Huston, Paul	MCC	1947,48
Inch, Chris	MCC	1987,88
Jacobs, Jeff	MCC	1982,83,84,86
Jacobson, John	MCC	1986,87
Janssen, Andrew	MCC	2001
Jewsbury, Walter	MCC	1948,49
Jirele, Jeff	MCC	1975,76
Johnston, Charles	MCC	1925
Jonsson, Karl	MCC	1955,56,57
Karkow, Waldemar	MCC	1947
Kelly, John	MCC	1968,69,70
Kivela, Paul	MCC	1982,84,85,86
Koers, Marko	MCC	1991,92,95
Krause, Dennis	MCC	1965
Kronforst, John	MCC	1999,01
Kurtz, Andrew	MCC	1998
LaBadie, Lee	MCC	1969,70,71
Lally, Rick	MCC	1962
Lamb, Lawton	MCC	1949
Lamoreux, John	MCC	1966,67,68
Landmeier, Verne	MCC	1933
Leuchtmann, Joe	MCC	1986,87
Lin, Richard	MCC	2000,01
Line, H. E.	MCC	1930,31,32
Lucchesi, Mike	MCC	1997,98,99,00
Luker, Tom	MCC	1954,55,56
Lynch, George	MCC	1950
Maddux, Scott	MCC	1989,90,91,92
Maddux, Troy	MCC	1990
Makeever, Sam J.	MCC	1923,29
Marzulo, Sam	MCC	1923
Mason, Arthur	MCC	1913
Mazur, Dan	MCC	1991,92,93
McClennan, Scott	MCC	1996,97,98,99
McClowry, Sean	MCC	1996
McElwee, Ermel	MCC	1925,26,27
McElwee, Jim	MCC	1960,61
McGinnis, Gordon	MCC	1921
Meier, Mike	MCC	1972
Mieher, Edward	MCC	1922,23,24
Miller, Harold	MCC	1924
Mitchell, Justin	MCC	1999,01
Moran, Tim	MCC	1999,01
Mumaw, Gary	MCC	1975,76
Munnis, James	MCC	1931
Myers, Les	MCC	1976
Nauta, Mike	MCC	1963
Nolan, Dan	MCC	1990,93
Novack, Joseph	MCC	1926,27
O'Connell, John	MCC	1935
Olszewski, John	MCC	1978,79,80
Painter, David	MCC	1979,80
Palumbo, Adam	MCC	2001
Patterson, Bruce	MCC	1921
Patton, Mike	MCC	1981,82,83,84
Pearman, Barry	MCC	1993,94
Petefish, William	MCC	1930
Peterson, Jim	MCC	1961
Pfeiffer, Brent	MCC	2000,01
Ponsonby, Charles	MCC	1966
Ponzer, Howard	MCC	1927
Powers, John	MCC	1985,87,88,89

Scott McClennan

Reasoner, Melton	MCC	1930
Rehberg, Robert	MCC	1941
Reynolds, Greg	MCC	1981,86
Rideout, Blaine	MCC	1935
Rideout, Wayne	MCC	1935
Ripskis, Stan	MCC	1962
Russell, Jon	MCC	1997,98,99
Saarima, Matt	MCC	1997
Saunders, Chris	MCC	1994
Scheirer, Mark	MCC	1988,89,90,91
Schmidt, Jon	MCC	1979,80,81
Scott, Russell	MCC	1921,22
Seib, Robert	MCC	1941,42
Seiwert, Tim	MCC	2000,01
Seldon, John	MCC	1928
Sheuring, Verland	MCC	1954,55,56
Siegel, Bill	MCC	1969
Siglin, Brett	MCC	1993,94,95,96
Sitko, Len	MCC	1987,88,89,90
Smaidris, Mike	MCC	1993,94,95
Sneberger, James	MCC	1937
Steinberg, Philip	MCC	1944
Stellner, Frank	MCC	1925
Stevens, Tom	MCC	1980,81,82
Stine, Francis	MCC	1927,28

Len Sitko

Jason Zieren

Swanson, Reuben	MCC	1921
Talbot, Paul	MCC	1993
Thanos, Jon	MCC	1984,85,86,87
Topper, Martin	MCC	1922
Twomey, John	MCC	1946,47
Twomey, Victor	MCC	1945,47,48,49
Ummel, Kregg	MCC	1989,90,91
VanSwol, Jason	MCC	1998,99
Virgin, Craig	MCC	1973,74,75,76
Wahls, Aaron	MCC	1999,00,01
Walker, George	MCC	1966,67
Walters, Dave	MCC	1974,76,77,78
Wells, Edwin	MCC	1922
Welsh, Roger	MCC	1912
Welyki, Joseph	MCC	1946
West, Jason	MCC	1991,92
West, William	MCC	1931,32,33
Wharton, Russell	MCC	1921
White, Charlie	MCC	1975,77,78
White, Harold	MCC	1925
Whitlow, Jamey	MCC	1993
Wieneke, Mark	MCC	1985
Wilson, Richard	MCC	1978
Winfield, Robert	MCC	1995,96,97
Winship, Harold	MCC	1977

Tsafrir Cohen

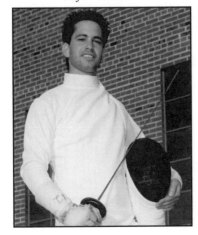

Wolf, Ty	MCC	1983,84
Wood, Arthur	MCC	1940,42
Woolsey, Robert	MCC	1930,31,32
Yarcho, Wayne	MCC	1938
Zieren, Jason	MCC	1994,95,96,97
Zimner, David	MCC	1988

Men's Fencing

Abel, Kevin J.	FN	1989,90,91,92
Abell, William A.	FN	1958
Abraham, William	FN	1967,68,69
Abraham, William J.	FN	1947
Acker, Alan S.	FN	1971,72,73,74
Albers, Daniel P.	FN	1981
Albrecht, A. J.	FN	1912,13
Aminzia, Norbert	FN	1993
Anderson, Truman O.	FN	1984
Armstrong, David T.	FN	1975,76,77
Arneborn, Mikael	FN	1992,93
Atkin, Leonard	FN	1951
Aufrecht, Ronald J.	FN	1965,66,67
Ausich, William I.	FN	1973,74
Ballard, Albert D.	FN	1970,71
Barousse, Ignacio C.	FN	1922
Barth, Frederic C.	FN	1981
Bartga-Nagy, Rudolfo	FN	1963,64
Baumann, Erich S.	FN	1991,92,93
Bebak, Arthur P.	FN	1981,82,83
Becker, Robert H.	FN	1958,59,60
Beebe, Kenneth J.	FN	1911,12
Beider, David	FN	1978,79
Bell, Craig	FN	1963,64,65
Bell, James F.	FN	1953,54,55
Bengard, E. Donald	FN	1948,49
Benham, Milford J.	FN	1935
Bennett, Austin H.	FN	1922
Bernstein, Lionel M.	FN	1942
Bishop, J. Scott	FN	1986,87
Blahouse Jr., Charles	FN	1955
Blazich, John L.	FN	1947
Bluhm, Ronald	FN	1970
Boland, Chester H.	FN	1940,41
Boland, John S.	FN	1936
Boyles, John K.	FN	1954
Brennan, Thomas M.	FN	1961,63
Brewer, Dave	FN	1968
Brooks, Eron B.	FN	1925
Brownlee, John J.	FN	1926
Bunting, William L.	FN	1923
Burke, Christopher J.	FN	1989,90,91,92
Bushche, Fred	FN	1965
Bye, Gary L.	FN	1975
Calderisi, Michael	FN	1987,88,89,90
Cameron, John K.	FN	1952,53
Camp, William F.	FN	1958
Campbell, Charles E.	FN	1959,60,61
Campoli, Douglas	FN	1983,84,85
Carlson, Carl E.	FN	1952
Carlson, David A.	FN	1970,71
Cawley, Kevin J.	FN	1977,78,79,80
Cha, Henry	FN	1964
Chaio, Richard	FN	1983,84,85
Chiprin, William	FN	1935,36,42

Cho, David J.	FN	1990,91,92,93
Choi, Charles Y.	FN	1982,83
Clinton, Edgar T.	FN	1928
Cohen, Tsafrir	FN	1991,92,93
Cohn, Richard D.	FN	1953,54
Cohn, Stuart L.	FN	1960,61,62
Cook, Eugene	FN	1915
Craig, Herbert W.	FN	1927
Crawford, David	FN	1972
Dammann, James E.	FN	1954,55,56
Dammers, Clifford R.	FN	1962,63,64
Danzer, Warren	FN	1958,59,60
Davis, Oral L.	FN	1940
Delaet, Thomas E.	FN	1975,76
Delismon, Ronald J.	FN	1957,58
Diamond, Arthur S.	FN	1976,77,78
D'Orazio, Vincent T.	FN	1950,51,52
Epstein, Ralph J.	FN	1932,33,34
Evans, David P.	FN	1964,65,66
Fleischer, Kenneth	FN	1970,71,73
Forhan, Richard M.	FN	1962
Fornof, John	FN	1963
Forsythe, Robert W.	FN	1948,49,50
Franke, Steven C.	FN	1980,81
Franklin, Richard	FN	1976,77
Franks, Robert D.	FN	1941
Frase, Robert C.	FN	1964,65
Fredericks, Brian	FN	1972
Fretz, Karl	FN	1967,68,69
Fricker, Donald P.	FN	1957
Friduss, Janvis H.	FN	1941,42
Friedberg, J. Frank	FN	1931
Frye, Richard N.	FN	1939
Garret, Roger	FN	1964,65,66
Garrett, T.C. Scott	FN	1971
Gates, Markland T.	FN	1964,65
Gelman, Max M.	FN	1938
Gerard, Gregory G.	FN	1977
Gerard, Michael R.	FN	1976,77
Gerten, Nicholas	FN	1916
Gillette, Steven M.	FN	1986,87,88,89
Gilman, Adam	FN	1993
Ginsburg, Marvin	FN	1956
Gladish, Ronald L.	FN	1963,64
Goddard, Robert F.	FN	1928
Golden, Craig	FN	1980,81
Gorin, James C.	FN	1932
Gorzowski, Jacek J.	FN	1990,91,92
Grahl, Carl H.	FN	1934
Green, Morris L.	FN	1936,37
Griffin, J. M.	FN	1912, 14
Gross, Chalmer A.	FN	1929,30
Grossman, Thomas	FN	1981,82,83,84
Guthrie, Russell D.	FN	1958
Guyton Jr., Fred F.	FN	1959
Haier, Otto C.	FN	1929,30
Hainsworth, Joseph	FN	1980,81,82,83
Handelman, Hyman	FN	1938
Harris, David	FN	1959
Harris, Harvey	FN	1968,69
Harter, Charles E.	FN	1965,66,67
Hartz, Sylvester H.	FN	1934,35
Haslhuhn, Gerald	FN	1956,57
Haslett, James M.	FN	1978,79,80

Arthur Diamond

Haywood, Nate	FN	1972,73
Heald, Paul J.	FN	1979,80,81
Hensley, Timothy T.	FN	1985,86,87,88
Hewitt, Ronald	FN	1955,56
Hochstrasser, Ronald	FN	1981,82,83,84
Howard, Joseph Omar	FN	1969,70,71
Hunt, Tyler R.	FN	1956,57
Ishu, Albert P.	FN	1983,84,85,86
Jackson, James L.	FN	1937
Jankowsky, Alexandre	FN	1961,62
Jebe, Tod A.	FN	1986,87
Jobson, Robert F.	FN	1942
Johnson, Karl E.	FN	1989,90,91,92
Johnson, Ken	FN	1972
Johnson, Steve	FN	1970
Johnston, Scott	FN	1969,70
Jones, Richard	FN	1973
Kadota, Paul	FN	1957
Kaihatsu, Edward J.	FN	1981,82,83
Kamper, Reiner H.	FN	1985,86,87
Kaplan, Hyman H.	FN	1936
Karnezis, Phillip P.	FN	1989,90,91
Katz, William B.	FN	1937
Kaufman, Larry L.	FN	1954,55,56
Kemner, Carl A.	FN	1973,74,75

Jin Kim

Nicholas Leever

Name		Years
Kennedy, Dan W.	FN	1963,64
Kennedy, David R.	FN	1959
Kim, Jin B.	FN	1988,89,90,91
Kim, Sukhoon	FN	1978,79,80,81
Knauff, Lawrence F.	FN	1962,63
Kniss, Steve E.	FN	1967,68
Knowles, Richard T.	FN	1941
Koshkarian, Kent A.	FN	1983,84,85,86
Kraft, Gerald G.	FN	1940
Kramer, Martin	FN	1958,59,60
Kriviskey, Bruce M.	FN	1960,61,62
Kronenfeld, Phillip	FN	1970,71,72
Kuhfuss, John D.	FN	1970,71
Larimer, Mark R.	FN	1948
Larkin, Erik	FN	1990
Laurence, Daniel L.	FN	1969
Lavelle, Kenneth E.	FN	1975,76,77,78
Laws, Joe W.	FN	1975,76,77
Leever, Nicholas J.	FN	1980,81,82,83
Lehmann, J. Dan	FN	1970,72,73,74
Leiken, Richard W.	FN	1962,63
Lempke, Duane A.	FN	1959
Lipson, Lee	FN	1948,49
Littell, David A.	FN	1972,73,74
Lucas, Anatole	FN	1948,49

Keith Mosser

Name		Years
Lynch, James R.	FN	1965,66
Malik, Warren C.	FN	1941,42
Manaois, Arnold C.	FN	1982,83,85
McDevitt, William	FN	1962,63
McDonald Jr., John	FN	1941
McRae, Thomas	FN	1993
Mench, Mark	FN	1976
Menke, Wilbur	FN	1929
Meyer, Ronald H.	FN	1950,51
Meyer, Werner	FN	1950,51
Miller, Jeff A.	FN	1980
Mills, Allen	FN	1950,51,52
Milstein, Sidney M.	FN	1971,72,73
Mohan, Edgar H.	FN	1921,22
Moll, William D.	FN	1956
Moore, Ron	FN	1970,72
Moreno, David R.	FN	1983,84,85,86
Mosser, Keith M.	FN	1984,85,86,87
Munson, Keith E.	FN	1983,84,85,86
Murowitz, Herbert	FN	1957
Neisz, W. Royce	FN	1964
O'Brien, Kevin	FN	1978,79
Oberrotman, Alan	FN	1971,72
O'Connell, James P.	FN	1984
Ofner, Clyde N.	FN	1971,72
Oliver, Alfonso L.	FN	1970,71,72,73
Olson, William E.	FN	1962,63
Orr, Charles R.	FN	1961,62
Osinski, Henry S.	FN	1948,49
Osness, James	FN	1982
Pacini, Michael S.	FN	1978,79,80,81
Palanca, Paul	FN	1980,81,82
Pengilly, H. E.	FN	1911,12,13
Perdue, Ralph P.	FN	1926
Perdue, Thomas W.	FN	1931
Pereira, Leonard	FN	1929
Perella, E.	FN	1933
Perella, P. J.	FN	1932
Perry, Michael	FN	1976
Perry, Russell A.	FN	1929
Phillips, Miles D.	FN	1985,86,87
Pianfetti, Brian M.	FN	1990,91,92,93
Pilenyi, Janos A.	FN	1990,91,92
Post, Warren M.	FN	1970,71
Priest, Edwim N.	FN	1976,77
Priest, Eric	FN	1977,78,79,80
Puccetti, Ronald P.	FN	1947
Quiros, Jorge L.	FN	1950,51,52
Rachmeler, Dale	FN	1970
Ramirez, Robin	FN	1991,92,93
Reamer, Owen J.	FN	1935
Reddish, Paul W.	FN	1932
Reed, Scott D.	FN	1975,76
Reilly, Edward F.	FN	1975
Roberts, Rodney	FN	1967,68,69
Ross, James E.	FN	1952,53
Rush, Scott	FN	1989,90,91,92
Sandstrom, James	FN	1954,55
Sayre, C. B.	FN	1911,12,13
Sawin, Frank L.	FN	1941
Scanlan, Robert W.	FN	1947,48,49
Schankin, Arthur A.	FN	1956,57,58
Schicker, Blake R.	FN	1986,87
Schicker, Eric	FN	1984,85,86,87

Name		Years
Schicker, Glenn R.	FN	1988,89
Schiller, Arthur M.	FN	1952,53
Schlicker, P. F.	FN	1929,31
Schrader, Henry C.	FN	1939
Schroeder, Michael	FN	1966,67,68
Schurecht, H. S.	FN	1914
Schwartz, Daniel	FN	1968,69
Schwartz, Larry	FN	1969,70
Schwartz, Michael	FN	1992,93
Schwartz, Steven H.	FN	1972,73,74,75
Sentman III, Lee H.	FN	1957,58
Sheffield, Jay	FN	1954,56
Shewchuk, William	FN	1953,54
Shipka, Ronald B.	FN	1958,59
Siebert, Fred W.	FN	1929,30,31
Silva, Hugo	FN	1988,89,90,91
Silverman, Lawrence	FN	1952,53
Silverman, Leslie	FN	1936
Silverstone, Abbey	FN	1958,59,60
Smith, Ronald C.	FN	1962,63
Snow, Mark P.	FN	1979,80,81,82
Socolof, Joseph D.	FN	1986,87,88,89
Song, Kenneth K.	FN	1986,87,88,89
Stahl, C. N.	FN	1921
Stammer, Steven E.	FN	1987,88,89
Stephenson, Robert	FN	1933
Stern, Simon H.	FN	1933,34
Sternfeld, Robert	FN	1937,38
Stevens, Terrence C.	FN	1990,91,92,93
Stoll, Steven G.	FN	1964,65
Streed, Jack A.	FN	1942
Stuebe, Louis F.	FN	1921
Stuebe, Louis M.	FN	1947,48,49
Sublette, Bruce M.	FN	1950,51,52
Sullivan, Warren	FN	1947
Suqui, Zeyad	FN	1984
Suritz, Charles S.	FN	1967
Sutton, Michael G.	FN	1977,78,79
Swensen, Charles C.	FN	1950,51
Szluha, Nicholas	FN	1960,61,62
Taliaferro, Mike	FN	1963
Taylor, C. B.	FN	1915
Thompson, Paul W.	FN	1976,77,78
Tibbetts, James D.	FN	1962,63,64
Tingley, Loyal	FN	1969
Tish, Allen I.	FN	1978,79,80,81
Titus, Rayburn L.	FN	1942
Tjaden Jr., Dean A.	FN	1969,70,71
Tocks, John H.	FN	1964,65,66
Todaro, Steven B.	FN	1976
Tolman, Robert G.	FN	1921
Tomars, Peter T.	FN	1956
Traynham Jr., Floyd	FN	1937,39
Tripp, Robert S.	FN	1959,60
Trobe, Pete	FN	1968,69,70
Urbanik, Edward J.	FN	1949
Urso, Philip J.	FN	1952,53
Van Aken, Harry	FN	1968
Van Matter, Francis	FN	1914,15,16
Vasaune, Steve	FN	1992,93
Veatch, David S.	FN	1977,78,79,80
Veatch, Paul D.	FN	1975
Velasco, Herman	FN	1954,55,56
Vitoux, Michael E.	FN	1968,69

Hugo Silva

Name		Years
Walker, Michael L.	FN	1968,69
Ward, Bruce N.	FN	1979
Warshaw, Lawrence	FN	1979,80,81,82
Weingartner, Harold	FN	1937,38,39
Weisman, Jonathan	FN	1982,83
West, Donald J.	FN	1942
Whalin, Brian G.	FN	1973,74,75
Wheeler Jr., Paul A.	FN	1930,31
White, David C.	FN	1965,66,67
Williamson, James	FN	1957,58,59
Wilmot, Ralph	FN	1939,40
Wolff, Leon V.	FN	1939
Wolfson, Robert H.	FN	1966,67
Zimmerman, Kenneth	FN	1962,63
Zindell, Lee H.	FN	1961
Zombolas, Anthony	FN	1953,54

Football

Name		Years
Abdullah, Muhammad	FB	1998,99,00,01
Abraham, George E.	FB	1932
Acks, Ron	FB	1963,64,65
Adams, Earnest	FB	1977,78,79,80
Adams, Conrad	FB	1995,96

Ron Acks

Mel Agee

Adams, Neil	FB	2000
Adams, Paul	FB	1956,57
Adeyemo, Ade	FB	2001
Adkins, Jason	FB	1994
Adsit, Bertram W.	FB	1898,99,00
Agase, Alex	FB	1941,42,46
Agase, Louis	FB	1944,45,46,47
Agee, Mel	FB	1987,88,89,90
Agnew, Lester P.	FB	1922
Agyeman, Nana	FB	2000,01
Aina, David F.	FB	1984,85
Allan, Chris	FB	2001
Allen, Derek	FB	1993,94
Allen, Larry	FB	1970,71,72
Allen, Lawrence T.	FB	1903
Allen, Robert	FB	1956,57,58
Allen, Steve	FB	1969
Allen, William M.	FB	1965
Allie, Glen	FB	1967
Amaya, Doug	FB	1987,88
Anders, Alphonse	FB	1939
Anderson, Harold B.	FB	1909
Anderson, Kai	FB	1965,66

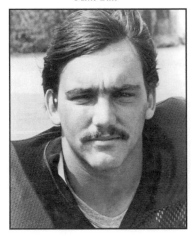

Mike Bass

Anderson, Neal	FB	1961,62
Anderson, Paul T.	FB	1921
Anderson, William W.	FB	1915,16
Antilla, Arvo A.	FB	1933,34,35
Antonacci, Rich	FB	1977
Applegate, Frank G.	FB	1903
Applegran, Clarence O.	FB	1915,19
Archer, Arthur E.	FB	1948
Argueta, Julio	FB	1995
Armstead, Charles	FB	1981,82
Armstrong, James W.	FB	1891,92
Armstrong, Lennox F.	FB	1913,14
Arneson, Jeff	FB	1991,92,93
Arvanitis, George	FB	1984
Ash, David	FB	1957,58,59
Ashley Jr., Richard	FB	1892
Ashlock, Dennis	FB	1976,77
Astroth, Lavere L.	FB	1939,40,41
Atherton, George H.	FB	1891,92,93
Atkins, Kelvin	FB	1979,80,81
Avery, Galen	FB	1972
Avery, Todd D.	FB	1984,85
Ayres, John	FB	1983,84
Babcock, Patrick	FB	2001
Babyar, Chris	FB	1981,82,83,84
Bachouros, Peter F.	FB	1950,51,52
Badal, Herbert	FB	1954
Baietto, Robert E.	FB	1954,55
Bailey, Gordon R.	FB	1931
Baker, Clarence	FB	1977
Bardwell, Roy	FB	1999
Bareither, Charles	FB	1967,68,69
Bargo, Ken	FB	1967,68,69
Barker, John K.	FB	1891
Barnes, Jeff	FB	1978
Barter, Harold H.	FB	1903
Baskin, Neil	FB	1969
Bass, Mike	FB	1980,81,82
Bassett, Denman J.	FB	1947
Bassey, Ralph C.	FB	1943
Batchelder, Robert (Bo)	FB	1964,65,66
Bateman, James M.	FB	1905
Bates, Melvin B.	FB	1953,54,55
Bauer, John A.	FB	1930
Bauer, John R.	FB	1951,52,53
Baughman, James	FB	1951
Baum, Benjamin F.	FB	1907,08,09
Baum, Harry, W.	FB	1893,94,95
Bauman, Frank	FB	1946
Baumgart, Tom	FB	1970,72
Beadle, Thomas B.	FB	1895,97
Beaman, Bruce	FB	1972,73,74,75
Beaver, Daniel	FB	1973,74,75,76
Beckmann, Bruce	FB	1958,59
Bedalow, John	FB	1970,71,72
Beebe, Charles, D.	FB	1894,95,96
Beers, Harley	FB	1902,03

Bell, Frank E.	FB	1936,37
Bell, Kameno	FB	1989,90,91
Bellamy, Mike	FB	1988,89
Bellephant, Joe F.	FB	1957
Belmont, Lou	FB	1980,81
Belting, Charles H.	FB	1910,11
Belting, Paul E.	FB	1911
Bennett, Caslon K.	FB	1930
Bennett, James	FB	1985
Bennett, Ralph E.	FB	1937,38,39
Bennett, Theodore (Tab)	FB	1970,71,72
Bennis, Charles W.	FB	1932,33,34
Bennis, William	FB	1937
Benson, Cam	FB	1980,81,82,83
Benson, Ivan	FB	1996,97,98
Bergeson, C. H.	FB	1928
Berner, John R.	FB	1935,36,37
Bernhardt, George W.	FB	1938,39,40
Bernstein, Louis S.	FB	1909,10
Berry, Gilbert I.	FB	1930,31,32
Berschet, Marvin	FB	1951
Bess, Bob	FB	1968,69
Bess, Ronald W.	FB	1965,66,67
Beverly, Dwight	FB	1982,83
Bevis, Joe	FB	2000,01
Beynon, Jack T.	FB	1932,33,34
Bias, Moe	FB	1982,83
Bierman, Randy	FB	1992,93
Bieszczad, Bob	FB	1968,69
Bingaman, Lester A.	FB	1944,45,46,47
Birky, David A.	FB	1984,85
Bishop, Dennis	FB	1981,82
Bishop, Robert E.	FB	1952,53
Blackaby, Ethan	FB	1959,60
Blackman, Ken	FB	1992,93,94
Blakely, David A.	FB	1977
Blondell, Jim	FB	1985,86,87
Bloom, Robert J.	FB	1932,33
Boatright, David	FB	1983,84,85
Bodman, Alfred E.	FB	1930,31,32
Bodman, Stanley L.	FB	1930
Boeke, Greg	FB	1978,80,81
Boeke, Leroy	FB	1977,78,79,80
Boerio, Charles	FB	1950,51
Bohm, Ron	FB	1983,84,85,86
Bonner, Bonjiovanna	FB	1978,79
Bonner, Lory T.	FB	1957,58
Booze, MacDonald C.	FB	1912
Borman, Herbert R.	FB	1951,52,53
Boso, Cap	FB	1984,85
Bostrom, Kirk	FB	1979,80
Boughman, James A.	FB	1951
Bourke, Timothy E.	FB	1984,85,86,87
Bowen, Herbert L.	FB	1890
Bowlay-Williams, Victor	FB	1988,89

Chuck Bennis

Boyer, Darren	FB	1990,91,92
Boykin, Rod	FB	1991,92,93,94
Boyle, Kenny	FB	2000,01
Boysaw, Greg	FB	1986,88,89
Bradley, John J.	FB	1905,06
Bradley, Kendall R.	FB	1935
Bradley, Theron A.	FB	1943
Brady, Edward	FB	1980,81,82,83
Braid, Ken	FB	1971,72,73
Branch, James M.	FB	1894,95,96
Bray, Edward C.	FB	1943,44,45
Brazas, Steven E.	FB	1984
Bremer, Lawrence H.	FB	1908
Breneman Amos L.	FB	1915
Brennan, Rich	FB	1969,70
Brewer, Melvin C.	FB	1937,38,39
Brewster, Tim	FB	1982,83
Brice, Romero	FB	1987,88,89,90
Briggs, Claude P.	FB	1900
Briley, Norman P.	FB	1899
Britton, Earl T.	FB	1923,24,25

Romero Brice

Chris Brown

Broerman, Richard FB 1952
Brokemond, George R. FB 1958
Bronson, George D. FB 1902
Brookins, Mitchell FB 1980,82,83
Brooks, Carson C. FB 1966,67,68
Brooks, Richard A. FB 1906
Brosky, Alfred E. FB 1950,51,52
Brown, Charles A. FB 1923,24,25
Brown, Charles E. FB 1948,49,50
Brown, Chico FB 1995
Brown, Chris FB 1995,96,97
Brown, Cyron FB 1995,96
Brown, Darrin I. FB 1984,85,86
Brown, Gary W. FB 1959,60,61
Brown, Horace T. FB 1909
Brown, James E. FB 1958,59,60
Brown, Joseph A. FB 1937
Brown, Julyon FB 1988,89,90,91
Brown, William D. FB 1958,59,60
Brownlow, Darrick FB 1987,88,89,90
Brundage, Martin D. FB 1901

Luke Butkus

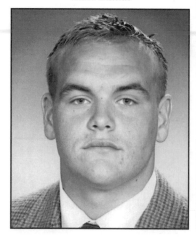

Brzuszkiewicz, Michael FB 1976
Bubin, Sean FB 2000,01
Bucheit, George C. FB 1918
Bucklin, Robert FB 1969,70,71
Bujan, George P. FB 1943,44,45
Bulow, Dan FB 1977
Bundy, Herman W. FB 1901,02
Burchfield, Brian FB 1986,87
Burdick, Lloyd S. FB 1927,28,29
Burgard, Peter FB 1980,81,82
Burkland, Theodore L. FB 1896
Burlingame, Keith FB 1978
Burman, Jon FB 1988
Burns, Bob FB 1968,69,70
Burrell, William G. FB 1957,58,59
Burris, Merlyn G. FB 1938
Burroughs, Wilbur G. FB 1904,05,06
Buscemi, Joseph A. FB 1946,47
Bush, Arthur W. FB 1891
Butkovich, Anthony J. FB 1941,42
Butkovich, William FB 1943,44,45
Butkus, Luke FB 1998,99,00,01
Butkus, Mark FB 1980,81,82,83
Butkus, Richard M. FB 1962,63,64
Butler, Charles FB 1954,56
Button, Lyle A. FB 1947,48,49
Butzer, Glenn D. FB 1908,09,10
Byrd, Darryl FB 1981,82
Byrd, Rodney FB 1993,94,95,96
Cabell, Kevin FB 1976
Cahill, Leo H. FB 1948,49,50
Callaghan, Richard T. FB 1962,63,64
Campbell, Robert A. FB 1939
Campbell, Tracy FB 1973,74
Campos, Lou, 1984 FB 1985,86,87
Cantwell, Francis R. FB 1934,35
Capel, Bruce FB 1962,63,64
Capen, Bernard C. FB 1902
Carbonari, Gerald M. FB 1965,66
Carlini, Perry FB 1983,84
Carlton, Matt FB 1998,99
Carmien, Tab FB 1978,80
Carney, Charles R. FB 1918,19,20,21
Caroline, J. C. FB 1953,54
Carpenter, Chris FB 1986
Carr, Chris FB 1979
Carr Jr., H. Eugene FB 1958
Carrington, Michael FB 1978,79,80,81
Carrithers, Ira T. FB 1904
Carson, W. Howard FB 1934,37
Carson, Paul H. FB 1931
Carter, Archie FB 1982,83
Carter, Donald H. FB 1911
Carter, Vincent FB 1978
Cast, Dick L. FB 1961

Castelo, Robert E. FB 1936,37,38
Catlin, James M. FB 1952
Cerney, Bill FB 1974,75,76
Chalcraft, Kenneth G. FB 1961
Chamblin, Jack FB 1953,54
Chapman, Ralph D. FB 1912,13,14
Charles, William W. FB 1936
Charpier, Leonard L. FB 1916,17
Chattin, Ernest P. FB 1930
Cheeley, Kenneth D. FB 1940,41
Cherney, Eugene K. FB 1957,58
Cherry, Robert S. FB 1940,41
Chester, Guy S. FB 1894
Christensen, Paul G. FB 1916
Christofilakos, Peter FB 2001
Chronis, Tony FB 1973
Chrystal, Jeff FB 1973,74,75
Cies, Jerry B. FB 1944,45
Ciszek, Ray A. C. FB 1943,44,45,46
Clark, Danny FB 1996,97,98,99
Clark, George (Potsy) FB 1914,15
Clark, Jamaal FB 2000,01
Clark, Robert FB 1922
Clark, Ronald FB 1949,50
Clarke, Curtis FB 1983,85
Clarke, Edwin B. FB 1890
Clarke, Frederick W. FB 1890
Claussen, Tom FB 1996
Clear, Samuel FB 1979,80
Clements, John H. FB 1930
Clements, Tony FB 1968,69
Clinton, Edgar M. FB 1896
Coady, Tom FB 1979,80
Cobb, Glenn FB 1987,88
Coffeen, Harry C. FB 1896,97
Colby, Greg FB 1971,72,73
Cole, E. Joseph FB 1949,50,51
Cole, Jewett FB 1935,36
Cole, Jerry FB 1969,70
Cole, Mike FB 1992,93
Cole, Terry FB 1980,81,82,83
Coleman, DeJustice FB 1957,58,59
Coleman, James FB 1976,77
Coleman, Roger FB 1973,74
Coleman, Norris FB 1969
Collier, Glenn FB 1969,70,71
Collier, Steve FB 1982
Collins, Clark FB 2000
Collins, John J. FB 1962
Collins, Michael E. FB 1976
Collins, Tyrone FB 1993
Connor, Rameel FB 1996,98,99
Conover, Robert J. FB 1930
Conradt, Greg FB 1988

Jeff Chrystal

Conroy, John FB 1996
Cook, David F. FB 1931,33
Cook, Jameel FB 1998,99,00
Cook, James F. FB 1898,00,01,02
Cook, James W. FB 1891,92
Cooledge, Marshall M. FB 1925
Cooper, Norm FB 1970
Cooper Jr., Paul H. FB 1893,94,95
Copher, Chad FB 1991,92,93,94
Correll, Walter K. FB 1941,42
Counts, John E. FB 1959
Coutchie, Stephen A. FB 1922,23
Covington, Jim FB 1981
Cox, Fred FB 1990,91,92
Cozen, Douglas FB 1978,79
Craciunoiu, Mike FB 1999
Craig, Ryan FB 1995,96,97
Cramer, Willard M. FB 1937,38
Crane, Russell J. FB 1927,28,29
Crangle, Walter F. FB 1919,20,21
Craven, Forest, I. FB 1932
Cravens, Robert D. FB 1961

Robert Crumpton

Matt Cushing

Crawford, Walter C.	FB	1923
Crum, Tom	FB	1968
Crumpton, Robert	FB	1991,92,93,94
Cruz, Ken	FB	1983,84
Cummings, Barton A.	FB	1932,33,34
Cunz, Robert W.	FB	1945,46,47
Curran, John	FB	1994
Curry, Jack C.	FB	1943
Curtis, Joe	FB	1980,81,82
Cushing, Matt	FB	1994,95,96,97
Custardo, Fred	FB	1963,64,65
Cutter, Dan	FB	1999,00,01
D'Ambrosio, Arthur L.	FB	1925,26,27
Dadant, Maurice G.	FB	1907
Dahl, Andres W.	FB	1934
Dallenbach, Karl M.	FB	1909
Damos, Donn	FB	1970
Damron, Tim	FB	1981,82
Daniel, Cullen	FB	1980
Daniels, Drew	FB	1990
Danosky, Anthony J.	FB	1958

Ty Douthard

Dardano, Rusty	FB	1981
Darlington, Dan	FB	1969,70,71
Daugherity, Russell S.	FB	1925,26
Davenport, Sedrick	FB	2001
Davis, Carey	FB	2000,01
Davis, Chester W.	FB	1910,11
Davis, John	FB	1966,67
Davis, Larry	FB	1998
Davis, Scott	FB	1983,85,86,87
Dawson, Bobby	FB	1986,87
Dawson, George	FB	1922
Day, Mark	FB	1996
Dean, Michael	FB	1996,97,98,99
DeDecker, Darrel	FB	1959,60
DeFalco, Steven	FB	1976
Deimling, Keston J.	FB	1927,28
dela Garza, Gabriel	FB	1987
Delaney, Robert F.	FB	1956,57
Deller, Dick	FB	1961,62,63
Delveaux, Jack	FB	1956,57,58
DeMoss, Clarence W.	FB	1952,53
Dennis, Mark	FB	1983,84,85,86
Dentino, Greg	FB	1980
DeOliver, Miguel	FB	1981,82
Depler, John C.	FB	1918,19,20
Derby, Sylvester R.	FB	1913,14
DesEnfants, Robert E.	FB	1954,55
Dickerson Jr., Charles F.	FB	1961
Diedrich, Brian	FB	1974,75,76
Diehl, Dave	FB	1999,00,01
Dieken, Doug	FB	1968,69,70
Diener, Walter G.	FB	1902,03,04
DiFeliciantonio, John	FB	1974,75,76
Dilger, Ken	FB	1991,92,93,94
Dillinger, Harry	FB	1903,04
Dillon, Chester C.	FB	1910,11,12
Dillon, David	FB	1939,40
Dimit, George	FB	1946
Dismuke, Mark	FB	1978
Dobrzeniecki, Mike	FB	1971
Dobson, Bruce	FB	1971,72,73
Doepel, Robert F.	FB	1920
Dollahan, Bruce E.	FB	1957,58
Dombroski, Jack	FB	1975,76
Dombrowski, Robert J.	FB	1984,85
Doney, Scott	FB	1979,80
Donnelly, George	FB	1962,63,64
Donnelly, Patrick	FB	1988,89,90
Donnelly, Tyler	FB	1993
Donoho, Louie W.	FB	1946
Donovan, Dan	FB	1988,89
Doolittle, Areal	FB	1986,87
Dorr, Dick	FB	1964
Doud, William O.	FB	1901
Douglass, Paul W.	FB	1949,50

Douthard, Talib (Ty)	FB	1993,94,95,96
Doxey, Samuel	FB	1891
Drayer, Clarence T.	FB	1921
Driscoll, Denny	FB	1970
Dubrish, Bob	FB	1973
Dufelmeier, Arthur J.	FB	1942,46,47
Dufelmeier, Jamie	FB	1969,70
Duke, Austin L.	FB	1952
Dulick, Jason	FB	1993,94,95,96
Dundy, Michael W.	FB	1961,63
Duniec, Brian J.	FB	1962,63,64
Durant, Philip S.	FB	1921
Durrell, Kenneth	FB	1978,79,80
Dusenbury, Marshall V.	FB	1951
Dwyer, Dave	FB	1979,80,81
Dykstra, Eugene R.	FB	1934,35,36
Dysert, Terry	FB	1970
Eason, Tony	FB	1981,82
Easter, Robert A.	FB	1961,62,63
Easterbrook, James C.	FB	1940
Easterbrook, John W.	FB	1958,59,60
Eberhart, Jason	FB	1997,98,99,00
Eddleman, T. Dwight	FB	1946,47,48
Edwards, Charles	FB	1994
Edwards, David	FB	1980,82,83,84
Edwards, Jason	FB	1993,94
Ehni, Ralph E.	FB	1938,39,40
Eichorn, Greg	FB	1988,89,90,91
Eickman, Gary	FB	1963,64,65
Eliot (Nusspickel), Raymond E.	FB	1930,31
Elliott, John	FB	1984,85
Ellis, Donald C.	FB	1949
Ellsworth, Sam	FB	1983,84,86,87
Elsner, Bernard W.	FB	1950,52
Elting, Donald N.	FB	1938,39
Ems, Clarence E.	FB	1917,20
Engel, Elmer H.	FB	1940,41,42
Engel, Greg	FB	1990,91,92,93
Engels, Donald J.	FB	1949,50,51
Enochs, Claude D.	FB	1897
Epps, Nick	FB	1982
Erb, Bruce	FB	1967,68,69
Erickson, Richard J.	FB	1965,66,67
Erlandson, Jim	FB	1981,82
Ernst, Donald W.	FB	1951,52,53
Evans, John C.	FB	1930,31
Fairweather, Charles A.	FB	1901,02,03,04
Falkenstein, Elry G.	FB	1952,53
Falkenstein, Robert R.	FB	1940
Fay, Richard B.	FB	1936,37
Feagin, Steve	FB	1989,90,91,92
Fearn, Ronald R.	FB	1961,62,63
Feeheley, Tom	FB	1974
Ferrari, Ron	FB	1980,81
Fields, Kenneth E.	FB	1928

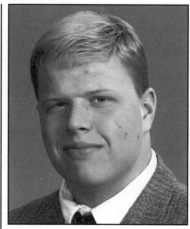
Greg Engel

Fields Jr., Willis E.	FB	1965,66,67
Finch, James	FB	1985,86
Finis, Jerry	FB	1974,75,76
Finis, Marty	FB	1980
Finke, Jeff	FB	1987,88,89,90
Finzer, David	FB	1977,78
Fischer, John	FB	1934
Fischer, Louis E.	FB	1895,96,97
Fisher, Fred D.	FB	1925
Fisher, Leon	FB	1986
Fisher, Shane	FB	1992,93,94,95
Fisher, William	FB	1975
Fit, Stan	FB	1985,86,87,88
Fitts, Steve	FB	1998,99,00,01
Fitzgerald, Richard J.	FB	1963
Flaar, Mike	FB	1997
Fletcher, Ralph E.	FB	1918,19,20
Fletcher, Robert H.	FB	1918,19,20
Flisakowski, Cory	FB	2001
Florek, Ray	FB	1946
Flynn, Dennis	FB	1977,78,81

Jeff Finke

Robert Franklin

Red Grange

Foggey, Erik	FB	1989,90,91,92
Follett, Dwight W.	FB	1924
Forbes, Stuart F.	FB	1897
Ford, Brian	FB	1974,75
Fordham, Mike	FB	1997
Forseman, Eric	FB	1981
Forst, Lawrence H.	FB	1943,45
Forte, Dominic J.	FB	1976
Foster, Dale W.	FB	1952
Foster, Greg	FB	1978,79,80
Fouts, L. H.	FB	1893
Fox, Charles M.	FB	1949,50
Fox, Wylie B.	FB	1962,63,64
Francis, Frank D.	FB	1899
Francis, Gary	FB	1954,55,56
Francis, Tony	FB	1996,97,98,99
Franklin, Robert	FB	1997,98,99,00
Franks, Willard G.	FB	1946,47
Frederick, George R.	FB	1935
French, A. Blair	FB	1926,27
Freund, Peter	FB	1987,88
Friel, Marty	FB	1974,75,76

Rick George

Frink, Frederick F.	FB	1931,33
Froschauer, Frank E.	FB	1932,33,34
Fulk, Robert T.	FB	1984,85
Fullerton, Theron B.	FB	1913
Fultz, Duane E.	FB	1939
Furber, William A.	FB	1890
Furimsky, Paul	FB	1954
Gabbett, William T.	FB	1961,62
Gabrione, Pete	FB	1992,93,94
Gal, Joe	FB	2001
Galbreath, Charles S.	FB	1933,34,35
Gallagher, Thomas B.	FB	1946,47,48
Gallivan, Raymond P.	FB	1924,25,26
Gann, John	FB	1971,72,73
Gano, Clifton W.	FB	1935
Gardiner, Lion	FB	1906,07,08
Gardner, Morris (Moe)	FB	1987,88,89,90
Garner, Donald S.	FB	1930
Garrett, Eric	FB	1998,99,00
Gartrell, Willie	FB	1974,75
Gates, Andrew W.	FB	1890,91
Gatton, Joe	FB	1996
Gaut, Robert E.	FB	1892,93,94
Gawelek, Mike	FB	2001
Gedman, Stacy	FB	1967
Genis, John E.	FB	1941,42,46
George, Jeff	FB	1988,89
George, Richard	FB	1978,79,80,81
Geraci, Joseph L.	FB	1959
Gerometta, Arthur L.	FB	1943
Gianacakos, Richard	FB	1990
Gibbs, Robert	FB	1940,42
Gibson, Alec	FB	1984,85
Giddings, Mike W.	FB	1984,85
Gillen, John	FB	1977,78,79,80
Gillen, Ken	FB	1979,80,82
Gilstrap, Charles	FB	2000,01
Glasson, Steve	FB	1986,87,88,89
Glauser, Glenn L.	FB	1961
Glazer, Herbert	FB	1935
Glielmi, Rob	FB	1982,83,84,85
Glosecki, Andy R.	FB	1936
Gnidovic, Donald J.	FB	1950,51
Gockman, John	FB	2001
Goelitz, Walter A.	FB	1917
Golaszewski, Paul P.	FB	1961
Goldberg, Jeff	FB	1976
Golden, Scott	FB	1981,82,83
Gongala, Robert B.	FB	1952,54
Good, Richard, J.	FB	1940,41,42
Gordon, James	FB	1986,87
Gordon, Louis J.	FB	1927,28,29
Gordon, Stephen M.	FB	1976
Gorenstein, Sam	FB	1931
Gosier, Harry	FB	1983

Gottfried, Charles	FB	1946,47,48,49
Gould, Dennis C.	FB	1961
Gould, Maurice	FB	1941
Gow, Mike	FB	1972,73,74
Grable, Leonard M.	FB	1925,26,27
Grabowski, Jim S.	FB	1963,64,65
Graeff, Robert E.	FB	1955
Gragg, Elbert R.	FB	1932,33
Graham, John	FB	1970,71
Graham, Walter	FB	1976
Grange, Garland A.	FB	1927
Grange, Harold E. (Red)	FB	1923,24,25
Grant, African	FB	1985,86,87
Grant, Randy	FB	1983,84
Graves, Perry H.	FB	1913,14
Greathouse, Forrest E.	FB	1925
Greco, Dale	FB	1964,65
Green, Chris	FB	1987,88,89,90
Green, Gordon	FB	1985
Green, Howard S.	FB	1906,07
Green, Robert K.	FB	1932
Green, Stanley C.	FB	1946
Green, Vivian J.	FB	1922,23
Green, William, J.	FB	1924,25
Greene, Earl B.	FB	1921
Greene, Steve	FB	1972,73,74,75
Greenwood, Donald G.	FB	1943,44
Gregus, Dan	FB	1980,81,82
Gregus, Kurt	FB	1986,87,88,89
Gremer, John A.	FB	1955,59
Grierson, Ray G.	FB	1941,42,46
Grieve, Robert S.	FB	1935,36
Griffin, Donald D.	FB	1941,42
Griffith, Howard	FB	1987,88,89,90
Grimmett, Richard	FB	1977
Grothe, Don	FB	1953,57,58
Gryboski, Edward	FB	1933,34,35
Guard, Jason	FB	1986,87,88,89
Guenther, Ron	FB	1965,66
Gumm, Percy E.	FB	1908,09
Gusich, Mike	FB	1995,96,97,98
Gustafsson, Jon	FB	1991
Hadsall, Harry H.	FB	1895
Hairston, Ray	FB	1984,85,86
Halas, George S.	FB	1917
Hall, Albert L.	FB	1911
Hall, Arthur R.	FB	1898,99,00
Hall, Charles V.	FB	1928,30
Hall, Harry A.	FB	1923,24,25
Hall, Joseph W.	FB	1950,52
Hall, Michael	FB	2001
Hall, Orville E.	FB	1944
Hall, Richard L.	FB	1923,24
Haller, Thomas F.	FB	1956,57
Halstrom, Bernhard C.	FB	1915

Hamner, Jerry	FB	1987,88,89,90
Hannum, P. E.	FB	1903
Hanschmann, Fred R.	FB	1915,18
Hansen, Don	FB	1963,64,65
Hansen, Jarrett	FB	1994
Hanson, Martin E.	FB	1900
Hanson, Rodney	FB	1955,56,57
Hanton, Jamie	FB	2001
Happenney, J. Clifford	FB	1922
Harbour, Dave	FB	1986,87
Hardy, Dale G.	FB	1976,77,78
Hardy, Kevin	FB	1992,93,94,95
Harford, Doug	FB	1965,66
Harkey, Lance	FB	1985,86
Harmon, Ivan G.	FB	1903
Harms, Frederick E.	FB	1965,66,67
Harper, William	FB	1965
Harris, Antoineo	FB	1999,00,01
Harris, Theron	FB	1994
Hart, R. W.	FB	1890,91,92
Hartley, Frank	FB	1988,89,90
Hartmann, Brad	FB	1990

Steve Greene

Bill Henkel

Harvey, Rocky	FB	1998,99,00,01
Haselwood, John M.	FB	1903,04
Hasenstab, Jeff	FB	1991,92,93,94
Hatfield, Joe	FB	1972,73,74
Hathaway, Ralph W.	FB	1938,39
Hauser, Bob	FB	1979
Havard, Steve	FB	1995,97,98,99
Hayer, Joseph C.	FB	1949
Hayes, Bob	FB	1972
Hayes, Erik	FB	1992
Haynes, Clint	FB	1982,83
Haywood, Brad	FB	2000,01
Hazelett, John	FB	1943
Heaven, Mike	FB	1981,82,83,84
Hedtke, William A.	FB	1931
Heinrich, Frank M. (Mick)	FB	1972,73
Heiss Jr., William C.	FB	1944,45,46
Helbling, James L.	FB	1943
Helle, Mark	FB	1980,81,82
Hellstrom, Norton E.	FB	1920
Hembrough, Gary	FB	1959,60,61
Henderson, William R.	FB	1956,57,58

Brian Hodges

Hendrickson, Richard W.	FB	1957
Henkel, Bill	FB	1987,88,89,90
Henry, Wilbur, L.	FB	1934,35,36
Herr, Rich	FB	1989
Hickey, Robert	FB	1957,58,59
Hickman, Robert Z.	FB	1928
Hicks, Tom	FB	1972,73,74
Higgins, Albert, G.	FB	1890
Higgins, Doug	FB	1987,88,89,90
Higgins, Jason	FB	1996
Hilderbrand, Dave	FB	2001
Hill, David	FB	1990,91
Hill, Sam H.	FB	1922
Hill, Stanley	FB	1912
Hill, LeRon W.	FB	1957,58
Hills, Otto R.	FB	1928,29,30
Hinkle, Robert	FB	1947
Hinsberger, Mike	FB	1973
Hodel, Nathan	FB	1997,98,99,00
Hodges, Aaron	FB	2000,01
Hodges, Brian	FB	1998,99,00,01
Hodges, James D.	FB	1937,38
Hoeft, Julius	FB	1932
Hoekstra, Mark	FB	1996,97,98
Hofer, Lance	FB	1980
Hoffman, Chris	FB	1996,97,98,99
Hoffman, James H.	FB	1966
Hoffman, Robert W.	FB	1912
Hogan, Mickey	FB	1967,68
Hogan, Richard	FB	1982
Holcombe, Robert	FB	1994,95,96,97
Holden, Lamont	FB	2001
Holecek, John	FB	1991,92,93,94
Hollenbach, Jeff	FB	1973,74
Holmes, Mike	FB	1979,80
Hood, Estus	FB	2001
Hood, Marcus	FB	2000
Hopkins, Brad	FB	1990,91,92
Hopkins, Michael	FB	1988,89,90,91
Horn, John	FB	1993
Horsely, Robert E.	FB	1931
Hotchkiss, R. J.	FB	1894,95
Howard, Dana	FB	1991,92,93,94
Huber, William W.	FB	1946
Huddleston, Thielen B.	FB	1930
Hudelson, Clyde W.	FB	1912
Huebner, Dave	FB	1976
Huff, George A.	FB	1890,92
Hughes, Henry L.	FB	1920
Huisinga, Larry	FB	1970,71,72
Hull, Walker F.	FB	1908,09
Humay, Daniel M.	FB	1966
Humbert, Fred H.	FB	1927,28,29
Hungate, Eddie	FB	1985
Huntoon, Harry A.	FB	1901,02,03,04

Hurley, O. Landis	FB	1940
Hurtte, Frank	FB	1944
Huston, William E.	FB	1966,67,68
Hyinck, Clifton F.	FB	1931
Ingle, Walden M.	FB	1938
Ingwersen, Burton A.	FB	1917,18,19
Iovino, Vito J.	FB	1956
Ivy, Mario	FB	2001
Jackson, Bobby	FB	1997,98,00,01
Jackson, Davis	FB	1967,68,69
Jackson, Earl A.	FB	1931
Jackson, Kevin	FB	1992,94
Jackson, Marc	FB	1999,00
Jackson, Trenton	FB	1962,65
Jacques, Virgus	FB	1973
James, Brad	FB	1987
James, David	FB	1994,95,96,97
Janata, John	FB	1981,82
Janecek, Bill	FB	1967,68
Janicki, Nick	FB	1969
Jansen, Earl	FB	1935
Janssen, Donald	FB	1944
Jefferson, Harry	FB	1954,55,56
Jenkins, Eddie	FB	1971,72,73
Jenkins, Richard H.	FB	1951
Jenkins, Terrence D.	FB	1984,85
Jenks, Charles N.	FB	1925
Jenner, Kris	FB	1983
Jensen, Stanley C.	FB	1930,31
Jerzak, Edward	FB	1957
Jeske, Thomas	FB	1971
Johnson, Bob	FB	1972
Johnson, Carl	FB	1956,57,58
Johnson, Donald T.	FB	1944
Johnson, Filmel	FB	1990,91,92,93
Johnson, Frank	FB	1973,74,75,76
Johnson, Garrett	FB	1995,96,97,98
Johnson Jr., Herschel E.	FB	1966,68
Johnson, Jackie	FB	1984,85
Johnson, Jay	FB	1976
Johnson, Johnny	FB	1993,94,95
Johnson, Kirk	FB	1998,99
Johnson, Mike	FB	1982,83
Johnson, Mikki	FB	1993,94,95
Johnson, Nathan E.	FB	1939,40,41
Johnson, Richard L.	FB	1966,67,68
Johnson, William M.	FB	1936
Johnston, Arthur R.	FB	1897,98,99
Jolley, Walter	FB	1927,28,29
Jones, Amos I.	FB	1949,50
Jones, Cliff	FB	1977
Jones, Henry	FB	1987,88,89,90
Jones, Keith	FB	1985,86,87,88
Jones, Mark	FB	1981,82
Jones, Martin	FB	1994,95

Garrett Johnson

Jones, Robert B.	FB	1945
Jones, Shawn	FB	1986
Jones, Tom	FB	1969,70
Joop, Lester	FB	1943,44,45
Jordan, Larry E.	FB	1965,66,67
Jordan, Stephen	FB	1987,88
Jordan, Taman	FB	2001
Julian, Anthony	FB	2000
Junghans, Brian	FB	1986
Jurczyk, Gary	FB	1975,76,77
Juriga, Jim	FB	1982,83,84,85
Jutton, Lee	FB	1901
Kaiser, John	FB	1969,70
Kane, John F.	FB	1943
Kanosky, John P.	FB	1935
Karras, John	FB	1949,50,51
Kasap, George	FB	1951
Kasap, Mike	FB	1942,46
Kassel, Charles E.	FB	1924,25,26
Kasten, Frederick W.	FB	1902,03,04
Kautter, Brett	FB	1999,00,01
Kavathas, Sam	FB	1974

Henry Jones

Jonathan Kerr

Brett Larsen

Kawal, E. J.	FB	1929
Kearney, Herschel P.	FB	1943
Kee, Dick	FB	1963,64,65
Kehoe, Scott	FB	1983,84,85,86
Keith, Alvin	FB	1970,71,72
Kelly, David J.	FB	1976,77,78,79
Kelly, Mark	FB	1985,86,87,88
Kelly, Moe	FB	1969,70,71
Kennedy Jr., John H.	FB	1931
Kent, David	FB	1993
Kerr, Jonathan	FB	1991,92,93,94
Kersulis, Walter T.	FB	1944,47,48,49
Khachaturian, John	FB	1976
Kiler, William H.	FB	1894,95
Kimbell, Steve	FB	1965
King, Harless W.	FB	1891
King, J. W.	FB	1898
Kingsbury, Brian G.	FB	1976,77
Kinney, Jeff	FB	1990,91,92
Kirk, Todd	FB	1904,05
Kirkpatrick, Jesse B.	FB	1918
Kirschke, John W.	FB	1938,39

Kirwan, Jim	FB	1975,76
Kisner, James W.	FB	1984,85
Kittler, Bud	FB	1973
Kittner, Kurt	FB	1998,99,00,01
Kleber, Doug	FB	1973,74,75
Kleckner, Bill	FB	1972,73,74
Klein J. Leo	FB	1915,16,17
Klein, Jim	FB	1992,93,94
Klemp, Joseph B.	FB	1937
Klimek, Anthony F.	FB	1948,49,50
Kmiec, Tom	FB	1968
Kmiec, Kenneth K.	FB	1965,66,67
Knapp, Clyde G.	FB	1926
Knell, Phil D.	FB	1965,66
Knop, Robert O.	FB	1916
Knox, Carl W.	FB	1937
Knox, Rodney	FB	1974
Koch, George W.	FB	1919
Koerwitz, Chris	FB	1994,95,96
Koester, Kraig	FB	1991,92,93
Kogut, Chuck	FB	1971,72,73
Kogut, James K.	FB	1976,77
Kohlhagen, Richard M.	FB	1952,53
Kolb, Gary A.	FB	1959
Kolens, S. William	FB	1940,45
Kolfenbach, Edwin J.	FB	1931
Kolloff, Thomas	FB	1977
Kopatz, Jim	FB	1974,75
Kopp, William K.	FB	1918,19
Kowalski, August J.	FB	1932
Kraft, Don	FB	1955
Kraft, Reynold R.	FB	1915,16,17
Krakoski, Joseph	FB	1960
Krall, William E.	FB	1945
Kreitling, Richard A.	FB	1957,58
Krueger, Bernard E.	FB	1946,47,48,49
Krueger, Kerry	FB	1980,82,83
Krueger, Kurt	FB	1981,83
Kruze, John J.	FB	1960,61
Kuchenbecker, Jay	FB	1995,96
Kuhn, Clifford W.	FB	1933,35,36
Kulaga, Jay	FB	2001
Kustock, Al	FB	1972,73
Kwas (Kwasniewski), Eugene S.	FB	1945,46
Lamb, Shane	FB	1986
Lange, Gary	FB	1969
Langhorst, Oliver M.	FB	1928
Lansche, Oral A.	FB	1913
Lantz, Simon E.	FB	1894
Lanum, Franklin B.	FB	1926,29
Lanum, Harold B.	FB	1910
Lanum, Ralph L.	FB	1918
Larimer, Floyd C.	FB	1917,20
Larsen, Brett	FB	1992,93,94,95
Lasater Jr., Harry A.	FB	1936,37

Laster, Tony	FB	1989,90,91
Lattimore, Carlos	FB	1999,00,01
Lauzen, Joe	FB	1997,98
Lavery, Larry B.	FB	1959,60
Lavery, Tim	FB	1997
Lawlor, Mike	FB	1983
Lawlor, Sean T.	FB	1984,86
Laz, Donald R.	FB	1950
Lazier, Murney	FB	1947,48
Leach, Todd	FB	1991,92,93
Lee, Gary	FB	1980,81
Lee, Willie	FB	1971
Leistner, Charles A.	FB	1943
Leitch, Neal M.	FB	1918
Lenich, William	FB	1937,38,39
Lennon, J. Patrick	FB	1960
Lenzini, Robert E.	FB	1951,52,53
Leonard, Marion R.	FB	1924,25
Lepic, Mike	FB	1974
Lester, Wagner	FB	1989,90
Levanti, John	FB	1971,72,73
Levanti, Louis	FB	1947,48,49
Levenick, Stu	FB	1974,75
Levitt, Lloyd	FB	1978,79
Lewis, Greg	FB	1999,00,01
Lewis, Ivery	FB	1999
Lewis, James W.	FB	1928
Lewis, Joe	FB	1970,71,72
Lifvendahl, Richard A.	FB	1919
Lindbeck, Emerit (Em) D.	FB	1953,54,55
Lindberg, Lester L.	FB	1933,34,35
Linden, Russell W.	FB	1920
Lindgren, Justa M.	FB	1898,99,00,01
Line, Jerry	FB	1967
Lingner, Adam	FB	1979,80,81,82
Litt, Leon B.	FB	1907
Little, Charles D.	FB	1984,85,86,87
Livas, Steve	FB	1969
Lloyd, Brandon	FB	1999,01
Logeman, Ron	FB	1976
Lollino, Frank V.	FB	1961,62
Lonergan, Charles P. A.	FB	1904
Long, Mon	FB	1997,98,99,00
Long, Robby	FB	1999,00,01
Lopez, John	FB	1979,80,81
Lovejoy, Charles E.	FB	1917,18,19
Lovelace, Curtis	FB	1987,88,89,90
Lovellette, Lindell J.	FB	1960
Lowe, Kevin	FB	1974
Lowenthal, Fred	FB	1898,99,00,01
Ludington, Lashon	FB	1993,94
Luhrsen, Paul H.	FB	1952,53
Lundberg, Albert J.	FB	1937,38,39
Lundgren, Carl L.	FB	1899,00
Lunn, Robert J.	FB	1945

Mon Long

Lyle, Duane	FB	1994,95
Lynch, Clinton	FB	1990,91,93
Lynch, James	FB	1985,86
Lynch, Lynn	FB	1949,50
Lyons, Thomas E.	FB	1909,10
MacArthur, John E.	FB	1942
Macchione, Rudolph J.	FB	1944
Machado, J.P.	FB	1996,97,98
MacLean, Dan	FB	1979,80
Macomber, F. B.	FB	1914,15,16
Madsen, Olav	FB	1914
Maechtle, Donald M.	FB	1946,47,48
Maggioli, Archille F.	FB	1946,47
Major Jr., Fred	FB	1950
Majoy, Rob	FB	1995,96,97,98
Malczyk, Mike	FB	2000,01
Malinsky, Robert E.	FB	1948
Marable, Terence	FB	1995
March, Dean	FB	1974,76
Marinangel, Jim	FB	1967
Markland, Jeff	FB	1986,87
Marlaire, Arthur G.	FB	1940

Paul Marshall

Mike Martin

Marshall, Paul	FB	1993,94,95,96
Marriner, Lester M.	FB	1925,26,27
Marriner, Scott T.	FB	1931
Martignago, Aldo A.	FB	1947,48,49
Martin, Jeffery C.	FB	1984,85,86
Martin, John	FB	1992
Martin, Mike	FB	1980,81,82
Martin, Robert W.	FB	1898
Martin, Russel	FB	1958
Martin, Wesley P.	FB	1938,39
Masar, Terry	FB	1969,70,71
Mason, Taylor	FB	1978
Mastrangeli, Al A.	FB	1946,47,48
Mathews, C. M.	FB	1900
Mathis, Mark	FB	1985,86
Mattiazza, Dominic L.	FB	1941
Mattison, Steve	FB	1994
Mauck, Jeff	FB	1985
Mauzey, John	FB	1968,69
May, Robert D.	FB	1931,32
Maze (Mazeika), Anthony	FB	1936,37
McAfee, Floyd H.	FB	1954,55

Tim McCloud

McAvoy, Tim	FB	1979,80,81
McBain, Mike	FB	1983,84,85
McBeth, Mike	FB	1979
McCarren, Larry	FB	1970,71,72
McCarthy, James P.	FB	1941,42
McCarthy, Tim	FB	1969,70
McCartney, Tom	FB	1972,73
McCaskill, Arthur	FB	1964
McCleery, Ben H.	FB	1909
McClellan, Anthony	FB	2001
McClellan, Lynn	FB	1987,88
McCloud, Tim	FB	1992,93,94,95
McClure, Robert T.	FB	1978,79
McClure, William E.	FB	1927,28
McCormick, Olin	FB	1892,93
McCormick, Roscoe C.	FB	1898
McCracken, Mac	FB	1975,76
McCray, Michael P.	FB	1976,77
McCullough, Lawrence	FB	1978,79
McCullough, Thomas M.	FB	1941
McCullum, Thomas	FB	1961
McDade, Richard L.	FB	1958,61
McDonald, George	FB	1995,96,97,98
McDonald, James W.	FB	1937,38
McDonald, Ken	FB	1979
McDonald, Mark	FB	1977
McDonald, Phil	FB	1974,75,76
McDonough, Mike	FB	1967,68
McGann, David G.	FB	1961
McGann, Mike	FB	1983
McGarry, Shawn	FB	1987,88
McGee, Michael	FB	1996,97,98,99
McGoey, Eric	FB	2000
McGovern, Edward F.	FB	1943
McGowan, Mark	FB	1985,86,87,88
McGregor, John L.	FB	1915,17
McGrone, Bryan	FB	1987
McIllwain, Wallace W.	FB	1922,23,24
McIntosh, Hugh	FB	1969
McKee, James H.	FB	1895,96
McKeon, Larry	FB	1969
McKinley, George H.	FB	1901,02
McKissic, Dan	FB	1967,69
McKnight, William A.	FB	1901,02,03
McLane, E. C.	FB	1897,98,99
McLaurin, Carlos	FB	1997
McMillan, Ernest	FB	1958,59,60
McMillen, James W.	FB	1921,22,23
McMillin, Kirk	FB	1969,70
McMillin, Troy	FB	1978,79,81
McMillin, Ty	FB	1972,73,74
McMullen, Rolla	FB	1955,56
McPartlin, Chris	FB	1994
McQuinn, Mike	FB	1980,81,82
Melsek, Daniel	FB	1976

Menkhausen, Brian	FB	1986,87,88,89
Merker, Henry F.	FB	1897
Merriman, John Riley	FB	1909,10,11
Meyer, John	FB	1977
Meyers, Curtis	FB	1980
Meyers, Melvin	FB	1959,60
Michel, Chris	FB	1985,86
Middleton, George E.	FB	1920
Miles, Joe	FB	1980,81,82,83
Miller, Bob	FB	1982,83,84
Miller, David H.	FB	1939
Miller, Kenneth R.	FB	1951,52,53
Miller, Richard R.	FB	1952,55,56
Miller, Roy A.	FB	1922,23,24
Miller, Terry	FB	1965,66,67
Mills, Douglas C.	FB	1961
Mills, Douglas R.	FB	1927,28,29
Milosevich, Paul	FB	1939,40,41
Minnes, Mason	FB	1970,71,72
Minor, James R.	FB	1955,56
Minor, William B.	FB	1962,63,64
Minsker, Robert S.	FB	1933
Mitchell, Bill	FB	1967
Mitchell, Robert C.	FB	1955,56,57
Mitchem, Rickie	FB	1975,76,77
Mitterwallner, Merwin H.	FB	1925,27
Mohr Jr., Albert W. T.	FB	1918,19,20,21
Mohr, Scott	FB	1987,88
Mongreig, Louis M.	FB	1917
Moore, Brandon	FB	1998,99,00,01
Moore, Craig	FB	1986,87
Moore, Paul	FB	1976
Moore, Ryan	FB	1995,96
Moorehead, Aaron	FB	1999,00,01
Morgan, Octavus	FB	1971,72,73
Morris, Harold H.	FB	1916
Morris, LaRue	FB	1936
Morris, Max	FB	1943
Morscheiser, Jack	FB	1971
Morton, Christian	FB	2000,01
Mosely, Marquis	FB	1993,94,96
Mosley, Larry	FB	1980,81
Moss, Perry L.	FB	1946,47
Mota, Joseph L.	FB	1961
Mountjoy, Earl L.	FB	1909
Mountz, Robert E. III	FB	1960,61
Moynihan, Charles J.	FB	1903,04,05,06
Muegge, Louis W.	FB	1925,27
Mueller, Dave	FB	1963,64
Mueller, Richard A.	FB	1948,49,50
Mueller, Steven	FB	1988,90,91,92
Muhl, Clarence A.	FB	1923,24,25
Muhl, Fred L.	FB	1903
Mulchrone, John	FB	1979,80
Mulchrone, Pete	FB	1979,81,82

Brandon Moore

Mullin, Tom	FB	1972,73
Munch, Donald C.	FB	1930
Murnick, Scott	FB	1987
Murphy, Mike	FB	1979,80,81,82
Murphy, Patrick	FB	1960,61
Murphy, Ryan	FB	1995,96,97,98
Murphy, Thomas W.	FB	1951,52
Murray, Edward	FB	1973,74
Murray, Lindley P.	FB	1931
Muti, Joe	FB	1990,91
Myers, Ty	FB	2000,01
Naponic, Robert	FB	1966,67,68
Navarro, Mike	FB	1970,71,72
Nawrocki, Nolan	FB	1998,99
Neathery, Herbert	FB	1950,51,52
Needham, James	FB	1891,92
Nelson, Evert F.	FB	1927
Nelson, Jesse W.	FB	1914,15
Nelson, Kenneth J.	FB	1934,35,36
Nelson, Ralph W.	FB	1956
Nelson, Steve	FB	1983,84
Nelson, Steve	FB	1989,91

Christian Morton

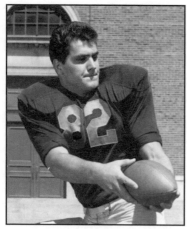

Ed O' Bradocich

Newell, Richard F.	FB	1960,61
Nicastro, Chip	FB	1998,99
Nichols, Sidney W.	FB	1917
Nickol, Edgar	FB	1926,28
Niedzelski, Clifford T.	FB	1941
Nietupski, Ronald	FB	1956,57,58
Nitschke, Ray E.	FB	1955,56,57
Noelke, Robert	FB	1978,79
Nordmeyer, Richard J.	FB	1955,56,57
Norman, Tim	FB	1977,78,80
Norton, John	FB	1977
Nosek, Stephen A.	FB	1951,53,54
Nowack, Albert J. (Butch)	FB	1926,27,28
Nowak, Bill	FB	1967,68
O'Bradovich, Edward	FB	1959,60
O'Brien, Mike	FB	1999,01
O'Connell, Thomas B.	FB	1951,52
O'Keefe, Arthur F.	FB	1931
O'Neal, Ronald D.	FB	1961
O'Neill, Dick A.	FB	1931
O'Neill, Robert J.	FB	1939
Oakes, Bernard F.	FB	1922,23

Quintin Parker

Offenbecher, Bill	FB	1956,57
Ogata, B.J.	FB	2000
Olander, Milton M.	FB	1918,19,20,21
Oliver, Chauncey B.	FB	1909,10,11
Oliver Jr., Percy L.	FB	1954,55,56
Olson, David	FB	1990,91,92,93
Oman, Steve	FB	1967,68
Ormsbee, Terry	FB	1974,76
Ornatek, Tony	FB	1968
Orr, John M.	FB	1944
Osby, Vince	FB	1982,83
Osley, Willie	FB	1970,71
Ovelman, John W.	FB	1930
Owen, Boyd W.	FB	1930
Owens, Isaiah H.	FB	1941,46,47
Pagakis, Chris N.	FB	1949,50
Palma, Gus	FB	1990,91
Palmer, Harry M.	FB	1933
Palmer, Peter	FB	1952,53
Palmer, Ralph W.	FB	1943
Pancratz, Kevin	FB	1975,76,77
Panique, Ken	FB	1971
Parfitt Jr., Alfred W.	FB	1943
Parker, Quintin	FB	1986,88,89,90
Parker, Roy S.	FB	1901,02
Parker, Walter A.	FB	1891,93
Parola, Jerry F.	FB	1961
Parola, Tony	FB	1964
Parrilli, Anthony K.	FB	1959,60,61
Pashos, Tony	FB	1999,00,01
Pasko, Larry	FB	1956
Pasko, William	FB	1961,62,63
Passmore, Don	FB	1981,82,83,84
Pater, Matt	FB	1987,88
Patrick, Gerald J.	FB	1958,59
Patterson, John D.	FB	1939
Patterson, Paul L.	FB	1944,46,47,48
Patton, Antwoine	FB	1992,93,94,95
Paulson, Wayne	FB	1963,64
Pavesic, Ray	FB	1977
Pawlowski, Joseph G.	FB	1940,41,42
Peach, John W.	FB	1976,77
Pearlman, Gavin	FB	1992
Peden, Don C.	FB	1920,21
Pepper, Cam	FB	1989,90
Perez, Peter J.	FB	1943
Perez, Richard B.	FB	1956,57
Perkins, Bernon G.	FB	1931
Perkins, Cecil	FB	1926,27
Perkins, Clyde M.	FB	1943,45
Perrin, Lonnie	FB	1972,73,75
Perry, Jemari	FB	2000,01
Pesek, James	FB	1990,91,92
Peters, Forrest I. (Frosty)	FB	1926,28,29
Peterson, Mark	FB	1972,73,74

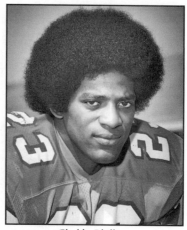

Chubby Phillips

Peterson, Clifford L.	FB	1938,40
Peterson, Daniel E.	FB	1951
Pethybridge, Frank H.	FB	1914
Petkus, Bob	FB	1965
Petraitis, Luke	FB	1989
Pettigrew, James Q.	FB	1906,07,08
Petty, Harold O.	FB	1932
Petty, Lawrence O.	FB	1916,19
Petty, Manley R.	FB	1914,15,16
Pezzoli, Phillip A.	FB	1938
Pfeffer, John E.	FB	1892,93,94,95
Pfeifer, Myron P.	FB	1940,41,42
Phillips, James E.	FB	1938,39,40
Phillips, Jim (Chubby)	FB	1973,74,75,76
Phipps, Thomas E.	FB	1903
Piatt, Charles L.	FB	1931,33
Piazza, Nick	FB	2000,01
Piazza, Sam J.	FB	1948,49,50
Pickering, Mike	FB	1969,71
Piel, Mike	FB	1986,87
Pierce, Alfred	FB	1992
Pierce, Jack B.	FB	1945,47,48
Pierce, Stephen	FB	1985,86
Piggott, Bert C.	FB	1946
Pike, David R.	FB	1962
Pillath, Jerry	FB	1968
Pillsbury, Arthur L.	FB	1890
Pinckney, Frank L.	FB	1905,06
Pinder, Cyril C.	FB	1965,66
Pittman Donald C.	FB	1947
Pitts, R. L.	FB	1902,03
Pixley, Arthur H.	FB	1893,94,95,96
Plankenhorn, James	FB	1961,62,63
Platt, Damien	FB	1993,94
Pleas, Asim	FB	1996,97,98,99
Pleviak, Anthony J.	FB	1966,67,68
Plummer, Ashley	FB	1980,81
Pnazek, Karl	FB	1969
Podmajersky, Paul	FB	1943
Pogue, Harold A.	FB	1913,14,15
Pokorny, Ray	FB	1976
Polaski, Clarence L.	FB	1936
Pollock, Dino	FB	1989
Poloskey, Michael	FB	1990,91
Popa, Elie C.	FB	1950,51
Pope, Jean A.	FB	1904
Portman, Crain P.	FB	1933,34
Postmus, Dave	FB	1987,88
Potter, Phil H.	FB	1916
Powell, Larry D.	FB	1978,79
Powell, Marwan	FB	1995
Powless, Dave	FB	1963,64
Price, Samuel L.	FB	1963,64,65
Priebe, Michael	FB	1978,79
Primous, Marlon	FB	1988,89,90,91

Prince, David C.	FB	1911
Prokopis, Alexander	FB	1944
Pruett, Eugene F.	FB	1913
Prymuski, Robert M.	FB	1946,47,48
Pugh, Dwayne	FB	1982,83,84,85
Purvis, Charles G.	FB	1939
Quade, John C.	FB	1893,94
Qualls, Mark	FB	1988,90
Quinn, Bob	FB	1969,71
Rackers, Neil	FB	1996,97,98,99
Raddatz, Russ	FB	1968
Radell Jr., Willard W.	FB	1965
Railsback, Fay D.	FB	1906,07,08
Raklovits, Richard F.	FB	1949,50
Ralph, Stanley	FB	1975,77,78,79
Ramein, Robert O.	FB	1982
Ramshaw, Jerry	FB	1977,78
Rathke, Phil	FB	1993
Rebecca, Sammy J.	FB	1950,51
Redmann, Doug	FB	1967,68,69
Redziniak, Ray	FB	1997,98,99,00
Reeder, James W.	FB	1937,38,39

Sammy Rebecca

Lloyd Richards

Name	Pos	Years
Reese, Jerrold A.	FB	1984,86
Reeves, Harley E.	FB	1892
Reichle, Richard W.	FB	1919,21
Reinhart, Rick	FB	1973
Reitsch, Henry O.	FB	1920
Reitsch, Robert	FB	1925,26,27
Renfro, Rick	FB	1983
Renn, Donald D.	FB	1954,55
Rettinger, George L.	FB	1938,39
Rhodes, Ora M.	FB	1896
Rice, Simeon	FB	1992,93,94,95
Richards, Edward J.	FB	1922,23
Richards, James V.	FB	1908,09
Richards, Lloyd	FB	1992,93,94
Richardson, Chris	FB	1991,92,93,94
Richie, James K.	FB	1908
Richman, Harry E.	FB	1927,28
Riehle, John	FB	1968
Riggs Jr., Thomas J.	FB	1938,39,40
Ringquist, Clarence L.	FB	1928
Roberson, Garvin	FB	1971,72,73
Roberts, Chester C.	FB	1909,10,11

Ryan Schau

Name	Pos	Years
Roberts, Clifford	FB	1958,59,60
Roberts, Gilbert J.	FB	1922,23,24
Roberts, Melvin	FB	1992,93,94,95
Robertson, Robert	FB	1966,67
Robinson, Darrell	FB	1969,70,71
Robinson, Olaf E.	FB	1929,30
Robinson, Roy	FB	1972,73,74
Robinson, Thomas	FB	1998
Robison, Morris W.	FB	1922
Rodgers, Randy	FB	1968
Rogers, Johnny	FB	1998,99
Rokusek, Frank E.	FB	1922,23,24
Romani, Melvin C.	FB	1959,60,61
Rooks, Thomas	FB	1982,83,84,85
Root, Clark W.	FB	1930
Root, George H.	FB	1893
Rose, Jerry	FB	1968
Ross, Steve	FB	1970,72
Rothgeb, Claude J.	FB	1900,02,03,04
Rotzoll Dan	FB	1970,71
Rouse, Eric V.	FB	1976,77,78
Rouse, Patrick	FB	1999,00,01
Roush, D. William	FB	1928, 29
Rowe, Enos M.	FB	1911,12,13
Royer, Joseph W.	FB	1892
Rucker, Derrick	FB	1990,91,92
Rucks, Jim	FB	1970,71,72
Rue, Orlie	FB	1913,14
Ruffin, Jeff	FB	2001
Rump, Charles A.	FB	1905
Rundquist, Elmer T.	FB	1915,16,17
Russ, Jerald B.	FB	1945
Russell, Eddie L.	FB	1963,64,65
Russell, Mike	FB	1992,93
Russell, W. Hunter	FB	1930,32
Rutgens, Joseph C.	FB	1958,59,60
Ryan Jr., Clement J.	FB	1955
Ryan, Corey	FB	1995
Ryan, John (Rocky)	FB	1951,52,53
Ryan, Mike	FB	1968,69
Rykovich, Julius	FB	1946
Ryles, Richard	FB	1982
Rylowicz, Robert A.	FB	1950,51
Saban, Joseph P.	FB	1945
Sabino, Daniel, F.	FB	1950,51,52
Sabo, John P.	FB	1918,20,21
Sajnaj, Chester B.	FB	1943
Samojedny, George	FB	1969,71
Samuels, Brian	FB	1990,91
Sanders, Bobby	FB	1993,94,95
Santini, Veto	FB	1969
Saunders, Don	FB	1964
Sayre, Elvin C.	FB	1934,35,36
Scarcelli, Tony	FB	1980,81,83
Schacht, Frederick W.	FB	1894,95,96

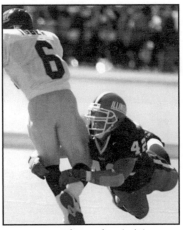

Jerry Schumacher (#42)

Name	Pos	Years
Schaefering, Brian	FB	2001
Schalk, Edward A.	FB	1931
Scharbert, Robert D.	FB	1961,62
Schau, Ryan	FB	1995,96,97,98
Schau, Tom	FB	1995,96,97,98
Schertz, Thomas	FB	1986,87
Schertz, Todd	FB	1986
Scheuplein, Bret	FB	1994,95,96
Schlosser, Merle J.	FB	1947,48,49
Schmidt, Burton J.	FB	1947,48,49
Schmidt, Gerald, C.	FB	1967
Schobinger, Eugene	FB	1912,13,14
Schoeller, Julies E.	FB	1905
Schooley, Thomas	FB	1977
Schnack, Jason	FB	1993
Schneider, Craig	FB	1986,87,88,89
Schrader, Charles	FB	1956
Schulte, Rick	FB	1981,82,83,84
Schultz, Arthur F.	FB	1930
Schultz, Emil G.	FB	1922,23,24
Schultz, Ernest W.	FB	1925,26,27
Schulz, Larry	FB	1974,75,76
Schumacher, Gregg H.	FB	1962,63,64
Schumacher, Henry N.	FB	1930
Schumacher, Jerry	FB	1999,00,01
Schwarzentraub, Jeff	FB	1993
Schustek, Ivan D.	FB	1931,32,33
Sconce, Harvey J.	FB	1894,95
Scott, Bob	FB	1975,76,77
Scott, Brian	FB	1999
Scott, John	FB	1977,78
Scott, Robert E.	FB	1952
Scott, Tom	FB	1968,69,70
Scully, Mike	FB	1983,84,85,87
Seamans, Frank L.	FB	1932
Searcy, Todd M.	FB	1984,85
Sebring, Bob	FB	1984,85
Seiler, Otto E.	FB	1909,10,11
Seliger, Vernon L. (Blinky)	FB	1946,47,48
Senneff, George F.	FB	1912,13
Serpico, Ralph M.	FB	1943,44,45,46
Sewall, Luke	FB	1980,81,82,83
Shaffer, Jim	FB	1989,90
Shapland, Earl P.	FB	1912
Shattuck, Walt F. Sr.	FB	1890
Shavers, Errol	FB	1989
Shaw, Kenny	FB	1979
Shea, Dan	FB	1980
Shelby, Aaron	FB	1990,91,92,93
Sheppard, Lawrence D.	FB	1904
Sherrod, Michael	FB	1978,79,80
Shively, Bernie A.	FB	1924,25,26
Shlaudeman, Harry R.	FB	1916,17,19
Short, William E.	FB	1927
Shuler, Hugh M.	FB	1897

Name	Pos	Years
Siambekos, Chris	FB	1986,89
Sidari, John	FB	1990,91,92,93
Siebens, Arthur R.	FB	1913
Siebold, Harry P.	FB	1937,40
Seigel, Kenneth C.	FB	1944
Siegert, Herbert F.	FB	1946,47,48
Siegert, Rudolph	FB	1954,55
Siegert, Wayne	FB	1949,50
Sigourney, Chris	FB	1979,81,82,83
Siler, Rich	FB	1981
Siler, Roderick W.	FB	1901
Silkman, John M.	FB	1912,13
Silva, Dave	FB	1989
Simpson, Tim	FB	1988,89,90,91
Sinclair, Matt	FB	2001
Singleton, Bobie	FB	2000
Singman, Bruce	FB	1962
Sinnock, Pomeroy	FB	1906,07,08
Skarda, Edward J.	FB	1936,37
Skubisz, Joe	FB	1987,88
Slater, William F.	FB	1890,91,92
Slimmer, Louis F.	FB	1923,24

Tim Simpson

Rex Smith

Sliva, Oscar	FB	1969
Slowinski, Art	FB	1991
Small, Terrance	FB	1998
Smalzer, Joe	FB	1974,75
Smerdel, Matthew T.	FB	1942
Smid, Jan	FB	1952,53,54
Smith, Bobby J.	FB	1976
Smith, Charles J.	FB	1944
Smith, Darrell	FB	1981
Smith, Donald I.	FB	1950
Smith, Dwayne	FB	2000,01
Smith, Eugene R.	FB	1920
Smith, J. Dale	FB	1956,57
Smith, James A.	FB	1939,41,42
Smith, Kevin	FB	1975
Smith, M. Rex	FB	1950,51,52
Smith, Marshall F.	FB	1948
Smith, Mick	FB	1965,66
Smith, Stuyvesant C.	FB	1919
Smith, Thomas D.	FB	1965,66
Smith, Wilbert	FB	1995,96
Smith, Willie	FB	1969

Revie Sorey

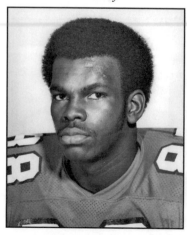

Smock, Walter F.	FB	1900
Snavely, Edwin R.	FB	1931
Snook, John K.	FB	1932,33
Soebbing, Mark H.	FB	1976
Somlar, Scott	FB	1980
Sorey, Revie	FB	1972,73,74
Sowa, Nick	FB	1979
Spencer, Brad	FB	1995
Spiller, John	FB	1969
Sprague, Stanley R.	FB	1945
Springe, Otto	FB	1909,10,11
Spurgeon, A. Lowell	FB	1935,36,37
Squier, George K.	FB	1914,15
Squirek, Jack S.	FB	1978,79,80,81
Stahl, Garland (Jake)	FB	1899,00,01,02
Stallings, Dennis	FB	1994,95,96
Standring, Bob	FB	1973
Stanley, Tim	FB	1982,85
Stapleton, John M.	FB	1959
Starghill, Trevor	FB	1994,95,96,97
Starks, Marshall L.	FB	1958,59,60
Stasica, Stanley J.	FB	1945
Stauner, Jim	FB	1974,75,76
Steele, James	FB	1890,91
Stefanski, Steve	FB	1993
Steger, Kurt	FB	1975,76,77
Steger, Russell W.	FB	1946,47,48,49
Steinhaus, Steve	FB	1994
Steinman, Henry J.	FB	1929
Stellwagen, Joel	FB	1966
Stelter, Chris	FB	1994
Stephenson, Lewis A.	FB	1901
Stern, Matt	FB	1991
Sternaman, Edward C.	FB	1916,17,19
Sternaman, Joseph T.	FB	1921
Stevens, Don	FB	1949,50,51
Stevens, Lawrence J.	FB	1951,52
Stevenson, Jeff	FB	1985
Stewart, Baird E.	FB	1952,53,54
Stewart, Charles A.	FB	1905,06
Stewart, David L.	FB	1957,58
Stewart, Frank	FB	1914,15,16
Stewart, James R. "Bud"	FB	1926,27
Stewart, Lynn	FB	1962,63,64
Stewart, Thomas C.	FB	1946,47,48,49
Stine, Mike	FB	1983
Stone, Clyde E.	FB	1902
Stone, Richard R.	FB	1965
Stotz, Charles H.	FB	1938
Stotz, James T.	FB	1966
Stotz, Richard A.	FB	1966
Stout, Hiles G.	FB	1954,55,56
Stowe, Bob	FB	1980,81,82,83
Strader, Wayne	FB	1977,78,79,80
Strauch, Donald J.	FB	1916

Straw, Thomas C.	FB	1931,32,33
Streeter, Sean	FB	1988,89,90,91
Strong, Manuel	FB	1996,97
Strong, David A.	FB	1936
Strong, Derrick	FB	2000,01
Strong, Jasper	FB	1992,93,94
Studley, Charles B.	FB	1949,50,51
Studwell, Scott	FB	1973,75,76
Stuessy, Dwight T.	FB	1926,27,28
Sturrock, Tom	FB	1968
Suarez, Mike	FB	1993,94
Sullivan, Bruce E.	FB	1965,66
Sullivan, Gerry	FB	1971,72,73
Sullivan, John	FB	1974,75,77,78
Sullivan, Marques	FB	1997,98,99,00
Sullivan, Mike	FB	1974,75
Summers, W. Michael	FB	1961,62,63
Suppan, Mike	FB	1974
Surdyk, Florian J.	FB	1937
Sutter, Kenneth F.	FB	1956
Sutton, Archie M.	FB	1962,63,64
Swanson, Mark B.	FB	1930
Sweney, Don	FB	1893,94,95,97
Swienton, Kenneth R.	FB	1952,53,54
Swoope, Craig	FB	1982,83,84,85
Tabloff, Ryan	FB	1997
Tabor, Hubert B.	FB	1921
Tackett, William C.	FB	1892,93
Tagart, Mark	FB	1984,85
Taliaferro, Mike	FB	1962,63
Tarnoski, Paul T.	FB	1905
Tarwain, John	FB	1928
Tate, Albert R.	FB	1948,49,50
Tate, Donald E.	FB	1951,52,53,54
Tate, Richard A.	FB	1965,66,67
Tate, William L.	FB	1950,51,52
Taylor, Brent	FB	1995,96,97
Taylor, Carooq	FB	1977,80
Taylor, Joseph W.	FB	1904
Taylor, Keith	FB	1983,85,86,87
Taylor, Randall R.	FB	1976,77,78
Teafatiller, Guy	FB	1984,85
Tee, Darrin	FB	1986,87
Tee, David	FB	1982
Tesdall, Seth	FB	1997,98,99
Theodore, James J.	FB	1934
Theodore, John A.	FB	1935
Thiede, John	FB	1977,78
Thomas, Calvin	FB	1978,79,80,81
Thomas, Karleton	FB	1997,98,99
Thomas, Ken	FB	1987,89
Thomas, Stephen K.	FB	1961
Thomases, Robert	FB	1938
Thompson, Darryl	FB	1982,83
Thompson, Herbert P.	FB	1911

Marques Sullivan

Thorby, Charles H. J.	FB	1895
Thornton, Bruce	FB	1975,76,77,78
Thorp, Don	FB	1980,81,82,83
Tilton, Harry W.	FB	1894
Timko, Craig S.	FB	1965,66,67
Timm, Judson A.	FB	1927,28,29
Tischler, Matthew	FB	1935
Tohn, Clarence G.	FB	1943
Tomanek, Emil	FB	1944
Tomasula, David G.	FB	1965,66,67
Tregoning, Wesley W.	FB	1941,45
Trigger, Jeff C.	FB	1966,67,68
Trudeau, Jack	FB	1983,84,85
Trumpy, Bob	FB	1964
Tubbs, J.J.	FB	2001
Tucker, Derwin	FB	1975,76,77,78
Tumilty, Richard J.	FB	1941
Tupper, James O.	FB	1913
Turek, Joseph J.	FB	1939,40
Turnbull, David	FB	1937
Turner, Elbert	FB	1988,90,91
Turner, Greg	FB	1986,87,88

Scott Turner

Jason Verduzco

Turner, E. Scott	FB	1991,92,93,94
Turner, Shawn	FB	1985,86,88
Twist, John F.	FB	1908,09,10
Uecker, Bill	FB	1972,73,74
Ulrich Jr., Charles	FB	1949,50,51
Umnus, Leonard	FB	1922,23,24
Uremovich, George	FB	1971,72,73
Usher, Darryl	FB	1983,84,85,87
Utz, George J.	FB	1956,57
Valek, James J.	FB	1945,46,47,48
Valentino, R. Rudolph	FB	1949,51
Van Dyke, Jos. A.	FB	1932
Van Hook, Forest C.	FB	1906,07,08
Van Meter, Vincent J.	FB	1932
VanOrman, Ellsworth G.	FB	1935
Vanosky, Brian	FB	1995
Varrige, Tom	FB	1980,81,82
Venegoni, John	FB	1978,80,81
Verduzco, Jason	FB	1989,90,91,92
Vernasco, Joseph P.	FB	1950,51
Vernasco, Walter L.	FB	1952,53,54
Veronesi, Don	FB	1993

Shawn Wax

Versen, Walter G.	FB	1944
Vierneisel, Phil	FB	1973,74,75,76
Voelker, Gary	FB	1992,93
Vogel, Otto H.	FB	1921
Vogel, Rob	FB	1993
Vohaska, William J.	FB	1948,49,50
Volkman, Dean E.	FB	1965,66,67
Von Oven, Fred W.	FB	1896,97
Vukelich, John J.	FB	1949
Vyborny, Julian	FB	1969,70
Wachter, John	FB	1986,88,90
Wadsworth, Albert M.	FB	1899
Wagner, Alexander	FB	1912,13,14
Wagner, Richard B.	FB	1922
Wainwright, Jack	FB	1964
Wakefield, Fred	FB	1997,98,99,00
Waldbeser, Clifford H.	FB	1951,52,53
Waldron, Ralph H.	FB	1966,68
Walker, David R.	FB	1955,56
Walker, Frank H.	FB	1927,28,29
Walker, Mike	FB	1970,72
Walker, Thurman	FB	1960,61,62
Wall, Joe	FB	1991
Wallace, Douglas A.	FB	1957,58,59
Wallace, Stanley H.	FB	1951,52,53
Waller, Mike	FB	1972,74,75
Waller, Trayvon	FB	1999,00
Waller, William H.	FB	1934
Wallin, Robert W.	FB	1940,42
Wallner, Neil	FB	1986,87
Walquist, Lawrence W.	FB	1918,19,20,21
Walser, Herman J.	FB	1931,32,33
Walsh, George	FB	1954,55
Walsh, L. Ed	FB	1965
Walters, Jay	FB	1967
Ward, Brian	FB	1982,83,85
Ward, Dustin	FB	2000,01
Ward, Raymond C.	FB	1943,44
Wardell, Roosevelt	FB	1988
Wardley Jr., George P.	FB	1936,37,38
Warren, James B.	FB	1962,63
Washington, Edward W.	FB	1962,63,64
Washington, Keith	FB	1997
Washington, Quincy	FB	1999
Washington, Terrell	FB	1999,00,01
Washington, Tyrone	FB	1992,93,94,95
Waters, Alan J.	FB	1964,65,66
Watson, Carl P.	FB	1908
Watson, Chauncey B.	FB	1911,12
Watson, John W.	FB	1913,14,15
Wax, Shawn	FB	1988,89,90
Weaver, Scott	FB	1993,94,95,96
Weber, Charles	FB	1977,78
Weddell Jr., Robert W.	FB	1951,52
Wehrli, Robert J.	FB	1937,38

Weingrad, Mike	FB	1982,83
Weiss, Richard M.	FB	1978
Weisse, Jeff	FB	195,96,97,98
Wells, Forry	FB	1990,91,92,93
Wells, John	FB	1982
Wells, Mike	FB	1970,71,72
Welsh, Jim	FB	1970,71
Wendryhoski, Joseph S.	FB	1959,60
Wendt, Pat	FB	1991,92
Wenskunas, Mac P.	FB	1942,45,46
West, Kevin	FB	1982
Westerlind, Dan R.	FB	1978
Wham, Charles	FB	1910
Wham, Fred L.	FB	1905,07,08
Wheatland, John A.	FB	1961,63
White, Chris	FB	1983,84,85
White, Earl A.	FB	1906,07
White, Edward L.	FB	1984,85,86
White, Ron	FB	1975,76
Whiteside, Jim	FB	1967,68
Whitman, Doug	FB	1967,68
Whitman, Josh	FB	1997,98,99,00
Wickhorst, George N.	FB	1925
Widner, Albert E.	FB	1943
Wietz, L. J.	FB	1927,28,29
Wile, Dan	FB	1955
Wiley, Francis R.	FB	1903
Williams, Anthony	FB	1984,85,86,87
Williams, Brian	FB	1988,89
Williams, Christopher	FB	1976
Williams, David	FB	1983,84,85
Williams, Greg	FB	1973,74
Williams, James	FB	1995,96,97
Williams, Melvin R.	FB	1984,85
Williams, Oliver	FB	1981,82
Williams, Rick	FB	1973,75
Williams, Scott	FB	1890,91
Williams, Steven	FB	1985,86,88,89
Willis, Lenny	FB	1995,97,98,99
Willis, Norman L.	FB	1960,62
Willis, Steve	FB	1995,96,97
Willis, William W.	FB	1949
Willmann, Dean E.	FB	1954
Wilmarth, George H.	FB	1897,98
Wilmoth, Fred	FB	1954
Wilson, Brett	FB	1983
Wilson, Darryl	FB	1979,80,81
Wilson, David C.	FB	1980
Wilson, David D.	FB	1921,22
Wilson, Eugene	FB	1999,00,01
Wilson, John	FB	1971
Wilson, Joseph W.	FB	1902
Wilson, Kenneth L. (Tug)	FB	1925
Wilson, Kirby	FB	1981,82
Wilson, Norman K.	FB	1912,13
Wilson, Ray	FB	1983,84,85,86

Eugene Wilson

Wilson, Robert A.	FB	1941,42
Wilson, Thomas P.	FB	1930,35,36
Wilson, Wendell S.	FB	1925,26
Wiman, Robert L.	FB	1953,54
Windy, Gary	FB	1970
Wineland, Harold S.	FB	1962
Wintermute, Bob	FB	1969,70
Winsper, Edwin S.	FB	1930
Wislow, Len	FB	1967,68
Witek, Roger	FB	1987
Wiza, John	FB	1970,71,72
Wodziak, Frank S.	FB	1950,51,52
Wolf, Fred	FB	1967,68
Wolf, Roger E.	FB	1952,53,54
Wolgast, Arnold E.	FB	1927,29
Wood, Gerald A.	FB	1959,60
Woods, Toriano	FB	1993,94,95,96
Woodson, Abraham B.	FB	1954,55,56
Woodward, Harold C.	FB	1921,22
Woody, Frederick W.	FB	1892,93,94
Woolston, William. H.	FB	1910,11,12
Worban, John C.	FB	1940
Worthy, Tyrone	FB	1979,80
Wrenn, John M.	FB	1946,47
Wright, Dave	FB	1970,71,72
Wright Jr., John	FB	1990,91
Wright Sr., John	FB	1965,66,67

*(left to right) John Wright Jr.,
Bob Wright, John Wright Sr.*

Walter Young

Wright, Richard	FB	1969,71
Wright, Robert C.	FB	1935
Wright, Royal	FB	1890,91,93
Wright, Sidney B.	FB	1908
Wyatt, R. D.	FB	1906
Wycoff, Eric	FB	1984,85
Yadron, Paul	FB	1973,74
Yanuskus, P. J.	FB	1929,30,32
Yavorski, Mike	FB	1962
Yeazel, Donald R.	FB	1957,58,59
Yochem, Ron	FB	1955
Young, Al	FB	1975
Young, Claude H. (Buddy) FB		1944,46
Young, Herbert T.	FB	1938
Young, Michael	FB	1997,98,99,00
Young, Roy M.	FB	1904,05
Young, W. Cecil	FB	1961,62
Young, Walter	FB	1999,00,01
Young, Willie	FB	1981
Yukevich Jr., Stanley F.	FB	1959,60,61
Zaborac, Thomas F.	FB	1945,46
Zatkoff, Samuel	FB	1944,46,47

Lia Biehl

Zeppetella, Anthony J.	FB	1961
Zimmerman, Albert G.	FB	1945
Zimmerman, Ken W.,Jr.	FB	1961,62
Zimmerman Kenneth W.	FB	1936,37,38
Zimmerman, Walter H.	FB	1895,96
Zirbel, Craig	FB	1980,81,82
Zitnik, Mark	FB	1988,89,90,91
Zochert, Dave	FB	1969,70,71
Zuppke, Robert E.	FB	1937

Women's Golf

Arnholt, Cheryl	WGO	1984,85,86,87
Beach, Becky	WGO	1976,77,78
Berto, Terrie	WGO	1981,82,83,84
Biehl, Becky	WGO	1992,93,94,95
Biehl, Lia	WGO	1988,89,90,91
Borbeck, Connie	WGO	1985,86,87
Campbell, Allison	WGO	1975
Campbell, Michelle	WGO	1984,85,87
Carroll, Michelle	WGO	2001,02
Cheney, Stephanie	WGO	2000,01,02
Cowell, Andrea	WGO	1996,97
Cox, Marla	WGO	2001,02
Eaton, Carol	WGO	1979
Eaton, Jane	WGO	1979
Eckols, Molly	WGO	1998
Evans, Wendy	WGO	1992,93,94
Garrett, Christine	WGO	1992,93,94,95
Grumish, Julie	WGO	1989,90,91
Gwillim, Linda	WGO	1976
Hannam, Gail	WGO	1975, 1976
Hayes, Jessica	WGO	1998
Heiken, Renee	WGO	1990,91,92,93
Ittersagen, Jill	WGO	1981,82,83,84
Johnson, Julie	WGO	1980
Johnston, Allison	WGO	1985,86,87,88
Kanda, Laurin	WGO	2000,01,02
Karmazin, Karen	WGO	1995,96,98
Kelleher, Elizabeth	WGO	1988,89,90
Kim, Sarah	WGO	1999
Kimpel, Janice	WGO	1975,76,77
Klein, Kristen	WGO	1988,90,91
Lang, Susan	WGO	1981,82,83,84
Larson, Laurie	WGO	1976,77,78,79
Leech, Rhonda	WGO	1975,76
Leishman, Jane	WGO	1983
Lin, Michelle	WGO	1996,97,98
Lynch, Jennifer	WGO	1992,93,94,95
Lyttle, Lorette	WGO	1997,98,99,00
Macconnachie, Brenda	WGO	1985,86,87,88
Macke, Nell	WGO	1997,98,99,00
Maxwell, Nancy	WGO	1977,78,79,80
McCloskey, Pam	WGO	1984,85,86
McKinzie, Laura	WGO	1976,77
Miller, Diane	WGO	1975,76,77,78
Miller, Justi Rae	WGO	1986,87,88,89
Murphy, Jane	WGO	1980,81,82,83
Murphy, Mary Ellen	WGO	1980,81,82,83

Mulcahy, Kourtney	WGO	1994,96
Pirk, Stacey	WGO	1991,92
Pope, Sally	WGO	1979,80
Redington, Nancy	WGO	1980
Reynolds, Shelly	WGO	1985
Rogala, Alexis	WGO	1991
Rubin, Jacqueline	WGO	1994,95,96,97
Scott, Christine	WGO	1999,00
Seyman, Sandy	WGO	1977,78,79
Sielicki, Carmel	WGO	2001,02
Sitter, Jillian	WGO	1996,97,98,99
Sutton, Christin	WGO	1997,99
Sutton, Sandy	WGO	1982,83,84
Tate, Barb	WGO	1981
Tex, Cathy	WGO	1977
Treseler, Kristie	WGO	1994
Walters, Mari	WGO	2000,02
Webb, Ashley	WGO	1995,96,97,98
Webb, Leslie	WGO	1997
Winkelman, Susan	WGO	1987,88,89,90
Wood, Shellie	WGO	1989,90
Young, Renata	WGO	2000,01,02
Zimmerman, Valerie	WGO	1993

Men's Golf

Alexander, Charles	MGO	1970,71,72
Allen, Mike	MGO	1990,91,92
Almquist, Robert	MGO	1959,60
Alpert, S. G.	MGO	1930,31,32
Anderson, E. J.	MGO	1927
Anderson, W. J.	MGO	1926
Arendt, James W.	MGO	1968
Atkinson, Brian	MGO	1994,95,96,98
Baker, Robert	MGO	1933,34
Bakke, Niles	MGO	1970,71,72,73
Barr, John	MGO	1934
Bartelstein, Alan	MGO	1977,78
Beard, Trevor	MGO	1990,91,92
Beck, Bruce	MGO	1970,71,72
Becker, William	MGO	1962
Beckman, Gary A.	MGO	1969
Billings, Albert F.	MGO	1938,39
Bishop, Danny H.	MGO	1967,68,69
Bootz, Harold	MGO	1946
Bridenthal, C. F.	MGO	1908
Briggs, Randy	MGO	1991,93
Brill, Tyson	MGO	2000
Bristol, R. S.	MGO	1921
Brown, James F.	MGO	1942
Brown, Lloyd	MGO	1946,47
Bruce, Ben	MGO	1989,90,91,92
Buenzli, James J.	MGO	1980,81,82,83
Burden, Joe	MGO	1970,71,72,73
Buzick, John W.	MGO	1941
Cable, Dave	MGO	1991,93,94,95
Campbell, Robert S.	MGO	1938
Carlson, Ralph O.	MGO	1937,38,39

Justi Rae Miller

Carlson, Roger W.	MGO	1982
Carter, W. E.	MGO	1928
Cashman, Dennis	MGO	1965,66,67
Cassady, Donald	MGO	1951,52,53
Castelo, Chip	MGO	1972,74
Chadwick, Michael	MGO	1979,80,81,82
Chaussard, Garrett	MGO	2002
Clark, Tom	MGO	1961
Cockrell, Paul F.	MGO	1927
Coghill, John R.	MGO	1938
Connell, Byron	MGO	1955,56
Correll, Charles R.	MGO	1956,57,58
Crawford, Heath	MGO	1987,88,89,90
Crowe, R. H.	MGO	1930,31,32
Culp, George	MGO	1949
Culp Jr., John D.	MGO	1947
Cwik, Ronald	MGO	1957,58,59
Cyboran, John V.	MGO	1982,83
Cyboran, Steve	MGO	1990
Davies, Richard	MGO	1955
Dawson, George	MGO	1924

Joe Burden

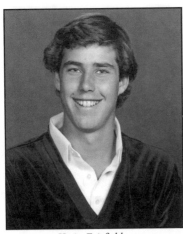
Kevin Fairfield

Dayiantis, George	MGO	1948,50
Dechert, Douglas R.	MGO	1981,82
Dilsaver, Carl	MGO	1953,54
Dixon	MGO	1908
Dobrovolny, Chris	MGO	2000,01
Dray, Don	MGO	1973,74,75,76
Edwards, Don	MGO	1985,86,87,88
Edwards, Richard	MGO	1978,80
Ellerbeck, Ron	MGO	1960
Emery, Eugene	MGO	1944,45
England, Joseph	MGO	1960,61,62
Evans, Terry L.	MGO	1966,67
Fairbanks, Jamie	MGO	1991,92,93,94
Fairfield, Kevin	MGO	1987,88,89,90
Fassnacht, Bill	MGO	1951
Fiser, Chuck	MGO	1985,86,87
Fish Jr., C. M.	MGO	1927,28
Fleming, John D.	MGO	1965,66,67
Fletcher, Pete	MGO	1950
Fletcher, Rodney	MGO	1950
Flood, Gerold	MGO	1950,51
Foley, Henry J.	MGO	1955

Kenneth Kellaney

Fornof, J.R.	MGO	1908
Foster, Douglas	MGO	1962,63,64
Frederickson, J. L.	MGO	1921,22
Funkhouser, Mark R.	MGO	1982
Garvin, Steve	MGO	1971
Georlett, Clem	MGO	1958,59
Gibala, Nick	MGO	1970,71,72
Gindler, Matt	MGO	1994,95
Goldstein, Jacob	MGO	1995,97
Goldwater, R.W.	MGO	1929
Goulding, Bob	MGO	1963,64,65
Graff, Ryan	MGO	1992,93,94,96
Green, Jim	MGO	1974
Haime, Kevin	MGO	1984,85,86
Hall, John	MGO	1961,62,63
Harder, Harold	MGO	1972,73,74,75
Hatch, Lemoine S.	MGO	1923
Haubold, Bill	MGO	1986
Hawkins, Burford H.	MGO	1952,53,54
Hayes, John C.	MGO	1941
Healy, Patrick	MGO	1979
Hedges, Elsum G.	MGO	1936
Henderson, Mark	MGO	1996,97,98,99
Hill, Elton	MGO	1934,35,36
Hirsch, Joel	MGO	1963
Hobart, John A.	MGO	1936,37,38
Hoffman, Lyle	MGO	1933,34
Holmes Jr., John A.	MGO	1966,67
Holmstrom, John T.	MGO	1940,41,42
Hougham, Kym	MGO	1973,74,75,76
Humphreys, John	MGO	1923,24,25
Hunt, L. D.	MGO	1924,25
Hurst, Joe	MGO	1964,65
Hutchinson, Edgar B.	MGO	1937,38,39
Iantorno, Tony	MGO	1974
Jaronik, Frank J.	MGO	1941,42
Jaronik, Stanley	MGO	1945
Jemsek, Gregory	MGO	1947,48
Keen, J. Patrick	MGO	1969,70
Kehlor, J. M.	MGO	1912
Kellaney, Kenneth	MGO	1975,76,77,78
Kennedy, Brian S.	MGO	1982
Kimpel, Raymond	MGO	1948,49,50
King, Andrew	MGO	1976,77,78
Kirchner, Peter A.	MGO	1968
Kisselburg, B. M.	MGO	1915
Kohr, Charles	MGO	1963,64,65
Kokes, Wilbert J.	MGO	1935,36,37
Kuntstadler, R. H.	MGO	1925,26,27
Kurz, W. C.	MGO	1928
LeBosquet, Maurice	MGO	1921,22
Leighty, Brad	MGO	1986,87
Lepp, James	MGO	2002
Lewis, Randy R.	MGO	1981,82,83,84
Logan, David	MGO	1948,49,50

Lound, Geoff	MGO	2000,01,02
Lukasik Jr., Fred	MGO	1968
Lyon, F. S.	MGO	1929,30,31
MacDonald, J. M.	MGO	1917
Mahon, John	MGO	1985
Malstrom, Gordon	MGO	1960
Mann, Philip	MGO	1977,78
Marquardt, Robert	MGO	1952
Martin, R. S.	MGO	1929,30,31
Mason, W. T.	MGO	1926
Mazzetta, Ozzie	MGO	1954
McCarthy, James P.	MGO	1942,43
McCloskey, Bob	MGO	2000
McKinzie, James	MGO	1951,52
Meier, Joseph	MGO	1979,80
Metcalf, Robert L.	MGO	1939
Mickelson, A. M.	MGO	1935
Miller, Stephen	MGO	1979,80
Modjeska, Eugene F.	MGO	1940,43
Moore, Ryan	MGO	2001
Mudrock, Mark	MGO	1979,80
Mueller, Roger	MGO	1955,56
Mulliken, John W.	MGO	1966,67,68
Murphy Jr., Frank	MGO	1947
Needler, L. Q.	MGO	1921
Newell, Lee	MGO	1964,65
Niva, George	MGO	1957,58
Novotny, A. L.	MGO	1921,22,23
Nuger, Larry	MGO	1998,99,00
O'Neal, Mike	MGO	2002
O'Neal, Robert D.	MGO	1934,35
Olsen, C. F.	MGO	1914,15
Olson, Evan	MGO	2000,01,02
Orsi, Tom	MGO	1957,58,59
Parga, Ed	MGO	1996,97,98,99
Pagoraro, Robert A.	MGO	1969,70,71
Parkhill, Thomas S.	MGO	1965,66,67
Patton, Herbert R.	MGO	1938,39,40
Pell, Robert	MGO	1957
Peressini, William	MGO	1975,76,77,78
Peressini, Tony	MGO	2001
Persin, Scott	MGO	1996,97
Petersen, Gregory A.	MGO	1981,82,84
Peterson, Eugene	MGO	1950
Peterson, James H.	MGO	1955
Pittenger, Greg	MGO	1997,2000
Points, D.A.	MGO	1998,99
Pray, Lee	MGO	1933
Prince, Tom	MGO	1988,89,90
Prouty, E. C.	MGO	1912,14
Quackenbush, Justin	MGO	1949
Ramey, F. W.	MGO	1917
Ramsey, R. W.	MGO	1915
Rascher, Vernon	MGO	1951,52
Rasmussen, Rich	MGO	1974,75

Ed Parga

Reed, Ross C.	MGO	1940,41,42
Reif, John P.	MGO	1947,48
Reitsch, Robert	MGO	1954,55,56
Renwick, F. W.	MGO	1932
Reston Jr., James B. (Scotty)	MGO	1931,32
Richart Jr., Frank E.	MGO	1939,40,46
Riley, Tim	MGO	1998,99,00,01
Ring, Wayne	MGO	1945,46,47
Ripley, C. T.	MGO	1908
Rolfe, Rial E.	MGO	1922,23,24
Rowader, Thomas	MGO	1952,53,54
Rugg, Robert F.	MGO	1976,77,78,79
Russo, Tony	MGO	1989
Schiene, Martin	MGO	1977,78,79,80
Schroder, Robert	MGO	1944,45
Scott, Jay	MGO	1992,93,94,95
Simon, Donald	MGO	1963,64
Simpson, J. M.	MGO	1915,16,17
Slattery, Edward T.	MGO	1983,84
Slothower, James B.	MGO	1956,57
Small, Mike	MGO	1985,86,87,88
Smith, Dale J.	MGO	1956,57

Jay Scott

Mike Small

Smith, Gerald	MGO	1961,62,1963
Smith, Harold R.	MGO	1949,50
Sparks, Frank	MGO	1960
Stasica, Stanley	MGO	1946
Stricker, Steve	MGO	1986,87,88,89
Suitor, Rick	MGO	1970,71,72,73
Sutin, L. R.	MGO	1928,29
Tanous, Jerry	MGO	1961
Tapscott, Robert A.	MGO	1943,48
Tendall, Ryan	MGO	2001,02
Tewksbury, W. J.	MGO	1925,26,27
Thompson, John	MGO	1974
Tolluszis, Mike	MGO	1960,61,62
Triebel Jr., Albert	MGO	1936
Turnbow, Charles R.	MGO	1943
Turner, T. R.	MGO	1985
Usinger, William A.	MGO	1940,41
Voyda, John F.	MGO	1956,57,58
Walch, Leo	MGO	1952
Walduck, C. L.	MGO	1912
Walker, John	MGO	1969
Wallace, Robert R.	MGO	1967,68,69

Lynn Devers

Walton, H. R.	MGO	1915
Weems, C. L.	MGO	1915
Weise, Robert W.	MGO	1942
Welsh, Alex	MGO	1940,41
West, Byron Kenneth	MGO	1952,53,54,55
Wheatland, Alan	MGO	1962
Whitacre, Andrew	MGO	1984,85
White, F. H.	MGO	1914,15
White, H. H.	MGO	1917
Whitelaw, J. C.	MGO	1914,15
Whyte, G. K.	MGO	1928
Wiley, D. F.	MGO	1928,29
Williams, R. C.	MGO	1912
Winters, C. P.	MGO	1915
Wolfley, Richard F.	MGO	1941
Woodcock, Scott	MGO	1994
Wyatt, Arthur R.	MGO	1946,47,48,49
Young	MGO	1908
Zahn, Dene W.	MGO	1936
Zambole, Nicholas	MGO	1979,80,81,82

Women's Gymnastics

Adams, Susan	WGY	1988,89,90,91
Althans, Tracey	WGY	1993,94,95,96
Amico, Mary	WGY	1981
Ashton, Becky	WGY	1996,97,98
Baffes, Kathy	WGY	1978,79,80
Bagel, Jean	WGY	1976
Barrow, Christine	WGY	1984
Bathke Kimberly	WGY	1991,92,93,94
Bedrosian, Tammy	WGY	1977
Berg, Allison	WGY	2000,01,02
Berres, Kim	WGY	1996,97,98,99
Brems, Karen	WGY	1981,82,83,84
Buranich, Michelle	WGY	2000,01,02
Carmichael, Patty	WGY	1977
Carr, Bridget	WGY	1980,81,82
Castle, Jennifer	WGY	1978
Charpentier, Mary	WGY	1978,79,80,81
Ciccarelli, Nicole	WGY	1994,95,96,97
Ciccarelli, Tracey	WGY	1996,97
Clisham, Mary Beth	WGY	1991,92,93,94
Collias, Emily	WGY	1984,85,86
Corso, Kara	WGY	1990,91,92,93
Danke, Cheryl	WGY	1985
Dann, Margaret	WGY	2002
Delact, Joan	WGY	1977
Devers, Lynn	WGY	1988,89,90,91
Dixon, Phaedra	WGY	1998,99,00
Dorwart, Melanie	WGY	1996,97,98,99
Drummond, Becky	WGY	1994
Durdil, Jennifer	WGY	1989,90,92
Eberle, Mimi	WGY	1980
Ericson, Carissa	WGY	1998,99,00
Farrar, Kelli	WGY	1995,96,97,98

Fernandez, Carmella	WGY	1997,98,99,00
Fleischmann, Gayle	WGY	1977,78,79,80
Forsthoefel, Natalie	WGY	1993,94,95,96
Gaa, Becky	WGY	1990,91,92,93
Gallagher, Jana	WGY	2000,01,02
Gardner, Laura	WGY	1978
Garrity, Allison	WGY	1984,85,86,87
Greathouse, Teresa	WGY	1975,76
Gruss, Gena	WGY	1997,98,99,00
Hamilton, Gail	WGY	1989
Hawley, Karen	WGY	2000,01,02
Helmke, Heidi	WGY	1981,82,83,84
Hicks, Laura	WGY	1985,86
Hogan, Kelly	WGY	1994,95,96,97
Howell, Lisa	WGY	1979
Johnson, Gaye	WGY	1978,79,80
Kalal, Randy	WGY	1975
Kapernekas, Kara	WGY	2002
Karubas, Kari	WGY	1994,95,96,97
Kaufman, Amanda	WGY	2000,02
Knutson, Laura	WGY	1987,88,89,90
Kontur, Tracy	WGY	1987,88,89,90
Lacki, Michelle	WGY	1998
Lamborn, Denise	WGY	1987,88
LaPlante, Liz	WGY	1978
Lundquist, Debra	WGY	1977
Maart, Michelle	WGY	1985,86,87,88
MacAdams, Maggie	WGY	1976,77,78
Matiya, Joellyn	WGY	1980,81,82
McGee, Cindy	WGY	1983
Mesik, Michelle	WGY	2000,01,02
Montero, Kristin	WGY	1995,97,98
Montgomery, Lisa	WGY	1982
Moore, Cindy	WGY	1982,83
Moradi, Mina	WGY	2000,01,02
Murin, Laura	WGY	1981
Neilson, Dotty	WGY	1983
Newcomb, Lauren	WGY	2002
Numrych, Charlene	WGY	1981,82,83,84
Osowski, Jan	WGY	1979,80,81
Pedregal, Marianne	WGY	1984,85,86,87
Pellegrinetti, Lisa	WGY	1998,99,00
Peterson, Anne	WGY	1978,79,80
Peterson, Karla	WGY	1992,93,95
Pollack, Allyson	WGY	1981,82
Polz, Laura	WGY	1990,91,92
Pontious, Joyce	WGY	1978,79,80,81
Powers, Terri	WGY	1978,79,80
Pullman, Peggy	WGY	1990,92
Rechenmacher, Jayne	WGY	1978,79,80,81
Rechenmacher, Jill	WGY	1986
Redmond, Stacy	WGY	1995,96
Reid, Connie	WGY	1983
Roberts, Luann	WGY	1983,84,85,86
Robinson, Deborah	WGY	1975

Laura Knutson

Rosenwinkel, Pam	WGY	1975
Roska, Sarah	WGY	1976
Rossetto, Karen	WGY	1989,90,91
Rudnicki, Patsy	WGY	1982,83,84,85
Ruf, Michelle	WGY	1985,86,87,88
Ruffolo, Laura	WGY	2002
Salinas, Maria	WGY	1975,76
Segers, Alicia	WGY	1976
Semeniuk, Tanya	WGY	1993
Sheppard, Sarah	WGY	1978,79,80
Shively, Debbie	WGY	1987,88
Simpson, Faith	WGY	1991
Singalewitch, Heather	WGY	1987,88,89,90
Slomski, Dina	WGY	1992,94,95
Smith, Karen	WGY	1975
Smith, Shari	WGY	1988,89
Sullivan, Kelcey	WGY	1991
Tex, Cathy	WGY	1975
Thies, Nancy	WGY	1976,77
Travis, Lee	WGY	1975,76,77
Viernes, Nicole	WGY	1994,95,96,97
Ward, Nicole	WGY	1992,93,94,95

Nicole Viernes

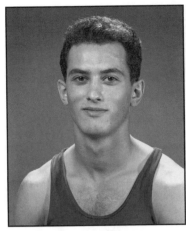

Gilberto Alburquerque

Wasserman, Sarah	WGY	1991,92
Weber, Cynthia	WGY	1975,76,77,78
Webster, Julie	WGY	1980
Wiechmann, Gina	WGY	1998,99,00
Williams, Ashley	WGY	2002
Wurtzel, Melissa	WGY	1997
Yonezuka, Natacha	WGY	1984,85

Men's Gymnastics

Adamson, Steve	MGY	1981,83,84,85
Adkins, John D.	MGY	1941,42
Adler, Leon	MGY	1917
Adler, M. A.	MGY	1922,23
Albuquerque, Gilberto	MGY	1981, 82,84,85
Almy, W. H.	MGY	1905
Antoniolli, Carl	MGY	1978
Aufrecht, Michael	MGY	1960,61,62
Austin, Jeffrey	MGY	1952,53,54,55
Ayalon, Yuval	MGY	1995,96,97,98
Baker, Nicholas	MGY	1990,91,92,93
Baley, James A.	MGY	1941
Ballou, Donald	MGY	1963,64
Barasch, Alvin	MGY	1960

Ricardo Cheriel

Bare, Frank	MGY	1952,53,54
Barmes, William	MGY	1950
Barr, Ken	MGY	1970,71,72
Barrett, Brad	MGY	1972
Bauer, Ronald	MGY	1966
Beck, Howard W.	MGY	1972,73,74,75
Bedard, Irvin	MGY	1950,51
Bennett, F.H.	MGY	1922
Bird, Patrick	MGY	1958,59,60
Black, William	MGY	1905
Blair, Gavin	MGY	1956,63
Blazek, Frank	MGY	1956
Blazek, James	MGY	1957,58,59
Bohaty, Zdenek A.	MGY	1942
Bralower, Leonard	MGY	1948
Bredfeldt, Charles	MGY	1920
Brinkmeyer, Gilbert	MGY	1952,53
Brockman, Robert A.	MGY	1975
Broome, Robert	MGY	1967,68
Brown, Harold J.	MGY	1941
Brown, Randall	MGY	1966,67
Browning, Richard	MGY	1953,54
Bucher, E. G.	MGY	1913,14
Buck, P. E.	MGY	1913,14
Buck, Steve	MGY	1977
Burgeson, Lennart B.	MGY	1937
Butler, Paul L.	MGY	1939
Butts, Larry	MGY	1968,69,70
Cadle, R.	MGY	1932,33
Calhoun, Dean	MGY	1966,67
Calvetti, Joseph A.	MGY	1942,48,49
Cannon, James	MGY	1951
Cason, Robert	MGY	1961
Chance, W.W.	MGY	1931
Chapple, Steve	MGY	1967,68,69
Cheriel, Ricardo	MGY	1990,91,92,93
Cherry, W.L.	MGY	1930,31
Chhay, Vuthik	MGY	1991,92,93
Christian, W.A.	MGY	1929,31
Claycomb, Gordon	MGY	1959
Cleary, James	MGY	1951
Clow, Robert J.	MGY	1940
Coats, Wayne	MGY	1968,69
Cobb, C. Caton	MGY	1941,42
Cook, Greg	MGY	1998,99,00
Corbitt, Jon	MGY	1998,99,00
Crawford, Sean-Paul	MGY	1999,00,01,02
Cress Jr., John M.	MGY	1939,40
Cryer, Walter	MGY	1950,52
Culbertson, Jon	MGY	1954,55,56
Dallenbach, John W.	MGY	1939
Danner, Richard M.	MGY	1958
Danzer, John	MGY	1929
Davis, John	MGY	1956,57,58
Davis, John	MGY	1968,69
Davis, John	MGY	1977,78,79
Deutschman, F. J.	MGY	1902
Dewey, C.	MGY	1928
Diamond, Robert N.	MGY	1958
Diamond, Scott	MGY	1988
Dillon, Andrew	MGY	1987,88,89
Dixon, A.	MGY	1924
Dolan, Francis (Frank)	MGY	1949,50,51

Dooley, Justin	MGY	1985,86
Draper, E. L.	MGY	1902
Echols, Holly	MGY	1949
Edwards. Robert W.	MGY	1937,38
Eliason, John	MGY	1964,65,66
Elkin, David	MGY	1993,94,95
Ensalaco, Robert	MGY	1964
Erwin, Frank K.	MGY	1973,74,75,76
Feinstein, Victor	MGY	1976,77,78,79
Fenske, Greg	MGY	1971,72,73
Field, David A.	MGY	1939,40
Filla, Mike	MGY	2001,02
Fina, John	MGY	1948,49
Fina, Joseph	MGY	1947,48,49,50
Fina, Louis R.	MGY	1940,41,42
Fina, Paul	MGY	1939,40,41
Fisher, Arthur E.	MGY	1935,36
Flood, William	MGY	1962,63
Forman, Marvin N.	MGY	1939
Fulton, W. J.	MGY	1927,28,29
Gardner, Thomas	MGY	1953,54,55
Garnett, Erik	MGY	2002
Geissler, Burkhard	MGY	1963,64
Geist, H. F.	MGY	1912
Giallombardo, Joseph J.	MGY	1938,39,40
Gill, Matt	MGY	1998,99,00
Glasser, J.	MGY	1931,32,33
Glomb, Robert	MGY	1961,62
Goldstein, William J.	MGY	1938,39,40
Gombos, Edward	MGY	1957,58,59
Goodrich, John	MGY	1960
Goone, David	MGY	1981,82,83
Gossett, W.P.	MGY	1922
Grace, Dale	MGY	1961,62
Grace, Sterling	MGY	1963
Grant, Kimp	MGY	1991,92,93
Gray, J. N.	MGY	1931,32,33
Grieb, Donald L.	MGY	1972,75
Grimes, Michael	MGY	1971,72,73,74
Grossfeld, Abie	MGY	1957,58,59,60
Grossi, George	MGY	1964
Hackleman, Michael	MGY	1963
Hadley, Raymond	MGY	1960,61,62
Hailand, Frank	MGY	1956,57,58
Hale, Clarence	MGY	1937
Halkin, Daniel	MGY	1979
Ham, Jonathan	MGY	1998,99,00
Hamman, James	MGY	1981
Hand, Nick	MGY	2002
Harrington, Peter J.	MGY	1947,48
Harvey, Allan F.	MGY	1957,58,59
Heil, Robert	MGY	1957
Heimovics, I.	MGY	1922
Henderson, Sean	MGY	1990,91,92
Hettinger, Kurt	MGY	1996,97,98,99
Highsmith, Charles	MGY	1955
Hirsch, Alan	MGY	1990,91
Hlinka, Anthony	MGY	1955
Hlinka, Charles	MGY	1950
Hoang, Linh	MGY	1998,99,00
Hochhauser, Daniel	MGY	1970,71,72
Hois, William	MGY	1977
Hollman, E.E.	MGY	1912

Victor Feinstein

Holmes, Harold	MGY	1961,62,63
Holveck, Gary	MGY	1967
Horimura, H.	MGY	1916,17
Hosfield, Mark	MGY	1976,77,78
Hoskins, R.N.	MGY	1926
Houser, Edwin	MGY	1951
Howorth, Ronald	MGY	1961
Hughes, Edgar O.	MGY	1936,38
Hughes, Gaylord	MGY	1948,49,50
Hunt, Paul	MGY	1971,72,73
Hutchings, Steven	MGY	1990
Iffland, Llewellyn	MGY	1963,64,65
Illingworth, Michael	MGY	1978
Im, Oscar	MGY	1985,86
Jenkinson, H. R.	MGY	1928,29,30
Jennings, Alpha M.	MGY	1935
Jirus, Richard	MGY	1954,55,56
Joudakin, Al	MGY	1961
Juengert, Steve	MGY	1983,84,86,87
Kalin, Gene	MGY	1970,71,72
Kamm, R.M.	MGY	1914
Kaplan, Mark	MGY	1967,68,69
Karon, Michael	MGY	1956,57
Karpen, William E.	MGY	1972,73,74,75
Katzman, Jesse	MGY	1994
Ketchen, J.G.	MGY	1999,00,01,02

Brian Kobylinski

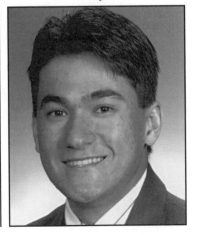

Steve Lechner

Kimball, Jason	MGY	1995
Kingsbury, F. L.	MGY	1924
Kirby, Eugene	MGY	1960,61
Klausman, Henry	MGY	1960,61,62
Kobylinski, Brian	MGY	1992,93,94,95
Koehnemann, Harry E.	MGY	1939,40,41
Komm, J.	MGY	1927
Komm, R.	MGY	1932
Koperski, Kevin	MGY	1995,97
Kostick, Andrew	MGY	1957
Kowalski, Charles	MGY	1992,93,94
Kraft, Michael	MGY	1980,81
Kratz, A. P.	MGY	1905
Kring, C. W.	MGY	1931,32
Kushner, Terry	MGY	1969
Lakes, Charles	MGY	1983,84,85
Landon, R. H.	MGY	1927,28
Landry, Jeremiah	MGY	1992,93,94,95
Lane, Randy	MGY	1986,87,88
Lat, Paul	MGY	1975,76,77,78
Lawler, William	MGY	1960,61,62
Lechner, Steven	MGY	1978,79,80,81
Ledvora, Joseph	MGY	1983,84,86
Lenke, E. H.	MGY	1902
Levitt, David	MGY	1973
Lifvendahl, R. A.	MGY	1920

Dominick Minicucci

Linder, Raymond	MGY	1947,48,50
Lindner, Paul	MGY	1987,88
Linhart, George	MGY	1990,91
Linnenburger, Paul	MGY	1999,00
Lirot, Daniel	MGY	1954,55,56
Lundien, Edwin	MGY	1950
Luyando, David	MGY	1984
Macedo, Goncalo	MGY	1993,94,95,96
Maher, Steve	MGY	1984,85
Mann, A. S.	MGY	1913
Marrero, Emilio	MGY	1988,89,92
Marshall, Douglas G.	MGY	1937
Matson, George A.	MGY	1942
McCarthy, John	MGY	1967,68,69
McDonald, B. A.	MGY	1925,26
McFarland, P. E.	MGY	1924
McGlaun, Gregory	MGY	1994,95,96,97
McGlone, Chris	MGY	1996,97
McKee, Christopher	MGY	1986,87,88,89
McMurchie, Kevin	MGY	1980,81,82,83
Mierzwa, Fred	MGY	1967,68
Mingle, David	MGY	1984,85,87,88
Mingle, Michael	MGY	1989
Minicucci, Dominick	MGY	1988,89
Mitchell, Jeffrey	MGY	1979,80,81,82
Mkchyan, Tigran	MGY	1985,86,87,88
Monk, Marvin E.	MGY	1937
Morf, F. P.	MGY	1925
Murchison, R. R.	MGY	1905
Murray, Robert	MGY	1951
Murray, William	MGY	1975
Nagel, Richard	MGY	1971,72
Newman, Ben	MGY	2002
Nilsen, P. J.	MGY	1914,15
Nishimoto, Eric	MGY	1998,99,00
Norwood, E. E.	MGY	1923,24,25
Oeler, R. C.	MGY	1928,29,30
O'Hare, John	MGY	1966
O'Heron, John	MGY	1947
Oka, Leo	MGY	1998,99,00
Olson, Carlton	MGY	1976,78,79,80
Oltendorf, Kevin	MGY	1981,82,83
Orr, R. V.	MGY	1914
Palmer, Richard	MGY	1950,51
Palmer, William	MGY	1964
Pangrle, Brian	MGY	1981,82,83
Panozzo, Brad	MGY	1995,96,97,98
Pearlstein, David	MGY	1990,91,92,93
Peltzer, A.	MGY	1927,30
Perlman, S. L.	MGY	1923,24
Peterson, David	MGY	1981,82
Petritis, Daniel	MGY	1990,91
Phillips, Oliver J.	MGY	1942
Phillips, R. J.	MGY	1925
Plante, Jonathan	MGY	2002
Pletta, D. H.	MGY	1925,26,27
Polaski, Kenneth	MGY	1964
Posey, Douglas	MGY	1962
Potter, Richard N.	MGY	1937
Prather, Paul	MGY	1935,37
Prochaska, Brad	MGY	1971,72
Quade, Charles (Chip)	MGY	1979,80
Rafaloski, Dennis	MGY	1971

Raymond, Edward	MGY	1968,69,70
Reali, Craig	MGY	1977,78,79,80
Redman, Matthew	MGY	1994,95,96,97
Redmond, John	MGY	1991
Reed, Robert	MGY	1965,66
Rehor Jr., Joseph	MGY	1932,35
Reiter, E. L.	MGY	1928,29,30
Rodriguez, Raul	MGY	1980,81,82,83
Roemer, John	MGY	1970,71,72
Rogers, Bob	MGY	2001,02
Rollo, Cook	MGY	1966,67,68
Romagnoli, Travis	MGY	1997,98,99,00
Romero, David	MGY	1986,87,89,90
Rosch, Frank	MGY	1980,81,82,83
Ross, H. A.	MGY	1917
Ruppert, Thomas	MGY	1959
Sader, Melvin	MGY	1935
Salemo, Charles	MGY	1981
Salemo, Lloyd	MGY	1980
Salter, John	MGY	1960,62
Samsten, Kari	MGY	1981,82,83,84
Sanches, Gilmarcio	MGY	1981,82,83,84
Sanchez, Victor	MGY	1964,65,66
Scanlan, John	MGY	1983,84
Schmeissing, Roy	MGY	1961
Schmidt, Michael	MGY	1976,78,79
Schreier, Marc	MGY	1995
Schroeder, John R.	MGY	1967
Schutt, Steve	MGY	1973,74
Schwitzer, G. B.	MGY	1922,23
Sepke, Arnold	MGY	1968,69
Seward, Ed	MGY	2002
Shapin, Paul	MGY	1966,67,68
Sharp, John	MGY	1949
Shaw, Harold	MGY	1966,67,68
Shostchuk, Peter	MGY	2002
Sidlinger, Bruce	MGY	1951
Silhan, William	MGY	1964,66,67
Silverman, David	MGY	1969
Sims, C. E.	MGY	1915
Singer, R. B.	MGY	1923,24
Smidl, E.	MGY	1917
Spelic, Bob	MGY	2000,01,02
Sperry, L. B.	MGY	1925
Spurney, Robert	MGY	1975,76,77,78
Stahl, Archie	MGY	1922,23
Stahl, Cecil	MGY	1922
Stoldt, David	MGY	1977,78,79,80
Stone, Kenneth	MGY	1954,55,56
Stuebe, L. F.	MGY	1921
Stuermer, Raymond J.	MGY	1937
Styles, Edward B.	MGY	1910,11,12
Su, Kenneth	MGY	1994,95
Sullivan, Robert	MGY	1951,52,53
Swonick, Robert	MGY	1970,71
Taylor, Jonathan	MGY	2002
Temple, H.	MGY	1934
Thompson, M.	MGY	1928
Ticknor, Anthony	MGY	1985,86
Tolmie, T. W.	MGY	1917
Tonry, Donald	MGY	1956,57,59
Torres, Nathan	MGY	2000,01,02
Torres, R.	MGY	1934

Travis Romagnoli

Trabert, M. L.	MGY	1935
Trujillo, Oscar	MGY	1994
Tucker, Brandon	MGY	1996,97,98
Tucker, Joel	MGY	1986,87,88,89
Turnbull, Jeffrey	MGY	1993
Valentino, John	MGY	1974
VanEtten, Gary	MGY	1971
VonEbers, Donald	MGY	1947,48,49
Wagner, Wayne	MGY	1963,64,65
Wagstaff, C. D.	MGY	1917
Wakerlin, Warren	MGY	1961,62,63
Walters, Michael W.	MGY	1956,57,58
Warga, F. J.	MGY	1928,29,30
Wasik, Jon	MGY	1994,95
Wayman, Leonard	MGY	1934,35
Weber, Charles	MGY	1965,66,67
Weintraub, Edward	MGY	1964
Weirsema, H. A.	MGY	1913
Weiss, Raymond	MGY	1938,39,40
Wetterling, Scott	MGY	2001,02
Whipple, G. B.	MGY	1928
White, Matthew	MGY	1992,93,94
Whitney, E. M.	MGY	1935
Wills, Eric	MGY	1998,99,00
Wolochuk, Lee	MGY	1988,90,91

Butch Zunich

Amo Bessone

Wolochuk, Mark	MGY	1990,91
Yahiro, Mark	MGY	1978
Yasukawa, Steven	MGY	1974,76,77,78
Yeaton, F. D.	MGY	1905
Yi, Theodore	MGY	1977,78
Zak, Kyle	MGY	1996,97,98,99
Zander, Anthony	MGY	1975,76,77
Zavell, Howard	MGY	1986,88,89
Zeddies, David	MGY	1986,87,88,89
Ziegler, A. W.	MGY	1920,21
Zinzi, Vito	MGY	1947,48
Zitzewitz, A. F.	MGY	1924
Zitzler, E.	MGY	1931,32
Zopf, William	MGY	1992
Zunich, Andreja (Butch)	MGY	1977,78,79,80

Ice Hockey

Austin Jr., Roswell M.	IHO	1943
Babbitt, Richard K.	IHO	1939
Balestri, George L.	IHO	1942,43
Beaumont, James D.	IHO	1939
Benson, Herschel G.	IHO	1942,43
Bessone, Amo	IHO	1941,42,43
Carlson, Edward H.	IHO	1939
Coupe Jr., Henry J.	IHO	1943

Sarah Aberle

Fee, Richard M.	IHO	1939
Ferranti, Louis	IHO	1942
Fieldhouse Jr., George	IHO	1939,40
Gannon, Joseph F.	IHO	1941
Gillan, John H.	IHO	1940,41,42
Jaworek, Thomas E.	IHO	1939,40,41
Karakas, Thomas J.	IHO	1943
Kaufmann, Eugene H.	IHO	1939
Killen, Ray T.	IHO	1941,42
Kopel, Howard F.	IHO	1940,41
Lotzer, Joseph J.	IHO	1940,41,42
McCune, Clinton C.	IHO	1941,42
McKibbin, Wayne J.	IHO	1940,41
Mettler, Charles W.	IHO	1940
Miller, Robert F.	IHO	1942
Owen, Starr H.	IHO	1941
Palazzari, Aldo	IHO	1941,42
Prentiss, William L.	IHO	1943
Priestley, Gilbert P.	IHO	1941
Priestley, Russell T.	IHO	1942
Rolle, Glenn L.	IHO	1943
Sigerson, Charles W.	IHO	1939
Slater, C. Paul	IHO	1940
Sterle, Norbert J.	IHO	1941
Stewart, Charles M.	IHO	1940
Thompson, Maurice P.	IHO	1939,40
Twitchell, Thomas H.	IHO	1942,43
Welsh, Alex	IHO	1939
White, John M.	IHO	1939,40
Ziemba, Chester J.	IHO	1939,40,41

Polo

Alyea, Lou	PO	1934
Anger, Edward	PO	1934
Bauer, Gene	PO	1936,37,38
Croninger, Carl	PO	1939
Cunningham, Thomas	PO	1941
Douglas, Art	PO	1935
Durfee, Ted	PO	1934
Ely, Graham	PO	1941
Garrett, Frank	PO	1938,39
Gordon, Michael J.	PO	1935,36
Harris, Bryan	PO	1941
Jaeger, Robert O.	PO	1939,40,41
Johnson, Robert	PO	1936,37,38
Kovacic, Ivan	PO	1934,35
Lord, Chester	PO	1941
Martin, James	PO	1939,40
McCrackin, Robert	PO	1941
Mercer, Frank	PO	1934,35
Peritz, Ray	PO	1940,41
Rodgers, Lee	PO	1936,38
Schaefer, Frank J.	PO	1937,38,39,40
Teeman, Hall	PO	1934,35
Walker, John	PO	1939
Wood, Harlington	PO	1941
Wright, Frederick W.	PO	1935,36,37,38

Women's Soccer

Aberle, Sarah	WSO	1997,98,00

Alcia, Leisha	WSO	2001
Anderson, Sarah	WSO	2000
Baldwin, Lisa	WSO	1998,99
Bessette, Amy	WSO	1997,98,99
Bergschneider, Kristin	WSO	1997
Brown, Emily	WSO	1998,99,00
Brown, Molly	WSO	1998
Buszkiewicz, Kelly	WSO	1997,98,99
Doetzel, Kim	WSO	1998,99
Freeman, Laura	WSO	1999,00,01
Fogelson, Kim	WSO	1997
Gordon, Ashley	WSO	1997
Green, Julie	WSO	1997
Gunville, Alaree	WSO	2001
Heggen, Sarah	WSO	1999
Hennes, Annemarie	WSO	2000
Hodson, Sue	WSO	1999,00
Holman, Kristen	WSO	1998,99,00
Holtzman, Heidi	WSO	1998,99,00,01
Hurless, Tara	WSO	2001
Johnson, Lindsay	WSO	1998,99,00,01
Joyce, Colleen	WSO	2000,01
Kann, Missy	WSO	1997
Keeler, Missy	WSO	1998
Kellett, Maggie	WSO	2000,01
Kenney, Robyn	WSO	1998
Kolze, Meghan	WSO	1999,00
Lantz, Laura	WSO	1997,98,99
Liang, Debbie	WSO	1998
Loechl, Erica	WSO	1997
Mitchell, Sarah	WSO	1997
Nadeau, Heather	WSO	1999
Patrick-Johnson, Rebecca	WSO	1998,99,00,01
Pyter, Leah	WSO	1997
Ridgeway, Andrea	WSO	2001
Rowland, Sarah	WSO	1999,00,01
Schueller, Julie	WSO	1997,98,99,00
Schuling, Tara	WSO	1999,00,01
Schurr, Hollie	WSO	1999,00,01
Sinak, Christine	WSO	2001
Sinisalo, Elina	WSO	1997
Smith, Jennifer	WSO	2000,01
Smith, Rachel	WSO	1997
Steinhoff, Stephanie	WSO	1997,98,99
Taccona, Leanne	WSO	1997
Twyning, Kris	WSO	1997,98
Tyler, Katie	WSO	1997
Walker, Kelly	WSO	2000
Walker, Tiffani	WSO	2000,01
Ward, Emily	WSO	2001

Men's Soccer

Ader, Richard F.	SOC	1930,31,32
Anderson, Wilbur H.	SOC	1932,33
Arkema, Edward L. S.	SOC	1927
Bert Jr., Vernon J.	SOC	1931
Borri, Robert P.	SOC	1934
Byman, Ellis	SOC	1928
Cassell, Charles W.	SOC	1927
Chamy, Luis F.	SOC	1927,28
Chen, Yu Hwa	SOC	1927

Kelly Buskiewicz

Cohn, P. E.	SOC	1933
Contratto, James	SOC	1930
Ehnborn, Gustave B.	SOC	1927,28,29
Fearey, Hiram D.	SOC	1928
Fencl, George S.	SOC	1929,30,31
Floreth, John	SOC	1928,29
Florio, A. E.	SOC	1933
Forsberg, Vernon A.	SOC	1932
Gasparich, Stephen J.	SOC	1928
Granata, William J.	SOC	1927
Hagen, Jack L.	SOC	1927
Hastings Jr., Douglas A.	SOC	1929,30,31
Hayes, Edwin R.	SOC	1931,32,33
Higgins, John Norris	SOC	1927
Hodge, John R.	SOC	1932
Hult, Bernard E.	SOC	1930,31
Hult, Richard E.	SOC	1930,31
Jackson Jr., Robert V.	SOC	1933
Kamin, Burt	SOC	1929
Kautt, Elmer C.	SOC	1927
Keys, John J.	SOC	1927
Kott, John H.	SOC	1930,31,32
Krakower, Irving	SOC	1929
Kwint, Joseph A.	SOC	1931

Stephanie Steinhoff

Alicia Hammel

Levine, Julius	SOC	1932
Lewin, Maxwell M.	SOC	1928,29
Lindall, Fred H.	SOC	1932
Locke, Seward C.	SOC	1932
MacLean, William P.	SOC	1934
McFadzean, John	SOC	1927,28,29
McMahon, John E.	SOC	1933,34
Mink, Ely H.	SOC	1930,31,32
Morse, Roger W.	SOC	1931,33
Patterson, James A.	SOC	1927,28
Pflager, Miller S.	SOC	1933,34
Piano, Louis J.	SOC	1930,31,32
Pinsley, H. H.	SOC	1929
Priddle, George H.	SOC	1932,33
Radebaugh, Gus H.	SOC	1934
Reston Jr., James B. (Scotty)	SOC	1929,30,31
Reynolds, Thomas E.	SOC	1928,29
Rumana, Henry	SOC	1932,33
Schachtman, Milton R.	SOC	1932,33,34
Siegal, Irving J.	SOC	1927
Simon, Frank	SOC	1928
Smith, Warren H.	SOC	1934
Strzepek, Alfred W.	SOC	1933
Vlach, William P.	SOC	1934
Walter, George	SOC	1929,30
Willig, Joseph H.	SOC	1932

Katie O'Connell

Wilson, A. Gordon	SOC	1931
Wright, Noel N.	SOC	1927
Young, Aitken F.	SOC	1928,29,30
Zbornik, Joseph J.	SOC	1932

Women's Softball

Almanza, Pam	SB	2000
Balicki, Julie	SB	2002
Baumgartner, Sarah	SB	2001,02
Bird, Karyn	SB	2001
Black, Heather	SB	2000
Bradley, Jami	SB	2002
Brocker, Mari Anne	SB	2000
Burchill, Christine	SB	2002
Butcher, LeeAnn	SB	2002
Cannizzo, Laura	SB	2000
Ceisel, Jessica	SB	2000
Christensen, Kelly	SB	2000
Colantuono, Kim	SB	2000
Creydt, Lindsey	SB	2000
Davis, Nickie	SB	2000
Evans, Reed	SB	2000
Floyd, Jenny	SB	2000
Fortune, Amanda	SB	2001,02
Gardner, Angie	SB	2000
Gronski, Lauren	SB	2001,02
Hamma, Lindsey	SB	2001,02
Hammel, Alicia	SB	2001,02
Hardwick, Abby	SB	2000
Hofert, Kim	SB	2000
Hubbard, Kim	SB	2000
Jones, Erin	SB	2001,02
Jones, Jean	SB	2000
Lindgren, Shannon	SB	2001
Lockett, Keri	SB	2001
Lovejoy, Abby	SB	2001
Lowry, Chris	SB	2000
Manley, Betty	SB	2000
Montgomery, Erin	SB	2001,02
O'Connell, Katie	SB	2001,02
Nevard, Kathryn	SB	2001
Pasquesi, Gina	SB	2000
Planinsek, Elene	SB	2001
Pluta, Bridget	SB	2001
Powaga, Jenny	SB	2000
Rymer, Annie	SB	2000
Sartini, Janna	SB	2001,02
Sauter, Kristie	SB	2001,02
Schaeffer, Lori	SB	2000
Tanner, Lindsey	SB	2001,02
Taylor, Sherri	SB	2001,02
Watson, Megan	SB	2001
Wheeler, Paige	SB	2000
White, Anitra	SB	2000
Williams, DeAnna	SB	2000

Women's Swimming

Ackermann, Mary	WSW	1991,92,93,94
Adair, Lorrie	WSW	1978,79,80
Adler, Darcy	WW	1998,99,00,01
Ahlsund, Annukka	WSW	1984,85
Apel, Patti	WSW	1977,78
Armstong, Sue	WSW	1979,80,81,82
Arnoff, Alison	WSW	1983,84
Auclair, Renee-Claude	WSW	1988,89
Aveyard, Jessica	WSW	1999,00,01,02
Beavis, Ann-Marie	WSW	1987,88,89,90
Beinke, Luann	WSW	1975
Benz, Adrienne	WSW	1997
Berg, Kristi	WSW	1993
Bergsma, Bonnie	WSW	1982,83,84,85
Bieryzchudek, Anne	WSW	1989,90
Billish, Teresa	WSW	1986,87
Binneboese, Kim	WSW	1998
Black, Marcie	WSW	1997,98,99,00
Blackwell, Amanda	WSW	1990
Bogle, Stacy	WSW	2001
Bollinger, Traci	WSW	1997,98,99,00
Bordwell, Amanda	WSW	2002
Bower, Allison	WSW	1997
Boyd, Casey	WSW	2001,02
Braun, Ashley	WSW	1999,00,01
Brecik, Deann	WSW	1984,85,86,87
Brown, Christy	WSW	1995,96,97,98
Brown, Michelle	WSW	1985,86,87,88
Burke, Brigid	WSW	1994
Busch, Molly	WSW	1998,99,00,01
Byars, Mary	WSW	1978
Canino, Toni	WSW	1983,84
Caraker, Lori	WSW	1995
Chiappe, Carole	WSW	1978,79
Christiansen, Anna	WSW	1998,99,00,01
Ciucci, Michelle	WSW	1990
Cordero, Jackie	WSW	1996
Costello, Sonya	WSW	1984,85,86,87
Cronin, Rosanne	WSW	1980,81,82,83
Cronin, Sheila	WSW	1981
Czmarko, Alison	WSW	2000,01,02
Daill, Kris	WSW	1976,77,78
David, Amy	WSW	1991,92
de Camp, Veronica	WSW	1997
Dempsey, Terry	WSW	1979,80,81,82
DesEnfants, Kate	WSW	1986,87
Didde, Erin	WSW	1996,97,98,99
Dietrich, Cathy	WSW	1991,92,93,94
Dikmen, Ilkay	WSW	2001,02
Dittmann, Martha	WSW	1977
Dixon, Michele	WSW	1988,89,90
Doll, Jill	WSW	1989,90,91,92
Domitrz, Cheri	WSW	1985,86,87,88
Dowdeswell, Marla	WSW	1992,93

Mary Ackermann

Downing, Amy	WSW	2002
Dudley, Sue	WSW	1975,76,77
Duffy, Robin	WSW	1979,80,81,82
Durbin, Cathy	WSW	1976
Eaton, Jessica	WSW	2000,01,02
Eckenroad, Susanne	WSW	1981
Eckert, Toni	WSW	1999,2001,02
Eichmeier, Katy	WSW	1976
Everaert, Christine	WSW	1992,93
Farrell, Colleen	WSW	1999,00,01
Feldman, Marla	WSW	1975,76
Fish, Lisa	WSW	2001,02
Flynn, Katy	WSW	1979,80,81,82
Fontaine, Simone	WSW	1990,91,93
Fransene, Sarah	WSW	1995,97
Galan, Anna	WSW	1988,89
Gamboa, Renee	WSW	1995,96
Gardiner, Allison	WSW	1986,87,88,89
Garrison, Emily	WSW	2001,02
Gatlin, Anne	WSW	1979
Gnade, Gail	WSW	1977
Gomery, Shannon	WSW	1996,97,98

Nicole Homenock

Kathy Kielty

Gorman, Colleen — WSW — 2002
Grandcolas, Sarah — WSW — 1985,86,87,88
Grant, Liz — WSW — 1985,86,87,88
Gregory, Melissa — WSW — 1978,79,80
Grenier, Adrienne — WSW — 1996
Guinn, Deb — WSW — 1975
Gullickson, Jennifer — WSW — 1987,88,89
Gutterridge, Theresa — WSW — 1985,86,87,88
Haag, Eileen — WSW — 1980
Hackett, Kady — WSW — 1993,94,95
Hackler, Sarah — WSW — 1995,96,97,98
Hamann, Carolyn — WSW — 1983,84,85,86
Hamann, Suzi — WSW — 1981,82,83
Handel, Kelly — WSW — 1997,98,99,00
Hansmann, Katie — WSW — 1995
Hartman, Sarah — WSW — 2001,02
Heck, Kirsten — WSW — 1995,96
Heckert, Monica — WSW — 1990
Hejnicki, Jennifer — WSW — 1992,93
Henry, Trisha — WSW — 1995,96,97,99
Hess, Jennifer — WSW — 1992,93
Hichhalter, Cheri — WSW — 1983

Jenny Patton

Hill, Barb — WSW — 1984
Holquist, Sue — WSW — 1975,76
Homenock, Nicola — WSW — 1996,97,98,99
Hooper, Jill — WSW — 1981,83
Hopkins, Kristine — WSW — 1984,85,86
Huttenlocher, Gail — WSW — 1985,86,87,88
Joesten, Holly — WSW — 1982,83
Jutton, Jerry — WSW — 1977,78
Kalafut, Christine — WSW — 1999
Karich, Sarah — WSW — 1987
Kats, Judith — WSW — 1988
Kelley, Melissa — WSW — 2001
Kelly, Jennifer — WSW — 1987
Kelly, Sue — WSW — 1980,81
Kerr, Marsha — WSW — 1975
Kielty, Kathy — WSW — 2000,01,02
Koepcke, Kristen — WSW — 2002
Lakatos, Trisha — WSW — 2002
LaMere, Dorothy — WSW — 1977
Landers, Kathleen — WSW — 1987
Lawson, Kris — WSW — 1999,00,01
Lazear, Jessica — WSW — 1999,00
Lee, Joyce Lynn — WSW — 1989,90,91,92
Lubeck, Kim — WSW — 1992
Lyons, Kristin — WSW — 2000,01
Macari, Molly — WSW — 2000
MacGregor, Ellen — WSW — 1985,86,87,88
Mackin, Beth — WSW — 1987,88
Madej, Diane (Tina) — WSW — 1976,77
Mainville, Tanya — WSW — 1997
Mamakos, Lisa — WSW — 2000,01
Matthews, Joyce — WSW — 1985
Matthias, Astrid — WSW — 2000,01,02
McAdam, Chrystal — WSW — 2001,02
McCarthy, Kathleen — WSW — 1987,88
McClain, Amy — WSW — 1985,86,87
McGauvran, Kelly — WSW — 2001
McSwine, Becky — WSW — 1977,78
Mercer, Lindy — WSW — 1995
Meriweather, Michele — WSW — 1987,88
Messmer, Natasha — WSW — 1997,98,99,00
Mowrer, Jessica — WSW — 2000
Mueller, Kristie — WSW — 1993,94,95
Musiek, Annette — WSW — 1979
Nagel, Betsy — WSW — 1997,98,99,00
Netzel, Denise — WSW — 1979
Nichols, Talyna — WSW — 1997
Noonan, Peggy — WSW — 1976
Nosal, Paula — WSW — 2001,02
Novotny, Meg — WSW — 1992,94
Nowak, Mary — WSW — 2002
Ochab, Jennifer — WSW — 2000,01,02
O'Connor, Laura — WSW — 2001
O'Fallon, Sara — WSW — 2000,01,02
Ohr, Jessica — WSW — 1998,99,00,01
Olech, Allison — WSW — 1998,99,00,01
Oostendorp, Heather — WSW — 1989,90
Oostendorp, Kristen — WSW — 1988,89,90

Palekas, Audrey — WSW — 1979,80,81
Palton, Mary — WSW — 1978
Patterson, Mary — WSW — 1975,76,77,78
Patton, Mary Andrea — WSW — 1978
Pasztor, Janna — WSW — 1999
Patton, Jenny — WSW — 1999,00,01,02
Paulson, Kirsten — WSW — 1991,92
Payette, Rebecca — WSW — 1986,87
Pederson, Laurie — WSW — 1981,82,83,84
Peters, Jennifer — WSW — 1999,00,01,02
Plattner, Sharon — WSW — 1992,93,94,95
Pogofsky, Marcy — WSW — 1997,98
Polanek, Eileen — WSW — 1980
Pottgen, Jennifer — WSW — 1994,95,96
Povey, Jeannine — WSW — 1996
Powelski, Andrea — WSW — 1999,00,01,02
Prasse, Erin — WSW — 1999
Prather, Allison — WSW — 2002
Quigley, Stephanie — WSW — 1980
Rakoski, Kristen — WSW — 1992,93,94,95
Rakoski, Lisa — WSW — 1990,91,92
Randell, Jillian — WSW — 1995
Reber, Dawn — WSW — 1995,96
Richards, Debby — WSW — 1989,90
Richart, Jane — WSW — 1986,87
Richter, Lori — WSW — 1990
Richter, Padra — WSW — 1989,90
Richter, Sandra — WSW — 1989,90
Richter, Susan — WSW — 1986
Roscetti, Erin — WSW — 1988
Roth, Barb — WSW — 1983,84,85
Ryan, Amy — WSW — 1994
Ryan, Kate — WSW — 1995
Ryan, Kristi — WSW — 1994
Sadler, Jenny — WSW — 1990,94
Salmon, Kalli — WSW — 1989,90,91,92
Sampey, Eileen — WSW — 1989,90
Sands, Jennifer — WSW — 1995,96,97,98
Scheurich, Katie — WSW — 1999,00,01
Schillmoeller, Renatta — WSW — 1983
Schofield, Jane — WSW — 1987,88,89,90
Schomer, Susan — WSW — 1980
Schwartz, Debbie — WSW — 1994,95,96
Scoville, Kristen — WSW — 2002
See, Tracy — WSW — 1990,91,92,93
Simmons, Jill — WSW — 1979,80
Skrna, Mary — WSW — 1980
Smith, Jodi — WSW — 1996,97,98,99
Snook, Erin — WSW — 2001
Sommerville, Jessica — WSW — 1993
Soucheck, Elizabeth — WSW — 1995,96
Staples, Stephanie — WSW — 1998,99
Stephens, Sarah — WSW — 1995,96,97,98
Sticha, Cherie — WSW — 1995,96,97,98
Stillwell, Jennifer — WSW — 1996
Stimpfle, Lisa — WSW — 1990,91,92,93
Suess, Frederica — WSW — 1986,87
Sullivan, Patricia — WSW — 1989,90

Jennifer Sands

Sundahl, Karen — WSW — 1987
Swann, Leeda — WSW — 1994
Taaffe, Sabine — WSW — 1989,90,92,93
Takata, Chris — WSW — 1981
Taylor, Kelli — WSW — 1989,90,91,92
Theil, Linda — WSW — 1976,77,78,79
Theobald, Nan — WSW — 1978,79,80
Tobin, Marni — WSW — 1994,95
Torchia, Meta Rose — WSW — 1985,86,87,88
Toth, Anne — WSW — 1995
Toth, Magdalena — WSW — 1983,84,85,86
Tratt, Kerrie — WSW — 1990
Treado, Kristine — WSW — 1987,88,89
Trenda, Pamela — WSW — 1989,90,91,92
Veerman, Beth — WSW — 1990
Wailing, Karen — WSW — 1983,84,85,86
Wang, Emily — WSW — 1997,98,99,00
Ward, Lindsey — WSW — 1995,96,97,98
Weber, Amanda — WSW — 1995
Weidner, Karla — WSW — 1986,87
Werder, Beth — WSW — 1979
Westhoff, Sue — WSW — 1980,81,82,83
Westohoff, Karen — WSW — 1981

Sabine Taaffe

James Barnett

Whitaker, Kim	WSW	1976
Wilhite, Noelle	WSW	1998,99,01
Williams, Janet	WSW	1976
Witte, Christy	WSW	2000
Wopat, Paula	WSW	1977
Worth, Carolyn	WSW	1984,85,86,87
Wylie, Mary	WSW	1982,83,84,85
York, Pam	WSW	1980,81,82,83
Yount, Amy	WSW	1975, 76

Men's Swimming

Ackerman, Owen	MSW	1957,58,59
Ahlem, Ted	MSW	1975,76
Albecker, Walter	MSW	1980
Alcorn, Stanley W.	MSW	1937,39
Alderson, E. W.	MSW	1920
Allen, Robert	MSW	1987,88,89
Anderson, Bob	MSW	1968,69,70
Anderson, Daniel C.	MSW	1941,42
Anderson, Darryl	MSW	1966
Anderson, H. B.	MSW	1910
Anderson, John V.	MSW	1938
Anderson, Richard F.	MSW	1941

Bob Carstensen

Anderson, Richard	MSW	1966,67,68
Anderson, Tom	MSW	1972
Andrew, Philip	MSW	1989
Andrews, L. E.	MSW	1917
Arrison, Kevin	MSW	1985
Ash, Homer	MSW	1950,51
Bachman, Bob	MSW	1965,66,67
Banks, Daniel	MSW	1982,83,85
Barber, Thomas	MSW	1946
Barnes, David	MSW	1974,75,76,77
Barnett, James	MSW	1983,84,85,86
Barry, G. W.	MSW	1929
Bartholomew, F. G.	MSW	1930,31,32
Bates, Pete	MSW	1965,66,67
Bates, Rob	MSW	1991
Baughter, George	MSW	1947
Beaumont, G. S.	MSW	1912,13,14
Beebe, H. K.	MSW	1923
Beebe, W. E.	MSW	1920,22
Bell, Brian	MSW	1992
Benner, Jeffery	MSW	1981
Berry, Mark	MSW	1981,82
Bezella, Bruce	MSW	1990,91
Bigger, Hamilton	MSW	1946
Bihl, Pete	MSW	1977
Bishop, David	MSW	1978,79
Blackman, E. O.	MSW	1926
Blankley, W. H.	MSW	1926,27
Block, F. L.	MSW	1930
Bockman, Ted	MSW	1950
Boedicker, Charles	MSW	1978,79,80,81
Boor, Alden K.	MSW	1941,42
Borman, Michael	MSW	1974
Borst, G. E.	MSW	1925
Boston, Bill	MSW	1962
Bouchard, Mike	MSW	1956,59,60
Bowen, C. L.	MSW	1922,23
Boyce, Chuck	MSW	1965,67
Branca, Tom	MSW	1963,64,65
Branch, Robert	MSW	1948,49,50
Brandt, Todd	MSW	1982,83,84
Brekke, William C.	MSW	1941,42,43
Brennan, William	MSW	1975
Brinck, Per Ake	MSW	1983
Brock, J.	MSW	1931,32,33
Brooks, H. M.	MSW	1908
Brouk, John J.	MSW	1937
Brown, James M.	MSW	1941,42,43
Bulaw, Adolph	MSW	1935
Burton, Gary	MSW	1961,62,63
Cady, G. H.	MSW	1930
Cajet, Arnold	MSW	1954,55,56
Carey, Robert	MSW	1955,56
Carnes, Brian	MSW	1978
Carpenter, Lee	MSW	1968,69,70
Carpenter, Tom	MSW	1972,73,74
Carstensen, Bob	MSW	1988,89,90,91
Cary, M. C.	MSW	1920
Castator, Alan	MSW	1965,66,67
Castles, Bryan	MSW	1980,83
Chadsey, C. P.	MSW	1923,24,25

Chaney, Dennis	MSW	1971
Chapman, E. N.	MSW	1915
Chapman, John	MSW	1963,64
Chase, Dean	MSW	1912
Chiappe, David	MSW	1982,83,84
Christ, G. P.	MSW	1920
Christensen. Gary	MSW	1970
Clemons, Robert	MSW	1952,53,54
Clooney, Donald	MSW	1949,50,51
Collora, N. A.	MSW	1928
Colwell, Gary	MSW	1978
Condon, V. H.	MSW	1922,23
Congreve, George	MSW	1973,74,75,76
Conrad, Joseph A.	MSW	1941
Cook, Ed	MSW	1964
Copeland, J. R.	MSW	1925
Cortis, R. P.	MSW	1923
Cramer, Curt	MSW	1968,69,70
Crane, D. W.	MSW	1916
Crosby, F. H.	MSW	1934
Cryer, Walter	MSW	1951,52
Cutter, Robert L.	MSW	1937
Cutter. W. C.	MSW	1910
Davey, Tim	MSW	1992
DeBord, Jim	MSW	1967,68,69
Dennett, Kenneth	MSW	1920,21
Denzler, Mike	MSW	1988
Deuss, E.	MSW	1927,28
Diamantos, Tony	MSW	1974,75
Dillman, Greg	MSW	1988,89
Dixon, Terence	MSW	1983,84,85,86
Dollins, Matthew	MSW	1989
Donohue, John	MSW	1958,59,60
Dooley, Dick	MSW	1961,62,63
Dowd, Donald	MSW	1955,56
Drake, Greg	MSW	1988,89,90,91
Driemeyer, Dan	MSW	1971
Driscoll, John	MSW	1944
Druz, Dave	MSW	1972,74,75
Dupon, Norm	MSW	1962
Dvorak, R. F.	MSW	1921
Eberhardy, Richard	MSW	1957,58,59,60
Ekstrom, Lee	MSW	1969
Eldredge, L. E.	MSW	1924,25
Ellis, Elias L.	MSW	1937,38
Engstrom, DeWayne	MSW	1980
Enochs, C. H.	MSW	1928,29
Erickson, Keith	MSW	1984,85
Erwin, John R.	MSW	1936
Essick, Raymond	MSW	1955
Essick, Raymond	MSW	1978,79,80,81
Etzbach, W. H.	MSW	1930
Faircloth, S. E.	MSW	1917,20
Falkenberg, G. V.	MSW	1920
Fieldhouse, Jim	MSW	1970,71,72,73
Fifield, C. W.	MSW	1916
Fisher, F. L.	MSW	1925,26,27
Fix, John	MSW	1957,58,59
Flachmann, Charles O.	MSW	1933,34,35
Flachmann, John M.	MSW	1941
Flanders, J. A.	MSW	1909

Peter Gruben

Fletemeyer, Richard	MSW	1957,59,60
Florio, Dave	MSW	1965,66,67
Folts, Thomas	MSW	1980,81,82,83
Fornof, John	MSW	1961
Forsythe, William	MSW	1957
Foster, Bruce	MSW	1969
Fox, A. L.	MSW	1922,23
Franks, Mark	MSW	1992
Frazier, Ernest	MSW	1945
Fulling, B. C.	MSW	1927
Funk, Mark	MSW	1981,82
Gale, E. O.	MSW	1922
Garland, John	MSW	1955,56,57
Gaynor, Allen	MSW	1974,75
Gaynor, Duffy	MSW	1972,73
Gelwicks, Greg	MSW	1988,89
Gerometta, Robert	MSW	1947,48
Gfroerer, George	MSW	1952,53,54,55
Gill, Richard J.	MSW	1942
Givot, Michael	MSW	1985,86,87,88
Gordon, N.	MSW	1931
Gore, Stanley A.	MSW	1944
Gossett, J. E.	MSW	1910,11
Gould, P. N.	MSW	1917

Kent Helwig

Reese Jones

Gray, J. M	MSW	1917
Green, Lonsdale	MSW	1910,11,12
Green, Ralph	MSW	1913,14
Grey, N. E	MSW	1916
Grider, Chris	MSW	1987
Griffin, J. M.	MSW	1913,14,15
Grimmer, Mike	MSW	1974,75,76,77
Groh, Harold	MSW	1927,28,29
Grossman, Jake	MSW	1954,55,56
Gruben, Peter	MSW	1987,89,90,91
Gruenberg. A. A.	MSW	1924
Gruenfeld, Julius J.	MSW	1943
Guerrera, Chris	MSW	1987,88,89
Gwin, Greg	MSW	1962,63,64
Haig, Thomas	MSW	1981,82
Hallden. John T.	MSW	1937
Hallerud, Dean	MSW	1959
Hammel, Jeff	MSW	1975,76
Hansen, David	MSW	1955,56
Hansen, Henry F.	MSW	1935,36
Hanson, Eric	MSW	1983
Hardacre, G. K.	MSW	1922
Harmeson, Terry	MSW	1969
Harrold, Norman M.	MSW	1942

Chris Lubeck

Hartman, Leo P.	MSW	1940,41,42
Hatfield, Doug	MSW	1969
Haulenbeck, John	MSW	1945,46
Haymaker, Chris	MSW	1989
Hays, Bill	MSW	1964
Hegeler, Edward	MSW	1944
Helwig, Kent	MSW	1981,82,83,84
Henry, C. D.	MSW	1911
Hewitt, F. E.	MSW	1932,33,34
Hickey, James J .	MSW	1935
Hill, Arthur	MSW	1982,84,85,86
Hines, N. W.	MSW	1932,33
Hoffman, Dennis	MSW	1960,61
Holbrook, F. W.	MSW	1928,29,30
Holbrook, Jim	MSW	1962,63,64
Holquist, Henry J.	MSW	1939,40,41
Hopwood, Milton T.	MSW	1937,38,39
Houcek, Richard	MSW	1946,47
Huebner, Louis H.	MSW	1944
Hunsaker, Joe	MSW	1957,58,59
Hunt, Robert	MSW	1956,57,58
Huyler, Joe	MSW	1959,60,61,62
Jager, William	MSW	1979,80,81
Janota, Neil	MSW	1972,73,74,75
Jansen, Earl	MSW	1934
Jensen, George	MSW	1947
Johns, D. C.	MSW	1916,17
Johnson, H. M.	MSW	1925
Johnson, Harlan	MSW	1946
Johnson, Roy	MSW	1946
Jones, Benton	MSW	1950,51,52
Jones, Billy M.	MSW	1938,39,40
Jones, John C.	MSW	1934
Jones, Reese	MSW	1989,90,91
Jones, Steven	MSW	1982,83,84
Jurgens, Carl	MSW	1971
Karafotas, Phil	MSW	1962,63,64
Karpinchik, Nick	MSW	1954,57
Keenan, Donald	MSW	1955,56
Keinlen, Tom	MSW	1963,64
Kelley, Bill	MSW	1991,92
Kennesey, George	MSW	1992
Kerr, John K.	MSW	1943
Kesler, Robert	MSW	1948,49
Keswick, Bruce	MSW	1970,71,72,73
Kieding, Ray	MSW	1928,29,30
Kienlen, Donlad L.	MSW	1939,40,41
Kireilis, Raymond W.	MSW	1939,41
Kirkland, Alfred Y.	MSW	1939,40,41
Kjellstrom, Theodore	MSW	1952
Klapperich, Andrew	MSW	1979,80,81,82
Klingel, Martin	MSW	1961,63
Kneesi, C. W.	MSW	1927
Konstant, Anthony	MSW	1945,46
Kosakiewicz, Anthony	MSW	1945
Kostick, Eugene	MSW	1958
Kozlowski, Aaron	MSW	1990,91
Kracen, Scott	MSW	1968,69
Kral, Ed	MSW	1961,62,63
Kramp, Robert	MSW	1952,53,54
Kratz, Paul	MSW	1950
Kuhlman, Erich	MSW	1991,92
Kunde, Mark	MSW	1988

Kurlak, Peter	MSW	1939,40,41
Kuypers, Bob	MSW	1974,75
Lakin, J. C.	MSW	1931
Lamb, F. W.	MSW	1925,26
Lane, Thomas	MSW	1948
Larsen, Eric M.	MSW	1934,35
Larson, Donald	MSW	1955,56,57
Lary, Brad	MSW	1947
Layne, Allen	MSW	1991,92
Lehman, Fred	MSW	1951,52
Lehmkuhl, Richard	MSW	1981
Lentz, Jac	MSW	1938
Levin, M .	MSW	1924
Levine, Bob	MSW	1968,69,70
Lewis, Norman B.	MSW	1936,37
Lewis, Tom I.	MSW	1942
Lichter, J. P.	MSW	1913
Linden, O. W.	MSW	1921
Lively, Thomas G.	MSW	1938
Loar, Ned	MSW	1955,56,57
Lockwood, W. W.	MSW	1930
Lopater, Dave	MSW	1971
Lovin, Christopher	MSW	1983,84,85,86
Lowe, George A.	MSW	1937,38,39
Lubeck, Chris	MSW	1988,89,90,91
MacDonald, Rod	MSW	1972,73,74,75
Mackie, Chris	MSW	1986,87
Mackin, James	MSW	1987,88,89
Madsen, Harry	MSW	1950,51
Maier, John	MSW	1977,78
Makielski, Ward	MSW	1988
Malmberg, Kenneth	MSW	1985,86,87,88
Maloney, Russ	MSW	1990,91,92
Mann, William E.	MSW	1944,45,46
Marine, Gar	MSW	1966
Marshall, John	MSW	1930
Mathieu, Bud	MSW	1976,77,78
Matten, Brad	MSW	1968,69,70
Matthei, L. P.	MSW	1931
Mauck, Eugene H .	MSW	1936
Mautner, Henry	MSW	1947
Mayer, S. R.	MSW	1924
McCarthy, Terence	MSW	1983,84,85
McConnell, Douglas	MSW	1976,77,78,79
McDonald, A. P	MSW	1914,16
McDyer, Dale	MSW	1958,59
McFarland, P. E.	MSW	1924
McGufficke, Graeme	MSW	1983,85,86,87
McKinley, Robert O.	MSW	1940,41
McLarty, Brandon	MSW	1992
McNally, Andrew	MSW	1920,21
McNamara, Brian	MSW	1991,92
McPheron, Ron	MSW	1984
McVey, Andrew	MSW	1987,88,89
Meeland, Tor	MSW	1942,43
Melnicove, Gary	MSW	1962,63
Mersbach, David	MSW	1953,54
Metcalf, Doug	MSW	1975
Meyer, Russ	MSW	1973,74,75,76
Michelson, Larry	MSW	1960
Middleton, James R.	MSW	1942
Milani, Anthony	MSW	1980
Miller, Robert	MSW	1955,56,57

Graeme McGufficke

Mix, M. l.	MSW	1912
Moench, R. G.	MSW	1931
Moore, Christopher	MSW	1982
Moore, Henry H.	MSW	1944,45
Moore, Merrill D.	MSW	1945
Moore, Tom	MSW	1991,92
Morley, George	MSW	1964
Moskiewicz, John	MSW	1954
Mottern, H. M.	MSW	1913
Mueller, William	MSW	1983,84,85,86
Mullins, George	MSW	1947,48,49
Mulloy, Chris	MSW	1991,92
Munro, Dan	MSW	1983,84,85
Musch, Tom	MSW	1969,70
Nedrud, Brad	MSW	1973,74,75
Nelson, John	MSW	1988,89
Nevels, Charles	MSW	1944
Newell, Bruce	MSW	1964,65
Neylon, Brian	MSW	1985,86,87,88
Nichols, Pete	MSW	1960
Nielsen, Kurt	MSW	1979
Niziolek, Frank	MSW	1990,91,92
Novosel, Brett	MSW	1991
Novosel, Scott	MSW	1988,89,90,91
Nowack, Carl	MSW	1978,79
Nowack, Steven	MSW	1980

Phillip Quigley

Don Sammons

O'Brien, W. C.	MSW	1925,26
Olcott, G. W.	MSW	1924
Olin, Jon	MSW	1964,65
Olsen, Hugh H.	MSW	1945
Olsen, R. S.	MSW	1921,22
Ott, George	MSW	1923
Ott, J. E.	MSW	1916
Overman , Warren C.	MSW	1935,36,37
Padgett, Christopher	MSW	1983,84,85
Pala, Steve	MSW	1990,91
Pashby, R. W.	MSW	1930
Paul, Jim	MSW	1974,75,76
Pauly, Patrick	MSW	1982,83,84,85
Pearson, Jack	MSW	1950
Pendleton, James	MSW	1951,52
Peragine, Tom	MSW	1989,90,91,92
Pertle, J. L.	MSW	1927
Peters, Scot	MSW	1984
Petersen, Neal	MSW	1971,72
Pierce, Steve	MSW	1985,86
Piggott, A.	MSW	1923
Pihera, Otto	MSW	1947
Pillinger, R. A.	MSW	1908
Piper, John	MSW	1928,29
Pope, Kip	MSW	1967,68,69

Joseph Tanner

Postle, D. E.	MSW	1921,22
Potter, Keith	MSW	1976,77,78,79
Powers, Robert	MSW	1983
Pribil, Martin	MSW	1976
Puchalski. Don	MSW	1959
Quackenbush, B. H.	MSW	1924
Quigley, Phillip	MSW	1976,77,78,79
Read, Phil	MSW	1969
Reitsch, Charles	MSW	1949,50,51
Rempert, John	MSW	1982
Rezab, Ray	MSW	1983
Richter, Gary	MSW	1986,87,88,89
Rick, Dickson	MSW	1926
Roach, James W.	MSW	1941,42,43
Roddick, Lawrence	MSW	1986
Roos, E. G	MSW	1916
Rosenbaum, Lee	MSW	1980
Ross, Roy	MSW	1950
Rotkis, Walter A.	MSW	1937
Rotteld, Herb	MSW	1971
Royal, T. E.	MSW	1921,22,23
Ruben, Benjamin	MSW	1953
Rubenstein, Allan	MSW	1956,57,58
Rucker, Douglas	MSW	1948,49
Rusackus, Charles J.	MSW	1936
Sammons, Donald	MSW	1954
Sandor, Bela	MSW	1960
Sarussi, Marty	MSW	1984,86,87
Sawicki, Tom	MSW	1965,66,67
Schanel, James	MSW	1976,77,78,79
Scherrer, Steve	MSW	1983,84,86
Scherwat, Don	MSW	1947,48,49
Schick, A. l.	MSW	1932
Schindehette, Russell	MSW	1980,81,82,83
Scholz, Robert	MSW	1953
Schroeder. F. R.	MSW	1928,29,30
Schwartz, Terry	MSW	1973,74
Scott, Greg	MSW	1973,74,75,76
Scotty, Brian	MSW	1980,84
Scotty, Matthew	MSW	1985,86,87,88
Scotty, Thomas	MSW	1983,85,86
Seaman, Glen	MSW	1977,78
Seaman, Richard	MSW	1986,87
Seidler, Burton A.	MSW	1943
Seiwert, Herb	MSW	1948,49
Seybold, Harvey	MSW	1974,75,76
Sharer, Rock	MSW	1959,60,61
Shattuck, W. F.	MSW	1926,27,28
Shea, Jeft	MSW	1963
Shoemaker, Kenn	MSW	1975
Shriner, William	MSW	1961,62,63
Siegert, Philip	MSW	1960,61
Simmons, G. E.	MSW	1924
Simpson, Ken	MSW	1967,68
Sims, Robert	MSW	1992
Sinnock, Pommery	MSW	1932
Skunberg, Craig	MSW	1982
Smiley, Larry	MSW	1967,68,69
Smith, Andrew	MSW	1983
Solbert, Michael	MSW	1983
Sommer, Joseph	MSW	1961,62,63
Spasott, Tom	MSW	1962
Spreitzer, Fred	MSW	1963
Spreitzer, James	MSW	1961,62,63

Staples, Paul	MSW	1988,89
Stapleton, Christopher	MSW	1986,87,88
Stark, Art	MSW	1966,67,68
Stelton, Peter	MSW	1960,61,62
Sterba, Tony	MSW	1970,71,72,73
Sterrett, David	MSW	1955,56,57
Stettensen, Jim	MSW	1970,71,72,73
Stluka, Gary	MSW	1970,71,72
Stout, W. H.	MSW	1928,29
Strange, Rob	MSW	1978,79
Stroker, Steven	MSW	1979,80,81
Sullivan, Robert	MSW	1953
Sutton, M.	MSW	1924
Swatek, E. T.	MSW	1907
Sweetman, Frank	MSW	1929
Taber, B. F.	MSW	1911,12,13
Tack, Joseph	MSW	1979,80
Tague, Chris	MSW	1977,78,79,80
Tait, Fred	MSW	1952,53
Tanner, Jim	MSW	1968
Tanner, Joseph R.	MSW	1970,71,72
Tanner, John	MSW	1972,73,74,75
Tanner, Tom	MSW	1977,78,79
Taylor, F. M.	MSW	1925
Taylor, W. H.	MSW	1921,22,23
Thompson, H. P.	MSW	1912
Thompson, Jett	MSW	1992
Thompson, O. H.	MSW	1914
Thompson, T. H.	MSW	1912
Tiedemann, Lance	MSW	1988,89,90,91
Tothero, Steve	MSW	1989,90,91,92
Trigger, Tom	MSW	1966,67
Turek, Marty	MSW	1992
Van Gunter, M. B.	MSW	1933
Van Heltebrake, Jerry	MSW	1971
Van Rossen, Donald	MSW	1953
Van Tuin, J. W.	MSW	1933,35
Vial, H. C.	MSW	1917
Vinke, Bob	MSW	1973,74,75
Voelkner, Alvin	MSW	1960
Vokac, Frank G.	MSW	1935,36
Vosburgh, William R.	MSW	1911,12,13
Wagner, E. H.	MSW	1929
Wahlstrom, Marvin	MSW	1946
Waldo, J. H.	MSW	1917,20
Walker, Rick	MSW	1979
Walker, Thomas	MSW	1957,58,59
Walker, Wesley	MSW	1980,81,82
Wannemanker, Bob	MSW	1970,72
Ward, Richard	MSW	1980,81
Warren, Kent	MSW	1990,91
Watson, James	MSW	1953
Weathertord, Harold	MSW	1976
Weber, Glenn	MSW	1946
Webster, G. A.	MSW	1928,29,30
Weiss, G. S.	MSW	1925
Werner, James	MSW	1978,79,80
Werner, Robert	MSW	1979,80,81,82
Werremeyer, Kit	MSW	1966,67,68
Wessberg, Tom	MSW	1986,87
Wheeler, R. L.	MSW	1922
White, Scott	MSW	1972
Whittaker Jr., Lorin	MSW	1957,58
Whittaker, Dick	MSW	1959

Camille Baldrich

Wich, Fred	MSW	1975,76,77,78
Williams, John	MSW	1974,75,76
Williamson, Esby	MSW	1932
Williamson, J. C.	MSW	1930,31
Willingham, Thomas	MSW	1983
Wilson, Anthony	MSW	1985,86,87
Wilson, Paul	MSW	1991,92
Wine, John	MSW	1984,85,86,87
Wollrab, James C.	MSW	1939,40,41
Wolters, Brett	MSW	1992
Woodbury, Ed	MSW	1973,74,75,76
Younger, Charles	MSW	1961,62
Zimmerman, Wessel	MSW	1984
Zitz, John	MSW	1990,91

Women's Tennis

Adsuar, Natalie	WTN	1995,96
Aguero, Liana	WTN	1997
Arildsen, Susan	WTN	1982,83,84,85
Baldrich, Camille	WTN	1992,93,94,95
Bareis, Barbara	WTN	1982,84,85
Basolo, Margaret	WTN	1977,78,79
Batt, Jaclyn	WTN	1994,96
Bjerknes, Lisa	WTN	1980
Boomershine, Kate	WTN	2002

Carrie Costigan

Lissa Kimmel

Brouder, Cynthia	WTN	1978,79
Bruce, Lindsey	WTN	1997
Buchanan, Lisa	WTN	1980,81
Burgess, Sandra	WTN	1980,81
Burgess, Sharon	WTN	1978,79,80
Burns, Sheila	WTN	1984,85,86,87
Buwick, Cynthia	WTN	1977,78,79
Cathrall, Jodi	WTN	1989
Cehajic, Leila	WTN	2002
Chambers, Cynthia	WTN	1988,89,90,91
Choe, Eva	WTN	2001,02
Clery, Colleen	WTN	1976,77
Corcoran, Maura	WTN	1988
Costigan, Carrie	WTN	1986,87,88,89
Crane, Donna	WTN	1980
Cunningham, Nancy	WTN	1978
Davis, Barbara	WTN	1975,76,
Daw, Jessie	WTN	1984,85,87,88
DeSilva, Gayathri	WTN	1980,81,82,83
Eichner, Astrid	WTN	1987,88,90
Eklov, Tiffany	WTN	2001,02
Ensslin, Sabine	WTN	1989,90,91
Faford, Ann	WTN	1976,77,78
Fazlic, Eldina	WTN	2000,01,02
Ferney, Brooke	WTN	1999,00

Jennifer Roberts

Flesvig, Christine	WTN	1983,84,85,86
Fraker, Elizabeth	WTN	2002
Gates, Linda	WTN	1989,90,92
Goecke, Michelle	WTN	1992
Goern, Sandra	WTN	1985,86,87,88
Gottlieb, Allison	WTN	1996,97,98,99
Goulet, Cynthia	WTN	2002
Harris, Jean	WTN	1975
Haubold, Lois	WTN	1977,78,79,80
Hogan, Dorothy	WTN	1980
Holmes, Kam	WTN	1976,77
Hoppmann, Rita	WTN	1981,82,83,84
Hutchinson, Susan	WTN	1981,82,83,84
Jackson, Nicole	WTN	1996
Johnson, Cathryn	WTN	1977
Johnson, Amy	WTN	1991
Jones, Kristen	WTN	1992,93,94,95
Kane, Laurie	WTN	1990,91
Kazarian, Stacey	WTN	1985,86
Kestly, Christie	WTN	1991
Kewney, Kathryn	WTN	1982
Kimmel, Lissa	WTN	1992,93,94,95
Klapper, Jessica	WTN	1994,95,96,97
Knowles, Stacey	WTN	1986,87,89
Kole, Kathy	WTN	1975,76,77,78
Kung, Simone	WTN	1998,99,00,01
Land, Susanne	WTN	1994,95,96,97
Loebnitz, Natascha	WTN	2000
Loffelmacher, Kara	WTN	1996,97,98
Manasova, Natalia	WTN	1999,00
Marshak, Sara	WTN	1993,94,95
Matz, Jenny	WTN	1982
McGaffigan, Jennifer	WTN	2001,02
McNamara, Colleen	WTN	1975,76,77
McNamara, Maura	WTN	1981,82,83,84
Mehlman, Romy	WTN	1996
Meola, Kristi	WTN	1992,93,94
Neil, Kathy M.	WTN	1985,86,87,88
Nelson, Maureen	WTN	1976,77,78,79
Nimmo, Lindsey	WTN	1991,92,93
Olson, Sara	WTN	1981
Panique, Lisa	WTN	1998
Pratt, Margaret	WTN	1975
Pullman, Cheri	WTN	1993,95
Rickard, Kelley	WTN	1982
Roberts, Jennifer	WTN	1982
Rosenberg, Carla	WTN	1998,99,00,01
Rydberg, Laura	WTN	1994,95,96,97
Salamone, Kristina	WTN	1975,76,77,78
Schapiro, Stacey	WTN	1996,97,98,99
Scherschligt, Barbra	WTN	1985,86
Smolensky, Loren	WTN	1987,88,90
Stout, Susan	WTN	1985,86,87,88
Strauss, Deborah	WTN	1978
Webb, Michelle	WTN	2000,01,02
Welsh, Barb	WTN	1978
Wentink, Nancy	WTN	1975
Wickiser, Jo	WTN	1983
Willey, Kristin	WTN	1990,91
Williams, Mary Beth	WTN	1990,91,92
Wise, Megan	WTN	1998,99,00
Wujek, Kathy	WTN	1975
Young, Amy	WTN	1978,79,80

Men's Tennis

Abrams, Jack	MTN	1952
Adams, Neil	MTN	1981,82,83,84
Alcock, Warren	MTN	1948
Amaya, Manuel	MTN	1973,74
Ambielli, Adam	MTN	1982
Appleman, Jim	MTN	1975
Archer, Corbin	MTN	1995,97,98
Basson, Michau	MTN	1993,94,95
Bauer, Tom	MTN	1964,65,66
Becker, Robert	MTN	1934
Bennorth, Robert	MTN	1950,51,52
Besant, Wilson	MTN	1949,50
Bielefeld, Roger	MTN	1954,55,58
Bishop, Lee	MTN	1951
Black, Todd	MTN	1979,80,81,82
Blain, Brady	MTN	1995,96,97,98
Boatman, Tom	MTN	1960,61,62
Bouton, Peter	MTN	1982,83,84,85
Bradley, Ed	MTN	1950,51
Brandt, Harry	MTN	1954,55,56
Braun, Cyril	MTN	1938
Breckenridge, Robert	MTN	1957,58,59
Brooke, Shawn	MTN	2000
Brown, David	MTN	1947,48,49
Brown, Neil	MTN	1988,89,90
Brown, Thurston	MTN	1962
Burkholder, Robert	MTN	1967
Bush, Roger	MTN	1940
Buwick, Eugene	MTN	1949,50,51
Calkins, Michael	MTN	2001,02
Chambers, Franklin	MTN	1961
Chanowitz, Harry	MTN	1938,39,40
Chaudhuri, Mickey	MTN	1991,92
Chiricosta, Anthony	MTN	1976,77,78,79
Clapper, Kenneth	MTN	1942,43
Clark, Keith	MTN	1945
Clark, Ryan	MTN	1991,92,93
Clatfelter, Jack	MTN	1943
Clements, Chip	MTN	1969,70,71
Confer, Warren	MTN	1938
Conlan, Jack	MTN	1981,82,83
Cook, Jeff	MTN	1968,69,70
Cordes, Rob	MTN	1993
Cossette, Bryan	MTN	1993
Crain, Delmar	MTN	1939,40
Crawmer, Charly	MTN	1993,94
Dankert, William	MTN	1952,53
Davis, Jared	MTN	1944,45
Davitz, Joel	MTN	1944
Daw, Joe	MTN	1981,82
Dawson, Jim	MTN	1965
Dean, Paul	MTN	1939
Delic, Amer	MTN	2001,02
DeVore, Adrian	MTN	1991,92
DeVore, Chris	MTN	1994,95,96
Dillman, Brian	MTN	1988,89,90
Downs, Roger	MTN	1946,47
Dunlap, Tom	MTN	1968,69,70
Earl, Robert	MTN	1976,77,78,79
Eberly, Mike	MTN	1991,92
Edidin, Norman	MTN	1941
Edwards, Jeffrey	MTN	1977,78,79,80
Elbl, Michael	MTN	1967,68

Carey Franklin

Epkins, Joe	MTN	1958,59,60
Farmer, Alan	MTN	1952
Fisher, Ben	MTN	1948
Franklin, Cary	MTN	1997,98,99,00
Franks, Bruce	MTN	1974,75,76,77
Freelove, Oliver	MTN	1996,97,98,99
Frei, Tom	MTN	1984,85,86
Garfield, Marvin	MTN	1949
Gates, James	MTN	1942,43,46
Geist, Harvey	MTN	1934
Gilmore, George	MTN	1957,58,59
Glass, Doyle	MTN	1954
Gottman, Jay	MTN	1986
Goodman, David	MTN	1983,84
Gorham, Sidney	MTN	1956
Gottman, Jay	MTN	1986
Greenberg, Scott	MTN	1984,86,87
Greenleaf, John	MTN	1954,55
Groppel, Jack	MTN	1973
Gudeman, Gene	MTN	1958
Gueche, Sadri	MTN	1990,92
Harris, Miles	MTN	1970,71,72,73
Hartenstein, Harvey	MTN	1952
Hawthorne, Jamison	MTN	1993,94
Hayne, Wilbur	MTN	1973,74,75

Jack Groppel

Mark Krajewski

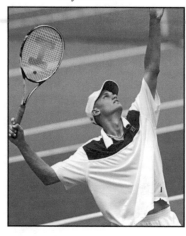

Graydon Oliver

Hedden, Dan	MTN	1963
Heller, Steve	MTN	1961,62
Henderson, Tom	MTN	1980,81,82
Hertz, Jed	MTN	1968,71
Hicks, Bruce	MTN	1935,36
Hill, Stephen	MTN	1953,54
Hobson, Alex	MTN	2000,01,02
Hoffman, Robert	MTN	1951,52
Holden, David	MTN	1966,67,68
Holtmann, Al	MTN	1957,58,59
Hoppenjans, Mark	MTN	1991
Howie, Bill	MTN	1953
Howie, Bill	MTN	1986,87
Hulvey, Walter	MTN	1953
Hummel, Glenn	MTN	1973,74,75,76
Isenburg, Orville	MTN	1940
Johnson, Howard	MTN	1939
Johnson, Jerry	MTN	1965,66
Johnson, Kenneth	MTN	1939,40
Jones, Arthur	MTN	1941
Jones, Ebon	MTN	1938,39,40
Karacan, Ercument	MTN	1945
Kell, Dick	MTN	1961
Kelso, Kevin	MTN	1972,73,74,75
Kennett, Greg	MTN	1988,89

Knowlton, Brett	MTN	1988
Kosta, Mike	MTN	1999,00,01,02
Kramer, Mike	MTN	1978,79,80,81
Krajewski, Mark	MTN	1989,90,91,92
Lambert, Andre	MTN	1983.84
Lansford, Bob	MTN	1959,60
Lantin, Arnaud	MTN	1998,99
Lapriore, Chris	MTN	1985
Laski, Jeff	MTN	1997,98,99,00
Leininger, Joseph	MTN	1980
Levenson, Steve	MTN	1966,67,68
Levy, Bertram	MTN	1944
Lewers, Richard	MTN	1935,36
Lewke, Bob	MTN	1965,66
Littell, Dave	MTN	1972
Little, Roger	MTN	1945,48,49,50
Lobb, Andrew	MTN	1986,87
Lombardi, Vince	MTN	1993
Long, Mark	MTN	1985,86.87.88
Losito, John	MTN	1984,85
Lothrop, James	MTN	1942,43
MacDonald, Don	MTN	1953
Manpearl, David	MTN	1994,95,96
Martin, Chris	MTN	2002
Maxwell, Barry	MTN	1970,71,72
McCollum, Tom	MTN	1963,64
McCoy, William	MTN	1937,38
McCraven, Steve	MTN	1988.89
McDonald, Richard	MTN	1956,57
McInich, Nelson	MTN	1935
McKenzie, Nick	MTN	1986
Mesch, Dan	MTN	1959,60
Meurisse, Charles	MTN	1975,76,77,78
Meyer, Mike	MTN	1983,84,86
Migdow, Ben	MTN	1946,47
Minkus, Marc	MTN	1974
Mioduski, Moseph	MTN	1939
Moll, Joe	MTN	1934,35.36
Morrey, Kevin	MTN	1971,72,73,74
Morrison, Wayne	MTN	1975
Moses, James	MTN	1949,50,51
Moss, Larry	MTN	1962,63
Most, Fred	MTN	1952,55
Muresan, Alex	MTN	2001,02
Murray, John	MTN	1988,89,90
Nair, Madhu	MTN	1985,86
Nasser, David	MTN	1989,90,91,92
Nasser, Mark	MTN	1993,94
Noble, Carl	MTN	1956,57,58
Noble, Frank	MTN	1962,63,64
O'Neal, George	MTN	1945
Olefsky, Jerry	MTN	1962,63
Oliver, Graydon	MTN	2000,01
Ortiz, Hector	MTN	1987,88,89,90
Parker, Drew	MTN	1995
Parker, Jamal	MTN	1999,00,01,02
Pearne, Gary	MTN	1987,88,89,90
Pechous, Ed	MTN	1954
Philiotis, Greg	MTN	1985
Pilz, Clifford	MTN	1942
Puentes, Rey	MTN	1992
Ramey, Royce	MTN	1999,00
Randoll, Melvin	MTN	1946,47,48
Rich, William	MTN	1936,38

Riepma, Paul	MTN	1944,45
Riley, James	MTN	1960,61
Rosborough, Terrill	MTN	1968,69
Saikley, Frank	MTN	1941,42,43
Sarkary, Xerxes	MTN	1991
Schalin, Guy	MTN	1981
Schantz, Eric	MTN	1985,86
Schreiber, Ben	MTN	2000,01
Schroeder, Rod	MTN	1970,71,72
Schuder, John	MTN	1938
Schunk, Charles	MTN	1947,48
Schwartz, Kevin	MTN	1995,96,97
Schwarz, Robert	MTN	1939,40,41
Shapiro, Richard	MTN	1974,75,77
Shineflug, Bob	MTN	1963,64
Simons, Steve	MTN	1965,66
Sisson, John	MTN	1963,64,65
Snyder, Matthew	MTN	1997,98,99,00
Sommers, Scott	MTN	1979,80,81,82
Sontag, Gavin	MTN	1996,97,98,99
Staake, Donald	MTN	1944
Stafford, Bruce	MTN	1960,61,62
Stafford, Harold	MTN	1952,53
Steers, Fred	MTN	1946,47,48
Stewart, Dave	MTN	1953
Stolt, Phil	MTN	2001,02
Sutter, Jeremy	MTN	1994,95,96
Teply, Jakub	MTN	1996,97,98,99
Thatcher, Chris	MTN	1993
Thompson, Edwin	MTN	1967,68,69
Turek, Jerry	MTN	1994,95,96,97
Van Tine, James	MTN	1955,56,57
Velasco, Manny	MTN	1986,88,89
Von Spreckelsen, Ray	MTN	1942,46
Voss, George	MTN	1969
Wack, Rick	MTN	1970,71,72
Waddell, Barry	MTN	1981,83
Wagner, Mark	MTN	1977
Weaver, Robert	MTN	1943
Weinstein, David	MTN	1978
Weiss, Joe	MTN	1947,48
Weiss, Jon	MTN	1956
Westberg, Carey	MTN	1979
Wilson, Brian	MTN	2002
Woods, Conrad	MTN	1954,55
Wright, Jack	MTN	1935
Wurtzel, Frederic	MTN	1965,66,67
Yeaton, Edward	MTN	1937
Zeder, Nathan	MTN	1999,00,01,02
Zych, Jon	MTN	1991,93,94

Women's Track

Ania, Emma	WTR	2000
Angel, Katherine	WTR	1979,80,81,82
Anderson, Linda	WTR	1980,81
Aschoff, Laura	WTR	1999
Baine, Shayla	WTR	1988,89,90
Baker, Yolanda	WTR	1991,92,93
Balagtas, Lisa	WTR	1987,88,89
Bass, Rachel	WTR	1983
Bayne, Jessica	WTR	2002
Bearfield, Chequetta	WTR	1999,00,01,02
Benson, Lisa	WTR	1980
Beverly, Leticia	WTR	1986,87,88,89

Shayla Baine

Bodden, Shirley	WTR	1986,87,88
Bodey, Kimberly	WTR	1987,89
Brown, Jana	WTR	1980
Brown, Mekelayaie	WTR	1991,92
Bruene, Carol	WTR	1986,87
Buciarska, Joanna	WTR	1999
Buford, Tonja	WTR	1990,91,92,93
Burkett, Aspen	WTR	1995,96,98
Carr, Renee	WTR	1986,87,88,90
Carver, Dorothy	WTR	1979,80
Christopher, Amy	WTR	1998
Conda, Rolanda	WTR	1985,86
Corbett, Carmel	WTR	1992,93,94,95
Crutchfield-Tyus, Terra	WTR	1993,94,95,96
Dale, Charlene	WTR	1980,81,82
Des Enfants, Laura	WTR	1979
Dickerson, Marianne	WTR	1981,82
Dietzen, Cecelia	WTR	2000,01
Drewes, Elizabeth	WTR	1979
Dunlap, Kim	WTR	1983,84,85,86
Dunnavan, Lyndsey	WTR	2000,01
Elsen, Virginia G.	WTR	1982
Estes, Carolyn	WTR	1999,01,02
Felicien, Perdita	WTR	2000,01,02
Fernandez, Juana	WTR	1985,86

Perdita Felicien

Gia Lewis

Fonzino, Danielle	WTR	1996,98
Ford, Mary	WTR	1981,82,83
Frakes, Erin	WTR	2002
Fulcher, Victoria	WTR	1987,88
Garrett, Rebekah	WTR	1992,94,95,96
Gentry, Gretchen	WTR	1984
Gilliean, Allisa	WTR	1995,96
Glade, Jayne	WTR	1981,82,83,84
Grant, Stacy Ann	WTR	1996,97,98,99
Grier, Gretchen Y.	WTR	1982,83
Greiner, Sue	WTR	1983
Gross, Samantha	WTR	1992,93
Gulick, Catherine	WTR	1979
Hackett, Colleen	WTR	1983,84,85
Hall, Pamela	WTR	1982,83,84
Hansen, Michelle	WTR	1991
Harpell, Danielle	WTR	1989,90,91,92
Harrison, Yvonne	WTR	1996,97,98
Hawkins, Leslie L.	WTR	1987
Heise, Jennifer	WTR	1995
Heitz, Angie	WTR	1984,85
Helfer, Cheryl	WTR	1979
Henry, Ann	WTR	1985,86
Hilmersson, Marie	WTR	2002
Howard, Gillian	WTR	1991

Collinus Newsome

Huffman, Shannon	WTR	1994,95,96
Hunt, Amber	WTR	2000,01
Hunziker, Janae	WTR	1979,81
Johnson, Janelle	WTR	1993,94
Jones, Bernette	WTR	1991,92
Kaiser, Becky	WTR	1979,80,81,82
Kallur, Jenny	WTR	2001,02
Kallur, Susanna	WTR	2001,02
Kelley, Benita	WTR	1995,96,97,98
Knop, Nancy	WTR	1979
Kopko, Amy	WTR	1980,81,82,83
Koster, Bridget	WTR	1985
Kraiss, Katherine	WTR	1995
Kuenne, Jill	WTR	1979,80,81
Latimer, Aleisha	WTR	1998,99,00,01
Lawrence, Cynthia	WTR	1987,88,89,90
Lantis, Julie	WTR	1983,84
Lewis, Gia	WTR	2000,01
Locascio, Sharon	WTR	1987,88,89
Long, Kelly	WTR	1980
Lottes, Jan	WTR	1983
Madsen, Wendy	WTR	1991,92,93
Marine, Jenny	WTR	1996,97
Martin, Lindsay	WTR	1998,99
Martin, Lyria	WTR	1997,98,99,00
Mason, Melissa	WTR	1982
Mastoris, Helen	WTR	1988,89,90
Mazikowski, Carol	WTR	1980,81,82,83
Mayer, Patricia	WTR	1979
McClatchey, Angela	WTR	1986,87,88,89
McGlone, Cathy	WTR	1981
McNee, Kelly	WTR	1983,84,85,86
Mendozza, Tara	WTR	1997,98,99,01
Meyer, Jordana	WTR	2000,01,02
Meyle, Wendy J.	WTR	1981,82,83,84
Miles, Kathy	WTR	1980
Miles, Donna	WTR	1982,85
Miller, Christine	WTR	1991,92
Mindcock, Laura	WTR	1994,95,96
Mondie-Milner, Celena	WTR	1987,88,89,90
Morris, Karen Jo	WTR	1992,94
Morris, Kathy Ann	WTR	1992,94
Moss, Tracy	WTR	2000,01
Moyer, Anita	WTR	1979
Neverstitch, Lisa	WTR	1979,80
Newsome, Collinus	WTR	1995,96,97,98
Nicholson, Candace	WTR	1998,99
Nuhsbaum, Tanja	WTR	1991,92
O'Brien, Kelly	WTR	1989,90,92
Oldham, Yvonne	WTR	1983,84,85,86
Oshinowo, Adeoti	WTR	1999,00,01,02
Palm, Stacy	WTR	1987
Pannier, Kathy	WTR	1980,81,82
Pickett, Shanna	WTR	2002
Piotrowski, Mary	WTR	1992
Plummer, Lisa	WTR	1980,81,82
Ponder, Tisha	WTR	1997,98,99,00
Powell, Shontel	WTR	1998,99
Pulcher, Victoria J.	WTR	1987
Richards, Kerry Ann	WTR	1996,98,99,00
Riggins, Pat	WTR	1980
Riley, Crystal	WTR	2000,01,02
Riley, Dawn	WTR	1993,94,95,96
Rimar, Jeanne C.	WTR	1993

Rogers, Rhea A.	WTR	1981
Russell, Donna	WTR	1987,88,89,90
Sabin, Beth	WTR	1980
Sanders, Hope	WTR	1992,93,94,95
Schwab, Jennifer	WTR	1992,93
Scigousky, Brooke	WTR	1995
Shimmon, Lauren	WTR	2002
Simmering, Laura	WTR	1989,91,92,93
Smith, Deborah	WTR	1988,89
Smith, Suzanne	WTR	1977,79
Smith, Terika	WTR	1991,92
Speer, Lindsay	WTR	1997,98
Sterneman, Ruth	WTR	1985,86
Stetson, Deborah	WTR	1984,85
Stecyk, Amy	WTR	1979
Stoltz, Terry	WTR	1987
Stone, Melissa	WTR	1989
Straza, Melissa	WTR	1987,88
Thomas, Althea	WTR	1989,90
Thurmon, Kimberly	WTR	1991,92
Tiffin, Donna	WTR	1977
Tochihara, Tama	WTR	1991,92,93,94
Tomlinson, Amy	WTR	1992,93,94
Tweedy, Jennifer	WTR	1990,91,92,93
Vogel, Margaret	WTR	1982,84,85
Wacaser, Jan	WTR	1980,82
Walling, Rochelle	WTR	1996
Walters, Kathy	WTR	1979
Walters, Vicki	WTR	1983
Waldinger, Beth	WTR	1982
Ward, Cheryl	WTR	1982,83,84,85
Washington, Bev	WTR	1976,77,78
Weber, Nora	WTR	1994,95,96,98
Welch, Wendy	WTR	1992
Werkowski, Amy	WTR	1987,88,89
Weygand, Tricia	WTR	1994,95
Whitman, Nicole	WTR	2002
Williams, Allison	WTR	2002
Williams, Camee	WTR	1999,00,01,02
Williams, Katherine	WTR	1991,92,93,94
Williams, Tonya	WTR	1993,94,95,96
Withrow, Loretta	WTR	1989,90
Yonke, Martha	WTR	1979
Zimmerman, Beth	WTR	1982

Men's Track

Abbot, Richard R.	MTR	1943
Abbott, David	MTR	1928,29
Adams, Alfred O.	MTR	1933,34
Agase, Louis	MTR	1945
Aihara, Henry K.	MTR	1945
Ainsworth, Walter W.	MTR	1912
Akers, Todd A.	MTR	1989
Alberts, Dewey V.	MTR	1921
Alexander, Joe	MTR	1996
Allen, James C.	MTR	1893
Allen, William	MTR	1974
Allman, John C.	MTR	1920,21
Allman, Omar L.	MTR	1933
Ames, Waldo B.	MTR	1915,16,17
Andersen, Harry E.	MTR	1947,48,49
Anderson, Samuel	MTR	1952
Angel, Wendell W.	MTR	1981
Angelo, Louis	MTR	1991,93

Kerry Ann Richards

Angier, Milton S.	MTR	1922,23,24
App, Benjamin R.	MTR	1973,74,75
Applequist, J. G.	MTR	1899
Aranda, Ezequiel	MTR	1891
Armstrong, Edward	MTR	1988
Armstrong, James W.	MTR	1893
Armstrong, Jay L.	MTR	1898
Armstrong, Sherman	MTR	1998,99,00,01
Arnold, Mark D.	MTR	1982,83,84,85
Arning, Louis H.	MTR	1932
Ascher, Vernon W.	MTR	1922
Ashley, Robert L.	MTR	1937,38,39
Asper, Orville W.	MTR	1930
Avery, Mark E.	MTR	1975,77,78
Axelrod, David J.	MTR	1974,75
Ayoub, David M.	MTR	1978,79,80,81
Ayres, Robert B.	MTR	1922,23,24
Baader, Richard P.	MTR	1982,83
Baietto, Michael E.	MTR	1972,73,74,75
Bailey, Donald	MTR	1940,41
Baird, William	MTR	1901
Bales, Edwards J.	MTR	1926
Banschbach, Edward A.	MTR	1893,94,95
Bareither, Charles	MTR	1968
Barmes, Andy	MTR	1982,83

Ben Beyers

Lee Bridges

Barnes, George H.	MTR	1925,26,27
Barnum, Robert V.	MTR	1948,50,51
Baron, Dan	MTR	1974
Barrett, Jesse L.	MTR	1905,06,07
Barron, James L.	MTR	1911
Barron, Oliver D.	MTR	1931
Barth, George B.	MTR	1978
Bates, Charles R.	MTR	1903
Bauer, John R.	MTR	1953,54
Bauer, Craig	MTR	1985
Baughman, V. Lynn	MTR	1934,35
Bear, Ernest R.	MTR	1900,02,03
Beary, Matt	MTR	1992,93,94,95
Beastall, Theodore W.	MTR	1959,60
Beck, H. Clint	MTR	1909
Becker, David L.	MTR	1963,64,65
Bedell, David T.	MTR	1946,47,48
Beebe, Charles D.	MTR	1894
Behan, Paul F.	MTR	1948
Behrensmeyer, George	MTR	1891,92
Beile, Charles W.	MTR	1943,47
Bekermeier, Herbert W.	MTR	1943
Bell, Oscar C.	MTR	1901
Bell, Richard	MTR	1973
Belnap, Nuel D.	MTR	1912,13
Belting, Charles H.	MTR	1911,12

Steve Bridges

Benberry, Hershel	MTR	1969,70,71
Bennett, Basil	MTR	1916,17,20
Benso, Bryan M.	MTR	1987,88
Bergstrom, Hugo E.	MTR	1927
Berschet, Marvin W.	MTR	1950,51,52
Bertelsman, George A.	MTR	1929,31
Best, David H.	MTR	1944,45
Beyers, Ben	MTR	1993,94,95
Biebinger, Isaac N.	MTR	1896,97
Bila, Michael S.	MTR	1984,86,87
Birks, John M.	MTR	1919
Bissell, Lonnie	MTR	1980
Blanchard, John	MTR	1968,69
Blanheim, Melvin L.	MTR	1962,63,64
Blankley, Alfred R.	MTR	1905
Blom, G. Peter	MTR	1945
Blomfeldt, Allen A.	MTR	1907
Blount, Walter P.	MTR	1919
Bobert, Dave	MTR	1968,69,70
Bolander, Harold B.	MTR	1912,13,14
Booker, Harry G.	MTR	1970,71,72
Borden, W. T.	MTR	1899
Boswell Jr., Thomas E.	MTR	1947
Bowe, Christopher L.	MTR	1986,87,88
Bowers, James S.	MTR	1958,59,60
Boyd, Edward P.	MTR	1899,00,01
Boyd, George E.	MTR	1896
Bradley, James C.	MTR	1897,98,99
Brede, Erwin C.	MTR	1921
Brenneman, G. Bruce	MTR	1946
Bridges, Dave	MTR	1968
Bridges, Jan M.	MTR	1964,65
Bridges, Lee A.	MTR	1986,87,88,89
Bridges, Michael R.	MTR	1975
Bridges, Steve	MTR	1990,92,93,94
Briggs, Thomas	MTR	1949
Brode, Luther D.	MTR	1893,94
Brooks, Arvella	MTR	1990,91
Brooks, Kevin U.	MTR	1984,85,86,87
Brooks, David	MTR	1974
Brooks, Richard	MTR	1974,75,76
Brookins, Mitchell	MTR	1981,83
Brown, David E.	MTR	1919,20,21
Brown, Edward W.	MTR	1908,10
Brown, Hamilton A.	MTR	1989,90
Brown, Joseph A.	MTR	1937
Brown, Kenneth	MTR	1942
Brown, Kenneth	MTR	1959,60
Brown, Lewis	MTR	1899,00
Brown, Park L.	MTR	1939,40,41
Brown, Wallace W.	MTR	1919
Brown, William D.	MTR	1959,60,61
Brownell, Dean G.	MTR	1923,24,25
Brubaker, James C.	MTR	1967,68,69
Bruder, Henry L.	MTR	1937
Brundage, M. D.	MTR	1899,00
Brundage, Avery	MTR	1908,09
Brunton, Richard W.	MTR	1936,37,38
Buchanan Jr., Gordon	MTR	1920
Buchheit, George C.	MTR	1919
Bullard, Edward W.	MTR	1911,13
Bullard, Robert I.	MTR	1895,96
Bunning, Walter F.	MTR	1928,29
Burch, Clarence	MTR	1967,68,69

Burgener, David B.	MTR	1979,71,72
Burgess, Oscar W.	MTR	1916
Burghardt, Charles A.	MTR	1945
Burgoon, David W.	MTR	1916
Burke, Ralph	MTR	1912,14
Burke, William H.	MTR	1894,95
Burkhart, George H.	MTR	1929
Burleigh, C. H.	MTR	1898
Burns, Joesph K.	MTR	1910,11
Burroughs, Wilbur G.	MTR	1905,06,07
Burton, Charles	MTR	1999,00,01,02
Burwash, Arthur E.	MTR	1911
Bush, Alexander T.	MTR	1916
Buster, William E.	MTR	1945,46,48,49
Butt, Harley M.	MTR	1912,13,14
Byrne, Lee	MTR	1896,97,98
Cabeen, Joshua	MTR	1897
Cadwallader, Douglas P.	MTR	1904
Caiazza, Theodore	MTR	1957,58
Caldwell, Randolph	MTR	1917
Calisch, Richard W.	MTR	1950,51,52
Campbell, Alvin C.	MTR	1988,89
Campbell, Laverne C.	MTR	1944
Cannon, Ward C.	MTR	1921,22
Capelle, Mark	MTR	1982
Carius, Allen B.	MTR	1962,63,64
Carlson, Herbert N. R.	MTR	1922
Carper, Robert J.	MTR	1977,78,79
Carr, Robert J.	MTR	1928,29,30
Carrison, Henry C.	MTR	1931
Carrithers, Ira T.	MTR	1905,07
Carroll, Charles	MTR	1918,19
Carroll, Robert C.	MTR	1932,33,34
Carson, Paul H.	MTR	1932
Carter, Dale	MTR	1923,24
Carter, William S.	MTR	1915,16
Case Jr., John R.	MTR	1912,13
Caskey, George R.	MTR	1919
Casner, Sidney	MTR	1913
Cave, James A.	MTR	1929,30,31
Cayou, F. M.	MTR	1900,01,02
Celaya, Robert	MTR	1931
Chambers, Alan R.	MTR	1928
Chambers, Robert L.	MTR	1929,30
Chandler, George A.	MTR	1922
Chatten, Melville C.	MTR	1893,94
Cheney, Howard L.	MTR	1912
Cherot, Anthony	MTR	1969,70
Christiansen, Harold A.	MTR	1932,33
Claar, Elmer A.	MTR	1913,14
Clancy, Timothy	MTR	1987,88,89,90
Clarida, T. W.	MTR	1915
Clark, A. C.	MTR	1892,93,94,95
Clark, Howard	MTR	1894,95,96,97
Clarke, Edwin B.	MTR	1890
Clarke, Frederick W.	MTR	1890
Clayton, C. M.	MTR	1899
Claypool, Mark J.	MTR	1978,79,80,81
Clinton, Edgar M.	MTR	1896,97
Cobb, Laurence J.	MTR	1970,71,72
Coffeen, Harry C.	MTR	1895,96
Colbrese, William L.	MTR	1969
Coleman, Delbert L.	MTR	1959,60
Coleman, Richard A.	MTR	1950,51,52

Mark Claypool

Collins, John H.	MTR	1922,23
Cook, David F.	MTR	1932,33,34
Cook, James W.	MTR	1892
Cook, William D.	MTR	1947,48
Cooley, William M.	MTR	1945,46
Cope, Walter A.	MTR	1911,12,13
Corley, Joseph W.	MTR	1952,53,54
Cornelius, William	MTR	1970
Correll, Walter K.	MTR	1942
Cortis, Frederic B.	MTR	1911,12,13
Costar, Lloyd	MTR	1912
Coughlin, John A.	MTR	1923
Courter, Anson O.	MTR	1927
Coxworth, James L.	MTR	1974,75,76
Crane, Robert L.	MTR	1942,43
Crumpton, Robert	MTR	1994
Cryer, Henry	MTR	1951,52,55
Cullinan, Duane A.	MTR	1935,36,37
Culp, John D.	MTR	1914,15,16
Cummings, Barton A.	MTR	1933
Currier, Donald E.	MTR	1914,15
Cutter, Scott C.	MTR	1893
Dadant, Louis C.	MTR	1899,00

Doug Dossey

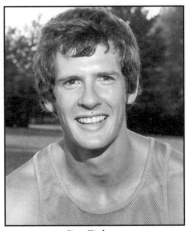

Jim Eicken

Dorian Green

Dailey, Bo	MTR	1993,96
Davies, Richard O.	MTR	1965
Davis, George F.	MTR	1893
Davis, James T.	MTR	1960
Decker, Gene W.	MTR	1950,51
deBeers, James	MTR	1989,90,91,92
DeLong, Edward	MTR	1956,57
DeMoss, Clarence	MTR	1953
DePuy, Orval C.	MTR	1905,06
Deuchler, Gustave H.	MTR	1918
Dickinson Jr., Charles F.	MTR	1930,31
Dickinson, Richard J.	MTR	1893
Dickinson, Roger F.	MTR	1926
Dickison, Marc	MTR	1994
Dickson, Kerry	MTR	1980,81,82,84
Diefenthaler, Robert J.	MTR	1937,38,39
Diettrich, Henry J.	MTR	1942
Dill, Arthur W.	MTR	1893
Dillavou, Lanny D.	MTR	1986
Dillon, Roy H.	MTR	1897
Dintelmann, Robert H.	MTR	1955,56,57
Dlesk, David C.	MTR	1979,80
Domantay, Gregory	MTR	1983
Donoghue, R. C.	MTR	1894,99
Donohoe, Philip H.	MTR	1920,21
Dossey, Doug	MTR	1992,93,94,95

Pharoah Gay

Dowling, Ralph	MTR	1944
Downey, William H.	MTR	1948,49
Downs, H. Burton	MTR	1938,39,40
Downs, Robert B.	MTR	1947,48,49,50
Dozier, Benjamin A.	MTR	1970,71,72
Drake, Elmo S.	MTR	1911
Drake, Waldo H.	MTR	1911
Dufresne, Jacques A.	MTR	1933,34,35
Dunbar, Harry B.	MTR	1903
Duncan, Earl J.	MTR	1931
Duncan, James F.	MTR	1926
Dundy, Michael W.	MTR	1962,63
Dunham, N. C.	MTR	1906,07
Dunn, Clarence L.	MTR	1942,43,47
Dunning, Frank W.	MTR	1905,07
Durham, Theo	MTR	1995,96
Durkin, John F.	MTR	1969,70,71
Durkin, Michael K.	MTR	1972,73,74,75
Durland, Clyde E.	MTR	1903,04
Dusenberry, Paul B.	MTR	1920,21
Dykstra, Greg	MTR	1968,69,70
Dykstra, Larry R.	MTR	1970,71,72
Eason, Ryan	MTR	1999,2001
East, Warren E.	MTR	1910
Eastin, Edward M.	MTR	1966
Eckert, Vernon M.	MTR	1934,35
Eckburg, David	MTR	1994,95
Eddleman,Thomas(Dike)	MTR	1943,46,47,48,49
Edwards, Charles F.	MTR	1940,42
Edwards, James F.	MTR	1967,68,69
Edwards, Steve	MTR	1973
Ehizuelen, Charlton O.	MTR	1974,75,76,77
Ehlers, Norman F.	MTR	1958
Eicken, James H.	MTR	1976,77,78,79
Elder, R. M.	MTR	1903
Elders, Gerald W.	MTR	1940,41
Elliott, John A	MTR	1984,85,86,87
Ely, Warren G.	MTR	1947,48
Emery, Robert S.	MTR	1918,19,20
Emrich, Jon B.	MTR	1982
Enck, James A.	MTR	1964,65,66
English, E. C.	MTR	1899,00
Enochs, Claude D.	MTR	1896,97,98
Enochs, Delbert R.	MTR	1898
Estes, Raymond A.	MTR	1975,76,77,78
Etnyre, Roy E.	MTR	1930,32
Evans Jr., Harry	MTR	1923,24,25
Evans, Paul B.	MTR	1930,31
Evans, Robert H.	MTR	1893,94,95
Evers, Walter A.	MTR	1940
Fairfield, David	MTR	1927,28
Fairweather, Charles	MTR	1903
Fasules, James W.	MTR	1971,72,73,74
Feldman, Ed	MTR	1968
Fell, Milan T.	MTR	1925,26
Fessenden, Douglas A.	MTR	1922,24
Fessenden, Ralph J.	MTR	1952,53,54,55
Ffitch, Peter B.	MTR	1982
Field, David E.	MTR	1917
Fields, David W.	MTR	1921
Finney, Damon W.	MTR	1975
Finney, Bruce	MTR	1972
Fiore, Phillip J.	MTR	1977
Fish, Julian L.	MTR	1914

Fisher, Ralph M.	MTR	1933
Fitch, Horatio M.	MTR	1922,23
Flannery, James M.	MTR	1977,79
Floto, E. C.	MTR	1903
Floyd, Thomas	MTR	1951,52,53
Flynn, Thomas F.	MTR	1893
Foreman, Paul L.	MTR	1959,60,61
Forman, Hamilton M.	MTR	1908
Foskett, Roy M.	MTR	1903,04,05
Foster, Alfred B.	MTR	1893
Foster, Duane	MTR	1958
Foster, Dale W.	MTR	1952,53,54,55
Fournier, Josh	MTR	2002
Fouts, L. H.	MTR	1892,94,95
Frandsen, Lee R.	MTR	1959
Franks, Willard G.	MTR	1946
Franz, Frederick W.	MTR	1977,78,79,80
Frary, C. Deane	MTR	1936,37,38
Frazier Jr., Leotis K.	MTR	1956
Freeland, Chesley B.	MTR	1909
Freese, John A.	MTR	1902
Frey, Hugh W.	MTR	1935
Fritz, Timothy	MTR	1984
Froom, Albert N.	MTR	1906
Fruin, Leon T.	MTR	1930
Fuller, Michael K.	MTR	1971,72
Fullerton, Thomas C.	MTR	1943,44
Fultz, Duane	MTR	1940
Furness, Carl N.	MTR	1921
Gage, John C.	MTR	1930,31
Gaines, Harry E.	MTR	1936,37,38
Gale, Eli P.	MTR	1901
Gallo, Michael P.	MTR	1964
Gantz, Howard S.	MTR	1915,17
Gardiner, Lion	MTR	1907,08
Gardiner, Robert P.	MTR	1918,19
Gardner, Robert	MTR	1970
Garrett, Richard P.	MTR	1897,99,00
Gassmann, Neal M.	MTR	1990
Gault, Ben	MTR	1999
Gay, Pharoah	MTR	1994,95,96
Gentry, Derrick L.	MTR	1981,82,83,84
Gerard, Kenneth C.	MTR	1928
Gerrish, William G.	MTR	1965,66
Gibson, Robert L.	MTR	1978,79,80
Gibson, Charles	MTR	1994,95,96,97
Gilbert, Dwight A.	MTR	1988,89
Gilbertson, Hunter	MTR	1950,51
Gilkerson, Thomas J.	MTR	1904,05
Gill, John S.	MTR	1936
Gillon, Randy	MTR	1997,98,99
Gladding, Donald K.	MTR	1942,43
Glass, Rufus C.	MTR	1928
Glesne, Kurt	MTR	2002
Glosecki, Andy R.	MTR	1936,38
Goelitz, William H.	MTR	1913,14,15
Gonzalez, Joseph A.	MTR	1951,52
Gonzalez, Marcelino	MTR	1943,44,45,46
Goodell Jr., Warren F.	MTR	1943
Goodspeed, Wilbur F.	MTR	1901
Goodspeed, A. C.	MTR	1903
Goretzke, Fritz A.	MTR	1964,65,66
Gould, William C.	MTR	1931
Gould, Maurice S.	MTR	1942

Gow, Nick	MTR	1999,00,01,02
Grady, Bernard	MTR	2000,01,02
Gragg, George L.	MTR	1938,39
Graham, Paul J.	MTR	1909,10,11
Grant, Wendell E.	MTR	1962,63,64
Greanias, Evon C.	MTR	1943
Grear, Sidney F.	MTR	1905,06
Greathouse, Forrest G.	MTR	1926
Green, Dorian	MTR	1994,95,96,97
Grieve, Robert S.	MTR	1935,36,37
Gross II, Richard G.	MTR	1970,71,72
Groves, James C.	MTR	1904
Guercio, Anthony M.	MTR	1983,84
Gunn, Charles A.	MTR	1890,91,92
Haas, Brian L.	MTR	1988,89,90,91
Hackett, Theodore N.	MTR	1936,37
Haisley, Ernle	MTR	1958,59
Hale, Clyde S.	MTR	1940,41
Hale, Hugh K.	MTR	1926,28
Haley, Arthur F.	MTR	1893
Halik Jr., Edwin J.	MTR	1968,69
Hall, Melvin E.	MTR	1923,24
Hall, Raymond T.	MTR	1927
Hall, Richard	MTR	1968
Hall, Seymour E.	MTR	1895

Bannon Hayes

Earl Jenkins

Halle, David A.	MTR	1985,86,87,88
Hamer, Charlton P.	MTR	1985,86,87,88
Hamer, Paul E.	MTR	1944,45
Hamlett, Robert T.	MTR	1927,28
Hammitt, Andrew B.	MTR	1913,14,15
Hammond, James	MTR	1960,61,62
Hampton, Keith	MTR	1930,31,32
Hanley, James T.	MTR	1908,09,10
Hanssen, G. A.	MTR	1889
Hanlon, James A.	MTR	1973,74,75,76
Harford, Douglas	MTR	1965,66,67
Harford, Josh	MTR	2002
Harney, J. M.	MTR	1901
Harper, Bueford R.	MTR	1929,30
Harper, Gordon K.	MTR	1929
Harris, Harold E.	MTR	1958,59,60
Harris, Mark	MTR	1976
Harshbarger, Terry L.	MTR	1962,63
Hart, William W.	MTR	1914
Harts, D. H.	MTR	1899
Hartman, William H.	MTR	1965,66
Haviland, William D.	MTR	1939
Hayes, Bannon D.	MTR	1986,87,88,89
Hayes, Joseph C.	MTR	1945

Tyrone Jones

Hedgcock, Frank M.	MTR	1956,57,58
Heinsen, Norman K.	MTR	1928
Heitmeyer, Troy A.	MTR	1988
Hellmich, Hudson A.	MTR	1932,33,34
Henderson, Fred	MTR	1912,13,14
Henson, Eric	MTR	1993,94,95,96
Henry, Smith T.	MTR	1901,02
Herrick, G. Wirt	MTR	1909,10,11
Herrick, Lyle G.	MTR	1899,02,03
Hill, Aaron	MTR	1932
Hill, Cliff	MTR	1977,81
Hill, Gregory H.	MTR	1982,83,84,85
Hill, Sam H.	MTR	1921,22,23
Hiller, William C.	MTR	1952,53
Hills, Otto R.	MTR	19931
Hinkle, Robert S.	MTR	1944,48,49,50
Hinton, Larry	MTR	1964
Hinman, Lawrence D.	MTR	1908
Hoagland, John C.	MTR	1897
Hoagland, John K.	MTR	1895,97,98,99
Hobble, Arthur C.	MTR	1899,00
Hobbs, Glenn M.	MTR	1889,90,91,92
Hobbs, Tim	MTR	2002
Hohman, Elmo P.	MTR	1914,15,16
Holbrook, Michael	MTR	1963,64
Hollingsworth, Elbert R.	MTR	1931,32
Homoly, Andy	MTR	1992
Hoover, H. Harold	MTR	1899
Houston, Edward N.	MTR	1960
Howard, Daniel O.	MTR	1920
Howard, Glen	MTR	1992,95
Howland, Dennis R.	MTR	1969,70,71
Howse, Kenneth R.	MTR	1969,70,71
Hughes, Eric L.	MTR	1946
Hughes, Seth M.	MTR	1923,24,25
Hugill, William	MTR	1939
Hull, W. H.	MTR	1912
Hunsley, Lorne E.	MTR	1924,25
Hunter, James A.	MTR	1911,12,13
Huntley, Osman H.	MTR	1936
Husted, Guy H.	MTR	1913
Husted, Merle R.	MTR	1916,17
Huston, Paul E.	MTR	1948
Hutchinson, Scott R.	MTR	1987
Hutchinson, Thomas W.	MTR	1978
Imrie, Earl D.	MTR	1958
Inch, Christopher A.	MTR	1988
Irons, Louis M.	MTR	1947,48,49,50
Jackson, Trenton	MTR	1963,64,65
Jacobs, Jeffrey P.	MTR	1983,84,85,86
Jacobson, John D.	MTR	1986,87,88
Jarboe, Marcus	MTR	1993,95
Jenkins, Earl A.	MTR	1990,91,92,93
Jenkins, Edwin M.	MTR	1906,07,08
Jenkins, Jerome J.	MTR	1986,87,88,89
Jenner, Kyle W.	MTR	1982
Jennings, Scott A.	MTR	1981,83
Jewsbury, Walter M.	MTR	1949,50,53
Jirele, Jeffrey S.	MTR	1976,77
Johnson, Clarence E.	MTR	1898
Johnson, A. M.	MTR	1900
Johnson, Franklin P.	MTR	1922,23,24
Johnson, Gerald P.	MTR	1950

Johnson, Joseph	MTR	1944,45
Jones, Anthony M.	MTR	1991,93,94
Jones, Bruce L.	MTR	1975
Jones, Chris	MTR	1997,98
Jones, Gordon E.	MTR	1934
Jones, Tyrone	MTR	1997,98,99,00
Jones, W. Ray	MTR	1908,09,10
Jones, William N.	MTR	1976
Jonsson, Karl	MTR	1955,56,57
Jordan, Arthur I.	MTR	1910
Jumper, T.J.	MTR	1998,99,00
Kabel, Robert L.	MTR	1953
Kaczkowski, Thomas H.	MTR	1974,75
Kaemerer, David W.	MTR	1972,73,74
Kamm, Albert C.	MTR	1933,34
Kamin, Mike	MTR	1994,95
Kaplan, Bruce S.	MTR	1972
Kariher, Harry C.	MTR	1898,99
Karkow, Waldemar	MTR	1947,48
Karnopp, E. B.	MTR	1903
Kats, Jerry H.	MTR	1951
Kay, Michael	MTR	1970
Kearney, Thomas	MTR	1974,75
Keator, Edward O.	MTR	1898,99,00,02
Keifer, Martin	MTR	2001,02
Keller, Charles I.	MTR	1938
Keller, Thomas O.	MTR	1974,75
Kelley, Jon	MTR	1990
Kelley, Robert L.	MTR	1942,43,44,45
Kenney, Wendell L.	MTR	1920
Kennicott, Robert M.	MTR	1933
Kerr, George E.	MTR	1958,59,60
Ketzle, Henry B.	MTR	1901,02
Keys, Melvin	MTR	1983,84,85
Kienlen, Donald L.	MTR	1940,41
Kimmel, Lyman B.	MTR	1925,28
Kimball, C. B.	MTR	1891
Kincaid, Brian V.	MTR	1990,91,92
Kinsey, Daniel C.	MTR	1924,25
Kirkpatrick, John W.	MTR	1906
Kivela, Paul	MTR	1984,86
Klima, Matt	MTR	1995,96,97,98
Kline, William G.	MTR	1903,05,06
Kloepper, Victor F. H.	MTR	1922
Knight, William A.	MTR	1933
Knight, E. J.	MTR	1905
Knox, J. H.	MTR	1905
Knuffman, Joe	MTR	1997,98
Kocian, Frederick M.	MTR	1981,82
Koenig, Thomas E.	MTR	1964,65
Kolasa, Richard J.	MTR	1987,89,90,91
Koonz, John C.	MTR	1924
Kopf, Frank A.	MTR	1912
Koers, Marko	MTR	1992,93,94,95
Koster, Mark R.	MTR	1969,70,71
Krainik, Anthony	MTR	1978,79,80,81
Kratz, J. P.	MTR	1899,00
Krause, Dennis W.	MTR	1966
Kreidler, Chester J.	MTR	1917,18
Kriegsmann, Michael	MTR	1990,93,94
Krivec, John J.	MTR	1939,40
Kronforst, John	MTR	2000,01,02
Kubala, Tom	MTR	1973

Michael Lehmann

Kueker, Brian A.	MTR	1975,76,77,78
Kusz, William	MTR	1937
La Badie, Lee D.	MTR	1970,71,72
La Frank, Samuel E.	MTR	1971,72,73
Lally, J. Richard	MTR	1963,64
Lamb, Courtney	MTR	1996,97,98,99
Lamb Jr., Lawton B.	MTR	1950,51,52
Lamoreax, John R.	MTR	1967,68
Landmeier, Vernon O.	MTR	1934
Lang, Alvin L.	MTR	1917,18
Langston, Donnell	MTR	1972
Lansche, Oral A.	MTR	1915
Larson, Lyman B.	MTR	1963
LasCasas, Vince A.	MTR	1952
Lasley, Matt	MTR	2000
Lattimore, John A.	MTR	1958,59,60
Lawrence, C. G.	MTR	1897,98,99
Lawton, Brad	MTR	1992,93
Laz, Donald R.	MTR	1949,50,51
Laz, Douglas L.	MTR	1976,77
Lazear, Weston B.	MTR	1907
Leach, William F.	MTR	1963
Leck, Walter C.	MTR	1932
LeCrone, Armand J.	MTR	1959,60,61
LeCrone, Charles M.	MTR	1958,59,60

Rob Mango

Scott McClennan

Lee, Omar C.	MTR	1928
Lehmann, Jeffery G.	MTR	1983,84,85
Lehmann, Michael H.	MTR	1979,80,81,82
Lehmann, William	MTR	1936,38
Leigh, William L.	MTR	1979,80
Lenington, Ernest	MTR	1931,32,33
Lenzini, James R.	MTR	1978,79,80,81
Lenzini, Robert E.	MTR	1952
Leo, Herbert T.	MTR	1910,11,12
Leuchtmann, Joseph W.	MTR	1986,87
Leuthold, Donald W.	MTR	1947,48,49,50
Levanti, Louis	MTR	1946
Lewis, Charles M.	MTR	1892,93,94,95,96
Lewis, Kenneth S.	MTR	1918
Lewis, William M.	MTR	1940,41,42
Lifvendahl, Richard A.	MTR	1919
Lindall, Fred H.	MTR	1931,32
Lindberg, Edward F. J.	MTR	1906,07,08,09
Linde, Gerald H.	MTR	1924
Lindley, Jake	MTR	1999,2001
Line, Harold E.	MTR	1932
Lloyd, Brandon	MTR	2000
Lloyd, R. C.	MTR	1901
Lohr, Lane	MTR	1984,85,86,87

Daren McDonough

Long, Harold D.	MTR	1932
Long, Troy L.	MTR	1901,05
Loughman, Philip G.	MTR	1971
Louis, Benjamin E.	MTR	1966
Luker, Thomas P.	MTR	1956,57
Lundeen, Jeffery	MTR	1964,65
Lyon, Daniel R.	MTR	1926,27,28
MacIntyre, James	MTR	1965
Mackay, J. J.	MTR	1904,05,06
Maddux, Scott	MTR	1992
Mail, Isaac P.	MTR	1941,42,43
Makeever, Samuel J.	MTR	1924,25,30
Malz, Peter J.	MTR	1951
Mango, Robert J.	MTR	1970,71,72,73
Mann, Arthur R.	MTR	1895
Marchese, Thomas	MTR	2001
Marczewski, Jeff	MTR	1981,82
Maris, Ronald W.	MTR	1957
Marley, James A.	MTR	1903,05
Martin, John D.	MTR	1946
Martin, Lorenzo E.	MTR	1956
Martin, Robert W.	MTR	1899,00,01
Marzulo, Sam C.	MTR	1923,24
Mason, Arthur H.	MTR	1914,15,16
Mason, Richard W.	MTR	1958,59
Masterson, Daniel	MTR	1966
Masterson, Donald J.	MTR	1966
Mathers, Manley B.	MTR	1913
Mathis, William	MTR	1946,47
Matter Jr., Herbert J.	MTR	1942,43,47
Maxwell, John R.	MTR	1893
May, William W.	MTR	1906,07,08,09
Maynard, Eugene E.	MTR	1952,53,54
Mazur, Dan	MTR	1994,95
McBride, Willis B.	MTR	1893
McCaskrin, Henry M.	MTR	1892,93,94
McClennan, Scott	MTR	1999,00,01
McClure, L. Milton	MTR	1936
McCord, Ralph N.	MTR	1908,09,10
McCown, Wilbur M.	MTR	1938,39,40
McCroy, Kendall	MTR	1999,00,01,02
McCulley, Daniel M.	MTR	1980,81
McCulley, C. T.	MTR	1903,04
McDermont, Verne A.	MTR	1929,30,31
McDonald-Ashford, George	MTR	1999
McDonough, Daren	MTR	1993,94,95
McElfresh, Fred M.	MTR	1893,94
McElwee Jr., Ermel J.	MTR	1961,62
McElwee Sr., Ermel J.	MTR	1926,27,28
McGinnis, Gordon F.	MTR	1921,22
McGraw, Arthur C.	MTR	1936
McHose, Joseph C.	MTR	1924
McKeever, Donald	MTR	1927
McKenley, Herbert H.	MTR	1946,47
McKeown, John L.	MTR	1913,14,15
McKinney, Norman	MTR	1917
McKown, Robert W.	MTR	1956,57,58
McLellan, Jeffery C.	MTR	1967,68,69
McNulty, Joel M.	MTR	1951,52,53
McNabb, Lou	MTR	1970
McSween, Cirilo A.	MTR	1951,52,54
Meharry, J. E.	MTR	1899
Mehock, Harry E.	MTR	1925,26
Meislahn, Arthur C.	MTR	1925,26,27

Melin, Carl A.	MTR	1903,04
Melton Jr., Albert	MTR	1974,75,76
Merigold, Julian S.	MTR	1925
Merrifield, Albert W.	MTR	1889,90,91,92
Merrill, Stillwell F.	MTR	1900
Merriman, John R.	MTR	1911
Mieher Jr., Edward C.	MTR	1924,25
Mies, Harold H.	MTR	1938
Mikolay, Mikel	MTR	1997
Miles, Rutherford T.	MTR	1899,1901
Miller, C. Marshall	MTR	1934
Miller, Clarence B.	MTR	1907,08
Miller, Harold R.	MTR	1925
Miller, Jr., V. Ward	MTR	1959
Miller, Terry	MTR	1966,67
Miller, Thomas S.	MTR	1928,30
Miller, William G.	MTR	1892
Mills, Morton J.	MTR	1919
Mills, Ralph	MTR	1897,99
Milne, Edward L.	MTR	1895,96,97
Missey, Matt	MTR	1993
Mitchell, George W.	MTR	1892
Mitchell, Robert	MTR	1957,58
Mitchell, Ronald L.	MTR	1952,54,58,59
Mitizia, Albert M.	MTR	1935,36
Mobarak, Aaron A.	MTR	1990,91
Mongreig, Louis M.	MTR	1917
Moore, Terrance D.	MTR	1985
Moorman, Anthony	MTR	2001,02
Moran, Mark A.	MTR	1898,99
Morehouse, Merritt J.	MTR	1889
Morrill, Guy L.	MTR	1910,11,12
Morris, George	MTR	1967,68,69
Morris, R. Jeffery	MTR	1976
Morrison, Heraldo E.	MTR	1986
Mors Jr., Robert J.	MTR	1960
Mullen, R. Patrick	MTR	1964,65,66
Murphy, Frank D.	MTR	1910,11,12
Murray, Oscar J.	MTR	1914
Muschler, George	MTR	1974
Myers, Carl	MTR	1993,94,95,96
Nagle, James	MTR	1954
Nagle, Perry I.	MTR	1921
Nast, Wayne A.	MTR	1951
Naughton, Jr., Frank U.	MTR	1920,21
Nauta, Michael	MTR	1965
Nelle, Richard S.	MTR	1932
Nevins, Arthur S.	MTR	1911,12,13
Nichols, David C.	MTR	1944,45
Nickol, Edgar	MTR	1927,28
Nipinak, Michael	MTR	1974
Nolan, Dan	MTR	1992
Norberg, Justin	MTR	1998,2000
Norris, Ralph V.	MTR	1905,06,07
Norton, James M.	MTR	1965,66,67
Novak, Joseph C.	MTR	1928
O'Connell, John J.	MTR	1936
O'Meara, Allan R.	MTR	1916
Oakes, Bernard F.	MTR	1924
Ockert, Carl	MTR	1946
Olesen, Robert J.	MTR	1986,87,89,90
Olsen, Donald E.	MTR	1940,41,42
Olson, Gail I.	MTR	1979,80,81,82
Olszewski, John M.	MTR	1978,80

Alvin Perryman

Orlovich, Michael G.	MTR	1937
Orlovich, Robert B.	MTR	1927,28,29
Orr, E. E.	MTR	1893,95
Osborn, Harold M.	MTR	1920,21,22
Osley, Willie	MTR	1970
Ostaszewski, Walter R.	MTR	1932
Ottoson, Eric R.	MTR	1987,88,89
Overbee, William B.	MTR	1917
Paden, J. C.	MTR	1905
Paetau, Gary	MTR	1970
Paetau, Holger	MTR	1972,74
Parham, Earl R.	MTR	1988,89
Parker, George T.	MTR	1915
Parola, J. Tony	MTR	1964
Paterson, James A.	MTR	1928,29,30
Patrick, Stanley A.	MTR	1944
Patterson, Asa E.	MTR	1991,93,94
Patterson, Bruce	MTR	1921,22
Patterson, Paul L.	MTR	1944
Pattison, Richard H.	MTR	1923
Patton, Michael K.	MTR	1982,83,84,85
Pearman, Barry	MTR	1995,96,97
Peck, Ken E.	MTR	1969,70,71
Peebles, Thomas A.	MTR	1904,05,06
Pellant, F. Robert	MTR	1956,57,58

Rudy Reavis

Babatunde Ridley

Pendarvis, Harry R.	MTR	1916,17
Peoples, Stephen	MTR	1982
Perryman, Alvin	MTR	1977,78,79,80
Petefish, William M.	MTR	1931
Peters, Forrest I. (Frosty)	MTR	1927
Peterson, James M.	MTR	1961,62
Peterson, Michael	MTR	1984
Peterson, Ralph	MTR	1954
Pettigrew, James Q.	MTR	1908,09
Pettinger, R. G.	MTR	1899,00
Phelps, John C.	MTR	1912,13
Phelps, Robert L.	MTR	1943,44,45,46
Phillips, Donald J.	MTR	1982,83
Phillips, Ronnie E.	MTR	1970,71,72
Pierce, Jack B.	MTR	1946
Pierre-Louis, Gandy	MTR	1995
Pierzynski, Thaddens	MTR	1945,47
Pike, Albert M.	MTR	1918
Pinder, Cyril C.	MTR	1966
Pivovar, Greg M.	MTR	1971,72,73
Plant, Francis B.	MTR	1899,00
Pogue, Harold A.	MTR	1914,15,16
Polakow, A. H.	MTR	1914
Pollard, Ray A.	MTR	1941
Pollensky, Chas	MTR	1935

Robert Shank

Ponzer, Etnest D.	MTR	1924,25
Ponzer, Howard S.	MTR	1927,28
Porter, Horace C.	MTR	1896,97
Portman, Crain P.	MTR	1934
Post, Clarence F.	MTR	1903
Powers, John P	MTR	1988,89
Prescott, John S.	MTR	1919,20,21
Prickett, F. W.	MTR	1897
Prince, Eric W.	MTR	1990
Purma, Frank L.	MTR	1931,32
Putnam, Edmund D.	MTR	1966
Radloff, Ronald L.	MTR	1979
Railsback, Fay D.	MTR	1908,09
Rapp, J. H.	MTR	1914
Rayburn, Cecil C.	MTR	1894,95
Read, E. N.	MTR	1899
Reavis Jr., Rudolf W.	MTR	1976,77,78,79
Redhed, William S.	MTR	1909,10
Redmon, G. Bogie	MTR	1963,64,65
Reeder, James W.	MTR	1938
Rehberg, Robert	MTR	1942,46,47
Rehm, Arthur C.	MTR	1923,25
Reising, Richard K.	MTR	1939,40
Replogle, Vernon L.	MTR	1929
Reynolds, Greg	MTR	1982,87
Reynolds, Richard W.	MTR	1951,52
Rice, James E.	MTR	1967
Richards, James V.	MTR	1908,09,10
Richards, Robert E.	MTR	1946,47
Richardson, Brad J.	MTR	1969
Richardson, William H.	MTR	1905,06,07
Richie, James K.	MTR	1908,09,10
Ricketts, C. Alan	MTR	1950
Ridley, Babatunde	MTR	1997,98,99,01
Riegel, Robert W.	MTR	1935,36
Ringquist, Mauritz E.	MTR	1935
Ripskis, Stanley	MTR	1962,63
Ritter, Michael G.	MTR	1989
Robinson, Herman	MTR	1931,32
Robinson, James O.	MTR	1939,40
Robinson, J. T.	MTR	1936,37,38
Rodgers, Robert A.	MTR	1928,29,30
Rodman, Charles S.	MTR	1901,02,03,04
Rodriguez, Matt	MTR	1997
Rogers, Aaron M.	MTR	1989,90,91
Rohrer, Carl J.	MTR	1909,10,11
Romein, Daniel C.	MTR	1977
Root, George H.	MTR	1894
Ropp, Franklin N.	MTR	1907
Rothlisberger, Curt	MTR	1984,86
Rothwell Jr., William F.	MTR	1966
Rothgeb, Claude J.	MTR	1902,03,04,05
Rowland, E. M.	MTR	1900
Royer, James M.	MTR	1927
Rudolph, David L.	MTR	1961
Rudolph, Leonard	MTR	1937
Rue, Doran T.	MTR	1925,26,27
Ruff, Robert	MTR	1976
Ruleau, John G.	MTR	1985
Runkle, Willard C.	MTR	1926
Ruscin, Mark J.	MTR	1989
Russell, Brian	MTR	1983
Russell, James T.	MTR	1985,86
Russell, Jon	MTR	1999,00

Russell, W. Hunter	MTR	1934
Ruther, Robert E.	MTR	1944,49
Saarima, Matt	MTR	1998
Salyers, R.	MTR	1905
Sandeen, John D.	MTR	1966,67,68
Sanders, Floyd W.	MTR	1929
Sanders, Ralph L.	MTR	1912,13,14
Sanner, J. David	MTR	1968,69
Sarros, James J.	MTR	1978
Saunders, Chris	MTR	1995,96
Sawtelle, Stephen E.	MTR	1978
Schellenberg, Steven	MTR	1977,78
Schildhauer, Fred J.	MTR	1923,24
Schilke, Renold E.	MTR	1962,63
Schlansker, D. Lynn	MTR	1932,33
Schlapprizzi, Fred H.	MTR	1921,22
Schleizer, Shawn M.	MTR	1990,93,94
Schmidt, Edward S.	MTR	1961
Schmidt, Jon	MTR	1979,80,81,82
Schmidt, Mark S.	MTR	1978,79
Schneck, Sereno W.	MTR	1894
Schnittgrund, Gary D.	MTR	1968,69
Schobinger, Eugene	MTR	1913,14,15
Schoch, Philip F.	MTR	1924,25,26
Schoeninger, Joseph F.	MTR	1934
Schubert, Wolfgang M.	MTR	1939
Schuh, Charles R.	MTR	1918,19,20
Schultz, Greg	MTR	1999,00
Scott, J. Russell	MTR	1922,23
Scott, Lawson	MTR	1892
Seely, Irving R.	MTR	1933,34,35
Seely, Ralph W.	MTR	1933
Seib, Robert C.	MTR	1942,43
Seiler, Otto E.	MTR	1910,11
Seldon, John M.	MTR	1929
Self, Bruce	MTR	1967,68,69
Sentman Jr., Lee H.	MTR	1929,30,31
Shepherd, John W.	MTR	1903
Shank, Robert	MTR	1988,89,90,91
Sherline, Charles H.	MTR	1986,88
Sherry, H. Raymond	MTR	1968,69,70
Shively, Bernie A.	MTR	1925,26,27
Shockey, Victor E.	MTR	1980,81,82,83
Shuman, Donald L.	MTR	1946,47,49
Sibbitt, J. P.	MTR	1928
Siders, Stacey A.	MTR	1951,52,53
Siegel, William	MTR	1970
Siglin, Brett	MTR	1995,96
Sikich, John	MTR	1939,40,41
Siler, R. W.	MTR	1900
Simon, Frank	MTR	1928,29
Simon, Joseph V.	MTR	1926,27,28
Simon, Timothy	MTR	1985,86,87,88
Sitko, Leonard J.	MTR	1988,89,90,91
Sittig, John F.	MTR	1925,26,27
Slack Jr., Jerry	MTR	1950,51
Slogan, John C.	MTR	1975,76,77,78
Smith, C. F.	MTR	1899
Smith, Claire H. W.	MTR	1905,06,07
Smith, Al	MTR	1971
Smith, Dave P.	MTR	1988
Smith, Dewitt	MTR	1893
Smith, Ed	MTR	1983,84
Smith, Fred D.	MTR	1903,05

Tim Simon

Smith, Harvey H.	MTR	1932
Smith, Leonard A.	MTR	1969
Smith, Russell W.	MTR	1923
Smith, Timothy C.	MTR	1975,76,77,78
Snyder, Ray E.	MTR	1945
Somers, Aloysius J.	MTR	1917
Spangler, Scott	MTR	1983
Spakowski, Scott	MTR	1988,89
Speer, Kenneth R.	MTR	1935,36,37
Spink, Phillip M.	MTR	1916,17,20
Sprague, Stanley R.	MTR	1945
Springe, Otto	MTR	1910
Spurlock, Albert C.	MTR	1936
Spurgeon, Lowell	MTR	1936,37
St. Clair, Tim	MTR	1984
Staff, Lawrence M.	MTR	1955,56,57
Stanners, Jerry K.	MTR	1955,56,57
Starck, Robert W.	MTR	1940,41,42
Starkey, Dean E.	MTR	1986,87,88,89
Stead, Charles B.	MTR	1917
Steinberg, Philip	MTR	1945
Stellner, Frank L.	MTR	1926
Stephenson, Roger A.	MTR	1909
Sterrenberg, Ronald K.	MTR	1977,78
Stevens, Thomas	MTR	1980,81,82,83
Stevenson, Amos M.	MTR	1899,00

Jeffrey Teach

Roderick Tolbert

Stewart, D. Larry	MTR	1957,58,59
Stine, Francis B.	MTR	1927,28,29
Stillwell, Al	MTR	1974
Stirton, James C.	MTR	1914,15,16
Stitzel, Clarence M.	MTR	1911,12
Stoddard, David	MTR	1973,74
Stone, Richard R.	MTR	1965,66
Stone, W. W.	MTR	1899
Stotlar, Samuel D.	MTR	1948,49
Stout, Lorence S.	MTR	1939,40,41
Stovall, David	MTR	1994
Stringfellow, Efrem Z.	MTR	1978,79,80,81
Studzinski, James D.	MTR	1950
Stuttle, Fred L.	MTR	1925,26,27
Sullivan, Harold F.	MTR	1926
Sutter, J. H.	MTR	1899
Swank, Roger L.	MTR	1950,51,52
Swanson, Reuben E.	MTR	1922
Swartzendruber, Frederick	MTR	1945
Sweeney, Marshall J.	MTR	1923,24,25
Sweney, Don	MTR	1893,94,95,98
Sweet, Gayln L.	MTR	1971,74
Sweet, Paul C.	MTR	1921,22,23
Swift, A. Dean	MTR	1938
Tackett, William C.	MTR	1893
Talbot, Paul	MTR	1994

Jason Van Swol

Tapping, Charles H.	MTR	1914,15
Taylor, Deryck L.	MTR	1961,62,63
Taylor, Kyle	MTR	1993,94,95,96
Teach, Jeffrey D.	MTR	1991,93,94,95
Thanos, Jon D.	MTR	1986,87,88
Thomas, Ranis	MTR	1944
Thompson, Frank L.	MTR	1900,01
Thompson, Fred B.	MTR	1898
Thompson, Harwell C.	MTR	1912,13
Thomson, Willard P.	MTR	1952,53,54,55
Tilton, Leon D.	MTR	1913
Timm, Judson A.	MTR	1928,29
Timmerhaus, Klaus	MTR	1948
Tjarksen, Donald E.	MTR	1958,59
Tockstein, L. A.	MTR	1929
Toerring, Christian J.	MTR	1891
Tolbert, Roderick L.	MTR	1986,87,88,89
Townsend, Rolla E.	MTR	1903
Trandel, Eugene J.	MTR	1946
Trapp, Harold F.	MTR	1896
Travis Jr., Foster L.	MTR	1964,65,66
Trimble, Leon	MTR	1929
Trimble, Ocie	MTR	1951,52,53
True, Bobby	MTR	1996,97,98,99
Turner III, Elbert L.	MTR	1989,90,91
Turner, E. Scott	MTR	1991,92,93,94
Turner, John H.	MTR	1940,41
Twardock, A. Robert	MTR	1951,52,53
Twomey, John E.	MTR	1946,47
Twomey, Vic L.	MTR	1946,48,49,50
Tyson, Steven M.	MTR	1984,85,86,87
Upton, Richard A.	MTR	1949,50
Urbanckas, Alfred	MTR	1956,57
Useman, Ernest M.	MTR	1930
Usher, Darryl C.	MTR	1985,86
Usrey, Vergil R.	MTR	1924
Utt, Arthur H.	MTR	1918
Van Inwagen, F.	MTR	1905,06,07
Van Kirk, William K.	MTR	1979,82
Van Meter, Vincent J.	MTR	1934,35
Van Oven, Frederick W.	MTR	1896,97,98
Van Swol, Jason	MTR	1999,00,01,02
Veirs, David C.	MTR	1899,00,01
Vieth, Wayne	MTR	1951
Virgin, Craig	MTR	1974,75,76
Vitalleto, Nick	MTR	1997,98
Voris, Alvin C.	MTR	1893
Vranek, Lee R.	MTR	1943,47,49
Waarich, Herman	MTR	1949,50,51
Wachowski, Theodore J.	MTR	1927,28
Wagner, Bertram E.	MTR	1950,51
Wagner, David A.	MTR	1978
Wahls, Aaron	MTR	2001
Walker, George	MTR	1966,67,68
Walker, George	MTR	1945,46,47,48
Walker, John A.	MTR	1949,50
Wallace, Henry S.	MTR	1921,22
Wallace, Samuel H.	MTR	1920,21,22
Wallace, William H.	MTR	1924,25,26
Wallace, Oscar	MTR	1973
Walters, David B.	MTR	1975,76,78,79
Walters, Thom D.	MTR	1963
Wanger Jr., David E.	MTR	1930
Ware, Paul R.	MTR	1952

Ware, J. W.	MTR	1905
Warner, Gale A.	MTR	1925
Warner, E. A.	MTR	1903
Washburn, Ludlow J.	MTR	1908,09,10
Washington, Lester	MTR	1983,84,85
Washington, Quincy	MTR	1999
Wasser, Norman	MTR	1947,48,49
Wasson, Roy A.	MTR	1941
Watson, Carl P.	MTR	1908
Watson, William A.	MTR	1966,67
Webb, Terrence	MTR	1969,70,71
Webster, Frederick F.	MTR	1916,17
Wedding, C. Nugent	MTR	1938
Weedman, Frederick J.	MTR	1892,93,94
Wehling, Fred J.	MTR	1935,36
Weiler, W. Richard	MTR	1946
Weiss, John N.	MTR	1918,20,21
Welker, Douglas J.	MTR	1977,78
Wells Jr., Edwin S.	MTR	1921,22,23
Welter, Cullen J.	MTR	1989,90,91
Welty, William R.	MTR	1936
Werner, Charles D.	MTR	1925,26
West, Jason D.	MTR	1991,92,93
West, William O.	MTR	1932,33
Wham, James B.	MTR	1940
Wham, Richard A.	MTR	1952,53,54
Wharton, Russell F.	MTR	1920,21,22
Wheeler, H. H.	MTR	1904
White, Charles V.	MTR	1975,76,77,78
White, Donald R.	MTR	1978,79
White, Earl C.	MTR	1926,27,28
White, Harold R.	MTR	1926,28,29
White Jr., James E.	MTR	1991
White Jr., Sylvester	MTR	1989
Whitehead, Donell	MTR	1984
Wieneke, Mark J.	MTR	1986
Wiley, Raymond S.	MTR	1899
Wilkerson, Michael R.	MTR	1985
Will, Larry D.	MTR	1977,78,79,80
Williams, Gil	MTR	1964,65
Williams, Tyrone	MTR	1995
Williams, Willie J.	MTR	1952,53,54
Willis, Stephen I.	MTR	1972
Wilson, Kenneth L.	MTR	1918,19,20
Wilson, Norman K.	MTR	1912
Winfield, Rob	MTR	1997,98
Winship, Harold L.	MTR	1977
Wolff, Gary L.	MTR	1962,63
Wolf, Ty	MTR	1984,85
Womick, John P.	MTR	1966
Wood, Arthur	MTR	1941
Wood, Charles H.	MTR	1904,08
Woodin, D. E.	MTR	1904,05,06
Woods, John T.	MTR	1978
Woods, Stanley W.	MTR	1957
Woodson, Abraham B.	MTR	1954,55,56
Woolsey, Robert D.	MTR	1931,32,33
Wright Jr., James W.	MTR	1953,54
Wright Sr., John W.	MTR	1966,67
Wright, Laurence S.	MTR	1923,24,25
Wright, Newton A.	MTR	1914,15
Wright, Robert	MTR	1936
Wright, Royal	MTR	1889
Wright, Wesley E.	MTR	1974,75,76

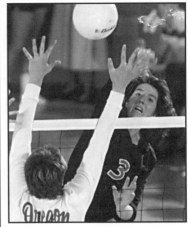

Laura Bush

Wyatt, Nathaniel C.	MTR	1977,78,79
Yarcho, Wayne B.	MTR	1938,39
Yarnall, Thomas C.	MTR	1925,26
Yates, Howard N.	MTR	1920,21,22
Yates, Robert W.	MTR	1926
Yavorski, Michael T.	MTR	1962,64
Yesko, Matt	MTR	1997,99
Young, Claude H. (Buddy)	MTR	1944
Young, Maurice	MTR	1995
Young, Richard	MTR	1944
Zieren, Jason	MTR	1995,96,97,98
Zimmerman, John H.	MTR	1919
Zimmerman, Al	MTR	1945

Volleyball

Anderson, Lori	VB	1984,85,86,87
Argabright, Lisa	VB	2000,01
Bailey, Ellen	VB	1980
Bazzetta, Kathleen	VB	2001
Beitz, Melissa	VB	1996,97,98,99
Belter, Jessica	VB	2001
Binkley, Elizabeth	VB	1984,85,86,87
Bochte, Sue	VB	1974,75,76
Borske, Erin	VB	1994,95
Bowers, Stephanie	VB	1988,89,90

Heidi Coulter

Shadia Haddad

Boyle, Bridget	VB	1986,87,88,89
Breen, Melissa	VB	1975,76,77,78
Brickley, Amy	VB	1991,92,93,94
Brookhart, Nancy	VB	1986,87,88,89
Bukenas, Dale R.	VB	1974
Bush, Laura	VB	1987,88,89,90
Calabrese, Vanessa	VB	1974
Carver, Dorothy	VB	1974,75,76
Cavato, Carrie	VB	1995,96,97,98
Chapman, Cristy	VB	1997,98
Chatterton, Amy	VB	1995
Clasey, Jody	VB	1979,80,81,82
Coleman, Mary	VB	1995,96,97,98
Collymore, Karen	VB	1979,80,81,82
Conway, Anne	VB	1989,90,91
Cook, Jennie	VB	1994,95
Coulter, Heidi	VB	1994,95,96,97
Dayton, Devin	VB	1975
Dikhoff, Carolien	VB	1995
Dillman, Lisa	VB	1987,88,89,90
Dippel, Kathy	VB	1982,83
Dluzak, Marijo	VB	1974
Douglass, Paula	VB	1984,85,86,87

Tracey Marshall

Dowdy, Chris	VB	1979,80,81,82
Dvorak, Gerry	VB	1982
Edwards, Julie	VB	1991,92,93,94
Eggers, Mary	VB	1985,86,87,88
Eiserman, Betsy	VB	1999,00,01
Falcon, Dee Dee	VB	1981
Firnhaber, Martha	VB	1988
Fracaro, Denise	VB	1982,83,84,85
Gard, Lydia	VB	1998,99,00,01
Gartland, Eileen	VB	1975,76,77
Gartland, Kathleen	VB	1976,77,78
Gleis, Kirsten	VB	1992
Glynn, Kathy	VB	1977,78,79
Greenwood, Brittney	VB	1995
Haddad, Shadia	VB	1998,99,00,01
Harkins, Eileen	VB	1991
Harks, Lauren	VB	2001
Haselhorst, Laura	VB	1995,96,97,98
Hebeisen, Kellie	VB	1990,91,92,93
Helfrich, Kim	VB	1974
Henderson, Lorna	VB	1989,90,91,92
Henriksen, Kristin	VB	1990,91,92,93
Hill, Kate	VB	2000
Holtz, Carla	VB	1974
Hrischuk, Amy	VB	1994
Johnson, Disa	VB	1984,85,86,87
Jones, Amy	VB	1990,91,92,93
King, Nancy	VB	1974
Kissinger, Molly	VB	1983
Koester, Anne	VB	1999,00
Krolik, Ann	VB	1976,77
Laverman, Petra	VB	1988,89,90
Lee, Jessica	VB	1994
Lenti, Kim	VB	1978,79,80,81
Lindner, Amber	VB	1998,99,00,01
Livingston, Mary	VB	1974
Lottes, Jan	VB	1979,83
Lourcey, Linnea	VB	1974,75
Marshall, Tracey	VB	1996,97,98,99
McArthur, Joan	VB	1974
Moeck, Peggy	VB	1974,75,76
Moskovitz, Bonnie	VB	1983
Mullis, Merrill	VB	1990,91,92,93
Neal, Melissa	VB	1994
Nemec, Carrie	VB	1978,79,80
Norris, Joan	VB	1984
Nucci, Sue	VB	1991,92,93,94
O'Bryan, Shelly	VB	2000,01
Owen, Holly	VB	1977,78,79
Parrish, Melissa	VB	1989
Pedelty, Amy	VB	1984
Podlecki, Karen	VB	1977
Pomeroy, Sarah	VB	2000
Prentice, Paul	VB	1995,96,97,98
Rea, Sally	VB	1985,86
Rimzdius, Nancy	VB	1975,76,77,78
Roberts, Janet	VB	1975,76,77,78
Rogers, Tina	VB	1990,91,92,93
Rumpel, Carol	VB	1985
Samuelson, Jill	VB	1983,84,85
Sanchez, Gina	VB	1993

Scherr, Kelly	VB	1993,94,95,96
Schlinkman, Jean	VB	1975,76,77
Scholtens, Sandy	VB	1985,86,87,88
Schorn, Dena	VB	1999
Schwarz, Chris	VB	1985,86,87,88
Schwarz, Liz	VB	1979,80,81
Schwarz, Margie	VB	1978,79,80,81
Schwarz, Rita	VB	1982,83,84,85
See, Kelly	VB	1981,82,83
Shannon, Kathleen	VB	1991,92,93
Shipman, Tracy	VB	1988
Skorus, Nina	VB	1980,81
Skudlarek, Mary	VB	1980,81
Smith, Joyce	VB	1988
Sorrell, Sara	VB	1996,97,98,99
Spicer, Betsy	VB	1997,98,99,00
Stecyk, Amy	VB	1977,78,79
Stettin, Megan	VB	1992,93,94,95
Stoessel, Annie	VB	1996,97,99
Sullivan, Jeanne	VB	1978,79,80,81
Temelli, Esra	VB	1982
Vandrey, Melissa	VB	2000,01
Venkus, Laura	VB	1978,79
Virtue, Erin	VB	2001
Wacaser, Jan	VB	1979
Watters, Laurie	VB	1981,82,83
Webber, Sue	VB	1999,00,01
Wheeler, Missy	VB	1984
Wilson, Heather	VB	1997,98,99,00
Wilson, Mary Ellen	VB	1975,76,77
Winsett, Barb	VB	1987,88,89,90
Yario, Sue	VB	1980,81,82,83
Yoss, Jeanne	VB	1984,85
Zenarosa, Rena	VB	1992,93

Wrestling

Abromovich, Phil	WR	1951
Adams, William	WR	1934,35
Agase, Alex	WR	1942,43
Agase, Louis	WR	1945
Alexander, Jeff	WR	1993
Alexander, Robert	WR	1955,56
Allen, Earl	WR	1981,82
Allen, Guy	WR	1981
Aloia, Alex	WR	1941,42
Ambler, Basil	WR	1931
Anastasia, Dana	WR	1985
Anderson, Darin	WR	1989
Anderson, Kerry	WR	1967,68
Anderson, Rob	WR	1996
Andrew, Arthur	WR	1954
Andrews, Charles	WR	1934,35
Anthonisen, Norman	WR	1942,46,47
Aprati, Fred	WR	1964,65,66
Archer, Arthur	WR	1948
Azinger, Kirk	WR	1985,86,87,88
Baird, Dave	WR	1984,85,86,87
Barbour, Dave	WR	1987,88
Barnes, Harvey	WR	1925
Bartley, John	WR	1943
Battaglia, Frank	WR	1937,38

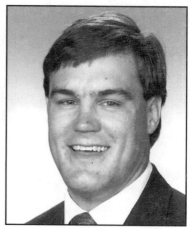

Kirk Azinger

Bauerle, Louis	WR	1929,30
Beam, Bruce	WR	1973,74,75
Beattie, Clayton	WR	1963,64,65
Beck, Denver	WR	1970,71,72
Benion, Ernest	WR	1994,95,96,97
Benson, Scott	WR	1994,95,96,97
Berbardoni, Edwin	WR	1943
Berger, Matt	WR	1985,86
Berger, Ryan	WR	2000,01,02
Bergren, Mark	WR	1973,74,75
Bernstein, Matt	WR	1989,92
Berry, Kenneth	WR	1940,41,42
Birkhiner, D. James	WR	1941
Blount, Al	WR	1981
Blum, Bill	WR	2001
Blum, Daniel	WR	1936,37
Bohannon, Edward	WR	1945
Bollman, Keith	WR	1991,92
Borland, Harold	WR	1922
Bower, Ed	WR	1944,45
Bowman, John	WR	1980
Boyd, Jesse	WR	1939,40
Brady, Seth	WR	1994,95,96,97

Ryan Berger

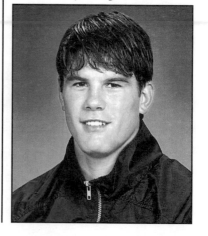

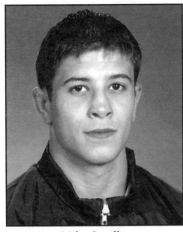

Mike Castillo

Brannan, Jon	WR	1961
Brennan, James	WR	1939
Brenne, Gary	WR	1968
Briggs, John	WR	1980
Briggs, Steve	WR	1977,78,79
Brittain, Alpheus	WR	1929
Brown, C. Addison	WR	1925
Brownridge, Enis	WR	1970,71,72
Brownstein, Harold	WR	1956,57,59
Brunkow, N.F.	WR	1912,13
Burdick, Lloyd	WR	1930
Burns, Bruce	WR	1965,66
Burwell, Robert	WR	1945
Bussey, Charles	WR	1926
Butler, Jason	WR	1999,00
Byrd, Tyrone	WR	2002
Callahan, Phil	WR	1982,84,85,86
Callaghan, Rich	WR	1963,64,65
Campbell, Albert	WR	1928
Carek, Frank	WR	1934
Carpenter, Kenneth	WR	1934,35,36
Carso, L.	WR	1931
Castillo, Anthony	WR	2001,02

Lindsey Durlacker

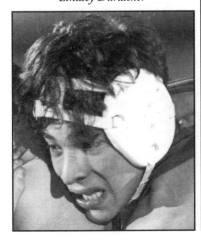

Castillo, Mike	WR	1998,99,00,01
Catarello, Dan	WR	1998,99
Catlett, Stan	WR	1965
Causey, Juan	WR	1978,79
Chamberlain, Jess	WR	1937
Check, Robert	WR	1974,75,76,77
Chirico, Doug	WR	1975,76
Chirico, Phillip	WR	1975,76
Chirico, Randy	WR	1973
Cianciarulo, Howard	WR	1962
Citron, Abraham	WR	1935
Claypool, Austin	WR	1928,29
Close, Greg	WR	1981,82
Cochran, R. Bruce	WR	1978,81,82
Collum, Paul	WR	2001
Columbo, J. B.	WR	1911,13
Compton, Norton	WR	1952,53
Cook, Shane	WR	2000
Cope, Lorin	WR	1915,16,17
Cortez, Ralph	WR	1978,80,81
Cosneck, Barney	WR	1932,33,34
Crane, Russell	WR	1928,29
Cravens, Brian	WR	2000,01,02
Crenshaw, Derrick	WR	1990
Crum, Edward	WR	1933
Cummins, J.R.	WR	1914
Curby, Nick	WR	2000,01,02
Cutler, John	WR	1912,13,14
Dahl, Andrew	WR	1934,35
Daugherty, Troy	WR	1983
Davis, Chris	WR	1981,82,83,84
DeAno, Jon	WR	1962,63
DeLong, George	WR	1944
DeMarco, Vic	WR	1964
Deutschman, Archie	WR	1937,38,39
Devor, Forest	WR	1958,59,64
Dick, C. D.	WR	1915
Dietzen, Anton	WR	2001,02
Diewald, Emil	WR	1955
Dillon, Edward	WR	1941
Doerrer. Steve	WR	1997,98,99
Domko, Joe	WR	1964
Dooley, Wilbur	WR	1929,30,31
Dowell, Wilbur	WR	1932
Drury, Ian	WR	1987,88
Ducato, Phil	WR	1987
Dunn, Merle	WR	1952
Durlacher, Dave	WR	1988,89
Durlacher, Lindsey	WR	1994,95,96,97
Dwyer, Robert	WR	1949,50
Dziedzic, Dave	WR	1993
Eagermann, Aaron	WR	1995,96,97
Echternacht, T. J.	WR	1930
Edgren, Thomas	WR	1974,75
Edison, Markwood	WR	1933
Emmons, Bob	WR	1931,32,33
Emmons, David	WR	1939
Emmons, James	WR	1940
Escobar, Ryan	WR	2000,01
Esslinger, Paul	WR	1922
Esterl, Jason	WR	1996,97,98

Ferrari, Patrick	WR	1977,78
Ferreira, Al	WR	1983
Ferrill, Dent	WR	1911
Fetherston, J. M.	WR	1913
Fiorini, Tim	WR	1978
Fitz, Eugene	WR	1928
Flood, Paul	WR	1929
Flostrom, Victor	WR	1922
Fonzino, Joe	WR	2000,01
Foor, Doug	WR	1988
Ford, Jay	WR	1993
Fotos, Paris	WR	2000,01
Frederick, E. M.	WR	1915
Fredericks, W. M.	WR	1933,34
Fregeau, John	WR	1968,69,70,71
Fricker, David	WR	1956
Froehlich, Peter	WR	1976,78,79,80
Fullerton, Willard	WR	1930
Furlong, Mark	WR	1976,77,78
Gabbard, Thomas	WR	1957,58,59
Gabbard, William	WR	1956,58
Garcia, Joe	WR	1946,47,48,49
Gary, Charles	WR	1992,93,94,95
Gaumer, Gilbert	WR	1948,49,50
Gaumer, Wayne	WR	1949,50
Geis, Clarence	WR	1925,26
Gerdes, Ken	WR	1991,93
Gibson, James	WR	1974,75,77
Gillespie, Conor	WR	2001,02
Ginay, John	WR	1936,37,38
Glassgen, Al	WR	1944
Glick, Sanford	WR	1932
Glynn, Brian	WR	2002
Gottfried, Charles	WR	1947,48,49
Goverdare, Paul	WR	1940,41
Gradman, Harold	WR	1930,31
Graham, James	WR	1978
Green, Richard	WR	1928
Greene, Joe	WR	1995
Grieshaber, Gary	WR	1973
Grunwald, Carl	WR	1946
Gudeman, Will	WR	1998
Gunlock, Virgil	WR	1926,27
Haas, Dan	WR	1969
Hale, LaDaryl	WR	1999,00,01
Hankenson, Lew	WR	1960,61,62
Hankenson, Steve	WR	1986,87,88,89
Hansen, Jay	WR	1993
Hanson, Tim	WR	1983,85
Harkness, Roland	WR	1945
Harp, Jeff	WR	1985,86
Harris, Andre	WR	1999
Harris, Robert	WR	1941
Harshbarger, Thad	WR	1959
Hart, Brett	WR	1994,95,96
Hatton, Troy	WR	1995,96,97,98
Hay, Ben	WR	2001,02
Hay, Chad	WR	1999,00,01,02
Hayes, John	WR	1942
Healy, Keith	WR	1985,86,87,88
Heffernan, Brendan	WR	2001,02

Charles Gary

Heffernan, Patrick	WR	2002
Helman, David	WR	1938,39
Helmick, Dave	WR	1981,83
Herman, Jevon	WR	1995,96,97,98
Hewitt, Wilfred	WR	1931
Hesmer, Theodore	WR	1927,28
Hestrup, Joel	WR	1976,77
Hewitt, Wilfred	WR	1931
Hill, Kimbrell	WR	1940
Hill, Robert	WR	1916
Hoerr, Blake	WR	1999,00
Hoffman, Harold	WR	1920
Holzer, Werner	WR	1957,58,59
Houghton, Eldon	WR	1932,33,34
Howell, Edward	WR	1936
Huddleson, Clyde	WR	1912
Hughes, John	WR	1940
Hughes, Robert	WR	1943,44
Hull, Wendell	WR	1957
Humphreys, Albert	WR	1926
Hurry, Tyler	WR	1997
Huth, William	WR	1939
Inman, Dave	WR	1970

Jevon Herman

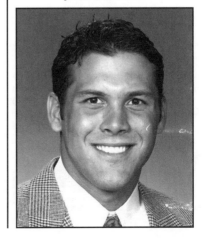

Ben King

Irle, Joseph	WR	1974
Irussi, Bruce	WR	1979,80
Jacobson, Ken	WR	1964
Jackson Jr., Edwin	WR	1951,54,55
Jacob, Paul	WR	1970,71
Jacobson, Ken	WR	1962,63
Jayne, Mark	WR	2001,02
Jeffery, Dan	WR	1964,66
Jeffery, John	WR	1964
Johnson, Rick	WR	1976,77,78,79
Johnson, Scott	WR	1978
Johnston, Jeff	WR	1983
Jurinek, George	WR	1961,62
Jurtzrock, E. V.	WR	1917
Kachiroubas, Lou	WR	1946,47,52
Kagen, Irving	WR	1941,42
Kahon, Don	WR	1966
Kakacek, John	WR	1979,81
Kanke, Tim	WR	1994,95
Kastor, Frank	WR	1954,55
Kays, William	WR	1977
Kelly, John	WR	1979
Kelly, Pat	WR	1962
Kenney, Gene	WR	1950

Matt Lackey

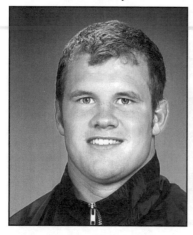

Kenney, Harold (Hek)	WR	1924,25,26
Kerestes, Tim	WR	1969
Keuhl, Doug	WR	1973
King, Andrew	WR	1976
King, Ben	WR	1999,99,00,01
Kirkpatrick, Bruce	WR	1968,69,70
Klaas, Palmer	WR	1972,73,74
Klass, Craig	WR	1973
Koenig, Tom	WR	1963
Korfist, Matt	WR	1990,92
Kranz, Richard	WR	1945
Kraml, Ken	WR	1959
Krom, Dave	WR	1965
Kummerow, Walter	WR	1966
Kusmanoff, Tony	WR	1963
Laase, F. H.	WR	1924
Lackey, Matt	WR	2000,01,02
Langdon, Bill	WR	1963
Lanning, John	WR	2000,01
Lansche, Oral	WR	1915
Law, Glenn	WR	1926
Layer, Bruce	WR	1968
Leasure, Scott	WR	1983
Ledbetter, George	WR	1934,35
Lee, Jamie	WR	1994,95
Lee, Stanley	WR	1943,48
Lee, Thomas	WR	1996,97
Lehnerer, Jim	WR	1964,65
Leischaruring, M. F.	WR	1913
Levanti, Mike	WR	2000,01,02
Levanti, Mike	WR	1970,71,72
Lembeck, Tom	WR	1983
Leverich, Wesley	WR	1939
Lewis, Chester	WR	1973
Lindy, Donald	WR	1940
Llewellyn, Chris	WR	1982,84
Llewellyn, Jon	WR	1988,89,90,91
Locascio, Victor	WR	1952
Lockhart, John	WR	1999,00,01,02
Loewe, Richard	WR	1948,50
Loffredo, Bob	WR	1966,67,68
Lorenz, Ed	WR	1969
Lukas, Peter	WR	1942
Luthringer, Marshall	WR	1924,25
Lutz, Charles	WR	1940
Lutz, Robert	WR	1952,53
Macomber, Bart	WR	1966,67,68
Madden, Kelly	WR	2000,01,02
Major, John	WR	1983,84
Maniar, Anuj	WR	1996,97,98
Mann, William	WR	1947,48,50
Manning, Joel	WR	2001,02
Marianetti, Steve	WR	1992,93,94,95
Marlin, Ken	WR	1946,47,49
Marshall, Chuck	WR	1968,69
Mathers, Manley	WR	1911,12
Mathis, Archie	WR	1924,25
Matlock, Gary	WR	1974,75,76,78
Matsumoto, Yukio	WR	1953,54
May, Roger	WR	1966,67,68
Mayer, Bob	WR	1970,71,72,73

McBride, Corey	WR	2001
McCabe, Dennis	WR	1972
McCarron, Dennis	WR	1955,56
McCracken, Brian	WR	1985,86,87
McCullum, Al	WR	1964,65,66
McDermith, Harry	WR	1933
McDonald, Mark	WR	1978
McIlvoy, Jack	WR	1935,37
McMillen, James	WR	1923,24
Mechling, Paul	WR	1953,54
Medley, Earl	WR	1970,71
Meeks, Richard	WR	1952,53,55
Mellen, William	WR	1953,55,56
Merzian, Chuck	WR	1951
Meyer, Wayne	WR	1953
Miller, Phil	WR	1972,73,74,75
Minot, George	WR	1926,29
Minsker, Bob	WR	1934
Mizue, Evan	WR	1997
Monson, Jeff	WR	1993
Moore, David	WR	1956,57,58
Morrissey, Don	WR	1959,60
Morrison, Allie	WR	1929,30
Morrison, R.C.	WR	1928
Mota, Dan	WR	1983,84,85
Mottlowitz, Kevin	WR	1987,88,89
Muegge, Louis	WR	1928
Mueller, Erik	WR	1987,88
Muther, William	WR	1956,57,58
Mutter, Charles	WR	1936,37,38
Nalls, Alonzo	WR	1987
Nelson, Dale	WR	1949
Nelson, Steve	WR	1984,85
Nichols, Mike	WR	1991,92,93
Nicoll, Shawn	WR	1980
Nordquist, Ken	WR	1953
Norman, Bob	WR	1957,58
Novak, Eric	WR	2001,02
Novak, Mike	WR	1990,91,92,93
Oaks, John	WR	1972,73
O'Brien, Dan	WR	1989,90,92
O'Brien, Mike	WR	1985,86,87,88
O'Laughlin, Mike	WR	1959,61
Ontiveros, John	WR	1953,54,55
Opiola, Anthony	WR	2000,01
Orth, Glen	WR	1932,33
Pakutinsky, Frank	WR	1936
Pakutinsky, Pete	WR	1934,35,36
Paloucek, Keith	WR	1980,81,82,83
Pancratz, Kevin	WR	1974,75,76,77
Parke, Glenn	WR	1969
Passaglia, Andy	WR	1971,72,73,74
Patrick, Nate	WR	1999,00,01
Paul, Victor	WR	1958
Paun, Joe	WR	2000,01,02
Pearson, Roland	WR	1961,62
Pelton, Lance	WR	1991,92,93,94
Pero, Jason	WR	1996,98
Perry, Carl	WR	1997,98,99,00
Perry, Joe	WR	1967
Perry, Thomas	WR	1942,43

Ken Nordquist

Petry, Jack	WR	1946
Petry, Paul	WR	1939,40,41
Pham, Twan	WR	2001,02
Picard, Richard	WR	1949,50,51
Pierre, Don	WR	1956,58
Pigozzi, Ray	WR	1950,51
Pillath, Jerry	WR	1967,79
Pineda, Ron	WR	1960
Player, John	WR	1923,24
Polkwalski, H.	WR	1912
Polz, Chris	WR	1990
Polz, Jeff	WR	1963,65
Polz, John	WR	1960,61,62
Ponder, Max	WR	1952
Porter, Tom	WR	1961
Potter, Jason	WR	2001,02
Powell, Griff	WR	1999,00,01,02
Powers, John	WR	1983
Preissner, Paul	WR	1994,95
Price, Dale	WR	1940
Price, Henry	WR	1951
Prout, Charles	WR	1936
Provinse, Jason	WR	1994,95,96

Kevin Pancratz

Griff Powell

Puebla, Kevin   WR 1976,77,78,79
Puerta, Joe   WR   1931,32,33
Purvin, Theodore   WR   1940,41
Pusey, Frank   WR   1911,12
Quirk Pat   WR 1998,99,00,01
Radell, Will   WR   1965
Rallo, Charlie   WR   1999,00,01
Rasmussen, Chuck   WR   1959
Ray, Andy   WR   2001
Rayburn, Roland   WR   1942,43
Read, Richard   WR   1951,52
Redman, Louis   WR   1933
Rehling, C. H.   WR   1915
Resner, Peter   WR   1977
Riggins, Paul   WR   1950,51
Ritz, John   WR   1926,27
Robinson, Darrell   WR   1970
Robinson, Frank   WR   1956
Roesler, Karl   WR 1996,97,98,99
Rome, Wade   WR   1990
Romersberger, Richard WR   1942
Romine, Wesley   WR   1999
Roth, Michael   WR   1973,75,76

Eric Ryan

Rott, Dennis   WR   1967,68,69
Rotter, G. E.   WR   1915
Roy, Willie   WR   1963
Rubiner, John   WR   1987
Rudin, Greg   WR   1989,90,91
Rundquist, Elmer   WR   1916
Runneberg, Elton   WR   1915
Rusk, Steve   WR   1994,95
Russell, Dave   WR   1963,64
Ryan, Dean   WR   1947,48
Ryan, Eric   WR 1995,96,97,98
Salata, Bob   WR   1959
Salomente, D.   WR   1931
Sapora, Allen   WR   1936,37,38
Sapora, Joe   WR   1928,29,30
Sargent, Norbert   WR   1955,56,57
Saric, Robert   WR   1978
Sauer, Andrew   WR   1943
Scamen, Warren   WR   1976
Schram, Bill   WR   1959
Schrieder, G. W.   WR   1912
Schroeder, Bill   WR   1971
Schroeder, G. W.   WR   1913,14
Schultz, Alfred   WR   1925
Schultz, Arthur   WR   1931
Schwartz, Martin   WR   1950,51
Schwartz, Richard   WR   1952
Seabrooke, Theodore WR   1940,41,42
Sears, John   WR   1999,00,01
Shapiro, David   WR   1946,47,48
Shatiko, Basil   WR   1924
Shaw, Ward   WR   1925
Sheahan, Pat   WR   1998
Sheahan, Tim   WR   1995,96,97
Shively, Bernie   WR   1926,27
Shively, Bob   WR   1965
Siebert, Eric   WR 1995,96,97,98
Sikich, John   WR   1939,40,41
Sikora, Brad   WR   1997,98,99
Silverstein, Ralph   WR   1935,36,37
Siml, Art   WR   1961
Sizer, Richard   WR   1941
Skisak, Chris   WR   1973,74
Slomski, Dennis   WR   1995
Smerdel, Matthew   WR   1943
Smith, George   WR   1970
Snyder, Ray   WR   1945
Soga, Susumu   WR   1926,27
Stangle, Solomon   WR   1926
Stelzer, Robert   WR   1960
Stewart, Brian   WR 1991,93,94,95
Stitzel, Stan   WR   1966
Stoltz, David   WR   1999,00,01
Stonitsch, Mike   WR 1991,92,93,94
Strange, Robert   WR   1949
Strong, H. D.   WR   1914
Struznik, Mark   WR   1993
Sulaver, Randy   WR 1972,73,74,75
Sullivan, Albert   WR   1977,78
Sullivan, Dave   WR   1992,93,94
Sullivan, Paul   WR   1990,91

Sullivan, Robert   WR   1976
Swartz, Joel   WR   1960
Szabo, Steve   WR   1955,56,57
Taylor, Trent   WR 1979,80,81,82
Temmler, Bernard   WR   1961
TenPas, Larry   WR   1954,55,56
Thacker, Edgar   WR   1926,27
Thomas, Harry   WR   1916
Thompson, Earl   WR   1942
Tiernan, Terry   WR   1962
Tirapelle, Adam   WR 1998,99,00,01
Tofft, Leonard   WR   1935
Tomala, Andy   WR   1978
Tomaras, William   WR   1941,42,46
Toncoff, Jean   WR   1929,30
Tosetti, Arthur   WR   1924,25
Townsell, William   WR   1988
Treadman, Jack   WR   1944
Trenkle, Howard   WR   1922
Trousil, Tom   WR   1959,60
Trowbridge, Sam   WR   1931
Turner, Bill   WR   1954,55
Unruh, Dan   WR   1979,80,81
Valvano, Dominic   WR   2000,01,02
Vandersteeg, Jeff   WR   1969,70
Vaughn, Jon   WR 1994,95,96,97
Veercruysee, Bob   WR   1973
Vestuto, Paul   WR   1977,78,79
Vincens, Jason   WR   2001,02
Vogt, Gary   WR   1962,63
Vohaska, William   WR   1949,50
Voorhees, George   WR   1944,45
Walker, Carl   WR   1961,62
Walsh, Kevin   WR   1989
Watts, James   WR   1945
Watts, Larry   WR   1966,67
Weber, Joe   WR   2001,02
Weber, Ron   WR   1994,95,96
Webster, Ralph   WR   1926,28
Wedel, John   WR   1952
Wedell, Mark   WR   1975
Weight, Matt   WR   2001
Weitz, L. J.   WR   1929
Welsh, Roger   WR   1915
Werner, Franklin   WR   1938
Whitelatch, Rex   WR   1958,59
Whitson, Herman   WR   1920
Wiesenborn, Kurt   WR   1977
Williams, Derrick   WR   1984,85,86
Williams, Elvie   WR   1976,77
Williams, Marty   WR   1978
Willman, Dean   WR   1952,53
Wilson, Bob   WR   1946
Witt, Terry   WR   1966
Wolff, Quentin   WR   1969,70,71
Woodcock, Geoff   WR   1990,92
Woodcock, Gregg   WR   1989,90
Wright, Ernie   WR   1967
Wyller, Tim   WR   1998,99
Yates, Michael   WR   1982,83,84
Zander, Andy   WR   1965,67

Eric Siebert

Zander, John   WR   1960,61,62
Zanetakos, William   WR   1952
Zeman, Bill   WR 1997,98,99,00
Zuidema, Greg   WR   1970,71,72

Year-by-Year Summaries

The Following is a year-by-year summary of University of Illinois athletic teams through the 2001-02 season. History has been documented more completely for some sports than others, but an attempt has been made to chart each of the 24 different sports that have attained varsity status. Big Ten championship teams are denoted in bold face.

Baseball

Year	Overall Record	Big Ten Record	Big Ten Finish
1879	1-0		
1880	1-0		
1881	0-1		
1882	No Team		
1883	3-0		
1884	1-1		
1885	1-0		
1886	4-2		
1887	4-4		
1888	3-4		
1889	1-2-1		
1890	5-3		
1891	8-2		
1892	8-3		
1893	14-8		
1894	8-6		
1895	10-4		
1896	15-4		
1897	8-9-1		
1898	12-9		
1899	13-11	10-4	2nd
1900	**12-2-1**	**11-2**	**1st**
1901	12-7	9-5	2nd
1902	12-4	8-3	2nd
1903	**17-1**	**13-1**	**1st**
1904	**23-4**	**11-3**	**1st**
1905	14-5	11-5	2nd
1906	**13-3**	**8-3**	**1st**
1907	**10-1**	**7-0**	**1st**
1908	**11-3**	**11-3**	**1st**
1909	11-3	9-3	2nd
1910	**14-0**	**11-0**	**1st**
1911	**18-2**	**14-1**	**1st**
1912	13-3-1	10-2-1	2nd
1913	11-5-1	8-4	3rd
1914	**11-7-1**	**7-3**	**1st**
1915	**18-1-1**	**9-1-1**	**1st**
1916	**13-1**	**8-1**	**1st**
1917	13-7	8-3	2nd
1918	13-6	7-3	2nd
1919	13-5	7-4	2nd
1920	16-8	6-4	3rd
1921	**17-3**	**10-1**	**1st**
1922	**17-2-1**	**8-2**	**1st**
1924	10-6-1	4-3-1	5th
1925	11-8-0	6-5	5th
1926	16-7-1	7-4	3rd
1927	**10-7-3**	**7-3-1**	**1st-T**
1928	32-12-5	6-6	N A
1929	13-7-2	6-5	4th
1930	15-5-0	8-2	2nd
1931	**15-4**	**8-2**	**1st**
1932	10-5	7-3	2nd
1933	13-3	8-2	2nd
1934	**15-3**	**9-1**	**1st**
1935	12-4	7-3	2nd
1936	13-4	10-2	2nd
1937	**14-3**	**9-1**	**1st**
1938	8-8	4-4	6th
1939	7-7-2	4-5	8th
1940	**16-5**	**9-3**	**1st-T**
1941	13-7	7-4	3rd
1942	9-9	5-7	5th
1943	8-6	5-3	3rd
1944	9-3-2	5-2-2	3rd
1945	10-10-1	6-5-1	3rd
1946	13-8-0	6-3	3rd
1947	**22-6**	**9-3**	**1st**
1948	**20-7-1**	**10-2**	**1st-T**
1949	9-8-1	6-5-1	5th
1950	13-6	6-5	4th
1951	16-9	8-3	2nd
1952	**20-11-1**	**10-5**	**1 St**
1953	**17-6**	**10-3**	**1st-T**
1954	16-15	4-11	9th
1955	14-10	7-6	4th
1956	15-18-1	4-11	10th
1957	17-9	7-4	2nd
1958	18-10	8-6	4th
1959	22-9	9-6	2nd
1960	21-10	6-8	7th
1961	22-8	9-4	4th
1962	**25-6**	**13-2**	**1 st**
1963	**18-13**	**10-5**	**1 st**
1964	9-22	1-14	10th
1965	14-9	8-6	5th
1966	14-14	5-7	6th
1967	17-21	5-11	9th
1968	18-19	7-10	6th
1969	22-20	11-7	2nd
1970	19-16-1	8-10	6th
1971	20-16-1	10-7-1	4th
1972	16-21	5-9	8th
1973	21-13	8-10	7th
1974	27-11	9-7	4th
1975	25-17-1	4-11-1	9th
1976	20-22	3-12	10th
1977	23-25	8-10	6th
1978	25-22-1	6-12	9th
1979	14-30-1	3-15	10th
1980	18-33	6-10	6th
1981	35-26	11-3	4th/0-2
1982	49-23	14-2	4th/0-2
1983	23-24-2	6-9	4th West/DNP
1984	46-21	3-10	5th West/DNP
1985	**46-21**	**12-4**	**1st West/0-2**
1986	34-19-2	8-8	4th West/DNP
1987	32-24	9-7	2nd-T West/DNP
1988	26-20	12-16	7th/DNP
1989	42-16	17-11	2nd-T/3-0
1990	43-21	19-9	2nd-T/3-0
1991	26-30	13-15	7th/DNP
1992	36-20	16-12	4th/1-2
1993	32-23	12-16	8th-T/DNP
1994	26-26	12-16	7th/DNP
1995	25-31	14-14	5th-T/DNP
1996	37-22	17-10	2nd/3-2
1997	32-27	17-11	3rd/1-2
1998	**42-21**	**19-5**	**1st/2-2**
1999	34-22	15-12	3rd/1-2
2000	**41-23**	**17-11**	**1st-T/4-1**
2001	29-28	13-14	5th/1-2
2002	32-19	14-15	6th-T

* Conference divided into East and West Divisions, with top two teams from each division competing in playoffs
** Divisional system eliminated, top four teams advanced to playoffs

Men's Basketball

Year	Overall Record	Big Ten Record	Big Ten Finish	Year	Overall Record	Big Ten Record	Big Ten Finish	Year	Overall Record	Big Ten Record	Big Ten Finish
1906	6-8	3-6	4th	1938	9-9	4-8	8th-T	1970	15-9	8-6	3rd-T
1907	1-10	0-8	5th	1939	14-5	8-4	3rd	1971	11-12	5-9	5th-T
1908	20-6	6-5	3rd	1940	14-6	7-5	4th-T	1972	14-10	5-9	8th-T
1909	7-6	5-6	4th	1941	13-7	7-5	3rd-T	1973	14-10	8-6	3rd-T
1910	5-4	5-4	4th	**1942**	**18-5**	**13-2**	**1st**	1974	5-18	2-12	10th
1911	6-6	6-5	4th	**1943**	**17-1**	**12-0**	**1st**	1975	8-18	4-14	9th-T
1912	8-8	4-8	5th	1944	11-9	5-7	6th	1976	14-13	7-11	7th-T
1913	10-6	7-6	5th	1945	13-7	7-5	3rd	1977	16-14	8-10	6th
1914	9-4	7-3	3rd	1946	14-7	7-5	5th-T	1978	13-14	7-11	7th
1915	**16-0**	**12-0**	**1st**	1947	14-6	8-4	2nd-T	1979	19-11	7-11	7th
1916	13-3	9-3	2nd-T	1948	15-5	7-5	3rd-T	1980	22-13	8-10	6th-T
1917	**13-3**	**10-2**	**1st-T**	**1949**	**21-4**	**10-2**	**1st**	1981	21-8	12-6	3rd
1918	9-6	6-6	4th-T	1950	14-8	7-5	3rd-T	1982	18-11	10-8	6th
1919	6-8	5-7	5th	**1951**	**22-5**	**13-1**	**1st**	1983	21-11	11-7	2nd-T
1920	9-4	8-4	3rd	**1952**	**22-4**	**12-2**	**1st**	**1984**	**26-5**	**15-3**	**1st-T**
1921	11-7	7-5	4th-T	1953	18-4	14-4	2nd	1985	26-9	12-6	2nd
1922	14-5	7-5	4th-T	1954	17-5	10-4	3rd-T	1986	22-10	11-7	4th-T
1923	9-6	7-5	4th-T	1955	17-5	10-4	2nd-T	1987	23-8	13-5	4th
1924	**11-6**	**8-4**	**1st-T**	1956	18-4	11-3	2nd	1988	23-10	12-6	3rd-T
1925	11-6	8-4	3rd-T	1957	14-8	7-7	7th	1989	31-5	14-4	2nd
1926	9-8	6_6	5th-T	1958	11-11	5-9	8th-T	1990	21-8	11-7	4th-T
1927	10-7	7_5	4th-T	1959	12-10	7-7	5th-T	1991	21-10	11-7	3rd-T
1928	5-17	2-10	9th-T	1960	16-7	8-6	3rd-T	1992	13-15	7-11	8th
1929	10-7	6-6	5th-T	1961	9-15	5-9	7th	1993	19-13	11-7	3rd-T
1930	8-8	7-5	4th-T	1962	15-8	7-7	4th-T	1994	17-11	10-8	4th-T
1931	12-5	7-5	5th	**1963**	**20-6**	**11-3**	**1st-T**	1995	19-12	10-8	5th-T
1932	11-6	7-5	5th	1964	13-11	6-8	6th-T	1996	18-13	7-11	9th
1933	11-7	6-6	5th-T	1965	18-6	10-4	3rd	1997	22-10	11-7	4th-T
1934	13-6	7-5	4th	1966	12-12	8-6	3rd-T	**1998**	**23-10**	**13-3**	**1st-T/1-1**
1935	**15-5**	**9-3**	**1st-T**	1967	12-12	6-8	7th-T	1999	14-18	3-13	11th/3-1
1936	13-6	7-5	3rd-T	1968	11-13	6-8	7th-T	2000	22-10	11-5	4th/2-1
1937	**14-4**	**10-2**	**1st-T**	1969	19-5	9-5	2nd-T	**2001**	**27-8**	**13-3**	**1st-T/1-1**
								2002	26-9	11-5	1st-T/1-1

Women's Basketball

Year	Overall Record	Big Ten Record	Big Ten Finish	Year	Overall Record	Big Ten Record	Big Ten Finish	Year	Overall Record	Big Ten Record	Big Ten Finish
1974-75	10-11			1983-84	12-16	6-12	8th	1992-93	12-15	7-11	7th
1975-76	15-10		5th*	1984-85	13-15	7-11	6th	1993-94	10-17	5-13	10th
1976-77	15-9		5th*	1985-86	20-10	12-6	3rd	1994-95	10-17	3-13	10th-T/0-1
1977-78	9-9		5th-T*	1986-87	19-10	11-7	4th	1995-96	13-15	6-10	8th/1-1
1978-79	9-12		DNP*	1987-88	9-19	3-15	6th-T	**1996-97**	**24-8**	**12-4**	**1st-T/2-1**
1979-80	6-21		5th*	1988-99	11-18	6-12	8th	1997-98	20-10	12-4	2nd/0-1
1980-81	20-11		DNP*	1989-90	11-17	5-13	8th	1998-99	19-12	10-6	3rd/2-1
1981-82	21-9		2nd*	1990-91	9-19	6-12	8th	1999-2000	23-11	11-5	4th/1-1
1982-83	14-14	9-9	6th	1991-92	9-19	6-12	8th	2000-01	17-16	9-7	6th/2-1
								2001-02	15-14	7-9	8th/0-1

*Tournaments from 1976-82 were not sanctioned by the Big Ten Conference

Men's Cross-Country

Year	Dual Meet Record	Big Ten Finish	NCAA Finish	Year	Dual Meet Record	Big Ten Finish	NCAA Finish	Year	Dual Meet Record	Big Ten Finish	NCAA Finish
1905	-	2nd		1938	1-2	UI did not place		1969	9-1	2nd	5th
1906	No team			1939	No team			1970	6-1-1	4th	25th
1907	No team			1940	1-1	UI did not place		1971	3-3	5th	
1908	No team			1941	2-2	4th	10th	1972	5-5	8th	
1909	No team			1942	0-3	2nd	5th	1973	4-1-1	4th	
1910	No team			1943	World War 11			1974	6-3	3rd	
1911	No team			1944	0-1	5th		1975	5-1	4th	10th
1912	-	7th		1945	0-1	4th		1976	3-1	2nd	5th
1913	1-1	2nd		1946	-	3rd		1977	5-0	2nd-T	22nd
1914	-	3rd		**1947**	**2-0**	**1st**		1978	4-1	5th	
1915	-	5th		1948	2-0-1	2nd		1979	2-3	4th	
1916	0-1			1949	1-2	2nd	8th	1980	1-0	3rd	21st
1917	World War 1			1950	0-2	6th		1981	1-0	2nd	
1918	World War 1			1951	-	UI did not enter		1982	1-1	4th	9th
1919	1-1	7th		1952	-	UI did not enter		1983	0-2	4th	14th
1920	1-1	2nd		1953	-	UI did not enter		**1984**	**1-0**	**1st**	
1921	**1-0**	**1st**		1954	1-1			1985	1-0	5th	
1922	1-0	4th		1955	1-1			1986	1-0	2nd	7th
1923	1-0	2nd		1956	3-1	2nd	4th	1987	-	2nd	
1924	0-0-1	5th		1957	3-1			1988	-	4th	
1925	0-1	3rd		1958	0-2			1989	-	2nd	
1926	0-1	4th		1959	1-0	UI did not enter complete team		1990	-	4th	
1927	2-0	2nd		1960	0-2	UI did not enter complete team		1991	-	5th	
1928	0-2	7th		1961	0-2	UI did not enter complete team		1992	-	4th	
1929	0-1	9th		1962	2-2			1993	0-1	8th	
1930	1-0	3rd		1963	4-1			1994	0-1	4th	
1931	-	4th		1964	No team			1995	-	4th	
1932	-	2nd		1965	0-4	7th		1996	1-0	4th	
1933	4-0	No meet held		1966	3-4	8th		1997	3-0	9th	
1934	1-2-1	No meet held		1967	4-7	10th		1998	-	8th	
1935	4-0	No meet held		1968	4-5	6th		1999	-	8th	
1936	0-5	No meet held						2000	-	10th	
1937	1-2	No meet held						2001	-	10th	

Women's Cross-Country

Year	Dual Meet Record	Big Ten Finish	Year	Dual Meet Record	Big Ten Finish
1978	5-0	4th*	1990	-	6th
1979	5-1	9th*	1991	-	7th
1980	2-1	9th*	1992	-	7th
1981	not available	9th	1993	-	6th
1982	1-1	6th	1994	1-0	4th
1983	1-0	6th	1995	-	9th
1984	1-0	2nd	1996	-	6th
1985	1-0	3rd-T	1997	-	6th
1986	-	7th	1998	-	8th
1987	-	8th	1999	-	10th
1988	-	8th-T	2000	-	4th
1989	-	7th	2001	-	7th

*Championships from 1978-80 were not sanctioned by the Big Ten Conference

Fencing

Year	Dual Meet Record	Big Ten Finish	NCAA Finish	Year	Dual Meet Record	Big Ten Finish	NCAA Finish	Year	Dual Meet Record	Big Ten Finish	NCAA Finish
1910-11	2-4	1st		1938-39	8-2	2nd		1966-67	12-3	2nd	12th
1911-12	2-2	1st		1939-40	4-5-1	4th		1967-68	11-6	1st	12th
1912-13	0-2	1st-T		1940-41	8-2	3rd	2nd	1968-69	13-4	2nd	14th
1913-14	0-1			1941-42	7-3	1st	3rd	1969-70	18-5	2nd	15th
1914-15	1-0			1942-43	0-0		1st	1970-71	14-4	4th	
1915-16	1-1			1943-44	World War II			1971-72	15-3	1st	6th
1916-17	2-0			1944-45	World War II			1972-73	17-2	1st	8th
1917-18	World War I			1945-46	World War II			1973-74	11-3	1st	13th
1918-19	World War I			1946-47	4-3	2nd	6th	1974-75	8-4	1st	
1919-20	1-0	1st		1947-48	3-6	2nd	15th	1975-76	14-5	4th	
1920-21	1-0			1948-49	7-2	2nd	10th	1976-77	15-4	2nd	16th
1921-22	1-1	1st		1949-50	6-3-1	1st	17th	1977-78	13-2	3rd	
1922-23	1-0	3rd		1950-51	9-0	1st	5th	1978-79	17-2	2nd-T	23rd
1923-24	2-0			1951-52	8-0	1st	5th	1979-80	20-4	1st	11th
1924-25	2-1	2nd		1952-53	9-0	1st	6th	1980-81	25-2	1st	15th
1925-26	2-0-1	4th		1953-54	8-2	1st	8th	1981-82	15-3	2nd	13th
1926-27	4-0	3rd-T		1954-55	9-2	2nd	5th	1982-83	17-2	1st	11th
1927-28	1-3	2nd		1955-56	10-0	1st	1st	1983-84	24-4	3rd-T	20th
1928-29	5-0	1st		1956-57	8-3	2nd	6th	1984-85	20-3	2nd	17th
1929-30	3-2	1st		1957-58	8-4	1st	1st	1985-86	15-1	1st*	13th
1930-31	4-0	1st		1958-59	8-4	2nd	4th	1986-87	22-1	8th	
1931-32	4-0-1	1st		1959-60	10-1	1st	8th	1987-88	25-0	7th	
1932-33	4-0-1	1st		1960-61	6-5	1st	9th	1988-89	23-1	11th	
1933-34	4-3	2nd		1961-62	11-1	1st	4th	1989-90	27-2	14th	
1934-35	5-2	1st		1962-63	10-2	2nd	8th	1990-91	24-2	13th	
1935-36	5-4	2nd		1963-64	12-0	1st	7th	1991-92	17-1	10th	
1936-37	6-1	2nd		1964-65	13-1	1st	6th	1992-93	22-3	10th	
1937-38	4-4	2nd		1965-66	7-7	1st	15th				

Football

Year	Overall Record	Big Ten Record	Big Ten Finish	Bowl	Year	Overall Record	Big Ten Record	Big Ten Finish	Bowl
1890	1-2-0				1942	6-4-0	3-2-0	3rd-T	
1891	6-0-0				1943	3-7-0	2-4-0	6th	
1892	9-3-2				1944	5-4-1	3-3-0	6th	
1893	3-2-3				1945	2-6-1	1-4-1	7th	
1894	5-3-0				**1946**	**8-2-0**	**6-1-0**	**1st**	**Rose Bowl**
1895	4-2-1				1947	5-3-1	3-3-0	3rd-T	
1896	4-2-1	0-2-1	6th-T		1948	3-6-0	2-5-0	8th	
1897	6-2-0	1-1-0	4th		1949	3-4-2	3-3-1	5th-T	
1898	4-5-0	1-1-0	4th		1950	7-2-0	4-2-0	4th	
1899	3-5-1	0-3-0	6th-T		**1951**	**9-0-1**	**5-0-1**	**1st**	**Rose Bowl**
1900	7-3-2	1-3-2	8th		1952	4-5-0	2-5-0	6th-T	
1901	8-2-0	4-2-0	4th		**1953**	**7-1-1**	**5-1-0**	**1st-T**	
1902	10-2-1	4-2-0	4th		1954	1-8-0	0-6-0	10th	
1903	8-6-0	1-5-0	7th		1955	5-3-1	3-3-1	5th	
1904	9-2-1	3-1-1	4th		1956	2-5-2	1-4-2	7th-T	
1905	5-4-0	0-3-0	6th-T		1957	4-5-0	3-4-0	7th	
1906	1-3-1	1-3-0	5th		1958	4-5-0	4-3-0	6th	
1907	3-2-0	3-2-0	3rd		1959	5-3-1	4-2-1	3rd-T	
1908	5-1-1	4-1-0	2nd		1960	5-4-0	2-4-0	5th-T	
1909	5-2-0	3-1-0	3rd		1961	0-9-0	0-7-0	9th-T	
1910	**7-0-0**	**4-0-0**	**1st-T**		1962	2-7-0	2-5-0	8th	
1911	4-2-1	2-2-1	4th-T		**1963**	**8-1-1**	**5-1-1**	**1st**	**Rose Bowl**
1912	3-3-1	1-3-1	6th-T		1964	6-3-0	4-3-0	4th-T	
1913	4-2-1	2-2-1	5th		1965	6-4-0	4-3-0	5th	
1914	**7-0-0**	**6-0-0**	**1st**		1966	4-6-0	4-3-0	3rd-T	
1915	**5-0-2**	**3-0-2**	**1st-T**		1967	4-6-0	3-4-0	5th-T	
1916	3-3-1	2-2-1	4th-T		1968	1-9-0	1-6-0	8th-T	
1917	5-2-1	2-2-1	5th-T		**1969**	**0-10-0**	**0-7-0**	**10th**	
1918	**5-2-0**	**4-0-0**	**1st**		1970	3-7-0	1-6-0	9th-T	
1919	**6-1-0**	**6-1-0**	**1st**		1971	5-6-0	5-3-0	3rd-T	
1920	5-2-0	4-2-0	4th		1972	3-8-0	3-5-0	6th-T	
1921	3-4-0	1-4-0	8th-T		1973	5-6-0	4-4-0	4th-T	
1922	2-5-0	2-4-0	6th		1974	6-4-1	4-3-1	5th	
1923	**8-0-0**	**5-0-0**	**1st**		1975	5-6-0	4-4-0	3rd-T	
1924	6-1-1	3-1-1	2nd-T		1976	5-6-0	4-4-0	3rd-T	
1925	5-3-0	2-2-0	4th-T		1977	3-8-0	2-6-0	8th-T	
1926	6-2-0	2-2-0	6th-T		1978	1-8-2	0-6-2	9th	
1927	**7-0-1**	**5-0-0**	**1st-T**		1979	2-8-1	1-6-1	9th	
1928	**7-1-0**	**4-1-0**	**1st**		1980	3-7-1	3-5-0	6th-T	
1929	6-1-1	3-1-1	2nd		1981	7-4-0	6-3-0	3rd-T	
1930	3-5-0	1-4-0	8th		1982	7-5-0	6-3-0	4th	Liberty Bowl
1931	2-6-1	0-6-1	9th-T		**1983**	**10-2-0**	**9-0-0**	**1st**	**Rose Bowl**
1932	5-4-0	2-4-0	7th		1984	7-4-0	6-3-0	2nd-T	
1933	5-3-0	3-2-0	5th		1985	6-5-1	5-2-1	3rd	Peach Bowl
1934	7-1-0	4-1-0	3rd		1986	4-7-0	3-5-0	6th-T	
1935	3-5-0	1-4-0	9th-T		1987	3-7-1	2-5-1	8th	
1936	4-3-1	2-2-1	6th		1988	6-5-1	5-2-1	3rd-T	All-American Bowl
1937	3-3-2	2-3-0	8th		1989	10-2-0	7-1-0	2nd	Citrus Bowl
1938	3-5-0	2-3-0	7th		**1990**	**8-4-0**	**6-2-0**	**1st-T**	**Hall of Fame Bowl**
1939	3-4-1	3-3-0	6th		1991	6-6-0	4-4-0	5th	John Hancock Bowl
1940	1-7-0	0-5-0	9th		1992	6-5-1	4-3-1	4th	Holiday Bowl
1941	2-6-0	0-5-0	9th		1993	5-6-0	5-3-0		

Football (cont.)

Year	Overall Record	Big Ten Record	Big Ten Finish	Bowl	Year	Overall Record	Big Ten Record	Big Ten Finish	Bowl
1994	7-5-0	4-4-0	5th-T	Liberty Bowl	1998	3-8-0	2-6-0	7th	
1995	5-5-1	3-4-1	7th-T		1999	8-4-0	4-4-0	6th-T	Micron PC
1996	2-9-0	1-7-0	9th-T		2000	5-6-0	2-6-0	9th-T	
1997	0-11-0	0-8-0	11th		**2001**	**10-1-0**	**7-1-0**	**1st**	**Sugar**

Men's Golf

Year	Dual Meet Record	Big Ten Finish	NCAA Finish	Year	Dual Meet Record	Big Ten Finish	NCAA Finish
1908	1-0			1956	5-6-1	6th-T	
1909	No team			1957	8-3	8th	
1910	No team			1958	7-6-2	7th	
1911	No team			1959	4-8	10th	
1912	1-0			1960	2-5-1	10th	
1913	-			1961	3-6	10th	
1914	1-0			1962	1-11	6th	
1915	1-0			1963	4-5	7th-T	
1916	2-0			1964	5-3	9th	
1917	1-0			1965	1-1	10th	
1918	World War I			1966	2-2	9th	
1919	World War I			1967	0-1	8th	
1920	-	3rd-T		1968	4-4	8th	
1921	1-2	3rd-T		1969	1-1	8th	
1922	0-3	4th		1970	2-1-1	7th	
1923	**5-0**	**1st**		1971	4-2	4th-T	
1924	5-0	3rd		1972	-	6th	
1925	2-2	4th		1973	-	3rd	
1926	2-2	2nd		1974	-	8th	
1927	**3-2**	**1st**		1975	-	5th-T	
1928	3-2	3rd		1976	-	7th	
1929	4-2	*		1977	-	6th	
1930	**6-0**	**1st**		1978	-	7th	
1931	**6-0**	**1st**	**5th**	1979	-	5th	
1932	2-1	4th		1980	-	8th	
1933	1-3-1	6th		1981	-	8th	
1934	2-3-1	4th		1982	1-0	3rd-T	
1935	3-1	6th		1983	1-1	7th	
1936	3-3	3rd		1984	1-1	5th	28th
1937	3-3-1	3rd		1985	2-1	10th	
1938	4-2	4th		1986	1-0	2nd	
1939	5-2	6th		1987	2-0	4th	
1940	**5-2**	**1st**	**4th**	**1988**	**-**	**1st**	**23rd-T**
1941	**7-1**	**1st**	**4th**	1989	-	2nd	
1942	3-3-1	5th		1990	-	2nd	
1943	5-2	5th		1991	-	4th	
1944	1-5	7th		1992	-	9th	
1945	1-1	5th		1993	-	6th	
1946	3-5	9th		1994	-	8th	
1947	3-4	5th		1995	-	5th	
1948	5-6	6th		1996	-	10th	
1949	0-9	8th		1997	-	9th	
1950	4-7	6th	7th	1998	-	7th	
1951	3-9	9th		1999	-	3th	
1952	1-9	9th		2000	-	11th	
1953	4-5	8th		2001	-	10th	
1954	3-8	5th		2002	-	2nd	18th
1955	5-6-1	8th					

Women's Golf

Year	Dual Meet Record	Big Ten Finish	NCAA Finish	Year	Dual Meet Record	Big Ten Finish	NCAA Finish	Year	Dual Meet Record	Big Ten Finish	NCAA Finish
1975	-	4th*		1984	-	6th		1993	-	3rd-T	
1976	-	2nd*		1985	-	5th		1994	-	3rd-T	
1977	-	4th*		1986	-	5th		1995	-	3rd	
1978	-	8th*		1987	-	6th		1996	-	11th	
1979	-	8th*		1988	-	5th		1997	-	11th	
1980	-	9th*		1989	-	5th		1998	-	10th	
1981	-	7th*		1990	-	6th		1999	-	11th	
1982	-	4th		1991	-	6th		2000	-	11th	
1983	-	5th		1992	-	3rd		2001	-	11th	
								2002	-	5th	

*Championships from 1975-81 were not sanctioned by the Big Ten Conference

Men's Gymnastics

Year	Dual Meet Record	Big Ten Finish	NCAA Finish	Year	Dual Meet Record	Big Ten Finish	NCAA Finish	Year	Dual Meet Record	Big Ten Finish	NCAA Finish
1898	-			1939	6-0	1st	1st	1971	7-3	3rd	
1902	-			1940	5-0	2nd	1st	1972	2-7	6th	
1905	-	3rd		1941	6-0	1st	1st	1973	2-12	6th	
1910	0-1	2nd		1942	5-1	1st	1st	1974	8-9	4th	
1911	1-0	1st		1943	World War II			1975	10-8	4th	
1912	1-0	1st		1944	World War II			1976	5-8	3rd	
1913	0-1	4th		1945	World War II			1977	6-5	2nd	
1914	0-1	3rd		1946	World War II			1978	9-6	2nd	
1915	1-1			1947	1-1	2nd		1979	8-7	4th	
1916	0-2	4th		1948	4-3	2nd	3rd	1980	10-5	4th	
1917	0-2	4th		1949	4-0	3rd	3rd	1981	7-3	1st	8th
1918	World War I			1950	7-1	1st	1st	1982	9-6	2nd	11th
1919	World War I			1951	7-0	1st	2nd-T	1983	9-1	1st-T	6th
1920	0-1	3rd		1952	4-1	1st	3rd	1984	8-3	4th	9th
1921	0-1	4th		1953	5-2	1st	2nd	1985	5-5	4th	11th
1922	0-1	4th		1954	6-0	1st	2nd	1986	11-3-1	3rd	12th
1923	0-2	5th		1955	7-1	1st	1st	1987	8-3	4th	12th
1924	0-2	5th		1956	4-3	1st	1st	1988	11-0	1st	2nd
1925	0-3	7th		1957	11-0	1st	2nd	1989	7-1	1st	1st
1926	0-3	7th		1958	10-1	1st	1st	1990	1-3	4th	
1927	3-1	3rd		1959	10-1	1st	2nd	1991	4-4	5th	
1928	2-1	3rd		1960	8-3	1st	3rd	1992	4-3	3rd	13th
1929	4-0	1st		1961	7-2	2nd	5th	1993	9-1	4th	6th
1930	3-1	2nd		1962	7-0	3rd	4th	1994	3-4	6th	
1931	3-0	3rd		1963	1-8	6th	11th-T	1995	4-5	5th	
1932	3-0	3rd		1964	3-6	5th		1996	3-3	6th	
1933	3-1	3rd		1965	1-8-1	6th		1997	2-4	5th	8th
1934	3-3	3rd		1966	6-2	3rd	4th	1998	13-5	5th	3rd
1935	3-0	1st		1967	8-2	4th	4th	1999	9-8	6th	7th
1936	4-1	3rd		1968	8-4	4th		2000	11-9	3rd	8th
1937	4-3	3rd		1969	4-6	3rd		2001	19-4	4th	8th
1938	4-2	2nd		1970	6-3	3rd		2002	18-2	9th	

Women's Gymnastics

Year	Dual Meet Record	Big Ten Finish	Year	Dual Meet Record	Big Ten Finish	Year	Dual Meet Record	Big Ten Finish
1974-75	-	4th*	1983-84	2-4	4th-T	1992-93	2-14	7th
1975-76	**7-1**	**1st***	1984-85	2-5	5th	1993-94	4-14	7th
1976-77	**4-4**	**1st***	1985-86	12-6	5th	1994-95	6-12	5th
1977-78	3-5	3rd*	1986-87	11-6	4th	1995-96	13-5	5th
1978-79	3-5	2nd*	1987-88	5-3	3rd	1996-97	7-11	6th
1979-80	4-2	2nd*	1988-89	9-5	4th	1997-98	12-5	6th
1980-81	1-3	4th	**1989-90**	**7-2**	**1st**	1998-99	10-7-1	6th
1981-82	2-3	6th	1990-91	3-8	4th-T	1999-2000	7-10	5th-T
1982-83	8-7	3rd	1991-92	2-14	6th	2000-01	3-16	7th
						2001-02	5-11	6th

*Championships from 1975-81 were not sanctioned by the Big Ten Conference

Ice Hockey

Year	Overall Record	Big Ten Record
1938	0-4	0-3
1939	3-7	0-6
1940	3-11	1-7
1941	17-3-1	6-1-1
1942	10-4-2	4-0
1943	10-2	5-1

Polo

Year	Overall Record
1934	0-7
1935	4-5
1936	2-2
1937	3-2
1938	7-4-1
1939	9-5
1940	8-6
1941	5-7

Men's Soccer

Year	Overall Record
1927	1-1
1928	3-0
1929	3-0
1930	4-0-1
1931	7-0-1
1932	4-2-3
1933	5-2-1
1934	5-2
1935	2-3-1

Women's Soccer

Year	Overall Record	Big Ten Record	Big Ten Finish/ Tournament
1997	7-10	1-8	10th
1998	12-8	3-6	8th/0-1
1999	12-8-2	3-5-2	6th/1-1
2000	14-8	6-4	4th/1-1
2001	12-8-1	6-3-1	3rd/2-1

Men's Swimming

Year	Dual Meet Record	Big Ten Finish	Year	Dual Meet Record	Big Ten Finish	Year	Dual Meet Record	Big Ten Finish
1910-11	**2-1**	**1st**	1938-39	5-0	4th	1966-67	5-3	7th
1911-12	**2-2**	**1st**	1939-40	2-4	6th	1967-68	4-4-1	7th
1912-13	**3-2**	**1st**	1940-41	3-4	6th	1968-69	3-6	8th
1913-14	1-3	2nd	1941-42	3-5	8th	1969-70	5-6	7th
1914-15	2-2	3rd	1942-43	3-2	8th	1970-71	2-5	7th
1915-16	2-2	3rd	1943-44	2-1	8th	1971-72	3-5	8th
1916-17	0-3	3rd	1944-45	3-3-1	7th	1972-73	7-3	8th
1917-18	World War 1		1945-46	4-4	6th	1973-74	7-3	5th
1918-19	World War 1		1946-47	0-6-1	8th	1974-75	6-5	6th
1919-20	2-2	3rd	1947-48	1-6	8th	1975-76	5-5	5th
1920-21	2-2	3rd	1948-49	2-4	9th	1976-77	3-4	6th
1921-22	2-2	4th	1949-50	4-2	9th	1977-78	3-1	8th
1922-23	4-2	4th	1950-51	2-7	9th	1978-79	4-5	7th
1923-24	1-4	8th	1951-52	-5	10th	1979-80	-2	8th
1924-25	2-1	5th	1952-53	1-6	8th	1980-81	4-4	8th
1925-26	3-2	6th	1953-54	8-2	4th	1981-82	4-5	9th
1926-27	3-3	5th	1954-55	7-3	8th	1982-83	4-2	7th
1927-28	6-0	4th	1955-56	6-4	7th	1983-84	6-2	5th
1928-29	5-0	3rd	1956-57	8-1	5th	1984-85	7-4	5th
1929-30	6-0	4th	1957-58	10-2	5th	1985-86	8-3	5th
1930-31	2-2	6th	1958-59	7-2	6th	1986-87	1-7	7th
1931-32	2-1	5th	1959-60	6-2	6th	1987-88	2-5	9th
1932-33	5-1	3rd	1960-61	5-4	7th	1988-89	2-4	9th
1933-34	3-2	4th	1961-62	4-5	8th	1989-90	4-7	8th
1934-35	3-2	2nd	1962-63	7-4	10th	1990-91	1-8	10th
1935-36	2-3	4th	1963-64	1-7	10th	1991-92	1-9	11th
1936-37	2-3-1	5th	1964-65	1-8	9th	1992-93	4-8	11th
1937-38	1-5	6th	1965-66	10-5	9th			

Women's Swimming

Year	Dual Meet Record	Big Ten Finish	Year	Dual Meet Record	Big Ten Finish	Year	Dual Meet Record	Big Ten Finish
1974-75	not available	6th*	1983-84	2-4	9th	1992-93	0-9	10th
1975-76	7-4	6th*	1984-85	5-7	8th	1993-94	3-9	10th
1976-77	3-9	7th*	1985-86	5-4	8th	1994-95	9-3	8th
1977-78	3-5	10th*	1986-87	4-3	5th	1995-96	8-7	8th
1978-79	3-2	9th*	1987-88	1-5	9th	1996-97	13-4	6th
1979-80	6-3	10th*	1988-89	2-5	9th	1997-98	9-3	6th
1980-81	7-5	10th*	1989-90	2-7	9th	1998-99	9-6	6th
1981-82	3-3	7th	1990-91	1-7	9th	1999-2000	8-5	7th
1982-83	3-3	6th	1991-92	2-6	11th	2000-01	4-7	9th
						2001-02	4-6-1	8th

*Championships from 1975-81 were not sanctioned by the Big Ten Conference

Men's Tennis

Year	Dual Meet Record	Big Ten Finish	Year	Dual Meet Record	Big Ten Finish	Year	Dual Meet Record	Big Ten Finish
1904	0-1		1937	2-8	8th	1969	4-12	5th
1905	1-2-1		1938	5-5	5th-T	1970	7-7	5th
1906	1-0-1		1939	9-2	4th	1971	12-6	5th
1907	-		1940	8-2	5th-T	1972	17-5	4th
1908	0-3		1941	3-8	Did not enter	1973	13-4	5th
1909	2-1		1942	7-4	4th	1974	19-5	6th-T
1910	-		943	4-0	2nd	1975	16-11-1	5th
1911			944	3-3	7th-T	1976	13-5-1	5th
1912	-		945	4-2-1	7th	1977	7-7	5th
1913	1-0		**1946**	**10-0**	**1st**	1978	8-10	10th
1914	2-2	2nd	1947	9-1	2nd	1979	5-16	9th
1915	3-3		1948	9-2	4th	1980	21-17	10th
1916	3-2		1949	3-2	5th-T	1981	18-12	7th
1917	**2-0**	**1st**	1950	8-1	2nd	1982	18-12	5th
1918	World War I		1951	9-1	4th-T	1983	16-16	5th
1919	World War 1		1952	3-5	6th	1984	23-9	2nd
1920	4-1-1		1953	1-5	7th	1985	20-16	3rd
1921	3-4		1954	7-3	5th	1986	12-20	6th
1922	**6-2**	**1st**	1955	12-2	3rd	1987	16-13	3rd
1923	4-4		1956	5-4	5th	1988	11-13	10th
1924	4-0-3	2nd	1957	14-2	4th	1989	11-16	8th
1925	3-1-1		1958	6-1	2nd	1990	8-17	7th
1926	**5-0**	**1st**	1959	12-3	2nd	1991	10-13	10th
1927	**4-1**	**1st**	1960	8-4	4th	1992	11-11	6th
1928	**4-1**	**1st**	1961	7-4	5th	1993	4-23	11th
1929	3-1		1962	5-5	4th	1994	13-15	5th
1930	4-1		1963	4-8	7th	1995	18-10	7th
1931	5-3		1964	9-10	7th	1996	14-10	2nd
1932	**8-3**	**1st**	1965	9-4	5th	**1997**	**18-10**	**1st**
1933	9-1-2		1966	15-5	4th	**1998**	**21-6**	**1st**
1934	4-5-2	5th	1967	9-12	6th	**1999**	**28-4**	**1st**
1935	4-1-1	3rd	1968	15-6	8th	**2000**	**25-4**	**1st**
1936	4-3	5th-T				**2001**	**22-7**	**1st**
						2002	**26-5**	**1st**

298

Women's Tennis

Year	Dual Meet Record	Big Ten Finish	Year	Dual Meet Record	Big Ten Finish	Year	Dual Meet Record	Big Ten Finish
1974-75	6-0	5th*	1982-83	16-21	8th	1992-93	14-6	3rd
1985-86	16-16	7th	1983-84	15-18	7th	1993-94	13-9	5th
1975-76	5- 3	9th*	1984-85	17-20	5th	1994-95	14-10	6th
1976-77	7-8	9th*	1986-87	12-18	7th	1995-96	12-4	7th
1977-78	6-6	10th*	1987-88	10-17	10th	1996-97	11-14	6th
1978-79	5-11	10th*	1988-89	6-22	7th	1997-98	8-3	9th
1979-80	18-9	10th*	1989-90	15-14	8th	1998-99	13-11	3rd
1980-81	21-21	10th*	1990-91	19-9	5th	1999-2000	12-13	2nd-T
1981-82	22-16	8th	1991-92	16-8	4th	2000-01	18-8	2nd
						2002	11-12	4th-T

*Championships from 1975-81 were not sanctioned by the Big Ten Conference

Women's Track and Field

Year	Big Ten Indoors	Big Ten Outdoors	NCAA Indoors	NCAA Outdoors	Year	Big Ten Indoors	Big Ten Outdoors	NCAA Indoors	NCAA Outdoors
1975	-	-			1989	1st	1st	13th	7th
1976	-	4th*			1990	2nd-T	2nd	40th-T	
1977	-	3rd*			1991	2nd	2nd	-	27th
1978	4th*	6th*			1992	1st	1st	-	13th-T
1979	9th*	6th*			1993	1st	2nd	16th-T	21st-T
1980	8th*	8th*			1994	2nd	2nd	12th-T	29th-T
1981	6th*	7th*			1995	1st	1st	24th	4th
1982	7th	6th	7th		1996	1st	2nd	6th	4th
1983	8th	4th			1997	4th	7th-T	18th	
1984	8th	10th			1998	3rd	3rd	31st	15th
1985	8th	9th			1999	6th	5th	19th	
1986	4th	3rd			2000	7th	8th	42nd	34th
1987	5th	2nd	46th		2001	8th	7th	27th	18th
1988	3rd	1st	14th	17th	2002	3rd	3rd	13th	10th-T

*Championships from 1975-81 were not sanctioned by the Big Ten Conference

Men's Track and Field

Year	Big Ten Indoors	Big Ten Outdoors	NCAA Indoors	NCAA Outdoors	Year	Big Ten Indoors	Big Ten Outdoors	NCAA Indoors	NCAA Outdoors
1901		5th			1952	1st	1st		6th-T
1902		5th			1953	1st	1st		2nd
1903		5th-T			1954	1st	1st		2nd
1904		5th			1955	4th	2nd		29th
1905		5th-T			1956	5th	7th		
1906		4th			1957	10th	4th		18th-T
1907		1st			1958	1st	1st		6th
1908		3rd			1959	2nd	1st		9th
1909		1st			1960	2nd	1st		10th
1910		1st			1961	4th	3rd		24th-T
1911	2nd	2nd			1962	5th	7th		
1912	1st	1st			1963	6th	5th		
1913	1st	1st			1964	6th	3rd		9th
1914	1st	1st			1965	5th	7th	25th-T	
1915	2nd	3rd			1966	7th	7th	39th-T	
1916	1st	2nd			1967	9th	8th		
1917	2nd	2nd			1968	9th	5th		
1918	4th	2nd			1969	5th	6th		
1919	3rd	3rd			1970	7th	4th		
1920	1st	1st			1971	7th	3rd	44th-T	33rd-T
1921	1st	1st		1st	1972	2nd	2nd	7th-T	20th
1922	1st	1st		4th	1973	5th	7th	24th-T	25th-T
1923	2nd	2nd		6th	1974	2nd-T	5th	6th	18th-T
1924	1st	1st		10th	1975	2nd	1st	20th	11th
1925	4th	5th		10th	1976	3rd	4th	4th	25th
1926	4th	2nd	8th		1977	1st	1st	4th	7th
1927	5th	1st		1st	1978	5th-T	4th		
1928	1st	1st		3rd	1979	6th	5th		40th
1929	2nd	1st		3rd	1980	3rd	3rd	46th-T	
1930	2nd	2nd		6th	1981	1st	3rd	27th-T	24th-T
1931	2nd	2nd		3rd	1982	4th	4th	14th-T	38th-T
1932	4th	4th		7th	1983	6th	3rd		58th-T
1933	3rd	3rd		18th	1984	5th	5th		56th-T
1934	3rd	1st		19th	1985	2nd	3rd	27th-T	58th-T
1935	5th	7th		32nd	1986	2nd	2nd	21st-T	51st
1936	4th	5th		32nd	1987	1st	1st	17th-T	8th
1937	5th	4th		32nd	1988	1st	1st	2nd	7th
1938	6th	6th			1989	1st	1st	14th	51st-T
1939	9th	7th		17th	1990	3rd	3rd	-	-
1940	5th	5th			1991	2nd	2nd	51st	71st
1941	4th	6th		44th	1992	6th	5th	30th-T	43rd
1942	2nd	2nd		15th	1993	2nd	2nd	15th-T	21st-T
1943	3rd	2nd		7th	1994	3rd	1st	17th-T	17th-T
1944	2nd	2nd		1st	1995	2nd	2nd	4th	41st
1945	2nd	1st		2nd	1996	4th	4th	18th	16th
1946	1st	1st		1st	1997	2nd	4th	43rd-T	
1947	1st	1st		1st	1998	4th	8th	17th	56th-T
1948	2nd	3rd		4th	1999	2nd	4th	40th	30th
1949	3rd	4th		36th	2000	2nd	5th	47th	36th
1950	3rd	2nd-T			2001	6th	10th	55th	
1951	1st	1st		14th	2002	Cancelled	10th	-	-

Volleyball

Year	Overall Record	Big Ten Record	Big Ten Finish	NCAA Finish	Year	Overall Record	Big Ten Record	Big Ten Finish	NCAA Finish
1974	19-9				1988	30-4	18-0	1st	3rd-T
1975	15-14-1		2nd*		1989	27-8	13-5	2nd	5th-T
1976	25-14		5th*		1990	21-12	11-7	4th	
1977	18-17-6		5th-T*		1991	19-10	14-6	4th	
1978	28-14		3rd*		1992	32-4	19-1	1st-T	5th-T
1979	18-20		5th-T*		1993	18-13	14--6	3rd-T	1-1 (2nd round)
1980	22-32		5th*		1994	23-14	12-8	4th	0-1 (1st round)
1981	17-27		9th*		1995	24-9	12-8	4th-T	1-1 (Reg.semifinal)
1982	17-20	8-5	3rd-T		1996	13-15	8-12	7th	
1983	5-25	2-11	10th		1997	17-13	8-12	7th	
1984	18-15	6-7	6th		1998	22-11	13-7	4th	2-1 (Reg. semifinal)
1985	39-3	16-2	2nd	9th	1999	17-11	12-8	4th	1-1 (2nd round)
1986	36-3	18-0	1st	5th-T	2000	13-18	4-16	10th	
1987	31-7	17-1	1st	3rd-T	2001	21-9	13-7	4th-T	1-1 (Round of 32)

*Championships from 1975-81 were not sanctioned by the Big Ten Conference

Wrestling

Year	Dual Meet Record	Big Ten Finish	NCAA Finish	Year	Dual Meet Record	Big Ten Finish	NCAA Finish
1911	0-1			1939	6-3	2nd-T	4th-T
1912	0-2			1940	6-4	4th-T	
1913	2-0	T-1 st*		1941	6-6	2nd-T	
1914	1-0			1942	8-0	2nd-T	8th
1915	2-0-1	4th		1943	4-1	3rd-T	
1916	1-2-1	4th		1944	4-3	4th-T	
1917	4-0	1st		1945	4-1	3rd	
1918	Did not compete in intercollegiate wrestling			1946	4-4	1st	3rd
1919	Did not compete in intercollegiate wrestling			1947	6-2-1	1st	6th
1920	3-0	1st		1948	4-4	2nd-T	3rd
1921	2-1	5th		1949	6-1-2	5th	10th-T
1922	6-0	1st		1950	8-2	9th	10th
1923	4-2			1951	5-4-1	4th	
1924	5-0	1st-T		1952	5-5-2	1st	
1925	5-0	1st-T		1953	7-5-2	4th	
1926	4-2	1st		1954	7-5	6th	12th-T
1927	6-0	1st		1955	11-2	3rd	9th
1928	7-0	1st		1956	6-6-1	8th	8th-T
1929	6-1	2nd		1957	6-3-1	4th	6th-T
1930	6-0	1st		1958	8-3-1	2nd	6th
1931	6-1			1959	4-7-1	5th	25th-T
1932	5-0	1st-T		1960	3-11	9th	
1933	5-3-1			1961	10-1	5th	21st-T
1934	7-2-1	2nd		1962	6-6	8th	19th-T
1935	5-1	1st	3rd-T	1963	6-6-2	10th	40th-T
1936	5-2	3rd		1964	7-6-1	7th	46th-T
1937	6-2	1st		1965	3-11	4th	22nd-T
1938	7-2	3rd	2nd	1966	2-11	10th	

Wrestling (cont.)

Year	Dual Meet Record	Big Ten Finish	NCAA Finish	Year	Dual Meet Record	Big Ten Finish	NCAA Finish
1967	2-10	9th		1985	11-10	6th	
1968	1-9	8th		1986	5-8	8th	38
1969	9-11-1	7th		1987	13-7	4th	40th-T
1970	6-8	9th		1988	3-9	7th	33rd
1971	2-13	10th		1989	3-10	10th	28th
1972	3-9	10th		1990	3-9	10th	19th
1973	8-8	10th		1991	3-11	10th	19th
1974	7-13	7th		1992	2-11	8th	54th-T
1975	10-9-1	7th		1993	9-4	8th	23rd-T
1976	10-8-1	9th		1994	7-5-1	9th	37th-T
1977	3-11	9th		1995	13-2	4th	9th
1978	8-8	9th		1996	11-6	4th	12th
1979	12-10	6th	24th-T	1997	14-1	3rd	9th
1980	8-12	8th		1998	11-3	6th	7th
1981	7-9-1	10th		1999	13-2	4th	12th
1982	9-8	9th		2000	14-1	3rd	6th
1983	1-13-1	8th		2001	12-2	2nd	5th
1984	4-8	9th		2002	12-4	5th	10th

Kenney Gym was named after famed Illini wrestling coach "Hek" Kenney.

Personnel History of the University of Illinois Division of Intercollegiate Athletics (Athletic Association)

This personnel history was compiled through research of University of Illinois souvenir athletic programs, its athletic summary books, UI staff directories and the Big Ten Conference record book. Some of the lists are incomplete due to insufficient information. Please contact the UI Athletic Public Relations office should you discover errors.

Faculty Representatives

1896-98	Henry H. Everett
1898-99	Jacob K. Shell
1899-1906	Herbert J. Barton
1906-29	George A. Goodenough
1929-36	Alfred C. Callen
1936-49	Frank E. Richart
1950-59	Robert B. Browne
1959-68	Leslie A. Bryan
1968-76	Henry S. Stillwell
1976-81	William A. Ferguson
1981-89	John Nowak
1981-87	Alyce T. Cheska
1988	Mildred B. Griggs
1989-2000	David L. Chicoine
1999-	Fred Delcomyn
2000-	Rose Mary Cordova-Wentling

Directors of Athletics

1892-94	Edward K. Hall
1894-95	Fred H. Dodge
1895-98	Henry H. Everett
1898-1901	Jacob K. Shell
1901-36	George A. Huff
1936-41	Wendell S. Wilson
1941-66	Douglas R. Mills
1966-67	Leslie Bryan (interim)
1967-72	E.E. (Gene) Vance
1972	Charles E. Flynn (interim)
1972-79	Cecil N. Coleman
1979	Ray Eliot (interim)
1980-88	Neale R. Stoner
1988	Ronald E. Guenther (interim)
1988	Dr. Karol A. Kahrs (interim)
1988-91	John Mackovic
1991-92	Robert Todd (interim)
1992-	Ronald E. Guenther

Associate/Assistant Athletic Directors

1958-67	Melvin Brewer
1960-78	Raymond Eliot
1973-78	Richard R. Tamburo
1973-79	Lynn J. Snyder
1974-99	Dr. Karol A. Kahrs
1978-99	Tom Porter
1984-	Dana Brenner
1987-97	Rick Allen
1989-92	Robert Todd
1993-	Terry Cole
1994-	Warren Hood
1994-96	Debbie Richardson
1994-99	William Yonan
1996-97	Lou Henson
1998-	Kelly Landry
1998-	Vince Ille
1999-	Harriet Weatherford
2000-	David Johnson
2000-02	Sally Ross
2001-	Lenny Willis
2002-	Tom Michael
2002-	Howard Milton
2002-	Mary Ann McChesney

Ron Guenther
Director of Athletics

Sports Information Directors

1922-43	L.M. (Mike) Tobin
1943-56	Charles E. Flynn
1956-70	Charles M. Bellatti
1970-74	Norman S. Sheya
1974-89	Theodore A. (Tab) Bennett
1980-85	Lani Jacobsen (women's SID)
1985-87	Thomas Boeh (women's SID)
1987-89	Mary Fowler (women's SID)
1989-96	Michael G. Pearson
1996-99	David Johnson
1999	Barbara Butler
2000-	Kent Brown (Asst. A.D.)

Athletic Trainers

Pre-1913	William (Willie) McGill
1913-16	Dr. Samuel Bilik
1916-47	David M. (Matt) Bullock
1947-51	Elmer (Ike) Hill
1951-57	Richard Klein
1957-69	Robert Nicollette
1969-73	Robert Behnke
1973-83	John (Skip) Pickering
1975-78	Dana Gerhardt (women's)
1978-80	Ellen Murray (women's)
1980-	Karen lehl-Morse (women's)
1983-	Al Martindale

Business Managers

1922-27	Frank D. Murphy
1927-30	Carl Lundgren
1930-42	Charles E. (Chilly) Bowen
1943-50	Clyde W. (Bud) Lyon*
1950-69	Henry Thornes
1969-74	R. William Sticklen
1975-76	Carl W. Freeman
1977-84	Thomas Johnson
1984-86	Terry Hearne
1986-87	Julie Frichtl
1987-99	Tim Tracy
1999-	Harriett Weatherford

*On leave of absence for war service from 1944-46

Richard "Itch" Jones
Baseball

Theresa Grentz
Women's Basketball

Bill Self
Men's Basketball

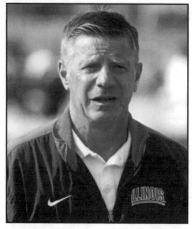
Gary Wieneke
Men's Cross-Country / Track & Field

Equipment Managers

1913-46	David M. (Matt) Bullock
1946-72	Paul Schaede
1973-81	Carl V. Rose
1981-85	Marion Brownfield
1985-	Andy Dixon

Facilities Director

1923-38	Ben Crackel
1938-47	Fred Brunner
1948-66	Fred J. Stipe
1966	William Hagerman
1966-73	Russell Mace
1973-87	Robert L. Wright
1987-94	John O'Donnell
1994-2001	Allan Heinze
2001-	Lenny Willis

Fighting Illini Scholarship Fund Directors

1969-92	T Dwight (Dike) Eddleman
1981-83	Carl Meyer (Chicago Operation)
1981-89	Wayne Williams (St. Louis Operation)
1983-89	Ronald E. Guenther (Chicago Operation)
1989-93	John Southwood (Chicago Operation)
1991-	Steven Greene (Chicago Operation)
1993-	Ken Zimmerman Jr. (Champaign Operation)
1999-	Shawn Wax (Director of Development)

Team Physicians

1933-71	Dr. Leland M.T Stilwell,M.D.*
1942-45	Dr. Irwin W. Bach, M.D.(acting)
1971-74	Dr. David Hamilton, M.D.
1975-78	Dr. L.M. Hursh, M.D.
1978-83	Dr. David Hamilton, M.D.
1983-	Dr. Robert Gurtler, M.D.
1983-	Dr. Stephen H. Soboroff, M.D.
1993-96	Dr. Michael Gernant, M.D.
2001-	Dr. Jeff Kyrouac, M.D.

*On leave of absence for war service from 1942-45

Ticket Managers

1924-27	L.M. (Mike) Stohrer
1927-42	Charles E. (Chilly) Bowen
1942-47	Clyde W. (Bud) Lyon*
1944-46	Jane Geiler (acting)
1947-75	George A. Legg
1976	Paul J. Foil
1977-89	Paul Bunting
1989-98	Mike Hatfield
1999	Cheryl Cain

*On leave of absence for war service from 1944-46

Baseball Coaches

1878-91	Student coaches appointed
1892-94	Edward K. Hall
1895	Student coach appointed
1896-1919	George A. Huff
1920	George (Potsy) Clark
1921-34	Carl L. Lundgren
1935-51	Walter H. Roettger
1952-78	Lee P. Eilbracht
1979-87	Thomas Dedin
1988-90	Augie Garrido
1991-	Richard (Itch) Jones

Basketball Coaches - Women's

1974-76	Steven Douglas
1976-79	Carla Thompson
1979-84	Jane Schroeder
1984-90	Laura Golden
1990-95	Kathy Lindsey
1995-	Theresa Grentz

Basketball Coaches - Men's

1906	Elwood Brown
1907	F.L. Pinckney
1908	Fletcher Lane
1909-10	Herbert V Juul
1911-12	TE. Thompson
1913-20	Ralph R. Jones
1921-22	Frank J. Winters
1923-36	J. Craig Ruby
1937-47	Douglas R. Mills
1948-67	Harry Combes
1967-74	Harv Schmidt
1974-75	Gene Bartow
1975-96	Lou Henson
1996-2000	Lon Kruger
2000-	Bill Self

Cross-Country Coaches - Men's

1938-60	Leo T. Johnson
1961	Edward Bernauer
1962-63	Phillip Coleman
1965-66	Robert C. Wright
1967-	Gary Wieneke

Gary Winckler
Women's Cross-Country / Track & Field

Ron Turner
Football

Mike Small
Men's Golf

Paula Smith
Women's Golf

Cross-Country Coaches - Women's

1977-81	Jessica Dragicevic
1981-83	Mary Beth Spencer
1984-85	Patty Bradley
1985-91	Gary Winckler
1992-93	Mary Beth Spencer-Dyson
1994-	Gary Winckler

Diving Coaches

1975-93	Fred Newport

Fencing Coaches

1911	R.N. Fargo
1912	K.J. Beebe
1913-16	H.E. Pengilly
1917-21	A.J. Schuettner
1922-23	R.G. Tolman
1924-28	Waldo Shurnway
1929-38	Herbert W. Craig
1939-40	James L. Jackson
1941-72**	Maxwell R. Garret
1973-93	Arthur Schankin

*Intercollegiate Fencing suspended from 1918-19 due to World War I
"Suspended from 1944-46 due to World War 11

Football Coaches

1890	Scott Williams
1891	Robert Lackey
1892-93	Edward K. Hall
1894	Louis D. Vail
1895-96	George Huff
1897-98	Fred L. Smith
1899	Neilson Poe
1900	Fred L. Smith
1901-02	Edgar G. Holt
1903	George Woodruff

Football Coaches cont.

1904	Arthur R. Hall,
	Justa M. Lindgren,
	Fred Lowenthal,
	Clyde Mathews
1905	Fred Lowenthal
1906	Justa M. Lindgren
1907-12	Arthur R. Hall
1913-41	Robert C. Zuppke
1942-59	Raymond Eliot
1960-66	Peter Elliott
1967-70	James Valek
1971-76	Robert Blackman
1977-79	Gary Moeller
1980-87	Mike White
1988-91	John Mackovic
1991-96	Lou Tepper
1997-	Ron Turner

Golf Coaches - Men's

1922-23	George Davis
1924	Ernest E. Bearg
1925-28	D.L. Swank
1929-32	J.H. Utley
1933	Robert Martin
1934	F.H. Renwick
1935-38	J.H. Utley
1939-43	W.W. Brown
1944-66	Ralph Fletcher
1967-71	Richard Youngberg
1972-80	Ladd Pash
1981-2000	Ed Beard
2001-	Mike Small

Golf Coaches - Women's

1974-78	Betsy Kimpel
1978-	Paula Smith

Gymnastics Coaches - Men's

1898	Adolph Kreikenbaum
1902	Adolph Kreikenbaum
1905	Leo G. Hana
1910-13	Leo G. Hana
1914-17*	R.N. Fargo
1921	A.J. Schuettner
1922	S.C. Staley
1924-25	J.C. Wagner
1926-29	R.C. Heidloff
1930-42**	Hartley D. Price
1947-48	Hartley D. Price
1949-61	Charles Pond
1961-62	Pat Bird (acting)
1962-73	Charles Pond
1973-93	Yoshi Hayasaki
1994-95	Don Osborn
1996-	Yoshi Hayasaki

Gymnastics Coaches - Women's

1974-75	Kim Musgrave
1975-77	Allison Milburn
1977-93	Beverly Mackes
1993	Lynn Crane
1994-99	Lynn Brueckman
2000-	Bob Starkell

Ice Hockey Coaches

1938-39	Raymond Eliot
1940-43	Victor Heyliger

Polo Coaches

1934	Pepper Clay
1935-39	Clifford B. Cole
1940	Alfred J. DeLorimer
1941	Philip R. Danley

Yoshi Hayasaki
Men's Gymnastics

Bob Starkell
Women's Gymnastics

Sue Novitsky
Women's Swimming & Diving

Sujay Lama
Women's Tennis

Soccer Coaches - Men's

1910	W.S. Strode
1927-33	Hartley D. Price
1934-35	King J. McCristal

Soccer Coaches - Women's

1996-98	Jillian Ellis
1999-2001	Trish Taliaferro
2002-	Janet Rayfield

Softball Coaches

2000-	Terri Sullivan

Strength & Conditioning Coaches

1980-88	William Kroll
1988-96	Leo Ward
1996	Greg Scanlan
1997-98	Pat Moorer
1999-	Jim Zielinski

Swimming Coaches - Women's

1974-75	Jeanne Hultzen
1975-80	Ann Pollock
1980-93	Donald Sammons
1993-99	Jim Lutz
2000-	Sue Novitsky

Swimming Coaches - Men's

1906-09	W.H. Hockmeister
1910-11	George B. Norris
1912-17*	Edward J. Manley
1920-52	Edward J. Manley
1953-70	Allen B. Klingel
1971-93	Donald Sammons

*Intercollegiate swimming suspended from 1918-19 due to World War I

Tennis Coaches - Men's

1908-13	P.B. Hawk
1914	W.A. Oldfather
1915-17*	Student coaches appointed
1920-24	E.E. Bearg
1925	B.P. Hoover
1926-29	A.R. Cohn
1930	E.A. Shoaff
1931-34	C.W. Gelwick
1935	Gerald Huff
1936-37	Casper H. Nannes
1938-42	Howard J. Braun
1943-46	Ralph Johnson
1946-64	Howard J. Braun
1965	Bob Lansford (acting)
1966-72	Dan Olson
1972-73	William Wright
1973-77	Bruce Shuman
1977	John Avallone Jr. (acting)
1978-81	Jack Groppel
1981-85	Brad Louderback
1986-92	Neil Adams
1992-	Craig Tiley

*Intercollegiate tennis suspended from 1918-19 due to World War I

Tennis Coaches - Women's

1974-75	Peggy Pruitt
1975-78	Carla Thompson
1978-81	Linda Pecore
1981-87	Mary Tredennick
1987-1998	Jennifer Roberts
1999-	Sujay Lama

Track and Field Coaches - Men's

1895	Harvey Cornish
1896-98	Henry H. Everett
1899-1900	Jacob K. Shell
1901-03	H.B. Conibear
1904-29	Harry L. Gill
1930	C.D. Werner
1931-33	Harry L. Gill
1934-37	Don C. Seaton
1938-65	Leo T. Johnson
1965-74	Robert C. Wright
1974-	Gary Wieneke

Track and Field Coaches - Women's

1974-75	Jerry Mayhew
1975-81	Jessica Dragicevic
1981-84	Mike Shine
1984-85	Patty Bradley
1985-	Gary Winckler

Craig Tiley
Men's Tennis

Janet Rayfield
Women's Soccer

Terri Sullivan
Softball

Don Hardin
Volleyball

Volleyball Coaches

1974-75	Kathleen Haywood
1975-77	Terry Hite
1977-80	Chris Accornero
1980-83	John Blair
1983-95	Mike Hebert
1996-	Don Hardin

Wrestling Coaches

1911	R.N. Fargo
1912-13	Alexander Elston
1914	Theodore Paulsen
1915-17*	Walter Evans
1921-28	Paul Prehn
1929-43	Harold E. (Hek) Kenney
1944-46	Glenn C. Law

Wrestling Coaches cont.

1946-47	Harold E. (Hek) Kenney
1948-50	Glenn C. Law
1950-68	B.R. Patterson
1968-73	Jack Robinson
1973-78	Thomas Porter
1978-83	Greg Johnson
1983-92	Ron Clinton
1992-	Mark Johnson

*Intercollegiate wrestling suspended from 1918-19 due to World War I

Mark Johnson
Wrestling

Photo Credits

Page iv   UI Athletic Media Relations
Page vi   UI News Bureau
Page viii   UI News Bureau
Page ix   UI Athletic Media Relations

Decade Page: UI Athletic Media Relations

1895-96
Moment: The Palmer House Hilton
Scrapbook: UI Athletic Media Relations
Item: UI Athletic Media Relations
List: UI Athletic Media Relations
Legend: UI Athletic Media Relations
Lore: UI Archives

1896-97
Moment: UI Athletic Media Relations
Scrapbook: UI Athletic Media Relations
Item: UI Athletic Media Relations
List: UI Athletic Media Relations
Legend: UI Athletic Media Relations
Lore: UI Archives

1897-98
Moment: UI Athletic Media Relations
Scrapbook: UI Archives
Item: UI Athletic Media Relations
List: UI Athletic Media Relations
Legend: UI Athletic Media Relations

1898-99
Moment: UI Athletic Media Relations
Scrapbook: UI Archives
Item: UI Athletic Media Relations
List: UI Athletic Media Relations
Legend: UI Athletic Media Relations
Lore: UI Archives

1899-1900
Moment: UI Athletic Media Relations
Scrapbook: Mark Jones
Item: UI Archives
List: UI Athletic Media Relations
Legend: UI Athletic Media Relations
Lore: UI Archives

1900-01
Moment: UI Athletic Media Relations
Scrapbook: UI Archives
Item: Author's collection
List: UI Illio
Legend: UI Athletic Media Relations
Lore: UI Archives

1901-02
Moment: UI Athletic Media Relations
Scrapbook: UI Illio
Item: UI Illio
List: UI Illio
Legend: UI Athletic Media Relations
Lore: UI Archives

1902-03
Moment: UI Athletic Media Relations
Scrapbook: UI Athletic Media Relations
Item: Mrs. Margaret Grange
List: UI Athletic Media Relations
Legend: UI Athletic Media Relations
Lore: UI Athletic Media Relations

1903-04
Moment: UI Athletic Media Relations
Scrapbook: UI Illio
Item: UI Athletic Media Relations
List: UI Athletic Media Relations
Legend: UI Athletic Media Relations
Lore: UI Archives

1904-05
Moment: UI Athletic Media Relations
Scrapbook: UI Archives
Item: UI Illio
List: UI Athletic Media Relations
Legend: UI Athletic Media Relations

Page 22   UI Athletic Media Relations

Decade Page: Author's collection

1905-06
Moment: The Palmer House Hilton
Scrapbook: UI Illio
Item: UI Athletic Media Relations
List: UI Athletic Media Relations
Legend: UI Archives
Lore: UI Archives

1906-07
Moment: UI Athletic Media Relations
Scrapbook: UI Illio
Item: UI Archives
List: UI Athletic Media Relations
Legend: UI Illio

1907-08
Moment: UI Athletic Media Relations
Scrapbook: UI Illio
Item: UI Athletic Media Relations
List: UI Athletic Media Relations
Legend: UI Athletic Media Relations
Lore: UI Archives

1908-09
Moment: UI Athletic Media Relations
Scrapbook: UI Illio
Item: UI Athletic Media Relations
Lists: UI Athletic Media Relations
Legend: UI Athletic Media Relations

1909-10
Moment: UI Athletic Media Relations
Scrapbook: UI Illio
Item: UI Illio
List: UI Illio
Legend: UI Archives
Lore: UI Archives

1910-11
Moment: UI Athletic Media Relations
Scrapbook: UI Archives
Item: UI Illio
List: UI Illio
Legend: UI Athletic Media Relations
Lore: UI Archives

1911-12
Moment: UI Athletic Media Relations
Scrapbook: UI Athletic Media Relations
Item: UI Athletic Media Relations
List: UI Athletic Media Relations
Legend: UI Illio

1912-13
Moment: UI Athletic Media Relations
Scrapbook: UI Illio
Item: Mrs. Margaret Grange
List: UI Athletic Media Relations
Legend: UI Illio
Lore: UI Illio

1913-14
Moment: UI Athletic Media Relations
Scrapbook: UI Illio
Item: UI Athletic Media Relations
List: UI Athletic Media Relations
Lore: UI Archives

1914-15
Moment: UI Illio
Scrapbook: UI Illio
Item: UI Illio
List: UI Athletic Media Relations
Legend: UI Athletic Media Relations
Lore: UI Archives

Decade Page: Jack Davis Graphics

1915-16
Moment: UI Illio
Scrapbook: UI Illio
Item: UI Athletic Media Relations
List: UI Athletic Media Relations
Legend: UI Athletic Media Relations
Lore: UI Illio

1916-17
Moment: UI Illio
Scrapbook: UI Illio
Item: UI Athletic Media Relations
List: UI Athletic Media Relations
Legend: UI Athletic Media Relations

1917-18
Moment: UI Athletic Media Relations
Scrapbook: UI Illio
Item: UI Athletic Media Relations
List: UI Athletic Media Relations
Legend: UI Athletic Media Relations

1918-19
Moment: UI Illio
Scrapbook: UI Athletic Media Relations
Item: UI Athletic Media Relations
List: UI Athletic Media Relations
Legend: UI Athletic Media Relations
Lore: UI Archives

1919-20
Moment: UI Athletic Media Relations
Scrapbook: UI Illio
Item: UI Athletic Media Relations
List: UI Athletic Media Relations
Legend: UI Athletic Media Relations
Lore: UI Athletic Media Relations

1920-21
Moment: UI Athletic Media Relations
Scrapbook: UI Archives
Item: Author's collection
List: UI Athletic Media Relations
Legend: UI Athletic Media Relations
Lore: UI Athletic Media Relations

1921-22
Moment: UI Athletic Media Relations
Scrapbook: UI Archives
Item: UI Athletic Media Relations
List: UI Athletic Media Relations
Legend: UI Athletic Media Relations
Lore: UI Archives

1922-23
Moment: UI Athletic Media Relations
Scrapbook: UI Athletic Media Relations
Item: UI Athletic Media Relations
List: UI Athletic Media Relations
Legend: UI Athletic Media Relations
Lore: UI Archives

1923-24
Moment: UI Athletic Media Relations
Scrapbook: UI Athletic Media Relations
Item: UI Athletic Media Relations
Legend: UI Athletic Media Relations
List: UI Athletic Media Relations

1924-25
Moment: UI Illio
Scrapbook: Author's collection
Item: UI Athletic Media Relations
List: UI Athletic Media Relations
Legend: UI Athletic Media Relations

Page 66:   Author's collection

Decade Page: Author's collection

1925-26
Moment: UI Athletic Media Relations
Scrapbook: Author's collection
Item: UI Athletic Media Relations
Legend: UI Athletic Media Relations
Lore: UI Athletic Media Relations

Red Grange: UI Athletic Media Relations

1926-27
Moment: UI Athletic Media Relations
Scrapbook: UI Athletic Media Relations
Item: UI Athletic Media Relations
List: UI Athletic Media Relations
Legend: UI Athletic Media Relations
Lore: UI Archives

1927-28
Moment: Author's collection
Scrapbook: UI Athletic Media Relations
Item: UI Athletic Media Relations
List: UI Athletic Media Relations
Legend: UI Athletic Media Relations
Lore: UI Archives

1928-29
Moment: UI Athletic Media Relations
Scrapbook: UI Illio
Item: UI Athletic Media Relations
List: UI Athletic Media Relations
Legend: UI Athletic Media Relations
Lore: UI Archives

1929-30
Moment: UI Athletic Media Relations
Scrapbook: UI Archives
Item: Author's collection
List: UI Athletic Media Relations
Legend: UI Athletic Media Relations
Lore: UI Archives

1930-31
Moment: UI Athletic Media Relations
Scrapbook: UI Athletic Media Relations
Item: UI Athletic Media Relations
List: UI Athletic Media Relations
Legend: UI Athletic Media Relations
Lore: UI Archives

1931-32
Moment: UI Athletic Media Relations
Scrapbook: UI Athletic Media Relations
Item: UI Athletic Media Relations
List: UI Athletic Media Relations
Legend: UI Athletic Media Relations
Lore: UI Archives

1932-33
Moment: UI Athletic Media Relations
Scrapbook: UI Athletic Media Relations
Item: UI Athletic Media Relations
List: UI Athletic Media Relations
Legend: UI Athletic Media Relations

1933-34
Moment: UI Athletic Media Relations
Scrapbook: UI Athletic Media Relations
Item: UI Athletic Media Relations
Legend: UI Athletic Media Relations
List: UI Athletic Media Relations
Lore: UI Archives

1934-35
Moment: UI Athletic Media Relations
Scrapbook: UI Athletic Media Relations
Item: University of Michigan
List: UI Athletic Media Relations
Legend: UI Athletic Media Relations

Decade Page: Jack Davis Graphics

1935-36
Moment: UI Athletic Media Relations
Scrapbook: UI Illio
Item: UI Athletic Media Relations
Legend: UI Athletic Media Relations

1936-37
Moment: UI Athletic Media Relations
Scrapbook: UI Athletic Media Relations
Item: UI Athletic Media Relations
List: UI Athletic Media Relations
Legend: UI Athletic Media Relations
Lore: UI Archives

1937-38
Moment: Author's collection
Scrapbook: UI Athletic Media Relations
Item: UI Athletic Media Relations
Legend: UI Athletic Media Relations
Lore: UI Archives

1938-39
Moment: UI Athletic Media Relations
Scrapbook: UI Athletic Media Relations
Item: UI Athletic Media Relations
List: UI Athletic Media Relations
Legend: UI Athletic Media Relations
Lore: UI Archives

1939-40
Moment: UI Athletic Media Relations
Scrapbook: UI Illio
Item: UI Athletic Media Relations
List: UI Athletic Media Relations
Legend: UI Athletic Media Relations
Lore: UI Archives

1940-41
Moment: UI Athletic Media Relations
Scrapbook: UI Athletic Media Relations
Item: UI Athletic Media Relations
List: UI Illio
Legend: UI Athletic Media Relations

1941-42
Moment: UI Athletic Media Relations
Scrapbook: UI Illio
Item: UI Athletic Media Relations
Legend: UI Athletic Media Relations

1942-43
Moment: UI Athletic Media Relations
Scrapbook: UI Athletic Media Relations
Item: UI Athletic Media Relations
List: Mark Jones
Legend: UI Athletic Media Relations

1943-44
Moment: UI Athletic Media Relations
Scrapbook: UI Athletic Media Relations
Item: UI Athletic Media Relations
Legend: UI Athletic Media Relations
List: UI Athletic Media Relations
Lore: UI Archives

1944-45
Moment: UI Athletic Media Relations
Scrapbook: UI Athletic Media Relations
Item: University of Michigan
List: UI Athletic Media Relations
Legend: UI Athletic Media Relations
Lore: UI Archives

Decade Page: Jack Davis Graphics

1945-46
Moment: UI Athletic Media Relations
Scrapbook: UI Athletic Media Relations
Item: UI Athletic Media Relations
List: UI Athletic Media Relations
Legend: UI Athletic Media Relations
Lore: UI Illio

1946-47
Moment: UI Athletic Media Relations
Scrapbook: UI Athletic Media Relations
Item: UI Athletic Media Relations
List: UI Athletic Media Relations
Legend: UI Athletic Media Relations
Lore: UI Archives

1947-48
Moment: UI Athletic Media Relations
Scrapbook: UI Athletic Media Relations
Item: UI Athletic Media Relations
List: UI Athletic Media Relations
Legend: UI Athletic Media Relations
Lore: UI Archives

1948-49
Moment: UI Athletic Media Relations
Scrapbook: UI Archives
Item: UI Athletic Media Relations
Legend: UI Athletic Media Relations
Lore: UI Archives

1949-50
Moment: UI Athletic Media Relations
Scrapbook: UI Athletic Media Relations
Item: UI Athletic Media Relations
List: UI Athletic Media Relations
Legend: UI Athletic Media Relations
Lore: UI Archives

1950-51
Moment: UI Athletic Media Relations
Scrapbook: UI Athletic Media Relations
Item: UI Athletic Media Relations
List: UI Athletic Media Relations
Legend: UI Athletic Media Relations
Lore: UI Illio

1951-52
Moment: UI Athletic Media Relations
Scrapbook: UI Athletic Media Relations
Item: UI Athletic Media Relations
List: UI Athletic Media Relations
Legend: UI Athletic Media Relations
Lore: UI Illio

1952-53
Moment: UI Athletic Media Relations
Scrapbook: UI Athletic Media Relations
Item: UI Athletic Media Relations
List: UI Athletic Media Relations

1953-54
Moment: UI Athletic Media Relations
Scrapbook: UI Illio
Item: UI Athletic Media Relations
Legend: UI Athletic Media Relations
Lore: UI Archives

1954-55
Moment: UI Athletic Media Relations
Scrapbook: UI Athletic Media Relations
Item: UI Athletic Media Relations
List: UI Athletic Media Relations
Legend: UI Athletic Media Relations
Lore: UI Archives

Decade Page: Jack Davis Graphics

1955-56
Moment: UI Athletic Media Relations
Scrapbook: UI Athletic Media Relations
Item: UI Athletic Media Relations
List: UI Athletic Media Relations
Legend: UI Athletic Media Relations

1956-57
Moment: UI Athletic Media Relations
Scrapbook: UI Athletic Media Relations
Item: UI Athletic Media Relations
List: UI Athletic Media Relations
Legend: UI Athletic Media Relations
Lore: UI Archives

1957-58
Moment: UI Athletic Media Relations
Scrapbook: UI Athletic Media Relations
Item: Green Bay Packers
List: UI Athletic Media Relations
Legend: UI Athletic Media Relations
Lore: UI Archives

1958-59
Moment: UI Athletic Media Relations
Scrapbook: UI Athletic Media Relations
Item: UI Athletic Media Relations
List: UI Athletic Media Relations
Legend: UI Athletic Media Relations

1959-60
Moment: UI Athletic Media Relations
Scrapbook: UI Athletic Media Relations
Item: UI Athletic Media Relations
Legend: UI Athletic Media Relations
Lore: UI Archives

1960-61
Moment: UI Athletic Media Relations
Scrapbook: University of Michigan
Item: UI Athletic Media Relations
Legend: UI Athletic Media Relations
Lore: UI Archives

1961-62
Moment: UI Athletic Media Relations
Scrapbook: UI Athletic Media Relations
Item: UI Athletic Media Relations
List: Purdue University
Legend: UI Athletic Media Relations
Lore: UI Archives

1962-63
Moment: Author's collection
Scrapbook: UI Athletic Media Relations
Item: UI Athletic Media Relations
Legend: UI Athletic Media Relations
Lore: UI Archives

1963-64
Moment: UI Athletic Media Relations
Scrapbook: UI Athletic Media Relations
Item: UI Athletic Media Relations
List: Duke University
Legend: UI Athletic Media Relations
Lore: UI Illio

1964-65
Moment: UI Athletic Media Relations
Scrapbook: UI Athletic Media Relations
Item: UI Athletic Media Relations
List: UI Athletic Media Relations
Legend: UI Athletic Media Relations
Lore: UI Archives

Decade Page: Jack Davis Graphics

1965-66
Moment: UI Athletic Media Relations
Scrapbook: UI Athletic Media Relations
Item: UI Athletic Media Relations
List: UI Athletic Media Relations
Legend: UI Athletic Media Relations
Lore: UI Illio

1966-67
Moment: UI Athletic Media Relations
Scrapbook: UI Athletic Media Relations
Item: UI Athletic Media Relations
List: Baltimore Colts
Legend: UI Athletic Media Relations

1967-68
Moment: UI Athletic Media Relations
Scrapbook: UI Archives
Item: UI Athletic Media Relations
List: Mark Jones
Legend: UI Athletic Media Relations
Lore: UI Archives

1968-69
Moment: UI Athletic Media Relations
Scrapbook: Author's collection
Item: UI Athletic Media Relations
List: UI Athletic Media Relations
Legend: UI Athletic Media Relations
Lore: UI Archives

1969-70
Moment: UI Athletic Media Relations
Scrapbook: UI Illio
Item: UI Athletic Media Relations
List: UI Athletic Media Relations
Legend: UI Athletic Media Relations

1970-71
Moment: UI Athletic Media Relations
Scrapbook: UI Athletic Media Relations
Item: UI Athletic Media Relations
List: UI Athletic Media Relations
Legend: UI Athletic Media Relations
Lore: UI Archives

1971-72
Moment: UI Athletic Media Relations
Scrapbook: UI Athletic Media Relations
Item: UI Athletic Media Relations
List: UI Athletic Media Relations
Legend: UI Athletic Media Relations
Lore: UI Archives

1972-73
Moment: UI Athletic Media Relations
Scrapbook: UI Athletic Media Relations
Item: UI Athletic Media Relations
List: UI Athletic Media Relations
Legend: UI Athletic Media Relations
Lore: UI Archives

1973-74
Moment: Phil Greer
Milestone: UI Athletic Media Relations
Item: UI Athletic Media Relations
List: UI Athletic Media Relations
Legend: UI Athletic Media Relations
Lore: UI Athletic Media Relations

1974-75
Moment: UI Athletic Media Relations
Milestone: UI Athletic Media Relations
Item: UI Athletic Media Relations
List: UI Athletic Media Relations
Legend: UI Athletic Media Relations

Decade Page: Jack Davis Graphics

1975-76
Moment: UI Athletic Media Relations
Milestone: UI Athletic Media Relations
Item: UI Athletic Media Relations
List: Michigan State University
Legend: UI Athletic Media Relations

1976-77
Moment: UI Athletic Media Relations
Milestone: UI Athletic Media Relations
Item: UI Illio
List: UI Athletic Media Relations
Legend: UI Athletic Media Relations

1977-78
Moment: UI Athletic Media Relations
Milestone: UI Athletic Media Relations
Item: UI Athletic Media Relations
List: UI Athletic Media Relations
Legend: UI Athletic Media Relations
Lore: UI Archives

1978-79
Moment: UI Athletic Media Relations
Milestone: UI Athletic Media Relations
Item: UI Athletic Media Relations
Legend: UI Athletic Media Relations
Lore: UI Archives

1979-80
Moment: UI Athletic Media Relations
Milestone: UI Athletic Media Relations
Item: UI Athletic Media Relations
List: UI Athletic Media Relations
Legend: UI Athletic Media Relations
Lore: UI Archives

1980-81
Moment: UI Athletic Media Relations
Item: UI Athletic Media Relations
List: UI Athletic Media Relations
Legend: UI Athletic Media Relations

1981-82
Moment: UI Athletic Media Relations
Milestone: UI Athletic Media Relations
Item: UI Athletic Media Relations
List: UI Athletic Media Relations
Legend: UI Athletic Media Relations

1982-83
Moment: Memphis Press
Milestone: UI Athletic Media Relations
Item: UI Athletic Media Relations
List: UI Athletic Media Relations
Legend: UI Athletic Media Relations

1983-84
Moment: UI Athletic Media Relations
Milestone: UI Athletic Media Relations
Item: UI Athletic Media Relations
List: UI Athletic Media Relations
Legend: UI Athletic Media Relations

1984-85
Moment: Basketball Times
Milestone: UI Athletic Media Relations
Item: UI Athletic Media Relations
List: UI Athletic Media Relations
Legend: UI Athletic Media Relations
Lore: UI Archives

Page 200: Mark Jones

Decade Page: Jack Davis Graphics

1985-86
Moment: UI Athletic Media Relations
Milestone: UI Athletic Media Relations
Item: UI Athletic Media Relations
List: UI Athletic Media Relations
Legend: UI Athletic Media Relations

1986-87
Moment: UI Athletic Media Relations
Milestone: UI Athletic Media Relations
Item: UI Athletic Media Relations
List: UI Athletic Media Relations
Legend: UI Athletic Media Relations

1987-88
Moment: UI Athletic Media Relations
Milestone: UI Athletic Media Relations
Item: UI Athletic Media Relations
List: UI Athletic Media Relations
Legend: UI Athletic Media Relations
Lore: UI News Bureau

1988-89
Moment: Mark Jones
Milestone: UI Athletic Media Relations
Item: Mark Jones
List: Mark Jones
Legend: UI Athletic Media Relations
Lore: UI Archives

1989-90
Moment: UI Athletic Media Relations
Milestone: UI Athletic Media Relations
Item: UI Athletic Media Relations
List: UI Athletic Media Relations
Legend: UI Athletic Media Relations
Lore: UI Archives

1990-91
Moment: Mark Jones
Milestone: Mark Jones
Item: UI Athletic Media Relations
List: Mark Jones
Legend: UI Athletic Media Relations

1991-92
Moment: Mark Jones
Milestone: UI Athletic Media Relations
Item: UI Athletic Media Relations
List: UI Athletic Media Relations
Legend: UI Athletic Media Relations
Lore: UI Athletic Media Relations

1992-93
Moment: Mark Jones
Milestone: UI Athletic Media Relations
Item: UI Athletic Media Relations
List: UI Athletic Media Relations
Legend: UI Athletic Media Relations
Lore: UI News Bureau

1993-94
Moment: Mark Jones
Milestone: UI Athletic Media Relations
Item: Mark Jones
List: UI Athletic Media Relations
Legend: UI Athletic Media Relations
Lore: Mark Jones

1994-95
Moment: Mark Jones
Milestone: UI Athletic Media Relations
Item: UI Athletic Media Relations
List: UI Athletic Media Relations
Legend: Butkus Award Committee

Page 222: UI Athletic Media Relations

Decade Page: UI Athletic Media Relations

1995-96
Moment: UI Athletic Media Relations
Milestone: UI Athletic Media Relations
Item: UI Athletic Media Relations
List: UI Athletic Media Relations
Legend: Mark Jones
Lore: UI News Bureau

1996-97
Moment: UI Athletic Media Relations
Milestone: UI Athletic Media Relations
Item: UI Athletic Media Relations
List: UI Athletic Media Relations
Legend: UI Athletic Media Relations
Lore: Authors Collection

1997-98
Moment: UI Athletic Media Relations
Milestone: UI Athletic Media Relations
Item: Mark Jones
List: UI Athletic Media Relations
Legend: UI Athletic Media Relations
Lore: Bill Wiegand, UI News Bureau

1998-99
Moment: UI Athletic Media Relations
Milestone: UI Athletic Media Relations
Item: Mark Jones
Legend: Mark Jones
Lore: UI News Bureau

1999-2000
Moment: Mark Jones
Milestone: Mark Jones
Item: UI Athletic Media Relations
List: UI Athletic Media Relations
Legend: UI Athletic Media Relations
Lore: UI Athletic Media Relations

2000-2001
Moment: Mark Jones
Milestone: Derrick Burson
Item: UI Athletic Media Relations
List: Mark Jones
Legend: UI Athletic Media Relations
Lore: Authors Collection

2001-02
Moment: Mark Jones
Item: Mark Jones
List: UI Athletic Media Relations
Legend: Mark Jones
Lore: Mark Jones

Page 239: Courtesy of Jim Turpin

Pages 241-297: UI Athletic Media Relations

Page 289: Mark Jones

Page 293: Mark Jones

Page 298: Mark Jones

Page 302: UI Athletic Media Relations

Pages 303-307: Mark Jones

Audio Credits

Audio editorial team:
Narration written by Mike Pearson, with the expert assistance of Brian Barnhart and Ed Bond of WDWS Radio in Champaign, Illinois.

Archival audio and audio research provided by: Ed Bond; Maynard Brichford and Chris Prom of University of Illinois Archives; Kent Brown, Athletic Public Relations Office, University of Illinois; Larry Miller; Jim Sheppard; WILL Radio, University of Illinois; Ted Patterson; Sid Rotz, WSOY Radio, Decatur, Illinois; Dave Eanet, WGN Radio, Chicago, Illinois; Bud Sports, St. Louis, Missouri; Robert M. Barnes, Jr.

Special thanks to: Ron Guenther, Division of Intercollegiate Athletics, University of Illinois; Stevie Jay, WDWS Radio; Keith Jackson, ABC Sports; James Keene, University of Illinois Bands; Dave Johnson, DIA, University of Illinois; Martin Kaufmann, DIA, University of Illinois; Roger Huddleston, Mahomet, Illinois; Mark and Julie Herman, Flushing Pheasant Video Productions.

Audio credits:
Brian Barnhart was recorded at WDWS Radio, Champaign, Illinois.
Audio production engineering by Ed Bond.
Some audio segments have been edited for time and content.

Archival audio provided by and copyright of:
The Illini Sports Network
University of Illinois Archives
CBS Radio Sports
NBC Radio Sports
Bud Sports
WGN Radio, Chicago, Illinois
WSOY Radio, Decatur, Illinois
WILL Radio, Champaign, Illinois
University of Illinois Bands
"The Proper State of Mind", courtesy of Athletic Enterprises,
    Sarasota, Florida

Announcers:
Our gratitude to these broadcasters whose exciting calls brought special magic to these moments. They are:
Brian Barnhart
Harry Creighton
Neil Funk
Jim Grabowski
Disa Johnson
Dave Loane
Dick Martin
Tom Michael
Sid Rotz
Bill Stern
Loren Tate
Jim Turpin

*C*elebrate the Heroes of Illinois Sports and Events

in These Other Acclaimed Titles from Sports Publishing!

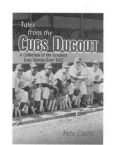

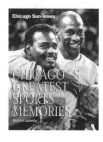

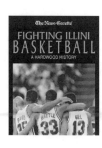

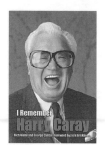